# DICEY, MORRIS AND COLLINS

ON

# THE CONFLICT OF LAWS



*FOURTH CUMULATIVE SUPPLEMENT*
*TO THE FOURTEENTH EDITION*

Up-to-date to October 1, 2010

UNDER THE GENERAL EDITORSHIP OF

LORD COLLINS OF MAPESBURY
P.C., LL.D., LL.M., F.B.A.

WITH

SPECIALIST EDITORS

SWEET & MAXWELL

THOMSON REUTERS

Published in 2011 by
Thomson Reuters (Legal) Limited
(Registered in England & Wales, Company No. 1679046.
Registered office and address for service:
100 Avenue Road, London NW3 3PF)
trading as Sweet & Maxwell.

For further information on our products and services,
visit *http://www.sweetandmaxwell.co.uk*

Computerset by Interactive Sciences Ltd, Gloucester
Printed in Great Britain by
Ashford Colour Press, Gosport, Hants.

No natural forests were destroyed to make this product. Only farmed timber was used and re-planted.

Main work ISBN: 978-0-421-88360-4
Supplement ISBN: 978-0-414-04369-5

**British Library Cataloguing in Publication Data**
A catalogue record for this book is available from the British Library.

# GENERAL EDITOR


LORD COLLINS OF MAPESBURY
P.C., LL.D. (Cantab.), LL.M. (Columbia Univ.), F.B.A.
*Justice of the Supreme Court of the United Kingdom*
*(and formerly Lord of Appeal in Ordinary);*
*Bencher, Inner Temple;*
*Honorary and Emeritus Fellow, Wolfson College, Cambridge;*
*Honorary Fellow, Downing College, Cambridge;*
*Visiting Professor, Queen Mary, London;*
*Sometime McNair Scholar and Whewell Scholar of International Law*
*in the University of Cambridge;*
*Member, Institut de droit international*


# EDITORS


ADRIAN BRIGGS
M.A., B.C.L. (Oxon.)
*Of the Middle Temple, Barrister;*
*Professor of Private International Law, Oxford University;*
*Fellow, St. Edmund Hall, Oxford*

ANDREW DICKINSON
M.A., B.C.L. (Oxon.)
*Solicitor;*
*Professor in Private International Law, University of Sydney;*
*Visiting Fellow, British Institute of International and Comparative Law*

JONATHAN HARRIS
M.A., B.C.L. (Oxon.), Ph.D. (Birm.)
*Of Lincoln's Inn, Barrister;*
*Professor of International Commercial Law,*
*University of Birmingham*

J.D. McCLEAN
C.B.E., Q.C. (Hon.), D.C.L. (Oxon.), F.B.A.
*Bencher, Gray's Inn;*
*Emeritus Professor of Law, University of Sheffield;*
*Chancellor of the Diocese of Sheffield;*
*Member, Institut de droit international*

PETER McELEAVY
B.Sc. (Surrey), Ph.D. (Aberdeen)
*Of Gray's Inn, Barrister;*
*Professor of International Family Law, University of Dundee*

CAMPBELL McLACHLAN
Q.C., LL.B. (Well.), Ph.D. (London)
*Barrister (New Zealand); Professor of Law,*
*Victoria University of Wellington*

C.G.J. MORSE
M.A., B.C.L. (Oxon.)
*Of the Middle Temple, Barrister;*
*Professor of Law, King's College, London*

# CONTENTS

PART THREE
## JURISDICTION AND FOREIGN JUDGMENTS

PART SIX
CORPORATIONS AND INSOLVENCY

# TABLE OF CASES

EUROPEAN CASES

# TABLE OF STATUTES

**UNITED KINGDOM**

2007 Arbitration Amendment Act
s.8 .......................................... 16–085

**OTHER COUNTRIES**

*Germany*

Code of Civil Procedure
para.890 .................................. 11–025

*Ireland*

Constitution
Art.41 ...................................... 19–122
Art.42 ...................................... 19–122

*Italy*

Civil Code
Art.1337 ................................. S35–242
Code of Civil Procedure
Art.382 .................................... 30–160

*Jersey*

1984 Trusts (Jersey) Law
Art.9 ........................................ 29–054
2006 Trusts (Amendment No.4) (Jersey) Law
Art.9 ........................................ 29–054
(4) ....................................... 29–054

*Guernsey*

2007 Guernsey (Trusts) Law
s.14(1) .................................... 29–054
(3) ....................................... 29–054
(4) ....................................... 29–054

*Switzerland*

1987 Private International Law Act
s.110(2) .................................. S35–229

*United States*

Constitution First Amendment .............................. 14R–141
United States Code 11 (Bankruptcy Code)
Ch.15 ................. 14–030, 30–108
United States Code, Title 28,
s.1782 .................................... 8–074
2008 Libel Terrorism Protection Act (New York) ........... 14R–141, 35–128
2010 Securing the Protection of our Enduring and Established Constitutional Heritage Act ................. 35–128

# TABLE OF STATUTORY INSTRUMENTS

# TABLE OF CIVIL PROCEDURE RULES

# TABLE OF EUROPEAN AND INTERNATIONAL TREATIES AND CONVENTIONS

# TABLE OF EC SECONDARY LEGISLATION

## CHAPTER 1

# NATURE AND SCOPE OF THE CONFLICT OF LAWS

NOTE 18. See also *Aziz v Aziz* [2007] EWCA Civ 712, [2008] 2 All E.R. 501. **1–008**

NOTE 21. See, on the United States Supreme Court's use of comity in judicial assistance cases, Collins (2006) 8 Yb. P.I.L. 53.

CPR, r.6.20 has been replaced by CPR PD6B, para.3.1: see CPR, r.6.36 (as substituted by SI 2008/2178, Sch.1). **1–010**

NOTE 31. See also *Masri v Consolidated Contractors International Company SAL (No.2)* [2008] EWCA Civ 303, [2009] Q.B. 450, at [36]–[39]. **1–013**

NOTE 49. See also Symeonides, *The American Choice-of-Law Revolution: Past, Present and Future* (2006). **1–018**

NOTE 53. Supreme Court Act 1981 is now renamed Senior Courts Act 1981: Constitutional Reform Act 2005, s.59 and Sch.11, in force October 1, 2009. **1–019**

On the impact of the European Convention on Human Rights see Fawcett (2007) 56 I.C.L.Q. 1; Juratowitch (2007) 3 J. Priv. Int. L. 173. **1–020**

NOTE 56. The European Community has become a member of the Hague Conference on Private International Law as from April 3, 2007.

See generally Harris (2008) 4 J. Priv. Int. L. 347. **1–021**

The EU Commission's action plan includes a timetable for the introduction of proposals in relation to these matters: a Regulation on the conflict of laws in matters concerning matrimonial property rights, including the question of jurisdiction and mutual recognition, and a Regulation on the property consequences of the separation of couples from other types of unions; a Regulation on improving the efficiency of the enforcement of judgments in the European Union: the attachment of bank accounts; a Regulation amending Council Regulation 2201/2003 (Brussels II *bis*); a Regulation on limitation periods in cross-border road traffic accidents; a Regulation amending Regulation (EC) No 1346/2000 on insolvency proceedings; a legislative proposal on mutual recognition of the effects of certain civil status documents (e.g. relating to birth, affiliation, adoption, name); a Regulation on improving the efficiency of the enforcement of judgments in the European Union: transparency of debtor's assets; a legislative proposal for dispensing with the formalities for the legalisation of documents between the Member States; and a legislative proposal aimed at improving the consistency of existing Union legislation in the field of civil procedural law.

NOTE 58. See now also Regulation (EC) 1896/2006 of the European Parliament and of the Council creating a European order for payment procedure: [2006] O.J. L399/1; Regulation (EC) 861/2007 of the European Parliament and of the Council establishing a European Small Claims Procedure: [2007] O.J. L199/1. For the revised Lugano Convention see entry at para.11R–001, below.

NOTE 59. See also Council Regulation (EC) 4/2009 on jurisdiction, applicable law, recognition and enforcement of decisions and co-operation in matters relating to maintenance obligations: [2009] O.J. L73/36.

NOTE 61. Regulation (EC) 593/2008 of the European Parliament and of the Council of June 17, 2008 on the law applicable to contractual obligations (Rome I) ("the Rome I Regulation") has replaced [2008] O.J. L177/6. It applies to contracts concluded after December 17, 2009 (Art. 28). The text is reproduced in Appendix 2 to this Supplement.

NOTE 62. See now the Rome II Regulation (Regulation (EC) 864/2007) of the European Parliament and of the Council on the Law Applicable to Non-Contractual Obligations: [2007] O.J. L199/40), which entered into force on January 11, 2009. The text is reproduced in Appendix 1 to this Supplement.

**1–027** NOTE 82. See also *Al-Skeini v Secretary of State for Defence* [2007] UKHL 26, [2008] 1 A.C. 153.

**1–029** NOTE 92. *Re Deep Vein Thrombosis and Air Travel Group Litigation* [2005] UKHL 72 is now reported at [2006] 1 A.C. 495.

**1–030** NOTE 97. *Re Deep Vein Thrombosis and Air Travel Group Litigation* [2005] UKHL 72 is now reported at [2006] 1 A.C. 495.

**1–036** NOTE 5. Add: Keyes (2008) 4 J. Priv. Int. L. 1.

**1–038** Text at note 7. On the force of the presumption see *Masri v Consolidated Contractors International Company SAL (No.4)* [2008] EWCA Civ 876, [2010] 1 A.C. 90, at [16], *per* Sir Anthony Clarke M.R. and [80], *per* Lawrence Collins L.J., revd. on other grounds [2009] UKHL 43, [2010] 1 A.C. 90 (noted Whomersley (2010) 126 L.Q.R. 171); *Serious Organised*

*Crime Agency v Perry* [2010] EWCA Civ 907; and also *Al-Skeini v Secretary of State for Defence* [2007] UKHL 26, [2008] 1 A.C. 153, at [11], [46]–[51]; *Office of Fair Trading v Lloyds TSB Bank plc* [2007] UKHL 48, [2008] 1 A.C. 316, at [4]; *Al Sabah v Grupo Torras SA* [2005] UKPC 1, [2005] 2 A.C. 333, at [13].

NOTE 10. *Agassi v Robinson* [2004] EWCA Civ 1518, [2005] 1 W.L.R. 1090 has been reversed: [2006] UKHL 23, [2006] 1 W.L.R. 1380.

NOTE 12. See also *Re Sovereign Marine & General Insurance Co Ltd* [2006] EWHC 1335 (Ch.), [2007] 1 B.C.L.C. 228.

Third Parties (Rights against Insurers) Act 2010, s.18 (not yet in force), provides that except as expressly provided, the application of the Act does not depend on whether there is a connection with a part of the United Kingdom; and in particular it does not depend on (a) whether or not the liability (or the alleged liability) of the insured to the third party was incurred in, or under the law of, England and Wales, Scotland or Northern Ireland; (b) the place of residence or domicile of any of the parties; (c) whether or not the contract of insurance (or a part of it) is governed by the law of England and Wales, Scotland or Northern Ireland; (d) the place where sums due under the contract of insurance are payable. Contrast *Ludgater Holdings Ltd v Gerling Australia Insurance Company Pty Ltd* [2010] NZSC 49, [2010] 3 N.Z.L.R. 713. **1–053**

NOTE 55. See also *Ravat v Halliburton Manufacturing & Services Ltd* [2010] CSIH 52. **1–057**

NOTE 79. Companies Act 1985 is replaced by Companies Act 2006. **1–064**

Contrary to the text, the Australian Capital Territory has a Legislative Assembly. **1–066**

NOTE 98. See also *Jersey Fishermen's Association Ltd v States of Guernsey* [2007] UKPC 30, [2007] Eur.L.R. 670. **1–074**

On connecting factors see *Dell Computer Corp v Union des consommateurs* 2007 SCC 34, (2007) 284 D.L.R. (4th) 577 (Sup. Ct. Can.). **1–078**

NOTE 26. See also Mills, *The Confluence of Public and Private International Law: Justice, Pluralism and Subsidiarity in the International Constitutional Ordering of Private Law* (2009). **1–088**

## Chapter 2

# CHARACTERISATION AND THE INCIDENTAL QUESTION

### A. Characterisation

**2–001** Note 1. See Forsyth (2006) 2 J. Priv. Int. L. 425.

**2–034** See also *Sweedman v Transport Accident Commission* [2006] HCA 8, (2006) 226 C.L.R. 362 (on which see Kourakis (2007) 28 Adelaide L.Rev. 23: characterisation in context of claim for reimbursement after compensation payment to victim of traffic accident). *Sweedman v Transport Accident Commission* was distinguished in *Gerling Australia Insurance Co Pty Ltd v Ludgater Holdings Ltd* [2009] NZCA 397, [2010] 2 N.Z.L.R. 145, as being inapplicable to the correct characterisation of a direct claim against the tortfeasor's insurer, which was held to be tortious in nature (appeal dismissed without specific reference to doctrine of characterisation: *Ludgater Holdings Ltd v Gerling Australia Insurance Co Pty Ltd* [2010] NZSC 49, [2010] 3 N.Z.L.R. 713). On characterisation issues raised by claim for contribution, see *Fluor Australia Pty Ltd v ASC Engineering Pty Ltd* [2007] VSC 262, at [39] *et seq*.

**2–035** On characterisation and choice of law in relation to equitable claims between parties to a contractual (including implied matrimonial contractual) relationship, see *Murakami v Wiryadi* [2010] NSWCA 7, which holds that even though the claim may be formulated as an equitable one, equity should simply act on the conscience of the party contractually bound, to enforce the expectations created by the contract, with the result that the claim is characterised (for the purposes of common law choice of law) as contractual in nature, and not as one which is independent of the contract. The question of how to characterise an equitable claim which alleged dishonest assistance of another's breach of trust arose, but was not directly answered, in *OJSC Oil Company Yugraneft v Abramovich* [2008] EWHC 2613 (Comm.). The conclusion at [221]–[223] was that such a claim had to satisfy the choice of law rules for a claim in tort, and that dishonest assistance "should" be characterised as a tort for the purposes of choice of law under the common law and under the Private International (Miscellaneous Provisions) Act 1995. This approach is consistent with the view expressed at para.2–035 of the main work, though the judgment does not purport to deal with choice of law for equitable claims in general, only going so far as was necessary to hold that the claimant was required to demonstrate civil liability under the law of Russia in order to sustain the personal claim based on dishonest assistance. (The judge had no need to consider the application of the Rome II Regulation, but it seems certain that a dishonest assistance claim would be seen as being based on a non-contractual obligation for the purposes of that Regulation.) The result is that, as para.2–035 of the main work suggests, there is no reason to suppose that "equitable claims" form a coherent characterisation category of their own at common law.

Personal restitutionary claims, and a claim for a proprietary lien or a constructive trust were characterised at [237]–[262] as restitutionary and therefore as falling within Rule 230 for the purpose of choice of law, despite their equitable character in domestic law; see further on this, paras 34–033 *et seq.*, below.

On the characterisation of claims for interest on damages as substantive or procedural, see *Maher v Groupama Grand Est* [2009] EWCA Civ 1191, [2010] 1 W.L.R. 1564 (holding that although the legal right to claim interest on damages in tort, sought in a direct action against the tortfeasor's insurer, was a matter of substantive tort law governed by the *lex causae*, the power conferred on the court by Senior Courts Act 1981, s.35A was a procedural one, which allowed the court to take into account any relevant principles of French law: at [40]). The decision was applied in *Abdel Hadi Abdullah Al Qahtani & Sons Beverage Industry Co v Antliff* [2010] EWHC 1735 (Comm.) (award of simple interest under s.35A a procedural matter unaffected by any prohibition in Saudi or sharia law which might otherwise have applied to the merits of the substantive claim). **2–036**

The approach in *Macmillan Inc v Bishopsgate Investment Trust Plc (No.3)*, and in *Raiffeisen Zentralbank Österreich AG v Five Star General Trading LLC* was applied in *Haugesund Kommune v Depfa ACS Bank* [2010] EWCA Civ 579, [2010] 2 Lloyd's Rep. 323 in which, at [47], the court held that the "capacity" of a corporation, to which Dicey's Rule 162 refers, was to be understood in a "broader, internationalist sense" than may be conveyed by the comparatively narrow meaning of the term in English domestic law. **2–037**

## CHAPTER 4

# RENVOI

**4–003** NOTE 2. *Neilson v Overseas Projects Corp of Victoria Ltd* is now reported at (2005) 233 C.L.R. 331, and on which see Briggs [2006] L.M.C.L.Q. 1; Dickinson (2006) 122 L.Q.R. 183; Mills [2006] C.L.J. 37; Mortensen (2006) 2 J. Priv. Int. L. 1.

**4–022** On the application of renvoi in the context of intestate succession to the rights created by a judgment, see *Re Haji-Ioannou, Haji-Ioannou v Frangos* [2009] EWHC 2310 (QB), [2010] 1 All E.R. (Comm.) 303 (judgment creditor died domiciled in Monaco; Monaco law on succession looks to the law of the nationality (British), and accepts a renvoi back to the domestic law of Monaco).

**4–024** *Cf.* the decision of the French Cour de Cassation, in *X v X* (June 23, 2010), holding, in a case concerning succession to land in Spain, that as the Spanish choice of law rule would make a renvoi to French law, it was appropriate for the French courts to exercise jurisdiction over the subject matter of the dispute, despite the fact that French courts ordinarily lack jurisdiction to determine title to foreign land. The decision illustrates a novel use of renvoi, ostensibly to increase the prospect of a true application of the law chosen by the rules for choice of law.

**4–025** So far as concerns the determination of title to tangible movables, recent first instance decisions have demonstrated little enthusiasm for the application of renvoi or for the approach taken by the High Court of Australia in *Neilson v Overseas Projects Corp of Victoria Ltd* (2005) 233 CLR 331.

Prior to the decision of the High Court of Australia, the approach of English law was not settled. In *Macmillan Inc v Bishopsgate Investment Trust Plc (No.3)* [1995] 1 W.L.R. 978, it had been held that priority of title to intangibles (registered shares in a New York company) was governed by the *lex loci actus*, excluding the doctrine of renvoi, but the Court of Appeal rejected the *lex loci actus* in favour of the law of the place of registration, and no argument was addressed to it on the application or otherwise of the doctrine of renvoi: [1996] 1 W.L.R. 387. However, in relation to tangible movables, it was said in *Glencore International AG v Metro Trading International Inc* [2001] 1 Lloyd's Rep. 284, 287, that the question of whether the *lex situs* allowed for a renvoi, if the evidence of foreign law established that the courts at the *situs* would not simply apply their domestic law, remained an open one.

A clearer trend became evident after the judgment in *Neilson*. In *Islamic Republic of Iran v Berend* [2007] EWHC 132 (QB), [2007] 2 All E.R. (Comm.) 132, the judge declined to admit the principle of renvoi in a claim to title to movables which was governed by French law as *lex situs* of the delivery. In *Dornoch Ltd v Westminster International BV* [2009] EWHC 889 (Admlty), [2009] 2 Lloyd's Rep. 191, the judge discussed, but did not decide, whether the reference to the *lex situs* in questions concerned with title to a ship located in Thailand was a reference to the domestic law of the *situs* or, if its content were proved, to that law including its private international law. The "provisional" answer, at [89], was that the reference was to domestic law. Though the judge recognised merit in the policy-sensitive, approach adopted in *Neilson*, there was no evidence of Thai private international law before the court, and therefore no material basis to allow him to undertake an analysis of the kind adopted in that case. In *Dornoch Ltd v Westminster International BV (No.2)* [2009] EWHC 1782 (Admlty), [2009] 2 Lloyd's Rep. 420, it was confirmed that as there was no evidence that a Thai court would do otherwise than apply Thai domestic law to the issue, the issue of renvoi required no further attention. In *Blue Sky One Ltd v Mahan Air* [2010] EWHC 631 (Comm.) (on which, see Knight (2010) 74 Conv. 61), the judge rejected (at [157] *et seq.*) any role for renvoi in the determination of the proprietary effect of a mortgage of an aircraft situated overseas. The balance of opinion at first instance is therefore that the choice of law rule for *inter vivos* transactions concerning movables is the *lex situs* without reference to renvoi.

NOTE 97. *Neilson v Overseas Projects Corp of Victoria Ltd* is now reported at (2005) 233 C.L.R. 331, and see entry at para.4–003, above. **4–033**

The opening sentence of this paragraph was approved in *Dornoch Ltd v Westminster International BV* [2009] EWHC 889 (Admlty), [2009] 2 Lloyd's Rep. 191 [88]. **4–034**

See also Hughes (2010) 6 J. Priv. Int. L. 195.

## Chapter 5

# THE EXCLUSION OF FOREIGN LAW

**5R–001** Note 1. Add: Mills (2008) 4 J. Priv. Int. L. 201

**5–009** Note 34. See also *Duarte v Black and Decker Corp* [2007] EWHC 2720 (QB), [2008] 1 All E.R. (Comm.) 401.

**5–010** See also *Westminster City Council v C* [2008] EWCA Civ 198, [2009] Fam. 11.

**5R–019** Note 84. See also *Pocket Kings Ltd v Safenames Ltd* [2009] EWHC 2529 (Ch.), [2010] 2 W.L.R. 1110.

Note 85. See also *Jamieson v Commissioner for Internal Revenue* [2007] NSWSC 324. For recent developments in the United States see *Attorney General of Canada v RJ Reynolds Tobacco Holdings, Inc*, 268 F.3d 103 (2d Cir. 2001) (RICO action by the Canadian Government against American and Canadian tobacco companies for damages based on lost revenues as a result of their participation in schemes to avoid taxes by smuggling cigarettes across the Canadian border: complaint was dismissed because the action was barred by the revenue rule); *Pasquantino v United States*, 544 U.S. 349 (2005) (conviction for federal wire fraud for scheme to smuggle alcohol into Canada from the United States: by a 5:4 majority, held that the conviction was not barred by revenue rule). *European Community v RJR Nabisco, Inc*, 424 F.3d 175 (2d Cir. 2005), cert. den 546 U.S. 1092 (2006) (RICO action by the European Community, Member States, and Colombia against tobacco manufacturers barred by revenue rule notwithstanding decision of the U.S. Supreme Court in *Pasquantino v United States*, *ante*).

Note 86. See also *Equatorial Guinea v Bank of Scotland International* [2006] UKPC 7; *Mbasogo v Logo Ltd* [2006] EWCA Civ 1370, [2007] Q.B. 846; *Islamic Republic of Iran v Barakat Galleries Ltd* [2007] EWCA Civ 1374, [2009] Q.B. 22; *United States Securities and Exchange Commission v Manterfield* [2009] EWCA Civ 27, [2009] 2 All E.R. 1009.

**5–021** Note 1. See also *Tasarruf Mevduati Sigorta Fonu v Demirel* [2006] EWHC 3354 (Ch.), [2007] 2 All E.R. 815, affirmed on other grounds: [2007] EWCA Civ 799, [2007] 1 W.L.R. 2508.

**5–026** Note 19. See *Islamic Republic of Iran v Barakat Galleries Ltd* [2007] EWCA Civ 1374, [2009] Q.B. 22, at [141] *et seq.* for discussion of these cases and for the conclusion that they are authority for the proposition that the court will recognise the title of the State to property in England held by revolutionaries or former governments, but do not touch on the question whether the property must have been reduced into possession by the foreign State. See also entry at para. 5–040, below.

See generally Collins (2007) 326 *Recueil des Cours* 11. **5–032—5–040**

NOTE 75. In *United States v Yemec* 2010 ONCA 414 the Ontario Court of Appeal enforced a United States federal judgment for $19 million arising out of the illegal cross-border telemarketing of Canadian and foreign lottery tickets to consumers in the United States. **5–038**

In March 2004 Zimbabwean police in Harare impounded a plane from South Africa with 64 alleged mercenaries on board, including Mr Simon Mann. The Government of Equatorial Guinea claimed that the individuals arrested were involved in an attempt to overthrow the Government by means of a privately hired force of mercenaries armed with weapons and to seize control of the State and its assets, in particular its substantial oil and gas reserves, to kill, severely injure or abduct the President, and to install Mr Severo Moto, who was in exile in Spain, as President. The Government alleged that this was pursuant to a conspiracy plotted and financed in England and elsewhere. The President of Equatorial Guinea then sued Simon Mann and his companies in England for damage caused by the unsuccessful attempt at revolution, and obtained orders in Guernsey for a bank to give information about the ownership of various companies and bank accounts which the Government had traced. **5–040**

*Equatorial Guinea v Bank of Scotland International* [2006] UKPC 7 concerned attempts by the Government of Equatorial Guinea to obtain information about bank accounts in Guernsey said to be owned by Simon Mann, in support of proceedings in England. The Government applied without notice to the Royal Court of Guernsey for an order requiring a bank in Guernsey to supply information and documents concerning the beneficial ownership of the accounts; and documents identifying incoming and outgoing transactions on bank accounts in the names of the interveners, Simon Mann and another individual.

The application was granted, and the Guernsey court gave the Government permission to use the information supplied to them to pursue others in Guernsey, Equatorial Guinea, Spain, Jersey, and England and Wales, in any civil actions but not in criminal proceedings. The Government gave an undertaking to use the information only for the purposes of civil legal action in the jurisdictions mentioned and specifically not to use it in any criminal proceedings.

The Privy Council, sitting on appeal from the Court of Appeal of Guernsey, decided that the order should be upheld, despite an argument by the interveners that disclosure should not be ordered in favour of the Government because the English court could not control the use made of it. But the Privy Council (in an opinion written by Lord Bingham and Lord Hoffmann) expressed disquiet at the fact that no argument was addressed, whether to the courts in Guernsey or to the Privy Council, on the question whether the Guernsey court lacked jurisdiction to make the order which it did on the ground that it could be regarded as the enforcement, direct or indirect, of the public law of a foreign State.

It was arguable that the claims which the Government said it wished to make in the English proceedings represented an exercise of sovereign authority, namely the preservation of the security of the State and its ruler. The apprehension and trial of suspects, the imposition of security measures, obtaining diplomatic assistance: these heads of damage alleged by in the English proceedings could all be regarded as aspects of sovereign authority. The Privy Council referred to what the High Court of Australia had said in *Att-Gen (United Kingdom) v Heinemann Publishers Australia Pty Ltd* (1988) 165 C.L.R. 30, at [46], namely that the application of the rule depends upon whether the "central interest" of the State bringing the action is governmental in nature. In that case the court held that notwithstanding the private law character of the cause of action (confidentiality) and the relief sought (an injunction), the claim arose out of "an exercise of the prerogative of the Crown, that exercise being the maintenance of the national security".

The Government had argued that its claims were personal and proprietary, involving threats to the safety of the President and the property of the State as well as the expense of suppressing a coup. But there could be few revolutions which were guaranteed not to cause any injury or damage or that could be suppressed without putting the ruling power to expense. It might therefore be that the question was not whether the claim was framed by reference to personal injury or damage to property but whether the "central interest" of the State in bringing the action was governmental in nature. Because of its doubts about the justiciability of the claim, and since the same questions in relation to English law were likely to come before the English Court of Appeal, the Privy Council decided that the order should be suspended until the Court of Appeal had decided whether the Government had a cause of action enforceable in English law. *Mbasogo v Logo Ltd* [2006] EWCA Civ 1370, [2007] Q.B. 846 was the decision of the English Court of Appeal anticipated by the Privy Council. The first claimant was the President of Equatorial Guinea, and the second claimant was the Republic of Equatorial Guinea. It was held that the critical question was whether in bringing a claim, the claimant was doing an act which was of a sovereign character or which was done by virtue of sovereign authority; and whether the claim involved the exercise or assertion of a sovereign right.

The appeal could be resolved without adopting the "governmental interest" approach enunciated by the majority of the High Court of Australia in *Att-Gen (United Kingdom) v Heinemann Publishers Australia Pty Ltd* (1988) 165 C.L.R. 30, and accordingly, it was not necessary to express a view as to whether that decision would be correct as a matter of English law. The mere fact that the claimants were the President and the Republic of Equatorial Guinea was not sufficient to make the claims non-justiciable. If the alleged coup had been successful and damage had been caused to buildings or other property owned by the claimants, a claim in tort to recover damages would have been justiciable in the English courts. In bringing such a claim, the claimants would not have been exercising or asserting sovereign authority or seeking relief to vindicate an act which might only be done by a sovereign in the capacity of sovereign. They would have been exercising the right of any person to bring private law proceedings to recover damages for loss suffered as a result of a civil wrong. Such a claim would have arisen solely from the fact that the claimants were owners of property that had been damaged by torts committed by the defendants. The claim would be a "patrimonial claim".

It was necessary to look at all the circumstances to see whether in substance the losses which were the subject of the claim had been suffered by virtue of an exercise of sovereign authority. If the losses had in truth been suffered as a result of the claimants' ownership of property, then the fact that the claimants were a foreign State and its President would not render their claims non-justiciable. But the claims which were pleaded were not founded on the claimants' property interests. The alleged losses arose as a result of decisions taken by the claimants to protect the State and citizens of Equatorial Guinea. The defence of a State and its subjects was a paradigm function of government. The special damages claimed by both claimants were in respect of losses incurred as a direct result of their response to the alleged conspiracy. They were: (i) costs incurred in investigating the conspiracy and attending meetings to discuss issues of national security; (ii) costs incurred in the detention of suspects; (iii) costs incurred in the prosecution of suspects; (iv) damage to the Republic's commercial interests and infrastructure as a result of the declaration of a state of emergency and security checks carried out on foreign nationals leading to economic disruption and delay; and (v) costs of increased security. It was impossible to characterise these heads of loss as property losses. With one possible exception, they were losses which could only be suffered by the governing body of the State. They arose as a direct result of the government's decisions as to how to respond to the conspiracy and (subject to the possible exception) were of a kind that could not be suffered by anyone else.

The possible exception was the allegation that, as a result of the defendants' actions, projects for roads and other civil engineering works were delayed by reason of the exodus of foreign nationals in the wake of the coup. But it was artificial to describe these losses as property losses caused by the defendants' actions and treat them as if they were similar in kind to, for example, the cost of repairing a government building damaged in the course of a coup. It was clear that it was not the defendants' action alone which caused the foreign nationals to leave. It was the claimants' declaration of a state of emergency and the security checks carried out by the Republic which affected the willingness and ability of foreign nationals to continue working in Equatorial Guinea.

If the claim were held to be justiciable it was likely that the defendants would seek to persuade the court to refuse relief on the grounds of the claimants' behaviour in responding to the alleged attempted coup. As the Privy Council said, to refuse relief on such grounds to the government of a State with which the United Kingdom had friendly diplomatic relations would be invidious. The court would be asked to decide whether some or all of the steps taken by the claimants were reasonable. That too could involve the court in making difficult judgments which it would be invidious to expect it to make, for example whether: the investigation into the alleged conspiracy was reasonably undertaken and the costs of doing so were reasonable; it was reasonable to detain all or any of the suspects, the cost of whose detention was claimed; the costs of the prosecution were reasonably incurred; it was reasonably necessary to declare and maintain the state of emergency which resulted in the alleged losses; it was reasonable to incur the costs of increased security. The claim was therefore not justiciable.

The House of Lords gave leave to appeal, and heard the appeal in part, but the appeal was subsequently withdrawn.

The decisions are noted by Dickinson (2006) 122 L.Q.R. 569; Briggs (2006) 77 B.Y.I.L. 554; Briggs (2007) 123 L.Q.R. 182; Mills [2007] C.L.J. 3; Scott [2007] L.M.C.L.Q. 296.

Contrast *Tasarruf Mevduati Sigorta Fonu v Demirel* [2006] EWHC 3354 (Ch.), [2007] 2 All E.R. 815 (affirmed on other grounds [2007] EWCA Civ 799), [2007] 1 W.L.R. 2508: claim by State-owned bank as successor to private banks was not a public law claim.

In *Islamic Republic of Iran v Barakat Galleries Ltd* [2007] EWCA Civ 1374, [2009] Q.B. 22 (noted Rushworth [2008] L.M.C.L.Q. 123, Rogerson [2008] C.L.J. 246; Briggs (2007) 78 B.Y.I.L. 628; Whomersly (2009) 125 L.Q.R. 227) the Court of Appeal decided, on preliminary issues, that Iran was not debarred by the penal law/public law rule from recovering ancient artefacts allegedly exported from Iran and belonging to the Iranian State, even though it was not claimed that the artefacts had been reduced into the possession of the State prior to export.

The fact that the law on the basis of which Iran claimed title created criminal offences with criminal penalties for unlawfully excavating or dealing with antiquities did not render penal all the other provisions of the law. The law altered the law as to the ownership of antiquities that had not yet been found, with the effect that these would all be owned by the State, subject to the entitlement of the chance finder to a reward. These were not penal provisions, and the claim did not fail on that ground: at [111].

On the enforcement of foreign public law the Court of Appeal said (at [123]) that the *Equatorial Guinea* case in the Court of Appeal was not in fact a case involving the attempted enforcement of foreign public law. Although the Court of Appeal in that case approved the residual category of "other public law" the ratio was that a claim involving the exercise or assertion of a sovereign right was not justiciable. That was not far removed from the test adopted by the High Court of Australia in the *Spycatcher* case. Nor was it far removed from the approach in civil law countries: *Duvalier v Etat haitien*, Cour de cassation, France, 1990, in 1991 *Clunet* 137.

The Court of Appeal said (at [125]) that the only category outside penal and revenue laws which was the subject of an actual decision, as opposed to dicta, was a claim which involves the exercise or assertion of a sovereign right. There was no decision which bound the court to find that there was a rule which prevented the enforcement of all foreign public laws. The test laid down by the High Court of Australia was not only consistent with the English authorities, including the *Equatorial Guinea* case in the Court of Appeal, but was a helpful and practical test.

The claim was not an attempt to enforce export restrictions, but to assert rights of ownership. The claim was maintainable even though Iran had not taken possession of the objects. Where the foreign State had acquired title under its law to property within its jurisdiction in cases not involving compulsory acquisition of title from private parties, there was no reason in principle why the English court should not recognise its title in accordance with the general principle that the *lex situs* governed. When a State owned property in the same way as a private citizen there was no impediment to recovery.

Where the foreign State has sought to confiscate or attach private property, the State's title will only be recognised in England if it has reduced the property into its possession. The distinction between the two categories of cases those where the foreign State will be able to claim its property in England even if it has not reduced it into its possession, and those where it may not claim unless it has reduced the property into its possession, depends on the way in which it has acquired ownership. If it has acquired title under public law by confiscation or compulsory process from the former owner, then it will not be able to claim the property in England from the former owner or his successors in title unless it has had possession. If it has taken the property into its possession, then its claim will be treated as depending on recognition; if it has not had possession it will be seeking to exercise its sovereign authority.

In that case Iran did not assert a claim based on its compulsory acquisition from private owners. It asserted a claim based upon title to antiquities which form part of Iran's national heritage. It was a patrimonial claim, not a claim to enforce a public law or to assert sovereign rights. It was not within the category of case where recognition of title or the right to possess under the foreign law depended on the State having taken possession.

In addition, the Court of Appeal said *obiter* that, even the claim were for enforcement of foreign public law, it was not precluded because there were positive reasons of policy why a claim by a State to recover antiquities which formed part of its national heritage and which otherwise complied with the requirements of private international law should not be shut out by the general principle. It was contrary to public policy for such claims to be shut out. There was international recognition that States should assist one another to prevent the unlawful removal of cultural objects including antiquities. There were a number of international instruments which had, in part, the purpose of preventing unlawful dealing in property which was part of the cultural heritage of States, although there still remains a question about their effectiveness. The United Kingdom is party to some of them, including the UNESCO Convention on the Means of Prohibiting and Preventing the Illicit Import, Export and Transfer of Ownership of Cultural Property of 1970; Council Directive 93/7 on the Return of Cultural Objects Unlawfully Removed from the Territory of a Member State, implemented by SI 1994/501, as amended.

See also *Brunei Investment Agency v Fidelis Nominees Ltd* [2008] JRC 152 (Royal Court, Jersey).

In *United States Securities and Exchange Commission v Manterfield* [2009] EWCA Civ 27, [2009] 2 All E.R. 1009 the the SEC had brought proceedings in the United States District Court in Massachusetts, alleging that the defendants, Manterfield and Anderson, fraudulently induced over 60 Taiwanese investors to invest approximately $34 million in a fund, and that they misappropriated millions of dollars, withdrawing $8 million of which it was alleged Manterfield received $2.35 million. The SEC made an application to the English court for interim freezing orders in support of their proceedings in Massachusetts, relying on s.25(1) of the Civil Jurisdiction and Judgments Act 1982, which gives the English court the power to grant interim relief in support of proceedings in foreign countries. It was argued on behalf of Manterfield that the SEC's action in Massachusetts was seeking to enforce a penal law and that thus any judgment obtained in Massachusetts would be unenforceable in England; and that no freezing order should be made at the interim stage which had as its object the enforcement of the penal law of a foreign State. The Court of Appeal looked to see the nature of the relevant part of the judgment which the SEC was seeking in Massachusetts. If in reality that part of the judgment was, in substance, a claim for damages which in England might have been brought in a civil case, the fact that it was all part of a judgment in a criminal case would not bring it within Rule 3. The substance of what the SEC would seek to enforce (if they were to prevail in the action), and in relation to which they sought to preserve the assets, was the disgorgement of what they alleged to be the proceeds of fraud. They also intended to seek orders, which would provide for the proceeds to be returned to the investors. Such a judgment would not, if obtained, fall foul of Rule 3.

In *Pocket Kings Ltd v Safenames Ltd* [2009] EWHC 2529 (Ch.), [2010] 2 W.L.R. 1110 the claimant had licensed the use of an internet domain name for online gaming purposes. The first defendant, an English company, was the registrar of that domain name. The Commonwealth of Kentucky brought a civil forfeiture claim in the Kentucky court against, inter alia, the claimant, alleging that the websites operated via the domain name were being used for illegal gambling in Kentucky, in contravention of local penal and public law, and seeking the penal forfeiture of the domain name. The Kentucky court held that the domain name was a gambling device within the meaning of Kentucky's criminal law and a seizure order was made requiring the domain name to be transferred by the first defendant to an account of the Commonwealth of Kentucky. The claimant brought proceedings in England against the first defendant and the Commonwealth of Kentucky seeking an injunction restraining the first defendant from complying with the seizure order made in the Kentucky proceedings and a declaration that the court would not recognise or enforce the order, or any subsequent order for the seizure or forfeiture of the domain name, since to do so would amount to the exercise of the sovereign authority of the Commonwealth of Kentucky within the jurisdiction. It was held that a foreign order requiring the forfeiture of assets used in the commission of crime under local foreign law, even if categorised by the foreign state as a civil remedy under its law, was penal in nature, requiring the confiscation without compensation of an asset on the ground that the owner, or user of it, was guilty of a criminal offence; that the fact that the purpose of the forfeiture was ostensibly to protect the public rather than punish the wrongdoer did not alter the position; that penal and public acts which would not be enforceable by virtue of the rule prohibiting the court from enforcing a penal or public foreign law if they were the acts of a sovereign state would not be enforceable if undertaken by a government which was a constituent part of a sovereign state but which did not act by virtue of the authority of that state; and that, accordingly, the Kentucky order was not enforceable in English law since the proceedings were penal or governmental in nature.

On the British act of state doctrine see *Al Jedda v Secretary of State for Defence* [2010] EWCA Civ 758, at [108] *et seq. per* Arden L.J. and contrast [127] *per* Sir John Dyson and [192] *et seq. per* Elias L.J.; *Habib v Commonwealth of Australia* [2010] FCAFC 12; Perreau-Saussine (2007) 78 B.Y.I.L. 176. **5–041—5–042**

NOTE 84. See also *R. (on the application of Kibris Turk Hava Yollari) v Secretary of State for Transport* [2009] EWHC 1918 (Admin), [2010] 1 All ER (Comm.) 253; *Christian v R.* [2006] UKPC 47, [2007] 2 A.C. 400 (executive's statement that a territory is a British colony conclusive). **5–041**

NOTE 85. See also *R. (on the application of Al Rawi) v Secretary of State for Foreign Affairs* [2006] EWCA Civ 1279, [2008] Q.B. 289.

NOTE 98. See also *Empresa Nacional de Telecomunicaciones SA v Deutsche Bank AG* [2009] EWHC 2579 (QB), [2010] 1 All ER (Comm.) 649; *cf. Short v Ireland* [2006] 3 I.R. 297. **5–044**

NOTE 4. See also *Al Jedda v Secretary of State for Defence* [2010] EWCA Civ 758, [74], [186] *et seq.* **5–046**

NOTE 11. See Sim (2009) 10 Melbourne J. Int. L. 102 **5–049**

**5–050** *Empresa Nacional de Telecomunicaciones SA v Deutsche Bank AG* [2009] EWHC 2579 (QB), [2010] 1 All ER (Comm.) 649 concerned a Bolivian nationalisation decree which nationalised shares in a Bolivian company held by a Dutch company. The question was whether a bank holding money on behalf of the nationalised company was bound to act on its instructions. It was held that the public policy exception to the act of state doctrine existed within very narrow limits. It was concerned with violations of international law or with very grave breaches of fundamental universal human rights. Where a foreign state had compulsorily acquired property there was scope for a range of views as to which rights of the expropriated party were such that they ought to be recognised in a domestic court. It had not been established that there was a rule of international law, whether in the nature of a human right or otherwise, that in no circumstances could property be compulsorily acquired by a state without compensation, at least where there was no element of racial or religious discrimination involved. The decree, on its face, provided for compensation. Whether the decree was in conformity with the domestic law of Bolivia was not a matter upon which the court could investigate or pronounce. The decree plainly did not fall within the public policy exception. The allegation that compensation had yet to be paid did not found an arguable public policy exception to the act of state doctrine.

NOTE 13. *cf. R. (on the application of Gentle & Clarke) v Prime Minister* [2008] UKHL 20, [2008] A.C. 1356, at [25].

NOTE 14. See also *Re AY Bank Ltd: AY Bank Ltd v Bosnia* [2006] EWHC 830 (Ch.), [2006] 2 All E.R. (Comm.) 463; *Att-Gen of Zambia v Meer Care & Desai* [2008] EWCA Civ 1007; *Korea National Insurance Corp v Allianz Global Corporate and Speciality AG* [2008] EWCA Civ 1355, [2008] 2 C.L.C. 837; *Republic of Croatia v Republic of Serbia* [2009] EWHC 1559 (Ch.), [2010] Ch. 200; *Republic of Serbia v ImageSat International NV* [2009] EWHC 2853) (Comm.), [2010] 1 Lloyd's Rep. 324; *Habib v Commonwealth of Australia* [2010] FCAFC 12; *cf. Total v Edmonds* [2006] EWHC 1136 (Comm.); *Tajik Aluminium Plant v Ermatov* [2006] EWHC 2374 (Comm.); *Gamogab v Akiba* [2007] FCAFC 74. On *Republic of Ecuador v Occidental Exploration & Production Co* [2005] EWCA Civ 1116, which is now reported at [2006] Q.B. 432, see O'Keefe [2006] C.L.J. 259.

NOTE 15. See now *Jones v Ministry of Interior of Saudi Arabia* [2006] UKHL 26, [2007] 1 A.C. 270.

## CHAPTER 6

# DOMICILE AND RESIDENCE

### 1. GENERAL PRINCIPLES

NOTE 51. Income Tax (Trading and Other Income) Act 2005, s.636 is amended by the Income Tax Act 2007, Sch.1, Pt 2, paras 492, 558. Inheritance Tax Act 1984, s.48 is amended, adding another reference to domicile in the United Kingdom, by the Finance Act 2006, s.157. More recent, and rather varied references to an individual being, or not being domiciled in the United Kingdom include: Finance Act 2008, s.809A; Finance Act 2009, s.52; Human Fertilisation and Embryology Act 2008, s.54; Political Parties and Elections Act 2009, s.10. **6–015**

NOTE 61. Add: *Holliday v Musa* [2010] EWCA Civ 335, [2010] W.T.L.R. 839 (balance of probabilities test applied to acquisition of a domicile of choice). **6–019**

NOTE 64. Add: *Munro v Munro* [2007] EWHC 3315 (Fam.), [2007] 1 F.L.R. 1613.

### 2. ASCERTAINMENT OF DOMICILE

#### B. *Domicile of choice*

##### (1) ACQUISITION

The authorities are reviewed in *Henwood v Barlow Clowes International Ltd* [2008] EWCA Civ 577, [2008] B.P.I.R. 778. **6R–033**

The criticism in the text of *Plummer v IRC* [1988] 1 W.L.R. 292 was said in *Henwood v Barlow Clowes International Ltd* [2008] EWCA Civ 577, [2008] B.P.I.R. 778, at [103], to be unjustified. **6–035**

NOTE 1. Add: *Gaines-Cooper v Commissioners for HM Revenue & Customs* [2007] EWHC 2617 (Ch.), [2008] S.T.C. 1665.

NOTE 13. The case cited as *Jablonski* is in fact *Jablonowski v Jablonowski* (1972) 28 D.L.R. (3d) 440 (Ont.). **6–037**

NOTE 15. On *Mark v Mark,* see Rogerson [2006] C.L.J. 35.

**6–040** NOTE 27. Add: *Holliday v Musa* [2010] EWCA Civ 335, [2010] W.T.L.R. 839 (expressed intention to retire to Cyprus was of the vague variety).

**6R–046** As Mummery L.J. observed in *Cyganik v Agulian* [2006] EWCA Civ 129, [2006] 1 F.C.R. 406, at [46], "the court must look back at the whole of the deceased's life, at what he had done with his life, at what life had done to him and at what were his inferred intentions in order to decide whether he had acquired a domicile of choice in England by [a particular date]. Soren Kierkegaard's aphorism that 'Life must be lived forwards, but can only be understood backwards' resonates in the biographical data of domicile disputes".

**6–049** NOTE 64. Add: *Holliday v Musa* [2010] EWCA Civ 335, [2010] W.T.L.R. 839, (long residence in England—48 years—was held by Waller L.J. to be a starting point); *Re Haji-Ioannou, Haji-Iannou v Frangos* [2009] EWHC 2310 (QB), [2010] 1 All E.R. (Comm.) 303 (lengthy uninterrupted residence may provide some evidence of the intentions of an individual as to domicile).

NOTE 84. Add: *R v R (Divorce: Jurisdiction: Domicile)* [2006] 1 F.L.R. 389 (failure to acquire residence or work permit or integrate into local society).

NOTE 93. Add: *F v F (Divorce: Jurisdiction)* [2009] EWHC 1448 (Fam.), [2009] 2 F.L.R. 1496.

**6–050** NOTE 3. Add: *F v F (Divorce: Jurisdiction)* [2009] EWHC 1448 (Fam.), [2009] 2 F.L.R. 1496.

**6–051** This paragraph was quoted with approval in *Henwood v Barlow Clowes International Ltd* [2008] EWCA Civ 577, [2008] B.P.I.R. 778, at [19].

NOTE 6. Add: *H v H (Validity of Japanese Divorce)* [2006] EWHC 2989 (Fam.), [2007] 1 F.L.R. 1318; *Holliday v Musa* [2010] EWCA Civ 335, [2010] W.T.L.R. 839 (declarations to the Inland Revenue by the *propositus* were to be treated with some caution).

NOTE 10. Add: In *F v F (Divorce: Jurisdiction)* [2009] EWHC 1448 (Fam.), [2009] 2 F.L.R. 1496, this was the case even though elements of the person's evidence were deemed to have been inaccurate and exaggerated.

NOTE 12. Add: *Kearly v Kearly* [2009] EWHC 1876 (Fam.), [2010] 1 F.L.R. 619.

**6–052** See *Cyganik v Agulian* [2006] EWCA Civ 129, [2006] 1 F.C.R. 406, and para.6R–046 above.

**6–054** NOTE 19. Add: *Re Haji-Ioannou, Haji-Iannou v Frangos* [2009] EWHC 2310 (QB), [2010] 1 All E.R. (Comm.) 303.

NOTE 46. *Cyganik v Agulian* is now reported at [2006] 1 F.C.R. 405. See McEleavy (2007) 56 I.C.L.Q. 453. **6–061**

NOTE 48. Add: *F v F (Divorce: Jurisdiction)* [2009] EWHC 1448 (Fam.), [2009] 2 F.L.R. 1496.

NOTE 59. Add: *Re Haji-Ioannou, Haji-Iannou v Frangos* [2009] EWHC 2310 (QB), [2010] 1 All E.R. (Comm.) 303 (residence in Greece for medical treatment); *Foote Estate (Re)*, 2009 ABQB 654 (residence in Alberta for medical treatment). **6–062**

This paragraph was quoted with approval in *Henwood v Barlow Clowes International Ltd* [2008] EWCA Civ 577, [2008] B.P.I.R. 778, at [20]. **6–076**

NOTE 10. Add: In a more recent decision from Alberta, *Foote Estate (Re)*, 2009 ABQB 654, [97], it was held that a common law judge had a residual authority to depart from the revival principle and find that a person had retained their last domicile of choice. **6–077**

C. *Domicile of dependency*

In Scotland the domicile of persons under 16 is now governed by the Family Law (Scotland) Act 2006, s.22 of which contains rules similar to those outlined in para.6–096 of the main work. **6E–098**

Many provisions of the Mental Capacity Act 2005 are now in force; they are noted in the entries below. **6–107**

See the comment on this paragraph by Thorpe L.J. in *Westminster City Council v C* [2008] EWCA Civ 198, [2009] Fam. 11, at [14]–[15]. **6–108**

NOTES 83, 85 and 86. The cited provisions of the Mental Capacity Act 2005 are now in force.

NOTE 93. The cited provisions of the Mental Capacity Act 2005 are now in force. **6–114**

Residence at a house for approximately fifty days a year was sufficient for that place to constitute a "usual residence" for the purposes of service under CPR, r.6.9(2): *Varsani v Relfo Limited (in liquidation)* [2010] EWCA Civ 560, [2010] 3 All E.R. 1045. Regard must be paid to the nature or quality of the use of the premises, which in the latter case were occupied permanently by the defendant's family. *Cf. Cherney v Deripaska* [2007] EWHC 965 (Comm.), [2007] 2 All E.R. (Comm.) 785, where the quality of residence of a Russian oligarch at his London property was "intermittent and generally fleeting". See also: *OJSC Oil Company Yugraneft (in liquidation) v Abramovich* [2008] EWHC 2613 (Comm.). **6–118**

## 3. RESIDENCE

6–119 A summary of the relevant features to be considered, provided in *Revenue and Customs Commissioners v Grace* [2008] EWHC 2708 (Ch.), [2009] S.T.C. 213, [3], was subsequently accepted by the Court of Appeal: *Grace v Commissioners for Her Majesty's Revenue & Customs* [2009] EWCA Civ 1082, [2009] S.T.C. 2707, [6].

NOTE 8. Add: As regards HMRC guidance see *R. (on the application of Davies) v Commissioners for Her Majesty's Revenue & Customs* [2010] EWCA Civ 83, [2010] S.T.C. 860.

6–120 NOTE 15. Add: *R v Secretary of State for Health* [2009] EWCA Civ 225, [2010] 1 W.L.R. 279 (entitlement to free NHS treatment).

6–121 NOTE 16. Income and Corporation Taxes Act 1988, s.334 is repealed and replaced by the Income Tax Act 2007, s.829. Add: *Shepherd v Revenue and Customs Commissioners* [2006] EWHC 1512 (Ch.), [2006] S.T.C. 1821.

6–123 In *Blair v Chung* (2006) 271 D.L.R. (4th) 311 (Alta.), the court was prepared to accept that an illegal resident could be said to be ordinarily resident for the purposes of divorce jurisdiction (though noting the divergence of authority in Canadian case law: *Bednar v Deputy Registrar of Vital Statistics* (1960) 24 D.L.R. (2d) 238 (Alta.); *Jablonowski v Jablonowski* (1972) 28 D.L.R. (3d) 440 (Ont.)); but it went on to refuse a divorce on public policy grounds related to immigration policy.

Add after note 26: whilst an asylum seeker cannot be ordinarily resident for the purposes of free NHS treatment,

6–125 For the autonomous meaning of habitual residence for the purposes of Council Regulation 2201/2003 (Brussels II *bis*), see the entry at para.18–003, and at para.19–031.

6–126 NOTE 39. Add: *Greenwich London Borough Council v S* [2007] EWHC 820 (Fam.), [2007] 2 F.L.R. 154 (where both concepts relevant).

NOTE 39. Add: *cf. Punter v Secretary for Justice* [2007] 1 N.Z.L.R. 40 (CA).

Text to notes 42 and 43. In *Re A (Abduction: Consent: Habitual Residence: Consent)* [2005] EWHC 2998 (Fam.), [2006] 2 F.L.R. 1, Sumner J. said that provided the stay is lawful, immigration status is unlikely to be of significance if there is residence for the necessary period with the required intent.

NOTE 43. Add: *Mendoza v Miranda (In re B del C S B)*, 559 F.3d 999 (9th Cir. 2009), (illegal immigrant acquired habitual residence in California); *cf. R v*

*Secretary of State for Health* [2009] EWCA Civ 225, [2010] 1 W.L.R. 279 (failed asylum seeker was deemed not to have become ordinarily resident in England).

NOTE 47. Add: Whilst this permanent or habitual centre of interests assessment of habitual residence has been held to apply to the matrimonial jurisdiction rules in Council Regulation 2201/2003 (*L-K v K (No.2)* [2006] EWHC 3280 (Fam.), [2007] 2 F.L.R. 729; *Marinos v Marinos* [2007] EWHC 2047 (Fam.); [2007] 2 F.L.R. 1018; *Z v Z (Divorce: Jurisdiction)* [2009] EWHC 2626 (Fam.), [2010] 1 F.L.R. 694; *Williamson v Williamson*, 2009 Fam. L.R. 44 (not challenged on appeal, 2010 S.L.T. (Sh Ct) 41); see above at para.18–003), the European Court has ruled that as regards the parental responsibility rules of the latter instrument it is the child's actual centre of interest which is determinative: Case C–523/07 *Proceedings Brought by A* [2009] E.C.R. I–2805. In this physical presence must be combined with factors which reflect some degree of integration in a social and family environment. **6–127**

Text to note 48. So, it is not possible for a person to acquire an habitual residence in one country while remaining physically in another: *Re A (Wardship: Habitual Residence)* [2006] EWHC 3338 (Fam.), [2007] 1 F.L.R. 1589.

NOTE 49. Add: Under the autonomous Community interpretation of the concept, immediate acquisition is possible: Case C–90/97 *Swaddling v Adjudication Officer* [1999] E.C.R. 1–1075; *Marinos v Marinos* [2007] EWHC 2047 (Fam.); [2007] 2 F.L.R. 1018.

Text to notes 49–50. A period of seven or eight days was held to be too short a period within which to acquire habitual residence in *Re A (Abduction: Habitual Residence)* [2007] EWHC 779 (Fam.), [2007] 2 F.L.R. 129.

NOTE 50. Add: *D v D*, 2002 SC 33 (6 weeks insufficient). Where the right of free movement is being exercised within the European Union, even where the purpose is temporary in nature and a home is maintained elsewhere, a habitual residence may be acquired after a relatively short period of time: *Re S (A Child) (Habitual Residence)* [2009] EWCA Civ 1021, [2010] 1 F.L.R. 1146 (7–8 weeks, in respect of an abducted child).

Material from this paragraph was cited with approval in *Punter v Secretary of* Justice [2007] 1 N.Z.L.R. 40 (CA). **6–128**

In *P v P* [2006] EWHC 2410 (Fam.) [2007] 2 F.L.R. 439 it was held that a woman who had been in Nepal for 15 months nonetheless retained her habitual residence in England, because she went there with a settled intent to return and was prevented from putting that intention into effect by illness and the removal of her passport by her husband. *Sed quaere*: this use of an intent to return seems more appropriate to domicile than habitual residence.

NOTE 52. Add: *LK v Director-General, Dept of Community Services* [2009] HCA 9, (2009) 253 A.L.R. 202.

**6–129** For the unusual case in which a child is born to parents then habitually resident in different countries, see *Re G (Abduction: Withdrawal of Proceedings: Acquiescence: Habitual Residence)* [2007] EWHC 2807 (Fam.), [2008] 2 F.L.R. 351.

NOTE 57. A child who had never lived in England was held not to be habitually resident there in *Re F (Abduction: Unborn Child)* [2006] EWHC 2199 (Fam.), [2007] 1 F.L.R. 627, where it was said that *B v H (Habitual Residence: Wardship)* [2002] 1 F.L.R. 388 was not to be taken as having laid down a principle to be followed. *cf.* the assertion, without full reasoning, in *S(PA) v S(AF)* [2004] IEHC 323, [2005] 1 I.L.R.M. 306, para.8.6, that "the habitual residence of a child is that of its parents and that, accordingly, children born abroad are deemed habitually resident in the jurisdiction of their parents". In *Re KJB and LRB (Adoption)* [2010] N.Z.F.L.R. 97 the child was held to have the habitual residence of the commissioning parents, who had cared for him since birth (New South Wales), even though he had been born in New Zealand and had lived nowhere else.

Text to note 58. This principle was extended in *Greenwich London Borough Council v S* [2007] EWHC 820 (Fam.), [2007] 2 F.L.R. 154. Children in the care of the local authority were allowed to go to Canada to live with their great aunt who was approved as their long-term foster-parent. They had lived in Canada for a year, with two short visits to England during that time. It was held that they remained habitually resident in England for the purposes of reg.50 of the Adoptions with a Foreign Element Regulations 2005 on the ground that the great aunt had never had parental responsibility for them and that their residence in Canada had always been at the behest of the local authority. That was held to be determinative. It is submitted that this is too strong a proposition: as the residence in Canada was with the consent of all concerned, the facts should have been allowed to govern, not questions of parental responsibility.

NOTE 61. Add: *A v N* [2007] Fam.L.R. 43 (O.H.).

NOTE 62. In *P v P* [2006] EWHC 2410 (Fam.), [2007] 2 F.L.R. 439 and *B v D (Abduction: Inherent Jurisdiction)* [2008] EWHC 1246 (Fam.), [2009] 1 F.L.R. 1015 residence abroad for the purposes of education did not lead to a change in habitual residence. Moreover in neither case was the mother aware of the father's underlying motives. However, where children were sent abroad to stay with relatives on an open ended basis, the parents remaining behind, the children were deemed to have acquired a habitual residence in the new jurisdiction after eighteen months. Contrasting the case with the traditional boarding school example, Sir Nicholas Wall P. relied on the fact the parents no longer shared a common intention as to the future care of the children: *ES v AJ* [2010] EWHC 1113 (Fam.), [2010] Fam. Law 786. Where a child is being voluntarily accommodated by a local authority under s. 20 of the Children Act 1989 and the parents decide to send him out of the jurisdiction with a relative, he will not imediately lose his English habitual residence; unreported decision of McFarlane J., May 21, 2010, followed by the Irish High Court in: *Coventry City Council* v *S* [2010] IEHC 303.

Text to note 63. In the case of the habitual residence of a child, even if the parents are agreed (or where one parent has accepted a decision made by the other) the legal focus is upon the factual position: *Re A (Abduction: Habitual Residence)* [2006] EWHC 3338 (Fam.), [2007] 2 F.L.R. 129.

The consequences flowing from time limited moves are more difficult to predict. Whilst a move of three months will not lead to a change: *Re C (A Child)* [2010] EWCA Civ 832, a move of six months may suffice to lead to a change in habitual residence: *Re R (Abduction: Habitual Residence)* [2003] EWHC 1968 (Fam.), [2004] 1 F.L.R. 216; *Cameron* v *Cameron*, 1996 S.C. 17; but equally stays of much longer duration have been held not to interrupt an existing habitual residence: *Re P-J (Children) (Abduction: Habitual Residence: Consent)* [2009] EWCA Civ 588, [2010] 1 W.L.R. 1237 ($11\frac{1}{2}$ months); *Re H. (Abduction: Habitual Residence: Consent)* [2000] 2 F.L.R. 294 (12 months, albeit in two locations). *cf.* the suggestions of Charles J. in *D v S (Abduction: Acquiescence)* [2008] EWHC 363 (Fam.), [2008] 2 F.L.R. 293.

NOTE 63. Add: *Re Z (Abduction)* [2008] 3473 (Fam.), [2009] 2 F.L.R. 298.

NOTE 64. Add: *Al Habtoor v Fotheringham* [2001] EWCA Civ 186, [2001] 1 **6–130**
F.L.R. 951; *D v D*, 2002 S.C. 33; *SK v KP* [2005] 3 N.Z.L.R. 590; *LK v Director-General, Dept of Community Services* [2009] HCA 9, (2009) 253 A.L.R. 202.

NOTE 68. Add: However, the principle that abandonment is ordinarily a central element in the acquisition of a new habitual residence has been endorsed by several Federal Courts of Appeals in the United States: *Mozes v Mozes*, 239 F.3d 1067 (9th Cir. 2001); *Gitter v Gitter*, 396 F.3d 124, 129–30 (2nd Cir. 2005); *Koch v Koch*, 450 F.3d 703 (7th Cir. 2006); *Ruiz v Tenorio*, 392 F.3d 1247, 1253 (11th Cir. 2004); *Maxwell* v *Maxwell*, 588 F.3d 245 (4th Cir. 2009). Effect may equally be given to agreements purporting to regulate habitual residence: *Vale v Avila*, 538 F.3d 581 (7th Cir. 2008). *Cf. Barzilay* v *Barzilay*, 600 F.3d 912 (8th Cir. 2010).

## Chapter 7

# SUBSTANCE AND PROCEDURE

**7–003** Note 4. See *Harding v Wealands* [2006] UKHL 32, [2007] 2 A.C. 1, where the House of Lords affirmed this distinction, albeit without specific reference to this paragraph.

Note 8. But see *Harding v Wealands* [2006] UKHL 32, [2007] 2 A.C. 1, discussed below, entry at para.7–043.

Note 10. But rules on the conduct of the parties prior to the instigation of proceedings are nonetheless procedural within the meaning of the *John Pfeiffer* test, since the rights and duties of the parties are unaffected: *Hamilton v Merck & Co Inc* [2006] NSWCA 55, (2006) 230 A.L.R. 156, (2006) 66 N.S.W.L.R. 48. See also *Hodgson v Dimbola Pty Ltd* [2009] ACTSC 59, at [24]; *Kok v Sheppard* [2009] NSWSC 1262, at [35]–[43]; *RACQ Insurance Ltd v Wilkins* [2009] QSC 365.

**7–004** Note 16. But this statement must now be viewed in the light of the decision of the House of Lords in *Harding v Wealands* [2006] UKHL 32, [2007] 2 A.C. 1, considered below, entry at para.7–043, where all matters of quantification of damages were regarded as procedural.

**7–005** The Rome Convention is superseded by the Rome I Regulation (Regulation (EC) 593/2008 of the European Parliament and of the Council on the law applicable to contractual obligations (Rome I): [2008] O.J. L177/6 (with *corrigendum* [2009] O.J. L307/87); reproduced in Appendix 2 of this supplement) and applies to contracts concluded on or after December 17, 2009. On the Rome I Regulation and the position of the United Kingdom, see entry at para.32–013, below.

**7–006** On the difficulty of distinguishing between rights and remedies, see the decision of the Queen's Bench for Saskatchewan in *Chrysler Financial Canada v Morris*, 2009 SKQB 510, at [122]–[123] and [140]–[143].

Note 20. *Harding v Wealands* [2006] UKHL 32, [2007] 2 A.C. 1.

**7–009** The law applicable to the contract is determined in the Rome I Regulation (entry at para.7–005, above) by Arts 3–8 and 14. The provision equivalent to Art.10(1)(c) of the Rome Convention is contained in Art.12(1)(c) of the

Regulation, which makes clear that that it applies both to the total and partial breach of obligations.

The Rome II Regulation (Regulation (EC) 864/2007 of the European Parliament and of the Council on the Law Applicable to Non-Contractual Obligations: [2007] O.J. L199/40), which entered into force on January 11, 2009, altered the law in respect of such obligations. Article 15 subjects the question of remedies to the *lex causae*. See entry at para.7–044, below.

On the impact of the Rome I and Rome II Regulations on the dichotomy between substance and procedure, see Illmer (2009) 28 C.J.Q. 237; see also Briggs (2009) 125 L.Q.R. 191, at 195. On the application of the distinction between substance and procedure to the Rome II Regulation, see Schoeman [2010] L.M.C.L.Q. 81.

Second paragraph. The same approach should be adopted where a constructive trust is imposed pursuant to the breach of a non-contractual obligation under the Rome II Regulation (entry at para.7–009, above). See further entries at paras 29–063 and 34–044, below. **7–010**

In *Gersec Pty Ltd v Sultan of Brunei* [2008] NSWCA 211, the New South Wales Court of Appeal had to consider the effect of an immunity from suit conferred on the Sultan by the Constitution of Brunei. The law of Brunei was the *lex causae*. Curiously, the court approached the matter not by considering the law on jurisdictional immunity before New South Wales courts but rather in terms of the distinction between substance and procedure. It held that the immunity was a substantive provision of the law of Brunei, with the effect that it was to be applied on the facts in the courts of New South Wales. **7–011**

On the proper parties to an action in the context of whether a direct action may be brought by an injured party in a road accident against the insurer of the allegedly negligent driver, see *Maher v Groupama Grand Est* [2009] EWCA Civ 1191, [2010] 1 W.L.R. 1564. **7–012**

See also *OJSC Oil Co Yugraneft v Abramovich* [2008] EWHC 2613 (Comm.), at [298]. **7–014**

The Rome II Regulation (entry at para.7–009, above) applies the governing law of the non-contractual obligation to determine: persons who may be held liable for acts performed by them (Art.15(a)); whether a right to claim damages or a remedy may be transferred, including by inheritance (Art.15(e)); persons entitled to compensation for damage sustained personally (Art.15(f)); and the liability for the acts of another person (Art.15(g)). See further Hay (2007) 4 Eu. L.F. 137; Beaumont and Tang (2008) 12 Edin. L.Rev. 131.

Note 69. The provision corresponding to Art.14(2) of the Rome Convention in the Rome I Regulation (entry at para.7–005, above) is Art.18(2). The rules **7–016** on formal validity are contained in Art.11 and are more liberal than those in Art.9 of the Rome Convention.

**7–018** Penultimate sentence. The provision corresponding to Art.14(2) in the Rome I Regulation (entry at para.7–005, above) is Art.18(2).

NOTE 76. The provision corresponding to Art.10(1)(a) of the Rome Convention in the Rome I Regulation (entry at para.7–005, above) is Art.12(1)(a).

**7–020** Final sentence. See entry at para.7–018, above.

**7–021** In *Tipperary Developments Pty Ltd v The State of Western Australia* [2009] WASCA 126, (2009) 258 A.L.R. 124, the Western Australian Court of Appeal held that the statute of frauds was to be treated as substantive and that, following the decision in *John Pfeiffer Pty Ltd v Rogerson* (2000) 203 C.L.R. 503, the ruling in *Leroux v Brown* (1852) 12 C.B. 801 no longer represented the law in Australia. However, as the proper law of the contract was Western Australian law, it made no difference on the facts.

**7–027** NOTE 3. In *Dawson v Broughton* (2007) 151 So. J. 1167 it was held in the Manchester County Court that the defence of contributory negligence to a claim in tort should be classified as substantive.

**7–028** The provision corresponding to Art.14(1) in the Rome I Regulation (entry at para.7–005, above) is Art.18(1).

The Rome II Regulation (entry at para.7–009, above) applies the *lex causae* of the non-contractual obligation to the extent that it contains rules in the law of non-contractual obligations, as opposed to the law of procedure, which determine the burden of proof (Art.22(1)).

**7–029** Third sentence. See entry at para.7–028, above.

**7–030** The Rome II Regulation (entry at para.7–009, above) applies the *lex causae* to the extent that it contains rules in the law of non-contractual obligations, as opposed to the law of procedure, which give rise to presumptions of law (Art.22(1)).

**7–031** This paragraph was considered by Tomlinson J. in *Dornoch Ltd v Westminster International BV* [2009] EWHC 1782 (Admlty), [2009] 2 Lloyd's Rep. 420, at [21].

**7–033** In *JP Morgan Chase Bank v Mystras Maritime Corp* [2008] FCA 399, (2008) 305 D.L.R. (4th) 442, the Canadian Federal Court of Appeal treated the question of whether a supplier of necessaries to a vessel had a maritime lien as substantive. Since, however, the contents of the relevant foreign law had not been proved, the court ultimately applied the *lex fori* to the matter. See also *World Fuel Services Corporation v The Nordems* (2010) FC 332, at [14].

See entry at para.7–009, above. **7–035**

Note 39. Final sentence. See the decision of the House of Lords in *Harding v Wealands* [2006] UKHL 32, [2007] 2 A.C. 1 (considered below, entry at para.7–043). *Re T& N Ltd* is now reported at [2006] 1 W.L.R. 1792.

Note 40. First sentence. See *Harding v Wealands* [2006] UKHL 32, [2007] 2 A.C. 1. **7–037**

Supreme Court Act 1981 is now re-named Senior Courts Act 1981: Constitutional Reform Act 2005, s.59 and Sch.11, in force October 1, 2009.

Second sentence. This point was not addressed in detail by the House of Lords in *Harding v Wealands* [2006] UKHL 32, [2007] 2 A.C. 1. It was held, however, that the entirety of the New South Wales Motor Accidents Compensation Act 1999 was inapplicable in an English court. The decision, accordingly, casts very considerable doubt on the correctness of the view of the Court of Appeal on this point. **7–039**

Note 50. In *Maher v Groupama Grand Est* [2009] EWCA Civ 1191, [2010] 1 W.L.R. 1564 (affirming [2009] EWHC 38 (QB), [2009] 1 W.L.R. 1752), the court considered and approved Rule 226 of the main work and the decision in *Somers v Fournier* (2002) 214 D.L.R. (4th) 611 (Ont. C.A.). It held that the availability of a claim for interest on damages should be regarded as a substantive issue and subject to the law applicable to the tort under the Private International Law (Miscellaneous Provisions) Act 1995, Pt III. The rate of interests was to be determined by English law; but, as para.33–398 of the main work indicates, these English principles of assessment are sufficiently flexible to allow the court to fix an appropriate rate, having due regard to both English and foreign law. The Court of Appeal's decision was followed in *Abdel Hadi Abdallah Al Qahtani & Sons Beverage Industry Co v Antliff* [2010] EWHC 1735 (Comm.), at [59]. The first instance decision in *Maher v Groupama Grand Est* was followed in *Knight v Axa Assurances* [2009] EWHC 1900 (QB), [2009] Lloyd's Rep. I.R. 667.

First sentence and note 51. Lord Hoffmann stated in *Harding v Wealands* [2006] UKHL 32, [2007] 2 A.C. 1 (at [46]), that this proposition was too broadly stated. He construed *Cope v Doherty* (1858) 4 K. & J. 367, (1858) 2 De G. & J. 614 as standing for the proposition that where a statute of limitation imposes a contractual term limiting the obligation to pay damages, this is to be treated as "an express limitation upon the substantive liabilities" (relying on the judgment of Street C.J. in *Allan J Panozza & Co Pty Ltd v* **7–040**

*Allied Interstate (Qld) Pty Ltd* [1976] 2 N.S.W.L.R. 192, 196–7). Where a statutory provision limiting liability does not operate as an imposed contractual term, such a provision should be classified as procedural. Lord Hoffmann observed (at [47]) that "Clarke J was right in *Caltex Singapore Pte Ltd v BP Shipping Ltd* [1996] 1 Lloyd's Rep. 286 to treat a modern limitation statute (in that case, of Singapore) as a procedural provision, limiting the remedy rather than the substantive right . . . ".

**7–042** On the dichotomy between substance and procedure in Australian law, see Davis, in Berryman & Bigwood (eds.), *The Law of Remedies: New Directions in the Common Law* (2010), Ch.19.

For a comparative analysis of the classification of financial remedies in tort, see Gray (2008) 4 J. Priv. Int. L. 279.

**7–043** The decision in *Harding v Wealands* [2004] EWCA Civ 1735, [2005] 1 W.L.R. 1539 has now been reversed by the House of Lords: [2006] UKHL 32, [2007] 2 A.C. 1 (noted by Dougherty and Wyles (2007) 56 I.C.L.Q. 443; Scott [2007] L.M.C.L.Q. 44; Seriki (2007) 26 C.J.Q. 28; Rogerson [2006] C.L.J. 515; Beaumont and Tang (2008) 12 Edin. L.Rev. 131. For a United States perspective on the decision, see Weintraub (2007) 42 Tex. Int. L.J. 311). It was held that the effect of *Boys v Chaplin* was that all matters relating to the quantification of damages were to be treated as procedural, with the effect that s.5 of the Motor Accidents Compensation Act 1999 (NSW) was inapplicable in the English courts. The introduction of statutory choice of law rules in tort in the Private International Law (Miscellaneous Provisions) Act 1995, Part III had not changed matters in this respect and the word "procedure" in s.14(3)(b) bore the same meaning as at common law. Lord Hoffmann explained that: "[S]ection 14(3) is expressed to be without prejudice to the generality of section 14(2), which says that nothing in Part III is to affect any rules of law except those abolished by section 10. Section 10 is concerned with the rules which determine 'whether a tort . . . is actionable' and not with the rules concerning the remedies available for actionable injury" (at [33]). If there had been any ambiguity on this point, *Pepper v Hart* [1993] A.C. 593 would have been applied, since the statements of Lord Mackay of Clashfern LC, who promoted the Bill, indicated that there had been no intention to change the law on damages, a view also expressed in the Joint Report of the Law Commission (Report No.193) and Scottish Law Commission (Report No.129), on which the legislation was based.

By contrast, the New South Wales Court of Appeal in *McNeilly v Imbree* [2007] NSWCA 156 refused to apply the Motor Accidents Compensation Act 1999 to a claim in respect of a car accident in the Northern Territory. The Court of Appeal concluded that the Northern Territory statute applied, on the basis that the assessment of damages was a question of substance governed by the law of the Northern Territory as the *lex loci delicti*. This was despite the fact that s.123 of the Motor Accidents Compensation Act 1999 provides that: "A Court cannot award damages to a person in respect of a motor accident contrary to this Chapter".

First sentence. The decision of the House of Lords in *Harding v Wealands* [2006] UKHL 32, [2007] 2 A.C. 1 has largely removed the uncertainty on this point. A reduction of damages on the basis of other benefits received relates to the quantification of damages and would almost certainly be treated as a procedural issue. **7–044**

Add at end: On the reduction of damages on the grounds of contributory negligence, see above, entry at para.7–027, n.3.

The Rome II Regulation (entry at para.7–009, above) makes a number of important changes to English law in the area of damages. Recital (33) of the Regulation provides that: "According to the current national rules on compensation awarded to victims of road traffic accidents, when quantifying damages for personal injury in cases in which the accident takes place in a State other than that of the habitual residence of the victim, the court seised should take into account all the relevant actual circumstances of the specific victim, including in particular the actual losses and cost of after-care and medical attention."

Article 15(c) provides that "the nature and assessment of damage" is a matter for the law applicable to the non-contractual obligation. In relation to the assessment of damages, this will reverse the effect of *Boys v Chaplin*, at least to the extent that application of that law does not infringe an overriding mandatory rule of English law (Art.16) or is not manifestly incompatible with the public policy of the forum (Art.26). Hence, it may be of critical importance to determine whether a damages claim falls within the ambit of the Rome II Regulation or the prior law: see *Homawoo v GMF Assurance SA* [2010] EWHC 1941 (QB); *Bacon v Nacional Suiza Cia Seguros Y Reseguros SA* [2010] EWHC 2017 (QB). See further *Maher v Groupama Grand Est* [2009] EWHC 38 (QB), [2009] 1 W.L.R. 1752, at [16] (affirmed without reference to this point [2009] EWCA Civ 1191, [2010] 1 W.L.R. 1564). See also Schoeman [2010] L.M.C.L.Q. 81.

Article 15(d) states that the *lex causae* applies "within the limits of powers conferred on the court by its procedural law" to "the measures which a court may take to prevent or terminate injury or damage or to ensure the provision of compensation". This constitutes a qualified reference to the *lex causae*, which should be applied provided that the remedy in question is known according to English law and that it is not unduly burdensome for the English court to grant it (*cf.* Art.10(1)(c) of the Rome Convention, discussed at para 32–203 of the main work).

The question whether a right to claim damages can be transferred (including by inheritance) is subject to the *lex causae* (Art.15(e)); as is the liability for the acts of another person (Art.15(g)).

The "limitation of any liability" is also a matter for the law applicable to the non-contractual obligation (Art.15(b)) and would lead to New South Wales law being applied on the facts of a case such as *Harding v Wealands.*

All these principles are subject to the overriding mandatory rules of the forum (Art.16) and should also not be applied if they are manifestly incompatible with the public policy of the forum (Art.26).

On the problems of awarding exemplary or punitive antitrust damages under the Rome II Regulation, see Danov (2008) 29 E.C.L.R. 430.

**7–047** See also the decision of the South African Supreme Court of Appeal in *Society of Lloyd's v Price; Society of Lloyd's v Lee* 2006 5 S.A. 393 (SCA) (noted by Forsyth (2006) 2 J. Priv. Int. L. 425) for discussion of the problem of a "gap" where limitation rules of the *lex causae* are classified as procedural but those of the *lex fori* are classified as substantive.

**7–048** The decision in *Castillo v Castillo* 2005 SCC 83, (2005) 260 D.L.R. (4th) 281 is considered by Walker (2006) 43 C.B.L.J. 487.

In *Vogler v Szendroi* (2008) 290 D.L.R. (4th) 642 (N.S.C.A.), the plaintiff was injured in a car accident in Wyoming. The law of Wyoming governed the case. The limitation period in Wyoming was four years. Three years after the accident, the plaintiff commenced proceedings in Nova Scotia. He did not, however, serve the defendant for a further three years. The law of Wyoming provides that an action is commenced by filing process with the court. It also states that if service has not been effected within sixty days, the action is not deemed to have been commenced until the date of service. The Nova Scotia Court of Appeal held that the Wyoming rule was procedural, since it determined the manner in which proceedings were to be instigated, and did not concern the rights of the plaintiff.

In *Hodgson v Dimbola Pty Ltd* [2009] ACTSC 59, the Supreme Court of the Australian Capital Territory considered whether an injured worker could recover under a statutory compensation scheme pursuant to Worker's Compensation and Rehabilitation Act 2003 (Queensland), s.324. That provision, in turn, referred to the law of New South Wales on the question of whether or not a claim for damages could be made, and, if so, on the determination of the claim. The court ruled that a limitation period in Limitation Act 1969 (NSW), s.18A(2), was not a law governing whether or not a claim for damages could be made; it merely prescribed the period within which the claim could be instituted. Accordingly, the limitation period of New South Wales law was inapplicable. See also the further proceedings: [2009] ACTSC 126.

**7–049** Law Applicable to Non-Contractual Obligations (England and Wales and Northern Ireland) Regulations (SI 2008/2986), Reg. 4 introduced a new s.8 of the Foreign Limitation Periods 1984 (in force from December 17, 2009). This provision disapplies sections 1, 2 and 4 of the Act where the rules of the Rome II Regulation are applicable. Law Applicable to Contractual Obligations (England and Wales and Northern Ireland) Regulations (SI 2009/3064), Reg. 3 further amends s.8 by introducing a new s.8(1)(A), extending the disapplication of sections 1, 2 and 4 of the Act where the rules of the Rome I Regulation apply. Hence, the public policy exception in s.2 of the Foreign Limitation Periods Act 1984 where a foreign limitation period causes undue hardship to a person who is, or might be made, a party to the action or proceedings, does not apply where either the Rome I or Rome II Regulation is applicable; and it will be necessary to refer exclusively to the public policy derogations in the Regulations.

Fifth sentence. In *Harley v Smith* [2009] EWHC 56 (QB), [2009] 1 Lloyd's Rep. 359, Foskett J. reviewed the authorities on Foreign Limitation Periods Act 1984, s.2(2), and the meaning and scope of the "undue hardship" exception. Although he concluded that the foreign limitation period had in fact not expired on the facts, he stated (at [94]) that the previous authorities established three propositions: (i) that the mere fact that the foreign limitation period is less generous than the equivalent English period is insufficient to trigger s.2(2); (ii) the claimant must satisfy the court that he would suffer particular hardship on the facts of the case; and (iii) that in considering (ii), the focus is on the claimant's interests rather than a balancing exercise between the interests of the claimant on the one hand and the defendant on the other. The Court of Appeal upheld the decision ([2010] EWCA Civ 78) and specifically endorsed this statement of the law. Whilst it agreed that the limitation period had not expired, it concluded, however, that the judge was wrong to say that the "undue hardship" exception would otherwise have been triggered and varied the order to that extent. In particular, it found that the judge had erroneously referred to two factors. First, the undue hardship must be caused by the foreign limitation period itself and not by allegedly erroneous legal advice as to what that limitation period was. Second, any uncertainty as to the applicable limitation period in the foreign law would normally be irrelevant, since it would encourage a claimant to bring proceedings sooner rather than later to avoid the risk of being out of time. See also *OJSC Oil Co Yugraneft v Abramovich* [2008] EWHC 2613 (Comm.), at [318]–[324]. **7–050**

The law applicable to the contract is determined in the Rome I Regulation (entry at para.7–005, above) by Arts 3–8 and 14. The equivalent provision to Art.10(1)(d) of the Rome Convention is contained in Art.12(1)(d) of the Regulation. The public policy provision is contained in Art.21 of the Regulation. Following the entry into force of the Rome I Regulation, consequential amendments to Foreign Limitation Periods Act 1984 have been made by Law Applicable to Contractual Obligations (England and Wales and Northern Ireland) Regulations (SI 2009/3064), Reg. 3. See entry at para.7–049, above. **7–052**

**7–053** Article 15(h) of the Rome II Regulation (entry at para.7–009, above) applies the law applicable to the non-contractual obligation to questions of prescription and limitation, including rules relating to the commencement, interruption and suspension of a period of prescription or limitation. Consequential amendments to the Foreign Limitation Periods Act 1984 have been made by Law Applicable to Non-Contractual Obligations (England and Wales and Northern Ireland) Regulations 2008 (SI 2008/2986), Regulation 4. See entry at para.7–049, above.

**7–054** Note 20. Delete second sentence.

Note 21. The equivalent provision in the Rome I Regulation (entry at para.7–005, above) is Art.12(1)(d).

**7–055** The Rome I Regulation (entry at para.7–005, above) contains a separate provision (Art.16) headed "multiple liability". It provides:

> "If a creditor has a claim against several debtors who are liable for the same claim, and one of the debtors has already satisfied the claim in whole or in part, the law governing the debtor's obligation towards the creditor also governs the debtor's right to claim recourse from the other debtors. The other debtors may rely on the defences they had against the creditor to the extent allowed by the law governing their obligations towards the creditor."

Second para. See also *OJSC Oil Co Yugraneft v Abramovich* [2008] EWHC 2613 (Comm.), at [298].

**7–056** See also *Inforica Inc. v CGI Information Systems and Management Consultants Inc.*, 2009 ONCA 642, at [23]–[28], where the Court of Appeal for Ontario suggested that the jurisdiction of an arbitrator to award security for costs is not "strictly speaking procedural in nature" (at [23]) and might fall within a special category; but that nonetheless "that category is much closer to procedure than to substance. Such orders are made to protect the integrity of the dispute resolution process by preventing parties from structuring their affairs in a manner that immunizes them from the discipline of costs. They do not decide rights, but rather serve to ensure that parties are governed by the rules of the game" (at [24]).

In *Hamilton v Merck & Co Inc* [2006] NSWCA 55, (2006) 230 A.L.R. 156, (2006) 66 N.S.W.L.R. 48, the New South Wales Court of Appeal ruled that provisions of the law applicable to the tort, Queensland law, contained in the Personal Injuries Proceedings Act 2002 (Qd), on providing notice before action, and on the need for a conference between the parties before starting proceedings, were procedural and hence inapplicable on the facts, since they did not affect the substantive rights or duties of the parties once proceedings were commenced. See also *Hodgson v Dimbola Pty Ltd* [2009] ACTSC 59, at

[24]; *Kok v Sheppard* [2009] NSWSC 1262, at [35]–[43]; *RACQ Insurance Ltd v Wilkins* [2009] QSC 365.

In *Uren v Neale* [2009] VSC 267, a provision in Magistrates' Court Act (Vic) 1989, s.30(3) stipulating that, in default of the filing of a summons within a prescribed period, "the Court must strike out the charge", was held to relate to the mode of proceedings and to be procedural in nature; and not to confer a substantive right on the person against whom the summons was issued.

Illustration 10. See entry at para.7–027, n.3, above. **7–061**

Illustration 17. Contrast *JP Morgan Chase Bank v Mystras Maritime Corp* [2008] FCA 399, (2008) 305 D.L.R. (4th) 442; *World Fuel Services Corporation v. Nordems (Ship)* (2010) FC 332, at [14]. **7–063**

Illustration 20. Following the decision of the House of Lords in *Harding v Wealands* [2006] UKHL 32, [2007] 2 A.C. 1, such provisions are procedural, so that the limits laid down by New South Wales law should not be applied. **7–064**

Illustration 21. Final sentence. In the light of the decision of the House of Lords in *Harding v Wealands* [2006] UKHL 32, [2007] 2 A.C. 1, the rule of State X should be classified as procedural and not applied by an English court.

The provision equivalent to Art.10(1)(d) of the Rome Convention is contained in Art.12(1)(d) of the Regulation. **7–065**

NOTE 58. The equivalent provision in the Rome I Regulation (entry at para.7–005, above) is Art.21.

## Chapter 8

# INTERNATIONAL LITIGATION: PROTECTIVE MEASURES AND JUDICIAL ASSISTANCE

**8–003** Note 3. On jurisdiction through attachment of assets in South Africa see *Bid Industrial Holdings (Pty) Ltd v Strang* [2007] SCA 144 (RSA), and Oppong (2008) 4 J. Priv. Int. L. 311; Sibanda (2008) 4 J. Priv. Int. L. 329.

**8–004** Note 7. See Valentine and Pitel (2006) 2 J. Priv. Int. L. 339.

**8–005** Supreme Court Act 1981 is now re-named Senior Courts Act 1981: Constitutional Reform Act 2005, s.59 and Sch.11, in force October 1, 2009.

**8–008** Note 21. Add: *Fourie v Le Roux* [2007] UKHL 1, [2007] 1 W.L.R. 320, at [2].

**8–009** Note 25. See also *The Capaz Duckling* [2007] EWHC 1630 (Comm.), [2008] 1 Lloyd's Rep. 54, at [28]–[31].

**8–010** On freezing orders against third parties see *Yukos Capital Sarl v OJSC Rosneft Oil Co* [2010] EWHC 784 (Comm.) and cases cited there.

Note 29. In *Kuwait Airways Corp v Iraq Airways Co* [2010] EWCA Civ 740 the Court of Appeal sanctioned an order against the Director General of Iraq Airways in support of a worldwide freezing order in aid of excecution preventing him from leaving the jurisdiction until he had sworn an affidavit of disclosure of assets, ordering handing over of his passport, and a Tipstaff order requiring the Tipstaff to attend upon him to obtain his passport with powers of arrest, entry and seizure.

Note 30. In *Commissioners of Customs & Excise v Barclays Bank plc* [2006] UKHL 28, [2007] 1 A.C. 181, it was held that a bank does not owe a duty of care in negligence to the person who has obtained a freezing injunction. The Commissioners sought to recover outstanding amounts of VAT from two companies, and obtained freezing injunctions in respect of their assets including funds held to specified accounts in Barclays Bank. The bank was given notice of the injunctions, but it failed to prevent payments out of the accounts in breach of the injunctions. It was held that since the bank on notification of the injunctions was obliged to comply with their terms and was exposed to the risk of punishment for contempt if it did not do so, and since there had been no relevant communication or act between the parties, or any reliance by the

Commissioners on the bank, it could not be understood as having voluntarily assumed responsibility for its actions so as to give rise to a duty of care towards them; that the court exercised its injunctive jurisdiction on the basis that its orders were enforceable only by its power to punish for contempt and the notified party's only duty was to the court; that it would not be analogous or incremental to any previous decision if a non-consensual court order were to be recognised as giving rise to a duty owed to the party who obtained it; and that, since its operation would be productive of unjust and unreasonable results, it would not be fair just and reasonable to recognise a duty of care in such circumstances. See Gee (2006) 122 L.Q.R. 535.

NOTE 32. See also Merrett [2008] L.M.C.L.Q. 71; Johnson [2008] C.J.Q. 433; Hartley (2010) 126 L.Q.R. 194. **8–011**

NOTE 33. Supreme Court Act 1981 is now re-named Senior Courts Act 1981: Constitutional Reform Act 2005, s.59 and Sch.11, in force October 1, 2009.

**Post-judgment freezing orders.** In *Masri v Consolidated Contractors International Company SAL (No.2)* [2008] EWCA Civ 303, [2009] Q.B. 450, the Court of Appeal confirmed that the effect of Case C–391/95 *Van Uden Maritime BV v Firma Deco-Line* [1998] ECR I–7091, [1999] Q.B. 1225 and Case C–99/96 *Mietz v Intership Yachting Sneek BV* [1999] ECR I–2277 was that the court with jurisdiction over the substance of the case had jurisdiction to grant any ancillary order. There was no reason to doubt that that included orders both pre-judgment and post-judgment, and would include a receivership order. In *Babanaft International Co SA v Bassatne* [1990] Ch. 13 Kerr L.J. considered (at 35) that a post-judgment provisional protective order fell within the scope of Art.24 of the 1968 Convention (now Art.31 of the Judgments Regulation): after judgment "the substance of the matter" referred to in Art.24 consisted of the "proceedings concerned with the enforcement of judgments" referred to in Art.16(5) (now Art.22(5)), which were within the exclusive jurisdiction of the State where the assets were; and Art.24 would be available in the interim, pending enforcement of the judgment there, to entitle the English court to grant a *Mareva* injunction over the foreign assets pending execution abroad. Nicholls L.J. shared this view: at 46. **8–014**

In *Masri v Consolidated Contractors International Company SAL (No.2)* the Court of Appeal held that *Babanaft International Co SA v Bassatne* did not bind the Court of Appeal to hold that, where a defendant/judgment debtor is domiciled in a Judgments Regulation State, post-judgment orders which are designed to assist, or preserve the position until, execution can only be made in circumstances permitted by Art.31 of the Judgments Regulation.

In *Banco Nacional de Comercio Exterior SNC v Empresa de Telecommunicaciones de Cuba SA* [2007] EWCA Civ 662, [2008] 1 W.L.R. 1936 (noted Merrett [2007] C.L.J. 495) it was held that a worldwide freezing order could not be made under Art.47(1) of the Judgments Regulation in support of the enforcement of an Italian judgment, and that it was inexpedient to grant such an injunction under s.25 of the Civil Jurisdiction and Judgments Act 1982. See also *Masri v Consolidated Contractors International Co SAL* [2008] EWHC 2492 (Comm.).

NOTE 42. Supreme Court Act 1981 is now renamed Senior Courts Act 1981: Constitutional Reform Act 2005, s.59 and Sch.11, in force October 1, 2009.

**8–017** In *Dadourian Group International Inc v Simms* [2006] EWCA Civ 399, [2006] 1 W.L.R. 2499 the Court of Appeal laid down guidelines for the grant of permission to enforce a worldwide freezing order abroad. First, the principle is that the grant of that permission should be just and convenient for the purpose of ensuring the effectiveness of the order, and in addition that it is not oppressive to the parties to the English proceedings or to third parties who may be joined to the foreign proceedings. Second, all the relevant circumstances and options need to be considered, and in particular consideration should be given to granting relief on terms, for example terms as to the extension to third parties of the undertaking to compensate for costs incurred as a result of the order and as to the type of proceedings that may be commenced abroad. Consideration should also be given to the proportionality of the steps proposed to be taken abroad, and in addition to the form of any order. Third, the interests of the applicant should be balanced against the interests of the other parties to the proceedings and any new party likely to be joined to the foreign proceedings. Fourth, permission should not normally be given in terms that would enable the applicant to obtain relief in the foreign proceedings which is superior to the relief given by the order. Fifth, the evidence in support of the application for permission should contain all the information (so far as it can reasonably be obtained in the time available) necessary to enable the judge to reach an informed decision, including evidence as to the applicable law and practice in the foreign court, evidence as to the nature of the proposed proceedings to be commenced and evidence as to the assets believed to be located in the jurisdiction of the foreign court and the names of the parties by whom such assets are held. Sixth, the standard of proof as to the existence of assets that are both within the order and within the jurisdiction of the foreign court is that the applicant must show that there is a real prospect that such assets are located within the jurisdiction of the foreign court in question. Seventh, there must be evidence of a risk of dissipation of the assets in question. Eighth, normally the application should be made on notice to the respondent, but in cases of urgency, where it is just to do so, the permission may be given without notice to the party against whom relief will be sought in the foreign proceedings but that party should have the earliest practicable opportunity of having the matter reconsidered by the court at a hearing of which he is given notice.

See also *Dadourian Group International Inc v Simms (No.2)* [2006] EWCA Civ 1745, [2007] 1 W.L.R. 2967 on the use in contempt proceedings of information obtained under a disclosure order. The principle was that it should be just and convenient for that information to be so used for the purpose of enforcing or policing the freezing order.

CPR, r.6.20(2) has been replaced by CPR PD6B, para.3.1(2): see CPR, r.6.36 (as substituted by SI 2008/2178, Sch.1). **8–022**

CPR, r.6.20 has been replaced by CPR PD6B, para.3.1: see CPR, r.6.36 (as substituted by SI 2008/2178, Sch.1). **8–023**

CPR, r.6.20(4) has been replaced by CPR PD6B, para.3.1(5): see CPR, r.6.36 (as substituted by SI 2008/2178, Sch.1). **8–024**

On the history see *Fourie v Le Roux* [2007] UKHL 1, [2007] 1 W.L.R. 320, at [26]–[31]. On the application of Art.31 of the Judgments Regulation see *SanDisk Corp v Koninklijke Philips Electronics NV* [2007] EWHC 332 (Ch.), [2007] Bus.L.R. 705 (relief refused because of insufficient connection with England).

See now revised Lugano Convention (entry at para. 11R–001, below.)

CPR, r.6.20(4) has been replaced by CPR PD6B, para.3.1(5): see CPR, r.6.36 (as substituted by SI 2008/2178, Sch.1). **8–025**

In *ETI Euro Telecom International NV v Republic of Bolivia* [2008] EWCA Civ 880, [2008] 1 W.L.R. 665 an order was sought under s.25 in support of a New York attachment which was itself made in support of the enforcement of an ICSID award. It was held (at [70] et seq.) that the foreign proceedings to which s.25 and the 1997 Order referred are proceedings on the substance of the matter, and it could not be used to supplement the New York attachment. But it was also accepted (at [76]) that the notion of substantive proceedings may have to be given a liberal interpretation to ensure international judicial co-operation.

Section 25 cannot be used in support of arbitration: *ETI Euro Telecom International NV v Republic of Bolivia* [2008] EWCA Civ 880, [2008] 1 W.L.R. 655, at [79] et seq.

Section 25 was applied in matrimonial proceedings in *Rhode v Rhode* [2007] EWHC 496 (Fam.), [2007] 2 F.L.R. 971; *N v R* [2008] EWHC 1347 (Fam.).

NOTE 83. See also *Kensington International Ltd v Republic of Congo* [2007] EWCA Civ 1128, [2008] 1 W.L.R. 1144, at [19]–[21]. **8–029**

NOTE 84. See also *Amedeo Hotels v Zaman* [2007] EWHC 295 (Comm.); *ETI Euro Telecom International NV v Republic of Bolivia* [2008] EWCA Civ 880, [2008] 1 W.L.R. 665, at [99] *et seq.*; *Belletti v Morici* [2009] EWHC 2316 (Comm.), [2010] 1 All ER (Comm.) 412. **8–030**

**8–031** Note 89. See also *Mobil Cerro Negro Ltd v Petroleos de Venezuela SA* [2008] EWHC 532 (Comm.), [2008] 1 Lloyd's Rep. 684, at [119].

**8–036** See now revised Lugano Convention (entry at para. 11R–001, below), Arts 23 and 27 to 28.

**8–040** Note 16. CPR, r.6.3(1)(b) has been replaced by CPR, r.6.4(1)(b).

**8–044** Note 20. CPR, r.6.25(2) has been replaced by CPR, r.6.42(1).

**8–045** A further Special Commission of the Hague Conference was held in 2009 to review the practical operation of a number of conventions, including the Service Convention.

Art.10(*a*) of the Hague Convention provides that the Convention does not interfere with the freedom to send judicial documents by postal channels directly to persons abroad, provided the State of destination does not object. Art.21(2)(*a*) requires each Contracting State to notify the depositary of its opposition to the use of methods of transmission pursuant to Articles 8 and 10. In *Fonexco Group Ltd (formerly Fonexco Ltd) v Manches* [2010] EWHC 493 (QB) (where Art.21 was not referred to) it was held (obiter) that although Italy was a party to the Convention and had not notified its objection to postal service, service in Italy under the Convention was subject to the requirements of national law including the need to obtain the permission of the local public prosecutor; it was therefore not sufficient to send a claim form by post from England to the defendant. It is submitted that this approach should not be followed: it undermines the certainty which the Convention sought to provide and requires claimants to look behind the Convention material to what were in the instant case unclear provisions of the law of the country of intended service. The court was influenced by the language of R.S.C. Ord. 11, r. 5, applicable at the relevant time. CPR r 6.40(3)(*b*) now expressly provides that a claim form may be served "by any method permitted by a Civil Procedure Convention", which term includes the Hague Convention. Service in Italy is now governed by the Service Regulation.

Note 21. A revised edition of the Practical Handbook was published in 2006.

Note 23. See *Bentinck v Bentinck* [2007] EWCA Civ 175, [2007] 2 F.L.R. 1, recording a "bizarre" attempt to effect personal service in Switzerland contrary to Swiss law. CPR, r.6.24(1)(a), (2) has been replaced by CPR, r.6.40(4).

**8–046** The Special Commission of 2009 re-affirmed the view "that the Service Convention is of a non-mandatory but exclusive character" (Conclusions and Recommendations, para.12). The terms used are to be understood as they are explained in Preliminary Document 10 for the Special Commission, which at para.6 observes:

"The language [in Art.1] 'where there is occasion to transmit' is understood as meaning that the Service Convention is non-mandatory in the sense that it is a matter for the *lex fori* to determine whether a document must be transmitted for service abroad. The use of the word 'shall' is understood as meaning that the Service Convention is exclusive, in the sense that once the law of the forum has determined that a document must be transmitted abroad for service, the channels of transmission expressly available or otherwise permissible under the Hague Service Convention are the *only* channels that may be used."

NOTE 29. CPR, r.6.8 has been replaced by CPR, r.6.15.

Council Regulation (EC) 1348/2000 is repealed and replaced, with effect from **8–048—**
November 13, 2008, by European Parliament and Council Regulation (EC) **8–053**
No 1393/2007 of 13 November 2007 on the service in the Member States of judicial and extrajudicial documents in civil and commercial matters (service of documents) and repealing Council Regulation (EC) 1348/2000. (For text see [2007] O.J. L324, p.79. The amendments to the CPR made with effect from October 1, 2008 already made reference to Regulation 1393/2007.) The new Regulation repeats many of the provisions of the Regulation it replaces, but makes a number of changes.

There is now an obligation on receiving agencies to take all necessary steps to effect the service of the document as soon as possible, and in any event within one month of receipt. If it has not been possible to effect service within one month of receipt, the receiving agency must immediately inform the transmitting agency by means of a certificate in a form set out in Annex I to the Regulation and continue to take all necessary steps to effect the service of the document, unless indicated otherwise by the transmitting agency, where service seems to be possible within a reasonable period of time (Regulation, Art.7(2)).

Article 8 is redrafted. The receiving agency must inform the addressee, using a standard form set out in Annex II to the Regulation, that he may refuse to accept the document to be served at the time of service or by returning the document to the receiving agency within one week if it is not written in, or accompanied by a translation into, a language which the addressee understands (which need no longer be that of the Regulation State of Transmission) or the official language of the State addressed (Art.8(1)). There is an express provision dealing with the consequences of a refusal to accept the document: the service of the document can be remedied through the service on the addressee in accordance with the provisions of this Regulation of the document accompanied by a translation into one of the above languages (Art.8(3), which also contains rules as to the effective date of service in such cases).

Also redrafted and simplified are the provisions as to the effective date of service in normal cases. The date of service of a document is the date on which it is served in accordance with the law of the State addressed (Art.9(1)). However, where according to the law of a State a document has to be served within a particular period, the date to be taken into account with respect to the applicant shall be that determined by the law of that State (Art.9(2)).

In the interests of transparency, it is provided that costs occasioned by recourse to a judicial officer or to a person competent under the law of the State addressed are to correspond to a single fixed fee laid down by that State in advance which respects the principles of proportionality and non-discrimination. Regulation States are required to communicate such fixed fees to the Commission (Art.11(3)).

Service by post and direct service are now governed by simplified rules. Each Regulation State is free to effect service of judicial documents directly by postal services (which term includes private operators) on persons residing in another Regulation State by registered letter with acknowledgement of receipt or equivalent (Art.14). Any person interested in a judicial proceeding may effect service of judicial documents directly through the judicial officers, officials or other competent persons of the State addressed, where such direct service is permitted under the law of that State (Art.15).

**8–048** An Agreement between the European Community and Denmark on the service of judicial and extrajudicial documents in civil or commercial matters, signed on October 19, 2005 ([2005] O.J. L300/55) entered into force on July 1, 2007.

In *Re Anderson Owen Ltd (in liquidation)* [2009] EWHC 2837 (Ch), the application, for relief under the Insolvency Act 1986, s.212, fell within the scope of "insolvency proceedings" to which the provisions of CPR Part 6 as to service of process out of the jurisdiction do not apply. The court assumed, on the basis of a concession by counsel, that Regulation No 1393/2007 did apply. The judge, correctly it is submitted, doubted the correctness of the concession, essentially because not all insolvency proceedings as defined in the Insolvency Rules 1986 would be within the category of "civil and commercial matters" for the purposes of the Service Regulation. In the particular circumstances of the case, the absence of a translation of the relevant documents into German was not such a defect as to require re-service.

The scope of Regulation 1348/2000 (and by implication of Regulation 1393/2007) in so far as "extra-judicial documents" are concerned was examined in Case C–14/08 *Roda Golf & Beach Resort SL* [2009] E.C.R. I–5439. The clerk of a Spanish court refused to serve, in the absence of legal proceedings, addressees in the United Kingdom and Ireland with a notarial act terminating a number of contracts for the sale of immovable property. The refusal was on the ground that no legal proceedings were in train. The European Court held that the concept of "extrajudicial document" was a Community law concept. A document could be regarded as an extrajudicial document even if there were no connection with current or contemplated legal proceedings, if the judicial co-operation governed by the Regulation had cross-border implications and was necessary for the proper functioning of the internal market.

In *Department of Civil Aviation of the Krygyz Republic v Finrep* [2006] EWHC 1722 (Comm.) it was held that an order for service upon a party's representative acting for him in the English arbitration could not be seen as "subversive of" the Service Regulation. The power under CPR r.6.8(1) to authorise service by an alternative method required there to be good reason for such an order. In the context of an arbitration which had its seat in England or Wales, where it was desired to serve an arbitration application relating to that arbitration on a party with an agent within the jurisdiction, who acted or had acted for him in the arbitration and whose authority did not appear to have been determined, there would very often be good reason to permit service to be made upon that agent rather than requiring service to be effected out of the jurisdiction.

Note 32. CPR, r.6.26A has been replaced by CPR, r.6.41. Practical details, based on the information provided to the Commission by Member States, are now published and updated continuously in the European Judicial Atlas in Civil Matters, available on the European Commission's website.

Text to note 43. In Case C–14/07 *Ingenieurburo Michael Weiss und Partner GbR v Industrie-und Handelskammer Berlin* [2008] E.C.R. I–3367 (see Franzina (2008) 10 Yb. P.I.L. 565), the European Court considered the interpretation of Art.8 of Regulation 1348/2000 in the case of documents instituting proceedings. It held that the term "document to be served" meant the document or documents which must be served on the defendant in due time in order to enable him to assert his rights in legal proceedings in the State of transmission. Such a document must make it possible to identify with a degree of certainty at the very least the subject-matter of the claim and the cause of action as well as the summons to appear before the court or, depending on the nature of the pending proceedings, to be aware that it is possible to appeal. Documents which had a purely evidential function and were not necessary for the purpose of understanding the subject-matter of the claim and the cause of action did not form an integral part of the document instituting the proceedings. It was for the national court to determine whether the content of the document instituting the proceedings is sufficient to enable the defendant to assert his rights or whether it is necessary for the party instituting the proceedings to remedy the fact that a necessary annex has not been translated. **8–050**

The fact that the addressee of a document served had agreed in a contract concluded with the applicant in the course of his business that correspondence was to be conducted in the language of the Member State of transmission did not give rise to a presumption of knowledge of that language, but was evidence which the court may take into account in determining whether that addressee understands the language of the Member State of transmission.

Where the addressee concluded a contract in the course of his business in which he agreed that correspondence was to be conducted in the language of the Member State of transmission and the annexes concerned that correspondence and were written in the agreed language, the addressee could not rely on Art.8(1) to refuse to accept the documents.

**8–054** In truly exceptional cases, the English court may take action to remedy a defect in service under the law of the country in which service was to be effected: *Phillips v Symes (No.3)* [2008] UKHL 1, [2008] 1 W.L.R. 180 (where a misunderstanding caused an essential document to be omitted from a bundle of documents served in Switzerland, though a translation was included; although the relevant limitation period had expired, the House held that CPR r.6.9 (now CPR, r.6.16) could be used to dispense with service, even though in that case the effect was to make the English court the one first seised for the purposes of jurisdiction under the Lugano Convention); *Olafsson v Gissurarson (No.2)* [2008] EWCA Civ 152, [2008] 1 W.L.R. 2016 (where the claim form and associated documents were served by personal service in Iceland; they were read and understood by the addressee but Icelandic law was not complied with as he was not asked to sign a receipt for the documents; the applicable limitation period had now expired, but the Court of Appeal applied CPR, r.6.9 (now CPR, r.6.16), noting that doing so would not subvert the provisions of the Convention).

In *Debt Collection London Ltd v SK Slavia Praha-Fotbal AS* [2009] EWHC 2726 (QB) the claim form and related documents were served in the Czech Republic twice: by a Czech lawyer on the defendant company at its registered office and on the following day by post. Both were said to be pursuant to the Convention between the United Kingdom and the Czechoslovak Republic relative to Legal Proceedings in Civil and Commercial Matters signed on November 11, 1924, and complied with the terms of that Convention. Art.20 of the Service Regulation, while providing (Art.20(1)) that it prevails over bilateral agreements between Member States, also provides (Art.20(2)) that it does "not preclude individual Member States from maintaining or concluding agreements or arrangements to expedite further or simplify the transmission of documents", provided that they are compatible with the Regulation. The 1924 Convention is so compatible. Art.20(3) provides that "Member States shall send to the Commission: (a) a copy of the agreements or arrangements referred to in paragraph 2 concluded between the Member States as well as drafts of such agreements or arrangements which they intend to adopt; and (b) any denunciation of, or amendments to, these agreements or arrangements." Tugendhat J. held that Art.20 applied to all agreements between what are now Member States, including those made before the accession of one or both States Parties to the EU (or indeed its creation). The fact that neither State had notified the 1924 Convention under Art.20(3)(a) did not mean that the Convention was not "maintained" under Art.20(2). He held that the Convention was so maintained and that service was validly effected on June 29, 2009. Leave to appeal was given on other issues: [2010] EWCA Civ 148.

Text to note 64. The sentence should begin "Except where it is allowed under an applicable Convention". In Note 64, delete the first sentence referring to CPR, r.6.8.

NOTE 59. Add: *Habib Bank Ltd v Central Bank of Sudan* [2006] EWHC 1767 (Comm), [2007] 1 All E.R. (Comm.) 53 (proper to authorise personal service in Sudan, which though not provided for in Sudanese law did not contravene that law). CPR, r.6.24(1)(a) has been replaced by CPR, r.6.40(3)(c).

NOTE 60. Substitute: CPR, rr.6.40(3)(a)(ii), 6.42(1), 6.43. For translation requirements, see CPR, r.6.45.

NOTE 61. Now CPR, rr.6.40(3)(a)(i), 6.41.

NOTE 62. Now CPR, rr.6.40(3)(b), 6.42(1).

NOTE 63. Substitute: CPR, rr.6.40(3)(a)(ii), 6.42(2). For service in Scotland or Northern Ireland, see CPR, r.6.40(2). For service in a Commonwealth State which is not a party to the Hague Convention, the Isle of Man, the Channel islands or a British overseas territory, see CPR, r.6.42(3).

NOTE 64. The CPR reference is now to CPR, r.6.15.

NOTE 65. Now CPR, r.6.40(3).

NOTE 66. Now CPR, r.6.40(4).

NOTE 68. The first CPR reference is now to CPR, r.6.11; the second to CPR, **8–055**
r.6.36.

NOTE 72. Now CPR, rr.6.48 to 6.52. **8–057**

A further Special Commission of the Hague Conference was held in 2009 to **8–059**
review the practical operation of a number of conventions, including the Evidence Convention.

For the implicit acceptance of the approach adopted in *Aérospatiale* by those **8–060**
States which allow evidence to be taken by audio or video conferencing across national borders, see Davis (2007) 55 Am. J. Comp.L. 205.

The Special Commission of 2009 recommended that States which have made **8–061**
a general, non-particularised declaration under Art.23 revisit their declaration taking into account terms such as those contained in the United Kingdom declaration or in Art.16 of the Additional Protocol of 1984 to the Inter-American Convention on the Taking of Evidence Abroad.

On the question whether the Regulation is the exclusive means of obtaining **8–063**
evidence, see Nuyts, 2007 *Rev. Crit.* 53.

In Case C–175/06 *Tedesco v Tomasoni Fittings SrL* (later removed from court register) Kokott A-G delivered an opinion on July 18, 2007 to the effect that measures for the preservation and collection of evidence (such as seizure of counterfeit goods under the Italian Industrial Property Code) constituted a request for the taking of evidence coming within the scope of Art.1 of Council Regulation 1206/2001 on cooperation between the courts of the Member States in the taking of evidence, which the competent court of a Member State must execute at the request of a court from another Member State.

In *Masri v Consolidated Contractors International (UK) Ltd (No.4)* [2008] EWCA Civ 876, [2010] 1 A.C. 90 the Court of Appeal emphasised that the Evidence Regulation only applies where a request is made by a court in one Member State either to take evidence in another Member State or that a court in that State should itself take evidence. An order under CPR r.71.2 against a judgment debtor to substantive proceedings over which the English court has jurisdiction, requiring the debtor to provide evidence to the English court as to nature and location of his assets did not fall within the Evidence Regulation, no such request being made. (On appeal the House of Lords held that an order under CPR r.71.2 could not be made against persons abroad: [2009] UKHL 43, [2010] A.C. 90 and see the entry at para.8–068). The Court of Appeal rejected an argument that the Evidence Regulation established a complete code, the sole and exclusive route by which evidence may be obtained from a non-party who is in the territory of another Member State. (This point was not reached in the House of Lords.) See Rushworth [2009] L.M.C.L.Q. 196.

**8–068** In *Masri v Consolidated Contractors International Company SAL* [2009] UKHL 43, [2010] 1 A.C. 90 the House of Lords confirmed that the service of a writ of subpoena under s.36 of the Supreme Court Act 1981 was only possible in respect of persons in one of the parts of the United Kingdom. (Supreme Court Act 1981 is now renamed Senior Courts Act 1981 (Constitutional Reform Act 2005, s.59 and Sch.11, in force October 1, 2009.)) No rule of court could require an ordinary witness outside the jurisdiction to attend for examination within the jurisdiction. The House examined the scope of CPR, r.71.2 which enables a judgment creditor to apply for an order requiring a judgment debtor, or if a judgment debtor is a company or other corporation, an officer of that body, to attend court to provide information about the judgment debtor's means or other matters needed for the enforcement of a judgment or order. Distinguishing *Re Seagull Manufacturing Co. Ltd* [1993] Ch. 345 (which concerned s.133 of the Insolvency Act 1986 and in which the Court of Appeal upheld an order made for the public examination of a former director of the relevant company living in Alderney), the House held that an order under CPR r.71.2 could not be made against persons abroad. Its scope was, however, not limited to assets within the jurisdiction.

**8–072** See Pengelley (2006) 85 Can.B.Rev. 345. Add: *Honda Giken Kogyou Kabushiki Kaisha v KJM Superbikes Ltd* [2007] EWCA Civ 313, [2007] C.P.

Rep. 28 applying on the "fishing" issue *First American Corp v Sheikh Zayed Al-Nahyan* [1999] 1 W.L.R. 1154. Sir Anthony Clarke M.R. indicated that a request might be refused where it was oppressive; where the proposed letter of request was too wide; where a case management judge concluded that the cost of obtaining the evidence would be disproportionate or that the evidence would not be necessary for the fair determination of the issues in the action; and in cases of delay in making the application.

In *Masri v Consolidated Contractors International Company SAL* [2008] EWHC 2492 (Comm.), in the context of the appointment of a receiver under s.37 of the Supreme Court Act 1981, the court made an order in the exercise of its discretion despite assertions that the obligations under the order would conflict with Lebanese criminal or company law, citing *Brannigan v Davison* [1997] A.C. 238 (P.C.) and *Morris v Banque Arab et Internationale d'Investissement* [2001] I.L.Pr. 37. (Supreme Court Act 1981 is now renamed Senior Courts Act 1981 (Constitutional Reform Act 2005, s.59 and Sch.11, in force October 1, 2009.)) See also *Michael Wilson & Partners Ltd v Nicholls* [2008] NSWSC 1230 (fact that compliance with an order for discovery may expose a party to penal sanctions under foreign law not an absolute objection to the making of an order for discovery; court will exercise its discretion).

Note 24. *Charman v Charman* is now reported at [2006] 1 W.L.R. 1053.

Note 31. The decision in *Morris v Banque Arab et Internationale d'Investissement* [2001] I.L.Pr.37 was a decision of the Commercial Court and not the C.A. as stated.

Text to note 44. To the same effect as *National Broadcasting Co. v Bear* **8–074**
*Stearns & Co Inc* is *Re the Application of Medway Power Ltd,* 985 F. Supp. 402 (S.D.N.Y. 1997). In *Re Application of Technostroyexport*, 853 F. Supp. 695 (S.D.N.Y. 1994) the court held that arbitrators could be a "tribunal" within 28 U.S.C., s.1782, but denied the application for assistance on discretionary grounds. In *Re Application of Roz Trading Ltd*, 469 F. Supp. 2d 1221 (N.D. Ga. 2006) the court held that an arbitral panel of the International Arbitral Centre of the Austrian Federal Economic Chamber in Vienna was a tribunal for the purposes of s.1782, regarding the matter as now to be governed by principles developed by the United States Supreme Court in *Intel Corp v Advanced Micro Devices Inc*, 542 U.S. 241 (2004) in holding that the Directorate-General of Competition for the Commission of the European Communities was a "tribunal" for that purpose. See Fellas (2007) 23 Arb.Int. 379; Knöfel (2009) 5 J. Priv. Int. L. 281.

For the approach of the Canadian courts, see *OPSEU Pension Trust Fund v* **8–082**
*Clark* (2006) 270 D.L.R. (4th) 429 (Ont. CA) (letters rogatory from a United States case sought the production of documents by an independent auditor and the oral examination of officers involved in the audit; it would require a minimum of 1500 person-hours to identify the documents sought; request

granted, applying the test that the evidence was relevant, not otherwise obtainable, and identified with reasonable specificity, and enforcement was consistent with Canadian public policy and not unduly burdensome). That case was distinguished in *Presbyterian Church of Sudan v Taylor* (2006) 275 D.L.R. (4th) 512 (Ont. CA), partly on public policy grounds, aspects of the litigation having been made the subject of a diplomatic protest by Canada, but also because a request seeking information about the defendant corporation's "operations in Sudan" was too wide and it had not been established that the evidence sought was relevant, necessary and not otherwise obtainable.

**8–086** See the examination of s.2(4) of the Evidence (Proceedings in Other Jurisdictions) Act 1975 in *Charman v Charman* [2005] EWCA Civ 1606, [2006] 1 W.L.R. 1053.

**8–088** See *Morgan, Lewis & Bockius LLP v Gauthier* (2006) 82 O.R. (3d) 189 (letter of request in part contrary to Canadian public policy opposing extra-territorial application by the United States of its embargo against Cuba).

**8–090** NOTE 7. Companies Act 1985, s.447 is amended by the Companies Act 2006, s.1038(2).

NOTE 12. Companies Act 1989, s.87 is amended by SI 1992/1315, SI 1993/1826, the Pensions Act 1995, Sch.3, para.19, SI 1997/2781, the Bank of England Act 1998, Sch.5, para.66(3), the National Lottery Act 1998, Sch.1, para.4, SI 1999/1820, SI 2001/1283, SI 2001/3649, the Enterprise Act 2002, Sch.25, para.21(1),(3), SI 2002/1889, the Pensions Act 2004, Sch.4, Pt 4, para.20 and Sch.12, para.6, the Companies (Audit, Investigations and Community Enterprise) Act 2004, Sch.2, Pt 1, para.1, 3(b) and Pt 3, para.29, SI 2005/1967 and SI 2006/1644.

**8–092** See also the power to require plaintiffs seeking interim injunctions to give undertakings in damages, and Gee [2006] L.M.C.L.Q. 181.

NOTE 18. CPR, r.25.13(2)(a)(ii) is amended by SI 2009/3131 so as to refer, inter alia, to claimants not resident in a State bound by the Lugano Convention 2007.

**8–093** NOTE 31. The reference should be to CPR, r.25.13(2)(a)(ii), now as amended by SI 2009/3131 so as to refer to claimants not resident in a State bound by the revised Lugano Convention.

NOTE 32. For the practice under the equivalent Scottish provision, see *Monarch Energy Ltd v Powergen Retail* 2006 S.L.T. 743 (O.H.). Companies Act 1985, s.726 is repealed by Companies Act 2006, Sch.16 (not yet in force).

NOTE 35. *Nasser v United Bank of Kuwait* [2001] EWCA Civ 556, [2002] 1 W.L.R. 1868 (CA) was followed in *Al-Koronky v Time-Life Entertainment*

*Group Ltd* [2006] EWCA Civ 1123 where an order for security for costs was upheld: it would be unlikely that a costs order would be enforced in Sudan, the plaintiff being a former Sudanese ambassador in London, owing to the influence of the Government of Sudan over its judiciary.

The Court of Appeal in *Gater Assets Ltd v NAK Naftogas Ukrainiy* [2007] EWCA Civ 988, [2007] 2 Lloyd's Rep. 588 considered whether security for costs could be ordered against an award creditor bringing enforcement proceedings in England under the New York Convention. It had been held in one previous case (*Dardana Ltd v Yukos Oil Ltd* [2002] 2 Lloyd's Rep. 261) that jurisdiction to make such an order existed, but an order was there refused in the exercise of discretion. Rix L.J. was prepared to assume, but not decide, that there was technical jurisdiction to order security for costs against any award creditor who brings enforcement proceedings pursuant to statute, but not where, as in the circumstances of the instant case, there was summary enforcement as that took the case outside CPR r.25.12. If the jurisdiction existed, it should be exercised only in exceptional cases. An award debtor seeking to resist enforcement on the ground of fraud was the substantive claimant. In the case of the enforcement of a domestic award under Arbitration Act 1996, s.66, an award debtor is not entitled to security for costs; to impose a security for costs regime upon an award creditor who seeks enforcement under s.101 would be to impose substantially more onerous conditions than are imposed in the case of the enforcement of domestic awards, in breach of Art.III of the New York Convention. To require an award creditor to provide security for the costs ran counter to the essential basis of the Convention. Moses L.J. on similar grounds held that the court did not have jurisdiction to make an order for security for costs. Buxton L.J. dissented. **8–097**

Companies Act 1985, s.726 is repealed by Companies Act 2006, Sch.16 (not yet in force). **8–102**

## Chapter 9

# PROOF OF FOREIGN LAW

**9–001** Article 30 of the Rome II Regulation (as to which, see paras S35–165 *et seq.*, below) requires the Commission to report on the effects of the way in which foreign law is treated in the different jurisdictions and the extent to which courts in the Member States apply foreign law in practice pursuant to the Regulation.

Note 1. See also Fentiman (2006) 59 Curr. Leg. Prob. 391.

**9–002** Note 3. For the view that the English approach may be more efficient or economical than an approach which permits parties to plead that foreign law applies and then leave it to the court to ascertain it, see Rühl (2007) 71 *RabelsZ* 559.

Note 8. See the cases set out in detail at the entry at para.9–025, below.

**9–003** Note 10. On incorporation of provisions of non-English *(in casu*, Jewish religious) law by reference, see also *Halpern v Halpern* (*Nos 1 & 2*) [2007] EWCA Civ 291, [2008] Q.B. 195.

**9–007** Note 28. But in *Oakley v Osiris Trustees Ltd* [2008] UKPC 2, (2007–8) I.T.E.L.R. 789 the Privy Council, sitting as the final court of appeal from the Isle of Man in a case in which the law of Jersey fell to be applied, preferred to leave the question open.

**9–008** Text under sub-para.(f): In *Islamic Republic of Iran v Berend* [2007] EWHC 132 (QB), [2007] 2 All E.R. (Comm.) 132, at [35], the judge was prepared to make a finding on the French (and Iranian) doctrine of *renvoi* even though he had received no evidence on the issue.

**9–010** See also *Abu Dhabi Investment Co v H Clarkson & Co Ltd* [2006] EWHC 1252 (Comm.). And see further, *General Motors Acceptance Corp of Canada Ltd v Town and Country Chrysler Ltd* (2007) 88 O.R. (3d) 666 (Ont. CA), holding that a finding of foreign law may be appealed on the ground that it is wrong, and that the appellate court may substitute its own conclusion for that of the judge.

**9–013** On the potential difficulties of proof of foreign law where Saudi Arabia is concerned, in particular, the relationship between Sharia principles and legislative decrees, see *Harley v Smith* [2009] EWHC 56 (QB), [2009] 1 Lloyd's

Rep. 359. The Court of Appeal subjected the judge's treatment of the evidence of foreign law to close analysis, but substantially approved the approach which he had taken and dismissed the appeal: [2010] EWCA Civ 78.

On the difficulty of making a finding as to Saudi law, in circumstances in which a Saudi judge has to decide for himself what the material principles of religious law require, he being bound neither by his own previous rulings nor by the opinions of others, and there is no tradition of textbook writing, see *Abdel Hadi Abdullah Al Qahtani & Sons Beverage Industry Co v Antliff* [2010] EWHC 1735 (Comm.).

On the assessment of expertise in witnesses, see *Dornoch Ltd v Westminster International BV* [2009] EWHC 1782 (Admlty), [2009] 2 Lloyd's Rep. 191, [49]. Likewise, evidence of foreign law given by a partisan "expert witness" may be accepted, but with considerable reserve: *Debt Collect London Ltd v SK Slavia Praha Fotbal AS* [2010] EWHC 57 (QB), [40]–[43]. **9–014**

On the weight to be attributed to foreign source material which appears to copy without attribution the view of other foreign sources, see *Dornoch Ltd v Westminster International BV* [2009] EWHC 1782 (Admlty), [37]. **9–015**

Note 84. See also *Catalyst Recycling Ltd v Nickelhütte Aue GmbH* [2008] EWCA Civ 541, [49]–[52]. **9–017**

See *Law Debenture Trust Corp plc v Elektrim SA* [2009] EWHC 1801 (Ch.), [100] on the use of foreign judicial decisions as evidence of the content of foreign law. **9–020**

On the difficulty of proving the law of the United States where the Circuit Courts of Appeal have given clear but contradictory decisions upon the legal issue in question, see *JP Morgan Chase Bank v Lanner (The)* [2008] FCA 399, (2008) 305 D.L.R. (4th) 442, [2009] 1 Lloyd's Rep. 566 (Can. Fed. CA): the majority accepted the most recent decision of an appellate court as representing the state of American law, while the minority concluded that proof of foreign law had failed and that the *lex fori* applied by default.

See also *Dallah Estate and Tourism Holding Co v Ministry of Religious Affairs, Government of Pakistan* [2009] EWCA Civ 755, [28]–[29] (the task of the judge is not just to ascertain the principles of foreign law but to understand their content and the way they are applied in the courts of the country in question), affd. [2010] UKSC 46, [2010] 3 W.L.R. 1472. On the difficulty of making a finding as to Iranian law, in circumstances in which the Supreme Court of Iran has not given guidance and the commentators are divided, the task for the judge is to "determine the trajectory of" the foreign law: *Blue Sky One Ltd v Mahan Air* [2010] EWHC 631 (Comm.), [88]. On the difficulty of making a finding as to Saudi law, in circumstances in which each Saudi judge has to decide for himself what the material principles of religious law require, he being bound neither by his own previous rulings nor by the opinions of others, and where there is no tradition of textbook writing, see

*Abdel Hadi Abdullah Al Qahtani & Sons Beverage Industry Co v Antliff* [2010] EWHC 1735 (Comm.).

**9–023** An English court may, in an appropriate case, give a ruling on a question of English law which will assist a foreign court to dispose of a case before it: see *Westacre Investments Inc v Yugoimport SDPR* [2008] EWHC 801 (Comm.), [2009] 1 All E.R. (Comm.) 780. A formal agreement between the Supreme Courts of New South Wales and Singapore will allow the courts of one, with the consent of the parties, to refer the parties to the other court to obtain a ruling on the law of the latter. This development may be extended; for the procedure, see Uniform Civil Procedure Rules (NSW) Part 6 Division 9.

**9–025** The presumption that foreign law is no different from the court's own law, and the circumstances in which it will and will not apply (and the consequence when the presumption is held not to apply) has produced a number of divergent decisions from which no single conclusion emerges.

In three cases the presumption was applied. In *Balmoral Group Ltd v Borealis UK Ltd* [2006] EWHC 1900 (Comm.), [2006] 2 C.L.C. 220, at [432]–[433], the Unfair Contract Terms Act 1977 was applied to a contract which was pleaded as being governed by Danish or Norwegian law although no evidence was led as to whether those laws contained provisions analogous to the 1977 Act. The presumption was pleaded; it had not been pleaded that the 1977 Act had no application to such contracts; and it would be unfair not to apply the Act. And in *Law Debenture Trust Corp plc v Elektrim SA* [2009] EWHC 1801 (Ch.), [55], the judge accepted the general principle that English law would apply unless it was shown to his satisfaction that Polish law was to different effect. In *Tisand Pty Ltd v Owners of the Ship MV Cape Morton* (2005) 219 A.L.R. 48, distinguishing *Damberg v Damberg* [2001] NSWCA 87, (2001) 52 N.S.W.L.R. 492, the Full Court of the Federal Court of Australia applied the presumption that foreign law was the same as local (Australian) law, to find that Liberian law on the registration and ownership of ships was the same as Australian law, as the relevant Australian Act had its roots in an international convention to which a large number of States were party.

By contrast, in *Global Multimedia International Ltd v Ara Media Services* [2006] EWHC 3107 (Ch.), [2007] 1 All E.R. (Comm.) 1160, a pleading alleged that a contract was governed by Saudi law, but the party making the assertion neither pleaded the content nor tendered evidence of Saudi law. The presumption was not applicable, and the pleading was liable to be struck out under CPR r.3.4(2)(a). (Likewise, according to Scots procedure, foreign law must be pleaded and its substance stated in the pleadings, failing which the pleading may be struck out: *Royal Bank of Scotland plc v Davidson* [2009] CSOH 134, 2010 S.L.T. 92, though the judgment, at [17], may mis-state the effect of the judgment in *Global Multimedia International Ltd v Ara Media Services*.) And in *Tamil Nadu Electricity Board v St CMS Electricity Co Ltd*

[2007] EWHC 1713 (Comm.) [2008] 2 Lloyd's Rep. 484, at [97]–[98], the presumption that foreign law is the same as English law was inapplicable where a party had adduced expert evidence of foreign law but had failed to deal with a particular point of that foreign law on which it later sought to rely.

In *National Auto-Glass Supplies (Australia) Pty Ltd v Nielsen & Moller Autoglass (NSW) Pty Ltd (No.8)* [2007] FCA 1625, at [41], the Australian authorities were considered to render the presumption that foreign law was the same as the *lex fori* "not inflexible". And in *TS Production LLC v Drew Pictures Pty Ltd* [2008] FCAFC 194, (2008) 252 A.L.R. 1, [18], the court applied the presumption that foreign law was the same as the *lex fori* only after checking that the presumption was in fact reliable. And on the Australian approach in general, see McComish (2007) 31 Melb. U.L.Rev. 400.

## CHAPTER 10

# JURISDICTIONAL IMMUNITIES

**10R–001** NOTE 1. See also *State Practice Regarding State Immunities*, ed. Hafner, Kohen and Breau (2006).

**10–002** In *Jurisdictional Immunities of the State (Germany v Italy)* (pending) Germany has brought proceedings in the International Court of Justice claiming that, by allowing claims to be brought in Italian courts arising out of acts by German forces in the Second World War, Italy had failed to respect Germany's immunity under international law.

**10–003** In *Jones v Ministry of Interior of Saudi Arabia* [2006] UKHL 26, [2007] 1 A.C. 270 (noted Seymour [2006] C.L.J. 479) Lord Bingham and Lord Hoffmann expressed doubts as to whether Art.6 of the European Convention on Human Rights was engaged by the grant of immunity under international law: see [14] and [64]. The House of Lords applied the decision of the European Court of Human Rights in *Al-Adsani v United Kingdom* (2002) 34 E.H.R.R. 273 (which was affirmed in *Kalogeropoulou v Greece and Germany* (App. No. 50021/00) (unreported, December 12, 2002)). See also *Entico Corp Ltd v United Nations Educational Scientific and Cultural Association* [2008] EWHC 531 (Comm.), [2008] 1 Lloyd's Rep. 673.

NOTE 6. *AIG Capital Partners Inc v Republic of Kazakhstan* [2005] EWHC 2239 (Comm.) is now reported at [2006] 1 W.L.R. 1420.

In Case C–292/05 *Lechouritou v Dimosio tis Omospondiakis Dimokratias tis Germanias* [2007] E.C.R. I–1519 (on which see Watt and Pataut, 2007 *Rev. Crit.* 61) it was not necessary to decide the question whether state immunity was compatible with the 1968 Convention on Jurisdiction and the Enforcement of Judgments in Civil and Commercial Matters. In *Grovit v Nederlandsche Bank* [2005] EWHC 2944, [2006] 1 W.L.R. 3323 (QB) (affirmed on other grounds: [2007] EWCA Civ 953, [2008] 1 W.L.R. 51) it was held to be compatible.

NOTE 8. See also McGregor (2006) 55 I.C.LQ. 437 (state immunity and *jus cogens*); Kloth, *Immunities and the Right of Access to Court under Article 6 of the European Convention on Human Rights* (2010).

On the history see *Jones v Ministry of Interior of Saudi Arabia* [2006] UKHL 26, [2007] 1 A.C. 270, at [8]. **10–004—10–005**

NOTE 13. On the UN Convention see Denza (2006) 55 I.C.L.Q. 395; Fox, *ibid.*, 399; Gardiner, *ibid.*, 407; Hall, *ibid.*, 411. For the use of the UN Convention as indicative of contemporary international law see *Jones v Ministry of Interior of Saudi Arabia* [2006] UKHL 26, [2007] 1 A.C. 270, at [8], *per* Lord Bingham, approving *AIG Capital Partners Inc v Republic of Kazakhstan* [2005] EWHC 2239 (Comm.), [2006] 1 All E.R. 284, at [80]. See also [26], [66]. **10–004**

CPR, r.6.20 has been replaced by CPR PD6B, para. 3.1: see CPR, r.6.36 (as substituted by SI 2008/2178, Sch.1). **10–007**

On immunity of the officials of a foreign State see *Jones v Ministry of Interior of Saudi Arabia* [2006] UKHL 26, [2007] 1 A.C. 270, where it was held that the immunity extends to officials in relation to acts, even if they are unauthorised, for which the State is internationally responsible. Reversing the decision of the Court of Appeal on this aspect (*Jones v Ministry of the Interior* [2004] EWCA Civ 1394, [2005] Q.B. 699), the House of Lords also held that immunity extends to allegations of torture. **10–008**

In *Samantar v Yousuf*, 130 S.Ct. 2278 (2010) the United States Supreme Court decided that the former Prime Minister of Somalia was not immune under the Foreign Sovereign Immunities Act in a claim brought by Somalis who claimed that the had authorised torture and killing of the claimants or their relatives. It was held that a State official is not to be regarded as an "agency or instrumentality" of the State. But the Court emphasised the narrowness of its holding (at pp 2292–2293): whether the official was entitled to immunity under the common law, and whether he had other valid defences to the charges against him, were matters to be addressed by the District Court on remand.

NOTE 28. See *Aziz v Aziz* [2007] EWCA 712, [2008] 2 All E.R. 501 for an unsuccessful application by a head of State to have judgments edited to remove references to himself on the ground that they amounted to an attack on his dignity. See also *Thor Shipping A/S v The Ship "Al Duhail"* [2008] FCA 1842, (2008) 252 A.L.R. 20 (noted Alderton (2009) 58 I.C.L.Q. 702).

NOTE 30. *Grovit v Nederlandsche Bank* [2005] EWHC 2944, [2006] 1 W.L.R. 3323 (QB) was affirmed on other grounds: [2007] EWCA Civ 953, [2008] 1 W.L.R. 51. See also *Pan v Bo* [2008] NSWSC 961, (2008) 220 F.L.R. 271.

In *Pocket Kings Ltd v Safenames Ltd* [2009] EWHC 2529 (Ch.), [2010] 2 W.L.R. 1110 (as to the facts of which see entry at para. 5–040, above) the claimant brought proceedings in England against the first defendant and the **10–009—10–010**

Commonwealth of Kentucky seeking an injunction restraining the first defendant from complying with the seizure order made in the Kentucky proceedings and a declaration that the court would not recognise or enforce the order, or any subsequent order for the seizure or forfeiture of the domain name, since to do so would amount to the exercise of the sovereign authority of the Commonwealth of Kentucky within the jurisdiction thus constituting the enforcement of the penal or public law of a foreign state. Although the Commonwealth of Kentucky was served with the proceedings in accordance with the requirements of the State Immunity Act 1978 it failed to acknowledge service. The claimant applied for summary judgment in default of acknowledgment of service. Before deciding whether to enter judgment, it was necessary for the court to satisfy itself as to whether the Commonwealth of Kentucky, which was not the subject of an Order in Council under 1978 Act, s.14(5), was immune from jurisdiction because it was either a "state", within the meaning of s.14(1), or a "separate entity" exercising sovereign authority, within the meaning of s.14(2)(a) of the Act. It was held that it was not possible for an entity to be both a constituent territory of a federal state and a State in its own right; that once a court had identified the recognised state any constituent territory of that state could not also to qualify as a state but had to be treated as a "separate entity" for the purposes of s.14; and that, accordingly, the Commonwealth of Kentucky, being one of the constituent territories of the United States of America which was a sovereign federal state, was not itself a state for the purposes of s.14(1). The phrase "sovereign authority" in s.14(2)(a) of the Act referred to the authority of the recognised state; that in order for a separate entity to attract immunity the act in respect of which immunity was claimed had to be the exercise of or manifestation of the sovereign authority of that recognised state; that there was no independent immunity for a separate entity or constituent territory since such immunity it enjoyed was parasitic on the immunity conferred on the recognised state; that the mere fact that the separate entity performed public functions was not of itself sufficient to attract immunity; that the proceedings which had been brought under local Kentucky law and by a Kentucky official were not therefore the exercise of or manifestation of any sovereign authority of the federal government of the United States but were the acts of the Commonwealth of Kentucky exercising its own non-sovereign authority; and accordingly, the Commonwealth of Kentucky was not entitled to state immunity under the Act and the court had jurisdiction to enter summary judgment against it.

**10–009** See *Koo Golden East Mongolia v Bank of Nova Scotia* [2007] EWCA Civ 1443, [2008] Q.B. 717 (state bank entered into contract in exercise of sovereign authority); *The Altair* [2008] EWHC 612 (Comm.), [2008] 2 Lloyd's Rep. 90, at [6] *et seq.*; *Wilhelm Finance Inc v Ente Administrador Del Astillero Rio Santiago* [2009] EWHC 1074 (Comm.) (state-owned shipyard a separate entity). See generally Dickinson (2009) 10 Bus. L. Int. 97.

State Immunity Act 1978, s.13(2), applies even if one of the jurisdictional exceptions applies. Thus, for example, by s.3 a State is not immune "as respects proceedings relating to . . . a commercial transaction entered into by the State." In such proceedings the State cannot be enjoined from breach of the contract: *ETI Euro Telecom International NV v Republic of Bolivia* [2008] EWCA Civ 880, [2008] 1 W.L.R. 665, at [113]. **10–014**

NOTE 54. See *Orascom Telecom Holding SAE v Republic of Chad* [2008] EWHC 1841 (Comm.), [2008] 2 Lloyd's Rep. 396. **10–015**

NOTE 58. *AIG Capital Partners Inc v Republic of Kazakhstan* [2005] EWHC 2239 (Comm.) is now reported at [2006] 1 W.L.R. 1420. See *also Continental Transfert Technique Ltd v Federal Government of Nigeria* [2010] EWHC 2898 (Comm.). **10–016**

NOTE 65. This procedure applies to an application under CPR, r. 62.18 to enforce an arbitral award: *Norsk Hydro ASA v State Property Fund of Ukraine*: [2002] EWHC 2120 (Comm.), [2009] Bus. L. R. 558.

State Immunity Act 1978, s.1(1) provides that the court must give effect to immunity even if the State does not appear and the issue of immunity would normally fall to be considered first: *ETI Euro Telecom International NV v Republic of Bolivia* [2008] EWCA Civ 880, [2008] 1 W.L.R. 665, at [110], [128] **10–018**

CPR, r.6.20 has been replaced by CPR PD6B, para.3.1: see CPR, r.6.36 (as substituted by SI 2008/2178, Sch.1). **10–019**

NOTE 64. See also *Mauritius Tourism Promotion Authority v Wong Min* [2008] UKEAT 0185/08/2411 (E.A.T.).

NOTE 65. CPR, r.6.27 has been replaced by CPR, r.6.44 (as substituted by SI 2008/2178, Sch.1).

NOTE 77. See *United States v Nolan* (2009) 153 S.J.L.B. 32 (E.A.T.) (where there was a waiver of immunity).

NOTE 1. In *Svenska Petroleum Exploration AB v Lithuania (No.2)* [2005] EWHC 2437 (Comm.), [2006] 1 Lloyd's Rep. 181; affd. [2006] EWCA Civ 1529, [2008] Q.B. 886, the contract between the parties contained an arbitration clause, and also the following provision: "GOVERNMENT and EPG hereby irrevocably waives [sic] all rights to sovereign immunity". EPG was at the material time a separate legal entity owned and controlled by the Government of Lithuania. Gloster J. distinguished *A Company Ltd v Republic of X* [1990] 2 Lloyd's Rep. 520 in which Saville J. had held that an agreement by the Ministry of Finance of the Republic to waive "whatever defence it may **10–028** have of sovereign immunity for itself or its property (present or subsequently acquired)" was a submission. She held that it was distinguishable on the grounds that the contract also contained an express choice of English law and an express submission to the jurisdiction of the English courts. The Court of Appeal, affirming her decision, held that there had been no submission, because the provision was too imprecise, and because it had to be read in the context of the Government's agreement to submit to ICC arbitration. See also *Republic of Argentina v NML Capital Ltd* [2010] EWCA Civ 41, [2010] 3 W.L.R. 874 (see Fox (2009) 125 L.Q.R. 544 on the decision at first instance, which was reversed).

**10–031** NOTE 10. *cf. Donegal International Ltd v Republic of Zambia* [2007] EWHC 197 (Comm.), [2007] 1 Lloyd's Rep. 397 (authority of Minister).

**10–033** NOTE 12. In *Svenska Petroleum Exploration AB v Lithuania (No.2)* [2006] EWCA Civ 1529, [2008] Q.B. 886 the Court of Appeal left open the question whether a joint venture agreement between a State organisation and a private investor to exploit a commercial opportunity relating to the State's natural resources on a profit-sharing basis was to be regarded as a commercial transaction for the purposes of the State Immunity Act 1978, s.3(3)(c). But proceedings to enforce an award were not proceedings which related to a commercial transaction, approving *AIC Ltd v Federal Government of Nigeria* [2003] EWHC 1357 (QB).

**10–035** CPR, r.6.20 has been replaced by CPR PD6B, para.3.1: see CPR, r.6.36 (as substituted by SI 2008/2178, Sch.1).

**10E–050** NOTE 45. See *The Altair* [2008] EWHC 612 (Comm.), [2008] 2 Lloyd's Rep. 90, at [56]–[59].

**10–051** NOTE 48. *Svenska Petroleum Exploration AB v Lithuania (No.2)* [2005] EWHC 2437 (Comm.), [2006] 1 Lloyd's Rep. 181 has been affirmed: [2006] EWCA Civ 1529, [2008] Q.B. 886. The Court of Appeal said that arbitration was a consensual procedure and the principle underlying the State Immunity Act 1978, s.9, was that, if a State has agreed to submit to arbitration, it rendered itself amenable to such process as might be necessary to render the arbitration effective. An application under the Arbitration Act 1996, s.101(2), for leave to enforce an award as a judgment was the final stage in rendering the arbitral procedure effective. That was confirmed by its parliamentary history.

**10–054** NOTE 55. Supreme Court Act 1981 is now re-named Senior Courts Act 1981: Constitutional Reform Act 2005, s.59 and Sch.11, in force October 1, 2009.

CPR, r.6.20 has been replaced by CPR PD6B, para.3.1: see CPR, r.6.36 (as substituted by SI 2008/2178, Sch.1). **10–071**

NOTE 18. See, e.g., *Entico Corp Ltd v United Nations Educational Scientific and Cultural Association* [2008] EWHC 531 (Comm.), [2008] 1 Lloyd's Rep. 673. **10R–078**

## CHAPTER 11

# JURISDICTION IN CLAIMS IN PERSONAM

**As from October 1, 2008 a new CPR Pt 6 has been substituted by the Civil Procedure (Amendment) Rules 2008 (SI 2008/2178), Rule 5 and Sch.1. The heads of jurisdiction in CPR, r.6.20 (the successor to RSC, Ord.11, r.1(1)) are now to be found in para.3.1 of Practice Direction B supplementing the new Pt 6 (PD6B): CPR, r.6.36 (in SI 2008/2178, Sch.1).**

**The revised Lugano Convention between the European Community, Iceland, Norway, Denmark and Switzerland ([2007] O.J. L339/1) entered into force between the Member States of the European Union (including Denmark) and Norway on January 1, 2010. It will be ratified by Switzerland with effect from January 1, 2011. The text of the previous Lugano Convention contained in Sch. 3C of the Civil Jurisdiction and Judgments Act 1982 has been repealed by the Civil Jurisdiction and Judgments Regulations 2009 (SI 2009/3131), which make consequential amendments to the 1982 Act and the Civil Procedure Rules. The terms of the revised Lugano Convention are substantially the same as those of the Judgments Regulation.**

## 1. GENERAL PRINCIPLE

**11R–001** Text at note 4. The revised Lugano Convention ([2007] O.J. L339/1) entered into force between the Member States of the European Union (including Denmark) and Norway on January 1, 2010. It will be ratified by Switzerland with effect from January 1, 2011. The text of the previous Lugano Convention contained in Sch. 3C of the Civil Jurisdiction and Judgments Act 1982 was repealed by Reg. 25 of the Civil Jurisdiction and Judgments Regulations 2009 (SI 2009/3131) as from January 1, 2010. There is no implementing legislation for the revised Lugano Convention on the basis that it is a treaty which has direct effect in the United Kingdom. For a report on the revised Lugano Convention by Professor Fausto Pocar see [1999] O.J. C319; and also Pocar (2008) 10 Yb. P.I.L. 1

**11–003** Text at note 6. A new CPR Pt 6 has been substituted: see CPR, r.6.36 (as substituted by SI 2008/2178, Sch.1).

NOTE 7. See also Magnus & Mankowski (eds.), *Brussels I Regulation* (2007). **11–004**

NOTE 18. The Judgments Regulation applies to Denmark by virtue of a parallel agreement ([2006] O.J. L120/22) with effect from July 1, 2007: SI 2007/1655. **11–009**

For the revised Lugano Convention see entry at para.11R–001, above. **11–010—11–011**

The European Commission has made a report to the European Parliament, the Council and the European Economic and Social Committee on the application of the Judgments Regulation: COM(2009) 174, April 21, 2009. The report was prepared in accordance with Art.73 of the Judgments Regulation on the basis of a general study ("the Heidelberg Report") commissioned by the European Commission: Hess, Pfeiffer and Schlosser, *Report on the Application of Regulation Brussels I in the Member States* (2007) (available at *http://ec.europa.eu/justice_home/doc_centre/civil/studies/doc_civil_studies_en.htm*), reprinted as Hess, Pfeiffer, and Schlosser, *The Brussels I-Regulation (EC) No.44/2001: The Heidelberg Report on the application of Regulation Brussels I in 25 Member States* (2008). **11–013**

The Commission Report was accompanied by a Green Paper which was intended to launch a broad consultation on possible ways to improve the Judgments Regulation with respect to the points raised in the Report: COM(2009) 175, April 21, 2009.

The Report estimated that the jurisdiction rules generally apply in a relatively small number of cases, ranging from less than 1 per cent of all civil cases to 16 per cent in border regions. The Regulation was considered to be a highly successful instrument, which had facilitated cross-border litigation through an efficient system of judicial co-operation based on comprehensive jurisdiction rules, co-ordination of parallel proceedings, and circulation of judgments. The system of judicial co-operation laid down in the Regulation had successfully adapted to the changing institutional environment (from intergovernmental co-operation to an instrument of European integration) and to new challenges of modern commercial life.

The principal points made in the Report are these. First, the main objective of the revision of the Judgments Regulation should be the abolition of the *exequatur* procedure in all matters covered by the Regulation.

Secondly, it recommends the consideration of the extension of the jurisdictional rules of the Regulation to defendants domiciled in non-Member States. The Report suggests that the absence of common rules determining jurisdiction against third State defendants may jeopardise the application of mandatory Community legislation, for example on consumer protection (e.g. time share), commercial agents, data protection or product liability. In Member States where no additional jurisdictional protection existed, consumers could not bring proceedings against third State defendants. The same was true for employees, commercial agents, victims of competition law infringements or of product liability torts, and individuals who intended to avail themselves of the rights afforded by EU data protection legislation. Where mandatory Community legislation existed, Community claimants might be deprived of the protection offered to them by the Community rules. In addition, the absence of common rules on the effect of third State judgments in the Community might in certain Member States lead to situations where third State judgments were recognised and enforced even where such judgments were in breach of mandatory Community law or where Community law provided for exclusive jurisdiction of Member States' courts. The absence of harmonised rules determining the cases where the courts of the Member States could decline jurisdiction on the basis of the Regulation in favour of the courts of third States generated a great deal of confusion and uncertainty.

Thirdly, the report draws attention to the problems caused by there being no uniform rule for the validity of jurisdiction agreements. This is said to lead to undesirable consequences, in that a choice of court agreement might be considered valid in one Member State and invalid in another. A party might seise the courts of a Member State in violation of the choice of court agreement, thereby obstructing proceedings before the chosen court in so far as the latter were brought subsequently to the first proceedings: Case C–116/02 *Erich Gasser GmbH v Misat Srl* [2003] E.C.R. I–14693, [2005] Q.B. 1. A tendency had been reported on the part of lenders in corporate loan transactions to institute proceedings prematurely so as to ensure the jurisdiction of the court designated in the agreement, with negative economic consequences in terms of triggering default and cross-default clauses in loan agreements. These situations were particularly resented in specific circumstances, such as when the first proceedings were limited to obtaining negative declaratory relief, which had the effect of completely blocking proceedings on the merits. The Commission proposed to sign the Hague Convention on choice of court agreements, and a coherent application of the rules of the Convention and those of the Regulation should be ensured.

Fourthly, the Commission draws attention to the problems caused by the *lis pendens* rules in intellectual property litigation, for example where pre-emptive proceedings are brought for negative declaratory relief.

Fifthly, the application of the *lis pendens* and related actions rules of the Regulation had also raised concerns in some other cases. With respect to exclusive jurisdiction under Art.22 of the Judgments Regulation, the study did not show an immediate practical need for exceptions to the priority rule. Nevertheless, the use of actions for negative declaratory relief had been reported in other specific areas such as corporate loan and competition cases.

As a result, it should be considered whether the need arose to improve the existing *lis pendens* rule in general in order to prevent abusive procedural tactics and ensure the good administration of justice in the Community.

Sixthly, provisional measures remained an area where the diversity in the national procedural laws of the Member States made the free circulation of such measures difficult. A first difficulty arose with respect to protective measures ordered without the defendant being summoned to appear and which were intended to be enforced without prior service of the defendant. In Case C–125/79 *Denilauler v SNC Couchet Frères* [1980] E.C.R. 1553 the European Court held that such *ex parte* measures fell outside the scope of the recognition and enforcement system of the Regulation. It was not entirely clear, however, whether such measures could be recognised and enforced on the basis of the Regulation if the defendant had the opportunity to contest the measure subsequently. A second difficulty arose with respect to protective orders aimed at obtaining information and evidence. In Case C–104/03 *St. Paul Dairy Dairy Industries NV v Unibel Exser BVBA* [2005] E.C.R. I–3481, the European Court held that a measure ordering the hearing of a witness for the purpose of enabling the applicant to decide whether to bring a case was not covered by the notion of provisional or protective measures. It was not entirely clear to what extent such orders were, as a general matter, excluded from the scope of Art.31 of the Regulation. It had been suggested that better access to justice would be ensured if the Regulation established jurisdiction for such measures in the courts of the Member State where the information or evidence sought was located, besides the jurisdiction of the courts having jurisdiction with respect to the substance of the matter. This was particularly important in intellectual property matters, where evidence of the alleged infringement must be secured by search orders, *saisies contrefaçon* or *saisies description* and in maritime matters. Further difficulties had been reported with respect to the application of the conditions set by the European Court in Case C–391/95 *Van Uden Maritime BV v Firma Deco-Line* [1998] E.C.R. I–7091, [1999] Q.B. 1225 and Case C–99/96 *Mietz Intership Yachting Sneek BV* [1999] E.C.R. I–2277 for the issue of provisional measures ordered by a court which did not have jurisdiction over the substance of the matter. In particular, it was unclear how the "real connecting link between the subject matter of the measure sought and the territorial jurisdiction" should be interpreted. This was the case, in particular, when the measure aimed at obtaining an interim payment or more generally did not concern the seizure of property. The requirement that repayment must be guaranteed in the case of interim payments had given rise to difficulties of interpretation and might lead to high costs if it was considered that such repayment might only be secured by the provision of bank guarantees on the part of applicants.

Finally, the Commission noted that procedural devices under national law aimed at strengthening the effectiveness of arbitration agreements (such as anti-suit injunctions) were incompatible with the Regulation if they unduly interfered with the determination by the courts of other Member States of their jurisdiction under the Regulation (Case C–185/07 *Allianz SpA v West Tankers Inc (The "Front Comor")* [2009] E.C.R. I–663, [2009] 2 A.C. 1138; there was no uniform allocation of jurisdiction in proceedings ancillary to or supportive of arbitration proceedings (Case C–190/89 *Marc Rich & Co AG v Società Italiana SpA* [1991] E.C.R I–3855, [1992] 1 Lloyd's Rep. 342); the recognition and enforcement of judgments given by the courts in disregard of an arbitration clause was uncertain; the recognition and enforcement of judgments on the validity of an arbitration clause or setting aside an arbitral award was uncertain; the recognition and enforcement of judgments merging an arbitration award was uncertain; and the recognition and enforcement of arbitral awards, governed by the NY Convention, was considered less swift and efficient than the recognition and enforcement of judgments. See further, entry at paras 16–089–16–093, below.

Additional points made by the Commission included these: the determination that a party was domiciled in another Member State in accordance with foreign law (Art.59(2)) was perceived as difficult. There might be a need for a non-exclusive jurisdictional ground based on the situs of movable assets. With respect to exclusive jurisdiction concerning rights *in rem*, the Heidelberg Report reported a need for choice of court in agreements concerning the rent of office space and a need for some flexibility concerning rent of holiday homes in order to avoid litigation in a forum which was remote for all parties. With respect to the exclusive jurisdiction in the area of company law, questions arose on the scope of the exclusive jurisdiction rule and the lack of uniform definition of the notion of "seat" of a company, leading to possible positive and negative conflicts of jurisdiction. The non-uniform application of Arts 6(2) and 11 on third party proceedings pursuant to Art.65 also raised difficulties: in particular, third parties as well as parties claiming against the third party were treated differently depending on the national procedural laws of the Member States; courts had difficulty in appreciating the effect of judgments issued by the courts of other Member States following a third-party notice. In maritime matters, difficulties were reported in the co-ordination of proceedings aimed at setting up a liability fund and individual liability proceedings. The reference to the law applicable to the transportation contract in order to determine the binding force of a jurisdiction agreement in a bill of lading for the third-party holder of the bill of lading (Case C–387/98 *Coreck Maritime GmbH v Handelsveem BV* [2000] E.C.R. I–9337) was reported to be artificial. In consumer matters, the types of consumer credit agreements covered by Arts 15(1)(a) and (b) of the Regulation no longer corresponded to the evolving consumer credit market where various other types of credit products had developed.

See also the Green Paper of the House of Lords European Union Committee, Sub-committee E (Law and Institutions, under the chairmanship of Lord

Mance), July 27, 2009, which is particularly supportive of proposals to increase the effectiveness of jurisdiction and arbitration agreements.

The European Commission has proposed the creation of an integrated jurisdictional system through the establishment of a unified European patent litigation system which would be entitled to deliver judgments on the validity and the infringement of European and future Community patents for the entire territory of the internal market: COM(2007)165.

Regulation (EC) 1896/2006 of the European Parliament and of the Council creating a European order for payment procedure (which applies to United Kingdom and Ireland, but not to Denmark) provides for the application to a court for an order for payment in the case of claims for a specific amount: [2006] O.J. L399/1. Article 6 provides that jurisdiction is to be determined in accordance with the relevant rules of the Judgments Regulation: Art.6(1). But in the case of claims against a consumer, for a purpose which could be regarded as being outside his trade or profession, only the courts of the Member State in which the defendant is domiciled will have jurisdiction: Art.6(2). The defendant is to be advised of his options to pay the amount indicated in the order or oppose the order by lodging with the court of origin a statement of opposition: Art.12. The Regulation is to apply from December 12, 2008. See Lopez de Tejada 2007 *Rev. Crit.* 717.

Regulation (EC) 861/2007 of the European Parliament and of the Council of July 11, 2007 establishes a European Small Claims Procedure, and will apply in the United Kingdom and Ireland, but not in Denmark: [2007] O.J. L199/1. It applies in cross-border cases to civil and commercial matters, whatever the nature of the court or a tribunal, where the value of a claim does not exceed 2000 Euros: Art.2. For the purposes of the Regulation a cross-border case is one in which at least one of the parties is domiciled or habitually resident in a Member State other than the Member State of the court or tribunal seised, and domicile is to be determined in accordance with Arts 59 and 60 of the Judgments Regulation: Art.3. The body of the Regulation does not deal expressly with the grounds of jurisdiction, but it is apparent from Annex 1, which sets out the claim form, that the tribunal must have jurisdiction in accordance with the rules of the Judgments Regulation: Annex 1, Form A, para.4. The Regulation will apply from January 1, 2009.

Directive 2008/52/EC of the European Parliament and of the Council of May 21, 2008 ([2008] O.J. L136/3) on certain aspects of mediation in civil and commercial matters is designed to facilitate access to alternative dispute resolution and to promote the amicable settlement of disputes by encouraging the use of mediation and by ensuring a balanced relationship between mediation and judicial proceedings. It has to be implemented by May 21, 2011. It requires the content of an agreement resulting from mediation which has been made enforceable in a Member State to be recognised and declared enforceable in the other Member States in accordance with applicable Community or national law. It applies to all civil and commercial matters (including family law), but not to revenue, customs or administrative matters or to the liability of the State for acts and omissions in the exercise of State authority (*acta iure imperii*) (Art.2). It does not apply to Denmark.

Council Regulation (EC) 664/2009 establishes a procedure for the negotiation and conclusion of agreements between Member States and third countries concerning jurisdiction, recognition and enforcement of judgments and decisions in matrimonial matters, matters of parental responsibility and matters relating to maintenance obligations, and the law applicable to matters relating to maintenance obligations.

NOTE 25. The Annexes to the Judgments Regulation have been amended to take account of the accession of the new Member States: Commission Regulation (EC) 280/2009: [2009] O.J. L93/13. The Judgments Regulation also now applies to Denmark by virtue of a parallel agreement ([2006] O.J. L120/22) with effect from July 1, 2007: SI 2007/1655.

**11–018** NOTE 32. See now revised Lugano Convention, Art.64(2).

**11–019** The revised Lugano Convention (see entry at para.11R–001, above) brings it into line with the Judgments Regulation.

**11–020** The Judgments Regulation applies to Denmark by virtue of a parallel agreement ([2006] O.J. L120/22) with effect from July 1, 2007: SI 2007/1655.

NOTE 46. In Opinion 1/03 *Competence of the Community to conclude the new Lugano Convention on jurisdiction and the recognition and enforcement of judgments (opinion pursuant to Article 300 EC)* [2006] E.C.R. I–1145, the European Court advised that the conclusion of the new Lugano Convention fell entirely within the sphere of exclusive competence of the European Community. Where common rules had been adopted, the Member States no longer had the right, acting individually or collectively, to undertake obligations with non-Member States which affected those rules. In such a case, the Community had exclusive competence to conclude international agreements.

The purpose of the Judgments Regulation was to unify the rules on jurisdiction in civil and commercial matters, not only for intra-Community disputes but also for those which had an international element, with the objective of eliminating obstacles to the functioning of the internal market which might derive from disparities between national legislation on the subject. The Judgments Regulation contained a set of rules forming a unified system which applied not only to relations between different Member States, since they concerned both proceedings pending before the courts of different Member States and judgments delivered by the courts of a Member State for the purposes of their recognition or enforcement in another Member State, but also to relations between a Member State and a non-member country.

The Judgments Regulation contained provisions governing its relationship with other existing or future provisions of Community law: Arts 67, 71(1), and 71(2)(a). Given the uniform and coherent nature of the system of rules on conflict of jurisdiction established by the Judgments Regulation, Art.4(1), which provides that "if the defendant is not domiciled in a Member State, the jurisdiction of the courts of each Member State shall, subject to Articles 22 and 23, be determined by the law of that Member State", must be interpreted as meaning that it forms part of the system implemented by the Regulation, since it resolved the situation envisaged by reference to the legislation of the Member State before whose court the matter is brought. Even if the reference to the national legislation in question could provide the basis for competence on the part of the Member States to conclude an international agreement, it was clear that, on the basis of the wording of Art.4(1), the only criterion which might be used is that of the domicile of the defendant, provided that there was no basis for applying Arts 22 and 23 of the Regulation. Even if it complied with the rule laid down in Art.4(1) of the Regulation, the agreement envisaged could still conflict with other provisions of that Regulation. Thus, in the case of a legal person which was the defendant in proceedings and not domiciled in a Member State, that agreement could, by using the criterion of domicile of the defendant, conflict with the provisions of the Regulation dealing with branches, agencies or other establishments lacking legal personality, such as Art.9(2) for disputes arising from insurance contracts, Art.15(2) for disputes arising from consumer contracts, or Art.18(2) for disputes arising from individual contracts of employment.

It was apparent from an analysis of the Judgments Regulation that, given the unified and coherent system of rules on jurisdiction for which it provided, any international agreement also establishing a unified system of rules on conflict of jurisdiction such as that established by the Regulation was capable of affecting those rules of jurisdiction.

The new Lugano Convention affected the uniform and consistent application of the Community rules on jurisdiction and the proper functioning of the system established by those rules. The rules of jurisdiction and those relating to the recognition and enforcement of judgments in the Judgments Regulation did not constitute distinct and autonomous systems but were closely linked. The Community rules on the recognition and enforcement of judgments were indissociable from those on the jurisdiction of courts, with which they formed a unified and coherent system, and the new Lugano Convention would affect the uniform and consistent application of the Community rules as regards both the jurisdiction of courts and the recognition and enforcement of judgments and the proper functioning of the unified system established by those rules. Accordingly, the Community has exclusive competence to conclude the new Lugano Convention. See Borrás (2006) 8 Yb. P.I.L. 37.

The revised Lugano Convention ([2007] O.J. L339/1) entered into force between the Member States of the European Union (including Denmark) and Norway on January 1, 2010. It will be ratified by Switzerland with effect from January 1, 2011. The text of the previous Lugano Convention contained in Sch.3C of the Civil Jurisdiction and Judgments Act 1982 was repealed by Reg. 25 of the Civil Jurisdiction and Judgments Regulations 2009 (SI 2009/3131) on January 1, 2010. There is no implementing legislation for the revised Lugano Convention on the basis that it is a treaty which has direct effect in the United Kingdom. For a report on the revised Lugano Convention by Professor Fausto Pocar see [1999] O.J. C319; and also Pocar (2008) 10 Yb. P.I.L. 1.

Belgium has initiated proceedings against Switzerland before the International Court of Justice which complain of the failure or refusal of the Swiss courts to apply the Lugano Convention in such a way as would result in a stay of Swiss proceedings in favour of the Belgian courts which were, according to the Belgian government, seised first of a dispute between the same parties and based on the same cause of action: Press Release 2009/36, International Court of Justice, December 22, 2009.

**11–023** Note 53. See also *Goshawk Dedicated Ltd v Life Receivables Irl Ltd* [2009] IESC 7, [2009] I.L.Pr. 435; *Catalyst Investment Group Ltd v Lewinsohn* [2009] EWHC 1964 (Ch.), [2010] 2 W.L.R. 839; *Skype Technologies SA v Joltid Ltd* [2009] EWHC 2783 (Ch.); *UBS AG v HSH Nordbank* [2009] EWCA Civ 585, [2009] 1 Lloyd's Rep. 272, [103]; *Lucasfilm Ltd v Ainsworth* [2009] EWCA Civ 1328, [2010] 3 W.L.R. 333, [105] *et seq.* (appeal to Supreme Court pending); *JKN v JCN* [2010] EWHC 843 (Fam.). See generally Kruger, *Civil Jurisdiction Rules of the EU and their impact on third States* (2008).

**11–024** See generally Scott (2007) 3 J. Priv. Int. L. 309.

**11–025** See generally Betlem and Bernasconi (2006) 122 L.Q.R. 124. In Case C–292/05 *Lechouritou v Dimosio tis Omospondiakis Dimokratias tis Germanias* [2007] E.C.R. I–1519 (on which see Muir Watt and Pataut, 2007 *Rev. Crit.* 61) a reference was made in proceedings by Greek nationals resident in Greece against the Federal Republic of Germany concerning compensation for the financial loss and non-material damage which the plaintiffs had suffered on account of acts perpetrated by the German armed forces and of which their parents were victims at the time of the occupation of Greece during the Second World War, namely the massacre of civilians by soldiers in the German armed forces in 1943 in Kalavrita. The European Court ruled that "civil matters" did not cover a legal action brought by natural persons in a Contracting State against another Contracting State for compensation in respect of the loss or damage suffered by the successors of the victims of acts perpetrated by armed forces in the course of warfare in the territory of the first

State. Operations conducted by armed forces were one of the characteristic emanations of State sovereignty, in particular inasmuch as they were decided upon in a unilateral and binding manner by the competent public authorities and were as inextricably linked to foreign and defence policy. The action for damages therefore resulted from the exercise of public powers on the part of the State concerned on the date when those acts were perpetrated, irrespective of whether those acts were lawful. *cf.* Case C–435/06 *C* [2007] E.C.R. I–10141, [2008] Fam. 27 (Council Regulation 2201/2003 is to be interpreted to the effect that a single decision ordering that a child be taken into care and placed outside his original home in a foster family is covered by the term "civil matters").

In Case C–406/09 *Realchemie Nederland BV v Bayer CropScience AG* (pending) the Dutch Hoge Raad has referred to the European Court the question whether "civil and commercial matters" in Art.1 of the Judgments Regulation is to be interpreted to apply to the recognition and enforcement of an order for payment of "Ordnungsgeld" (an administrative fine) pursuant to para.890 of the German Code of Civil Procedure.

NOTE 57. *Cf. Criminal Assets Bureau v JWPL* [2007] IEHC 177, [2008] I.L.Pr. 298 (Irish High Ct.)

NOTE 59. See also *Grovit v Nederlandsche Bank* [2005] EWHC 2944, [2006] 1 W.L.R. 3323 (QB), affirmed [2007] EWCA Civ 953, [2008] 1 W.L.R. 51.

See now revised Lugano Convention (entry at para.11R–001, above), Art.1(1). **11–026**

See now revised Lugano Convention, Arts 1(2) and 5(2). **11–028**

NOTE 67. See now revised Lugano Convention, Arts 18–21.

See now revised Lugano Convention, Art.1(2). **11–029**

NOTE 74. See now revised Lugano Convention, Art.5(6). **11–032**

Companies Act 1985, s.630 was replaced by Insolvency Act 1986, s.213. **11–033**

NOTE 76. In Case C–111/08 *SCT Industri AB i likvidation v Alpenblume AB* [2009] E.C.R. I–5655, [2010] Bus. L.R. 559, a Swedish liquidator transferred to Alpenblume shares situate in Austria owned by the insolvent company, SCT. An Austrian court held that the liquidator appointed in Sweden had no power to dispose of assets situated in Austria and that consequently Alpenblume's acquisition of the shares was invalid. Alpenblume brought proceedings before a Swedish court against SCT Industri for restitution of title to the shares in question. The Swedish court asked the European Court in effect whether the exclusion in Art.1(2)(b) applied to a judgment of the Austrian court that, in the absence of an international agreement on the mutual recognition of insolvency proceedings, it did not recognise the liquidator's powers to dispose of property situated in Austria. The European Court ruled that it was the closeness of the link, in the sense of Case 133/78 *Gourdain v Nadler* [1979] E.C.R. 733, between a court action such as that at issue in the main proceedings and the insolvency proceedings that was decisive for the purposes of deciding whether the exclusion in Art.1(2)(b) was applicable. The dispute concerned solely the ownership of the shares which were transferred in insolvency proceedings by the liquidator on the basis of provisions, such as those enacted by the Swedish Law on insolvency, which derogated from the general rules of private law and, in particular, from property law. In particular, such provisions provided that, in the case of insolvency, debtors lose the right freely to dispose of their assets and the liquidator has to administer the assets in insolvency on behalf of the creditors, which includes effecting any necessary transfers. The transfer and the action for restitution of title to which it gave rise, were the direct and indissociable consequence of the exercise by the liquidator—an individual who intervenes only after the insolvency proceedings have been opened—of a power which he derived from the provisions of national law governing that type of proceedings. The ground on which the Austrian court held invalid the transfer of the related, specifically and exclusively, to the extent of the powers of that liquidator in insolvency proceedings and, in particular, his power to dispose of the assets situated in Austria. The content and scope of that decision were therefore intimately linked to the conduct of the insolvency proceedings. Consequently, the action derived directly from insolvency proceedings and was closely linked with them, so that it did not fall within the scope of the Judgments Regulation. See also C–339/07 *Seagon v Deko Marty Belgium NV* [2009] I.LPr. 409 (action to set aside transaction by reason of debtor's insolvency).

In C–292/08 *German Graphics Graphische Maschinen GmbH v van der Schee* [2009] E.C.R. I–8421 the European Court ruled that the exception for bankruptcy does not apply to an action brought by a seller based on a reservation of title against a purchaser who is insolvent, where the asset covered by the reservation of title is situated in the Member State of the opening of those proceedings at the time of opening of those proceedings against that purchaser. The link between the claim and the insolvency proceedings was neither sufficiently direct nor sufficiently close to exclude the application of the Judgments Regulation. The only question before the German court related to the ownership of machines situated on the premises of the defendant in the Netherlands. The answer to that question of law was independent of the opening of insolvency proceedings, and the action brought by German Graphics sought only to ensure the application of the reservation of title clause in its favour. The concerning the reservation of title clause constituted an independent claim, as it was not based on the law of the insolvency proceedings and requires neither the opening of such proceedings nor the involvement of a liquidator.

See also *Byers v Yacht Bull Corp* [2010] EWHC 133 (Ch.), [2010] B.C.C. 368 (a claim by the liquidators of Madoff Securities International Ltd to a sports yacht was a claim to ownership under the general law and was not within the exception); *Choudhary v Bhatter* [2009] EWCA Civ 510, [2010] 2 All ER 1031.

In Case C–185/07 *Allianz SpA v West Tankers Inc* [2009] E.C.R. I–663, [2009] 2 A.C. 1138 (noted Peel (2009) 125 L.Q.R. 365, Briggs [2009] L.M.C.L.Q. 161) proceedings were brought in Italy in breach of an English arbitration agreement. An anti-suit injunction was sought in England. The European Court accepted that, because the English proceedings were designed to vindicate the arbitration agreement, they were not within the scope of the Judgments Regulation. But, even though proceedings did not come within the scope of the Judgments Regulation, they might nevertheless have consequences which undermined its effectiveness, namely preventing the attainment of the objectives of unification of the rules of conflict of jurisdiction in civil and commercial matters and the free movement of decisions in those matters. That was so where such proceedings prevented a court of another Member State from exercising the jurisdiction conferred on it by the Judgments Regulation. The Italian proceedings came within the scope of the Regulation, and consequently a preliminary issue in those proceedings concerning the applicability of an arbitration agreement, including in particular its validity, also came within its scope of application. Consequently, the objection of lack of jurisdiction raised by West Tankers before the Italian court on the basis of the existence of an arbitration agreement, including the question of the validity of that agreement, came within the scope of the Regulation and it was therefore exclusively for that court to rule on that objection and on its own jurisdiction, pursuant to Arts 1(2)(d) and 5(3). The use of an anti-suit injunction to prevent a court of a Member State, which had jurisdiction to resolve a dispute under Art.5(3) from ruling, in accordance with Art.1(2)(d), on the applicability of the Regulation to the dispute brought before it, necessarily amounted to stripping that court of the power to rule on its own jurisdiction under the Regulation. Consequently, an anti-suit injunction was contrary to the general principle that every court seised should itself determines whether it had jurisdiction to resolve the dispute before it. In obstructing the court of another Member State in the exercise of the power to decide, on the basis of the rules defining the material scope of the Regulation, including Art.1(2)(d), whether the Regulation was applicable, such an anti-suit injunction also ran counter to the trust which the Member States accorded to one another's legal systems and judicial institutions and on which the system of jurisdiction under the Regulation was based. **11–035— 11–040**

In *Youell v La Réeunion Aérienne* [2009] EWCA Civ 175, [2009] 1 Lloyd's Rep. 586 it was held that the fact that claims in England were the mirror image of claims in a French arbitration did not make them claims to which the arbitration exclusion applied.

See also *The Wadi Sudr* [2009] EWHC 196 (Comm.), [2009] 1 Lloyd's Rep. 666, where it was held that an action for a declaration that foreign proceedings were within the scope of a London arbitration agreement was not incompatible with the Judgments Regulation system; *DHL GBS (UK) Ltd v Fallimento Finmatica* [2009] EWHC 291 (Comm.), [2009] 1 Lloyd's Rep. 430; *National Navigation Co v Endesa Generacion SA* [2009] EWCA Civ 1397, [2010] 1 Lloyd's Rep. 193, at [40], [46] (noted Fentiman [2010] C.L.J. 242) (preliminary ruling by the court as to the applicability of an arbitration clause in proceedings in which the main subject of the proceedings was within the Judgments Regulation was to be categorised as within the Regulation).

Regulation (EC) 1896/2006 of the European Parliament and of the Council creating a European order for payment procedure does not have an arbitration exception in Art.2, by contrast with Art.2 of Regulation (EC) 861/2007 of the European Parliament and of the Council establishing a European Small Claims Procedure.

**11–038** NOTE 89. See also Van Houtte (2005) 21 Arb. Int. 509.

**11–040** NOTE 95. See also *A v B* [2006] EWHC 2006 (Comm.), [2007] 1 Lloyd's Rep. 237.

**11–041** See also *Republic of Congo v Groupe Antoine Tabet* (July 4, 2007); 2007 *Rev. Crit.* 822 (note Usunier); [2008] I.L.Pr. 367n.

**11–042** See now revised Lugano Convention, Art.31.

NOTE 96. See also *CMA CGM SA v Hyundai Mipo Dockyard Co Ltd* [2008] EWHC 2791 (Comm.), [2009] 1 Lloyd's Rep. 213; *DHL GBS (UK) Ltd v Fallimento Finmatica* [2009] EWHC 291 (Comm.), [2009] 1 Lloyd's Rep. 430.

**11–044** See now revised Lugano Convention, Art.64(2).

**11–046** See now revised Lugano Convention, Art.67.

**11–048** See now revised Lugano Convention, Art.67.

**11–049** In C–533/08 *TNT Express Nederland BV v AXA Versicherung AG* [2010] I.L.Pr. 663 the European Court ruled that the effect of Art.71 of the Judgments Regulation was that the rules governing jurisdiction, recognition and enforcement which were laid down by a convention on a particular matter, such as the *lis pendens* rule set out in Art.31(2) of the Convention on the Contract for the International Carriage of Goods by Road, and the rule relating to enforceability set out in Art.31(3) of that Convention, apply provided that they are highly predictable, facilitate the sound administration of justice and enable the risk of concurrent proceedings to be minimised and that they ensure, under conditions at least as favourable as those provided for by the Regulation, the free movement of judgments in civil and commercial matters and mutual trust in the administration of justice in the European Union (*favor executionis*). It also ruled that it did not have jurisdiction to interpret Art.31 of the Convention on the Contract for the International Carriage of Goods by Road.

NOTE 16. See now revised Lugano Convention, Art.21. **11–053**

NOTE 20. See now revised Lugano Convention, Art.79. **11–055**

The House of Lords in its judicial capacity has been replaced by the Supreme Court of the United Kingdom: Constitutional Reform Act 2005, Part 3 (in force October 1, 2009). **11–057**

The Treaty of Lisbon (2009) repeals Art.68 of the EC Treaty. The consequence is that courts from whom there is an appeal may make references. See also C–278/09 *Martinez v MGN Ltd*, November 20, 2009 (jurisdiction declined because Art.267 not in force). **11–058**

In Case C–533/07 *Falco Privatstiftung v Weller-Lindhorst* [2009] E.C.R. I–3327, [2010] Bus. L.R. 210 the European Court held that Art.5(1)(a) of the Judgments Regulation was to interpreted in accordance with its jurisprudence on Art.5(1) of the 1968 Convention. The Community legislature aimed to ensure continuity, and the Judgments Regulation sought to retain the structure and basic principles of the 1968 Convention. See also C–167/08 *Draka NK Cables v Omnipol Ltd* [2009] E.C.R. I–3477; Case C–180/06 *Ilsinger v Dreschers* [2009] E.C.R. I–3961; Case C–111/08 *SCT Industri AB i likvidation v Alpenblume AB* [2009] E.C.R. I–5655, [2010] Bus. L.R. 559; Case C–189/08 *Zuid-Chemie BV v Philippo's Mineralenfabriek NV/SA* [2009] E.C.R. I–6917; Case C–386/05 *Color Drack GmbH v Lexx International Vertriebs GmbH* [2007] E.C.R.I–3699, [2010] 1 W.L.R. 1909, [24] and [26]; C–381/08 *Car Trim GmbH v Key Safety Systems Srl* [2010] 2 All E.R. 770, at [49] and [50]; Case C–19/09 *Wood Floor Solutions Andreas Domberger GmbH v Silva Trade SA* [2010] 1 W.L.R. 1900, at [22]. **11–060**

Text at note 33. The provisions of the Judgments Regulation must be interpreted independently, by reference to its scheme and purpose: Case C–103/05 *Reisch Montage AG v Kiesel Baumaschinen Handels GmbH* [2006] E.C.R. I–6827. See also Case C–372/07 *Hassett v South Eastern Health Board* [2008] E.C.R. I–7403 (Judgments Regulation, Art.22(2), "decisions of their organs"). **11–061**

NOTE 34. Add: Case C–292/05 *Lechouritou v Dimosio tis Omospondiakis Dimokratias tis Germanias* [2007] E.C.R. I–1519.

NOTE 35. See also Case C–204/08 *Rehder v Air Baltic Corporation* [2009] E.C.R. I–6073 (Art.5(1)(b)).

NOTE 37. Add: Case C–189/08 *Zuid-Chemie BV v Philippo's Mineralenfabriek NV/SA* [2009] E.C.R. I–6917.

NOTE 40. See also Case C–343/04 *Land Oberösterreich v CEZ a.s.* [2006] E.C.R. I–4557.

NOTE 43. See also Case C–4/03 *Gesellschaft für Antriebstechnik mbH & Co. KG v Lamellen und Kupplungsbau Beteiligungs KG* [2007] E.C.R. I–6509.

NOTE 47. Add: Case C–167/08 *Draka NK Cables v Omnipol Ltd* [2009] E.C.R. I–3477 (Judgments Regulation, Art.43(1)).

**11–062** NOTE 52. See also Case C–433/01 *Feistaat Bayern v Blijdenstein* [2004] E.C.R. I–981; Case C–168/02 *Kronhofer v Maier* [2004] ECR I–6009; Case C–533/07 *Falco Privatstiftung v Weller-Lindhorst* [2009] E.C.R. I–3327, [2010] Bus. L.R. 210; Case C–189/08 *Zuid-Chemie BV v Philippo's Mineralenfabriek NV/SA* [2009] E.C.R. I–6917.

**11–063—11–064** See now revised Lugano Convention, Protocol 2. The Pocar Report (see entry at para.11R–001, above) is very full, and indicates (at para.3) that its purpose is to provide courts with a point of reference to clarify the meaning of the revised Lugano Convention and facilitate its uniform aplication.

NOTE 57. EC Treaty, Art.234, has been replaced by Art.267, TFEU.

**11–066** On the Scottish provisions of the Civil Jurisdiction and Judgments Act 1982 see *Tehrani v Secretary of State for the Home Department (Scotland)* [2006] UKHL 47, [2007] 1 A.C. 521, at [37]–[44].

**11–070** CPR, r.6.20 has been replaced by CPR PD6B, para.3.1.

NOTE 75. See now revised Lugano Convention, Arts 25 and 26.

NOTE 76. See now revised Lugano Convention, Art.22.

**11–071** NOTE 78. See now Judgments Regulation and revised Lugano Convention, Art.26.

## 2. DOMICILE

**11R–072** For the provisions for the purposes of the revised Lugano Convention (including Art.22(2)) see Civil Jurisdiction and Judgments Act 1982, ss 41A, 43A and 44A (as inserted by Civil Jurisdiction and Judgments Regulations 2009 (SI 2009/3131)).

NOTE 93. CPR, r.6.18(g) has been replaced by CPR, r.6.31(i).

NOTES 94 to 98. See now revised Lugano Convention, which mirrors the Judgments Regulation. **11–073**

See now revised Lugano Convention, Arts 59 and 60. **11–074**

See now revised Lugano Convention, Art.59. **11–075**

NOTE 7. See now revised Lugano Convention, Art.59(1). **11–078**

NOTE 2. CPR, r.6.20 has been replaced by CPR PD6B, para.3.1. CPR, r.6.18(g) has been replaced by CPR, r.6.31(i).

NOTE 10. See also *Cherney v Deripaska* [2007] EWHC 965 (Comm.), [2007] 2 All E.R. (Comm.) 785; *High Tech International AG v Deripaska* [2006] EWHC 3276 (QB), [2007] E.M.L.R. 15; *OJSC Oil Company Yugraneft v Abramovich* [2008] EWHC (Comm.) 2613.

NOTE 11. See now revised Lugano Convention, Art.59(2). **11–079**

See now revised Lugano Convention, Art.59(2). **11–081**

CPR, r.6.20(5) has been replaced by CPR PD6B, para.3.1(6).

See *Ministry of Defence and Support of the Armed Forces of Iran v FAZ Aviation Ltd* [2007] EWHC 1042 (Comm.), [2007] I.L.Pr. 538, at [32]: the "domicile" of a company in the Judgments Regulation is a different and autonomous concept: not only does it offer three alternative "domiciles", one of which (the statutory seat) is almost always going to exist and be relatively easy to identify, but all three may exist at the same time. See also *889457 Alberta Inc v Katanga Mining Ltd* [2008] EWHC 2679 (Comm.), [2009] I.L.Pr. 175: central administration did not necessarily mean the same as central management and control, and central administration and principal place of business were alternatives, and not necessarily to be found in the same place. **11–083**

NOTE 25. Companies Act 1985, ss.690A, 691 will be replaced by Companies Act 2006, ss.1139–1142 when they come fully into force. **11–085**

NOTE 26. CPR, r.6.5(6) has been replaced by CPR, r.6.9 (as substituted by SI 2008/2178, Sch.1).

See now revised Lugano Convention, Art.60. **11–087—11–089**

**11–088** Note 33. *cf. Royal & Sun Alliance Insurance plc v MK Digital FZE (Cyprus) Ltd* [2006] EWCA Civ 629, [2006] 2 Lloyd's Rep. 110.

**11–091** CPR, r.6.20 has been replaced by CPR PD6B, para.3.1. CPR, r.6.18(g) has been replaced by CPR, r.6.31(i).

**11–092** Note 38. See now revised Lugano Convention, Arts 9(2), 15(2).

**11–093** See Civil Jurisdiction and Judgments Act 1982, s.44A, as added by SI 2009/3131.

**11–094** See now revised Lugano Convention, Art.60(3). The reference to the Judgments Regulation should be to Art.60(3).

**11–095** Note 45. See now revised Lugano Convention, Art.59(2).

## 3. RULES RELATING TO JURISDICTION

### A. *Where the Judgments Regulation, the 1968 Convention and the Lugano Convention do not apply or where the defendant is not domiciled in the United Kingdom or any part thereof or in any other State which is a Judgments Regulation State or a State which is party to the 1968 Convention or the Lugano Convention*

**11R–096** Note 53. CPR, r.6.20 has been replaced by CPR PD6B, para.3.1.

**11–099** See now revised Lugano Convention, Art.24.

Note 61. See now revised Lugano Convention, Art.22(2).

**11–100** See now revised Lugano Convention, Art.23.

**11–103** See generally Oppong (2007) 3 J. Priv. Int. L. 321.

Note 67. *cf. Richman v Ben-Tovim*, 2007 2 S.A. 283.

**11–104** CPR, r.6.20 has been replaced by CPR PD6B, para.3.1.

**11–105** Note 75. In *City & Country Properties Ltd v Kamali* [2006] EWCA Civ 1879, [2007] 1 W.L.R. 1219 it was held, disapproving *Chellaram v Chellaram (No.2)* [2002] EWHC 632 (Ch.), [2002] 3 All E.R. 17, and applying *Rolph v Zolan* [1993] 1 W.L.R. 1305 (CA), that there is not, or is no longer, any fundamental principle that the defendant must be in England at the time of service. For criticism see Briggs (2007) 78 B.Y.I.L. 600. See also *Cherney v Deripaska* [2007] EWHC 965 (Comm.), [2007] 2 All E.R. (Comm.) 785.

**11–106** Note 76. CPR, r.6.8 has been replaced by CPR, r.6.15 (and see also r.6.27) (as substituted by SI 2008/2178, Sch.1).

NOTE 78. See also *Phillips v Symes (No.3)* [2008] UKHL 1, [2008] 1 W.L.R. 180; *Habib Bank Ltd v Central Bank of Sudan* [2006] EWHC 1767 (Comm.), [2007] 1 W.L.R. 470; *Olafsson v Gissurarson* [2006] EWHC 3162 (QB), [2007] 2 All E.R. 88; *Olafsson v Gissurarson (No.2)* [2008] EWCA Civ 152, [2008] 1 W.L.R. 2016.

NOTE 87. CPR, r.6.4(5) has been replaced by CPR, r.6.5(5). CPR, r.6.5(6) has been replaced by CPR, r.6.9. 6PD, para.4, has been replaced by CPR, r.6.5(3)(c). **11–110**

CPR, r.6.20 has been replaced by CPR PD6B, para.3.1. **11–111**

CPR, r.6.20 has been replaced by CPR PD6B, para.3.1. **11–113**

CPR, r.6.20 has been replaced by CPR PD6B, para.3.1. **11–114**

Companies Act 1985, ss.690A, 691, 694A, 695, 698, 699A, 725, and Sch.21A will be replaced by Companies Act 2006, ss.1139–1142 when they come fully into force. **11–115—11–128**

NOTE 2. CPR, r.6.2(2)(a) has been replaced by CPR, r.6.3(2)(b). CPR, r.6.5(6) has been replaced by CPR, r.6.9. **11–115**

CPR, r.6.2(2) has been replaced by CPR, r.6.3(2). A new CPR Pt 6 has been substituted: see CPR, r.6.36 (as substituted by SI 2008/2178, Sch.1). **11–120**

CPR, r.6.5(6) has been replaced by CPR, r.6.9. **11–122**

NOTE 36. CPR, r.6.2(2) has been replaced by CPR, r.6.3(2); CPR, r.6.5(6) has been replaced by CPR , r.6.9. **11–128**

CPR, r.6.20 has been replaced by CPR PD6B, para.3.1. **11–131**

NOTE 43. CPR, r.6.20 has been replaced by CPR PD6B, para.3.1. On submission generally add: *SMAY Investments Ltd v Sachdev* [2003] EWHC 474 (Ch.), [2003] 1 W.L.R. 1973; *Burns-Anderson Independent Network plc v Wheeler* [2005] EWHC 575 (QB), [2005] 1 Lloyd's Rep. 580; *Global Multimedia International Ltd v ARA Media Services* [2006] EWHC 3612 (Ch.), [2007] 1 All E.R. (Comm.) 1160; *Marketmaker Technology Ltd v CMC Group plc* [2008] EWHC 1556 (QB). See also on interpleader proceedings *Commonwealth of Australia v Peacekeeper International FZC UAE* [2008] EWHC 1220 (QB).

NOTE 47. CPR, r.6.4(2) has been replaced by CPR, r.6.7. **11–132**

NOTE 54. See also *United Group Resources Pty Ltd v Calabro (No 4)* [2010] FCA 791. **11–134**

**11–136** Text and note 62. CPR, r.6.20(5)(d) has been replaced by CPR PD6B, para.3.1(6)(d).

Text and note 65. CPR, r.6.15 has been replaced by CPR, r.6.11.

Note 65. See also *McCulloch v Bank of Nova Scotia* [2006] EWHC 790 (Ch.), [2006] 2 All E.R. (Comm.) 714.

**11R–140** Note 80. CPR, r.6.19(2) has been replaced by CPR, r.6.33(3).

Note 95. See also *The Wadi Sudr* [2009] EWHC 196 (Comm.), [2009] 1 Lloyd's Rep. 666.

**11–141** CPR, r.6.19(2) has been replaced by CPR, r.6.33(3).

**11–142** CPR, r.6.19(2) has been replaced by CPR, r.6.33(3). CPR, r.6.20 has been replaced by CPR PD6B, para.3.1.

Note 85. CPR, r.6.20(18) has been replaced by CPR PD6B, para.3.1(20). There is no equivalent in the new version of CPR Pt 6 and the Practice Direction to 6PDB, para.5.1.

**11R–145** Note 89. CPR, r.6.20 has been replaced by CPR PD6B, para.3.1. See also *Vitol AS v Capri Marine Ltd* [2008] EWHC 378 (Comm.), [2009] Bus. L.R. 271; *Masri v Consolidated Contractors International Co SAL (No 4)* [2009] UKHL 43, [2009] 3 W.L.R. 385.

**11–146** CPR, r.6.20 has been replaced by CPR PD6B, para.3.1.

On the extent of the rule-making power see *Masri v Consolidated Contractors International Co SAL (No 4)* [2009] UKHL 43, [2009] 3 W.L.R. 385.

Note 90. CPR, r.6.8 has been replaced by CPR, r.6.15. CPR, rr.6.24–6.26 are replaced by CPR, rr.6.40–6.43. CPR, r.6.24(2) has been replaced by CPR, r.6.40(4).

Permission to serve out of the jurisdiction may be granted retrospectively: *Nesheim v Kosa* [2006] EWHC 2710 (Ch.), applying *National Justice Compania Naviera v Prudential Assurance Co Ltd (No.2)* [2000] 1 W.L.R. 603 (CA). On the effect of procedural defects see further *Phillips v Symes (No.3)* [2008] UKHL 1, [2008] 1 W.L.R. 180; *Olafsson v Gissurarson (No.2)* [2008] EWCA Civ 152, [2008] 1 W.L.R. 2016.

**11–148** Text and note 94. CPR, r.6.20 has been replaced by CPR PD6B, para.3.1.

Note 95. See also *Islamic Republic of Pakistan v Zardari* [2006] EWHC 2411 (Comm.), [2006] 2 C.L.C. 667, at [185].

Note 96. See also *Sharab v Al-Saud* [2009] EWCA Civ 353, [2009] 1 Lloyd's Rep. 160.

CPR, r.6.21(2A) has been replaced by CPR, r.6.37(3). **11–151**

CPR, r.6.2(1)(b) has been replaced by CPR, r.6.3(1)(b). CPR, r.6.20 has been replaced by CPR PD6B, para.3.1. **11–152**

Note 11. See also *Islamic Republic of Pakistan v Zardari* [2006] EWHC 2411 (Comm.), [2006] 2 C.L.C. 667. *Cf. Hague v Nam Tai Electronics Inc* [2008] UKPC 13, [2008] B.C.C. 295.

Note 12. In *Canada Trust Co v Stolzenberg (No 2)* [1998] 1 W.L.R. 547 (affd [2002] 1 A.C. 1, Waller L.J. (at 555–556) said that "good arguable case" reflected the point that one side had "a much better argument" on the material available. See also *Konkola Copper Mines plc v Coromin Ltd* [2006] EWCA Civ 5, [2006] 1 Lloyd's Rep. 410, at [79]–[81]; *Royal & Sun Alliance Insurance plc v MK Digital FZE (Cyprus) Ltd* [2006] EWCA Civ 629, [2006] 2 Lloyd's Rep. 110; *WPP Holdings Italy SRL v Benatti* [2007] EWCA Civ 263, [2007] 1 W.L.R. 2316, at [42]–[44]; *Kolden Holdings Ltd v Rodette Commerce Ltd* [2008] EWCA Civ 10, [2008] Bus. L.R. 1051, at [49]–[52]; *Masri v Consolidated Contractors International Company SAL (No.2)* [2008] EWCA Civ 303, [2009] 2 W.L.R. 621, at [88]; *Sharab v Al-Saud* [2009] EWCA Civ 353, [2009] 2 Lloyd's Rep. 160; *Cecil v Bayat* [2010] EWHC 641 (Comm.), at [36].

In *Bols Distilleries v Superior Yacht Services* [2005] UKPC 45, [2007] 1 W.L.R. 12, Lord Rodger, speaking for the Privy Council, said (at [26]–[28]) that what the court is endeavouring to do is to find a concept not capable of very precise definition which reflects that the claimant must properly satisfy the court that it is right for the court to take jurisdiction. That may involve in some cases considering matters which go both to jurisdiction and to the very matter to be argued at the trial, e.g. the existence of a contract, but in other cases a matter which goes purely to jurisdiction, e.g. the domicile of the defendant. The concept also reflects that the question before the court is one which should be decided on affidavits from both sides and without full discovery and/or cross-examination, and in relation to which therefore to apply the language of the civil burden of proof applicable to issues after full trial is inapposite. Although there is power to order a preliminary issue on jurisdiction, it is seldom that the power is used because trials on jurisdiction issues are to be strongly discouraged. The phrase which reflects the concept "good arguable case" was originally employed in relation to points which related to jurisdiction but which might also be argued about at the trial. The court in such cases must be concerned not even to appear to express some concluded view as to the merits, e.g. as to whether the contract existed or not. The "good arguable case" test, although obviously applicable to the *ex parte* stage, becomes of most significance at the *inter partes* stage where two arguments are being weighed in the interlocutory context which must not become a "trial". "Good arguable case" reflects in that context that one side has a much better argument on the material available. It is the concept which the phrase reflects on which it is important to concentrate, i.e. of the court being satisfied or as satisfied as it can be having regard to the limitations which an interlocutory process imposes that factors exist which allow the court to take jurisdiction.

**11–153** CPR, r.6.20 has been replaced by CPR PD6B, para.3.1.

**11–154** NOTE 17. See also *ED & F Man Sugar Ltd v Lendoudis* [2007] EWHC 2268 (Comm.), [2008] 1 All E.R. 952.

**11–155** CPR, r.6.20 has been replaced by CPR PD6B, para 3.1.

**11–156** CPR, r.6.20 has been replaced by CPR PD6B, para.3.1. CPR, r.6.20(5)(c) has been replaced by CPR PD6B, para.3.1(6)(c).

**11–157** CPR, r.6.20 has been replaced by CPR PD6B, para.3.1.

**11–158** CPR, r.6.20 has been replaced by CPR PD6B, para.3.1. CPR, r.6.21(3) has been replaced by CPR, r.6.37(4).

**11R–159** NOTE 26. CPR, r.6.20(1) has been replaced by CPR PD6B, para.3.1(1).

**11–160** CPR, r.6.18(g) has been replaced by CPR, r.6.31(i).

**11–161** CPR, r.6.20 has been replaced by CPR PD6B, para.3.1.

**11R–162** CPR, r.6.20(2) has been replaced by CPR PD6B, para.3.1(2).

**11R–165** NOTES 44 and 45. CPR, rr.6.20(3) and (3A) are replaced by CPR PD6B, para.3.1(3) and (4). See also *889457 Alberta Inc v Katanga Mining Ltd* [2008] EWHC 2679 (Comm.) [2009] I.L.Pr. 175.

**11–168** CPR, r.6.20 has been replaced by CPR PD6B, para.3.1. CPR, r.6.19(2) has been replaced by CPR, r.6.33(3).

**11–169** NOTE 52. CPR, r.6.20(3)(a) has been replaced by CPR PD6B, para.3.1(3)(a).

NOTE 53. *cf. Walanpatrias Stiftung v Lehman Brothers* [2006] EWHC 3034 (Comm.)

**11–170** NOTE 59. See also *Konkola Copper Mines plc v Coromin Ltd (No.2)* [2006] EWHC 1093 (Comm.), [2006] 2 Lloyd's Rep. 446.

CPR, r.6.20(3) has been replaced by CPR PD6B, para.3.1(3). **11–171**

CPR, r.6.20(4) has been replaced by CPR PD6B, para.3.1(5). **11–179**

NOTE 77. CPR, r.6.20(4) has been replaced by CPR PD6B, para.3.1(5). **11–180**

NOTE 78. CPR, r.6.20(5) has been replaced by CPR PD6B, para.3.1(6). **11R–181**

CPR, r.6.20 has been replaced by CPR PD6B, para.3.1. See also *Albon v Naza Motor Trading* [2007] EWHC 9 (Ch.), [2007] 1 W.L.R. 249 (restitutionary claim for overpayment "in respect of a contract"); *Greene Wood & McLean v Templeton Insurance Ltd* [2008] EWCA Civ 65, [2009] I.L.Pr. 779 (claim for contribution or indemnity pursuant to Civil Liability (Contribution) Act 1978 "in respect of a contract") (noted Dickinson [2010] L.M.C.L.Q. 1); *Cecil v Bayat* [2010] EWHC 641 (Comm.) (quantum meruit, but not in respect of a contract which is legally unconnected with the contract between the parties). **11–184**

NOTE 92. CPR, r.6.20(7) has been replaced by CPR PD6B, para.3.1(8). **11–185**

NOTE 94. See also *Sharab v Al-Saud* [2009] EWCA Civ 353, [2009] 1 Lloyd's Rep. 160; *Chunilal v Merrill Lynch International Inc* [2010] EWHC 1467 (Comm.). **11–186**

NOTE 97. CPR, r.6.20(9) has been replaced by CPR PD6B, para.3.1(10).

CPR, r.6.16 has been replaced by CPR, r.6.12. CPR, r.6.20 has been replaced by CPR PD6B, para.3.1. **11–190**

NOTE 10. See also *Novus Aviation Limited v Onur Air Tasimacilik AS* [2009] EWCA Civ 122, [2009] 1 Lloyd's Rep. 576; *Pablo Star Ltd v Emirates Integrated Telecommunications Co PJSC* [2009] EWCA Civ 1044; *Royal & Sun Alliance Insurance Plc v Rolls-Royce Plc* [2010] EWHC 1869 (Comm.). **11–192**

NOTE 30. CPR, r.6.20(6) has been replaced by CPR PD6B, para.3.1(7). **11R–199**

CPR, r.6.20(6) has been replaced by CPR PD6B, para.3.1(7). **11–202**

NOTE 34. See also *Sharab v Al-Saud* [2009] EWCA Civ 353, [2009] 1 Lloyd's Rep. 160. **11–203**

NOTE 71. CPR, r.6.20(7) has been replaced by CPR PD6B, para.3.1(8). **11R–213**

NOTE 73. CPR, r.6.20(7) has been replaced by CPR PD6B, para.3.1(8). **11–215**

**11R–216** Note 74. CPR, r.6.20(8) has been replaced by CPR PD6B, para.3.1(9).

Note 78. See also *Puttick v Fletcher Challenge Forests Pty Ltd* [2007] VSCA 264 (leave to appeal to High Court of Australia has been granted).

**11–218** See also *FFSB Ltd v Seward & Kissel LLP* [2007] UKPC 16.

**11–221** Note 87. For Canada see now *Muscutt v Courcelles* (2002) 213 D.L.R. (4th) 577 (Ont. C.A.), and its companion cases; *Doiron v Bugge* (2005) 258 D.L.R. (4th) 716 (Ont. C.A.); Walker, in *Annual Review of Civil Litigation* (2002), 61. For Australia see also *Heilbrunn v Lightwood Plc* [2007] FCA 433.

Note 88. See also *Cooley v Ramsey* [2008] EWHC 129 (QB), [2008] I.L.Pr. 345. In that case an English claimant was seriously injured in a traffic accident in New South Wales while working in Australia. It was held that the English court had jurisdiction in his claim for damages, because the pain and suffering, and loss of income and amenities of life, was damage sustained within the jurisdiction: *sed quaere*.

**11–222** CPR, r.6.20 has been replaced by CPR PD6B, para.3.1.

**11–223** On "libel tourism" see Hartley (2010) 59 I.C.L.Q. 25.

**11–224** Note 84. See also *Metropolitan International Schools Ltd v Designtechnica Corp* [2009] EWHC 1765 (QB), [2009] E.M.L.R. 27.

**11R–227** Note 5. CPR, r.6.20(9) has been replaced by CPR PD6B, para.3.1(10).

The claimant does not have to show that there are assets in England available for execution: *Tasarruf Mevduati Sigorta Fonu v Demirel* [2006] EWHC 3354 (Ch.), [2007] 2 All E.R. 815, affirmed [2007] EWCA Civ 799, [2007] 1 W.L.R. 2508.

**11–228** An application for the examination of the foreign officer of a judgment debtor is not within this clause: *Masri v Consolidated Contractors International Co SAL (No.4)* [2009] UKHL 43, [2009] 3 W.L.R. 385.

**11R–230** Note 13. CPR, r.6.20(10) has been replaced by CPR PD6B, para.3.1(11).

**11–231** CPR, r.6.20(10) has been replaced by CPR PD6B, para.3.1(11).

**11–232** Note 15. See also *Islamic Republic of Pakistan v Zardari* [2006] EWHC 2411 (Comm.), [2006] 2 C.L.C. 667 (constructive claim to land in England); *Ashton Investments v OJSC Russian Aluminium* [2006] EWHC 2545 (Comm.), [2007] 1 Lloyd's Rep. 311.

**11R–234** Note 19. CPR, r.6.20(11) has been replaced by CPR PD6B, para.3.1(12).

NOTE 24. CPR, r.6.18(g) has been replaced by CPR, r.6.31(i). **11R–237**

NOTE 25. CPR, r.6.20(12) has been replaced by CPR PD6B, para.3.1(13).

NOTE 26. CPR, r.6.20(13) has been replaced by CPR PD6B, para.3.1(14). **11R–238**

NOTE 28. CPR, r.6.20(14) has been replaced by CPR PD6B, para.3.1(15). **11R–240**

NOTE 29. See *Cecil v Bayat* [2010] EWHC 641 (Comm.); *Astrazeneca UK Ltd v Albemarle International Corp* [2010] EWHC 1028 (Comm.), [2010] 2 Lloyd's Rep. 61. CPR, r.6.20(15) has been replaced by CPR PD6B, para.3.1(16). **11R–241**

NOTE 38. See also *Islamic Republic of Pakistan v Zardari* [2006] EWHC 2411 (Comm.), [2006] 2 C.L.C. 667. **11–244**

NOTE 39. CPR, r.6.20(16) has been replaced by CPR PD6B, para.3.1(17). **11R–245**

Supreme Court Act 1981 is now re-named Senior Courts Act 1981: Constitutional Reform Act 2005, s.59 and Sch.11, in force October 1, 2009. **11R–246**

NOTE 40. CPR, r.6.20(17) has been replaced by CPR PD6B, para.3.1(18).

Supreme Court Act 1981 is now renamed Senior Courts Act 1981: Constitutional Reform Act 2005, s.59 and Sch.11, in force October 1, 2009. **11–247**

CPR, r.6.20(17) has been replaced by CPR PD6B, para.3.1(18).

NOTE 45. CPR, r.6.20(17A) has been replaced by CPR PD6B, para.3.1(19). **11R–249**

NOTE 46. CPR, r.6.20(18) and 6PDB, para.5.2 are replaced by CPR PD6B, para.3.1(20). **11R–251**

CPR, r.6.20(18) has been replaced by CPR PD6B, para.3.1(20). **11–252**

### B. *Where the Defendant is domiciled in a Judgments Regulation State, in a 1968 Convention or Lugano Convention State, or in Scotland or Northern Ireland*

See now revised Lugano Convention, Art.23. **11–264**

NOTE 52. See now revised Lugano Convention, Art.31

CPR, r.6.19 has been replaced by CPR, r.6.33. **11–265**

NOTE 53. CPR, r.6.20(4) has been replaced by CPR PD6B, para.3.1(5).

NOTE 55. CPR, r.6.19(3) has been replaced by CPR, r.6.34(1).

NOTE 57. See also *Royal & Sun Alliance Insurance plc v MK Digital FZE (Cyprus) Ltd* [2006] EWCA Civ 629, [2006] 2 Lloyd's Rep. 110; *Bols Distilleries v Superior Yacht Services* [2005] UKPC 45, [2007] 1 W.L.R. 12; *WPP Holdings Italy SRL v Benatti* [2007] EWCA Civ 263, [2007] 1 W.L.R. 2316.

**11–267** NOTE 64. See Civil Jurisdiction and Judgments Act 1982, s.44A, added by SI 2009/3131.

**11R–270** NOTE 72. See now revised Lugano Convention, Art.2.

**11–273** NOTE 77. See now revised Lugano Convention, Arts 5(2), 9(1)(b), 16(1).

NOTE 78. See now revised Lugano Convention, Arts 9(2), 15(2), 22, 23.

**11–274** See now revised Lugano Convention, Art.23.

**11–275** NOTE 86. See now revised Lugano Convention, Art.3.

**11R–276** Text at note 91. The revised Lugano Convention provisions are the same as those in the Judgments Regulation.

NOTE 89. See also Zheng Tang (2008) 4 J. Priv. Int. L. 35.

**11–277** See entry at para.11R–276, above.

**11–278—11–279** See entry at para.11R–276, above.

**11–283** CPR, r.6.20(5)(c) has been replaced by CPR PD6B, para.3.1(6)(c).

**11–284** In *WPP Holdings Italy SRL v Benatti* [2007] EWCA Civ 263, 1 W.L.R. 2316 it was held that a claim by a third party under the Contracts (Rights of Third Parties) Act 1999 was a claim "in matters relating to a contract" for the purposes of Art.5 of the Judgments Regulation.

**11–288** NOTE 27. CPR, r.6.20(7) has been replaced by CPR PD6B, para.3.1(8).

**11–289** NOTE 24. But see Case C–533/07 *Falco Privatstiftung v Weller-Lindhorst*, April 23, 2009, where it was held that Art.5(1)(a) of the Judgments Regulation was to be interpreted in accordance with the jurisprudence on Art.5(1) of the 1968 Convention.

**11–292** NOTE 36. See also *Royal & Sun Alliance Insurance plc v MK Digital FZE (Cyprus) Ltd* [2006] EWCA Civ 629, [2006] 2 Lloyd's Rep. 110; *WPP Holdings Italy SRL v Benatti* [2007] EWCA Civ 263, [2007] 1 W.L.R. 2316;

*Crucial Music Corp v Klondyke Management AG* [2007] EWHC 1782 (Ch.), [2007] I.L.Pr. 733; *Commercial Marine Piling Ltd v Pierse Contracting Ltd* [2009] EWHC 2241 (T.C.C.), [2009] 2 Lloyd's Rep 659; *Gard Marine & Energy Ltd v Tunnicliffe* [2009] EWHC 2388 (Comm.), [2010] Lloyd's Rep. I.R. 62, affd. [2010] EWCA Civ 1052; *J.S. Swan (Printing) Ltd v Kall Kwik UK Ltd*, [2009] CSOH 99, 2009 S.C.L.R. 688.

See now revised Lugano Convention, Art.5(1)(b), in line with the Judgments Regulation. **11–294—11–296**

NOTE 44. See also *Universal Steels Ltd v Skanska Construction UK Ltd* [2003] ScotCS 271. **11–294**

NOTE 46. See also *7E Communications v Vertex Antennentechnik* [2007] EWCA Civ 140, [2007] 1 W.L.R. 2175. See now revised Lugano Convention, Art.23. **11–295**

In Case C–386/05 *Color Drack GmbH v Lexx International Vertriebs GmbH* [2007] E.C.R. I–3699, [2010] 1 W.L.R. 1909 (noted Harris (2007) 123 L.Q.R. 522) the Austrian Supreme Court referred the question whether Art.5(1)(b) of the Judgments Regulation was to be interpreted as meaning that a seller of goods domiciled in one Member State who, as agreed, has delivered the goods to the purchaser, domiciled in another Member State, at various places within that other Member State, can be sued by the purchaser regarding a claim under the contract relating to all the (part) deliveries—if need be, at the plaintiff's choice—before the court of one of those places (of performance). The European Court ruled that Art.5(1)(b) applied whether there was one place of delivery or several. It determined both international and local jurisdiction. Where there were several places of delivery within a single Member State and the claim related to all those deliveries, the plaintiff could sue the defendant in the court for the place of delivery of its choice on the basis of Art.5(1)(b), but one court must have jurisdiction to hear all the claims arising out of the contract. Where there were several places of delivery of the goods, the "place of delivery" must be understood, for the purposes of application of Art.5(1)(b), as the place with the closest linking factor between the contract and the court having jurisdiction. In such a case, the point of closest linking factor will, as a general rule, be at the place of the principal delivery, which must be determined on the basis of economic criteria. If it were not possible to determine the principal place of delivery, each of the places of delivery had a sufficiently close link of proximity to the material elements of the dispute and, accordingly, a significant link as regards jurisdiction. In such a case, the plaintiff could sue the defendant in the court for the place of delivery of its choice on the basis of Art.5(1)(b). **11–296**

In Case C–533/07 *Falco Privatstiftung v Weller-Lindhorst* [2009] E.C.R. I–3327, [2010] Bus. L.R. 210, it was held that a contract under which the owner of an intellectual property right grants its contractual partner the right to use the right in return for remuneration is not a contract for the provision of services within the meaning of Art.5(1)(b) of the Judgments Regulation. The concept of service implies, at the least, that the party who provides the service carries out a particular activity in return for remuneration. It cannot be inferred from a contract under which the owner of an intellectual property right grants its contractual partner the right to use that right in return for remuneration that such an activity is involved. By such a contract, the only obligation which the owner of the right granted undertakes with regard to its contractual partner is not to challenge the use of that right by the latter. The owner of an intellectual property right does not perform any service in granting a right to use that property and undertakes merely to permit the licensee to exploit that right freely. It is immaterial whether the licensee of an intellectual property right holder is obliged to use the intellectual property right licensed.

In Case C–204/08 *Rehder v Air Baltic Corporation* [2009] E.C.R. I–6073, [2010] Bus. L.R. 549 (noted George and Harris (2009) 125 L.Q.R. 30), the European Court ruled that Art.5(1)(b) of the Judgments Regulation was to be interpreted as meaning that, in the case of air transport of passengers from one Member State to another Member State, carried out on the basis of a contract with only one airline, which was the operating carrier, the court having jurisdiction to deal with a claim for compensation founded on that transport contract and on Regulation (EC) No.261/2004 of the European Parliament and of the Council of February 11, 2004 establishing common rules on compensation and assistance to passengers in the event of denied boarding and of cancellation or long delay of flights, is that, at the applicant's choice, which has territorial jurisdiction over the place of departure or place of arrival of the aircraft, as those places are agreed in that contract.

In Case C–381/08 *Car Trim GmbH v KeySafety Systems SRL* [2010] 2 All E.R. (Comm.) 770 the European Court ruled that Art.5(1)(b) was to be interpreted as meaning that where the purpose of contracts was the supply of goods to be manufactured or produced and, even though the purchaser has specified certain requirements with regard to the provision, fabrication and delivery of the components to be produced, the purchaser had not supplied the materials and the supplier was responsible for the quality of the goods and their compliance with the contract, those contracts were to be classified as a sale of goods within the meaning of Art.5(1)(b). In the case of a sale involving carriage of goods, the place where, under the contract, the goods sold were delivered or should have been delivered must be determined on the basis of the provisions of that contract. Where it was possible to determine the place of delivery on that basis, without reference to the substantive law applicable to the contract, that place was the place where the physical transfer of the goods took place, as a result of which the purchaser obtained, or should have obtained, actual power of disposal over those goods at the final destination of the sales transaction.

In C–19/09 *Wood Floor Solutions Andreas Domberger GmbH v Silva Trade SA* [2010] 1 W.L.R. 1900 the European Court ruled that Art.5(1)(b) (second indent) was applicable where services were provided in several Member States. First, applying *Color Drack* (above) to the provision of services, the Court ruled that where there are several places of delivery of the goods the "place of performance" must be understood as the place with the closest linking factor, which, as a general rule, will be at the place of the main provision of services. Second, in a commercial agency contract, it was the commercial agent who performed the obligation which characterised that contract and who, for the purpose of applying the second indent of Art.5(1)(b) of the regulation, provided the services. Where there were several places where services were provided by the agent the place of performance must, in principle, mean the place of the main provision of services by the agent. Third, the place of the main provision of services must be deduced, in so far as possible, from the provisions of the contract itself. In the context of a commercial agency contract, the place where the agent was to carry out his work on behalf of the principal, consisting in particular in preparing, negotiating and, where appropriate, concluding the transactions for which he had authority had to be identified, on the basis of that contract. If the provisions of a contract do not enable the place of the main provision of services to be determined, either because they provide for several places where services are provided, or because they do not expressly provide for any specific place where services are to be provided, but the agent has already provided such services, it is appropriate, in the alternative, to take account of the place where he has in fact for the most part carried out his activities in the performance of the contract, provided that the provision of services in that place is not contrary to the parties' intentions as it appears from the provisions of the contract. For that purpose, the factual aspects of the case may be taken into consideration, in particular, the time spent in those places and the importance of the activities carried out there. It is for the national court seised to determine whether it has jurisdiction in the light of the evidence submitted to it. Fourth, if the place of the main provision of services cannot be determined on the basis of the provisions of the contract itself or its actual performance, the place must be identified by another means which respects the objectives of predictability and proximity pursued by the legislature. For that purpose, it will be necessary for the purposes of the application of the second indent of Art.5(1)(b) to consider, as the place of the main provision of the services provided by a commercial agent, the place where that agent is domiciled. That place can always be identified with certainty and is therefore predictable. Moreover, it has a link of proximity with the dispute since the agent will in all likelihood provide a substantial part of his services there. The operative ruling was that Art.5(1)(b) "must be interpreted as meaning that where services are provided in several Member States, the court having jurisdiction to hear and determine all the claims based on the contract is the court within whose jurisdiction the place of the main provision of services is situated. For a commercial agency contract, that place is the place of the main provision of services by the agent, as it appears from the provisions of the contract or, in the absence of such provisions, the actual performance of that contract or, where it cannot be determined on that basis, the place where the agent is domiciled."

In Case C–87/10 *Electrosteel Europe SA v Edil Centro SpA* (pending) an Italian court has referred to the European Court the question whether the relevant place of delivery is the place of final destination of the goods covered by the contract or the place in which the seller is discharged from his obligation to deliver, in accordance with the substantive rules applicable to the individual case.

In *Scottish & Newcastle International Ltd v Othon Ghalanos Ltd* [2008] UKHL 11, [2008] Bus. L.R. 583 (noted Merrett [2008] C.L.J. 244; Hart and Hinks [2008] L.M.C.L.Q. 353; Briggs (2008) 79 B.Y.I.L. 508) it was held that the place of delivery in a contract for the sale of cider CFR (cost and delivery), to Limassol, Cyprus, was Liverpool, from which the goods were shipped, and where the sellers had performed all their obligations. Accordingly the English court had jurisdiction in a claim by the sellers for the price. In a CIF or C&F contract the seller has no obligation to deliver to destination, only to procure the shipment of goods for carriage to destination.

See also *General Monitors Ireland Ltd v SES-ASA Protection SpA* [2006] 1 I.L.R.M. 63; *Soc ND Conseil SA v Le Meridien Hotels et Resorts World Headquarters* [2007] I.L.Pr. 524 (French Cour de cassation, 2007).

A reference to the European Court on the meaning of "the provision of services" has been made in Case C–533/07 *Falco Privatstiftung v Weller-Lindhorst* (pending).

**11R–298** Note 54. See now revised Lugano Convention, Art.5(3).

**11–299** Note 56. See now revised Lugano Convention, Art.5(3).

Note 58. See also *Hewden Tower Cranes Ltd v Wolfkran GmbH* [2007] EWHC 857 (T.C.C.), [2007] 2 Lloyd's Rep. 138 (claim for contribution under Civil Liability (Contribution) Act 1978 within Article 5(3)).

Note 60. *Burke v UVEX Sports GmbH* is now reported at [2005] 4 I.R. 452.

**11–300** Note 61. CPR, r.6.20(8) has been replaced by CPR PD6B, para.3.1(9).

**11–301** In Case C–189/08 *Zuid-Chemie BV v Philippo's Mineralenfabriek NV/SA* [2009] E.C.R. I–6917, the claim by the plaintiff was that the defendant had contaminated the planitiff's fertilizer. The first question was whether the words "place where the harmful event occurred" designated the place where the defective product was delivered to the purchaser or whether they referred to the place where the initial damage occurred following normal use of the product for the purpose for which it was intended. It was held that Art.5(3) of the Judgments Regulation was to be interpreted as meaning that the words "place where the harmful event occurred" designated the place where the initial damage occurred as a result of the normal use of the product for the purpose for which it was intended. The second question was whether that damage had to consist of physical damage to persons or goods, or whether it might consist (at that stage) of purely financial damage. Since there had been physical damage in any event, that question was hypothetical and the European Court would not deliver advisory opinions on general or hypothetical questions.

In Case 509/09 *eDate Advertising GmbH v X* (pending) the German Bundesgerichtshof has referred these questions (inter alia) to the European Court: (1) whether Art.5(3) is to be interpreted as meaning, in the event of infringements of the right to protection of personality by means of content on an Internet website, that the person concerned may also bring an action for an injunction against the operator of the website, irrespective of the Member State in which the operator is established, in the courts of any Member State in which the website may be accessed, or (2) whether the jurisdiction of the courts of a Member State in which the operator of the website is not established require that there be a special connection between the contested content or the website and the State of the court seised going beyond technically possible accessibility? (3) If such a special domestic connecting factor is necessary, what are the criteria which determine that connection. (4) Does it depend on whether the intention of the operator is that the contested website is specifically (also) targeted at the Internet users in the State of the court seised or is it sufficient for the information which may be accessed on the website to have an objective connection to the State of the court seised, in the sense that in the circumstances of the individual case, in particular on the basis of the content of the website to which the applicant objects, a collision of conflicting interests—the applicant's interest in respect for his right to protection of personality and the operator's interest in the design of his website and in news reporting—may actually have occurred or may occur in the State of the court seised? (5) Does the determination of the special domestic connecting factor depend upon the number of times the website to which the applicant objects has been accessed from the State of the court seised? (6) If no special domestic connecting factor is required in order to make a positive finding on jurisdiction, or if it is sufficient for the presumption of such a special domestic connecting factor that the information to which the applicant objects has an objective connection to the State of the court seised, in the sense that in the circumstances of the individual case, in particular on the basis of the content of the website to which the applicant objects, a collision of conflicting interests may actually have occurred or may occur in the State of the court seised and the existence of a special domestic connecting factor may be presumed without requiring a finding as to a minimum number of times the website to which the applicant objects has been accessed from the State of the court seised.

NOTE 65. *cf.* also *London Helicopters Ltd v Heliportugal LDA-INAC* [2006] EWHC 108, [2006] I.L.Pr. 614; *SanDisk v Koninklijke Philips* [2007] EWHC 332 (Ch.), [2007] Bus. L.R. 705. See Case C–189/08 *Zuid-Chemie BV v Philippo's Mineralenfabriek NV/SA* (pending) for a reference to the European Court on the place of damage in product liability claims.

NOTE 66. *Dolphin Maritime and Aviation Ltd v Sveriges Angfartygs Assurans Forening* [2009] EWHC 716 (Comm.), [2009] 2 Lloyd's Rep. 123 (place where benefit should have been received was place where damage occurred).

**11–302** In Case C–584/08 *Real Madrid Football Club v Sporting Exchange Ltd* (pending), a Belgian court has referred a number of questions to the European Court on the applicability of Art.5(3) of the Judgments Regulation to harm allegedly caused by the availability of betting websites to the Belgian public, where none of the companies being sued, which run the websites, has its seat in Belgium; none of the websites is hosted in Belgium; none of the claimants is domiciled in Belgium; the betting websites are available to Belgian internet users, who can place their bets on those sites, to the same extent as they are available to internet users in other Member States since they are ".com" websites which have the purpose of extending their market to the whole of Europe, and they do not have the extension ".be" which is specific to Belgium; those websites are available in a number of languages without the two most commonly used languages in Belgium always being among them; those websites offer, inter alia, bets on Belgian matches, in the same way as for foreign championships, the use of a particular technology or canvassing technique aimed at the Belgian public has not been proved, the number of bets placed by the Belgian public is entirely marginal in comparison with the total number of bets taken by those sites.

On "libel tourism" see Hartley (2010) 59 I.C.L.Q. 25.

**11–303** NOTE 69. See also *Newsat Holdings Ltd v Zani* [2006] EWHC 342 (Comm.), [2006] 1 Lloyd's Rep. 707; *London Helicopters Ltd v Heliportugal LDA-INAC* [2006] EWHC 108, [2006] I.L.Pr. 614; *The Seaward Quest* [2007] EWHC 1460 (Comm.), [2007] 2 Lloyd's Rep. 308; *Crucial Music Corp v Klondyke Management AG* [2007] EWHC 1782 (Ch.), [2007] I.L.Pr. 733; *Maple Leaf Marro Volatility Master Fund v Rouvray* [2009] EWHC 257 (Comm.), [2009] 1 Lloyd's Rep. 475.

**11–304** See now revised Lugano Convention, Art.5(3).

**11R–308** NOTE 76. See now revised Lugano Convention, Art.5(5).

NOTE 79. See now revised Lugano Convention, Art.8(2).

NOTE 80. See now revised Lugano Convention, Art.15(2).

NOTE 81. See now revised Lugano Convention, Art.18(2).

NOTE 93. CPR, r.6.20(11) has been replaced by CPR PD6B, para.3.1(12). **11–316**

See *Gómez v Gómez-Monche Vives* [2008] EWCA Civ 1065, [2009] Ch. 245 for the meaning of the expression "sued . . . as . . . beneficiary or trustee." It was held that where the governing law of the trust had been expressly chosen by the parties, this would almost always be the system of law with which the trust had its closest and most real connection for the purposes of determining its domicile within the meaning of Art.5(6) of the Judgments Regulation. **11–317**

NOTE 94. See also *Gómez v Gómez-Monche Vives* [2008] EWCA Civ 1065, [2009] Ch. 245, at [79].

NOTE 98. See now revised Lugano Convention, Art.60(3).

NOTE 2. See now revised Lugano Convention, Art.23(4). **11–318**

NOTE 7. See now revised Lugano Convention, Art.7. **11R–323**

NOTE 10. See now revised Lugano Convention, Art.6(1). **11R–325**

CPR, r.6.20(3) has been replaced by CPR PD6B, para.3.1(4). **11–326**

In Case C–462/06 *GlaxoSmithkline v Rouard* [2008] E.C.R. I–3965 (on which see Harris (2008) 124 L.Q.R. 523) the national court asked whether Art.6(1) was applicable to an action brought by an employee against two companies established in different Member States which he considered to have been his joint employers. The European Court ruled that Art.6(1) could not be applied to a dispute falling under the special jurisdictional rules in section 5 of Chapter II applicable to individual contracts of employment. That conclusion was supported by the consideration that sound administration of justice would imply that any possibility of relying on Art.6(1) should be open, as in the case of counter-claims, both to employees and to employers. Such an application of Art.6(1) could give rise to consequences contrary to the objective of protection, which the insertion of a specific section for contracts of employment sought specifically to ensure. Reliance by an employer on Art.6(1) could deprive the employee of the protection afforded to him by Art.20(1) under which proceedings can be brought against an employee only in the courts of the Member State in which he is domiciled.

There must be a real issue between the claimant and the co-defendant domiciled outside the jurisdiction: *Cooper Tire & Rubber Company Europe Ltd v Dow Deutschland Inc* [2010] EWCA Civ 864, [28]; *FKI Engineeering*

*Ltd v De Wind Holdings Ltd* [2008] EWCA Civ 316, [2009] 1 All E.R. (Comm.) 118.

**11–327** In Case C–98/06 *Freeport plc v Arnoldsson* [2007] E.C.R. I–839, [2008] Q.B. 634 (noted Scott [2008] L.M.C.L.Q. 113) the European Court ruled that Art6(1) applies where claims brought against different defendants are connected when the proceedings are instituted, that is to say, where it is expedient to hear and determine them together to avoid the risk of irreconcilable judgments resulting from separate proceedings, without there being any further need to establish separately that the claims were not brought with the sole object of ousting the jurisdiction of the courts of the Member State where one of the defendants is domiciled.

The European Court said (at [51]) that Art.6(1), unlike Art.6(2), does not expressly make provision for a case in which an action is brought solely in order to remove the party sued from the jurisdiction of the court which would be competent in his case. The Court recalled that in Case 189/87 *Kalfelis v Schröder* [1988] E.C.R. 5565, after mentioning the possibility that a plaintiff could bring a claim against a number of defendants with the sole object of ousting the jurisdiction of the courts of the Member State where one of the defendants was domiciled, the Court ruled that it was necessary, in order to exclude such a possibility, for there to be a connection between the claims brought against each of the defendants. The requirement of a connection did not derive from the wording of Art.6(1) of the 1968 Convention but was inferred from that provision by the Court in order to prevent the exception to the principle that jurisdiction is vested in the courts of the State of the defendant's domicile laid down in Art.6(1) from calling into question the very existence of that principle. That requirement, subsequently confirmed by Case C–51/97 *Réunion européenne SA v Splithoff's Bevrachtingskantoor BV* [1998] E.C.R. I–6511, at [48] was expressly enshrined in the drafting of Art.6(1) of the Judgments Regulation. Accordingly Art.6(1) applies where claims brought against different defendants are connected when the proceedings are instituted, that is to say, where it is expedient to hear and determine them together to avoid the risk of irreconcilable judgments resulting from separate proceedings, without there being any further need to establish separately that the claims were not brought with the sole object of ousting the jurisdiction of the courts of the Member State where one of the defendants is domiciled. The Court did not follow the opinion of Mengozzi A-G, or its previous decision in Case C–103/05 *Reisch Montage AG v Kiesel Baumaschinen Handels GmbH* [2006] E.C.R. I–6827: see entry at para.11–330, below.

NOTE 16. *Daly v Irish Group Travel Ltd* is reported at [2007] 4 I.R. 423. See also Case C–539/03 *Roche Nederland BV v Primus* [2006] E.C.R. I–6535, at [20]; *ET Plus SA v Welter* [2005] EWHC 2115 (Comm.), [2006] 1 Lloyd's Rep. 251; *FKI Engineering Ltd v Dewind Holdings Ltd* [2008] EWCA Civ. 316, [2009] 1 All E.R. (Comm.) 118; *Gard Marine & Energy Ltd v Tunnicliffe*

[2009] EWHC 2388 (Comm.), [2010] Lloyd's Rep. I.R. 62, affd. [2010] EWCA Civ 1052.

In Case C–98/06 *Freeport plc v Arnoldsson* [2007] E.C.R. I–839, [2008] Q.B. 634 (noted Scott [2008] L.M.C.L.Q. 113) the reference was made in the context of proceedings in Sweden where an English company had been joined to proceedings against its Swedish subsidiary by the plaintiff who claimed to be entitled to a fee. The claim against the English company was for breach of contract and the claim against the Swedish company was based in tort. The European Court ruled that the fact that claims brought against a number of defendants have different legal bases did not preclude application of Art.6(1). **11–329**

The European Court said (at [42] *et seq.*) that Case C–51/97 *Réunion européenne SA v Splithoff's Bevrachtingskantoor BV* [1998] E.C.R. I–6511, at [50] was to be distinguished. That case concerned Arts 5(1) and (3), and concerned overlapping special jurisdiction based on Art.5(3) to hear an action in tort or delict and special jurisdiction to hear an action based in contract, on the ground that there was a connection between the two actions. It related to an action brought before a court in a Member State where none of the defendants to the main proceedings was domiciled, and it was in the context of Art.5(3) that the Court was able to conclude that two claims in one action, directed against different defendants and based in one instance on contractual liability and in the other on liability in tort or delict could not be regarded as connected. To accept that jurisdiction based on Art.5, which constituted special jurisdiction limited to an exhaustive list of cases, could serve as the basis on which to hear other actions would undermine the scheme of the Judgments Regulation.

In the present case the action was brought, in application of Art.6(1), before the court for the place where one of the defendants in the main proceedings had its head office. Where a court's jurisdiction was based on Art.2 (domicile), the application of Art.6(1) of the Regulation becomes possible if the conditions set out in that provision, without there being any need for the actions brought to have identical legal bases.

In Case C–103/05 *Reisch Montage AG v Kiesel Baumaschinen Handels GmbH* [2006] E.C.R. I–6827 the European Court ruled that Art.6(1) may be relied on in the context of an action brought in a Member State against a defendant domiciled in that State and a co-defendant domiciled in another Member State even when the action is regarded under a national provision as inadmissible from the time it is brought in relation to the first defendant. Proceedings had been brought in Austria against the first defendant, who was domiciled in Austria, and against the second defendant, who was domiciled in Germany. Under Austrian law it was not permissible to commence or continue proceedings to enforce or secure claims to assets forming part of a bankrupt's estate after the commencement of bankruptcy proceedings. The first defendant **11–330** had been declared bankrupt prior to the Austrian proceedings, and the proceedings were dismissed as against him. The European Court ruled that Art.6(1) of the Regulation could not be interpreted in such a way as to make its application dependent on the effects of domestic rules. It re-iterated that Art.6(1) could not be interpreted in such a way as to allow a plaintiff to make a claim against a number of defendants for the sole purpose of removing one of them from the jurisdiction of the courts of the Member State in which that defendant was domiciled, but that did not appear to be the case in the Austrian proceedings.

But this view was not followed in Case C–98/06 *Freeport plc v Arnoldsson* [2007] E.C.R. I–839, [2008] Q.B. 634 (noted Scott [2008] L.M.C.L.Q. 113): see entry at para.11–327, above. In that case the European Court did not rule on the question put by the national court, as to whether the likelihood of success of an action against a party before the courts of the State where he is domiciled is relevant in the determination of whether there is a risk of irreconcilable judgments for the purposes of Art.6(1). Mengozzi A-G's opinion on that point was that that assessment may also include an evaluation of the likelihood that the claim brought against the defendant who is domiciled in the forum Member State will succeed. That evaluation will be of real practical relevance for the purpose of excluding the risk of irreconcilable judgments only if that claim proves to be manifestly inadmissible or unfounded in all respects. But he recognised that this conclusion was inconsistent with the ruling in Case C–103/05 *Reisch Montage AG v Kiesel Baumaschinen Handels GmbH* [2006] E.C.R. I–6827, in which the Court ruled (at [42]) that the manifest inadmissibility of the claim brought against a defendant domiciled in the forum Member State, as a result of a procedural bar under national law, did not preclude reliance on the basis for jurisdiction under Art.6(1) in relation to a defendant domiciled in another Member State.

NOTE 21. See also *Deforche SA v Tomacrau SA* [2007] I.L.Pr. 367 (French Cour de cassation, 2006).

**11R–332** NOTE 23. Supreme Court Act 1981 is now renamed Senior Courts Act 1981: Constitutional Reform Act 2005, s.59 and Sch.11, in force October 1, 2009.

NOTE 24. See now revised Lugano Convention, Art.6(2).

**11–333** NOTE 26. CPR, r.6.20(3) has been replaced by CPR PD6B, para.3.1(4).

NOTE 27. For further proceedings see *GIE Réunion Européenne v Zurich Seguros* [2007] I.L.Pr. 301 (French Cour de cassation, 2006).

**11R–338** NOTE 38. See now revised Lugano Convention, Art.6(3).

See now revised Lugano Convention, Art.6(4). **11R–342**

See now revised Lugano Convention, Arts 5(5), 8 to 13. **11R–343— 11–360**

See entry at 11R–401, below. **11R–343**

NOTE 59. Case C–112/03 *Société financière et industrielle du Peloux v AXA Belgium* is now reported at [2005] E.C.R. I–3707, [2006] Q.B. 251. **11–344**

In Case C–463/06 *FBTO Schadeverzekeringen NV v Odenbreit* [2007] E.C.R. I–11321 Mr Odenbreit, a German domiciliary, had been involved in a road traffic accident in the Netherlands with a person insured with FBTO, a Dutch insurer. He brought a direct action against the insurer before a German court, on the basis of Art.11(2) and 9(1)(b) of the Judgments Regulation. The prevailing view in Germany was that such direct actions are not matters relating to insurance within the meaning of Arts 8 *et seq*. of the Judgments Regulation, since the right of action of the injured party in German private international law is regarded as a right in tort and not as a right under an insurance contract; Art.9(1)(b) covers only matters relating to the insurance policy, in the strict sense, and the concept of "beneficiary" in that provision does not include the injured party; and the latter cannot become a main party to the proceedings under Art.11(2). But the German Bundesgerichtshof took the view that the reference to Art.9 in Art.11(2) indicated that the courts for the place where the injured party is domiciled has jurisdiction to hear an action brought by the injured party directly against a liability insurance provider. **11–355**

The European Court agreed. The Court ruled that the reference in Art.11(2) to Art.9(1)(b) is to be interpreted as meaning that the injured party may bring an action directly against the insurer before the courts for the place in a Member State where that injured party is domiciled, provided that a direct action is permitted and the insurer is domiciled in a Member State. To interpret the reference in Art.11(2) to Art.9(1)(b) as permitting the injured party to bring proceedings only before the courts having jurisdiction under that latter provision, namely the courts for the place of domicile of the policy holder, the insured or the beneficiary, would run counter to the actual wording of Art.11(2). The reference leads to a widening of the scope of that rule to categories of plaintiff other than the policy holder, the insured or the beneficiary of the insurance contract who sue the insurer. The role of that reference is to add injured parties to the list of plaintiffs contained in Art.9(1)(b). The application of that rule of jurisdiction to a direct action brought by the injured party cannot depend upon the classification of that injured party as a "beneficiary" within the meaning of Art.9(1)(b), since the reference to that provision in Art.11(2) allows that rule of jurisdiction to be extended to such disputes without the plaintiff having to belong to one of categories in Art.9(1)(b). The application of the rule of jurisdiction provided for by Art.9(1)(b) to a direct action is not precluded by its classification, in national law, as an action in tort relating to a right extrinsic to legal relations of a contractual nature. The nature of the action in national law is of no relevance for the application of the provisions of the Judgments Regulation, since those rules of jurisdiction are contained in a section (Section 3 of Chapter II) which concerns, in general, matters relating to insurance and is distinct from those relating to special jurisdiction in matters relating to a contract or to tort or delict. The only condition which Art.11(2) lays down for the application of that rule of jurisdiction is that such a direct action must be permitted under the national law.

In Case C–347/08 *Vorarlberger Gebietskrankenkasse v WGV-Schwäbische Allgemeine Versicherungs AG* [2009] E.C.R. I–8661, the European Court ruled that the reference in Art.11(2) to Art.9(1)(b) meant that a social security institution, acting as the statutory assignee of the rights of the directly injured party in a motor accident, could not bring an action directly in the courts of its State of establishment against the insurer of the person allegedly responsible for the accident, where that insurer was established in another Regulation State.

See also *Maher v Groupama Grand Est* [2009] EWCA Civ. 1191, [2010] 1 W.L.R. 1564, [17]–[21]: Art.11(3) not limited to joinder of the insured as a third party at the suit of the insurer, and insured can be joined by claimant as an additional defendant to an action against the insurer.

NOTE 75. Third Parties (Rights against Insurers) Act 1930 is repealed by Third Parties (Rights against Insurers) Act 2010 (not yet in force).

**11–357** NOTE 89. Case C–112/03 *Société financière et industrielle du Peloux v AXA Belgium* is now reported at [2005] E.C.R. I–3707, [2006] Q.B. 251.

**11R–363— 11–371** See now revised Lugano Convention, Arts 13 to 17.

**11R–363** See generally Hill, *Cross-Border Consumer Contracts* (2008).

On clause (14)(3) and the proviso to clause (14) see Case C–585/08 *Pammer v Reederei Karl Schlüter GmbH & Co KG* and Case C–144/09 *Hotel Alpenhof GesmbH v Heller*, opinion of Trstenjak A-G, May 18, 2010. On the meaning of directing activities, her opinion was that the notion was not broad enough to cover the mere accessibility of a website in the country where the consumer is domiciled. The national judge must, in the light of all the circumstances, decide if the person who exercises a commercial and professional activity directs his activity towards the member states where the consumer is domiciled.

The relevant factors would include: the contents of the website at the time the contract was concluded; whether the seller intended to form a contract with consumers domiciled in other Regulation States and whether the seller invited or encouraged them to conclude a contract, and in particular whether international dialling codes or a special number for foreigners were included with telephone numbers on the site; indications of how to get to the place of business of the seller e.g. road, rail, airports; existence of the possibility for a consumer to check the availability of stock or of a service; the possibility for a consumer from another Regulation State to sign up to receive news about the goods/services on offer; the possibility for the consumer when indicating his/her delivery address to chose between different Regulation States (but simply displaying an email address was not sufficient); whether the seller has previously done business with consumers in other Regulation States; if the website is in a language of only one Regulation State, and which is not widely spoken, this may be an indication that the site is only directed towards that Regulation State; the fact that the website permits the consumer to change language suggests that the seller consciously sought to direct business to other Regulation States; whether the seller uses a "top-level domain" (e.g. co.uk / .fr); the type of business; and the use of advertisements by the seller.

In Case C–585/08 *Pammer* her opinion was that a journey on a cargo ship including accommodation, opportunity of shore leave and leisure facilities on board (swimming pool, gym, deck-chairs, etc.) constituted a contract which, for an inclusive price, provides for a combination of travel and accommodation according for the purposes of Art.15(3) of the Judgments Regulation.

NOTE 20. Case C–464 *Gruber v BayWa AG* is now reported at [2005] E.C.R. I–439, [2006] Q.B. 204. **11–365**

NOTE 21. But in Case C–80/06 *Ilsinger v Dreschers* [2009] E.C.R. I–3961, the European Court ruled that Art15(1)(c) of the Judgments Regulation applied even if the claiming of the prize was not made conditional upon actually ordering goods or placing a trial order and where no goods were actually ordered. Art.15(1)(c) was drafted in more general and broader terms. It covered all contracts, whatever their purpose, if they had been concluded by a consumer with a professional and fell within the latter's commercial or professional activities. But it did not apply if the professional did not undertake contractually to pay the prize promised to the consumer who requested its payment. Art.15(1)(c) was applicable only on condition that the misleading prize notification was followed by the conclusion of a contract by the consumer with the mail-order company evidenced by an order placed with the latter. The ruling was that Art.15(1)(c) applied if the professional vendor had undertaken in law to pay the prize to the consumer; and where that condition had not been fulfilled, such proceedings were covered by Art.15(1)(c) only if the consumer had in fact placed an order with that professional vendor. **11–367**

NOTE 25. See also Case C–234/04 *Kapferer v Schlank & Schick GmbH* [2006] E.C.R. I–2585; *Maple Leaf Marro Volatility Master Fund v Rouvray* [2009] EWHC 257 (Comm.), [2009] 1 Lloyd's Rep. 475.

**11–368** NOTE 27. See Farah (2008) 33 Eur. L. Rev. 257.

**11R–374— 11–381** See now revised Lugano Convention, Arts 18 to 21.

**11–379** In Case C–462/06 *GlaxoSmithkline v Rouard* [2008] E.C.R. I–3965 (noted Harris (2008) 124 L.Q.R. 523) the national court asked whether Art.6(1) was applicable to an action brought by an employee against two companies established in different Member States which he considered to have been his joint employers. The European Court ruled that Art.6(1) could not be applied to a dispute falling under the special jurisdictional rules in section 5 of Chapter II applicable to individual contracts of employment. That conclusion was supported by the consideration that sound administration of justice would imply that any possibility of relying on Art.6(1) should be open, as in the case of counter-claims, both to employees and to employers. Such an application of Art.6(1) could give rise to consequences contrary to the objective of protection, which the insertion of a specific section for contracts of employment sought specifically to ensure. Reliance by an employer on Art.6(1) could deprive the employee of the protection afforded to him by Art.20(1) under which proceedings can be brought against an employee only in the courts of the Member State in which he is domiciled.

In *WPP Holdings Italy SRL v Benatti* [2007] EWCA Civ 263, [2007] 1 W.L.R. 2316 the arrangement between the parties was held to be a management consultancy rather than a contract of employment.

**11R–383— 11–389** See now revised Lugano Convention, Art.22(1) and Art.22(2).

**11–387** In Case C–372/07 *Hassett v South Eastern Health Board* [2008] E.C.R. I–7403 two Irish doctors claimed in proceedings in Ireland an indemnity and/or a contribution from the Medical Defence Union (a professional association, established as a company incorporated under English law and having its registered office in the United Kingdom) in respect of any sum which, in the context of medical negligence actions brought against the health boards for which those doctors worked, either doctor might be ordered to pay by way of indemnity to the health board concerned. The Board of Management of the MDU, relying on the company's Articles of Association, under which any decision concerning a request for an indemnity comes within its absolute discretion, refused to grant their requests.

The MDU, having been joined in the Irish proceedings as a third party, maintained that, since the claims against it concerned in essence the validity of decisions adopted by its Board of Management, they fell within the scope of Art.22(2) of the Judgments Regulation, with the result that jurisdiction lay solely with the English courts and not with the courts of Ireland.

On a reference from the Supreme Court of Ireland, the European Court held that it was not sufficient for the application of Art.22(2) that a legal action involve some link with a decision adopted by an organ of a company. If all disputes involving a decision by an organ of a company had to be treated as coming within the scope of Art.22(2) that would in reality mean that all legal actions brought against a company—whether in matters relating to a contract, or to tort, or other—would almost always come within the jurisdiction of the courts of the Member State in which the company had it seat. Such an interpretation would make the exceptional jurisdiction in question applicable in the case of disputes which would not give rise to conflicting judgments as regards the validity of the decisions of the organs of a company, in that their outcome would have no bearing on that validity, and also in the case of disputes which did not require any examination of the publication formalities applicable to a company. Such an interpretation would extend the scope of Art.22(2) beyond what was required by its objective. It covered only disputes in which a party was challenging the validity of a decision of an organ of a company under the company law applicable or under the provisions governing the functioning of its organs, as laid down in its Articles of Association, which was not the case in the proceedings. The doctors were challenging the manner of exercise of powers. The European Court ruled that Art.22(2) was to be interpreted as meaning that proceedings, in the context of which one of the parties alleged that a decision adopted by an organ of a company had infringed rights that it claimed under that company's Articles of Association, did not concern the validity of the decisions of the organs of a company within the meaning of Art.22(2).

In *JP Morgan Chase Bank NA* v *Berliner Verkehrsbetriebe (BVG) Anstalt des Offentlichen Rechts* [2010] EWCA Civ 390, [2010] I.L.Pr. 529 BVG was responsible for the provision and operation of the public transport system of Berlin. BVG entered into credit default swap arrangements with the bankers JP Morgan. The terms of the transaction contained English law and jurisdiction clauses. JP Morgan began proceedings in the Commercial Court, claiming declarations and US$112 million pursuant to the terms of the swap. BVG claimed that BVG's board decisions were ultra vires and therefore void with the result that the subsequent contracts for the credit default swap arrangements were void. It was common ground that the issue of whether any decisions of the management and supervisory boards were ultra vires was a matter of German law. BVG applied for an order that the English court had no jurisdiction, because the proceedings had, for the purposes of Art.22(2) of the Judgments Regulation, "as their object the validity of the decisions" of the organs of a legal person, BVG, whose seat was in Germany.

BVG also commenced proceedings against JP Morgan in the Berlin Regional Court, claiming that the swap was invalid, that JP Morgan should release BVG from its obligations (if any) under the swap and a declaration that JP Morgan was obliged to compensate BVG for damages incurred. The German court stayed those proceedings under Art.27, pending the decision of the English court on whether it had jurisdiction, and on appeal the Berlin Kammergericht (Court of Appeal) referred to the European Court a number of questions which may be summarised as follows: (1) Does Art.22(2) apply to actions in which the defendant disputes liability on the ground that the transaction has been entered into as a result of invalid resolutions by its organs in breach of its constitution? (2) if so, does Art.22(2) apply to public law bodies? (3) if so, is the court second seised obliged to stay its proceedings under Art.27 if it is claimed that the jurisdiction clause is also invalid because of the invalidity of the resolution of the public body's organ?

In the Court of Appeal in England it was conceded that Art.22(2) applied to public bodies, but it was held that the English proceedings were not principally concerned with the validity of decisions of BVG's organs. The fact that proceedings raised an issue within Art.22(2) was not sufficient to make the proceedings "principally concerned with" that issue, even if that issue might be dispositive. The Court of Appeal also rejected BVG's application for the English proceedings to be stayed pending the ruling by the European Court on the German appeal court's reference, and refused to make a reference itself.

See also *Depfa Bank Plc v Provincia di Pisa* [2010] EWHC 1148 (Comm.).

NOTE 74. See also *FKI Engineering Ltd v Dewind Holdings Ltd* [2008] EWCA Civ 316, [2008] I.L.Pr. 492.

**11–388** Companies Act 1985 is replaced by Companies Act 2006.

**11R–393— 11–394** See now revised Lugano Convention, Art.22(4).

**11R–397— 11–398** See now revised Lugano Convention, Art.22(5).

**11–395** In Case C–4/03 *Gesellschaft für Antriebstechnik mbH & Co. KG v Lamellen und Kupplungsbau Beteiligungs KG* [2007] [2006] E.C.R. I–6509 the European Court ruled that Art.16(4) of the 1968 Convention applied to all proceedings relating to the registration or validity of a patent, irrespective of whether the issue is raised by way of an action or a plea in objection.

GAT and LuK, both German companies, are competitors in the field of motor vehicle technology. GAT made an offer to a motor vehicle manufacturer, also established in Germany, with a view to winning a contract to supply mechanical damper springs. LuK alleged that the spring which was the subject of GAT's proposal infringed two French patents of which LuK was the proprietor. GAT brought a declaratory action before the Landgericht (Regional Court), Düsseldorf, to establish that it was not in breach of the patents, maintaining that its products did not infringe the rights under the French patents owned by LuK and, further, that those patents were either void or invalid.

The Landgericht Düsseldorf considered that it had international jurisdiction to adjudicate upon the action relating to the alleged infringement of the rights deriving from the French patents. It considered that it also had jurisdiction to adjudicate upon the plea as to the alleged nullity of those patents. The Landgericht dismissed the action brought by GAT, holding that the patents at issue satisfied the requirements of patentability.

The Oberlandesgericht (Higher Regional Court) Düsseldorf referred to the European Court the question whether Art.16(4) concerned all proceedings concerned with the registration or validity of a patent, irrespective of whether the question is raised by way of an action or a plea in objection, or whether its application is limited solely to those cases in which the question of a patent's registration or validity is raised by way of an action.

The European Court recalled that proceedings relating to the validity, existence or lapse of a patent or an alleged right of priority by reason of an earlier deposit are to be regarded as proceedings "concerned with the registration or validity of patents": Case 288/82 *Duijnstee v Goderbauer* [1983] E.C.R. 3663, at [24]. But if the dispute did not concern the validity of the patent or the existence of the deposit or registration and these matters are not disputed by the parties, the dispute will not be covered by Art.16(4) of the Convention (*Duijnstee*, at [25]–[26]). Such would be the case, for example, with an infringement action, in which the question of the validity of the patent allegedly infringed is not called into question. But in practice the issue of a patent's validity was frequently raised as a plea in objection in an infringement action, the defendant seeking to have the claimant retroactively denied the right on which the claimant relies and thus have the action brought against him dismissed. The issue could also be invoked, as in the case in the main proceedings, in support of a declaratory action seeking to establish that there had been no infringement, whereby the claimant sought to establish that the defendant.

The exclusive jurisdiction in proceedings concerned with the registration or validity of patents conferred upon the courts of the Contracting State in which the deposit or registration has been applied for or made was justified by the fact that those courts are best placed to adjudicate upon cases in which the dispute itself concerns the validity of the patent or the existence of the deposit or registration (*Duijnstee*, at [22]). The courts of the Contracting State on whose territory the registers are kept may rule, applying their own national law, on the validity and effects of the patents which have been issued in that State. This concern for the sound administration of justice becomes all the more important in the field of patents since, given the specialised nature of this area, a number of Contracting States have set up a system of specific judicial protection, to ensure that these types of cases are dealt with by specialised courts. That exclusive jurisdiction is also justified by the fact that the issue of patents necessitates the involvement of the national administrative authorities.

In the light of the position of Art.16(4) within the scheme of the 1968 Convention and the objective pursued, the exclusive jurisdiction provided for by that provision should apply whatever the form of proceedings in which the issue of a patent's validity is raised, be it by way of an action or a plea in objection, at the time the case is brought or at a later stage in the proceedings. To allow a court seised of an action for infringement or for a declaration that there has been no infringement to establish, indirectly, the invalidity of the patent at issue would undermine the binding nature of the rule of jurisdiction laid down in Art.16(4) of the Convention. The claimant would be able, simply by the way it formulates its claims, to circumvent the mandatory nature of the rule of jurisdiction laid down in that article. Second, the possibility which this offers of circumventing Art.16(4) of the Convention would have the effect of multiplying the heads of jurisdiction and would be liable to undermine the predictability of the rules of jurisdiction laid down by the Convention, and consequently to undermine the principle of legal certainty, which is the basis of the Convention. Third, to allow, within the scheme of the Convention, decisions in which courts other than those of a State in which a particular patent is issued rule indirectly on the validity of that patent would also multiply the risk of conflicting decisions which the Convention seeks specifically to avoid.

In several Contracting States a decision to annul a patent has *erga omnes* effect. In order to avoid the risk of contradictory decisions, it is therefore necessary to limit the jurisdiction of the courts of a State other than that in which the patent is issued to rule indirectly on the validity of a foreign patent to only those cases in which, under the applicable national law, the effects of the decision to be given are limited to the parties to the proceedings. Such a limitation would, however, lead to distortions, thereby undermining the equality and uniformity of rights and obligations arising from the Convention for the Contracting States and the persons concerned.

On this case see Briggs [2006] L.M.C.L.Q. 447. *cf.* Case C–539/03 *Roche Nederland BV v Primus* [2006] E.C.R. I–6535 (entry at para.11–329, above). See also *Knorr-Bremse Systems for Commercial Vehicles Ltd v Haldex Brake Products GmbH* [2008] EWHC 156 (Pat.), [2008] 2 All E.R. (Comm.) 448.

**11R–397** NOTE 2. See Cuniberti, 2008 *Clunet* 963.

**11–398** NOTE 3. See also *Masri v Consolidated Contractors International Company SAL (No.2)* [2008] EWCA Civ 303, [2009] 2 W.L.R. 621.

**11R–399—11–400** See now revised Lugano Convention, Art.23.

See now revised Lugano Convention, Art.24. **11R–401—11–402**

In Case C–111/09 *Ceská podnikatelská pojišt'ovna, a.s. v Bílas*, May 20, 2010, the European Court ruled that the effect of Art.24 of the Judgments Regulation was that the court seised, where the rules in s.3 of Chapter II of the Judgments Regulation were not complied with, must declare itself to have jurisdiction where the defendant entered an appearance and did not contest that court's jurisdiction, since entering an appearance in that way amounted to a tacit prorogation of jurisdiction. **11R–401**

Note 12. See also *Maple Leaf Marro Volatility Master Fund v Rouvray* [2009] EWHC 257 (Comm.), [2009] 1 Lloyd's Rep. 475. **11–403**

See now revised Lugano Convention, Art.31. **11R–406—11–408**

Note 20. CPR, r.6.20(4) has been replaced by CPR PD6B, para.3.1(5). **11–407**

See now revised Lugano Convention, Art.22. **11–409**

Note 21. See now revised Lugano Convention, Art.22(1). **11R–410**

See now revised Lugano Convention, Art.27. The reference to Judgments Regulation, Art.23, should be to Art.27. **11R–412—11–413**

Final sentence. Companies Act 1985 is replaced by Companies Act 2006. **11–413**

Note 29. See now revised Lugano Convention, Art.22(3). **11R–414**

Note 30. See now revised Lugano Convention, Art.22(4). **11R–415**

See now revised Lugano Convention, Art.22(5). **11R–417—11–418**

See now revised Lugano Convention, Art.23. **11R–419—11–420**

# CHAPTER 12

# FORUM NON CONVENIENS, LIS ALIBI PENDENS, ANTI-SUIT INJUNCTIONS AND JURISDICTION AGREEMENTS

## 1. FORUM NON CONVENIENS, ANTI-SUIT INJUNCTIONS AND LIS ALIBI PENDENS

**12R–001** NOTE 1. The reference to Bell should read *Forum Shopping and Venue in Transnational Litigation.* See also Kruger, *Civil Jurisdiction Rules of the EU and Their Impact on Third States* (2008); de Vareilles-Sommières (ed), *Forum Shopping in the European Judicial Area* (2007). See also Magnus & Mankowski (eds.), *Brussels I Regulation* (2007); Von Mehren, *Adjudicatory Authority in Private International Law: A Comparative Study* (2007); McLachlan, *Lis Pendens in International Litigation* (2009); Briggs, *Revue de Droit Suisse*, Vol. 124 (2005) II 231.

NOTE 4. The European Commission has published a Report and Green Paper on the revision of the Judgments Regulation: COM(2009) 174 and COM(2009) 175. See entry at para.11–013, above.

**12–006** On the power to stay proceedings by reference to the inherent jurisdiction of the court, see *Texan Management Ltd v Pacific Electric Wire & Cable Co Ltd* [2009] UKPC 46 (BVI), esp at [49]–[57] (even though an application for a stay of proceedings, especially one which is based on the principle of *forum non conveniens*, must normally be made within the procedural framework and time-limits set out in CPR, Part 11, if the circumstances which justify the application for a stay arise outside the time limited by CPR, Part 11, or after the defendant has acknowledged service and so accepted the jurisdiction of the court to try the claim against him, an application for a stay may be made by reference to CPR, r.3(1)(2)(f), or advanced by reference to the inherent jurisdiction of the court: at [77]).

Final paragraph. Neither the European Patents Convention nor national legislation implementing it makes express provision for a stay of proceedings where there is parallel litigation in national court and European Patent Office. As the statutory scheme makes this possible, there is in this context no basis for a presumption against parallel proceedings: *Glaxo Group Ltd v Genentech Inc* [2008] EWCA Civ 23, [2008] Bus. L.R. 888.

NOTE 18: Supreme Court Act 1981 is now renamed Senior Courts Act 1981 (Constitutional Reform Act 2005, s.59 and Sch.11, in force October 1, 2009).

NOTE 19. See *Prifti v Musini SA de Seguros y Reaseguros* [2005] EWHC 832 (Comm.), [2006] Lloyd's Rep. I.R. 221 (stay ordered); *ET Plus SA v Welter* [2005] EWHC 2115 (Comm.), [2006] 1 Lloyd's Rep. 215 (stay ordered); *cf. Mabey & Johnson Ltd v Danos* [2007] EWHC 1094 (Ch.) (stay refused); *Curtis v Lockheed Martin UK Holdings Ltd* [2008] EWHC 260 (Comm.), [2008] 1 C.L.C. 219 (stay would reduce but not eliminate risk of conflicting decisions: refused); *Equitas Ltd v Allstate Insurance Co* [2008] EWHC 1671 (Comm.), [2009] Lloyd's Rep. I.R. 227 (English proceedings brought on basis of exclusive jurisdiction clause: stay refused). See also *Jefferies International Ltd v Landsbanki Islands* [2009] EWHC 894 (Comm.) (no stay, even on case management grounds, when express choice of English law and jurisdiction, and no way of telling how long the process of insolvency in Iceland would last); *Cooper Tire & Rubber Co Europe Ltd v Shell Chemicals UK Ltd* [2009] EWHC 1529 (Comm.) (no stay of proceedings to dispute jurisdiction to await outcome of appeal in Italy, which would take years to determine), affd. [2010] EWCA Civ 864; *Pacific International Sports Clubs Ltd v Pacific International Sports Clubs Ltd v Surkis* [2010] EWCA Civ 753 (case management may avert the risks resulting from uncoordinated judicial procedures in different countries).

NOTE 23. See also *Hatzl v XL Insurance Co* [2009] EWCA Civ 223, [2010] 1 W.L.R. 470 (CMR Convention; no power to stay).

In *Abbassi v Abbassi* [2006] EWCA Civ 355, [2006] 1 F.C.R. 648 (a matrimonial case) it was held that the judge had power to adjourn proceedings to allow the validity of a Muslim religious divorce to be determined in Pakistan.

NOTE 47. For analysis of the developed Australian jurisprudence, see *Murakami v Wiryadi* [2010] NSWCA 7. *Reinsurance Australia Corp Ltd v HIH Casualty and General Insurance Ltd* [2003] FCA 56, (2003) 254 A.L.R. 29 (Fed. Ct.) must now be read in the light of *Comandate Marine Corp v Pan Australia Shipping Pty Ltd* (2006) 157 F.C.R. 45, [2008] 1 Lloyd's Rep. 119 (Fed. Ct. Aust.) esp. at [241]. **12–011**

For the revised Lugano Convention, which supersedes the 1988 Lugano Convention, and the dates of its coming into force as between the European Union and Norway, and the European Union and Switzerland, see entry at para.11R–001, above. **12–013**

The decision in Case C–281/02 *Owusu v Jackson* [2005] E.C.R. I–1383 applies equally where jurisdiction is founded on Art.5 of the Judgments Regulation: *Gómez v Gómez-Monche Vives* [2008] EWHC 259 (Ch), [2008] 3 W.L.R. 309, revd on other aspects [2008] EWCA Civ 1065, [2009] Ch. 245 (there was no appeal on this point). **12–020**

Text to note 92. The issues were debated, but no decision was necessary, in *Antec International Ltd v Biosafety USA Inc* [2006] EWHC 47 (Comm.). **12–022**

However, in *Samengo-Turner v J&H Marsh & McLennan (Services) Ltd* [2007] EWCA Civ 723, [2008] I.C.R. 18 (on which see Briggs [2007] L.M.C.L.Q. 433), an agreement conferring jurisdiction on the courts of New York was annulled on the ground that the Regulation deprived it of legal effect: *sed quaere.*

It was held in *Lucasfilm Ltd v Ainsworth* [2009] EWCA Civ 1328, [2010] 3 W.L.R. 333 (on which see Dickinson [2010] L.M.C.L.Q. 181, Rogerson [2010] C.L.J. 245) that where proceedings were brought alleging an infringement of foreign copyright, an English court lacked jurisdiction over the subject matter of the claim, and the fact that the defendant was domiciled in England did not mean that the claim was one which the Judgments Regulation required the English court to adjudicate. The court considered the jurisdictional rule in *British South Africa Co v Companhia de Moçambique* [1893] A.C. 602, which it held to be applicable to copyright, as confirming the lack of subject-matter jurisdiction over claims concerning foreign copyright. It interpreted this rule as being unaffected by the decision in Case C–281/02 *Owusu v Jackson* [2005] E.C.R. I–1383, reaching this conclusion as a matter of English private international law rather than by attributing any form of "reflexive effect" to Art.22(4) of the Judgments Regulation. The Supreme Court has given permission to appeal.

The reasoning in *Lucasfilm Ltd v Ainsworth* was relied on and applied in *JKN v JCN* [2010] EWHC 843 (Fam.). The case examined in detail the potential application of *Owusu* in the context of a divorce and financial relief case, in which the English court had jurisdiction under Art.3 of the Brussels II*bis* Regulation but parallel proceedings were before the courts of New York. The conclusion was that *Owusu* should not be "extended" to cases in which there were parallel proceedings before the courts of a non-Member State, and that it should not be held to apply to family proceedings cases covered by the Brussels II *bis* Regulation. (It followed that the question whether to stay proceedings was determined in accordance with the principles set out in the main work at para.18–245.) See further, entry at para.18–245, below.

In *Choudhary v Bhatter* [2009] EWCA Civ 1176, [2010] 1 All E.R. (Comm.) 1031, [48]–[54] the Court of Appeal declined to express a view on whether a court with exclusive (*sic*) jurisdiction over a defendant by reason of Art.22 of the Judgments Regulation had power to stay its proceedings for the courts of a non-Member State. The question whether *Owusu* prevented a stay of proceedings in favour of the courts of a non-Member state where the jurisdiction of the English court was founded on Art.12 of the Regulation was raised but not decided (as the foreign court was not shown to be the natural forum) in *Royal & Sun Alliance Insurance plc v Rolls-Royce plc* [2010] EWHC 1869 (Comm.).

Text to note 94. In *Winnetka Trading Corp v Julius Baer International Ltd* [2008] EWHC 3146 (Ch.), [2009] Bus. L.R. 1006 it was held that a court was not precluded from granting a stay to give effect to an agreement on jurisdiction for the courts of Guernsey. See also *UBS AG v HSH Nordbank AG* [2009] EWCA Civ 585, [2009] 2 Lloyd's Rep. 272, [102]–[103], where the point was also discussed but was not required to be decided.

Notwithstanding the view advanced in the main work, the Irish Supreme Court considered it necessary to refer the question whether the existence of a *lis alibi pendens* in a non-Member State had any effect on proceedings before an Irish court brought against a defendant domiciled in Ireland to the European Court: *Goshawk Dedicated Ltd v Life Receivables Ireland Ltd* [2009] IESC 7, [2009] I.L.Pr. 435: the reference was, nevertheless, not made. The question was raised, but was not decided, in *Pacific International Sports Clubs Ltd v Soccer Marketing International Ltd* [2009] EWHC 1839 (Ch.) (appeal dismissed without reference to this point: *Pacific International Sports Clubs Ltd v Surkis* [2010] EWCA Civ 753). See generally Briggs (2009) 80 B.Y.I.L. 601.

In *Catalyst Investment Group Ltd v Lewinsohn* [2009] EWHC 1964 (Ch.) [2010] Ch. 218 it was held that the existence of a *lis alibi pendens* in a non-Member State was irrelevant to, and had no effect on, the jurisdiction of an English court in proceedings brought against a defendant domiciled in England (Art.27 could not be applied with strict reflexive effect, as the court in Utah, seised first, would not ask itself whether its jurisdiction was confirmed by the Judgments Regulation; Art.27 did not permit an English court to apply a principle of *forum non conveniens* to determine what effect to give to the Utah proceedings, as the principle was wholly inconsistent with the scheme of the Regulation; *Coreck* was distinguished as being confined to cases of prorogation of the courts of a non-Member State).

Note 92. See also Hare [2006] J.B.L. 157; Rodger (2006) 2 J. Priv. Int. L. 71, Fentiman (2006) 59 Curr. Leg. Prob. 391; Fentiman, in de Vareilles-Sommières (ed), *Forum Shopping in the European Judicial Area* (2007), chap.1.

Note 95. See also *The Seaward Quest* [2007] EWHC 1460 (Comm.), [2007] **12–024**
2 Lloyd's Rep. 308.

Note 97. In *Ivax Pharmaceuticals UK Ltd v AKZO Nobel BV* [2005] EWHC 2658 (Comm), [2006] F.S.R. 888, and in *The Seaward Quest* [2007] EWHC 1460 (Comm.), [2007] 2 Lloyd's Rep. 308, it was held that the doctrine of *forum non conveniens* was applicable generally in questions concerning the courts of England and Scotland. See also *Royal Bank of Scotland plc v Davidson* [2009] CSOH 134, 2010 S.L.T. 92 (though declining to stay Scottish proceedings in favour of the English courts).

However, the judgment of the European Court in Case C–386/05 *Color Drack GmbH v Lexx International Vertriebs GmbH* [2007] E.C.R. I–3699, [2010] 1 W.L.R. 1909 (a case on Art.5(1) of the Judgments Regulation) states at [30] that Art.5(1) determines both international and national jurisdiction, and serves to "designate the court having jurisdiction directly, without reference to the domestic rules of the Member States", which view is consistent with the suggestion referred to in note 97 in the main work.

On the operation of *forum non conveniens* as between the courts of England and Scotland in a matter excluded from the Civil Jurisdiction and Judgments Act 1982 and the Judgments Regulation, see *Tehrani v Secretary of State for the Home Department* [2006] UKHL 47, [2007] 1 A.C. 521.

**12–026** Text to note 9. But in *Cherney v Deripaska* [2009] EWCA Civ 849, [2010] 2 All E.R. (Comm.) 456 (a case on service out of the jurisdiction) it was held that the court might authorise service even though England was not (and Russia was) the natural forum, on the ground that a proper trial of the issues was not possible in Russia.

**12–027** *Pacific International Sports Clubs Ltd v Surkis* [2010] EWCA Civ 753, at [17], [23], reiterates the limited powers of the court hearing the appeal. By contrast, for an Australian suggestion that the decision at first instance should not be seen as discretionary (in the sense that it may not be reviewed on appeal unless clearly wrong) but as an exercise in judgment (on which an appellate court is just as well placed as the judge below to make the evaluation), see *Murakami v Wiryadi* [2010] NSWCA 7, [32]–[34].

**12–028** See also *Cecil v Bayat* [2010] EWHC 641 (Comm.), esp at [144]–[156] (US courts apparently not an available forum, as earlier proceedings had been dismissed and the file sealed, the grounds for this being unknown, with the result that England was the only available forum, and therefore was the natural forum, for the action; service out permitted).

NOTE 16. However, if the defendant undertakes to submit to the jurisdiction of the foreign court only during the hearing of an appeal against the decision of the judge to authorise service out, it is too late and will not be accepted, for the appeal is an appeal against the decision which was made by the judge at the time he made it: *Sharab v Al-Saud* [2009] EWCA Civ 353, [2009] 2 Lloyd's Rep. 160.

NOTE 19. In *Attorney General of Zambia v Meer Care & Desai* [2006] EWCA Civ 390, [2006] 1 C.L.C. 436 the fact that certain of the defendants were unable to attend trial in England, because they had been required to surrender their passports, did not mean that England was unavailable as a forum, or that it would necessarily be unjust for the trial to take place there. But a contrary view appears to have been taken in *Cherney v Deripaska* [2008] EWHC 1530 (Comm.), [2009] 1 All E.R. (Comm.) 333 (a case on service out of the jurisdiction) (appeal dismissed [2009] EWCA Civ 849, [2010] 2 All E.R. (Comm.) 456, without specific reference to this point).

Second paragraph. The fact that very complicated issues of foreign law would require decision was a powerful reason in favour of a stay, even in a case in which there were reasons to question the quality of justice available from the foreign court: *Pacific International Sports Clubs Ltd v Soccer Marketing International Ltd* [2009] EWHC 1839 (Ch.) (appeal dismissed, approving the detailed analysis of this issue by the judge below: *Pacific International Sports Clubs Ltd v Surkis* [2010] EWCA Civ 753) (shareholder dispute about the ownership of Dinamo Kiev Football Club). On the weight to be given to the fact that insurance was written in London, see also *Royal & Sun Alliance Insurance plc v Rolls-Royce plc* [2010] EWHC 1869 (Comm.). **12–029**

In *Novus Aviation Ltd v Onur Air Tasimacilik AS* [2009] EWCA Civ 122, [2009] 1 Lloyd's Rep. 576, it was held that the possibility that issues of English law might arise did not by itself serve to make England the natural forum, though if those issues raised questions of English public policy, that would make it more likely that England would be the natural forum for the trial. However, it would be contrary to principle to equate a choice of English law with a choice of English court: at [76].

The fact that the part of a claim which could be framed in tort might, if tried in England, be governed by English law, would not have prevented the UAE being seen as the natural forum for the whole of the claim: *Middle Eastern Oil LLC v National Bank of Abu Dhabi* [2008] EWHC 2895 (Comm.), [2009] 1 Lloyd's Rep. 251, [19]–[21].

By contrast, the fact that a personal injury claim might have been governed by the law of New Zealand did not, in the opinion of the High Court of Australia, serve to make Australia a clearly inappropriate forum for the trial, for this would be tantamount to denying the very purpose of choice of law rules: *Puttick v Tenon Ltd* [2008] HCA 54, (2008) 238 C.L.R. 265, [31]–[32]. However, as the Australian test is significantly different from that applied in England (see the main work, para.12–011), this is probably not to be understood as representing English law.

Third paragraph. The natural forum for the judicial interpretation of a will governed by English law and expressed in English terminology is England: *Dellar v Zivy* [2007] EWHC 2266 (Ch.), [2007] I.L.Pr. 868; see also *Jaiswal v Jaiswal* [2007] Jersey L.R. 305.

Note 28. *Cadre SA v Astra Asigurari SA* is now reported at [2006] 1 Lloyd's Rep. 560. Likewise, if the parties agreed on a particular foreign law, and the courts of that country would not recognise the order sought from the Ontario court, the Ontario court will lean against permitting service to be made out of the jurisdiction: *Kolibri Capital Corp v LSOF Canada I* [2004] CanLII 11509 (Ont).

Note 31. See also *Reeves v Sprecher* [2007] EWHC 117 (Ch.), [2008] B.C.C. 49. But it is otherwise if the companies are not being wound up compulsorily, and no other issue of corporate governance arises: *Pakistan v Zardari* [2006]

EWHC 2411 (Comm.), [2006] 2 C.L.C. 667. The English authorities on company law issues were distinguished in *Virgtel Ltd v Zabusky* [2006] QSC 66. See also *Re Krug International (UK) Ltd* [2008] EWHC 2256 (Ch.), [2008] B.P.I.R. 1512 (England proper place for claim arising out of misfeasance in context of insolvency in the United Kingdom).

**12–030** The "Cambridgeshire" factor was considered, but was not given decisive effect in *Royal & Sun Alliance Insurance plc v Rolls-Royce plc* [2010] EWHC 1869 (Comm.).

**12–031** It has been held that if the evidence shows that the courts of a foreign country which is proposed as the natural forum are not in practice available to the claimant for the hearing of the claim because law and order has wholly collapsed, a stay of English proceedings will not be granted: *889457 Alberta Inc v Katanga Mining Ltd* [2008] EWHC 2679 (Comm.), [2009] I.L.Pr. 175. It has also been held that if the court accepts that there is a demonstrable risk that the claimant will not obtain a fair trial in the foreign court, it may decline to stay its proceedings in favour of the foreign court: under the second limb of the *Spiliada* test: *Pacific International Sports Clubs Ltd v Surkis* [2010] EWCA Civ 753), approving the detailed analysis of this issue by the judge below. The court may even allow service out of the jurisdiction, even though the foreign court is the natural forum and the English court is not (*Cherney v Deripaska* [2009] EWCA Civ 849, [2010] 2 All E.R. (Comm.) 456, on which see Briggs (2009) 80 B.Y.I.L. 575) (*cf. Pacific International Sports Clubs Ltd v Soccer Marketing International Ltd* [2009] EWHC 1839 (Ch.), affd. [2010] EWCA Civ 753). To this extent, at least, the proposition that there may be no comparison and adverse assessment of the quality of justice available from a foreign court does not apply.

See also *Korea National Insurance Co v Allianz Global Corporate and Specialty AG* [2008] EWCA Civ 1355, [2008] 2 C.L.C. 837 (a case on the recognition of foreign judgments, permitting allegations of unjudicial behaviour by foreign court to be made to oppose recognition of the judgment as *res judicata*).

Note 39. See *Crown Resources Corp SA v National Iranian Oil Corp* (2006) 273 D.L.R. (4th) 65 (Ont. CA), enforcing agreement conferring jurisdiction on Iranian courts. *cf. Al-Koronky v Time-Life Entertainment Group Ltd* [2006] EWCA Civ 1123 (not illegitimate to adduce evidence to question impartiality of judges in Sudan, as the issue is properly justiciable, and doubting *Jayaretnam v Mahmood* on this point).

**12–032** First sentence. See also *R (on the application of Smith) v Secretary of State for Defence* [2010] UKSC 29, [301].

NOTE 41. *Cf. EM (Lebanon) v Secretary of State for the Home Department* [2008] UKHL 64, [2009] A.C. 1198 (refusal to deport individual to Lebanon as this would result in a flagrant breach of applicant's civil rights).

Text following note 46. See *Garsec v Sultan of Brunei* [2008] NSWCA 211, (2008) 250 A.L.R. 682: Australian proceedings were stayed even though there would be no justiciable claim in the alternative forum, as an Australian court would itself have applied the rule of substantive Brunei law and the Australian claim was therefore doomed. Had the rule of Brunei law been characterised as procedural, and as inapplicable in an Australian court, the Australian proceedings might still, though not necessarily, have been stayed. **12–033**

NOTE 49. See also *Sharab v Al-Saud* [2009] EWCA Civ 353, [2009] 2 Lloyd's Rep. 160 (but where the greater enforceability of an English judgment was held to contribute to making England the natural forum for the proceedings, and a reason to uphold an order granting permission for service out of the jurisdiction. It is doubtful whether such reasoning is generally available in support of an application for permission to serve out, but that the case was influenced by the fact that there appeared to be no other available forum anywhere).

The existence of proceedings before a foreign court is not decisive factor which should cause a court to stay its own proceedings: *Teck Cominco Metals Ltd v Lloyd's Underwriters* [2009] SCC 11, [2009] 1 S.C.R. 321, (2009) 303 D.L.R. (4th) 385 (applying the statutory version of the doctrine of forum non conveniens of the law of British Columbia); it does not make the bringing of the foreign proceedings oppressive or vexatious: *Deutsche Bank AG v Highland Crusader Offshore LP* [2009] EWCA Civ 725, [2010] 1 W.L.R. 1023 (especially where the English court has jurisdiction under an agreement on jurisdiction which does not support the contention that the bringing of the foreign proceedings involves a breach of contract). **12–036**

NOTE 60. See *Pfizer Ltd v Dai Nippon Sumitomo Pharma Co Ltd* [2006] EWHC 1424 (Ch.).

NOTE 62. See also *Galaxy Special Maritime Enterprise v Prima Ceylon Ltd* [2006] EWCA Civ 528, [2006] 2 Lloyd's Rep. 27.

Final sentence. Where the parties have made an agreement which expressly accepts that proceedings may be brought in more than one jurisdiction, it will be only rarely that it may be said to be wrong for there to be litigation in two courts at the same time: *Deutsche Bank AG v Highland Crusader Offshore Partners LP* [2009] EWCA Civ 725, [2010] 1 W.L.R. 1023. **12–037**

The question whether a court should grant relief in the form of an injunction when proceedings are brought in two jurisdictions and can be seen to be likely to lead to irreconcilable judgments has recently been answered in the negative: the fact of parallel proceedings may be objectively regrettable, but unless it can be said that one party has behaved so wrongfully that an English court is justified in imposing (directly or indirectly) its view to this effect on the foreign court, there will be no basis for the injunction: *Deutsche Bank AG v Highland Crusader Offshore Partners LP* [2009] EWCA Civ 725, [2010] 1 W.L.R. 1023; *TS Production LLC v Drew Pictures Pty Ltd* [2008] FCAFC 194, (2008) 252 A.L.R. 1; to cause or contribute to the bringing about of a situation of parallel litigation is not automatically wrongful. It is different where the foreign proceedings have been brought in breach of contract.

No election is called for when the claimant has brought proceedings before the Iranian courts as well as the English courts if the refusal of the defendant to submit to the Iranian proceedings means that any Iranian judgment could be enforced in Iran but not in England: *Karafarin Bank v Mansoury-Dara* [2009] EWHC 1217 (Comm.), [2009] 2 Lloyd's Rep. 289.

**12–038** It was confirmed by the Privy Council in *Texan Management Ltd v Pacific Electric Wire & Cable Co Ltd* [2009] UKPC 46, at [66]–[77], that applications for a stay of proceedings would be, in principle, required to be brought within the procedural framework and time-limits set out in CPR, Part 11. However, though it is reasonable to require that an application to set aside service out of the jurisdiction be made within those time-limits, it may not always be so where the relief sought is a stay of proceedings on the ground of *forum non conveniens*. If the application is not made within the time period set out in CPR, Part 11, the court may regard this, in accordance with CPR, r.3(1)(2)(f), as a curable irregularity which does not invalidate the application. If the circumstances which justify the application for a stay arise outside the time limited by CPR, Part 11, or even arise after the defendant has acknowledged service and so accepted the jurisdiction of the court to try the claim against him, an application for a stay may be still be entertained by reference to CPR, r.3(1)(2)(f), or advanced by reference to the inherent jurisdiction of the court. See also *Cooper Tire & Rubber Co v Shell Chemicals UK Ltd* [2009] EWHC 2609 (Comm.), [2009] I.L.Pr. 886, [96]–[103] (accepting that a stay of proceedings under Art.28 of the Judgments Regulation may be applied for outside the period of 28 days provided for such applications in the Commercial Court); *Bilta UK Ltd v Nazir* [2010] EWHC 1086 (Ch.) (application for extension of time for service of defence, to allow more time to seek information about the claim made, in order to take a decision whether to apply for a stay for arbitration, did not amount to the taking of a step in the proceedings such as would forfeit the right to apply for a stay under Arbitration Act 1996, s.9).

**12–041** In *Standard Bank plc v Agrinvest International Inc* [2007] EWHC 2595 (Comm.), [2008] 1 Lloyd's Rep. 532 the court made declarations as to the exclusive jurisdiction and governing law, as well as of non-liability, presumably to assist the claimant in a subsequent plea of issue estoppel.

NOTE 83. See also *Ark Therapeutics Ltd v True North Capital Ltd* [2005] EWHC 1585 (Comm.), [2006] 1 All E.R. (Comm.) 138.

Text to note 1. For service of the claim form in Scotland or Northern Ireland in cases in which the permission of the court is required, now see CPR, r.6.37(4). **12–043**

Text to note 8. A claimant may be able to demonstrate that England is clearly the appropriate forum for the trial of the action (or, in the language of CPR r.6.37(3), that England is the proper place in which to bring the claim), even though the courts of another country would be the natural forum, if there is a serious risk that a trial of the action in that other country would be subject to State interference or other cause amounting to a serious risk of injustice: *Cherney v Deripaska* [2009] EWCA Civ 849, [2010] 2 All E.R. (Comm.) 456. **12–044**

For the revised Lugano Convention, which supersedes the 1988 Lugano Convention (which on this point mirrors the provisions of Arts 27–30 of the Judgments Regulation), and the dates of its coming into force as between the European Union and Norway, and the European Union and Switzerland, see entry at para.11R–001, above. **12–045**

A contention that a court seised first should stay its proceedings pending a reference to the European Court of Justice (Case C–144/10 *BVG v JP Morgan Chase Bank NA*, pending) from a court seised second was rejected in *Berliner Verkehrsbetriebe (BVG) Anstalt des Offentlichen Rechts v JP Morgan Chase Bank NA* [2010] EWCA Civ 390, [2010] I.L.Pr. 529, [111].

Belgium has initiated proceedings against Switzerland before the International Court of Justice which complain of the failure or refusal of the Swiss courts to apply the Lugano Convention in such a way as would result in a stay of Swiss proceedings in favour of the Belgian courts which were, according to the Belgian government, seised first of a dispute between the same parties and based on the same cause of action: Press Release 2009/36, International Court of Justice, December 22, 2009.

Article 71 of the Judgments Regulation, and its application where the specialist convention contains its own provisions for the regulation of *lis alibi pendens* and the enforcement of judgments which may conflict with those of the Judgments Regulation, was considered by the European Court in Case C–533/08 *TNT Express Nederland BV v AXA Versicherung AG* [2010] I.L.Pr. 663. The Court ruled that "Article 71 of [the Judgments Regulation] must be interpreted as meaning that, in a case such as the main proceedings, the rules **12–046** governing jurisdiction, recognition and enforcement that are laid down by a convention on a particular matter, such as the *lis pendens* rule set out in Art.31(2) of the Convention on the Contract for the International Carriage of Goods by Road, signed at Geneva on 19 May 1956, as amended by the Protocol signed at Geneva on 5 July 1978, and the rule relating to enforceability set out in Article 31(3) of that convention, apply provided that they are highly predictable, facilitate the sound administration of justice and enable the risk of concurrent proceedings to be minimised and that they ensure, under conditions at least as favourable as those provided for by the Regulation, the free movement of judgments in civil and commercial matters and mutual trust in the administration of justice in the European Union (*favor executionis*)".

On the assumption that the ruling would be empty of content unless there were a difference between the provisions of the Judgments Regulation and the specialist convention, and notwithstanding the words used by the European Court in its ruling, it is hard to identify the cases in which the rules of the specialist convention on *lis alibi pendens* would be denied application as a result of this ruling.

NOTE 13. The Judgments Regulation applies to Bulgaria and Romania which were Member States from January 1, 2007 (Council Regulation (EC) 1791/2006); and to Denmark by virtue of a parallel agreement ([2006] O.J. L120/22) with effect from July 1, 2007: SI 2007/1655.

NOTE 14. See also *Sony Computer Entertainment Ltd v RH Freight Services Ltd* [2007] EWHC 302 (Comm.), [2007] 2 Lloyd's Rep. 463.

12–047 NOTE 23. Where the jurisdiction of a court is challenged, the court remains seised pending the final determination of any appeal; it is not dis-seised when a jurisdictional application succeeds, only to be (re-)seised, and possibly seised second as a result, when an appeal reverses the earlier decision: *Moore v Moore* [2007] EWCA Civ 361, [2007] I.L.Pr. 481. See also (on cure of procedural irregularity in service and date of seisin) *Phillips v Symes (No.3)* [2008] UKHL 1, [2008] 1 W.L.R. 180.

12–048 Where proceedings are before the courts of two Regulation states, the applicable rules are those in Arts 27–30 of the Regulation, and not those of Arts 21–23 of the (old) Lugano Convention, even if the relevant parties are domiciled only in a Convention state: *Cooper Tire & Rubber Company Europe Ltd v Dow Deutschland Inc* [2010] EWCA Civ 864, approving *Trademark Licensing Co v Leofelis SA* [2009] EWHC 3285, [2010] I.L.Pr. 290.

12–049 NOTE 30. Article 27 is not excluded or overridden when the jurisdiction of the court would otherwise have been founded on Art.24: *Popely v Popely* [1996] IEHC 134, [2006] I.R. 356.

NOTE 42. The Full Court of the Federal Court of Australia disapproved of this analysis of the admiralty action *in rem* in *Comandate Marine Corp v Pan Australia Shipping Pty Ltd* (2006) 157 F.C.R. 45, [2008] 1 Lloyd's Rep. 119. 12–051

NOTE 44. Case C–351/96 *Drouot Assurances SA v Consolidated Metallurgical Industries* [1998] E.C.R. I–3075, [1999] Q.B. 497 was applied in *Sony Computer Entertainment Ltd v RH Freight Services Ltd* [2007] EWHC 302 (Comm.), [2007] 2 Lloyd's Rep. 463 (no identity between insurer and insured). 12–052

NOTE 46. The test was applied in *Kolden Holdings Ltd v Rodette Commerce Ltd* [2008] EWCA Civ 10, [2008] Bus. L.R. 1051 to conclude that the assignee of a cause of action counted as the same party as the assignor for the purpose of Article 27 of the Judgments Regulation; the test of identity of parties requires the court to look to the substance, not the form, of the two claims: at [85]. Further, the court was seised as from the date of the original action, not the date of the assignment or consequential amendment. The Oberlandesgericht Köln came to the same conclusion: Case 16 U 110/02, September 8, 2003, IPRax 2004, 521 (and see Geimer, *ibid.*, 505).

On the question whether the parties to English and Italian proceedings were "the same parties", the court in *Cooper Tire & Rubber Co v Shell Chemicals UK Ltd* [2009] EWHC 2609 (Comm.), [2009] I.L.Pr. 886 (appeal dismissed without reference to this point *sub nom Cooper Tire & Rubber Company Europe Ltd v Dow Deutschland Inc* [2010] EWCA Civ 864) held that the test established by *Kolden Holdings Ltd v Rodette Commerce Ltd* was not satisfied because the interests of the principal participant in a cartel, whose exposure to liability was great, were not identical to those of minor participants who were less exposed. A common interest in defending proceedings will not by itself be sufficient to establish identity of interest. See also *Mölnlycke Health Care AB v BSN Medical Ltd* [2009] EWHC 3370 (Pat.), [2010] I.L.Pr. 171 (rights not identical and indissociable as licensee has an additional, not an assigned, right).

See *Secret Hotels 2 Ltd v EA Traveller Ltd* [2010] EWHC 1023 (Ch.), [2010] I.L.Pr. 616: Art.27 applied, as the claims made in the second-seised jurisdiction could be raised as defences to the claim in the first-seised court (and if that were not so, a stay under Art.28 was inevitable). 12–053

A complex question may arise when proceedings in the two courts involve claims which overlap, and may require the two courts to rule on issues which the two actions have in common, for it is unsettled whether the requisite comparison is made between individual causes of action, or between the two sets of proceedings in a broader sense. See *Underwriting Members of Lloyd's Syndicate 980 v Sinco SA* [2008] EWHC 1842 (Comm.) [2009] Lloyd's Rep. I.R. 365 (English proceedings including claim for damages for breach of 12–054 jurisdiction clause by bringing proceedings in Greek court: Art.27 not applicable), following *Evialis SA v SIAT* [2003] EWHC 863 (Comm.), [2003] 2 Lloyd's Rep. 377 and *Bank of Tokyo-Mitsubishi Ltd v Baskan Gida Sanayi ve Pazarlama AS* [2004] EWHC 945 (Ch.), [2004] 2 Lloyd's Rep. 395.

**12–055** NOTE 54. On the application of Art.27 of the Judgments Regulation where there is a risk of contradictory orders in contractual litigation, see *Jacobs & Turner Ltd v Celsius Sarl*, 2007 S.L.T. 722.

**12–057** NOTE 59. When the English court cures a procedural irregularity in service and declares that process was validly served notwithstanding the irregularity, the court is regarded as having been seised, and without subsequent hiatus, from the date of original imperfect service. It follows that the foreign court before which proceedings instituted after service but before the irregularity is dealt with is seised second: *Phillips v Symes (No.3)* [2008] UKHL 1, [2008] 1 W.L.R. 180 (a case on the Lugano Convention). The case is quite different where the claimant seeks to use the CPR in a "naked attempt . . . to subvert" the Convention: at [39]. See also *Olafsson v Gissurarson (No.2)* [2008] EWCA Civ 152, [2008] 1 W.L.R. 2016 (a case on the Lugano Convention): justice required an order dispensing with service, and there was no suggestion that making such an order would subvert the Hague Convention on the service of process.

**12–058** NOTE 61. In *Phillips v Symes (No.3)* [2008] UKHL 1, [2008] 1 W.L.R. 180 a minority would have been prepared to overrule *Dresser UK Ltd v Falcongate Freight Management Ltd* [1992] Q.B. 502 (CA) and *The Sargasso* [1994] 3 All E.R. 180 and hold the court to be seised on issue or on the first making of an order against the defendant, but the majority found no need to do so.

**12–059** NOTE 65. See also *Bentinck v Bentinck* [2007] EWCA Civ 175, [2007] I.L.Pr. 391 (stay of English proceedings to allow Swiss court to determine the date of seisin of proceedings pending before it).

**12–060** On the operation of Art.30 of the Judgments Regulation, and the (non-)effect of minor irregularities in service, see *WPP Holdings Italy srl v Benatti* [2007] EWCA Civ 263, [2007] 1 W.L.R. 2316; *Weiner v Weiner* [2010] EWHC 1843 (Fam.) (a case on the Brussels II*bis* Regulation). See also *Debt Collection London Ltd v SK Slavia Praha Fotbal AS* [2009] EWHC 2726 (QB), [2010] I.L.Pr. 114, holding that on a proper construction of Art.30(1) of the Regulation, and the provisions of Czech law on the institution of civil proceedings, the Czech court had not been seised before English court, for though Czech process was issued earlier than the English claim form, the claimant did not pay the Czech court fee, meaning that the Czech process was not in a position to be served, until after the English court had been seised.

**12–061** NOTE 69. But where the "new party" is in law the assignee of the pending cause of action, the date of seisin remains that of the original action, not that of the amendment: *Kolden Holdings Ltd v Rodette Commerce Ltd* [2008] EWCA Civ 10, [2008] Bus. L.R. 1051. But on the more complex difficulties which arise from amendment to add new causes of action, see *Underwriting Members of Lloyd's Syndicate 980 v Sinco SA* [2008] EWHC 1842 (Comm.), [2009] Lloyd's Rep. I.R. 365 (date of seisin when claim added by amendment).

Add in further support of this conclusion: *DT v FL* [2006] IEHC 98, [2007] I.L.Pr. 763 at [63] (Irish High Ct). **12–062**

See *FKI Engineering Ltd v Stribog Ltd* [2010] EWHC 1160 (Comm.), [2010] I.L.Pr. 711 (where an action in a court first-seised, which is not related to proceedings in a court second seised, undergoes amendment to add a claim which is related to the proceedings in the court second seised, it is the proceedings in the court second seised which are regarded as being the first-seised proceedings for the purposes of considering relief under Art.28. The amendment to the proceedings before the first court was not made to elucidate something which had already been pleaded, but was a substantively new claim, which was asserted after the (related) proceedings in the other court and to which it therefore took second place in point of time). **12–064**

NOTE 74. To determine whether actions are related for the purpose of Art.28 the court may look at the defences as well as the claims; but (either) the granting of relief is not automatic on finding the actions to be related, (or) if it is not expedient that the two actions be tried together, they are not related after all: *Research in Motion UK Ltd v Visto Corp* [2008] EWCA Civ 153, [2008] F.S.R. 499. See also *Prazic v Prazic* [2006] EWCA Civ 497, [2007] I.L.Pr. 381; *Prifti v Musini SA de Seguros y Reaseguros* [2005] EWHC 832 (Comm), [2006] Lloyd's Rep. I.R. 221; *Landis + Gyr Ltd v Scaleo Chip ET* [2007] EWHC 1880 (QB), [2007] I.L.Pr. 719; *Popely v Popely* [2006] IEHC 134, [2006] I.R. 356.

For the purposes of Art.28, a judge is not required to ignore the fact that proceedings in the court seised first in time are expected to take several years before coming to judgment, and so to refuse to stay proceedings: *Cooper Tire & Rubber Company Europe Ltd v Dow Deutschland Inc* [2010] EWCA Civ 864 (generally approving the analysis of the issues in a factually-complex cartel case by the judge *sub nom. Cooper Tire & Rubber Co v Shell Chemicals UK Ltd* [2009] EWHC 2609 (Comm.), [2009] I.L.Pr. 886: the judge had refused to order a stay, partly by reference to the anticipated slowness of proceedings before the first-seised court, and partly by reference to the overall organisational advantages of allowing the English proceedings to continue notwithstanding that the Italian courts were first seised of related proceedings). See also *Trademark Licensing Co v Leofelis SA* [2009] EWHC 3285 (Ch.), [2010] I.L.Pr. 290 (refusing to stay in favour of Italian court if the two actions were related, not least because the Italian proceedings would be slow, **12–065** but also because the Italian court would be assisted by a judgment in the English proceedings; and disagreeing with the proposition in Jenard that there was a presumption in favour of a stay of related proceedings before the court seised second in time).

**12–067** See generally, Raphael, *The Anti-suit Injunction* (2008).

**12–068** NOTE 93. See also *Starlight Shipping Co v Tai Ping Insurance Co Ltd* [2007] EWHC 1893 (Comm), [2008] 1 Lloyd's Rep. 230.

**12–069** In *Masri v Consolidated Contractors International Co SAL (No.3)* [2008] EWCA Civ 625, [2009] Q.B. 503 the Court of Appeal upheld the grant of a post-judgment anti-suit injunction ordered to restrain the judgment debtor from taking steps overseas to undermine an English judgment or its enforcement. Such an order was to be understood as ancillary to the exercise of jurisdiction to determine the merits of the dispute. This brought it within the requirement in *Turner v Grovit* [2002] UKHL 65, [2002] 1 W.L.R. 107 (as to which, see the main work, para.12–076), that it protect the jurisdiction of the court, and within the principle of the Judgments Regulation (Case C–391/95 *Van Uden Maritime BV v Deco-Line* [1998] E.C.R. I–7091) that a court exercising jurisdiction on the merits was entitled to make any order, whether provisional or protective or otherwise, which was ancillary to that adjudication, as it was in "full possession" of the litigation. For further application of this principle, see also *Masri v Consolidated Contractors International Co SAL (No.4)* [2008] EWCA Civ 876, [2010] 1 A.C. 90 (order for examination of officer of judgment debtor) (the decision of the Court of Appeal was reversed, *sub nom Masri v Consolidated Contractors International Co SAL* [2009] UKHL 43, [2010] 1 A.C. 90 on the ground that CPR r.71(2)(b) did not apply to persons not present within the jurisdiction; the impact of European law was not discussed).

The basis for the exercise of discretion was that the behaviour of the respondent was unconscionable and that this was sufficient to render it liable to restraint. It was possible to say that the applicant had an equitable "right" not be vexed by the overseas action if it was understood that "right" in this sense meant no more than a "thing which gives rise to a remedy".

**12–070** NOTE 6. See also *Goshawk Dedicated Ltd v ROP Inc* [2006] EWHC 1730 (Comm.), [2006] Lloyd's Rep. I.R. 711.

NOTE 8: See also *Harms Offshore AHT Taurus GmbH & Co KG v Bloom* [2009] EWCA Civ 632, [2010] Ch. 187 (injunction to restrain foreign attachment of assets of company in administration prior to sale as going concern: respondent's behaviour unconscionable; injunction granted).

**12–072** Text to note 17. The observation in the main work, that the approach of Australian law was somewhat narrower than the corresponding English law on the grant of anti-suit injunctions was questioned in *TS Production LLC v Drew Pictures Pty Ltd* (2008) 172 F.C.R. 433, [32], and in *Sunland Waterfront (BVI) Ltd v Prudentia Investments Pty Ltd (No 2)* [2010] FCA 312, [22]: the material difference, however, lies not in the wording of the respective tests, but in the results of their application. A contention that there was any symmetry between the rules governing recognition of foreign judgments and the rules governing the ordering of an anti-suit injunction was rejected in *Sunland Waterfront (BVI) Ltd v Prudentia Investments Pty Ltd (No.2)* at [45].

NOTE 16. See also *OT Africa Line Ltd v Magic Sportswear Corp* (2006) 273 D.L.R. (4th) 302, [2007] 1 Lloyd's Rep. 85 (Can. Fed. CA).

The question whether a court should grant relief in the form of an injunction when proceedings are brought in two jurisdictions and can be seen to be likely to lead to irreconcilable judgments has recently been answered in the negative: the fact of parallel proceedings may be objectively regrettable, but unless it can be said that one party has behaved so wrongfully that an English court is justified in imposing (directly or indirectly) its view to this effect on the foreign court, there will be no basis for the injunction: *Deutsche Bank AG v Highland Crusader Offshore Partners LP* [2009] EWCA Civ 725, [2010] 1 W.L.R. 1023; *TS Production LLC v Drew Pictures Pty Ltd* [2008] FCAFC 194, (2008) 252 A.L.R. 1; to cause or contribute to the bringing about of a situation of parallel litigation is not automatically wrongful. It is different where the foreign proceedings have been brought in breach of contract. **12–073**

But where the parties have made an agreement which expressly accepts that proceedings may be brought in more than one jurisdiction, it will be only rarely that it may be said to be wrong for there to be litigation in two courts at the same time: *Deutsche Bank AG v Highland Crusader Offshore Partners LP* [2009] EWCA Civ 725, [2010] 1 W.L.R. 1023.

First paragraph. An English court may order an injunction against proceedings which aim to nullify a London arbitral award, but there is a discretion to not do so: *Noble Assurance Co v Gerling-Konzern General Insurance Co—UK Branch* [2007] EWHC 253 (Comm.), [2008] Lloyd's Rep. I.R. 1; *C v D* [2007] EWCA Civ 1282, [2008] 1 Lloyd's Rep. 239. See also *Shashoua v Sharma* [2009] EWHC 957 (Comm.), [2009] 2 All E.R. (Comm.) 477 (injunction granted by court at the seat of the arbitration proper to defend the integrity of the agreement to arbitrate); *Midgulf International Ltd v Groupe Chimiche Tunisien* [2009] EWHC 963 (Comm.) (interim anti-suit injunction on grounds of case management to allow English court time to decide whether there was a binding agreement to arbitrate).

NOTE 24. See also *Albon v Naza Motor Trading Sdn Bhd* [2007] EWCA Civ 1124, [2008] 1 Lloyd's Rep. 1.

NOTE 25. *cf. Weinstock v Sarnat* [2005] NSWLR 744, (2005) 3 I.E.T.L.R. 141.

NOTE 27. *Cadre SA v Astra Asigurari SA* [2005] EWHC 2626 (Comm.) is now reported at [2006] 1 Lloyd's Rep. 549. *cf. Trafigura Beheer BV v Kookmin Bank Co* [2006] EWHC 1921 (Comm.), [2007] 1 Lloyd's Rep. 669 (on which Briggs (2007) 123 L.Q.R. 18), where the injunction was ordered even though English law had not been chosen but was the law with the closest connection to the contractual claims. See also *Standard Bank plc v Agrinvest International Inc* [2007] EWHC 2595 (Comm.), [2008] 1 Lloyd's Rep. 532.

**12–076** NOTE 39. In *Standard Bank plc v Agrinvest International Inc* [2007] EWHC 2595 (Comm.), [2008] 1 Lloyd's Rep. 532 an injunction restrained non-parties to an agreement on jurisdiction and choice of law from bringing foreign proceedings designed to subvert or frustrate the English proceedings between parties to that agreement.

**12–077** On "single forum" cases, see *Masri v Consolidated Contractors International Co SAL (No.3)* [2008] EWCA Civ 625, [2009] Q.B. 503, at [43] and [56].

**12–081** In *Masri v Consolidated Contractors International Co SAL (No.3)*, above, it was held at [66] (*obiter*) that an interim anti-suit injunction was a provisional or protective measure, falling within the scope of Art.31 of the Judgments Regulation (always supposing it was not made in respect of proceedings before another Member State). However, the respondent to such an injunction was not "sued" for the purposes of the Judgments Regulation, and the jurisdictional rules of Chapter II of the Regulation therefore furnished no impediment to the making of the order. (For further consideration of the meaning of "sued", see *Masri v Consolidated Contractors International Co SAL (No.4)* [2008] EWCA Civ 876, [2010] 1 A.C. 90 (order for examination of officer of judgment debtor: not sued): the decision of the Court of Appeal was reversed, [2009] UKHL 43, [2010] 1 A.C. 90 on the ground that CPR r.71(2)(b) did not apply to persons who were not present within the jurisdiction; the impact of European law was not discussed).)

Text to note 70. See C–185/07 *Allianz SpA v West Tankers Inc* [2009] E.C.R. I–663, below, entry at para.12–141.

**12–082** For CPR, r.6.20, now see CPR, r.6.36 and PD6B, para.3.1.

**12–083** For CPR, r.6.20, now see CPR, r.6.36 and PD6B, para.3.1.

## 2. JURISDICTION AGREEMENTS

**12R–086** For the revised Lugano Convention, which supersedes the 1988 Lugano Convention (which in relation to agreements on jurisdiction mirrors Article 23 of the Judgments Regulation), and the dates of its coming into force as between the European Union and Norway, and the European Union and Switzerland, see the entry at para.11R–001, above. See also Briggs, *Agreements on Jurisdiction and Choice of Law* (2008); Kruger, *Civil Jurisdiction Rules of the EU and Their Impact on Third States* (2008).

NOTE 84. For CPR, r.6.15, now see CPR, r.6.11; for CPR, r.6.20(5)(d), now see CPR PD6B, para.3.1(6)(d).

The European Union signed the Hague Convention on Choice of Court Agreements on April 1, 2009; the Convention has also been signed by Mexico and the United States, though only Mexico has ratified it. Papers examining various aspects of the Convention are published in (2009) 5 J. Priv. Int. L., at 125 (Beaumont), 161 (Garnett), 181 (Keyes), 517 (Svantesson), and 357 (Briza). See also (for an Australian perspective) Spigelman (2009) 83 A.L.J. 386. On the Convention, see also Kessedjian, 2006 *Clunet* 813; Kruger (2006) 55 I.C.L.Q. 447; Schulz (2006) 2 J. Priv. I.L. 243; Brand and Jablonski, *Forum Non Conveniens: History, Global Practice and Future under the Hague Convention on Choice of Court Agreements* (2007); Brand and Herrup, *The 2005 Hague Convention on Choice of Court Agreements* (2008). **12–088**

A basis for the reconciliation of the competing lines of authority was identified in *Habaş Sinai ve Tibbi Gazlar Isthisal Endustri AS v Sometal SAL* [2010] EWHC 29 (Comm.), [2010] Bus.L.R. 880. Where is it alleged that a jurisdiction clause has been incorporated into a contract from another contract to which they were also party, general words will suffice to do it. But where a jurisdiction agreement is to be incorporated from another contract which was not between the same parties (as in the context of charterparties and bills of lading), the test for incorporation is stricter, and general words will be less likely to suffice. **12–091**

NOTE 5. The appeal in *Dornoch Ltd v Mauritius Union Assurance Co Ltd* [2006] EWCA Civ 389, [2006] 2 Lloyd's Rep. 475 was dismissed; general words did not incorporate a jurisdiction clause from one reinsurance to the other (the question appears to have been answered by reference to the *lex fori* and English canons of construction).

NOTE 6. *cf. Sea Trade Maritime Corp v Hellenic Mutual War Risks Association (Bermuda) Ltd (The Athena) (No.2)* [2006] EWHC 2530 (Comm.), [2007] 1 Lloyd's Rep. 280, disapproving the distinction between provisions germane and ancillary to the risk, and regarding the question of incorporation as one to be answered simply one of construction of the words of incorporation; also *Axa Re v Ace Global Markets Ltd* [2006] EWHC 216 (Comm.), [2006] Lloyd's Rep. I.R. 683.

NOTE 9. See also *Nestorway Ltd v Ambaflex BV* [2006] IEHC 235, [2007] I.L.Pr. 633.

**12–092** See also *Middle Eastern Oil LLC v National Bank of Abu Dhabi* [2008] EWHC 2895 (Comm.), [2009] 1 Lloyd's Rep. 251 (construed as exclusive so far as borrower was concerned, non-exclusive so far as Bank was concerned); *Breitenbücher v Wittke* [2008] CSOH 145 (construction of jurisdiction agreement expressed to be limited in its effect to those with status of "Kaufmann", or "merchant" a matter for German law as law governing the contract); *Bank of New York Mellon v GV Films Ltd* [2009] EWHC 2328 (Comm.), [2010] 1 Lloyd's Rep. 365 (exclusive for one party, non-exclusive for the other).

Further, the question of who is party to and bound by the jurisdiction agreement is a matter for the law which governs that agreement: *Starlight Shipping Co v Tai Ping Insurance Co Ltd (Hubei Branch)* [2007] EWHC 1893 (Comm.), [2008] 1 Lloyd's Rep. 230 (a case on arbitration agreements).

NOTE 13. On the contextual construction of ambiguous words, *General Motors Corp v Royal & Sun Alliance Insurance plc* [2007] EWHC 2206 (Comm.), [2007] 2 C.L.C. 507. See also *Ace Insurance Ltd v Moose Enterprise Pty Ltd* [2009] NSWSC 724, [33] (on which see Yeo [2010] L.M.C.L.Q. 194) (ambiguously-worded clause may be non-exclusive on the footing that it is easy to draft the clause as exclusive if that were to be what the parties wanted).

NOTE 14. See also *Standard Bank plc v Agrinvest International Inc* [2007] EWHC 2595, [2008] 1 Lloyd's Rep. 532; *Armacel Pty Ltd v Smurfit Stone Container Corp* [2008] FCA 592, (2008) 248 A.L.R. 573.

**12–093** A non-exclusive jurisdiction clause which expressly provides that it is not to prevent the bringing of proceedings in any other court is not breached when proceedings are brought in another court. It is possible to breach a non-exclusive jurisdiction agreement, but everything depends on the construction of the clause in its entirety and the particular acts of the respondent in relation to it: *Deutsche Bank AG v Highland Crusader Offshore LP* [2009] EWCA Civ 725, [2010] 1 W.L.R. 1023.

NOTE 18. See also *Antec International Ltd v Biosafety USA Inc* [2006] EWHC 47 (Comm.), allowing service out on basis of non-exclusive jurisdiction agreement; *HIT Entertainment Ltd v Gaffney International Licensing Pty Ltd* [2007] EWHC 1282 (Ch.), refusing to stay where this would defeat non-exclusive jurisdiction agreement; *BP plc v Aon Ltd* [2005] EWHC 2554 (Comm.), [2006] 1 Lloyd's Rep. 549. It appears that only those factors which were not foreseeable at the time the agreement was made will have any real weight on an application which seeks to allow litigation to take place outside the non-exclusive chosen forum.

The approach to construction of arbitration agreements, which must apply equally to jurisdiction clauses, and which has invited courts to pay close attention to earlier decisions on the distinction between particular verbal formulae was strongly disapproved in *Comandate Marine Corp v Pan Australia Shipping Pty Ltd* (2006) 157 F.C.R. 45, [2008] 1 Lloyd's Rep. 119 (Aust Fed Ct), and in *Fiona Trust & Holding Corp v Privalov* [2007] UKHL 40, [2007] Bus. L.R. 1719 (on which see Briggs, [2008] L.M.C.L.Q. 1, (2007) 78 B.Y.I.L. 588, Rushworth (2008) 124 L.Q.R. 195). See also *Mabey & Johnson Ltd v Danos* [2007] EWHC 1094 (Ch.). 12–094

But the decision in *Fiona Trust* has limited application to the questions which arise where parties are bound by several contracts which contain jurisdiction agreements for different countries. There is no presumption that a jurisdiction (or arbitration) agreement in contract A, even if expressed in wide language, was intended to capture disputes arising under contract B; the question is entirely one of construction: *Satyam Computer Services Ltd v Upaid Services Ltd* [2008] EWCA Civ 487, [2008] 2 All E.R. (Comm.) 465. The same approach to the construction of potentially-overlapping agreements on jurisdiction (but there will, in this respect, be no difference between the construction of agreements on jurisdiction, arbitration agreements, and service of suit clauses) was taken in *UBS AG v HSH Nordbank AG* [2009] EWCA Civ 585, [2009] 2 Lloyd's Rep. 272, and in *Sebastian Holdings Inc v Deutsche Bank AG* [2010] EWCA Civ 998 (a question of construction in context of financial relationship constituted by multiple contracts case was answered by asking whether the claim brought by the claimant bank was one which the particular jurisdiction clause relied on by the bank allowed the bank to bring, the court not favouring an alternative approach which would have meant that the particular jurisdiction clause relied on would cease to be available if the defendant were to raise by way of defence a matter which, taken in isolation, more naturally fell within the scope of a jurisdiction clause in a related contract). See also, at first instance, *ACP Capital Ltd v IFR Capital plc* [2008] EWHC 1627 (Comm.); *ACE Capital Ltd v CMS Energy Corp* [2008] EWHC 1843 (Comm.), [2008] 2 C.L.C. 318; *Choil Trading SA v Addax Energy SA* [2009] EWHC 2742 (Comm.) (a case in which any agreement on jurisdiction would have been subject to Art.17 of the Lugano Convention, but it was not shown, clearly and precisely, that the parties had agreed to the jurisdiction of the English courts in respect of the particular contractual claim.). *Cf. Douglas v Glenvarigill Co Ltd* [2009] CSOH 17, 2009 S.C.L.R. 379 (jurisdiction agreement in umbrella agreement, expressed in wide terms, applied to dispute arising out of contract made under that agreement but which did not contain its own agreement on jurisdiction).

A number of cases have also re-examined the question, which was aired in *Credit Suisse First Boston (Europe) Ltd v MLC (Bermuda) Ltd* [1999] 1 All

E.R. (Comm.) 237, and considered by Lord Scott in *Donohue v Armco Inc* [2001] UKHL 64, [2002] 1 Lloyd's Rep. 425, whether a jurisdiction clause in a contract between A and B can bind A so as to oblige him not to bring proceedings against C outside the jurisdiction of a specified court. It is, in some instances, another aspect of the problem created when a number of linked contracts have distinct jurisdiction clauses. The answer to the question is, accordingly, also derived from the true construction of the words of the jurisdiction agreement itself, and it is to be doubted whether any general principles or presumptions are to be derived from the cases, which are no more than interpretations of specific wordings in specific contexts. See, for example, *Morgan Stanley & Co International plc v China Haisheng Juice Holdings Co Ltd* [2009] EWHC 2409 (Comm.), [2010] 1 Lloyd's Rep. 265; *Skype Technologies SA v Joltid Ltd* [2009] EWHC 2783 (Ch.); *Whitesea Shipping & Trading Corp v El Paso Rio Clara Ltda (The "Marielle Bolten")* [2009] EWHC 2552 (Comm.), [2010] 1 Lloyd's Rep. 648; *Cinnamon European Structured Credit Master Fund v Banco Comercial Portugues SA* [2009] EWHC 3381 (Ch.); *Global Partners Fund Ltd v Babcock & Brown Ltd (in liq)* [2010] NSWCA 196; *cf. Cavell USA Inc v Seaton Insurance Co* [2008] EWHC 3043 (Comm.).

In the final analysis, as the Court of Appeal has now made plain on several occasions (most recently, in *Sebastian Holdings Inc v Deutsche Bank AG* [2010] EWCA Civ 998, at [49], approving the version of this paragraph which appeared in the Third Cumulative Supplement), the question simply requires the careful and commercially-minded construction of the various agreements providing for the resolution of disputes, the point of departure being that agreements which appear to have been deliberately and professionally drafted are to be given effect so far as it is possible and commercially rational to do so, even where this may result in a degree of fragmentation in the resolution of disputes. It may be necessary to enquire under which of a number of interrelated contractual agreements a dispute actually arises; this may be answered by seeking to locate its centre of gravity.

The same approach, namely to focus on the commercially-rational construction, governs the interpretation of agreements on jurisdiction as exclusive or non-exclusive, and of agreements which specifically provide that the parties will not take objection to the bringing of proceedings if proceedings are brought in more courts than one: *Deutsche Bank AG v Highland Crusader Offshore Partners LP* [2009] EWCA Civ 725, [2010] 1 W.L.R. 1023. See further, *Astrazeneca UK Ltd v Albemarle International Corp* [2010] EWHC 1028 (Comm.), [2010] 2 Lloyd's Rep. 61. Likewise, if the parties have made an agreement on jurisdiction which applies to some, but not to all, disputes which may arise, it will not be very persuasive for one of them to seek to restrain proceedings brought before another court which fall outside the terms of the jurisdiction agreement: *Morgan Stanley & Co International plc v China Haisheng Juice Holdings Co Ltd* [2009] EWHC 2409 (Comm.), [2010] 1 Lloyd's Rep 265; *Skype Technologies SA v Joltid Ltd* [2009] EWHC 2783 (Ch.).

It is not a breach of a jurisdiction clause for the English courts for a judgment creditor to being proceedings to enforce the English judgment before a foreign court (*in casu*, New York) against an entity which is not a party to the clause but which is, as the judgment creditor alleges, the *alter ego* of the defendant if on a true construction of the jurisdiction clause, the claim advanced in the New York proceedings does not fall within it: *Brave Bulk Transport Ltd v Spot On Shipping Ltd* [2009] EWHC 612 (QB), [2009] 2 Lloyd's Rep. 115. And to the same effect: *Vitol SA v Capri Marine Ltd (No.2)* [2010] EWHC 458 (Comm.), [34].

A clause which provides for English law and exclusive jurisdiction over claims of "fraud" requires claims arising from the tort of deceit to be brought in England: *Cavell USA Inc v Seaton Insurance Co* [2009] EWCA Civ 1363, [2009] 2 C.L.C. 991.

It follows from the principle of separability that an arbitration agreement may be found to have been made, and may be binding on the parties, even though the main contract had not come into existence: *UR Power GmbH v Kuok Oils & Grains Pte Ltd* [2009] EWHC 1940 (Comm.), [2009] 2 Lloyd's Rep. 495, [40]. But if there is a dispute between the parties as to whether the contract which it is alleged that they made between them contained a written agreement to arbitrate, the principle of separability is irrelevant, for the issue is to ascertain the terms of the contract in order to see whether there was a written agreement to arbitrate: *Midgulf International Ltd v Groupe Chimiche Tunisien* [2010] EWCA Civ 66, [2010] 1 C.L.C. 113. Likewise, an application for permission to serve out under CPR PD6B, para.3.1(6) requires the claimant to show a good arguable case that the parties concluded a substantive agreement: it is not sufficient to show that there may be a (separable) agreement for the jurisdiction of the English court: *Rimpacific Navigation Inc v Daehan Shipbuilding Co Ltd* [2009] EWHC 2941 (Comm.), [2010] 2 Lloyd's Rep. 236.

NOTE 19. An exclusive jurisdiction clause even in wide terms may as a matter of construction not apply to proceedings taken within the insolvency procedure of a foreign court: *AWB Geneva SA v North America Steamships Ltd* [2007] EWCA Civ 739, [2007] 1 C.L.C. 749. *Leo Laboratories v Crompton BV* is now reported at [2005] 2 I.R. 225.

NOTE 21. The same principle was applied (and the clause held to be applicable) where the claimant framed his claim as one for restitution: *Mackays Stores v Topward Ltd*, 2006 S.L.T. 716. *cf. Noble v Carnival Corp* (2006) 80 O.R. (3d) 392 (claim in tort not within jurisdiction agreement which was in a contract of adhesion and which was construed *contra proferentem*).

On the interpretation of an agreement for English law and jurisdiction which allowed one party to opt for foreign law and jurisdiction (a "service of suit" clause), see *Catlin Syndicate Ltd v Adams Land & Cattle Co* [2006] EWHC 2065 (Comm.), [2006] 2 C.L.C. 425 (option upheld; English proceedings **12–095** stayed in consequence; *Excess Insurance Co Ltd v Allendale Mutual Insurance Co* [2001] Lloyd's Rep. I.R. 524 applied).

**12–096** Note 31. In Canada, Marine Liability Act 2001 s.46 (applied in *OT Africa Line Ltd v Magic Sportswear Corp* (2006) 273 D.L.R. (4th) 302, [2007] 1 Lloyd's Rep. 85 (Can. Fed. CA).

Note 33. It was implicitly held in *Samengo-Turner v J&H Marsh & McLennan (Services) Ltd* [2007] EWCA Civ 723, [2008] I.C.R. 18 that the limitations on jurisdiction clauses in employment contracts apply equally to jurisdiction agreements in relation to a non-Member State, and expressly that an employer who brings proceedings in a non-Member State on the basis of a clause which is not expressly validated by Art.21 may be restrained by an anti-suit injunction: *sed quaere*. Case C–112/03 *Société financière et industrielle du Peloux v AXA Belgium* [2006] Q.B. 251 is now reported at [2005] E.C.R. I–3707.

On jurisdiction clauses in consumer contracts, see also Tang (2005) 1 J. Priv. Int. L. 237.

**12–099** Text to note 44. The principle of separability was decisively approved by the House of Lords in *Fiona Trust & Holding Corp v Privalov* [2007] UKHL 40, [2007] Bus. L.R. 1719 (on which see Briggs, [2008] L.M.C.L.Q. 1, (2007) 78 B.Y.I.L. 588; Rushworth (2008) 124 L.Q.R. 195; Gee (2008) 24 Arb. Int. 467; Samuel, *ibid.* 489; Styles and Knowles, *ibid.* 499. Moreover, the Cour de Cassation has applied a principle of severability to uphold the validity of a jurisdiction agreement for a foreign court even though the substantive contract was objectionable as being contrary to French public policy and it appears that the foreign court would not apply the particular provisions of French law: *Monster Cable Products Inc v Audio Marketing Services* (October 22, 2008) [2009] I.L.Pr. 158.

Text following note 44. The reference in the main work to "excellent reasons of policy" was approved in *El Nasharty v J Sainsbury plc* [2007] EWHC 2618 (Comm.), [2008] 1 Lloyd's Rep. 360.

Note 38. The approach canvassed in *Konkola Copper Mines plc v Coromin Ltd* [2006] EWCA Civ 5, [2006] 1 Lloyd's Rep. 410 was applied in *Astrazeneca UK Ltd v Albemarle International Corp* [2010] EWHC 1028 (Comm.), [2010] 2 Lloyd's Rep. 61: it is for the party who relies on a foreign jurisdiction clause to displace a jurisdiction which is otherwise established in the English court to bear the burden of proof.

Note 40. *Ferris v Plaister* was approved by the Full Court of the Federal Court of Australia in *Comandate Marine Corp v Pan Australia Pty Ltd* (2006) 157 F.C.R. 45, [2008] 1 Lloyd's Rep. 119.

NOTE 44. The approach in *Scherk* was confirmed by the US Supreme Court in *Buckeye Check Cashing Inc v Cardegna*, 546 U.S. 440 (2006).

Text after note 48. The Judgments Regulation applies to Denmark with effect from July 1, 2007: [2006] O.J. L120/22; SI 2007/1655. **12–100**

NOTE 51. In deciding whether there has been an agreement which complies with Art.23, an English court should apply its own law and ask whether the party seeking to show that there is an agreement conferring jurisdiction on the English courts, or on the courts of another Member State, has "much the better of the argument" that such a term was agreed to. Such a test will generally satisfy the requirement that consent be demonstrated clearly and precisely: *Bols Distilleries BV v Superior Yacht Services Ltd* [2006] UKPC 45, [2007] 1 W.L.R. 12 (a case on the identical law of Gibraltar). See also *Hewden Tower Cranes Ltd v Wolffkran GmbH* [2007] EWHC 857 (TCC), [2007] 2 Lloyd's Rep. 138.

And for further application of the "much the better of the argument" test in determining whether there is an agreement on jurisdiction which meets the requirements of Art.23, see *Knorr-Bremse Systems for Commercial Vehicles Ltd v Haldex Brake Products GmbH* [2008] EWHC 156 (Pat.), [2008] I.L.Pr. 326; *Deutsche Bank AG v Asia Pacific Broadband Wireless Communications Inc* [2008] EWCA Civ 1091, [2008] 2 Lloyd's Rep. 619; *Kolmar Group AG v Visen Industries Ltd* [2009] EWHC 3765 (QB), [2010] I.L.Pr. 449.

NOTE 52. See also *7E Communications Ltd v Vertex Antennentechnik GmbH* [2007] EWCA Civ 140, [2007] 1 W.L.R. 2175.

NOTE 53. International character is required at the date of the agreement: *Soc Keller Grundbau v Eléctricité de France,* 2006 *Rev. Crit.* 413 (French Cour de cassation, 2005), note Audit, [2007] I.L.Pr. 8. *cf. Snookes v Jani-King (GB) Ltd* [2006] EWHC 289 (QB), [2006] I.L.Pr. 433 (holding that Art.23 applied to a case wholly internal to the United Kingdom, and that the validity of a clause under Art.23 was subject to Unfair Contract Terms Act 1977: *sed quaere*).

Article 71 of the Judgments Regulation, and its application where the specialist convention contains its own provisions for the regulation of lis alibi pendens and the enforcement of judgments which may conflict with those of the Judgments Regulation, was considered by the European Court in Case C–533/08 *TNT Express Nederland BV v AXA Versicherung AG* [2010] I.L.Pr. 663. On the assumption that the ruling will have no content unless there is a difference between the provisions of the Judgments Regulation and the specialist convention, and notwithstanding the words used by the European Court in its ruling (which seem to suggest that if the Regulation would have led to the recognition but the specialist convention not, then the latter is disapplied **12–102** in favour of enforcement), it is hard to identify specific cases in which the rules of the specialist convention would be denied application on the ground that they are not "highly predictable, facilitate the sound administration of justice and enable the risk of concurrent proceedings to be minimised". See entry at para.12–046, above.

**12–103** The question whether a court, seised of proceedings on the basis of Chapter II of the Regulation, may stay its proceedings if there are proceedings in respect of the same cause of action and between the same parties before the courts of a non-Member State arose but was not decided in *Goshawk Dedicated Ltd v Life Receivables Ireland Ltd* [2009] IESC 7, [2009] I.L.Pr. 435 (the reference to the European Court was nevertheless, not made). The question was raised, but was not decided, in *Pacific International Sports Clubs Ltd v Soccer Marketing International Ltd* [2009] EWHC 1839 (Ch) (appeal dismissed without reference to this point: *Pacific International Sports Clubs Ltd v Surkis* [2010] EWCA Civ 753). In *Catalyst Investment Group Ltd v Lewinsohn* [2009] EWHC 1964 (Ch.), [2010] Ch. 218 it was held that the existence of such a *lis alibi pendens* was irrelevant: entry at para. 12–022, above.

In *Winnetka Trading Corp v Julius Baer International Ltd* [2008] EWHC 3146 (Ch.), [2009] Bus. L.R. 1006 it was held that a court was not precluded from granting a stay to give effect to an agreement conferring jurisdiction on the courts of Guernsey.

**12–104** The fact that the claimant contends (in the alternative) that a contract was void and that relief should be ordered on the basis of unjust enrichment does not mean that the claim falls outside a disputed agreement on jurisdiction but which was in writing. If there is a good arguable case that the parties made an agreement on jurisdiction, which complies with Art.23, it will cover and apply to claims which are founded on the invalidity of the substantive contract in which it is contained: *Deutsche Bank AG v Asia Pacific Broadband Wireless Communications Inc* [2008] EWCA Civ 1091, [2008] 2 Lloyd's Rep. 619 (a case in which the objection was one of excess of, rather than absence of, authority by the corporate officer who committed the defendant to the agreement).

*Fiona Trust & Holding Corp v Privalov*, and *Deutsche Bank AG v Asia Pacific Broadband Wireless Communications Inc* were applied in the context of Art.23 of the Regulation in *Maple Leaf Macro Volatility Master Fund v Rouvroy* [2009] EWHC 257 (Comm.), [2009] 1 Lloyd's Rep. 475.

**12–105** For a summary of the law with special regard to the distinction between those issues determined by a national law, and those to which Art.23 applies an autonomous interpretation, see *Knorr-Bremse Systems for Commercial Vehicles Ltd v Haldex Brake Products GmbH* [2008] EWHC 156 (Pat.), [2008]

I.L.Pr. 326. See also *Breitenbücher v Wittke* [2008] CSOH 145 (construction of jurisdiction agreement expressed to be limited in its effect to those with status of "Kaufmann" or "merchant" a matter for German law as law governing the contract: it does not appear to have been argued that as the agreement was in writing there was no role for national law to play); *Nursaw v Dansk Jersey Eksport* [2009] I.L.Pr. 63 (provision "Court: DK–6100 Haderslev, Denmark" was an agreement on jurisdiction).

See also *Africa Express Line Ltd v Socofi SA* [2009] EWHC 3223 (Comm.), [2010] 2 Lloyd's Rep. 181 (approaching the question as one simply requiring "clear and precise acceptance" of the clause originally contained in a separate contract as binding the parties to the contract in dispute). **12–106**

First sentence. But *cf. Snookes v Jani-King (GB) Ltd* [2006] EWHC 289 (QB), [2006] I.L.Pr. 433 (holding validity of jurisdiction clause otherwise compliant with Article 23 was subject to the control imposed by Unfair Contract Terms Act 1977: *sed quaere*). **12–107**

Second sentence. It was held in *Andromeda Marine SA v O W Bunker & Trading A/S* [2006] EWHC 777 (Comm.), [2006] I.L.Pr. 739 that a claimant for negative declaratory relief, who denied being bound to a contract at all, could not rely on Art.23 to found jurisdiction, at least where the defendant did not make the contrary assertion that his substantive claim derived from the alleged contract. *cf. Equitas Ltd v Wave City Shipping Co Ltd* [2005] EWHC 923 (Comm.), [2006] Lloyd's Rep. I.R. 646 (negative declarations and special jurisdiction); Case II ZR 329/03, 2006 N.J.W. 689, [2006] I.L.Pr. 424 (German Fed. Sup. Ct.). **12–108**

Text to note 76. The statement in the main work, that the principle of good faith may serve to prevent unwarranted reliance on a jurisdiction agreement which satisfies the formal requirements of Art.23, is also supported by Merrett (2009) 58 I.C.L.Q. 545.

The proposition in the main work that, where one party denies that a jurisdiction clause was agreed to, the question whether there was a sufficient consensus was predominantly one of fact, was approved in *Polskie Ratownictwo Okretowe v Rallo Vito & C snc* [2009] EWHC 2249 (Comm.), [2010] 1 Lloyd's Rep. 384, [36].

The principle of separability may also lead to the conclusion that a defendant, who denies that he is bound by a contract, may still rely on Art.23 to challenge the jurisdiction of the court seised, if it is shown that there is sufficient evidence of consensus upon the jurisdiction of the courts of a Member State. The defendant who denies that he is bound by a contract in which a jurisdiction clause was written is not, by that fact, prevented from arguing that there was an agreement on jurisdiction on which he may rely: *Ryanair Ltd v Bravofly* [2009] IEHC 41, [2009] I.L.Pr. 701.

NOTE 78. See also *Stryker Corp v Sulzer Metco AG* [2006] IEHC 60, [2007] I.L.Pr. 616.

**12–111** See also *O'Connor v Masterwood Ltd* [2009] IESC 49 (jurisdiction agreement in document which was signed satisfied requirements of Art.23(1)(a)).

**12–113** On "in writing or evidenced in writing", see *Polskie Ratownictwo Okretowe v Rallo Vito & C snc* [2009] EWHC 2249 (Comm.), [2010] 1 Lloyd's Rep. 384, [55]–[62] (oral agreement, despatch of written copy, absence of immediate objection: requirements satisfied); *Kolmar Group AG v Visen Industries Ltd* [2009] EWHC 3765 (QB), [2010] I.L.Pr. 449 (agreement by telephone followed by confirmatory written document with jurisdiction agreement in it: requirements satisfied especially where parties had dealt on this basis before).

**12–114** See also *Ryanair Ltd v Billigfleuge.de GmbH* [2010] IEHC 47, [2010] I.L.Pr. 439 (jurisdiction clause on airline's website binding on entity which used the service or information provided on the website).

**12–115** NOTE 94. On practices which the parties have established between themselves, see *Calyon v Wytwornia Sprzetu Komunikacynego PZL Swidnik SA* [2009] EWHC 1914 (Comm.), [2009] 2 All E.R. (Comm.) 603.

**12–116** NOTE 2. Case C–112/03 *Société financière et industrielle du Peloux v AXA Belgium* is now reported at [2005] E.C.R. I–3707, [2006] Q.B. 251.

**12–121** See *M v V* [2010] EWHC 1453 (Fam.), [49].

**12–122** Third sentence. See also *Deforche SA v Tomacrau SA* [2007] I.L.Pr. 367 (French Cour de cassation, 2006).

**12–125** NOTE 21. For CPR, r.6.15, now see CPR, r.6.11.

NOTE 22. For CPR, r.6.16, now see CPR, r.6.12.

NOTE 23. For CPR, r.6.19(2), now see CPR, rr.6.32 (service of claim form in Scotland or Northern Ireland) and 6.33 (service of claim form outside the United Kingdom).

**12–126** For CPR, r.6.20(5)(d), now see CPR PD6B, para.3.1(6)(d).

**12–131** Where the jurisdiction clause, which is breached by the bringing of proceedings outside England, extends to only part of what has become a complex dispute, *Donohue v Armco Inc* [2001] UKHL 64, [2002] 1 All E.R. 749, suggests that there may be good reason to withhold the injunction which would otherwise go to enforce the jurisdiction agreement, particularly where the consequence of not ordering the injunction would be to allow the dispute to be concentrated before the foreign court, and especially where the respondent to the application for an injunction has accepted that he may in principle be liable in damages for breach of the jurisdiction agreement. However, where the contracting parties were or should have been aware that their jurisdiction agreement was not comprehensive and where the English court has (by reason of the Judgments Regulation) no power to stay the proceedings before it, with the result that a concentration of jurisdiction cannot be achieved, the court may fall back on the principle that negative covenants should be enforced by injunction, and enforce the jurisdiction agreement according to its terms (*Skype Technologies SA v Joltid Ltd* [2009] EWHC 2783 (Ch.)). And the fact that proceedings have been brought in a foreign court does not, by itself, provide good reason to stay English proceedings which were brought in the court with exclusive jurisdiction: *Bank of New York Mellon v GV Films Ltd* [2009] EWHC 2328 (Comm.), [2010] 1 Lloyd's Rep. 365. On fears of an unfair trial, see *Crown Resources Corp SA v National Iranian Oil Corp* (2006) 273 D.L.R. (4th) 65 (Ont. CA; leave to appeal refused), enforcing Iranian jurisdiction agreement despite allegations concerning judicial process in that country. But *cf. Al-Koronky v Time-Life Entertainment Group Ltd* [2006] EWCA Civ 1123 (where the context whether an English costs order would be enforceable against the claimant in Sudan). It has been held in a series of cases that if the evidence shows that the courts of a foreign country, which is proposed as the natural forum, are not in practice available to the claimant for the hearing of the claim because law and order has wholly collapsed, a stay of English proceedings will not be granted. One possible analysis of these cases is that the prima facie case for a stay may be overcome by the demonstration of well-founded of fears of unjudicial behaviour in the foreign court: see *889457 Alberta Inc v Katanga Mining Ltd* [2008] EWHC 2679 (Comm.), [2009] I.L.Pr. 175 (Congo: stay refused); *Pacific International Sports Clubs Ltd v Soccer Marketing International Ltd* [2009] EWHC 1839 (Ch.) (appeal dismissed, *sub nom: Pacific International Sports Clubs Ltd v Surkis* [2010] EWCA Civ 753) (Ukraine: a service out case: service out refused); *Cherney v Deripaska* [2009] EWCA Civ 849, [2010] 2 All E.R. (Comm.) 456 (Russia: a service out case: service out authorised, even though England was not the natural forum). To this extent, at least, the proposition that there may be no comparison and adverse assessment of the quality of justice available from a foreign court does not apply. See also *Korea National Insurance Co v Allianz Global Corporate and Specialty AG* [2008] EWCA Civ 1355, [2008] 2 C.L.C. 837 (North Korea: a case on the recognition of foreign judgments, permitting allegations of improper behaviour by foreign court to be made to oppose recognition of the judgment as *res judicata*).

NOTE 40. But *cf. Konkola Copper Mines plc v Coromin Ltd (No 2)* [2006] EWHC 1093 (Comm.), [2006] 2 Lloyd's Rep. 446 (holding parties to jurisdiction agreement despite fragmentation of proceedings, which should have been foreseen at the time the contract was made).

**12–136** And see entry under para.12–131, above.

**12–137** It is no part of the decisions of the European Court in Case C–116/02 *Erich Gasser GmbH v Misat srl* [2003] E.C.R. I–14693 and Case C–281/02 *Owusu v Jackson* [2005] E.C.R. I–1383, and does not follow, that a court with jurisdiction under Art.23 of the Judgments Regulation may or must order an anti-suit injunction to restrain proceedings before the courts of a non-Member State: *Skype Technologies SA v Joltid Ltd* [2009] EWHC 2783 (Ch.), [26].

For CPR, r.6.20(5)(d), now see CPR PD6B, para.3.1(6)(d).

**12–139** Note 66. For the possibility of an injunction to restrain a London arbitration (refused) see *Elektrim SA v Vivendi Universal SA (No.2)* [2007] EWHC 571 (Comm.), [2007] 2 Lloyd's Rep. 8; *cf. A v B* [2006] EWHC 2006 (Comm), [2007] 1 Lloyd's Rep. 280 (refusing injunction to restrain foreign arbitration).

Note 69. The Court of Appeal for Bermuda held that an anti-suit injunction may be granted to reinforce a non-Bermudian arbitration agreement: *IPOC International Growth Fund Ltd v OAO "CT Mobile"* [2007] Bermuda L.R. 43.

In *Samengo-Turner v J&H Marsh & McLennan (Services) Ltd* [2007] EWCA Civ 723, [2008] I.C.R. 18 (on which see Briggs [2007] L.M.C.L.Q. 433), a New York jurisdiction agreement was annulled on the ground that the Judgments Regulation deprived it of legal effect, and that this gave the claimant a legal right to be sued in England which was susceptible to protection by injunction against suit in the nominated court: *sed quaere.*

**12–140** See also *Elektrim SA v Vivendi Holdings 1 Corp* [2008] EWCA Civ 1178, [2009] 1 Lloyd's Rep. 59 (proceedings brought contrary to a "no action" clause were brought in breach of contract and were liable to be restrained under the principle in *Donohue v Armco Inc*) [2001] UKHL 64, [2002] 1 All E.R. 749.

Note 71. In *Skype Technologies SA v Joltid Ltd* [2009] EWHC 2783 (Ch.), at [33], it was observed that damages for breach of a jurisdiction agreement were not likely to be adequate where the party in breach had demanded trial by jury in the foreign court, with the result that the outcome of a finding of liability was impossible to quantify.

Note 72. See *Verity Shipping SA v NV Norexa* [2008] EWHC 213 (Comm.), [2008] 1 C.L.C. 45 (refusing the injunction; lack of promptness).

Note 75. On *OT Africa Line Ltd v Magic Sportswear Corp* [2005] EWCA Civ 710, [2005] 2 Lloyd's Rep. 170, see Baatz [2006] L.M.C.L.Q. 143.

NOTE 76. See also *Horn Linie GmbH v Panamericana Formas e Impresos SA* [2006] EWHC 373 (Comm.), [2006] 2 Lloyd's Rep. 44 (injunction to enforce agreement on choice of law and jurisdiction notwithstanding related litigation before the other court); *Starlight Shipping Co v Tai Ping Insurance Co Ltd* [2007] EWHC 1893 (Comm.), [2008] 1 Lloyd's Rep. 230 (a case on arbitration agreements; injunction despite related proceedings before foreign court).

It was held in Case C–185/07 *Allianz SpA v West Tankers Inc (The "Front Comor")* [2009] E.C.R. I–663, [2009] 1 A.C. 1138 (on which see Muir Watt, 2009 *Rev. Crit.* 373, Briggs [2009] L.M.C.L.Q. 161, Peel (2009) 125 L.Q.R. 365, Fentiman [2009] C.L.J. 278) that: (i) the English proceedings, which were for an injunction to restrain a party bound by an arbitration agreement from breaching it, had arbitration as their subject matter and therefore fell outside the material scope of the Regulation; (ii) the proceedings before the Italian court for damages for damage done by a ship were brought in a civil or commercial matter, even though it had been contended before that court that the parties were bound to arbitrate; and (iii), notwithstanding point (i), it was inconsistent with the scheme of the Regulation for the English court to issue an injunction by way of enforcement of the obligation of the parties to arbitrate. The result is that the principle laid down in *Turner v Grovit* was held to apply to injunctions which related to civil and commercial proceedings before the courts of other Member States, even if (as the court accepted) the proceedings before the English court were themselves outside the material scope of the Regulation. If the adverse impact of this decision on the law and practice of arbitration means that reform of the law is necessary, this will be a matter for to be dealt with on the review of the Regulation. See also the original reference by the House of Lords: *West Tankers Inc v Ras Riunione Adriatica di Sicurta SpA* [2007] UKHL 4, [2007] 1 Lloyd's Rep. 319. 12–141

But even if a court has no authority to grant an injunction to restrain proceedings before the courts of another Member State, the fact that there has been a reference to arbitration in Paris does not deprive the court of jurisdiction to adjudicate the substantive claim: *Youell v La Réunion Aerienne* [2009] EWCA Civ 75, [2009] 1 Lloyd's Rep. 586, as the subject matter of the proceedings in England was not arbitration; see also *National Navigation Co v Endesa Generacion SA (The "Wadi Sudr")* [2009] EWHC 196 (Comm.), [2009] 1 Lloyd's Rep. 666 (revd. on other grounds [2009] EWCA Civ 1397, [2010] 1 Lloyd's Rep. 193). By contrast with these developments, in *Beverage International SA v In Zone Brands Inc* [2010] I.L.Pr. 598 (on which see Muir Watt, 2010 *Rev. Crit.* 158, Clavel, 2010 *Clunet* 146, Perreau-Saussine (2010) 59 I.C.L.Q. 519), the French Cour de Cassation agreed to give conclusive effect to a decision of the Superior Court of the State of Georgia which ordered the respondent, by means of an anti-suit injunction, not to seise the courts of France in breach of its agreement on jurisdiction.

**12–142** See also the reference to *National Navigation Co v Endesa Generacion SA* (*The "Wadi Sudr"*) [2009] EWCA Civ 1397, [2010] 1 Lloyd's Rep. 193, entry para.14–195, below.

**12–143** *cf. National Westminster Bank plc v Rabobank Nederland* [2007] EWHC 1056 (Comm.), applying the principle in *Union Discount Co Ltd v Zoller* [2001] EWCA Civ 1755, [2002] 1 W.L.R. 1517 and ordering damages in the context of a claim brought in California in breach of a broad contractual promise not to bring proceedings anywhere.

The principle that damages were recoverable for breach of a contractual promise not to bring particular proceedings was further approved in *Sunrock Aircraft Corp Ltd v SAS Denmark-Norway-Sweden* [2007] EWCA Civ 882, [2007] 2 Lloyd's Rep. 612. The only decision to consider the specific measure of damages for breach of a jurisdiction agreement, appears to be *National Westminster Bank plc v Rabobank Nederland* [2007] EWHC 1742 (Comm.), [2008] 1 Lloyd's Rep. 16 (costs of the foreign proceedings assessed as though on the indemnity basis); referred to but not otherwise discussed in *C v D* [2007] EWCA Civ 1282, [2008] Bus. L.R. 843.

On the relationship between substantive proceedings and a claim for damages for breach of a jurisdiction agreement, see *Underwriting Members of Lloyd's Syndicate 980 v Sinco SA* [2008] EWHC 1842 (Comm.), [2009] Lloyd's Rep. I.R. 365.

According to *The Kallang* [2008] EWHC 2761 (Comm.), [2009] 1 Lloyd's Rep. 124 and *The Duden* [2008] EWHC 2762 (Comm.), [2009] 1 Lloyd's Rep. 145, proceedings brought in a non-Member State to undermine an English law and arbitration agreement were liable to be seen as breaches of contract by the parties bound by the contracts in question, and as torts by the non-party who induced it. It is not difficult to see how a claim for damages might follow from this analysis.

So far as breach of an arbitration agreement is concerned, if the scope of the reference to arbitration is sufficiently widely drawn, an arbitral tribunal may award damages, for breach of the agreement to arbitrate, against a party who has seised the French courts and has obtained judgment and thereby caused the applicant financial loss; the damages may extend to what was needed to reverse the judgment which *ex hypothesi* should not have been sought and which, because the Judgments Regulation does not apply to arbitration proceedings, is not required by the Regulation to be recognised: *CMA CGM SA v Hyundai Mipo Dockyard Co Ltd* [2008] EWHC 2791 (Comm.), [2009] 1 Lloyd's Rep. 213. However, the decision was doubted in *National Navigation Co v Endesa Generacion SA* (*The "Wadi Sudr"*) [2009] EWCA Civ 1397, [2010] 1 Lloyd's Rep. 193. See entry at para.14–195, below.

The Spanish Supreme Court has held that an award of damages for breach of a jurisdiction agreement is permissible: *USA Sogo Inc v Angel Jesús: TS sentencia nº 6/2009* (January 12, 2009); [2009] Repertorio de Jurisprudencia 542. And on damages for breach of jurisdiction agreements in civil law systems generally, see also Takahashi (2008) 10 Yb.P.I.L. 57.

See further *Ace Insurance Ltd v Moose Enterprise Pty Ltd* [2009] NSWSC 724 (on which see Yeo [2010] L.M.C.L.Q. 194) (declining to treat a contractual choice of law, as distinct from a choice of jurisdiction, as routinely giving rise to promissory obligations, though not excluding the possibility that more precise drafting could produce an agreement on choice of law which was also promissory in nature).

NOTE 88. See also Merrett (2006) 55 I.C.L.Q. 315.

The jurisdiction to restrain a party to an arbitration agreement from bringing proceedings in breach of it extends to restraining foreign proceedings brought (or threatened) to undermine or challenge the award otherwise than in the courts of the seat of the arbitration: *C v D* [2007] EWCA Civ 1282, [2008] Bus. L.R. 843 (on which see Briggs (2007) 78 B.Y.I.L. 595); *Steamship Mutual Underwriting Association (Bermuda) Ltd v Sulpicio Lines Inc* [2008] EWHC 914 (Comm.). See also *Shashoua v Sharma* [2009] EWHC 957 (Comm.), [2009] 2 All E.R. (Comm.) 477 (injunction granted by court at the seat of the arbitration proper to defend the integrity of the agreement to arbitrate); *Midgulf International Ltd v Groupe Chimiche Tunisien* [2009] EWHC 963 (Comm.) (interim anti-suit injunction on grounds of case management to allow English court time to decide whether there was a binding agreement to arbitrate); *Midgulf International Ltd v Groupe Chimiche Tunisien* [2010] EWCA Civ 66, [2010] 1 C.L.C. 113, [52] (final injunction to restrain party to agreement to arbitrate from pursuing foreign proceedings which breach or are designed to undermine, derail or by-pass the arbitration and any award made in it). **12–144**

NOTE 93. For CPR, r.6.15, now see CPR, r.6.11. **12–145**

NOTE 94. For CPR, r.6.20(5)(d), now see CPR PD6B, para.3.1(6)(d).

## Chapter 13

# JURISDICTION IN ADMIRALTY CLAIMS IN REM

**13R–001— 13–005** Supreme Court Act 1981 is now renamed Senior Courts Act 1981: Constitutional Reform Act 2005, s.59 and Sch.11, in force October 1, 2009. Consequential amendments are made to CPR, r.61.1(2)(a), r.61.1(2)(d), r.61.2(1)(a)(v), r.61.4(7)(a), and r.61.11(5)(a). PD CPR PD61.5(3)(2) is also amended accordingly.

**13R–001** The revised Lugano Convention ([2007] O.J. L339/1) entered into force between the Member States of the European Union (including Denmark) and Norway on January 1, 2010. It will be ratified by Switzerland with effect from January 1, 2011. The text of the previous Lugano Convention contained in Sch.3C of the Civil Jurisdiction and Judgments Act 1982 was repealed by Regulation 25 of the Civil Jurisdiction and Judgments Regulations (SI 2009/3131) on January 1, 2010.

Note 6. SI 2007/1655 gives the force of law to the Agreement for the application of the Judgments Regulation to Denmark: see above, entry at para.11–020.

**13–002** In *The Elusive* [2010] NSWSC 525 (at [37]), the New South Wales Supreme Court referred to the view propounded in *Republic of India v India Steamship Co Ltd (No.2)* [1998] A.C. 878 that the distinction between *in rem* and *in personam* claims is somewhat artificial. It noted that this view was not shared in Australia and pointed to the clear distinction drawn between *in rem* and *in personam* proceedings in the Admiralty Act 1988 (Cth) and to earlier remarks in *Comandate Marine Corp v Pan Australia Shipping Pty Ltd* (2006) 157 F.C.R. 45, [2008] 1 Lloyd's Rep. 119, at [99] and [120]–[128]; and *Rail Equipment Leasing Pty Ltd v CV Scheepvaartonderneming Emmagracht* [2008] NSWSC 850, at [33].

On the distinction between foreign judgments *in rem* and *in personam*, see *Cambridge Gas Transportation Corp v Official Committee of Unsecured Creditors of Navigator Holdings Plc* [2006] UKPC 26, [2007] 1 A.C. 508; *Pattni v Ali* [2006] UKPC 51, [2007] 2 A.C. 85. Both cases are noted by Chee Ho Tham [2007] L.M.C.L.Q. 129.

**13–004** See also *The Vasiliy Golovnin* [2008] SGCA 39, [2008] 4 S.L.R. 994.

Note 24. On the interpretation of the phrase "damage done by a ship" in the Australian Admiralty Act 1988, see *Elbe Shipping SA v The Ship "Global*

*Peace"* [2006] FCA 954, (2006) 232 A.L.R. 694, at [80]; considering, in particular *The Eschersheim* [1976] 2 Lloyd's Rep. 1, 8.

NOTE 25. In *Heilbrunn v Lightwood Plc* [2007] FCA 1518, (2007) 243 A.L.R. 343, the Federal Court of Australia held that an obligation could arise "out of an agreement relating to the carriage of goods or persons by a ship or to the use or hire of a ship" within the meaning of the Admiralty Act 1988 (Cth), s.4(3)(f) even where there was no contract between the parties and the claim was in tort or bailment. The relevant test was whether there was a reasonably direct connection between the claim and an agreement for use of a ship or carriage by ship. It also noted that it could assert jurisdiction on this basis wherever the damage arose (s.5).

The *Heilbrunn* test was considered and applied by the New South Wales Supreme Court in *Cargill International SA v Peabody Australia Mining Ltd* [2010] NSWSC 887, at [112]–[137].

NOTE 25. In *The Catur Samudra* [2010] SGHC 18, [2010] 1 Lloyd's Rep. 305 (noted Thomas (2010) 16 J.I.M.L. 97), the High Court of Singapore held that a claim under a guarantee in relation to a charterparty was not a claim arising out of an agreement relating to the carriage of goods for the purposes of the Singapore legislation.

A new Pt 6 of the CPR has been substituted by SI 2008/2178, Sch.1. As a result, some minor amendments to the wording of CPR, r.61 and CPR PD 61 have been made. **13–006**

In *Kallang Shipping SA Panama v AXA Assurances Senegal ("The Kallang")* [2008] EWHC 2761 (Comm.), [2009] 1 Lloyd's Rep. 124, Jonathan Hirst Q.C., sitting as a Deputy High Court Judge, held that an English court would not restrain a party to an English arbitration agreement from arresting a vessel in a foreign jurisdiction if the sole purpose of the arrest was to obtain reasonable security for the claim to be arbitrated in England. However, where the actions of the claimant went beyond this, this would amount to a breach of an arbitration agreement which would be restrained by the court. See also the judgment handed down simultaneously in *Sotrade Denizcilik Sanayi Ve Ticaret AS v Amadou LO ("The Duden")* [2008] EWHC 2762 (Comm.), [2009] 1 Lloyd's Rep. 145.

Supreme Court Act 1981 is now re-named Senior Courts Act 1981: Constitutional Reform Act 2005, s.59 and Sch.11, in force October 1, 2009. Consequential amendments to CPR, r.61 and CPR PD61 are made. **13–009—13–021**

In *JP Morgan Chase Bank v Mystras Maritime Corp* [2008] FCA 399, (2008) 305 D.L.R. (4th) 442, the Canadian Federal Court of Appeal treated the question of whether a supplier of necessaries to a vessel had a maritime lien as substantive. It went on to hold that although a maritime lien was a right *in* **13–010** *rem* arising by operation of law, it would normally be appropriate for the law stipulated in the supply contract to govern the rights arising from such a transaction, unless a maritime transaction was so strongly connected to another jurisdiction that that other State's substantive law, rather than the law chosen in the contract, should govern the transaction. In the event, no other law was more closely connected. Since, however, the contents of the relevant foreign law, United States law, had not been proven, the court applied the *lex fori*.

In *World Fuel Services Corporation v The Nordems* (2010) FC 332, the Canadian Federal Court considered the distinction between a maritime lien and a statutory right *in rem*. It went on to consider the law applicable to the existence of a maritime lien in a situation where there was no contractual relationship between the parties and ruled (at [67]) that: "Absent a contract, we must tote up the points of contact. In a fact situation which has contact with several jurisdictions, pride of place must be given to the place where the necessaries were provided." See further *Alpha Trading Monaco Sam v The Sarah Desgagnés* (2010) FC 695.

In *Mazda Canada Inc. v Mitsui O.S.K. Lines Co* [2009] 2 F.C.R. 382, the Canadian Federal Court of Appeal held that the fact that *in rem* proceedings might be available in Canada but not in an alternative forum was not a relevant factor in deciding whether to stay Canadian proceedings.

On the application of the *forum non conveniens* test in Hong Kong to *in rem* proceedings, see *The Hui Rong* [2008] HKCA 504.

**13–011** For the position under Australian law see *Elbe Shipping SA v The Ship "Global Peace"* [2006] FCA 954, (2006) 232 A.L.R. 694, at [130].

**13–012** For discussion of the meaning of the word "charge" in the context of *in rem* proceedings, see *The Altair II* [2009] NZHC 734.

In *Elbe Shipping SA v The Ship "Global Peace"* [2006] FCA 954, (2006) 232 A.L.R. 694 (noted Forrest (2007) 38 J.M.A.R.L.C. 309), three ships were contaminated by oil escaping from the ship *Global Peace* while she was being towed to berth by a tug. The claimants asserted that the damage resulted from defective navigation of the *Global Peace* and also of the tug. The defendants challenged the *in rem* jurisdiction of the court. The Federal Court of Australia ruled that it had jurisdiction under s.17 of the Australian Admiralty Act 1988, since this was a general maritime claim, as defined in s.4(3) of the Act. See also *Heilbrunn v Lightwood Plc* [2007] FCA 1518, (2007) 243 A.L.R. 343; *CSL Australia Pty Limited v Formosa* [2009] NSWCA 363.

**13–015** On the arrest of sister ships in Australia, see Glover (2008) 22 A.N.Z.M.L.J. 11.

**13–016** In *Thor Shipping A/S v The Ship "Al Duhail"* [2008] FCA 1842 (noted Alderton (2009) 58 I.C.L.Q. 702), *in rem* proceedings were commenced against a vessel arrested in Brisbane. The ship had been built in New Zealand for the Amir of Qatar and registered in Qatar. At the time of the alleged breach, the ship was under construction. Pursuant to Admiralty Act 1988 (Cth), s.17, it was necessary to show that the Amir of Qatar was the owner or charterer of, or in possession or control of, the ship, both at the time when proceedings were commenced and when the cause of action arose. This gave rise to a dispute as to whether the Amir of Qatar owned the vessel when the cause of action arose which, in turn, raised the question as to which law should decide the matter. In *Tisand Pty Ltd v Owners of the Ship MV Cape Moreton* [2005] FCAFC 68, the court had suggested *obiter* that the law of the place of registration should apply. In that case, however, the registered owner had already sold the ship and received the purchase price. In the present case, whilst the ship was under construction, it was alleged that the very act of registration in Qatar was sufficient to transfer ownership to the buyer. In such circumstances, Dowsett J. inclined to the view that New Zealand law should determine this matter, as the law of the place where the ship was located prior to registration. However, he went on to rule that the Amir enjoyed sovereign immunity pursuant to Foreign States Immunity Act 1985 (Cth), s.36, and Diplomatic Privileges and Immunities Act 1967 (Cth), notwithstanding that he had not actually entered Australia. That finding meant that Dowsett J. did not need to determine the choice of law question. See also *Dornoch Ltd v Westminster International BV* [2009] EWHC 889 (Admlty), [2009] 2 Lloyd's Rep. 191, considered at para.22–058, below.

In *The Catur Samudra* [2010] SGHC 18, [2010] 1 Lloyd's Rep. 305 (noted Thomas (2010) 16 J.I.M.L. 97), the High Court of Singapore held that a guarantor of a charterparty agreement could only be considered to be in possession or control of the chartered ship for the purposes of the Singapore legislation, if that possession or control arose "as an independent legal right" (at [60]). Mere physical possession or control of the vessel would not suffice.

On the threshold for determining whether a party is a beneficial owner in an application to set aside a warrant of arrest and to strike out a statement of claim, see the Canadian Federal Court of Appeal's decision in *Kremikovtzi Trade v Phoenix Bulk Carriers Ltd ("The Swift Fortune" (No.2))* [2007] FCA 381

Note 72. On the interpretation of the Australian Admiralty Act 1988, see *Elbe Shipping SA v The Ship "Global Peace"* [2006] FCA 954, (2006) 232 A.L.R. 694, at [74].

In *The Convenience Container* [2007] HKCA 302 (with *corrigendum* [2007] HKCA 379) (noted Thomas (2007) 13 J.I.M.L. 13), the applicant shipowners in liquidation applied to set aside claim forms issued *in rem* in admiralty actions following the sale of four of its vessels which had been arrested by the **13–017**

Hong Kong Admiralty Court after it went into voluntary liquidation in Singapore. The applicant contended that, whilst it had owned the vessels when the causes of action arose (and would have been liable on the claims *in personam*), the winding-up proceedings in Singapore had divested it of the beneficial ownership of the vessels. This meant that it was not the owner of the vessels when the claim forms were issued. The court rejected the application. It ruled that the phrase "beneficial owner" focused on title and the right to sell or dispose of a ship, and not merely on control or enjoyment of a vessel. It went on to hold that there had been no change of beneficial ownership, since the liquidation did not create a trust in favour of the liquidator.

**13–021** First sentence. See *Conocophillips (UK) Ltd v Partnereederei Ms Jork* [2010] EWHC 1214 (Comm.), at [38].

**13–022** The revised Lugano Convention entered into force between the EU Member States (including Denmark) and Norway on January 1, 2010. See entry at para.13R–001, above.

See above, entry at para.11–020, for the Agreement for the application of the Judgments Regulation to Denmark.

**13–026** On the difference between Art.71 of the Judgments Regulation and Art.57 of the 1968 Convention, see Case C–533/08 *TNT Express Nederland BV v AXA Versicherung AG* [2010] I.L.Pr. 663, at [38]. The European Court ruled that, pursuant to Art.71 of the Judgments Regulation, the rules of an international convention apply only if they are "highly predictable, facilitate the sound administration of justice and enable the risk of concurrent proceedings to be minimised"; and on condition "that they ensure, under conditions at least as favourable as those provided for by the regulation, the free movement of judgments in civil and commercial matters and mutual trust in the administration of justice in the European Union."

**13–030** Final sentence. See *Kallang Shipping SA Panama v AXA Assurances Senegal ("The Kallang")* [2008] EWHC 2761 (Comm.), [2009] 1 Lloyd's Rep. 124, at [72]–[73].

**13–037** Supreme Court Act 1981 is now renamed Senior Courts Act 1981: Constitutional Reform Act 2005, s.59 and Sch.11, in force October 1, 2009. Consequential amendments to CPR, r.61 and CPR PD61 are made.

## CHAPTER 14

# FOREIGN JUDGMENTS

## 1. INTRODUCTORY

NOTE 1. See also Von Mehren, *Adjudicatory Authority in Private International Law: A Comparative Study* (2007); Briggs, *Agreements on Jurisdiction and Choice of Law* (2008), chap.9. 14–001

As to the 2005 Hague Convention on Choice of Court Agreements, Mexico is currently the only State to have acceded to it; however, the European Union also signed the Convention on April 1, 2009. See also Spigelman (2009) 83 A.L.J. 386; Beaumont (2009) 5 J. Priv. Int. L. 125; Garnett, *ibid.* 161. On the negotiations preceding the Convention, see Barcelo and Clermont (eds), *A Global Law of Jurisdiction and Judgments: Lessons from The Hague* (2002). For its final conclusions see American Law Institute, *Recognition and Enforcement of Foreign Judgments: Analysis and Proposed Federal Statute* (2006), on which, and generally on the American approach to enforcement and recognition, see Silberman (2008) 19 King's L.J. 235.

However, on the distinction between judgments *in rem* and *in personam*, and for the possibility that a judgment not entitled to recognition as one *in rem* may be recognised as one binding parties *in personam*, see *Pattni v Ali* [2006] UKPC 51, [2007] 2 A.C. 85 (on which see Briggs (2006) 77 B.Y.I.L. 575; Tham [2007] L.M.C.L.Q. 129). 14–003

## 2. ENFORCEMENT AND RECOGNITION AT COMMON LAW

### A. *Enforcement and Recognition*

NOTE 62. In *Pro-Swing Inc v Elta Golf Inc* (2006) 273 D.L.R. (4th) 663, [2006] 2 S.C.R. 612 (Can. Sup. Ct.) (on which see Oppong (2007) 70 M.L.R. 670; Pitel (2007) 3 J. Priv. Int. L. 241) the Supreme Court of Canada unanimously accepted that in certain cases, of which (by a majority) this was not one, an equitable decree from a foreign court could be enforced in Canada. In *Minera Aquiline Argentina SA v IMA Exploration Inc* [2007] 10 W.W.R. 648 (B.C.C.A.), at [89]–[94], the court considered *Pro-Swing* to lend support to its decision to enforce equitable personal obligations undertaken in respect of foreign land. The Ontario Court of Appeal followed and applied *Pro-Swing Inc v Elta Golf Inc*, and ordered the enforcement in Canada of a US injunction 14–018 ordering a cessation of telemarketing activity which was directed to the United States, in *United States of America v Yemec* [2010] ONCA 414.

**14–020** On whether an English judgment granting equitable relief might be enforced in the US, in *Tandrin Aviation Holdings Ltd v Aero Toy Store LLC* [2010] EWHC 40 (Comm.), the court was evidently referred to the passage in the main work as indirect authority for the submission that the answer may be negative, but not to the later material in the Supplement which illustrates a different possible outcome. And see also *United States of America v Yemec* [2010] ONCA 414.

NOTE 75. On *Pro-Swing Inc v Elta Golf Inc* (2006) 273 D.L.R. (4th) 663, [2006] 2 S.C.R. 612 see entry at para.14–018, above.

NOTE 83. See also *US Securities and Exchange Commission v Manterfield* [2009] EWCA Civ 27, [2010] 1 W.L.R. 172 (on which see Briggs (2009) 80 B.Y.I.L. 623), generally approving the principle in *Robb Evans v European Bank Ltd* (2004) 61 N.S.W.L.R. 75.

**14–021** *Nouvion v Freeman* (1889) 15 App. Cas. 1 was applied in *Bank Polska Kasa Opieki SA v Opara* [2010] QSC 93 (Polish "execution title" not final and conclusive, as it did not constitute a judicial decision upon the underlying merits of the claim, and the proceedings which could subsequently be brought in Poland would be the first occasion on which the merits would be the subject of investigation).

NOTE 90: ; *Dallah Estate and Tourism Holding Co v Ministry of Religious Affairs, Government of Pakistan* [2009] EWCA Civ 755, [2010] 2 W.L.R. 805 (no estoppel against defendant whose contention was that it never agreed to arbitrate the matter and who had not submitted that issue to the final determination of a foreign court), affd. without reference to this point [2010] UKSC 46, [2010] 3 W.L.R. 1472.

NOTE 92. See also *CLE Owners Inc v Wanlass* [2005] 8 W.W.R. 559 (Man. CA). For a less strict interpretation of the requirement of finality, see *Re Cavell Insurance Co* (2006) 269 D.L.R. (4th) 663 (Ont. CA).

When the foreign default judgment is set aside, it is no longer entitled to recognition, and a local judgment will be set aside on application: *Benefit Strategies Group Ltd v Prider* [2007] SASC 250.

**14–025** If a foreign state may be entitled to immunity from the jurisdiction of the English courts in respect of proceedings to enforce a foreign judgment, an applicant for permission to serve it out of the jurisdiction must identify the ground on which it is contended that the court has jurisdiction over the state; and if that basis cannot be sustained, permission to serve process on the state

must be set aside: *Republic of Argentina v NML Capital Ltd* [2010] EWCA Civ 41, [2010] 3 W.L.R. 874, at [58]–[69]. (The Supreme Court has given permission to appeal.)
Note 8. *Tasarruf Mevduati Sigorta Fonu v Demirel* [2007] EWCA Civ 799, [2007] 1 W.L.R. 2508 (permission to serve out under CPR r.6.20(9) not dependent upon showing assets within the jurisdiction). See also *Belletti v Morici* [2009] EWHC 2316 (Comm.), [2009] I.L.Pr. 960 (service out of a claim for an order freezing assets, and requiring delivery up against a respondent alleged to be implicated in the concealment of assets (a "*Chabra*" order: see *TSB Private Bank International SA v Chabra* [1992] 1 W.L.R. 231) is not available under CPR PD6B, para.3.1(10) unless a judgment has been given against those respondents, or a judgment has been given against other persons but proceedings are brought to enforce it against the respondents).

For CPR, r.6.20(9), now see CPR PD6B, para.3.1(10).

A foreign judgment from a court which has dismissed a claim by the application of the principle that a court has no jurisdiction to enforce a foreign revenue law is not a decision on the merits of the claim, and no issue estoppel arises from it: *Relfo Ltd v Varsani* [2009] EWHC 2297 (Ch.) (the ruling on this point was not challenged on the appeal to the Court of Appeal, *sub nom. Varsani v Relfo Ltd* [2010] EWCA Civ 560, [2010] 3 All E.R. 1045). **14–027**

Note 12. The neutral citation for *Phillips v Avena, The Times*, November 22, 2005 is [2005] EWHC 3333.

*Carl Zeiss Stiftung v Rayner & Keeler Ltd (No.2)* [1967] 1 A.C. 853 was applied in *Abdel Hadi Abdullah Al Qahtani & Sons Beverage Industry Co v Antliff* [2010] EWHC 1735 (Comm.) (no issue estoppel arising from decision of Saudi Primary Commission). **14–029**

Note 19. There is no credible basis for contending, on the basis of existing law, that an English court could recognise a US class action judgment or settlement as precluding a person, invited to become a class member but who made no response to the invitation, from bringing proceedings in the English courts against a defendant. The conclusion of French law is the same, though the reasoning is distinctive: Lemontey & Michon, 2009 *Clunet* 535. By contrast, the Dutch courts have accepted that such preclusion is possible, subject to conditions, as a matter of Dutch private international law. In *Re Royal Ahold NV* (June 23, 2010), the Amsterdam District Court recognised as binding, in principle but subject to defences, on all class members who had not taken steps to opt out of the proposed class, a worldwide class-action settlement entered before the US courts. Such a judgment by the Dutch courts is, as a "judgment-on-a-judgment", not susceptible to recognition under Chapter III of the Judgments Regulation.

On the recognition of class action judgments within Canada (Quebec), see *Canada Post Corp v Lépine* [2009] SCC 16, (2009) 304 D.L.R. (4th) 539.

NOTE 21. See also *HJ Heinz Co Ltd v EFL Inc* [2010] EWHC 1203 (Comm.).

**14–030** But orders or requests made in bankruptcy proceedings before a foreign court may not be seen as judgments, and a court may make an order which responds to a judicial request for co-operation with the procedure before the foreign court even though a foreign judgment in similar terms and circumstances would be refused recognition: *Cambridge Gas Transport Corp v Official Committee of Unsecured Creditors of Navigator Holdings plc* [2006] UKPC 26, [2007] 1 A.C. 508 (on which see Briggs (2006) 77 B.Y.I.L. 575).

*Cambridge Gas Transport Corp v Official Committee of Unsecured Creditors of Navigator Holdings plc* was considered in *Rubin v Eurofinance SA* [2010] EWCA Civ 895 (on which, Briggs [2010] L.M.C.L.Q. 523). A US court, conducting proceedings under Ch.11 of the US Bankruptcy Code, made orders against individuals connected to the insolvent company, requiring them to pay damages and make restitution of certain sums received by them. The defendants did not appear in or defend the proceedings, and judgments were entered in default. It was held that as the US proceedings were to be recognised as foreign main proceedings, the orders made in those proceedings for the restitution of unjust enrichments and for the return of improperly preferential payments, were liable to be recognised and enforced in England as part and parcel of the insolvency proceedings, which were recognised, notwithstanding that the US court did not have jurisdiction to give a judgment *in personam* capable of recognition or enforcement within the Cases set out in Rule 36 of the main work.

In *New Cap Reinsurance Corp Ltd v Grant* [2009] NSWSC 662, (2009) 257 A.L.R. 740, a bankruptcy court in New South Wales issued a letter of request to the English court, asking it to enforce an Australian order requiring a creditor who had received an unfair preference to repay sums to the company. In the case of an insolvency administration in Australia, Insolvency Act 1986, s.426 provided a statutory basis to require the English court to assist the foreign court. This was taken to allow the NSW court "proceed with confidence" that the English court would make the orders requested by it.

On the degree of preclusion attributable to the foreign judgment, see *Barrett v Universal Island Records* [2006] EWHC 1009 (Ch.), [175] at [190] (foreign judgment will not be given greater preclusive effect than it has under its own law).

It may appear from *Deutsche Bank AG v Highland Crusader Offshore Partners LP* [2009] EWCA Civ 725, [2010] 1 W.L.R. 1023, at [22]–[29], that the English court may have been prepared, in principle at least, to give effect to findings made in the course of a motion to dismiss on jurisdictional grounds before the courts of Texas, though whether this may be taken as a form of recognition in the strict sense is doubtful. For the practical difficulty presented by the contention that one may "accord deference" to the reasons given by another tribunal, see *Dallah Estate and Tourism Holding Co v Ministry of Religious Affairs, Government of Pakistan* [2009] EWCA Civ 755, [2010] 2 W.L.R. 805, [20]–[21] affd. [2010] UKSC 46, [2010] 3 W.L.R. 1472.

Final sentence. See *Republic of Kazakhstan v Istil Group Ltd* [2006] EWHC 448 (Comm), [2006] 2 Lloyd's Rep. 370 (affd. [2007] EWCA Civ 471, [2008] Bus. L.R. 878, holding that estoppel may issue from implied determination by foreign court (application for permission to appeal refused without reference to this point: [2007] EWCA Civ 471, [2008] Bus. L.R. 878; for further proceedings, see *Republic of Kazakhstan v Istil Group Inc (No.2)* [2007] EWHC 2729 (Comm.), [2008] 1 Lloyd's Rep. 382); *Liebinger v Stryker Trauma GmbH* [2006] EWHC 690, applying *The Sennar (No.2)* [1985] 1 W.L.R. 490 (HL)) to a German decision as to validity of appointment of arbitrator. In *Armacel Pty Ltd v Smurfit Stone Container Corp* [2008] FCA 592, (2008) 248 A.L.R. 573, issue estoppel was held to operate against a party who, as defendant, had made an unsuccessful jurisdictional challenge before a foreign court. The observation at [66] that the case was "indistinguishable from *The Sennar*" does not appear to be correct, at least from the perspective of English law and s.33 of Civil Jurisdiction and Judgments Act 1982.

Note 36. See also *Enterprise Oil Ltd v Strand Insurance Co Ltd* [2006] EWHC 58 (Comm.), [2006] 1 Lloyd's Rep. 500; *Korea National Insurance Corp v Allianz Global Corporate & Specialty AG* [2007] EWCA Civ 1066, [2008] Lloyd's Rep. I.R. 413. **14–033**

See *Karafarin Bank v Mansoury-Dara* [2009] EWHC 1217 (Comm.), [2009] 2 Lloyd's Rep. 289 (Iranian judgment not entitled to recognition in England; neither Civil Jurisdiction and Judgments Act 1982, s.34, nor doctrine of abuse of process, a bar to proceedings in England). **14–034**

Note 41. *cf. Messer Griesheim GmbH v Goyal MG Gases Pvt Ltd* [2006] EWHC 79 (Comm.), holding that the principle of merger did not prevent an application for summary judgment after judgment had been entered in default of appearance. **14–035**

For the approach to judgments given against individuals in the context of a foreign main insolvency proceeding, see entry at para.14–030, above. **14–049**

### B. *Jurisdiction Of Foreign Courts at Common Law*

#### (1) Jurisdiction in Personam

The fact that the defendant advertises and sells goods on an internet website which is accessible from a foreign country provides no support for a contention that the defendant was present within the jurisdiction of the foreign court, **14–059** which is to be established by traditional means and in accordance with the law established by *Adams v Cape Industries plc* [1990] Ch. 433. In *Lucasfilm Ltd v Ainsworth* [2009] EWCA Civ 1328, [2010] 3 W.L.R. 333 (on which see Briggs (2009) 80 B.Y.I.L. 606; Dickinson [2010] L.M.C.L.Q. 181; Rogerson [2010] C.L.J. 245), the court was not inclined to accept that internet trading activity had, in itself, any relevance to the question whether the defendant had demonstrated the kind of personal allegiance to the foreign jurisdiction which was conveyed by or implicit in the traditional requirements of presence or residence within the jurisdiction of a court. The Supreme Court has given permission to appeal.

Once a corporation is in liquidation and ceases the carrying on business, it will not be regarded as present within the jurisdiction of the foreign court: *Re Flightlease (Ireland) Ltd* [2006] IEHC 193, [2008] 1 I.L.R.M. 53. An appeal to the Supreme Court of Ireland is pending.

**14–062** On submission by participation in procedures for disclosure of evidence, see *Walker v Newmont Australian Ltd* [2010] FCA 298 (not a case on foreign judgments).

**14–063** An English court may stay its proceedings to allow a foreign court to determine by way of preliminary issue whether it has jurisdiction under a dispute resolution agreement, on condition that it not be alleged that the defendant's participation in the procedure before the foreign court amounted a submission to its jurisdiction: *Winnetka Trading Corp v Julius Baer International Ltd* [2008] EWHC 2146 (Ch.), [2009] Bus. L.R. 1006.

**14–064** Note 42. In relation to *Starlight International Inc v Bruce* [2002] EWHC 374 (Ch.), [2002] I.L.Pr. 617, see (to similar effect, though not a case on the recognition of judgments) *Maple Leaf Macro Volatility Master Fund v Rouvroy* [2009] EWHC 257 (Comm.), [2009] 1 Lloyd's Rep. 475.

**14–066** In *AES Ust-Kamenogorsk Hydropower Plant LLP v Ust-Kamenogorsk Hydropower Plant JSC* [2010] EWHC 722 (Comm.), [2010] 1 C.L.C. 519, [42]–[52], it was accepted that a party to foreign proceedings, which had lodged and argued, under protest, a defence on the merits, while at the same time seeking to persuade the foreign court that the proceedings before it should be referred to arbitration, had at least a good arguable case that its behaviour was not to be seen as submission to the foreign court, with the result that Civil Jurisdiction and Judgments Act 1982, s.33(1) applied to it. The fact that the foreign court might have characterised the steps taken as a submission to its jurisdiction was not decisive to the application of s.33 of the 1982 Act. See also *United Group Resources Pty Ltd v Calabro (No.4)* [2010] FCA 791 (a case on the common law principle).

**14–080** Text to note 6. For CPR, r.6.20, now see CPR, r.6.36 and PD6B, para.3.1.

Text to note 8. For CPR, r.6.20, now see CPR, r.6.36 and PD6B, para.3.1. **14–081**

On jurisdictional competence, see *Long Beach Ltd v Global Witness Ltd* [2007] EWHC 1980 (QB), at [26].

Text to note 20. For CPR, r.6.20, now see CPR, r.6.36 and PD6B, para.3.1. **14–082**

See also *King v Drabinsky* (2008) 92 O.R. (3d) 616 (Ont. CA) (US judgment recognised in Ontario on basis that transaction had been entered into in US capital markets, and that comity therefore required its recognition). **14–084**

On the flexibility or unpredictability inherent in *Morguard Investments Ltd v De Savoye* [1990] S.C.R. 1077 (Can. Sup. Ct.), see *Disney Enterprises Inc v Click Enterprises Inc* (2006) 267 D.L.R. (4th) 291 (Ont.) (a case on wrongful commercial activity on the internet). However, the recognition of judgments in Quebec is governed by the Civil Code. According to that, recognition is not to be withheld on the ground that the adjudicating court, (*in casu*, Ontario) should have applied the principle of *forum non conveniens* to dismiss the proceedings before it: *Canada Post Corp v Lépine* [2009] SCC 16, [2009] 1 S.C.R. 549, (2009) 304 D.L.R. (4th) 539. In *Re Flightlease (Ireland) Ltd* [2006] IEHC 193, [2008] 1 I.L.R.M. 53 it was held that it was not yet appropriate for Ireland to adopt the new approach taken by the Supreme Court of Canada. An appeal to the Supreme Court of Ireland is pending.

NOTE 24. See also Pitel and Dusten (2006) 85 Can. B. Rev. 61.

On s.32, see *AES Ust-Kamenogorsk Hydropower Plant LLP v Ust-Kamenogorsk Hydropower Plant JSC* [2010] EWHC 722 (Comm.), [2010] 1 C.L.C. 519, [37]–[41]. **14–091**

It was held in *Republic of Argentina v NML Capital Ltd* [2010] EWCA Civ 41, [2010] 3 W.L.R. 874 approving the decision in *AIC Ltd v Federal Government of Nigeria* [2003] EWHC 1357 (QB), that the question whether a foreign judgment given against a state could be enforced in England was determined solely by the principles of state immunity in general and the State Immunity Act 1978 in particular, and that these were not materially affected or altered by Civil Jurisdiction and Judgments Act 1982, s.31; and para.14–095 of the main work is to be understood in this sense. If none of the other exceptions in the 1978 Act was applicable to the proceedings before the English courts, the only basis for finding the state to be subject to the jurisdiction of the English courts was for it to be found to have submitted to the jurisdiction of the English courts in accordance with s.2 of the 1978 Act: at [93]. As to that, for it to be concluded that the state had submitted to the jurisdiction of the English courts in relation to the enforcement in England of a New York judgment, it was necessary for the judgment creditor to show that this was the true construction of the terms of the bond which was said to provide the basis for **14–095** the contention that it had submitted: at [100], following *Svenska Petroleum Exploration AB v Government of the Republic of Lithuania (No.2)* [2006] EWCA Civ 1529, [2007] Q.B. 886, [128]. Even though the foreign state may have submitted to the jurisdiction of a foreign court, unless the terms of the bond amounted to a submission in advance to the adjudicative jurisdiction of the English court, the state was entitled to plead its immunity from the jurisdiction of the English court. On a true construction of the bond, the state had not submitted to the jurisdiction of the English courts in respect of the enforcement proceedings: even if the words of the clause in the bond could be interpreted as a waiver of immunity, or an undertaking to waive immunity, they did not amount to a submission to the jurisdiction of the English court: at [104]. An appeal to the Supreme Court is pending.

### (3) Judgments In Rem

**14R–099** On meaning of judgment *in rem*, see *Pattni v Ali* [2006] UKPC 51, [2007] 2 A.C. 85 (on which see Briggs (2006) 77 B.Y.I.L. 575; Tham [2007] L.M.C.L.Q. 129). Rule 40 deals with recognition of judgment as one *in rem*, as distinct from the separate question whether a judgment *in rem*, which may not be recognised, may still be recognised as binding the parties to the proceedings as a judgment *in personam.*

**14–100** An order made by a foreign court which is exercising insolvency jurisdiction, which orders a repayment of money to the insolvent company to undo a fraudulent preference, may be seen as a judgment *in personam*, and its recognition governed by Rule 36 rather than Rule 40: *Re Flightlease (Ireland) Ltd* [2006] IEHC 193, [2008] 1 I.L.R.M. 53. An appeal to the Supreme Court of Ireland is pending. See also entry at para.14–030, above.

**14–103** Supreme Court Act 1981 is now renamed Senior Courts Act 1981: Constitutional Reform Act 2005, s.59 and Sch.11, in force October 1, 2009.

### C. *Conclusiveness of Foreign Judgments: Defences*

**14R–109** Note 97. On whether a foreign order refusing or granting recognition to a judgment from a third State is a final judgment on the merits, see *Cortés v Yorkton Securities Inc* (2007) 278 D.L.R. (4th) 740, at [49]; *Morgan Stanley & Co International Ltd v Pilot Lead Investments Ltd* [2006] 4 H.K.C. 93 (on which see Smart (2007) 81 A.L.R. 349).

**14–128** It was the opinion of the House of Lords in *Clarke v Fennoscandia Ltd* [2007] UKHL 56, 2008 S.C. (H.L.) 122, at [23]–[24], that where a Scottish court declares that a foreign judgment was obtained by fraud and for that reason may not be recognised or enforced in Scotland, such a decision has no effect *in rem*, and "no conceivable effect" outside Scotland. There is no reason to suppose that English private international law is to different effect; and the decision suggests that estoppel by *res judicata* is inapplicable to such a ruling.

NOTE 54. See also *Korea National Insurance Corp v Allianz Global Corporate & Specialty AG* [2007] EWCA Civ 1066, [2008] Lloyd's Rep. I.R. 413 (a case on the recognition of foreign judgment as founding a claim for reimbursement by a reinsurer): to challenge a foreign judgment for fraud, it must be shown that the party putting forward a false claim knew of its falsity.

NOTE 55. See also *Yeager v Garner* [2007] 4 W.W.R. 469 (B.C.). **14–129**

See *Korea National Insurance Co v Allianz Global Corporate and Specialty AG* [2008] EWCA Civ 1355, [2008] 2 C.L.C. 837 (allegations that foreign judgment was procured by fraudulent conspiracy between judgment creditor, foreign court and foreign State were properly justiciable, given that the foreign State had been notified of the allegations and had made no response; such serious allegations needed to be advanced with caution). **14–133**

By contrast with the narrow conception of English (and Canadian) public policy as a basis for refusal to recognise foreign judgments, various legislative acts in the United States have been adopted to justify the refusal to recognise English judgments in libel actions which, had they been brought before the American courts, would have been defeated by reference to the First Amendment to the US Constitution and its guarantee of free speech. Notable examples are the Libel Protection Terrorism (*sic*) Act 2008 (New York), and the Securing the Protection of our Enduring and Established Constitutional Heritage Bill, which goes so far as to allow a US court to award claw-back damages, which was approved by the Senate of the United States in July 2010. For a different analysis of the merits of these developments, see the 5th Dame Anne Ebsworth Memorial Lecture by Lord Hoffmann, available at http://www.indexoncensorship.org/2010/02/the-libel-tourism-myth/ **14R–141**

See also *Jenton Overseas Investment Pte Ltd v Townsing* [2008] VSC 470, (2008) 21 V.R. 241, [22] (public policy objection will be very hard to sustain). **14–144**

On the question of whether a party bringing proceedings outside England which are designed to undermine an English judgment may be restrained from bringing those proceedings, see *Masri v Consolidated Contractors International Co SAL (No.3)* [2008] EWCA Civ 625, [2009] Q.B. 503, where *ED & F Man (Sugar) Ltd v Haryanto (No.2)* was distinguished. **14–145**

But in the matrimonial context, where a spouse has obtained a divorce in defiance of an order (a *Hemain* order) that no step be taken in the foreign proceedings until after the English hearing, non-recognition of the foreign divorce pursuant to Family Law Act 1986, s.53 (1)(c) (recognition manifestly contrary to public policy) was not regarded as the inevitable consequence of a breach of the order: *A v L* [2010] EWHC 460 (Fam.) (relying on other grounds to refuse recognition of Egyptian decree); *Golubovich v Golubovich* [2010] EWCA Civ 810 (refusing to withhold recognition of a Russian divorce obtained by a husband in defiance of a *Hemain* order, on the ground that the obligation to respect the decision of a Russian court, which had simply proceeded in accordance with its own law, would not materially affect the wife's claim for financial relief from the English courts).

**14–146** According to the New Zealand Court of Appeal, recognition may be denied on grounds of public policy where recognition would offend a reasonable New Zealander's sense of morality, but may not be denied simply because the case would have been decided differently in New Zealand: *Reeves v One World Challenge LLC* [2006] 2 N.Z.L.R. 184, [50]–[67]; applied in *Questnet Ltd v Lane* [2008] NZHC 710 (a case also rejecting a complaint of lack of notification of the hearing of an application as a plea sufficient to establish a want of natural justice). See also *Purdie v Mikkelsen* [2009] NZHC 756.

**14–148** See Fawcett (2007) 56 I.C.L.Q. 1.

**14–149** Note 32. *Drozd & Janousek v France and Spain* (1992) 14 E.H.R.R. 745 was examined in *R (on the application of Smith) v Secretary of State for Defence* [2010] UKSC 29, but without specific reference to the issue of recognition by the courts of a Contracting State of foreign judgments given by the courts of non-Contracting states.

**14R–151** Note 32. Canadian case-law places more emphasis on the principle of natural justice as a result of the wider approach to rules of jurisdictional competence established by its Supreme Court. See *Oakwell Engineering Ltd v Enernorth Industries Inc* (2007) 81 O.R. (3d) 288 (CA) (on which Sullivan and Woolley (2006) 85 Can. B. Rev. 605; *United States of America v Shield Development Co* (2004) 74 O.R. (3d) 585 (appeal dismissed May 18, 2005); *Angba v Marie* (2004) 263 D.L.R. (4th) 562 (Fed. Ct.); *CLE Owners Inc v Wanlass* [2005] 8 W.W.R. 559 (Man. CA). But an invitation to extend the defence of breach of natural justice to a rather broader "lack of meaningful opportunity to be heard" was rejected by the Ontario Court of Appeal in *United States of America v Yemec* [2010] ONCA 414.

**14–156** Note 65. On whether the objection needs to be taken before the foreign court (held sometimes, but not where the complaint is founded on the absence of due service), see *Cortés v Yorkton Securities Inc* (2007) 278 D.L.R. (4th) 740; *Marx v Balak* [2008] BCSC 195.

**14–157** See *Bank of Scotland plc v Wilson* (2008) 295 D.L.R. (4th) 128 (B.C.) (refusal of recognition in Canada of English default judgment under UK–Canada

Convention as English claim form found not to have been served on defendant in accordance with English law).

## 3. ENFORCEMENT AND RECOGNITION UNDER STATUTE

### (1) Administration of Justice Act 1920

NOTE 95. See also *Svenska Petroleum Exploration AB v Lithuania (No.2)* [2006] EWCA Civ 1529, [2007] Q.B. 886. **14–164**

The decision in *AIC Ltd v Federal Government of Nigeria* [2003] EWHC 1357 (QB) was approved in *Republic of Argentina v NML Capital Ltd* [2010] EWCA Civ 41, [2010] 3 W.L.R. 874. (The Supreme Court has given permission to appeal.)

### (2) Foreign Judgments (Reciprocal Enforcement) Act 1933

NOTE 34. A court may set aside a default judgment and give summary judgment instead if the latter, but not the former, would be enforceable in India under the bilateral treaty: *Messer Griesheim GmbH v Goyal MG Gases Pvt Ltd* [2006] EWHC 79 (Comm.). **14–172**

NOTE 52. Companies Act 1985, s.425 was replaced by Companies Act 2006, ss.895–896. **14–173**

See also (on judgments against States): *Re Ivory*, 2006 S.L.T. 758 (which was not a judgment in the sense of the 1920 or 1933 Acts). Likewise, an order of the California courts entering as a judgment a decision of the courts of Nevada as a "sister-state judgment" is, as a "judgment on a judgment", excluded from registration in British Columbia under the Court Order Enforcement Act 1996 (BC): *Owen v Rocketinfo Inc* [2008] BCCA 502, (2008) 305 D.L.R. (4th) 370.

The view has been judicially expressed that the definition in the 1933 Act (probably) excludes an order, made by a foreign court exercising insolvency jurisdiction, requiring a defendant to pay sums in respect of an unfair preference given to a creditor of the company: *New Cap Reinsurance Corp Ltd v Grant* [2009] NSWSC 662, (2009) 257 A.L.R. 740 (interpretation of s.11(1) of the 1933 Act by a judge of the Supreme Court of New South Wales: *sed quaere*). See, however, entry at para.14–030, above.

The decision in *AIC Ltd v Federal Government of Nigeria* [2003] EWHC 1357 (QB) was approved in *Republic of Argentina v NML Capital Ltd* [2010] EWCA Civ 41, [2010] 3 W.L.R. 874. An appeal to the Supreme Court is pending.

An appeal against the decision in *Re Cavell Insurance Co* (2005) 25 C.C L.I. (4th) 245 was dismissed: (2006) 269 D.L.R. (4th) 679 (Ont. CA).

### (3) Schedule 1 to the Civil Jurisdiction and Judgments Order 2001, Part 1 of the Civil Jurisdiction and Judgments Act 1982 and Council Regulation (EC) 805/2004

An amended version of the Lugano Convention (for practical purposes identical with the Judgments Regulation) was signed on October 30, 2007: [2007] O.J. L.339/3. See above, entry at para. 11–020.

**14R–185** The revised Lugano Convention entered into effect as between the Member States of the European Union and Norway on January 1, 2010. Switzerland will adopt the new Convention on January 1, 2011. Regulations which provide for its taking effect in England are made by SI 2009/3131. See entry at para.11R–001, above.

Note 7. See also Magnus and Mankowski (eds.), *Brussels I Regulation* (2007).

Note 8. On the new Lugano Convention, see Pocar (2008) 10 Yb.P.I.L. 1.

The European Commission has published a Report and Green Paper on the revision of the Judgments Regulation: COM(2009) 174 and COM(2009) 175. See entry at para. 11–013, above.

**14–187** Belgium has initiated proceedings against Switzerland before the ICJ which complain of the failure or refusal of the Swiss courts to apply the Lugano Convention to recognise judgments given in Belgian proceedings which were, according to the Belgian government, given in a civil or commercial matter not otherwise excluded from the material scope of the Lugano Convention: see entry at para.12–045, above.

Note 12. The Judgments Regulation applies to Romania and Bulgaria, which become Member States with effect from January 1, 2007 (Council Regulation (EC) 1791/2006); and to Denmark by virtue of a parallel agreement (at [2006] O.J. L120/22) with effect from July 1, 2007: SI 2007/1655.

Note 14. On the transitional arrangements see also *T v L* [2008] IESC 48, [2009] I.L.Pr. 46.

**14–189** In further pursuit of the aim of simplifying the recovery of debts, see the following instruments, and proposals for further legislation:

(a) Regulation (EC) 1896/2006, [2006] O.J. L399/1 (the "EOP Regulation"), in force December 12, 2008 (on which, see Lopez de Tejada, 2007 Rev. Crit. 717). This creates the European Order for Payment procedure, which at Art.19 *et seq.* provides for enforcement of orders by certification with restricted opportunity for opposition. The procedure for the enforcement of such orders in England is governed by CPR Pt 78, in particular rr.78.9–11.

(b) Regulation (EC) 861/2007, [2007] O.J. L199/1 (the "ESCP Regulation"), in force January 1, 2009. This creates the European Small Claims Procedure. Chapter III of the Regulation provides for enforcement of judgments made under the ESCP Regulation to be by certification. The procedure for enforcement of such judgments in England is governed by CPR Pt 78, in particular rr.78.20–22.

(c) Council Directive 2008/52/EC, [2008] O.J. L136/3, to be implemented by May 20, 2011. This provides for certain aspects of mediation in civil and commercial matters and may, according to Recital 20, make provision for an agreement resulting from mediation to be enforced as though it were a judgment.

(d) European Commission Green Paper on Improving the Efficiency of the Enforcement of Judgments in the European Union: The Attachment of Bank Accounts: COM (2006) 618 Final, October 24, 2006.

(e) European Commission Green Paper on Effective Enforcement of Judgments in the European Union: The Transparency of Debtors' Assets: COM (2008) 128 Final, March 6, 2008.

A judgment from the courts of Cyprus which had as its subject matter trespass **14–191** to the claimant's land in the occupied northern part of the Republic of Cyprus, and which sought various forms of relief, was not excluded from recognition under Chapter III of the Judgments Regulation even though certain aspects of the Cypriot judgment could not be carried into effect in the place where the land was situated: Case C–420/07 *Apostolides v Orams* [2009] E.C.R. I–3571. (The decision in *Orams v Apostolides* [2006] EWHC 2226 (QB), [2007] 1 W.L.R. 241, on which see Briggs (2006) 77 B.Y.I.L. 561, is therefore to be taken as overruled.) In further proceedings, an argument that, notwithstanding the decision on the European Court, recognition of the Cypriot judgment could still be refused on grounds of English "international" public policy (based, in some way, on a contention that refusal to recognise the judgment would encourage the communities on the island of Cyprus to resolve their political differences) was rejected: *Apostolides v Orams* [2010] EWCA Civ 9, [2010] 1 All E.R. (Comm.) 992.

A judgment entered when a defendant is debarred from defending is still a judgment for the purpose of Chapter III: Case C–394/07 *Gambazzi v Daimler Chrysler Canada Inc* [2009] E.C.R. I–2563 (on which, see Cuniberti, 2009 *Rev. Crit.* 685).

Note 32: In relation to Case 145/86 *Hoffmann v Krieg* [1988] E.C.R. 645, and in particular for the view that it does not authorise a court to withhold recognition from a foreign judgment ruling on the validity of an arbitration agreement in a manner which would contradict the answer given by English law, see *National Navigation Co v Endesa Generacion SA (The "Wadi Sudr")*

[2009] EWCA Civ 1397, [2010] 1 Lloyd's Rep. 193; see also entry at para.14–197, below.

NOTE 33. An appeal to the House of Lords in *Clarke v Fennoscandia Ltd* was dismissed on other grounds: [2007] UKHL 56, 2008 S.C. (H.L.) 122.

NOTE 34. The same principle will be applied to exclude from Chapter III a "judgment" from a court in a Member State recognising the preclusive effect of a US class action settlement, of the type illustrated by the decision of the Amsterdam District Court in *Re Royal Ahold NV* (June 23, 2010).

On whether the enforcement of a fine for contempt of court falls within the scope of Chapters I and III of the Judgments Regulation, see Case C–406/09 *Realchemie Nederland BV v Bayer CropScience AG* (pending).

**14–192** See also on the exclusion of arbitration, *ETI Euro Telecom NV v Republic of Bolivia* [2008] EWCA Civ 880, [2009] 1 W.L.R. 665 [81]–[87].

**14–195** See Case C–185/07 *Allianz SpA v West Tankers Inc (The "Front Comor")* [2009] E.C.R. I–663.

It was held in *National Navigation Co v Endesa Generacion SA (The "Wadi Sudr")* [2009] EWCA Civ 1397, [2010] 1 Lloyd's Rep. 193 (on which see Briggs (2009) 80 B.Y.I.L. 594; Fentiman [2010] C.L.J. 242) that where a Spanish court had dismissed a challenge to its jurisdiction by making a ruling that the parties had not bound themselves to arbitrate their differences, the Spanish judgment on the validity or invalidity of the arbitration agreement was required to be recognised in accordance with Chapter III of the Judgments Regulation. Such a judgment was given in a civil or commercial matter, and as a result fell within, and was not excluded from, the material scope of the Judgments Regulation. It was not contrary to public policy to recognise a Spanish judgment which concluded, contrary to the view which would have been reached by an English court, that the alleged agreement to arbitrate was not binding on the parties, for Civil Jurisdiction and Judgments Act 1982, s.32(3) could not be regarded as a rule of English law of fundamental importance in English law sufficient to bring it within the principle in Case C–7/98 *Krombach v Bamberski* [2000] E.C.R. I–1935.

The issue which arise on enforcement were mentioned but not discussed on the decision not to stay the proceedings in *DHL GBS (UK) Ltd v Fallimento Finmatica SpA* [2009] EWHC 291 (Comm.), [2009] 1 Lloyd's Rep. 430, [23].

NOTE 44. *cf. A v B* [2006] EWHC 2006 (Comm.), [2007] 1 Lloyd's Rep. 280.

However, the French Cour de Cassation has ruled that a judgment may be presented for enforcement under the Lugano Convention even though it appears to be irreconcilable with an arbitral award, as arbitration falls outside the material scope of the Convention and therefore can furnish no obstacle to the enforcement of civil or commercial judgments under the Convention. (The judgment refers only to Art.27(3) of the Lugano Convention; it is unclear whether an objection to registration on the ground of public policy is to be considered as excluded as well, but if it were, the consequences would be unacceptable: *Republic of Congo v Groupe Antoine Tabet* (July 4, 2007); 2007 Rev. crit. 822 (note Usunier); [2008] I.L.Pr. 367n. **14–196**

The decision in Case C–185/07 *Allianz SpA v West Tankers Inc (The "Front Comor")* [2009] E.C.R. I–663, [2009] 1 A.C. 1138 (on which, also see Muir Watt, 2009 *Rev. Crit.* 373) was interpreted and applied by the Court of Appeal in *National Navigation Co v Endesa Generacion SA (The "Wadi Sudr")* [2009] EWCA Civ 1397, [2010] 1 Lloyd's Rep. 193 (on which see Briggs (2009) 80 B.Y.I.L. 594; Fentiman [2010] C.L.J. 242). It was held that where a Spanish court had dismissed a challenge to its jurisdiction by making a ruling that the parties had not bound themselves to arbitrate their differences, the Spanish judgment on the validity or invalidity of the arbitration agreement was required to be recognised in accordance with Chapter III of the Judgments Regulation. Such a judgment was given in a civil or commercial matter, and was for that reason not excluded from, but was included within, the material scope of the Judgments Regulation. It was not contrary to public policy to recognise a Spanish judgment which concluded, contrary to the view which would have been reached by an English court, that the alleged agreement to arbitrate was not binding on the parties, for Civil Jurisdiction and Judgments Act 1982, s.32(3) could not be regarded as a rule of English law of fundamental importance in English law sufficient to bring it within the principle in Case C–7/98 *Krombach v Bamberski* [2000] E.C.R. I–1935. **14–197**

To the extent that the decision of the Commercial Court in *CMA CGM SA v Hyundai Mipo Dockyard Co Ltd* [2008] EWHC 2791 (Comm.), [2009] 1 Lloyd's Rep. 213 supported a contradictory view, and held that arbitrators applying English law were nevertheless not obliged to give effect to the ruling in *Allianz SpA*, it was doubted. Moreover, a court was obliged to apply the ruling in that case, even when hearing an appeal under Arbitration Act 1996, s.32(1).

First paragraph. The court hearing the enforcement proceedings is not obliged to stay them pending the determination of an ordinary appeal against the judgment in the Member State of origin: *DHL GBS (UK) Ltd v Fallimento Finmatica SpA* [2009] EWHC 291 (Comm.), [2009] 1 Lloyd's Rep. 430. **14–199**

Note 56. Where the extent to which the foreign judgment is enforceable is itself uncertain, the application may be adjourned to allow clarification to be given by procedural methods available in the foreign court: *La Caisse Régional du Crédit Agricole de France v Ashdown* [2007] EWCA Civ 574.

NOTE 59. See also *Banco Nacional de Comercio Exterior SNC v Empresa de Telecomunicaciones de Cuba* [2007] EWHC 2322 (Comm.), [2007] 2 C.L.C. 690.

NOTE 82. On whether a court may refuse to recognise a default judgment given against a defendant who was debarred from defending by reason of contempt, see Case C–394/07 *Gambazzi v Daimler Chrysler Canada Inc* [2009] E.C.R. I–2563.

**14–208** It is not contrary to English public policy to recognise a judgment from the courts of Cyprus dealing with trespass to land in the occupied northern part of Cyprus: Case C–420/07 *Apostolides v Orams* [2009] E.C.R. I–3571. In further proceedings an argument that, notwithstanding the decision on the European Court, recognition of the Cypriot judgment could still be refused on grounds of English "international" public policy (derived, in some form, from a contention that refusal to recognise the judgment would encourage the communities on the island to resolve their differences) was rejected: *Apostolides v Orams* [2010] EWCA Civ 9, [2010] 1 All E.R. (Comm.) 992.

On the stringent requirements for a judgment to be refused recognition on grounds of public policy under Art.34(1), see Case C–394/07 *Gambazzi v Daimler Chrysler Canada Inc* [2009] E.C.R. I–2563: where the objection is founded on the fact that the defendant was debarred from defending, there would need to be a manifest and disproportionate infringement of the right to be heard before non-recognition was justified.

The Greek Supreme Court has apparently refused to recognise an English costs order on the ground that the costs were clearly disproportionate to the sum at stake in the claim and hence enforcement of the order was contrary to Greek public policy: Case 1829/2006, [2008] I.L.Pr. 608.

NOTE 88. See also *Masson v Ottow, Union Discount Ltd v Casamata*, 2007 *Clunet* 543 (French Cour de cassation, 2006), note Péroz; *cf. Material Auxiliare d'Informatique v Printed Forms International* [2006] I.L.Pr. 803 (French Cour de cassation, 2006). To the same effect, refusing to recognise an English judgment given summarily and without what the French courts considered to be sufficient reasons, see *Society of Lloyd's v X* (Cour de Cassation, October 22, 2008) [2009] I.L.Pr. 161. On the French practice, see also Cuniberti (2008) 57 I.C.L.Q. 25.

NOTE 90. See also *Habib Bank Ltd v Central Bank of Sudan* [2006] EWHC 1767 (Comm.), [2007] 1 W.L.R. 470.

On the documents the service of which is material for the purposes of Art.34(2), and for the requirement of service according to the Service Regulation, see Case C–14/07 *Ingenieurbüro Weiss & Partner GbR v Industrie- und Handelskammer Berlin* [2008] E.C.R. I–3367. **14–211**

On the omission of "duly" from Art.34(2), see *Tavoulareas v Tsavliris (No.2)* [2006] EWCA Civ 1772, [2007] 1 W.L.R. 1573 (some sort of service is still required; omission of "duly" did not make a radical change to the law); Case C–283/05 *ASML Netherlands BV v Semiconductor Industry Services GmbH* [2006] E.C.R. I–12041 (if the defendant was aware of the judgment and its content, a technical irregularity in service did not excuse a failure to take steps to challenge it). **14–214**

When the hearing resumed before the referring court, it was held that the defendant had not forfeited the protection of Art.34(2) because, having been served only with the notice of registration for enforcement, and not with the judgment itself, he could not be said to have failed to take steps to challenge the judgment when it was possible for him to do so: [2009] I.L.Pr. 487 (Austrian Sup. Ct.).

The European Court has since confirmed that the changes made to what was Art.27(2) of the Brussels Convention were deliberate and substantial: see Case C–14/07 *Ingenieurbüro Weiss & Partner GbR v Industrie- und Handelskammer Berlin* [2008] E.C.R. I–3367; Case C–420/07 *Apostolides v Orams* [2009] E.C.R. I–3571. It is therefore sensible to take Art.34(2) at face value, and not to read back to its predecessor provision in the Convention. By contrast, on the stricter wording of Art.27(2) of the (old) Lugano Convention, and the consequent non-recognition of judgments resulting from proceedings in which due service was not duly made, see *Ólafsson v Foreign and Commonwealth Office* [2009] EWHC 2608 (QB).

Note 9. For discussion of Case C–522/03 *Scania Finance France SA v Rockinger Spezialfabrik* [2005] E.C.R. I–8639, and whether Art.IV of the First Protocol to the Lugano Convention imposes a mandatory form for service of process in the cases to which it applies, see *Olafsson v Gissurarson (No.2)* [2008] EWCA Civ 152, [2008] 1 W.L.R. 2016, at [67] *et seq.*

See also *British Seafood Ltd v Kruk* [2008] EWHC 1528 (Comm.). **14–215**

If the defendant applies to have a default judgment set aside, and the application is dismissed after a full hearing, Art.34(2) is inapplicable and the judgment may not be refused recognition by reference to its original default character: Case C–420/07 *Apostolides v Orams* [2009] E.C.R. I–3571. (The decision in *Orams v Apostolides* [2006] EWHC 2226 (QB), [2007] 1 W.L.R. 241, on which see Briggs (2006) 77 B.Y.I.L. 561, is therefore overruled.) **14–216**

**14–217** NOTE 19. See also *SA AGF Kosmos Assurance Générale v SA Surgil Trans Express* [2007] I.L.Pr. 363 (French Cour de cassation, 2006).

**14–220** In *T v L* [2008] IESC 48, [2009] I.L.Pr. 46, it was held that a Dutch maintenance decree was liable to be refused recognition on the ground that it was incompatible with the status of the parties according to Irish law; and that the decision in Case 145/86 *Hoffmann v Krieg* [1988] E.C.R. 645 was still effective.

**14–221** The question whether Art.34(4) has any bearing on whether a court, seised of proceedings on the basis of Chapter II of the Regulation, may or should stay its proceedings if there are proceedings in respect of the same cause of action and between the same parties before the courts of a non-Member State arose before but was not decided by the Irish Supreme Court in *Goshawk Dedicated Ltd v Life Receivables Ireland Ltd* [2009] IESC 7, [2009] I.L.Pr. 435. The court decided that a reference should be made to the European Court, but the reference was, however, not made. However, in *Catalyst Investment Group Ltd v Lewinsohn* [2009] EWHC 1964 (Ch.), [2010] Ch. 218 it was held that the existence of a *lis alibi pendens* in a non-Member State, and the possibility that those proceedings may resulting in a judgment which would be required to be recognised in England, had no effect on the jurisdiction of an English court in proceedings brought against a defendant domiciled in England, and that the English court had no power to stay the proceedings before it.

**14–223** It was held in *Re Haji-Ioannou, Haji-Ioannou v Frangos* [2009] EWHC 2310 (QB), [2009] I.L.Pr. 936 (on which see Briggs (2009) 80 B.Y.I.L. 583), that where the judgment creditor died after the application, but before the order, for registration had been made, the application could not be continued by his successor, who would not be an "interested party", unless he or she had succeeded to the judgment in accordance with the law which governed the intestate succession to the deceased's estate (*in casu*, the law of Monaco, including its principles of private international law including renvoi).

The court hearing the appeal against the making of an order for registration is not obliged to stay the proceedings on the enforcement application: *DHL GBS (UK) Ltd v Fallimento Finmatica SpA* [2009] EWHC 291 (Comm.), [2009] 1 Lloyd's Rep. 430.

The listing of courts in Annexes II, to which the application for enforcement is made, and the courts in Annexes III and IV, to which the appeals lie, is amended and corrected by Council Regulation (EC) 280/2009, [2009] O.J. L93/13.

NOTE 39. See Case C–3/05 *Verdoliva v J M Van der Hoeven BV* [2006] E.C.R. I–1579 (service of decision authorising enforcement must be in accordance with procedural law of State in which service is made; informal knowledge of the decision to authorise enforcement is not enough to cause time to start to run: a case on the 1968 Convention, Art.36).

NOTE 40. The Annex V certificate, confirming that the judgment is enforceable, is conclusive: *Schmitz v Schmitz* [2006] I.L.Pr. 896 (French Cour de cassation, 2006).

NOTE 41. See also Case C–167/08 *Draka NK Cables Ltd v Omnipol Ltd* [2009] E.C.R. I–3477 (there is no possibility under the Regulation for non-parties to appeal, even if they have an interest in the judgment, if they had not formally appeared in the proceedings).

NOTE 50. See *Banco Nacional de Comercio Exterior SNC v Empresa de Telecomunicaciones de Cuba SA* [2007] EWCA Civ 662, [2008] 1 W.L.R. 1936, [2008] Bus. L.R. 1265 (no right to particular protective measures, the grant of which is a matter for national law and discretion).

NOTE 52. See also *Banco Nacional de Comercio Exterior SNC v Empresa de Telecomunicaciones de Cuba* [2007] EWHC 2322 (Comm.), [2007] 2 C.L.C. 690.

For problems which may arise when an application to register a judgment is **14–225**
made, but the foreign court then varies the original judgment, see *D'Hoker v Tritan Enterprises* [2009] EWHC 949 (QB) (on which see Briggs (2009) 80 B.Y.I.L. 583) (setting aside the original order for registration of an asset-freezing injunction on the ground that the original judgment was no longer in force in the state of origin). On the power to vary (on the ground that circumstances have changed) a foreign judgment ordering maintenance which has been registered, see *M v V* [2010] EWHC 1453 (Fam.).

On whether an order for enforcement may be revoked on the basis of facts which arose after the judgment was declared to be enforceable, see Case C–139/10 *Prism Investments BV v JA Van Der Meer qq Arilco Holland BV* (pending).

**Orders made to assist the enforcement of English judgments**. Though **14–225A**
this Rule deals with the enforcement in England of judgments from another Member State, the question has recently arisen whether the Judgments Regulation places any restrictions on the power of a English court to make orders which are designed to assist a judgment creditor obtain the enforcement of his English judgment where those orders are made against persons (whether the judgment debtor or those associated with the judgment debtor) domiciled in other Member States, or relate in some way to assets located in other Member or non-Member States. In three separate judgments the Court of Appeal considered various orders which might be made, after final judgment on the merits had been given against a defendant, to assist the judgment creditor in

enforcing that judgment. It held that where the court had exercised jurisdiction on the merits of the claim over a defendant domiciled in another Member State, the jurisdictional rules of the Regulation were no obstacle to: (i) ordering the judgment debtor to refrain from bringing proceedings in the courts of a non-Member State designed to frustrate the enforcement of the judgment: *Masri v Consolidated Contractors International Co SAL (No.3)* [2008] EWCA Civ 625, [2009] Q.B. 450, or to (ii) the appointment of a receiver by way of equitable execution: *Masri v Consolidated Contractors International Co SAL (No.2)* [2008] EWCA Civ 303, [2009] Q.B. 503 or to (iii) making an order under CPR, r.71.2 against a director of the judgment debtor who was himself domiciled in another Member State: *Masri v Consolidated Contractors International Co SAL* [2008] EWCA Civ 876, [2010] 1 A.C. 90. In each case the measure was one ancillary to the exercise of substantive jurisdiction of the English court, and the decision in Case C–391/95 *Van Uden Maritime BV v Deco-Line* [1998] E.C.R. I–7091 confirmed that a court with substantive jurisdiction could (subject only to the decision in Case C–159/02 *Turner v Grovit* [2004] E.C.R. I–3565, [2005] 1 A.C. 101) make any order which was ancillary to that jurisdiction. Neither was the making of such order contrary to comity or to the general principles of private international law. However, the decision of the Court of Appeal in *Masri v Consolidated Contractors International Co SAL (No.4)* [2008] EWCA Civ 876, [2010] 1 A.C. 90 was reversed by the House of Lords, [2009] UKHL 43, [2010] 1 A.C. 90 on the ground that CPR r.71(2)(b) did not apply to persons not present within the jurisdiction. The impact of European law was not discussed.

And see also the entry under para. 24–086, below.

**14–226** See *Re Baden-Wurttembergische Bank AG* [2009] CSIH 47 (registration of authentic instrument).

**14–229** Note 65. CPR Pt 74, Section V, is supplemented by Practice Direction 74B. On the EEO generally, see Crifò, *Cross-Border Enforcement of Debts in the EU* (2009).

For further legislation and proposals for legislation, see entry at para 14–189, above.

**14–233** Note 86. See also Cuniberti (2008) 57 I.C.L.Q. 25 (non-recognition of unreasoned judgments in France).

**14–241** See also *Parkes v MacGregor* [2008] CSOH 43, 2008 S.C.L.R. 345 (enforcement under Sch.6).

**14R–252** On the award of punitive (which may mean multiple) damages by American courts, see *Exxon Shipping Co v Baker* 128 S. Ct. 2605, at 2623–24 (2008).

But in *Lucasfilm Ltd v Ainsworth* [2008] EWHC 1878 (Ch.), [2009] F.S.R. 103 (on which see Briggs (2008) 79 B.Y.I.L. 537) the court considered (*obiter*) that the "untainted compensatory element" (which is to say, the sum before multiplication), in a foreign judgment for multiple damages, should be recoverable notwithstanding the actual wording of s.5 of the Act. The point was not pursued before the Court of Appeal. **14–255**

Note 46. CPR, r.6.19(2) is replaced by CPR, rr.6.32(2) (service of claim form in Scotland or Northern Ireland), 6.33(3) (service of claim form out of the United Kingdom). **14–256**

## Chapter 15

# JURISDICTION AND ENFORCEMENT OF JUDGMENTS UNDER MULTILATERAL CONVENTIONS

**15–002** Note 5. Supreme Court Act 1981 is now renamed Senior Courts Act 1981: Constitutional Reform Act 2005, s.59 and Sch.11, in force October 1, 2009.

**15–003** On the difference between Art.71 of the Judgments Regulation and Art.57 of the 1968 Convention, see Case C–533/08 *TNT Express Nederland BV v AXA Versicherung AG* [2010] I.L.Pr. 663, at [38]. The European Court held that the overarching aims of the Judgments Regulation cannot be compromised by an international convention. Hence, the European Court ruled (at [56]) that pursuant to Art.71 of the Judgments Regulation, the rules of an international convention can only prevail, for matters also falling within the ambit of the Judgments Regulation, if they are "highly predictable, facilitate the sound administration of justice and enable the risk of concurrent proceedings to be minimised"; and on condition "that they ensure, under conditions at least as favourable as those provided for by the regulation, the free movement of judgments in civil and commercial matters and mutual trust in the administration of justice in the European Union." See also entry at para.15–025, below.

Note 9. SI 2005/2092 entered into force on July 1, 2006.

**15–005** A new Pt 6 of the CPR has been substituted by SI 2008/2178, Sch.1. CPR, r.6.19(2) has been replaced by CPR, r.6.33(3).

**15–006** In *Laroche v Spirit of Adventure (UK) Ltd* [2009] EWCA Civ 12, [2009] Q.B. 778, the Court of Appeal ruled that a broad and purposive approach should be adopted to the ambit of the Warsaw Convention; and that a hot air balloon designed for the carriage of passengers was an "aircraft" within the meaning of Carriage by Air Acts (Application of Provisions) Order 1967, Sch.1, Art.1.

**15–008** Third sentence and note 31. The Montreal Convention 1999 has now entered into force in Uruguay, and so a flight from London-Montevideo no longer falls within the provisions of the unamended Convention given effect by the Order in Council. Indonesia is an example of a State which has succeeded to the 1929 Convention but which is not party to the 1955 Hague Protocol or the Montreal Convention of 1999. Hence, a flight from London-Jakarta does not fall within the amended text as given effect by the Carriage by Air Act 1961, but does fall within the provisions of the unamended Convention given effect by the Order in Council.

NOTE 37. But see, in this respect, *Ashad v Deutsche Lufthansa Aktiengesellschaft (Lufthansa German Airlines)*, 2009 Carswell Ont 7251, at [45]–[49]. **15–010**

NOTE 41. In *Gulf Air Company GSC v Fattouh* [2008] NSWCA 225, a passenger was injured en route to Sydney, some two hours flying time before arrival. The injured passenger's ticket was for a round trip from Beirut to Bahrain to Sydney. The injured party was due to stay in Sydney for three months. Beirut was identified as the "destination" on the ticket. The question arose as to whether the New South Wales courts could exercise jurisdiction under Art.28 of the Montreal Protocol of 1975, on the basis that Sydney was the place of destination. It was held (approving the decision in *Vertzyas v Singapore Airlines Ltd* (2000) 50 N.S.W.L.R. 1) that the New South Wales courts did not have jurisdiction, since Beirut was the place of destination by agreement of the parties. Such a choice could only be rebutted if it could be demonstrated that the agreed terms of the concluded contract were other than as stated on the ticket. See also *Ashad v Deutsche Lufthansa Aktiengesellschaft (Lufthansa German Airlines)*, 2009 Carswell Ont 7251. **15–011**

On the scope of application of the Convention to claims for personal injury and for delay, see *Kandiah v Emirates* Carswell Ont. 4192, June 28, 2007. **15–012**

NOTE 43. SI 1998/1058 was repealed by Carriage by Air Acts (Application of Provisions) Order (SI 2004/1899).

CPR, r.6.19(2) is now CPR, r.6.33(3): see SI 2008/2178, Sch.1. **15–013**

NOTE 46. CPR, r.6.27 is now CPR, r.6.44.

NOTE 51. CPR, r.6.19(2) is now CPR, r.6.33(3). **15–014**

In *Ashad v Deutsche Lufthansa Aktiengesllschaft (Lufthansa German Airlines)*, 2009 Carswell Ont 7251, it was held that the 1999 Convention would be inapplicable where a State was not party to the Convention at the time when the alleged cause of action accrued but had subsequently become a party before the proceedings were heard. **15–015**

See Carriage by Air (Revision of Limits of Liability under the Montreal Convention) Order (SI 2009/3018).

In Case C–204/08 *Rehder v Air Baltic Corp* [2009] E.C.R. I–6073 (noted George and Harris (2010) 126 L.Q.R. 30), the European Court ruled that a **15–016** passenger's claim for a standardised and lump-sum payment following the cancellation of a flight, which was based on Regulation (EC) 261/2004 of the European Parliament and Council establishing common rules on compensation and assistance to passengers in the event of denied boarding and of cancellation or long delay of flights, was independent of a claim for compensation for damage under the Montreal Convention, Art.19 (relying upon Case C–344/04 *IATA and ELFAA* [2006] E.C.R. I–403). Accordingly, the claim was subject to the jurisdiction rules in the Judgments Regulation, rather than those in the Montreal Convention. See also Case C–402/07 *Sturgeon v Condor Flugdienst GmbH* [2010] 2 C.M.L.R. 12.

Note 60. CPR, r.6.19(2) is now CPR, r.6.33(3).

**15–018** The 1999 Protocol entered into force in respect of the United Kingdom on July 1, 2006.

Note 66. SI 2005/2092 came into force on July 1, 2006.

Note 66. SI 2005/2092 is modified by Rail Passengers' Rights and Obligations Regulations 2010 (SI 2010/1504, in force from June 25, 2010), which provide for the effective implementation of Regulation (EC) No. 1371/2007 of the European Parliament and of the Council on rail passengers' rights and obligations [2007] O.J. L315/14. The European Regulation harmonises the rules regarding the rights and obligations of rail passengers in the European Union. Where there is a conflict between the European Regulation and the COTIF Convention (as modified by the Vilnius Protocol of 1999), the former prevails. The European Regulation, however, largely replicates the COTIF Convention, as modified. The European Regulation does not contain rules on jurisdiction and arbitration. Where there is no incompatibility with the European Regulation, the United Kingdom must continue to apply the COTIF Convention, as modified by the Vilnius Protocol.

**15–023** Note 78. Substitute: Article 5 of the Convention with Title V, Arts 28 to 32 of the Convention.

Note 79. The 1999 Protocol is now in force, however, the Expert Committee for the Carriage of Dangerous Goods has yet to produce an Annex to the Rules.

**15–024** In *Hatzl v XL Insurance Co Ltd* [2009] EWCA Civ 223, [2010] 1 W.L.R. 470, the Court of Appeal ruled that an assignee who was resident in England could not be sued in England on this basis under Art.31 of the CMR Convention, where the assignor who was party to a carriage by road contract was not itself resident in England. The court ruled that a purposive approach to Art.31 was required and that Art.31 was concerned with jurisdiction as between parties to the carriage contract and sought to confer jurisdiction on a court which had some connection to the dispute. Jacob and Rix L.JJ. also held that the assignor should be regarded as standing in the shoes of the assignor. Since the assignor could not have been sued in England under Art.31, the assignee was similarly entitled not to be sued in England.

An additional Protocol to the Convention on the Contract for the International Carriage of Goods by Road (CMR) Concerning the Electronic Consignment Note, was concluded on February 20, 2008. The United Kingdom is yet to ratify this.

NOTE 81. In *Datec Electronic Holdings Ltd v United Parcels Service Ltd* [2007] UKHL 23, [2007] 2 Lloyd's Rep. 114 (noted Clarke [2008] J.B.L 184), certain packages had exceeded the maximum value stipulated in the terms of conditions of carriage. Nonetheless, the carrier did not exercise its right, contained in its standard terms and conditions, to refuse to carry, or to suspend carriage of the packages. The House of Lords ruled that there was a "contract for . . . carriage" within the meaning of the Convention, since the natural interpretation of the carrier's terms and conditions was that, unless and until it exercised its right to refuse to transport goods or to suspend carriage, there was a contract that it would carry the packages. This would give effect to the parties' expectations and reflect the commercial reality of the agreement.

In Case C–533/08 *TNT Express Nederland BV v AXA Versicherung AG* [2010] **15–025**
I.L.Pr. 663, the question arose whether a Dutch court, which was first seised of proceedings under the CMR Convention (and whose judgment was the subject of a pending appeal) was required to enforce a German judgment ostensibly given in defiance of the court first seised rule in Art.31(2) of the CMR Convention. TNT alleged that the Dutch court could decline to enforce the German judgment on public policy grounds. AXA argued that this would be incompatible with Art.35(3) of the Judgments Regulation, which precludes the use of the public policy defence in Art.34(1) of the Judgments Regulation to review the jurisdiction of the court of origin. This, in turn, gave rise to questions as to the meaning of Art.71(2)(b) of the Judgments Regulation and the extent to which the rules on the enforcement of foreign judgments in the CMR Convention could prevail over rules in the Judgments Regulation. The European Court ruled that the effect of Art.71(2)(b) of the Judgments Regulation was that the CMR rules on enforcement of foreign judgments would prevail, provided that they did not compromise the fundamental aims of free movement and the sound administration of justice in the Judgments Regulation; and, in particular, provided that the rules on enforcement of foreign judgments in the CMR Convention were not less favourable than those in the Judgments Regulation. The European Court declined to determine whether this was the case, on the basis that it lacked competence to interpret the CMR Convention. See also entry at para.15–003, above.

In *Sony Computer Entertainment Ltd v RH Freight Services Ltd* [2007] EWHC 302 (Comm.), [2007] 2 Lloyd's Rep. 463, Sony brought a claim against various companies in England for the loss of a consignment of its goods during its carriage by road from England to the Netherlands. The carriage had been carried out by a driver employed by one of the companies. Sony's potential claim for damages was substantially larger than the amount for which it was insured. One of the companies, K, issued Dutch proceedings seeking a declaration of non-liability or, alternatively, a declaration limiting its liability under the CMR Convention. Sony's insurers were named as a defendant in those proceedings; but Sony itself was not named. When Sony subsequently brought English proceedings, K then sought the same relief in the Dutch proceedings against Sony itself. Sony contended that the English court was first seised of the dispute between it and K and that, although the first Dutch action was a related action, the Dutch court should stay its proceedings under Art.28 of the Judgments Regulation. The English court ruled (at [27]), that as the CMR was silent on the treatment of related actions, Art.28 of the Judgments Regulation was applicable. It then held that the Dutch court was first seised, since the action became pending when it was issued, considerably before the English action became pending. It held that although the parties in the English action were not the same parties as in the first Dutch action, the English court should decline jurisdiction pursuant to Art.28 of the Judgments Regulation.

NOTE 94. *Royal & Sun Alliance Insurance plc v MK Digital FZE (Cyprus) Ltd* [2006] EWCA Civ 629 is now reported at [2006] 2 Lloyd's Rep. 110.

**15–026** NOTE 98. CPR, r.6.19(2) is now CPR, r.6.33(3).

NOTE 1. CPR, r.6.27 is now CPR, r.6.44.

## **15–028** THE UNITED NATIONS CONVENTION ON CONTRACTS FOR THE INTERNATIONAL CARRIAGE OF GOODS WHOLLY OR PARTLY BY SEA (THE ROTTERDAM RULES)

On December 11, 2008, the General Assembly of the UN adopted the UN Convention on Contracts for the International Carriage of Goods Wholly or Partly by Sea. On September 23, 2009, a ceremony for the opening for signature was held in Rotterdam. The new Convention will enter into force once it has been adopted by at least twenty states. It will replace the Hague Rules, the Hague-Visby Rules and the Hamburg Rules, and establish a single international set of rules. For an overview and discussion of the drafting history of the Convention, see Sturley (2008) 14 J.I.M.L. 461.

Unlike the Hague and Hague-Visby Rules, the Rotterdam Rules contain detailed provisions on jurisdiction and arbitration. However, Ch.14 on jurisdiction and Ch.15 on arbitration will only apply if a Contracting State declares its intention to be bound by either or both sets of rules (pursuant to Art.91 of the Rules) and such a declaration may be withdrawn at any time. For discussion, see Baatz (2008) 14 J.I.M.L. 608; Baatz, in *The Rotterdam Rules: A Practical Annotation* (2009), Chs 14 and 15; Baatz, in Thomas (ed), *A New Convention for the Carriage of Goods by Sea—The Rotterdam Rules* (2009); Alvarez Rubio (2009) 11 Yb. P.I.L. 171. See also Diamond [2008] L.M.C.L.Q. 135, at pp.183–186; [2009] L.M.C.L.Q. 445.

NOTE 14. CPR, r.6.19(2) is now CPR, r.6.33(3). **15–031**

See also the Civil Aviation Act 2006, which is in force. **15–032**

NOTE 22. CPR, r.6.19(2) is now CPR, r.6.33(3). **15–034**

Supreme Court Act 1981 is now re-named Senior Courts Act 1981: Constitutional Reform Act 2005, s.59 and sch.11, in force October 1, 2009 (SI 2009/1604). **15–036**

On the possible differences between the jurisdiction provisions applicable to collisions between ships, on the one hand, and collision by a ship with an oil platform, on the other, see *Conocophillips (UK) Ltd v Partnereederei Ms Jork* [2010] EWHC 1214 (Comm.), at [38].

Merchant Shipping (Liner Conferences) Act 1982, ss.2–4, 11–13 are repealed by SI 2008/163 Merchant Shipping (Liner Conferences) Act 1982 (Repeal) Regulations 2008. The Explanatory Provisions state: **15–037**

> "These Regulations provide for the mandatory provisions of the United Nations Code of Conduct for Liner Conferences, as implemented in the United Kingdom by the Merchant Shipping (Liner Conferences) Act 1982, the Merchant Shipping (Liner Conferences) (Conditions for Recognition) Regulations 1985 and the Merchant Shipping (Liner Conferences) (Mandatory Provisions) Regulations 1985, to cease to have effect, and make consequential repeals.
>
> Council Regulation (EC) No 1419/2006 of 25 September 2006 (O.J. L269, 28.9.2006, p.1) repealed Council Regulation (EEC) No 4056/86 and thereby removed the block exemption from Arts 81 and 82 of the EC Treaty granted to liner shipping conferences, subject to a transitional period of two years for conferences which complied with the requirements of Regulation 4056/86 on 18th October 2006. As a consequence, Council Regulation (EEC) No 954/79 of 15 May 1979 (O.J. L121, 17.5.1979, p.1), which gave effect to the Code within the European Union, has become inapplicable. The present Regulations repeal the provisions giving effect to Regulation 954/79."

Most of the provisions will enter into force on October 18, 2008, although some entered into force on February 26, 2008.

NOTES 27 and 29. See entry at para.15–036, above.

**15–039** Compare Merchant Shipping (Prevention of Pollutions by Sewage and Garbage from Ships) Regulations 2008 (SI 2008/3257), Regulation 45 (in force February 1, 2009).

NOTE 37. The Merchant Shipping (Pollution) Act 2006, which is in force, enables effect to be given to the Supplementary Fund Protocol 2003 and to future revisions of the international arrangements relating to compensation for oil pollution from ships.

**15–040** CPR, r.6.27 is now CPR, r.6.44: see SI 2008/2178, Sch.1.

NOTE 44. The provisions on service out of the jurisdiction formerly contained in CPR, r.6.20 are now found in CPR PD6B, para.3.1. CPR, r.6.20(17A)(b) is now CPR PD6B, para.3.1(19)(b).

**15–041** The International Convention on Civil Liability for Bunker Oil Pollution Damage 2001 entered into force on November 21, 2008 (see Jacobsson (2009) 15 J.I.M.L. 21). The Convention is designed to fill a gap in the international regime for dealing with oil spillage, as the 1992 Convention does not include bunker oil spills from vessels other than tankers. Merchant Shipping (Oil Pollution) (Bunkers Convention) Regulations 2006 (SI 2006/1244) amend Merchant Shipping Act 1995, ss.152–71 accordingly. These Regulations amend Ch.3 of Pt 6 of Merchant Shipping Act 1995 in order to implement Council Decision 2002/762/EC authorising the Member States, in the interests of the Community, to sign, ratify or accede to the Convention. The Regulations introduce a new s.153A into Merchant Shipping Act 1995, which concerns liability for pollution by bunker oil. Regulation 20 supplements the rules on jurisdiction and registration of foreign judgments in s.166 of the 1995 Act. Section 166(3)(A) of the Act provides that:

"Where—

(a) there is a discharge or escape of bunker oil falling within section 153A(1) which does not result in any damage caused by contamination in the territory of the United Kingdom and no measures are reasonably taken to prevent or minimise such damage in that territory, or

(b) any relevant threat of contamination falling within section 153A(2) arises but no measures are reasonably taken to prevent or minimise such damage in the territory of the United Kingdom,

no court in the United Kingdom shall entertain any action (whether in rem or in personam) to enforce a claim arising from any relevant damage or cost—

(i) against the owner of the ship, or
(ii) against any person to whom section 156(2A)(ii) applies, unless any such damage or cost resulted from anything done or omitted to be done as mentioned in that provision."

ILLUSTRATION 1. The Montreal Convention 1999 is now in force in Uruguay, so that this illustration is no longer valid (see entry at para.15–008, above). However, a contract between A and X & Co, an Indonesian company, for a return flight Jakarta-London-Jakarta would fall within this illustration, as Indonesia has succeeded to the 1929 Convention but is party to neither the 1955 Hague Protocol nor the Montreal Convention of 1999. **15–045**

ILLUSTRATION 4. The relevant provisions of the Companies Act 1985 will be replaced by the Companies Act 2006 when they are fully in force: see entry at para.11–115, above.

Supreme Court Act 1981 is now re-named Senior Courts Act 1981: Constitutional Reform Act 2005, s.59 and Sch.11, in force October 1, 2009. **15R–046**

See entry at para.15R–046, above. **15–048**

NOTE 74. 2004 Protocol to amend the Paris Convention on Third Party Liability in the field of Nuclear Energy of July 29, 1960, as amended by the additional Protocol of January 28, 1964 and by the protocol of November 16, 1982, contains in Part M more detailed provisions on jurisdiction. The 2004 Protocol has yet to enter into force. **15–049**

Sections 152 to 171 of the Merchant Shipping Act 1995 are amended by the Merchant Shipping (Oil Pollution) (Bunkers Convention) Regulations 2006, with effect from November 21, 2008. See entry at para.15–041. **15–051**

NOTE 83. The revised Lugano Convention ([2007] O.J. L339/1) entered into force on January 1, 2010 between the Member States of the European Union (including Denmark) and Norway on January 1, 2010. It will be ratified by Switzerland with effect from January 1, 2011. The text of the previous Lugano Convention contained in Sch.3C of the Civil Jurisdiction and Judgments Act 1982 was repealed by Reg. 25 of the Civil Jurisdiction and Judgments Regulations 2009 (SI 2009/3131). See entry at para.11R–001, above.

NOTE 97. The 1999 Protocol entered into force in respect of the United Kingdom on July 1, 2006. **15–054**

On the enforcement of CMR judgments and their relationship to the Judgments Regulation, see Case C–533/08 *TNT Express Nederland BV v AXA Versicherung AG* [2010] I.L.Pr. 663 (considered at paras 15–003 and 15–025, above). **15–055**

**15–057** THE UNITED NATIONS CONVENTION ON CONTRACTS FOR THE INTERNATIONAL CARRIAGE OF GOODS WHOLLY OR PARTLY BY SEA (THE ROTTERDAM RULES)

The Rotterdam Rules (considered above, at para.15–028) contain provisions on the recognition and enforcement of foreign judgments (Art.73). These Rules would only apply if the State of origin and the State where recognition was sought were both Contracting States that had declared their intention to be bound by the rules in Ch.14 of the Regulation.

**15–060** The Convention entered into force on November 21, 2008. See entry at para.15–041, above. Regulation 20(4) of SI 2006/1244 amends s.166(4) of the 1995 Act so as to extend Part I of the Foreign Judgments (Reciprocal Enforcement) Act 1933 to relevant judgments given by courts in Bunker Convention countries.

NOTE 21. See above, entry at para.11–020, for the Agreement for the application of the Judgments Regulation to Denmark.

**15–062** The 2004 Protocol, which further amends the Paris Convention on Third Party Liability in the field of Nuclear Energy (1960), is not yet in force. See entry at para.15–049, n.74, above.

## Chapter 16

# ARBITRATION AND FOREIGN AWARDS

## 1. GOVERNING LAW

Note 1. Add *C v D* [2007] EWHC 1541 (Comm.), affirmed [2007] EWCA Civ 1282, [2008] 1 Lloyd's Rep. 239, (noted Briggs (2008) 78 B.Y.I.L. 595); Arzandeh and Hill (2009) 5 J. Priv. Int. L. 425; Bantekas (2010) 27 J. Int. Arb. 1. **16R–001**

Note 4. Add Park, *Arbitration of International Business Disputes* (2006); Born, *International Commercial Arbitration* (2009). **16–002**

Note 7. See Caron, Caplan and Pellonpää, *The UNCITRAL Arbitration Rules: A Commentary* (2006). **16–003**

Note 8. Law Reform (Miscellaneous Provisions) (Scotland) Act 1990, s.66 and Sch.7, have now been repealed and replaced by Arbitration (Scotland) Act 2010.

Note 15. Add Derains and Schwartz, *A Guide to the ICC Rules of Arbitration*, (2nd ed., 2005). **16–009**

Note 21. In *Fiona Trust and Holding Corp v Privalov* [2007] EWCA Civ 20, [2007] 2 Lloyd's Rep. 267 (noted Berg (2007) 123 L.Q.R. 352), the Court of Appeal (approving a passage to this effect in para.12–099 of this work) held that the principle of separability applied even in a case where it was alleged that the main contract was invalid, having been procured by bribery. There had to be some special reason for saying that the bribery impeached the arbitration clause in particular to remove the question from the competence of the arbitral tribunal. The decision was affirmed by the House of Lords [2007] UKHL 40, [2007] Bus. L.R. 1719 (noted Briggs [2008] L.M.C.L.Q. 1, Rushworth (2008) 124 L.Q.R. 195, Gee (2008) 24 Arb. Int. 467; Samuel (2008) 24 Arb. Int. 489; Style and Knowles (2008) 24 Arb. Int. 499; Briggs (2008) 78 B.Y.I.L. 595) Lord Hope observed that, in cases where the litigant claimed that he was entitled to rescind the arbitration agreement on grounds that the contract as a whole was procured by bribery: **16–011**

> "The doctrine of separability requires direct impeachment of the arbitration agreement before it can be set aside. This is an exacting test. The argument must be based on facts which are specific to the arbitration agreement.

Allegations that are parasitical to a challenge to the validity of the main agreement will not do" [35].

*Fiona Trust* was applied in *El Nasharty v J Sainsbury plc* [2007] EWHC 2618 (Comm.), [2008] 1 Lloyd's Rep. 360.

Add Joseph, *Jurisdiction and Arbitration Agreements and their Enforcement* (2005).

NOTE 22. The principle has been approved by the United States Supreme Court: *Buckeye Check Cashing Inc v Cardegna*, 546 U.S. 440 (2006) (noted Samuel (2006) 22 Arb. Int. 477); and by the Full Court of the Federal Court of Australia: *Comandate Marine Corp v Pan Australia Shipping Pty Ltd* [2006] FCAFC 192, (2006) 157 F.C.R. 42.

**16–013** The Supreme Court of Canada has upheld the primacy of the autonomy of the parties in both arbitration and jurisdiction clauses, subject to operation of mandatory rules of the forum and the construction of the clause itself: *Gre-Con Dimter Inc v J R Normand Inc* [2005] 2 S.C.R. 401, 255 D.L.R. (4th) 257, especially at [20]–[27].

The law governing the arbitration agreement must be that of a national legal system: *Halpern v Halpern* [2006] EWHC 603 (Comm.), [2006] 2 Lloyd's Rep. 83, at [47]–[58] (reversed in part, but not on this point [2007] EWCA Civ 291, [2008] Q.B. 195).

**16–014** Thus, in *Dallah Estate and Tourism Holding Co v Ministry of Religious Affairs, Government of Pakistan* [2009] EWCA Civ 755, [2010] 2 W.L.R. 805, affd [2010] UKSC 46, [2010] 3 W.L.R. 1472, an ICC arbitral award made in France was held unenforceable in England, since the arbitration agreement was not effective to bind the award debtor as a matter of French law.

**16–016** A passage to this effect in the previous edition of this work was approved in *Halpern v Halpern* [2006] EWHC 603 (Comm.), [2006] 2 Lloyd's Rep. 83, at [55] (reversed in part, but not on this point [2007] EWCA Civ 291, [2008] Q.B. 195, applied in *Musawi v R E International (UK) Ltd* [2007] EWHC 2981 (Ch.), [2008] 1 Lloyd's Rep. 326).

This paragraph noted with approval in *National Navigation Co v Endesa Generacion SA (The "Wadi Sudr")* [2009] EWHC 196 (Comm.), [2009] 1 Lloyd's Rep. 666, [107].

**16–017** NOTE 34. Add: *Tamil Nadu Electricity Board v ST-CMS Electric Co Pvt Ltd* [2007] EWHC 1713 (Comm.), [2008] 1 Lloyd's Rep. 93.

**16–019** The parties are free, under s.46(1)(b) of the 1996 Act, to choose a non-national system of law to govern the substance of their contract. The arbitration agreement, on the other hand, must be governed by a national legal system, which is determined to be the proper law of that agreement. This may lead to a different applicable law for the arbitration agreement, even where the parties have made an express choice of law to govern the substantive contract: *Halpern v Halpern* [2006] EWHC 603 (Comm.), [2006] 2 Lloyd's Rep. 83 (reversed in part, but not on this point [2007] EWCA Civ 291, [2008] Q.B. 195, applied in *Musawi v R E International (UK) Ltd* [2007] EWHC 2981 (Ch.), [2008] 1 Lloyd's Rep. 326).

Note 42. Add: *Midgulf International Ltd v Groupe Chimiche Tunisien* [2010] EWCA Civ 66, [2010] 1 C.L.C. 113, [56]. **16–022**

Note 43. Add: *Abu Dhabi Investment Co v H Clarkson & Co Ltd* [2006] EWHC 1252 (Comm.), [2006] 2 Lloyd's Rep. 381; *ET Plus SA v Welter* [2005] EWHC 2115 (Comm.), [2006] 1 Lloyd's Rep. 251; *Midgulf International Ltd v Groupe Chimiche Tunisien* [2010] EWCA Civ 66, [2010] 1 C.L.C. 113, [56].

In *Emmott v Michael Wilson & Partners Ltd* [2008] EWCA Civ 184, [2008] 1 Lloyd's Rep. 616, [84], [110], the tentative view was expressed *obiter* that the extent and scope of any obligation of confidentiality in an arbitration were matters of substance, which were governed by the law applicable to the arbitration agreement, and ought therefore to be determined by the arbitral tribunal, rather than by application to court.

Note 54. In *Svenska Petroleum Exploration AB v Lithuania (No.2)* [2006] EWCA Civ 1529, [2007] Q.B. 886 (noted Kawharu [2007] L.M.C.L.Q. 136), the Court of Appeal considered the reverse situation, in which a foreign State sought to rely on general principles of law applied by international tribunals, rather than its own law, as grounds for a submission that it was not bound by an arbitration agreement. The choice of law clause in the agreement provided for the application of the law of Lithuania "... supplemented, where required, by rules of international business activities generally accepted in the petroleum industry if they do not contradict the laws of the Republic of Lithuania". The court applied the law governing the arbitration agreement to the question. It held that effect had to be given to both parts of the clause in interpreting the arbitration agreement. It upheld the finding at first instance that the agreement did bind the State as a matter of Lithuanian law, and found no general principle of law applied by international tribunals which was inconsistent with that conclusion. **16–027**

Powerful support to the delocalisation theory has recently been given by the final courts of appeal in Canada and France. The Supreme Court of Canada has held, in *Dell Computer Corp v Union des consommateurs* 2007 SCC 34, (2007) 284 D.L.R. (4th) 577, at [51], that: **16–032**

> "Arbitration is part of no state's judicial system . . . The arbitrator has no allegiance or connection to any single country . . . In short, arbitration is a creature that owes its existence to the will of the parties alone."

The French Cour de Cassation held in *PT Putrabali Adyamulia v Est Epices* (June 29, 2007) (2008) 24 Arb. Int. 293, 295 (noted Pinsolle (2008) 24 Arb. Int. 277) that " . . . an international arbitral award—which is not anchored to any national legal order—is an international judicial decision whose validity must be ascertained with regard to the rules applicable in the country where its recognition and enforcement is sought."

NOTE 62. Add: Gaillard, *Legal Theory of International Arbitration* (2010).

**16–033** The wide degree of party autonomy in arbitration conferred by many domestic arbitration laws, such as the 1996 Act, (including a power for the parties to waive their general right of appeal to the courts) does not in principle offend Art.6 of the European Convention on Human Rights, especially where, as in the case of the 1996 Act, the domestic courts of the seat retain some measure of control of the arbitration proceedings: *Sumukan Ltd v Commonwealth Secretariat* [2007] EWCA Civ 243, [2007] 3 All E.R. 342, at [57].

**16–034** Thus, where the parties have expressly chosen the seat of their arbitration, it is the courts at the seat which have exclusive supervisory jurisdiction to determine claims for a remedy going to the existence or scope of the arbitrator's jurisdiction, or to allegations of bias. Proceedings seeking to determine these issues in a court elsewhere than the seat would amount to a breach of the arbitration agreement and should be stayed. So held in the context of a claim which had been brought in England on the grounds that the arbitration agreement was liable to be avoided for fraudulent misrepresentation, but the parties had chosen Swiss law to govern their arbitration agreement and Switzerland as the seat of the arbitration. In this situation, the English courts would: (a) refuse to grant an injunction restraining the arbitrator from determining his own jurisdiction on the principle of *Kompetenz-Kompetenz*: *Weissfisch v Julius* [2006] EWCA Civ 218, [2006] 1 Lloyd's Rep. 716; (b) grant a stay of English proceedings against the arbitrator personally in the exercise of the court's inherent powers: *A v B* [2006] EWHC 2006 (Comm.), [2007] 1 Lloyd's Rep. 237; and (c) make an award of damages or of indemnity costs against the party bringing proceedings otherwise than in the courts of the seat: *A v B (No.2)* [2007] EWHC 54 (Comm.), [2007] 1 Lloyd's Rep. 358, at [15]–[19] (noted Briggs (2007) 78 B.Y.I.L. 595).

Where the parties have expressly chosen England as the seat of their arbitration, the English court will restrain by injunction foreign court proceedings seeking to challenge, vacate or review an English arbitral award: *C v D* [2007] EWHC 1541 (Comm.), affirmed [2007] EWCA Civ 1282, [2008] Bus. L.R. 843. Choice of the seat of the arbitration confers upon the courts of that country exclusive jurisdiction for remedies seeking to attack the award (other than in the course of its enforcement in other countries under the New York Convention or otherwise) even if the arbitration agreement itself were governed by another law: *Shashoua v Sharma* [2009] EWHC 957 (Comm.), [2009] 2 All E.R. (Comm.) 477.

The same approach applies where the foreign proceedings are before an arbitral review tribunal, rather than a judicial forum: *Sheffield United Football Club Ltd v West Ham United Football Club plc* [2008] EWHC 2855 (Comm.), [2009] 1 Lloyd's Rep. 167.

This paragraph was applied in *Shashoua v Sharma* [2009] EWHC 957 (Comm.), [2009] 2 All E.R. (Comm.) 477, [32]. **16–035**

Section 4(5) requires an express choice of a different *lex arbitri*. It does not refer to an express choice of the *lex causae* governing the main contract of which the arbitration agreement forms a part: *C v D* [2007] EWHC 1541 (Comm.), at [38]. The fact that the 1996 Act allows parties to contract out of its non-mandatory provisions does not mean that the proper law of an arbitration agreement can constitute an agreement to the contrary importing a method of challenge to the award not permitted by the seat of the arbitration. Section 4(5) requires a choice of law with regard to the specific provision of the Act which the parties agree is not to apply: *C v D* [2007] EWCA Civ 1282, [2008] Bus. L.R. 843. **16–038**

Note 74. A similar approach was also taken even where the parties had by their contract expressly nominated a seat for the arbitration in Scotland, when it was clear from all of the other express terms that they wished English law to be the *lex arbitri*, and the choice of a Scottish seat must therefore be treated as a convenient place for hearings only: *Braes of Doune Wind Farm (Scotland) Ltd v Alfred McAlpine Business Services Ltd* [2008] EWHC 426 (TCC), [2008] 1 Lloyd's Rep. 608. **16–041**

Note 92: The same result of excluding the right to appeal to the courts was validly achieved through the incorporation by reference into the arbitration agreement of the Statute of an international organisation: *Sumukan Ltd v Commonwealth Secretariat* [2007] EWCA Civ 243, [2007] 3 All E.R. 342. **16–044**

Where such an application is made, the Court has power to order substituted service, pursuant to CPR PD62, para.3.1, upon the solicitors or attorneys acting for the party in the arbitration, whether within or outside the jurisdiction. In the absence of special circumstances, it will commonly do so where the authority of such solicitors does not appear to have been terminated: *Kyrgyz Republic Ministry of Transport Department of Civil Aviation v Finrep GmbH* [2006] EWHC 1722 (Comm.), [2006] 2 C.L.C. 402. **16–045**

Where the parties have chosen England as the seat of their arbitration, England is almost always likely to be the appropriate forum, as the parties **16–046** have already submitted themselves to the supervisory jurisdiction of the English court: *Kyrgyz Republic Ministry of Transport Department of Civil Aviation v Finrep GmbH* [2006] EWHC 1722 (Comm.), [2006] 2 C.L.C. 402.

**16–047** This paragraph was approved and applied in *Musawi v R E International (UK) Ltd* [2007] EWHC 2981 (Ch.), [2008] 1 Lloyd's Rep. 326.

**16–052** NOTE 12. It has been held that s.46(1)(a) does not affect the approach which the arbitral tribunal is entitled to take to the ascertainment of the content of the *lex causae*. Thus, an arbitral tribunal sitting in England may, if there is no suggestion by the parties that there is an issue under the applicable system of law which is different from English law, or the tribunal does not itself raise a specific issue, decide the matter on the basis of English law: *Hussman (Europe) Ltd v. Al Ameen Development & Trade Co* [2000] 2 Lloyd's Rep. 83. But, for a general comparative analysis of the ascertainment of the content of the applicable law (doubting the value of applying a presumption as to the similarity of the *lex causae* with the law of the seat) see: ILA Committee on International Commercial Arbitration *Ascertaining the Contents of the Applicable Law in International Commercial Arbitration* (2008) 73 ILA Conf. Rep. 850, (2010) 26 Arb. Int. 191.

**16–053** NOTE 16. In an award between the Channel Tunnel concessionaires and Britain and France seeking recovery of losses in relation to the problem of clandestine migrants in the Tunnel, the tribunal found that its jurisdiction was strictly limited to breaches of the Concession Agreement, but held that it could apply a mixed choice of law clause in determining the issues subject to its jurisdiction. The clause provided: " . . . the relevant provisions of the Treaty and of this Agreement shall be applied. The rules of English law or the rules of French law may, as appropriate, be applied when recourse to those rules is necessary for the implementation of particular obligations under English law or French law. In general, recourse may also be had to the relevant principles of international law and, if the parties in dispute agree, to the principles of equity.": *Channel Tunnel Group Ltd v Secretary of State for Transport of the United Kingdom of Great Britain and Northern Ireland* Award under Treaty of Canterbury 1986 (Crawford, Fortier, Guillaume, Millett and Paulsson, January 30, 2007, available at *http://www.pca-cpa.org*), para.151.

See also *Svenska Petroleum Exploration AB v Lithuania (No.2)* [2006] EWCA Civ 1529, [2007] Q.B. 886.

**16–061** NOTE 32. *Lesotho Highlands Development Authority v Impregilo SpA* [2005] UKHL 43, [2006] 1 A.C. 221 was applied in *B v A* [2010] EWHC 1626 (Comm.), where it was suggested that a conscious disregard of the provisions of the chosen law would be a necessary, but not sufficient, requirement to challenge an award under s.68(2)(b) for excess of powers in the determination of the applicable law. It is no ground for review under s.68 that the arbitrator might have expressed his conclusions on foreign law at greater length: *ABB AG v Hochtief Airport GmbH* [2006] EWHC 388 (Comm.), [2006] 2 Lloyd's Rep. 1.

## 2. STAYING OF PROCEEDINGS AND INJUNCTIONS TO RESTRAIN FOREIGN PROCEEDINGS

RULE 58(2). Delete existing text and replace as follows. **16R–065**

**(2) The English court has jurisdiction *in personam* to restrain by injunction foreign proceedings in breach of an arbitration agreement, save where those proceedings are brought in the courts of a State to which Council Regulation (EC) 44/2001 on jurisdiction and the enforcement of judgments in civil and commercial matters, or the 1968 or Lugano Conventions on jurisdiction and the enforcement of judgments in civil and commercial matters, applies.**

NOTE 50. Supreme Court Act 1981 is now renamed Senior Courts Act 1981: Constitutional Reform Act 2005, s.59 and Sch.11, in force from October 1, 2009. **16–067**

Section 6(2) of the 1996 Act provides: "The reference in an agreement to a written form of arbitration clause or to a document containing an arbitration clause constitutes an arbitration agreement if the reference is such as to make that clause part of the agreement". The effect of this subsection is to make the incorporation of an arbitration agreement by reference a matter of contractual construction according to the law applicable to the arbitration agreement. Where English law is the applicable law, a reference in the primary contractual document to a set of rules which include an arbitration clause will be sufficient to constitute an arbitration agreement: *Sea Trade Maritime Corp v Hellenic Mutual War Risks Association (Bermuda) Ltd (The Athena) (No.2)* [2006] EWHC 2530 (Comm.), [2007] 1 Lloyd's Rep. 280; *Sumukan Ltd v Commonwealth Secretariat* [2007] EWCA Civ 243, [2007] 3 All E.R. 342. **16–069**

Where the cross-claim is subject to an arbitration agreement, the court will grant a stay in respect of that claim, even if it could, under its governing law, constitute a set-off to the principal claim before the English court: *Prekons Insaat Sanayi AS v Rowlands Castle Contracting Group Ltd* [2006] EWHC 1367 (Comm.), [2007] 1 Lloyd's Rep. 98. **16–070**

NOTE 65. It follows that where, by their arbitration agreement, the parties have limited the tribunal's jurisdiction over defences of set-off to counterclaims arising out of the same contract, the court will give effect to the limitation: *Econet Satellite Services Ltd v VEE Networks Ltd* [2006] EWHC 1664 (Comm.), [2006] 2 Lloyd's Rep. 423 (construing Art.19(3) LCIA Rules to this effect).

Note 68. Section 9(3) makes exclusive provision for the time within which an application to stay must be made. It is not necessary to comply in addition with the requirements of CPR Part 11 (as to which see para.11–133 of the main work): *Bilta (UK) Ltd (In Liquidation) v Nazir* [2010] EWHC 1086 (Ch.).

**16–075** It will in general be right for the arbitral tribunal to be the first tribunal to consider whether it has jurisdiction, unless the arbitration agreement itself is directly impeached: *Fiona Trust and Holding Corp v Privalov* [2007] EWCA Civ 20, [2007] 2 Lloyd's Rep. 267, at [34], affirmed [2007] UKHL 40, [2007] Bus. L.R. 1719.

Note 78. Add: *ASM Shipping Ltd of India v TTMI Ltd of England* [2005] EWHC 2238 (Comm.), [2006] 1 Lloyd's Rep. 375 (a case on apparent bias of arbitrator), application for leave to appeal dismissed [2006] EWCA Civ 1341, [2007] 1 Lloyd's Rep. 136; *Republic of Kazakhstan v Istil Group Inc* [2006] EWHC 448 (Comm.), [2006] 2 Lloyd's Rep. 370, at [41] affd. [2007] EWCA Civ 471, [2008] Bus. L.R. 878.

The Supreme Court of Canada has held, interpreting the law of Quebec consistently with Art.II(3) of the New York Convention, that the application of the competence-competence principle requires that a challenge to the arbitrator's jurisdiction should in general be referred first to the arbitral tribunal. The court should only depart from that general principle where the challenge (e.g. as to the nullity of the arbitration agreement) is based solely on a question of law (or involves questions of fact which require only superficial consideration from the record). Even then, the court must be satisfied that hearing the challenge itself would not lead to unnecessary delay or impair the conduct of the arbitral process: *Dell Computer Corp v Union des consommateurs* 2007 SCC 34, (2007) 284 D.L.R. (4th) 577, [84]–[87], applied in *Jean Estate v Wires Jolley LLP* 2009 ONCA 339, where it was held (by majority, Jurianz JA dissenting on this ground) that the question whether an agreement to arbitrate disputes over a contingency fee arrangement was unenforceable for reasons of public policy was a question of law, which the court need not refer to the arbitrator.

**16–076** Note 80. Add *Albon v Naza Motor Trading SDN Bhd (No.3)* [2007] EWHC 665 (Ch.), [2007] 2 All E.R. 1075; *Accentuate Ltd v ASIGRA Inc* [2009] EWHC 2655 (QB), [2009] 2 Lloyd's Rep. 599, [71].

**16–078** Note 89. The issue of Admiralty proceedings *in rem* does not, without more, amount to the repudiation of an arbitration agreement between the owner and charterer, since the arrest of the ship may be maintained as a provisional measure pending the outcome of the arbitration: *Comandate Marine Corp v Pan Australia Shipping Pty Ltd* [2006] FCAFC 192, (2006) 157 F.C.R. 42.

NOTE 92. Add *ET Plus SA v Welter* [2005] EWHC 2115 (Comm.), [2006] 1 Lloyd's Rep. 251. 16–079

However, where English law applies to the construction of the arbitration agreement, the court will adopt a liberal approach, so as to include within the common phrase "arising out of" every dispute relating to the contract (including claims in tort) except a dispute as to whether there was ever a contract at all, as, for example, if where it was procured by impersonation or forgery: *Fiona Trust & Holding Corp v Privalov* [2007] EWCA Civ 20, [2007] 2 Lloyd's Rep. 267, at [17]–[18]; affirmed [2007] UKHL 40, [2007] Bus. L.R. 1719, [2007] UKHL 40. A similar approach has now also been taken in the Australian Federal Court, so as to include within the same phrase claims relating to alleged misleading or deceptive conduct or misrepresentation in contract formation: *Comandate Marine Corp v Pan Australia Shipping Pty Ltd* [2006] FCAFC 192, (2006) 157 F.C.R. 42 (departing from its earlier decision in *Hi-Fert Pty Ltd v KiuKiang Maritime Carriers Inc* (1998) 159 A.L.R. 142).

NOTE 95. While the proposition advanced in the text of this work at note 95 has not been doubted, *Roussel-Uclaf v GD Searle Ltd* [1978] 1 Lloyd's Rep. 225 was overruled by the Court of Appeal in *City of London v Sancheti* [2008] EWCA Civ 1283, [2009] 1 Lloyd's Rep. 117 to the extent that it had held that s.9 of the 1996 Act could apply to a person who was not a party to the arbitration agreement. In *Sancheti,* the Court of Appeal considered that the City of London was not bound by an arbitration agreement contained in a bilateral investment treaty entered into by the United Kingdom, such that the court was obliged to stay proceedings brought by the City against Mr Sancheti.

NOTE 3. "Dispute" also includes admitted but unpaid claims: *Exfin Shipping (India) Ltd v Tolani Shipping Co Ltd* [2006] EWHC 1090 (Comm.), [2006] 2 Lloyd's Rep. 389. 16–081

Examples of where s.9 of the 1996 Act does not apply, but where the inherent power to stay may be exercised include: (a) where the claim is not within the arbitration agreement, because it is brought against the arbitrator personally: *A v B* [2006] EWHC 2006 (Comm.), [2007] 1 Lloyd's Rep. 237; (b) where the court cannot be sure, on the evidence before it, whether there is a valid arbitration agreement, and it is in the interests of justice for the arbitral tribunal to decide that question: *Albon v Naza Motor Trading SDN Bhd (No.3)* [2007] EWHC 665 (Ch.), [2007] 2 All E.R. 1075; (c) where it is appropriate to do so on a temporary basis in the exercise of the court's case management powers, in the light of a pending related arbitration: *ET Plus SA v Welter* [2005] EWHC 2115 (Comm.), [2006] 1 Lloyd's Rep. 251, at [91]. 16–082

NOTE 6. *Roussel-Uclaf v GD Searle Ltd* [1978] 1 Lloyd's Rep. 225 was overruled by the Court of Appeal in *City of London v Sancheti* [2008] EWCA Civ 1283, [2009] 1 Lloyd's Rep. 117, see entry at para. 16–079, n. 95.

**16–084** Where, however, the claimant takes action in a foreign court which goes beyond simply seeking reasonable security for the arbitration proceedings, and seeks instead to secure the jurisdiction of the court in breach of the arbitration agreement, the court will, if necessary, restrain the claimant by injunction from further pursuit of the foreign proceedings: *Sotrade Denizcilik Sanayi Ve Ticaret AS v Amadou Lo (The "Duden")* [2008] EWHC 2762 (Comm.), [2009] 1 Lloyd's Rep. 145; *Kallang Shipping SA Panama v AXA Assurances Senegal (The "Kallang") (No.2))* [2008] EWHC 2761 (Comm.), [2009] 1 Lloyd's Rep. 124.

**16–085** The arbitral tribunal may, where the parties so agree, grant its own provisional measures, either in the form of an order, or an interim Award: 1996 Act, s.39(1), and see ICC Rules Art.23(1), applied in an arbitration in England: *ICC Case No. 11443 of 2001* (2005) 30 Yb. Comm. Arb. 85.

Australia and New Zealand have given effect to the elaborate and controversial amendments to the UNCITRAL Model Law (as amended in 2006 UN Doc A/61/17, annex I) on the power of the arbitral tribunal to order interim measures and *ex parte* preliminary orders. In Australia, the Model Law has the force of law, save as expressly otherwise provided: International Arbitration Act 1974 (Cth.), s.16. International Arbitration Amendment Act 2010 (Cth.) substitutes the 2006 revised Model Law for this purpose (but see ss.18B and 19 of the principal Act for respects in which the interim order regime of the 2006 revised Model Law is qualified in its application in Australia).

In New Zealand, Arbitration Amendment Act 2007 s.8, adds new ss.17–17M to the Arbitration Act 1996 (noted Kawharu (2008) 24 Arb. Int. 405, 413–9). Article 9(2) of Schedule 1 of the principal Act (as amended) now provides that the court will have the same powers as an arbitral tribunal to grant interim measures. Article 9(2) does not follow the corresponding provision in the Model Law (Art.17J). It has the surprising effect that the New Zealand court now does have power to order security for costs (*cf.* the position in England noted at [8–097] in the main work), but apparently does not have the power to grant *ex parte* relief in aid of arbitration.

NOTE 10. Section 25 does not otherwise apply to the grant of interim relief in aid of arbitration; specific provision for this having been made by s.44 of the 1996 Act: *ETI Euro Telecom International NV v Republic of Bolivia* [2008] EWCA Civ 880, [2009] 1 W.L.R. 665. In that case, an attempt to use s.25 in support of foreign judicial proceedings, which were themselves only for interim relief in aid of arbitration, was also held outside the scope of the statutory section. Section 25 required foreign proceedings on the substance of the matter: *ibid.*, at [70].

NOTE 13. Add *Permasteelisa Japan KK v Bouyguesstroi* [2007] EWHC 3508 (QB), where it was held that, in principle, the court could utilise its limited power under this section to grant an injunction against a third party bank restraining payment under a performance bond, where the arbitral tribunal had not yet been constituted.

The court may also exercise its powers in support of arbitration by enforcing the peremptory order of an arbitral tribunal under s.42 of the 1996 Act. The court should generally enforce such an order, unless there has been a material change of circumstances, or the arbitral tribunal has exceeded its powers, or acted unfairly as between the parties: *Emmott v Michael Wilson & Partners Ltd (No.2)* [2009] EWHC 1 (Comm.), [2009] 1 Lloyd's Rep. 233. This power only applies where the seat of the arbitration is in England (or the seat has not been determined and the court is satisfied that by reason of the connection of the matter with England, it is appropriate to do so): s.2.

NOTE 15. Add *Econet Wireless Ltd v VEE Networks Ltd* [2006] EWHC 1568 (Comm.), [2006] 2 Lloyd's Rep. 428 (injunction in aid of foreign arbitration). **16–086**

NOTE 17. This principle was also applied in a case where the seat of the arbitration was in New York: *Mobil Cerro Negro Ltd v Petroleos de Venezuela SA* [2008] EWHC 532 (Comm.), [2008] 2 All E.R. (Comm.) 1034, [2008] 1 Lloyd's Rep. 684. The court held that it would only be prepared to grant an application for a freezing injunction in aid of a foreign arbitration affecting assets not located in England if the respondent or the dispute had a sufficiently strong link with England: [119], [135].

NOTE 18. In Australia, where an action *in rem* is stayed on account of an arbitration agreement, the arrested property may be retained, or released on condition of provision of equivalent security, pending the outcome of the arbitration: *Comandate Marine Corp v Pan Australia Shipping Pty Ltd* [2006] FCAFC 192, (2006) 157 F.C.R. 42. **16–087**

The application must be made without delay and before the proceedings in the foreign court are too far advanced: *Verity Shipping SA v NV Norexa (The "Skier Star")* [2008] EWHC 213 (Comm.), [2008] 1 Lloyd's Rep. 652, and see the further references cited in the main work at para.12–078, n.47. **16–088**

In *Starlight Shipping Co v Tai Ping Insurance Co Ltd Hubei Branch* [2007] EWHC 1893 (Comm.), [2008] 1 Lloyd's Rep. 230, the court considered the question whether the court's power to grant an injunction to restrain a foreign action brought in breach of an arbitration agreement was derived from the general terms of s.37 of the Supreme Court Act 1981 or was limited by the narrower terms of s.44 of the 1996 Act, which deals *inter alia* with interim injunctions in aid of arbitration (as to which see paras 16–085–16–086 in the main work). The court proceeded (without finally deciding the point) on the basis that it did have general power under s.37, but that, in exercising its discretion, it would have regard to the factors enumerated in s.44. See also: *Elektrim SA v Vivendi Universal SA (No.2)* [2007] EWHC 571 (Comm.), [2007] 2 Lloyd's Rep. 8, at [67]–[79]. The Court of Appeal has not yet had an opportunity to decide this point, but has noted on a number of recent occasions that it would at some stage require detailed consideration: *Cetelem SA v Roust Holdings Ltd* [2005] EWCA Civ 618, [2005] 1 W.L.R. 3555, at [74]; *Emmott v Michael Wilson & Partners Ltd* [2008] EWCA Civ 184, [2008] 1 Lloyd's Rep. 616, at [110] and [123]; and *ETI Euro Telecom International NV v Republic of Bolivia* [2008] EWCA Civ 880, [2009] 1 W.L.R. 665, at [97].

The court has jurisdiction to grant an anti-suit injunction to restrain foreign proceedings brought in breach of an arbitration agreement, even where there are no actual or intended arbitration proceedings, since the purpose of the relief is to restrain breach of the contractual promise not to be sued in a foreign court: *AES Ust-Kamenogorsk Hydropower Plant LLP v Ust-Kamengorsk Hydropower Plant JSC* [2010] EWHC 772 (Comm.).

Moreover, where the arbitration agreement is governed by English law and provides for arbitration in England, such an injunction will be issued to restrain pursuit of declaratory proceedings in the foreign court as to the validity of the arbitration agreement. The issue of an anti-suit injunction in aid of arbitration does not infringe the New York Convention on the Recognition and Enforcement of Foreign Arbitral Awards 1958: *Midgulf International Ltd v Groupe Chimique Tunisien* [2010] EWCA Civ 66, [2010] 1 C.L.C. 113.

By contrast to the position in relation to foreign actions, the court should be very slow to restrain a party from continuing with an arbitration, properly brought under an arbitration agreement, whether the seat of the arbitration is in England or abroad, and even if there are related concurrent proceedings: *Elektrim S.A. v Vivendi Universal S.A. (No.2)* [2007] EWHC 571 (Comm.), [2007] 2 Lloyd's Rep. 8, (doubting *Intermet FZCO v Ansol Ltd* [2007] EWHC 226 (Comm.), where the point was not fully argued). In view of the priority to be accorded to the parties' choice of arbitration, and the limited nature of the court's powers to intervene under the 1996 Act save in support of the arbitral process, the court should not simply apply the same approach as for the grant of an anti-suit injunction.

Two such situations may be: (a) where the arbitral tribunal's determination of its jurisdiction has already been reviewed by the court of the seat, and that court has decided that the tribunal lacked jurisdiction, yet one party is still claiming the right to pursue the arbitration: *Republic of Kazakhstan v Istil Group Inc (No.2)* [2007] EWHC 2729 (Comm.), [2008] 1 Lloyd's Rep. 382; and (b) where the essence of the challenge to the arbitral tribunal's jurisdiction is that the arbitration agreement is a forgery, and it has been agreed that the English court may determine that question: *Albon v Naza Motor Trading Sdn Bhd* [2007] EWCA Civ 1124, [2008] 1 Lloyd's Rep. 1, affirming [2007] 2

Lloyd's Rep. 420. Neither of these cases is a true exception to the principle stated above, since, in both cases, the essential claim was that there was no arbitration agreement at all, and the English court either had determined, or was entitled to determine, that point. Such cases are likely to be very rare.

NOTE 21. Add Gaillard, *Reflections on the use of Anti Suit Injunctions in International Arbitration*, in *Pervasive Problems in International Arbitration* (ed. Mistelis and Lew, 2006), p.201. Raphael, *The Anti-suit Injunction* (2008), Ch. 6; McLachlan, *Lis Pendens in International Litigation* (2009), Ch. 3.

NOTE 22. Add: *Goshawk Dedicated Ltd v ROP Inc* [2006] EWHC 1730 (Comm.), [2006] Lloyd's Rep. I.R. 711; *Noble Assurance Co v Gerling-Konzern General Insurance Co* [2007] EWHC 253 (Comm.), [2007] 1 C.L.C. 85 (restraining post-award foreign proceedings, where the seat of the arbitration was London).

NOTE 24. Add *Kallang Shipping SA v AXA Assurances Senegal (The Kallang)* [2006] EWHC 2825 (Comm.), [2007] 1 Lloyd's Rep. 160.

See now Case C–185/07 *Allianz SpA v West Tankers Inc (The "Front Comor")* **16–089—**
[2009] E.C.R. I–663, [2009] 1 A.C. 1138; noted Peel (2009) 125 L.Q.R. 365, **16–093**
Fentiman [2009] C.L.J. 278, McLachlan *Lis Pendens in International Litigation* (2009), 228–237, Grierson (2009) 26 J. Intl. Arb. 891. The case came to the European Court on a reference from the House of Lords *sub nom. West Tankers Inc v Ras Riunione Adriatica di Sicurta SpA (The Front Comor)* [2007] UKHL 4, [2007] 1 Lloyd's Rep. 391 (noted Bollée [2007] *Revue de l'Arbitrage* 223; Fentiman [2007] C.L.J. 493), following a decision of Colman J. granting an injunction: [2005] 2 Lloyd's Rep. 257.

The *Front Comor*, a vessel owned by West Tankers and chartered to Erg Petroli SpA, collided with a jetty owned by Erg. The charterparty provided for arbitration of disputes in London. While Erg began arbitration to recover the losses not covered by their insurers, the insurers exercised their statutory right of subrogation under Italian law to commence proceedings against West Tankers in Italy for the insured losses. West Tankers responded with proceedings in England, seeking a declaration that, as the dispute being litigated in Italy arose out of the charterparty, the insurers inherited the obligation to refer it to arbitration. West Tankers sought an injunction that the insurers not pursue the claim further except by way of arbitration, and in particular that they discontinue the Italian proceedings.

Colman J. held that the insurers' claim was subject to the arbitration clause and that the court had jurisdiction to grant the injunction because arbitration was excluded from the Judgments Regulation. The House of Lords referred to the European Court the question whether it was consistent with the Judgments Regulation 44/2001 for a court of a Member State to make an order to restrain a person from commencing or continuing proceedings in another Member State on the ground that such proceedings were in breach of an arbitration agreement. Lord Hoffmann (with whom all other members agreed) expressed the view that an injunction would be consistent with the Regulation. He said (at [16]):

> "The arbitration agreement lies outside the system of allocation of court jurisdictions which the Regulation creates. There is no dispute that, under the Regulation, the Tribunale di Siracusa has jurisdiction to try the delictual claim. But the arbitration clause is an agreement not to *invoke* that jurisdiction. . . . [A]n arbitration clause takes effect outside the Regulation and its enforcement is not subject to its terms."

The European Court accepted that the English proceedings as a whole, which sought declaratory as well as injunctive relief, did not come within the scope of the Judgments Regulation. The delictual proceedings before the Italian Court came within the scope of the Regulation. Since they did, the effect of the arbitration agreement, including its validity, were an incidental question, which also came within the scope of the Regulation: Judgment, [26]. Accordingly, it was the Italian court which had the exclusive power under the Regulation to rule on the effect of the arbitration agreement on its jurisdiction. The English proceedings, to the extent that they sought an anti-suit injunction, might have consequences which undermined the effectiveness of the Regulation, being "the attainment of the objectives of unification of the rules of conflict of jurisdiction in civil and commercial matters and the free movement of decisions in those matters:" [24].

The decision of the European Court in *West Tankers* has a number of important subsidiary consequences. First, the mere fact that a claim is the subject of an arbitration agreement does not deprive a court, which could otherwise determine the substance of the claim, of its jurisdiction under the Judgments Regulation. The remedy for the party which claims that the proceedings are brought in breach of an arbitration agreement is to seek a stay pursuant to s.9 of the 1996 Act, or its equivalent in other countries, giving effect to Article II of the New York Convention: applied in *Youell v La Réunion Aérienne* [2009] EWCA Civ 175, [2009] 1 Lloyd's Rep. 586.

Secondly, the decision of the Court in no way affects the power of the arbitral tribunal to determine its own jurisdiction under the principle of *Kompetenz-Kompetenz.* Thus, the judgment has the effect, as Kokott A-G recognised ([70]–[73]) that there could be parallel determinations, by the arbitral tribunal and by a national court in another Judgments Regulation State, on the validity and scope of the arbitration agreement, and its effect on the pending court proceedings. That could, in turn, lead to inconsistent decisions.

Thirdly, given the current scope of the arbitration exclusion in the Judgments Regulation, there can be no objection to declaratory proceedings as to the validity of the arbitration agreement in the courts of the seat: *National Navigation Co v Endesa Generacion SA (The "Wadi Sudr")* [2009] EWHC 196 (Comm.), [2009] 1 Lloyd's Rep. 666 (noted Knight [2009] L.M.C.L.Q. 285), reversed [2009] EWCA Civ 1397, [2010] 1 Lloyd's Rep. 193, but not on this point. As such proceedings fall outside the Regulation, they will not be caught by the first-in-time *lis pendens* rule in Art.27.

Fourthly, however, the judgment of another Regulation State on the scope or validity of an arbitration agreement, when made in the course of proceedings the main scope of which brings them within the Regulation, is required to be recognised and enforced under the Regulation: *National Navigation Co v Endesa Generacion SA (The "Wadi Sudr")* [2009] EWCA Civ 1397, [2010] 1 Lloyd's Rep. 193 (noted Fentiman (2010) 69 C.L.J. 242), reversing [2009] EWHC 196 (Comm.), [2009] 1 Lloyd's Rep. 666.

The solution proposed in the Heidelberg Report, reviewing the operation of the Judgments Regulation (Hess, Pfeiffer, Schlosser *The Brussels I-Regulation (EC) No.44/2001* (2008) [133]), is to add to the Judgments Regulation a new Art.27A, which would provide:

> "A court of a Member State shall stay the proceedings once the defendant contests the jurisdiction of the court with respect to existence and scope of an arbitration agreement if a court of the Member State that is designated as place of arbitration in the arbitration agreement is seized for declaratory relief in respect of the existence, the validity and/or the scope of that arbitration agreement."

The Commission, in its Report to the European Parliament on the Application of the Judgments Regulation dated April 21, 2009 (COM (2009) 174) has pointed to the difficulties which may arise from the exclusion of arbitration from the scope of the Regulation: [3.7]. In its Green Paper dated April 21, 2009 (COM (2009) 175), the Commission seeks consultation, *inter alia,* on the above proposal: [7].

The Committee on Legal Affairs of the European Parliament, which issued its Report on the Judgments Regulation on June 29, 2010 (A7–0219/2010), has recommended to the European Parliament that the exclusion of arbitration from the scope of the Regulation should remain in place; that "a rule providing that the courts of the Member State of the seat of the arbitration should have exclusive jurisdiction could give rise to considerable perturbations"; and that:

> "[T]he various national procedural devices developed to protect arbitral jurisdiction (anti-suit injunctions so long as they are in conformity with free movement of persons and fundamental rights, declaration of validity of an arbitration clause, grant of damages for breach of an arbitration clause, the

negative effect of the '*Kompetenz-Kompetenz* principle', *etc.)* must continue to be available and the effect of such procedures and the ensuing court decisions in the other Member States must be left to the law of those Member States as was the position prior to the judgment in *West Tankers*."

## 3. ENFORCEMENT OF FOREIGN AWARDS

### A. *At Common Law*

**16–101** NOTE 53 As from October 1, 2008, CPR, r.6.20(9) has been replaced in the same terms by CPR PD6B, para.3.1(10).

NOTE 55. Supreme Court Act 1981 is now renamed Senior Courts Act 1981: Constitutional Reform Act 2005, s.59 and Sch.11, in force from October 1, 2009.

**16–113** NOTE 81. In *Weizmann Institute of Science v Neschis*, 421 F. Supp. 2d 654 (S.D.N.Y. 2005), the New York Federal Court confirmed that a foreign arbitral award was capable of recognition at common law in the United States so as to give rise to a collateral estoppel precluding subsequent re-litigation of an issue necessarily and conclusively determined in the arbitration (recognition of a Liechtenstein award not covered by the New York Convention).

**16–121** NOTE 8. Add: *Weizmann Institute of Science v Neschis*, 421 F. Supp. 2d 654 (S.D.N.Y. 2005) (parties to be afforded a full and fair opportunity to be heard on the relevant issue in the arbitration).

### B. *New York Convention Awards*

**16–124** The provision in s.101(3) to the effect that judgment may be entered "in terms of the award" does not preclude the court from requiring the payment of interest at the judgment rate from the date upon which judgment has been entered on the award, even if the arbitral tribunal did not provide for the payment of interest in its award: *Gater Assets Ltd v Nak Naftogaz Ukrainy (No.3)* [2008] EWHC 1108 (Comm.), [2008] 2 Lloyd's Rep. 295

NOTE 15. The court's jurisdiction to enforce a New York Convention award is limited strictly to the party against whom the award was made. Save in the case of a slip or a change of name, the court has no discretion to change the respondents as named in the award. Thus, an order for enforcement against each of (1) the Republic of Ukraine and (2) the State Property Fund of Ukraine was set aside on the application of the Republic of Ukraine, the award having been entered against "the Republic of Ukraine, through the State Property Fund of Ukraine": *Norsk Hydro ASA v State Property Fund of Ukraine* [2002] EWHC 2120 (Comm.), [2009] Bus. L.R. 558.

A Convention award includes a part award. Thus, where part of a Convention award was the subject of challenge in the courts of the seat, it was still permissible to order enforcement of the unchallenged part of the award, provided that the part to be enforced could be ascertained from the face of the award and judgment could be given in the same terms as the award: *Nigerian National Petroleum Corp v IPCO (Nigeria) Ltd (No.2)* [2008] EWCA Civ 1157, [2009] 1 Lloyd's Rep. 89. **16–126**

Limitation Act 1980, s.7 provides: "An action to enforce an award, where the submission is not by an instrument under seal, shall not be brought after the expiration of six years from the date on which the cause of action accrued." The imposition of such a local requirement at the place of enforcement is not inconsistent with the New York Convention, since the obligation in Article III to enforce Convention awards is "in accordance with the rules of procedure of the territory where the award is relied on", subject to the proviso that no substantially more onerous conditions are imposed than apply to domestic awards. So held unanimously (considering the point in relation to s.2 of the Alberta Limitations Act 2000) by the Supreme Court of Canada in *Yugraneft Corp v Rexx Management Corp* [2010] SCC 19. **16–131**

Note 36. A challenge to an award invoking one of the grounds under s.103 (Rule 62) is by way of rehearing not review: *Dallah Estate and Tourism Holding Co v Ministry of Religious Affairs, Government of Pakistan* [2009] EWCA Civ 755, [2010] 2 W.L.R. 805, affd. [2010] UKSC 46, [2010] 3 W.L.R. 1472. Moreover, the principle of estoppel of record does not preclude the court from coming to a different view on the relevant issues under s.103 to that reached by the arbitral tribunal: *ibid.*, and, to like effect in French law: *République tchèque v Nreka* (Fr. Cour d'Appel de Paris, September 25, 2008) [2009] *Revue de l'arbitrage* 337, 339, note Fadlallah; Duprey (2009) 26 J. Int. Arb. 591. **16–133**

Note 37. That discretion is not, however, open-ended. Where one of the grounds stated under s.103 has been made out, the court would normally only enforce the award if the right to rely upon one of the stated grounds had been lost, for example by another agreement or estoppel: *Kanoria v Guinness* [2006] EWCA Civ 222, [2006] 1 Lloyd's Rep. 701, at [25], approving a statement to this effect in *Yukos Oil Co v Dardana Ltd* [2002] EWCA Civ 543, [2002] 2 Lloyd's Rep. 326, at [8]. This approach was further approved in *Dallah Estate and Tourism Holding Co v Ministry of Religious Affairs, Government of Pakistan* [2009] EWCA Civ 755, [2010] 2 W.L.R. 805, affd. [2010] UKSC 46. The court considered that it would be unlikely to exercise its discretion where the award in question was subject to a fundamental or structural defect. But the court added *obiter* the caveat that it might be necessary to revisit the question whether the discretion to permit enforcement might be broader in a case under Rule 62(f) (where the award has been set aside by the supervisory court).

**16–135** Where the parties have not chosen the law applicable to the arbitration agreement, the reference to the law of the country where the award was made denotes the substantive law rules of that country, and not its conflict of laws rules: *Dallah Estate and Tourism Holding Co v Ministry of Religious Affairs, Government of Pakistan* [2010] UKSC 46, [2010] 3 W.L.R. 1472, at [123]–[125].

**16–136** NOTE 44. Where, however, a party was not informed of the case which he was called upon to meet, this ground for refusal will be made out: *Kanoria v Guinness* [2006] EWCA Civ 222, [2006] 1 Lloyd's Rep. 701.

**16–140** On the application of Art.V(1)(e) of the New York Convention to the paradigm case, see *TermoRio SA v Electranta SP*, 487 F. 3d 928 (D.C. Cir. 2007).

**16–141** NOTE 61. Where, however, a severable part of the award is not subject to credible challenge in the courts of the seat, it has been held that the court may enter judgment for that part of the award, maintaining a stay in respect of the balance: *IPCO (Nigeria) Ltd v Nigerian National Petroleum Corp* [2008] EWHC 797 (Comm.), [98]–[105].

**16–142** It has been held that the court also has power to order security for costs to be provided by the award creditor seeking an order for the enforcement of the award, and that this is not a breach of Art.III of the New York Convention, since the jurisdiction applies in the same manner to domestic and foreign awards: *Gater Assets Ltd v Nak Naftogaz Ukrainiy* [2007] EWHC 697 (Comm.), [2007] 1 Lloyd's Rep. 522, following *Dardana Ltd v Yukos Oil Co (No.2)* [2002] 2 Lloyd's Rep. 261.

In *Gater Assets Ltd v Nak Naftogaz Ukrainiy* [2007] EWCA Civ 988, [2007] 2 Lloyd's Rep. 588, the Court of Appeal considered the reverse question of whether an award debtor could obtain security for costs against an award creditor, who was seeking enforcement of his award in England under the New York Convention. The court was divided on the matter. A majority (Rix and Moses L.JJ., Buxton L.J. dissenting) held that the order of Field J. awarding security for costs ([2007] EWHC 697 (Comm.), [2007] 1 Lloyd's Rep. 522) ought to be discharged. Rix L.J. was prepared to assume, without deciding, that the court had jurisdiction. But he held that the court should not exercise the jurisdiction, save in an exceptional case, since it would normally be contrary to the principles underlying the enforcement of awards under the New York Convention to do so (disapproving *Dardana Ltd v Yukos Oil Co (No.2)* [2002] 2 Lloyd's Rep. 261). Moses L.J. held that the court had no jurisdiction to award security against an award creditor seeking enforcement under the New York Convention. No such provision was made in the Convention itself, and to insert such a requirement would be to impose upon a Convention creditor a more onerous requirement than applies in the case of domestic awards, contrary to Art.III of the Convention.

NOTE 64. Add *PT Putrabali Adyamulia v Est Epices* (French Cour de cassation, June 29, 2007), (2008) 24 Arb. Int. 293 (noted Pinsolle (2008) 24 Arb. Int. 277); Ghikas (2006) 22 Arb. Int. 53; Slater (2009) 25 Arb. Int. 271. **16–143**

See *Dallah Estate and Tourism Holding Co v Ministry of Religious Affairs, Government of Pakistan* [2010] UKSC 46, [2010] 3 W.L.R. 1472, at [129]–[130]. **16–144**

NOTE 67. Add: *World Duty Free Co Ltd v Kenya* (2007) 46 Int. Leg. Mat. 339, at para.138; Radicati di Brozolo (2005) 315 *Recueil des Cours* 265. **16–145**

See also *Gater Assets Ltd v Nak Naftogaz Ukrainiy (No.2)* [2008] EWHC 237 (Comm.), [2008] 1 Lloyd's Rep. 479. **16–146**

NOTE 70. Add: *R v V* [2008] EWHC 1531 (Comm.), [2009] 1 Lloyd's Rep. 97 (a challenge under s.68, where the *lex causae* and *lex arbitri* were English law).

NOTE 71. Add: *World Duty Free Co Ltd v Kenya* (2007) 46 Int. Leg. Mat. 339 (holding that a contract procured by a bribe was contrary both to the international public policy of English law, as well as being contrary to transnational public policy, and accordingly was unenforceable by the arbitral tribunal); Sayed, *Corruption in International Trade and Commercial Arbitration* (2004).

NOTE 73. Add: *Bad Ass Coffee Company of Hawaii Inc v Bad Ass Enterprises Inc* 2007 ABQB 581, [2008] 1 W.W.R. 738.

NOTE 76, applied in *R v V* [2008] EWHC 1531 (Comm.), [2009] 1 Lloyd's Rep. 97.

NOTE 77. See also: Gee (2006) 22 Arb. Int. 337. **16–147**

NOTE 78. See also *Accentuate Ltd v ASIGRA Inc* [2009] EWHC 2655 (QB), [2009] 2 Lloyd's Rep. 599, [88]. The French Court of Cassation has held that a breach of a mandatory provision of European law may constitute a ground of international public policy upon which a French court may refuse to enforce an arbitral award. But the court is entitled to limit its review to an examination of whether the arbitral tribunal considered the issue of European law. Where it did so, the court should only refuse to enforce the resulting award if the tribunal misapplied European law in a flagrant manner: *SNF v Cytec Industries BV* (June 4, 2008). **16–148**

This paragraph was noted with approval in *ED & F Man Sugar Ltd v Lendoudis* [2007] EWHC 2268 (Comm.), [2008] 1 All E.R. 952, where, however, it was also observed (*obiter*) that the right to enforce a foreign judgment on an arbitral award may be important where an action on the award **16–160** is already barred by limitation. In such a case, it is not contrary to public policy to allow an action to enforce a judgment on the award: [53]–[55].

E. *Arbitration And Investment Disputes*

**16–169** NOTE 28. Add: McLachlan, Shore and Weiniger, *International Investment Arbitration: Substantive Principles* (2007); Muchlinski, Ortino and Schreuer, *The Oxford Handbook of International Investment Law* (2008); Newcombe and Paradell, *Law and Practice of Investment Treaties: Standards of Treatment* (2008); Dolzer and Schreuer, *Principles of International Investment Law* (2008); Douglas, *The International Law of Investment Claims* (2009).

NOTE 29. The International Law Commission has now concluded its work: *Diplomatic Protection: Text of the Draft Articles with Commentaries thereto* (Dugard, Special Rapporteur) in Report of the International Law Commission on its Fifty-eighth Session (2006), Official Records of the General Assembly Sixty-first Session, Supp. No.10, UN Doc. A/61/10, 22–100.

NOTE 30. See also *Case concerning Ahmadou Sadio Diallo (Republic of Guinea v Democratic Republic of Congo)*, I.C.J., Preliminary Objections, Judgment of May 24, 2007.

NOTE 37. See also *City of London v Sancheti* [2008] EWCA Civ 1283, [2009] 1 Lloyd's Rep. 117.

**16–171** The future of BITs entered into by Member States of the European Union has been called into question by two important developments in Europe.

First, the European Court was called upon to consider the compatibility of BITs with Member States' obligations under European law in three cases: Case C–205/06 *Commission of the European Communities v Republic of Austria* [2009] E.C.R. I–1301; Case C–249/06 *Commission of the European Communities v Kingdom of Sweden* [2009] E.C.R. I–1335; Case C–118/07 *Commission of the European Communities v Republic of Finland*, November 19, 2009. Prior to their accession to the European Union, the Respondent States had entered into BITs with third states, containing free transfer of capital provisions. The European Court held that these provisions were incompatible with the powers of the European Council to impose restrictions on the free transfer of capital. Accordingly the Respondent states were in breach of the obligations which they had assumed under EC Treaty, Art.307, to take all appropriate steps to eliminate incompatibilities with Community law found in agreements with third states entered into prior to accession to the Union.

Second, under Art.207 of the Lisbon Treaty on the Functioning of the European Union (December 13, 2007), the Member States transferred to the Union competence in investment matters. On July 7, 2010, the European Commission issued a Communication and a Proposal for a Regulation as to implementation of Art.207: European Commission, *Towards a comprehensive*

*European international investment policy*, COM(2010)343; *Proposal for a Regulation of the European Parliament and of the Council establishing transitional arrangements for bilateral investment agreements between Member States and third countries*, COM(2010)344. The proposed Regulation would, during a transitional period of five years, authorise Member States to maintain existing BITs in force, provided that they have been notified to the Commission. But it would give the Commission the power to decide whether to authorize negotiation and conclusion of future BITs in light of their compatibility with European law. In its policy statement, the Commission proposes that the European Union should negotiate investment agreements directly with third states. The statement endorses investor-state arbitration as a means of dispute settlement and supports EU accession to the ICSID Convention (noting that this would require an amendment to the ICSID Convention).

NOTE 39. Add: McLachlan, Shore and Weiniger, *International Investment Arbitration: Substantive Principles* (2007); Paulsson, *Denial of Justice in International Law* (2005); Muchlinski, Ortino and Schreuer, *The Oxford Handbook of International Investment Law* (2008); Newcombe and Paradell, *Law and Practice of Investment Treaties: Standards of Treatment* (2008); Dolzer and Schreuer, *Principles of International Investment Law* (2008).

NOTE 41. For recent examples of hybrid choices of law to govern State contracts see: *Channel Tunnel Group Ltd v Secretary of State for Transport of the United Kingdom of Great Britain and Northern Ireland* (entry at para. 16–053, above) and *Svenska Petroleum Exploration AB v Lithuania (No.2)* [2006] EWCA Civ 1529, [2007] Q.B. 886. **16–173**

NOTE 46. On choice of law in investment treaty arbitration generally see: McLachlan (2008) 14 ICCA Congress Series 95. **16–175**

NOTE 49. Add *Azurix Corp v Argentina,* Decision on Annulment (September 1, 2009), [136]–[137], and *Yukos Universal Ltd (Isle of Man) v Russian Federation* (Interim Award on Jurisdiction and Admissibility, PCA, November 30, 2009, (2010) 22 World Trade & Arb. Mat. 279). In the latter decision (following *Kardassopoulos v Georgia* (Decision on Jurisdiction, ICSID, July 6, 2007), the Tribunal applied Energy Charter Treaty ("ECT"), Art.45, so as to find that it had jurisdiction over the Russian Federation in respect of a dispute which had arisen during the period within which the ECT was provisionally applied in Russia and before Russia had formally notified its intention not to ratify the ECT.

NOTE 50. Add: *Aguas del Tunari SA v Bolivia* (Decision on Jurisdiction) (2005) 20 ICSID Rev.–FILJ 450 (noted Vandevelde (2007) 101 A.J.I.L. 179); *LG&E Energy Corp v Argentina* (2006) 18 World Trade & Arb. Mat. 199 (noted Fouret [2007] *Revue de l'arbitrage* 249) (applying the doctrine of necessity under international law in the construction of the obligations of the host State under a BIT) but *cf. Enron Corp v Argentine Republic* (ICSID Case No. ARB/01/3, May 22, 2007); and *Siemens AG v Argentina* (2007) 19 World Trade & Arb. Mat. 103.

Add: *CMS Gas Transmission Co v Argentine Republic* (Decision on Annulment) (2007) 19 World Trade & Arb. Mat. 227, at [128]–[136]; *Sempra Energy International v Argentine Republic* (2008) 20 World Trade & Arb. Mat. 117, at [325]–[391]. On the relationship between investment treaties and general international law in investment treaty arbitration see: McLachlan (2008) 57 I.C.L.Q. 361.

**16–177** The distinction between contract claims and treaty claims will be affected by a clause (found in a number of BITs) pursuant to which the host State agrees to observe any undertakings which it has entered into with regard to investments (sometimes referred to as an "umbrella clause"). The proper construction of such a clause is a controversial question (see the authorities cited in n.58 of the main work and below). Subject to the specific wording of the clause, it is submitted that the following general observations are consistent with principle. First, such a clause is effective to confer jurisdiction upon the investment arbitral tribunal in relation to contractual claims: *Siemens AG v Argentina* (2007) 19 World Trade & Arb. Mat. 103, at para.204. Second, however, where the parties have by contract chosen a specific forum to resolve their contractual dispute (for example, the courts of the host State), the arbitral tribunal should ordinarily hold the parties to that part of their contractual bargain as *lex specialis* and stay its proceedings pending a determination of the contractual dispute in the parties' chosen forum: *SGS Soc Gen de Surveillance SA v Philippines* (2004) 8 ICSID Rep. 515, at pp.557–558. Third, nevertheless, if the State has, in the exercise of its sovereign authority, subsequently altered fundamentally the nature of the contractual bargain, such conduct could constitute a free-standing claim in international law under the umbrella clause, irrespective of any contractual submission clause. To this extent, the decision of the tribunal in *El Paso Energy Intl Co v Argentina*, Decision on Jurisdiction (ICSID Case No. ARB/03/15, April 17, 2006) (followed in *Pan American Energy Int Co v Argentina*, Decision on Preliminary Objections (ICSID Case No.ARB/03/13 and *Sempra Energy International v Argentine Republic* (2008) 20 World Trade & Arb. Mat. 117, at [310]) can be accepted. But it is submitted that those decisions may have gone too far to the extent that they held that an umbrella clause can never be effective to submit contractual claims generally to the jurisdiction of an investment arbitral tribunal, unless the contract includes a stabilization clause. Fourth, an umbrella clause which protects "any obligations it may have entered into with regard to investments" protects specific consensual obligations arising independently of the BIT itself. It does not cover general requirements of host state law. Fifth, such a clause does not change the proper law or the content of the obligation in question, nor confer benefits on persons other than the parties to that obligation: *CMS Gas Transmission Co v Argentine Republic* (Decision on Annulment) (2007) 19 World Trade & Arb. Mat. 227, at [95]. See further: McLachlan, Shore and Weiniger, *International Investment Arbitration: Substantive Principles* (2007), Ch.4, especially at paras 4.93–4.116; Crawford (2008) 24 Arb. Int. 351.

NOTE 57. Add *Azurix Corp v Argentina,* Decision on Annulment (September 1, 2009), [146]–[147].

NOTE 60. For an example of the enforcement of an ICSID Additional Facility award under NAFTA in the United States see *International Thunderbird Gaming Corp v United Mexican States*, 473 F. Supp. 2d 80 (D.C. 2007). **16–178**

NOTE 64. This statement of the law has now been considered and approved in England: *ETI Euro Telecom International NV v Republic of Bolivia* [2008] EWCA Civ 880, [2009] 1 W.L.R. 665 at [108]. **16–179**

On *Republic of Ecuador v Occidental Exploration & Production Co* [2005] EWCA Civ 1116, [2006] 1 W.L.R. 70 see O'Keefe [2006] C.L.J. 259; Carr [2006] L.M.C.L.Q. 257. On the subsequent hearing of the challenge under Arbitration Act 1996, ss.67 and 68, the Court upheld the award: *Republic of Ecuador v Occidental Exploration & Production Co (No.2)* [2006] EWHC 345 (Comm.), [2006] 1 Lloyd's Rep. 773, affirmed [2007] EWCA Civ 656. So, too, in *Czech Republic v European Media Ventures SA* [2007] EWHC 2851 (Comm.), [2008] 1 Lloyd's Rep. 186, the court entertained an application under s.67(1)(a) of the 1996 Act to set aside an award on jurisdiction in a non-ICSID investment treaty arbitration. It approved the test applied in *Republic of Ecuador v Occidental Exploration & Production Co (No.2)*, above, namely that the question was whether the arbitral tribunal was correct in its decision on jurisdiction, not whether it was entitled to reach the decision that it did. The court found, construing the applicable BIT in accordance with Public International Law principles, that the tribunal's decision was correct. So too, the Paris Court of Appeals, in considering its first challenge to an award under a BIT, has held that it must conduct an independent examination, in fact and in law, of the arguments of the parties as to the jurisdiction of the arbitral tribunal: *République tchèque v Nreka* (entry at para.16–133, n.36, above). In *Republic of Argentina v BG Group plc*, 2010 WL 2925946 (D.D.C. 2010), a United States District Court held the standards of the Federal Arbitration Act applicable to review of an arbitral award issued in Washington by an ICC Tribunal under a BIT. It considered that the Court was entitled to review the merits of the award in order to determine whether the tribunal had exceeded its powers, but, applying *Stolt-Nielsen SA v AnimalFeeds International Corp*, 130 S. Ct. 1758 (2010) that the question was whether the "arbitrator stray[ed] from interpretation and application of the agreement and effectively dispense[d] his own brand of industrial justice." **16–181**

**16–183** NOTE 71. Add: *MTD Equity Sdn. Bhd. v Chile,* Decision on Annulment (2007) 19 World Trade Arb. Mat. 3, (2007) 13 ICSID Rep. 500; *Azurix v Argentina* (Decision on Annulment) ICSID Case No ARB/01/12 (September 1, 2009); *MCI Power Group LC v Ecuador* (Decision on Annulment) ICSID Case No ARB/03/6 (October 19, 2009); *Rumeli Telekom A/S v Kazakhstan* (Decision on Annulment) ICSID Case No ARB/05/16 (March 25, 2010); *Helnan International Hotels AS v Egypt* (Decision on Annulment) ICSID Case No ARB/05/19 (June 14, 2010); *Sempra Energy International v Argentina* (Decision on Annulment) ICSID Case No ARB/02/16 (June 29, 2010); *Enron Creditors Recovery Corp v Argentina* (Decision on Annulment) ICSID Case No ARB/01/3 (July 30, 2010); *Compañia de Aguas del Aconquija SA and Compagnie Générale des Eaux/ Vivendi Universal ('Vivendi') v Argentina (No 2)* (Decision on Annulment) ICSID Case No ARB/97/3 (August 10, 2010).

NOTE 73. On the enforcement of ICSID awards see: Baldwin, Kantor and Nolan (2006) 23 J. Int. Arb. 1.

## Chapter 17

# MARRIAGE

### 1. FORMAL VALIDITY

The Rule was cited with approval by Sir Mark Potter P. in *Wilkinson v Kitzinger (No.2)* [2006] EWHC 2022 (Fam.), [2007] 1 F.C.R. 183 (as to which see entry at para.17–088 below). **17R–001**

In *Alfonso-Brown v Milwood* [2006] EWHC 642 (Fam.), [2007] 2 F.L.R. 265, a ceremony took place in Ghana. If it were a marriage it was void for bigamy, but in proceedings for nullity the court examined whether what occurred was indeed a marriage ceremony under Ghanaian custom or an engagement ceremony. The nature of the ceremony and the intentions of the parties were treated as governed by local law; there was no finding as to domicile and no separate treatment of the issue of consent. **17–004**

Note 17. See also *Veleta v Canada (Minister of Citizenship and Immigration)* 254 D.L.R. (4th) 484 (Fed. Ct.) (reversed on other grounds, 268 D.L.R. (4th) 513). **17–005**

In *Burns v Burns* [2007] EWHC 2492 (Fam.), [2008] 1 F.L.R. 813 (ceremony in hot air balloon over California), as in *Gereis v Yagoub* [1997] 1 F.L.R. 854, the marriage was held void but the court recognised the existence of a category of a "non-marriage" or a "non-existent marriage". In *Hudson v Leigh* [2009] EWHC 1306 (Fam.), [2009] 2 F.L.R. 1129 which concerned a religious ceremony in South Africa intended by the parties and the officiant to have no legal effect and to be a precursor to a civil marriage in England, the court held that the ceremony came within the category of "non-existent marriage". Reliance was placed on *A-M v A-M (divorce: jurisdiction: validity of marriage)* [2001] 2 F.L.R. 6 (recognising that the relevant material was obiter) and *Gandhi v Patel* [2002] 1 F.L.R. 603 and academic writings including Probert (2000) 22 Legal Studies 398. *Kassim v Kassim* [1962] P. 224 and *Corbett v Corbett (otherwise Ashley)* [1971] P. 83 were distinguished, both being cases in which the parties clearly wished and intended by the ceremonies concerned to become married. The court observed that questionable ceremonies should be classified on a case by case basis, relevant factors including (but not being limited to): (a) whether the ceremony or event set out or purported to be a lawful marriage; (b) whether it bore all or enough of the hallmarks of marriage; (c) whether the three key participants (most **17–007** especially the officiating official) believed, intended and understood the ceremony as giving rise to the status of lawful marriage; and (d) the reasonable perceptions, understandings and beliefs of those in attendance. An Islamic marriage in England was held to be a "non-marriage" in *A v H* [2009] EWHC 636 (Fam.), [2010] 1 F.L.R. 1. *Cf. Ben Hasem v Al Shayif* [2008] EWHC 2380 (Fam.), [2009] 1 F.L.R. 115, where a nullity decree was granted in the case of a marriage which both parties knew to be bigamous and therefore of no legal effect; but the "non-existent marriage" point was not argued. On the grant of a declaration in a "non-existent marriage" case, see entry at para.18R–159, below.

**17–011** *Apt v Apt* [1948] P. 83 (CA) was applied in *CB (Validity of marriage: proxy marriage) Brazil* [2008] UKAIT 00080, where both parties were domiciled in England and the marriage was celebrated by proxy in Brazil. The tribunal rejected an argument that in the immigration context the law of the domicile was to be applied to govern the formal validity of a marriage.

**17–013** The marriage in *Westminster City Council v C* [2008] EWCA Civ 198, [2009] Fam. 11 was by telephone, the bride, the bridegroom's father (who was possibly acting as proxy for the husband) and many relatives being in Bangladesh and the husband in England. Counsel argued the case on the assumption that the marriage took place in Bangladesh; the court proceeded on that footing but expressed the wish that the issue be fully argued in an appropriate case.

For discussion of the validity of a marriage by telephone between parties in Saudi Arabia and Somalia, see Shah (2010) 6 Utrecht L. R. 17 at 24–25.

**17–020** The English case-law extends to cases in which the form of marriage available under the *lex loci* is morally unacceptable to the parties. A decision of the Family Court of Australia, *Nygh & Kasey* [2010] FamCA 145, held that a sincerely held conscientious objection to the registration (as opposed to the celebration) of a marriage excused compliance with the *lex loci*. The wife's feminist principles led to her objecting to the registration of an otherwise valid marriage in Thailand as this would require her under Thai law to have her husband's surname; this was held a sufficient basis on which the marriage could be recognised under the common law rules applicable under Marriage Act 1961 (Cth), s.88E.

**17–029** Section 22 of the Foreign Marriage Act 1892 now applies where at least one of the parties to the marriage is a person who is: (a) a member of HM Forces serving in the foreign territory concerned; or (b) a civilian subject to service discipline (within the meaning of the Armed Forces Act 2006) of a description prescribed by Order in Council and who is employed in that territory; or (c) a child of such a person who has his home with that person in that territory. Other conditions may be prescribed by Order in Council. Foreign Marriage

Act 1892, s.22 as amended by the Foreign Marriage (Amendment) Act 1988, s.6 and the Armed Forces Act 2006, Sch.16, para.5.

The Registration of Births, Deaths and Marriages (Scotland) Act 1965 is amended by the Local Electoral Administration and Registration Services (Scotland) Act 2006, ss.37–47. **17–040**

Simple cohabitation has effects in the law of some countries. See Carruthers (2008) 12 Edin.L.Rev. 51. **17–045**

It was held in *Lester and Lester* [2007] Fam. CA 186 that in the absence of a finding that a marriage ceremony took place, even one of questionable validity, the evidence in relation to cohabitation and repute needs to be substantial to allow the presumption to operate. **17–047**

Note 60. Add: *Cf. A v H* [2009] EWHC 636 (Fam.), [2010] 1 F.L.R. 1 where the cohabitation after an Islamic ceremony not constituting a valid marriage was too brief to attract the presumption.

## 2. CAPACITY

The Rule was cited with approval by Sir Mark Potter P. in *Wilkinson v Kitzinger (No.2)* [2006] EWHC 2022 (Fam.), [2007] 1 F.C.R. 183 (as to which see entry at para.17–088 below). **17R–054**

Note 77. Marriage (Scotland) Act 1977, s.2, is amended by SI 2009/1892, Sch.1, para.1.

The Rule is of general application and is not limited to cases in which the marriage was precluded in the country of the domicile of one of the parties: *Westminster City Council v C* [2008] EWCA Civ 198, [2009] Fam. 11. **17–056**

The possibility that a marriage, invalid under the dual domicile test, might be recognised as valid under the alternative tests of intended matrimonial home and real and substantial connection was considered in *Westminster City Council v C* [2008] EWCA Civ 198, [2009] Fam. 11, where however all tests led to the same result, that the marriage was invalid. **17–063**

Note 21. Marriage (Scotland) Act 1977, s.2 is amended by SI 2009/1892, Sch.1, para.1. **17–070**

In *B v United Kingdom* (App. No. 36536/02) (2005) 19 B.H.R.C. 430, [2006] 1 F.L.R. 35 the European Court of Human Rights held that the inability under English law of a father-in-law and daughter-in-law to marry after their previous marriages had ended in divorce violated their right to marry under Art.12 of the European Convention on Human Rights. Such a marriage is now **17–072** possible in England (SI 2007/438 repealing Marriage Act 1949, subs.1(4)–(8)), Scotland (Family Law (Scotland) Act 2006, s.1) and Northern Ireland (Law Reform (Miscellaneous Provisions) (Northern Ireland) Order 2006 (NI 14), Art.3 amending the Family Law (Miscellaneous Provisions) (Northern Ireland) Order 1984 (NI 14)).

**17–078** *Pugh v Pugh* [1951] P. 482 was cited, without disapproval, in *Re X (Children) (Parental Order)* [2008] EWHC 3030 (Fam.), [2009] Fam. 71.

**17–088** In *Wilkinson v Kitzinger (No.2)* [2006] EWHC 2022 (Fam.), [2007] 1 F.C.R. 183 two persons of the same sex, both domiciled in England, married under the law of British Columbia. Under the Civil Partnership Act 2004, s.215 this was a valid overseas relationship and fell to be treated in England as a civil partnership. The court held that the parties, being domiciled in England, lacked capacity to marry one another. It rejected an argument that the ordinary rules that capacity be governed by the law of the domicile of the parties be set aside on the basis of the Human Rights Act 1998 (holding that there was no incompatibility with any Convention right). It also held that the Matrimonial Causes Act 1973, s.11(c) was clear and that it would be contrary to public policy to recognise the marriage as such. See Scherpe [2007] C.L.J. 32 and on the general issue of the recognition of foreign relationships, Norrie (2006) 2 J. Priv. Int. L. 137.

**17–093** See on the Royal Marriages Act 1772 generally, Cretney (2008) 124 L.Q.R. 218.

**17–101** See now the Family Law (Scotland) Act 2006, s.38(3).

**17–116** In *Westminster City Council v C* [2008] EWCA Civ 198, [2009] Fam. 11, where the marriage was invalid under the dual domicile test, the court also based its decision not to recognise it on public policy grounds; the mental state of the husband was such that the marriage would be potentially highly injurious to him.

## 3. CONSENT OF THE PARTIES

**17R–118** See *Alfonso-Brown v Milwood* [2006] EWHC 642, [2007] 2 F.L.R. 265 and entry at para.17–004, above. In *Torfehnejad v Salimi* (2006) 276 D.L.R. (4th) 733 (Ont.) fraud as to the intentions of one party was treated (wrongly, it is submitted) as a matter of formalities; but in *Davison v Sweeney* (2005) 255 D.L.R. (4th) 757 (BC) it was held that alleged absence of consent (on account of intoxication) was a matter for the domicile of the party concerned.

**17–119** Under Pt 4A of the Family Law Act 1996, as inserted by the Forced Marriage (Civil Protection) Act 2007, the High Court or a county court has power to make a forced marriage protection order for the purposes of protecting a person from being forced into a marriage or from any attempt to force a person into a marriage; or to protect a person who has been forced into a marriage (Family Law Act 1996, s.63A as inserted by the Forced Marriage (Civil Protection) Act 2007). Force includes coercion by threats or other psychological means (s.63A(6)). A forced marriage protection order may contain such prohibitions, restrictions or requirements and such other terms as the court considers appropriate for the purposes of the order; the terms of an order may relate to conduct outside England and Wales as well as (or instead of) conduct within England and Wales (s.63B(1),(2)(a)).

For a comparative study of English and French approaches to the issue of forced marriages, see Clark and Richards (2008) 57 I.C.L.Q. 501.

NOTE 41. *Singh v Singh*, 2005 S.L.T. 749 was decided before the Family Law (Scotland) Act 2006 was enacted; see now s.38(2) of that Act. **17–121**

## 4. POLYGAMOUS MARRIAGES

British Nationality Act 1981, s.6(2), is amended by Borders, Citizenship and Immigration Act 2009, s.40(1) (not yet in force). It no longer refers expressly to marriage but speaks of a "relevant family association", to be defined by regulations. **17–199**

Council Directive 2003/86/EC of September 22, 2003 on the right to family reunification ([2003] O.J. L215/12), Art.4(4) provides that in the event of a polygamous marriage, where the sponsor already has a spouse living with him in the territory of a Member State, the Member State concerned must not authorise the family reunification of a further spouse. The United Kingdom is not bound by this Directive but follows the same policy on this point. See Shah (2003) 52 I.C.L.Q. 359.

A decision as to the validity of a marriage for one purpose (e.g., immigration) does not preclude a different agency from reaching a different conclusion for another, e.g. social security: *R (on the application of Nahar) v Social Security Commissioners* [2001] EWHC 1049 (Admin), [2002] 2 F.C.R. 442 (affirmed on different grounds, [2002] EWCA Civ 859) (which did not involve polygamy).

National Assistance Act 1948, s.42 is repealed by Health and Social Care Act 2008, Sch.15 Pt 5. **17–201**

National Assistance Act 1948, ss. 42 and 43 are repealed by Health and Social Care Act 2008, Sch.15 Pt 5. **17–206**

## 5. CIVIL PARTNERSHIPS

The Registration of Births, Deaths and Marriages (Special Provisions) Act 1957 is amended by the Armed Forces Act 2006, Sch.16, paras 39 to 42. **17R–207**

**17–209** For Scots law, see Carruthers, Electronic J. Comp. L. 10.3 (December 2006).

**17–211** Note 58. The Army Act 1955, the Armed Forces Act 1966 and the cited provisions of the Armed Forces Acts 1976 and 1981 are repealed, and the definition of "Her Majesty's forces" is now in the Armed Forces Act 2006, s.374 (not yet in force). Section 245(2) of the Civil Partnerships Act 2004 is amended accordingly by the Armed Forces Act 2006, Sch.16, para.241. The Registration of Births, Deaths and Marriages (Special Provisions) Act 1957 is amended by the Armed Forces Act 2006, Sch.16, paras 39 to 42 (not yet in force).

**17–212** The question of the recognition of rights accorded in some legal systems to unmarried cohabitants who are not within a civil partnership or equivalent relationship has yet to be considered in England. See Devers (2003) 5 Yb. P.I.L. 191. For the rights given to cohabitants in Scotland, see the Family Law (Scotland) Act 2006, ss.25–31.

The Civil Partnership Act 2004, s.213 is amended by SI 2007/2914.

**17–213** On Netherlands partnerships, see Boele-Woelki, Curry-Sumner, Jansen and Schrama (2006) 8 Yb. P.I.L. 27. For a wider comparative study, see Curry-Sumner, *All's well that ends registered? The Substantive and Private International Law Aspects of Non-Marital Registered Relationships in Europe* (Antwerp: European Family Law Series No. 11, Intersentia, 2005).

**17–214** See *Wilkinson v Kitzinger (No.2)* [2006] EWHC 2022 (Fam.), [2007] 1 F.C.R. 183 and entry at para.17–088, above.

## Chapter 18

# MATRIMONIAL CAUSES

## 1. DIVORCE, NULLITY AND JUDICIAL SEPARATION

### A. *Jurisdiction of the English courts*

See Boele-Woelki and González Beilfuss (eds.), *Brussels IIbis: Its impact and application in the Member States* (Antwerp: European Family Law Series No. 14, Intersentia). **18–003**

The constitutionality in Ireland of Brussels II and Brussels II Revised was established in *YNR v MN* [2005] 4 I.R. 552.

The exercise of jurisdiction is subject to the rule giving priority to the court first seised, as to which see Clause (2) of Rule 94 and para.18–244. **18–004**

Although the making of Regulation 2201/2003 gives the European Union exclusive competence in certain areas, Council Regulation No 664/2009 of July 7, 2009 ([2009] L 200/46) establishes a procedure for the negotiation and conclusion of agreements between Member States and third countries concerning jurisdiction, recognition and enforcement of judgments and decisions in matrimonial matters, matters of parental responsibility and matters relating to maintenance obligations, and the law applicable to matters relating to maintenance obligations.

In the context of Art.3 of Council Regulation 2201/2003, habitual residence is to be given an autonomous definition developed by the European Court, in other contexts, and by the French Cour de Cassation: *L-K v K (No.2)* [2006] EWHC 3280 (Fam.), [2007] 2 F.L.R. 729; *Marinos v Marinos* [2007] EWHC 2047 (Fam.), [2007] 2 F.L.R. 1018; *Munro v Munro* [2007] EWHC 3315 (Fam.), [2007] 1 F.L.R. 1613; *Z v Z (Divorce: Jurisdiction)* [2009] EWHC 2626 (Fam.), [2010] 1 FLR 694. The decisions of the European Court cited were Case 13/73 *Angenieux v Hakenberg* [1973] E.C.R. 935, Case 76/76 *Di Paolo v Office National de L'Emploi* [1977] E.C.R. 315, Case C–297/89 *Rigsadvokaten v Ryborg* [1991] E.C.R. I–1943, Case C–102/91 *Knoch v Bundesanstalt für Arbeit* [1992] E.C.R. I–4341, Case C–452/93 *Magdalena Fernández v European Commission* [1994] E.C.R. I–4295 and Case C–90/97 *Swaddling v Adjudication Officer* [1999] E.C.R. I–1075; the Cour de Cassation decision was *Moore v Moore* (First Civil Chamber, December 14, 2005). The definition of habitual residence in *Swaddling v Adjudication Officer* was **18–005** cited in *PM v Devins* [2007] IEHC 380, [2008] 2 I.R. 707, but the matter was not the subject of a clear decision.

The meaning derived from these authorities is that a person is habitually resident in the place which is the habitual centre of his interests. On the interests to be weighed, the importance of which will vary from case to case: see *Marinos v Marinos* at [80] to [83]; they may include employment, educational, emotional, personal and family interests, a balancing exercise more difficult than the assessment undertaken by the English courts in considering habitual residence in other contexts. See Lamont (2007) 3 J. Priv.Int.L. 261.

In this context, a person may only have one habitual residence: *Marinos v Marinos* [2007] EWHC 2047 (Fam.), [2007] 2 F.L.R. 1018; *Munro v Munro* [2007] EWHC 3315 (Fam.), [2007] 1 F.L.R. 1613; *Re A; HA v MB (Brussels II Revised; Article 11(7) Application)* [2007] EWHC 2016 (Fam.), [2008] 1 F.L.R. 289.

In Case C–523/07 *Proceedings Brought by A* [2009] E.C.R. I–2805, at [38], the European Court indicated that decisions on the meaning of habitual residence in one area of European Union law could not always be transposed so as to apply in another area (in the instant case the question of the habitual residence of a child). That case was distinguished in *Z v Z (Divorce: Jurisdiction)* [2009] EWHC 2626 (Fam.), [2010] 1 FLR 694, where the context was Art.3 of Brussels II *bis* rather than Art.8.

Differing judicial opinions have been expressed as to the correctness of the assumption in the text to note 20 that in the fifth and sixth indents of Art.3(1) of Council Regulation 2201/2003 (reflected in the Rule at (e) and (f)), "resided" means "habitually resided". In *Marinos v Marinos* [2007] EWHC 2047 (Fam.), [2007] 2 F.L.R. 1018 at [45] to [49], Munby J. took the view that the authors of the Regulation had deliberately distinguished between the two concepts, so that for the period of six or twelve months only residence *simpliciter* need be established. In *Munro v Munro* [2007] EWHC 3315 (Fam.), [2007] 1 F.L.R. 1613 at [45] to [53], Bennett J. expressed the contrary view, relying essentially on the dominant role given to habitual residence in Art.3 as stressed in the Borrás report on the equivalent material in the earlier draft Convention. In neither case was a resolution of this issue essential.

**18–006** That British nationality is irrelevant in this context, that of Art.3(1)(b) of Regulation 2201/2003, was confirmed in *Re N (Jurisdiction)* [2007] EWHC 1274 (Fam.), [2007] 2 F.L.R. 1196.

In C–168/08 *Hadadi v Hadadi* [2009] E.C.R. I–6871, the European Court had to consider the case in which both spouses were dual nationals of the same two Member States. Rejecting an argument that the parties could only rely on the more "effective" nationality, the court held that under Art.3(1)(b) of Regulation 2201/2003 the parties were free to invoke the jurisdiction of either State. The case arose under the transitional provisions in Art.64(4) which exceptionally require a court to rule on the jurisdiction of a court in another Member State, but the decision must apply more generally.

The correct interpretation of Arts 6 and 7 of Regulation 2201/2003 was the subject of a decision of the European Court in Case C–68/07 *Lopez v Lizazo* [2007] E.C.R. I–10403, [2008] Fam. 21 (see Requejo Isidro (2008) 10 Yb. P.I.L. 579). A wife, of Swedish nationality but habitually resident in France, sought a divorce in the Swedish courts from her husband, of Cuban nationality and habitually resident in Cuba. The Swedish court asked for a preliminary ruling: were Arts 6 and 7 to be interpreted as meaning that where, in divorce proceedings, a respondent is not habitually resident in a Member State and is not a national of a Member State, the courts of a Member State can base their jurisdiction to hear the petition on their national law, even though the courts of another Member State have jurisdiction under Art.3 of the Regulation? **18–010**

An affirmative answer to that question would be based on Art.6 ("A spouse who: (a) is habitually resident in the territory of a Member State; or (b) is a national of a Member State, or, in the case of the United Kingdom and Ireland, has his or her 'domicile' in the territory of one of the latter Member States; may be sued in another Member State only in accordance with Arts 3, 4 and 5.")

In the instant case, the respondent spouse did not fall within the terms of this Article, and it was therefore arguable that the jurisdiction created by Arts 3 to 5 was not exclusive. The European Court gave a negative answer. In its view the clear words of Art.7(1) ("Where no court of a Member State has jurisdiction pursuant to Arts 3, 4 and 5, jurisdiction shall be determined, in each Member State, by the laws of that State") meant that national grounds of jurisdiction could be relied upon only if no court in a Member State had jurisdiction. In the instant case, the habitual residence of the wife gave the French courts jurisdiction under the fifth indent to Art.3(1)(a) and Swedish national law could not be relied upon.

The court held that Art.6 did not affect that position. It accepted that Art.6 does not prohibit a respondent who has neither his habitual residence in a Member State nor the nationality of a Member State from being sued before a court of a Member State pursuant to the rules of jurisdiction provided for by the national law of that State. That might be the case in accordance with Art.7(1) where no court of a Member State had jurisdiction pursuant to Arts 3 to 5. However, it could not be inferred from this that Art.6 laid down a general rule that the jurisdiction of the courts of a Member State to hear questions relating to divorce in respect of a respondent who did not have his habitual residence in a Member State and was not a national of a Member State is to be determined, in all cases, under national law, including where a Member State had jurisdiction pursuant to Arts 3 to 5 of the regulation.

In effect, priority is given to Art.7 where there appears to be some inconsistency between its language and that of Art.6. The court offers an explanation which, it is submitted, is wholly unconvincing. It argues that a different view would be contrary to the objective pursued by Regulation 2201/2003, which "aims to lay down uniform conflict of law rules for divorce in order to ensure a free movement of persons which is as wide as possible". It follows that Regulation 2201/2003 applies also to nationals of non-Member States whose links with the territory of a Member State were sufficiently close, in keeping with the grounds of jurisdiction laid down in the Regulation, grounds which, according to Recital 12 in the preamble to the predecessor Regulation 1347/2000, were based on the rule that there must be a real link between the party concerned and the Member State exercising jurisdiction. Such a link existed in the instant case with France and not with Sweden.

### B. *Choice of law*

**18–028** In July 2006, the European Commission made a proposal (COM (2006) 399 final) for a Council Regulation amending Regulation (EC) No 2201/2003 as regards jurisdiction and introducing rules concerning applicable law in matrimonial matters ("Rome III"). See Gaertner (2006) 2 J. Priv. Int. L. 99, Fiorini (2008) 22 Int. J. Law, Policy and the Family 178, and Clarkson (2008) 4 J. Priv. Int. L. 421; and for the discussions which led to the United Kingdom's decision not to participate the account given by Thorpe L.J. in *Radmacher v Granatino* [2009] EWCA Civ 649, [2009] 2 F.C.R. 645 at [6]–[9]. See also *Granatino v Radmacher* [2010] UKSC 42, [2010] 3 W.L.R. 1367, at [104]–[105]. In June 2008 the Council noted the lack of the unanimity needed to proceed with the proposal Regulation, but it became clear that some Member States (eventually Austria, Bulgaria, France, Hungary, Italy, Luxembourg, Romania, Slovenia and Spain) wished to proceed with certain aspects of the proposal by way of enhanced cooperation. In March 2010, the Commission presented a proposal for a Council Regulation implementing enhanced cooperation in the area of the law applicable to divorce and legal separation (COM (2010) 105 final/2). The proposal concerns only applicable law and not jurisdiction. The proposed Regulation would introduce an element of party autonomy, with the parties being able to designate the applicable law, subject to certain safeguards, from a list of options: (a) the law of the State of the spouses' habitual residence at the time of conclusion of the agreement; (b) the law of the State of the spouses' last habitual residence if one of them still lives there at the time of conclusion of the agreement; (c) the law of the State of nationality of one of the spouses at the time of conclusion of the agreement; and (d) the *lex fori*. In the absence of a choice by the parties, a "cascade" of possibly applicable laws would be established. Divorce and legal separation would be subject to the law of the State: (a) where the spouses are habitually resident at the time the court is seised; or, failing that, (b) where the spouses were last habitually resident, provided that the period of residence did not end more than one year before the court was seised, in so far as one of the spouses still resides in that State at the time the court is seised; or, failing that, (c) of which both spouses are nationals at the time the court is seised; or, failing that, (d) where the court is seised.

A few States in the United States have introduced "covenant marriages" the parties to which limit the grounds of divorce to fault-based grounds. It is submitted that the English courts would not treat this as a distinct from of marriage, and would apply the ordinary rules of English divorce law to any petition for the dissolution of such a marriage. See Ng (2007) 44 Alta.L.Rev. 815.

Provision equivalent to that in the Divorce (Religious Marriages) Act 2002 is made in Scotland by the Divorce (Scotland) Act 1976, s.3A as inserted by the Family Law (Scotland) Act 2006, s.15. **18–030**

See also *R (on the application of Baiai) v Secretary of State for the Home Department* [2008] UKHL 53, [2009] 1 A.C. 287 where the House of Lords re-affirmed the rule of public policy that a "sham" marriage is still a valid marriage in English law. **18–041**

*Burns v Burns* [2007] EWHC 2492 (Fam.), [2008] 1 F.L.R. 813 concerned a marriage in California (aboard a hot air balloon) before the relevant licence had been issued. The marriage was invalid in the law of California, being classified as "putative" rather than either void or voidable. An English decree of nullity was granted, declaring the marriage void. **18–042**

### C. *Recognition of foreign decrees*

#### (2) Decrees Obtained in other Regulation States

Directive 2008/52/EC on certain aspects of mediation in civil and commercial matters (see entry at para.11–013, above) applies to family law matters within its scope. It is limited to cross-border disputes as defined in Art.2. **18–056**

Text to note 95. "Judgment" in this context means the written order issued by the court: *Re A; HA v MB (Brussels II Revised; Article 11(7) Application)* [2007] EWHC 2016 (Fam.), [2008] 1 F.L.R. 289.

Text to notes 97 and 98. For the interpretation of Art.64 in the case of new Member States, see *D v D* [2007] EWCA Civ. 1277, [2008] 1 F.L.R. 1003.

Except where the procedure concerns a decision certified pursuant to Arts 11(8) and 40 to 42 of the Regulation, any interested party can apply for non-recognition of a decision, even if no application for recognition of the decision has been submitted beforehand: Case C–195/08 PPU *Inga Rinau (applicant)* [2008] E.C.R. I–5271, [2009] Fam. 51. **18–057**

#### (3) Decrees Obtained Elsewhere

In this context "appearance" requires something more than mere proof of service; there must be active participation in the proceedings of the party **18–073** concerned, either in person or through a representative, or at the very least some formal step at least equivalent to the entry of an appearance in English proceedings: *A v L* [2010] EWHC 460 (Fam.) at [70]. In that case the wife had not appeared and the English court was satisfied that the finding of the foreign court that she was resident there was incorrect.

(4) Non-proceedings Divorces and Annulments

**18–099** See *A v L* [2010] EWHC 460 (Fam.) at [60].

**18–102** It was held in *H v H (Validity of Japanese Divorce)* [2006] EWHC 2989 (Fam.), [2007] 1 F.L.R. 1318, where the equivalent passage from the 13th Edition of this work was cited with approval, that a Japanese *kyogi rikon* was a divorce obtained by proceedings: there was State regulation of the process and registration with the State authorities had substantive and not merely probative force.

A Pakistani talak was recognised in *H v H (Talaq Divorce)* [2007] EWHC 2945 (Fam.), [2008] 2 F.L.R. 857, Sumner J. citing both the dictum of Lord Scarman in *Quazi v Quazi* [1980] A.C. 744, 824 (quoted in para.18–099) and *El Fadl v El Fadl* [2000] 1 F.L.R. 175.

**18–103** In *A v L* [2010] EWHC 460 (Fam.) a talak was pronounced by telephone but the judgment does not indicate the whereabouts of the parties. It was subsequently confirmed by an Egyptian court on the basis that it was valid under the law of Libya applicable under the Egyptian rules of the conflict of laws. Sir Mark Potter P held that it was immaterial that the judicial proceedings were in a country other than that of the law applying to the talak. Recognition was refused on other grounds.

**18–113** Note 21. The reference should be to s.51(1).

**18–116** In the usual case, notice of the commencement of proceedings will suffice. In the special circumstances of *A v L* [2010] EWHC 460 (Fam.), where the husband was restrained by a *Hemain* injunction from taking further steps in the foreign court, he should have given notice to the wife of his intention, despite the injunction, to revive the foreign proceedings after their earlier adjournment. Recognition of the foreign decree was refused primarily on the basis of Family Law Act 1986, s.51(3)(ii) (see para.18–117).

**18–117** Recognition of a foreign decree was refused recognition on this ground in *A v L* [2010] EWHC 460 (Fam.).

**18–118** See *H v H (Validity of Japanese Divorce)* [2006] EWHC 2989 (Fam.), [2007] 1 F.L.R. 1318 (where there was proper notice and an appropriate opportunity to take part in the *kyogi rikon*) and *H v H (Talaq Divorce)* [2007] EWHC 2945

(Fam.), [2008] 2 F.L.R. 857 (where the wife, though brought up in Pakistan, was habitually resident and probably domiciled in England at the time of the divorce).

Recognition of a foreign decree would have been refused recognition in *A v L* [2010] EWHC 460 (Fam.) had the material before the English court established that the foreign decree had been obtained by deception; but as recognition was refused on other grounds, this point was not relied upon. In *Golubovich v Golubovich* [2010] EWCA Civ 810, divorce proceedings were commenced by W in England and shortly after by H in Moscow. H prevented the grant of a decree in the English proceedings by relying on a forged Russian decree. In order to preserve the status quo before the trial in England of an issue as to the validity of the supposed decree, the English court issued a *Hemain* injunction restraining H from taking any further steps in relation to any proceedings between the parties in Russia. In breach of that injunction, H obtained a divorce decree in Moscow. The Court of Appeal held that the decree was entitled to recognition in England and declined to refuse recognition under Family Law Act 1986, s.51(1)(c), on the ground of public policy. The Moscow court was made aware of the injunction and there were no procedural defects in that court. To refuse recognition of a divorce decree pronounced by the court in another jurisdiction within the Council of Europe, absent breach of natural justice, must be regarded as truly exceptional: at [78]. If an English judge concluded that recognition would be manifestly contrary to public policy, refusal of recognition must follow; there was no further discretion: [69]. **18–120**

### D. *Effect in England of foreign decrees*

A foreign decree recognised in England as ending the parties' marriage will prevent either party obtaining an English divorce decree purporting to dissolve the same marriage. This is the case even if the foreign decree refers to a ceremony taking place in the foreign country after an earlier ceremony in England, for what is dissolved is the marital status not a particular ceremony: *D v D (Nature of Recognition of Overseas Divorce)* [2005] EWHC 3342 (Fam.), [2006] 2 F.L.R. 825, citing the corresponding passage in the 13th edition of this work and *Thynne v Thynne* [1955] P. 272 (similar issue in domestic context, the parties having two successive ceremonies in England, the decree of divorce referring to the second). *cf. Syed v Ahmed* [2005] CSIH 72, 2006 S.C. 165, where the Inner House of the Court of Session refused, on the facts of the case, to quash a Scottish decree given after a foreign divorce between the parties which was entitled to recognition in Scotland. **18–136**

## 3. DECLARATIONS AS TO STATUS

In exceptional cases, it may be possible for the court to make other declarations relevant to a person's status. So, in *X City Council v MB* [2006] EWHC **18R–159**

168 (Fam.), [2006] 2 F.L.R. 968 the court made a declaration that an autistic adult, whose parents were contemplating his removal to Pakistan to marry his cousin, lacked capacity to marry (so that the proposed marriage would not be capable of recognition in England). As declaration that a person lacked capacity to marry on account of her mental condition was made in *Local Authority X v MM* [2009] 1 F.L.R. 443 and in *Ealing LBC v S* [2008] EWHC 636 (Fam.).

In *Hudson v Leigh* [2009] EWHC 1306 (Fam.), [2009] 2 F.L.R. 1129 a "non-existent marriage" case (see entry at para.17–007), a declaration was made in the inherent jurisdiction of the High Court that that the ceremony did not create the status of marriage as between the parties. The court held that Family Law Act 1986, s.58(5) (which forbids any declaration that a marriage was at its inception void) did not prevent the making of such a declaration.

NOTE 50. Domicile and Matrimonial Proceedings Act 1975, s.7 is amended by the Family Law (Scotland) Act 2006, Sch.2, para.1.

**18–161** NOTE 57. Add: *Westminster City Council v C* [2008] EWCA Civ 198, [2009] Fam. 11. *Cf. Hudson v Leigh* [2009] EWHC 1306 (Fam.), [2009] 2 F.L.R. 1129 (see entry at para.18R–159, above).

**18–163** It may sometimes be appropriate to adjourn an application for a declaration to enable issues to be tried in a foreign court better suited to deal with them. This course was taken in *Abbassi v Abbassi* [2006] EWCA Civ 355, [2006] 2 F.L.R. 415, where the issue concerned the alleged forgery of documents issued in Pakistan, a matter better addressed by a Pakistani court.

## 4. FINANCIAL RELIEF

### A. *Jurisdiction of the English courts*

**18R–169** Council Regulation (EC) 4/2009 of December 18, 2008 on jurisdiction, applicable law, recognition and enforcement of decisions and cooperation in matters relating to maintenance obligations ([2009] O.J. L7) ("the Maintenance Regulation") replaces the provisions of the Judgments Regulation applicable to maintenance obligations. It applies to proceedings instituted, to court settlements approved or concluded, and to authentic instruments established after June 18, 2011, subject to transitional provisions enabling the continued application of the Judgments Regulation to procedures for recognition and enforcement under way on that date (Art.75). Although the United Kingdom originally decided to opt out of the application of the Regulation, it subsequently decided to accept it (see Commission Decision 2009/451/EC of June 8, 2009, [2009] O.J. L149).

Recital (11) states: "The scope of this Regulation should cover all maintenance obligations arising from a family relationship, parentage, marriage or affinity, in order to guarantee equal treatment of all maintenance creditors. For the purposes of this Regulation, the term 'maintenance obligation' should be interpreted autonomously". This leaves unchanged the position under the Judgments Regulation, that many property issues between spouses, including property adjustment orders between spouses after a divorce, and some lump sum orders not made with maintenance in mind, remain outside the scope of the European legislation (see main work, para.18–203).

For the provisions of the Maintenance Regulation dealing with recognition and enforcement, see entry at para.18–233, below.

*Jurisdiction*

So far as the rules of jurisdiction in Chapter II (Arts 3 to 14) are concerned, the Maintenance Regulation makes more comprehensive provision. The Community rules apply even where the defendant is habitually resident in a third State; choice of court by the parties is allowed in many cases; the Regulation provides for a forum necessitatis; and there is a special rule, derived from the Hague Convention on the International Recovery of Child Support and Other Forms of Family Maintenance (2007, as to which see entry at para.18–232, below), as to jurisdiction over applications by the debtor to modify an existing maintenance decision or to have a new decision given.

The Regulation provides (Art.3) that in matters relating to maintenance obligations in Member States, jurisdiction is to lie with:

(a) the court for the place where the defendant is habitually resident; or
(b) the court for the place where the creditor is habitually resident; or
(c) the court which, according to its own law, has jurisdiction to entertain proceedings concerning the status of a person if the matter relating to maintenance is ancillary to those proceedings, unless that jurisdiction is based solely on the nationality (domicile in the case of the United Kingdom and Ireland: Art.2(3)) of one of the parties; or
(d) the court which, according to its own law, has jurisdiction to entertain proceedings concerning parental responsibility if the matter relating to maintenance is ancillary to those proceedings, unless that jurisdiction is based solely on the nationality (domicile in the case of the United Kingdom and Ireland: Art.2(3)) of one of the parties.

For jurisdiction to order provisional, including protective, measures, see Art.14.

The principle of party automony is introduced, the parties being able to agree that certain courts chosen from a prescribed list are to have jurisdiction to settle any disputes in matters relating to a maintenance obligation which have arisen or which may arise between them. The agreement must be in writing, or by a communication by electronic means which provides a durable record of the agreement (Art.4(2)). The parties may select:

(a) a court or the courts of a Member State in which one of the parties is habitually resident;

(b) a court or the courts of a Member State of which one of the parties has the nationality (in which one of the parties is domiciled in the case of the United Kingdom and Ireland: Art.2(3));

(c) in the case of maintenance obligations between spouses or former spouses: (i) the court which has jurisdiction to settle their dispute in matrimonial matters; or (ii) a court or the courts of the Member State which was the Member State of the spouses' last common habitual residence for a period of at least one year.

The relevant connecting factors have to be satisfied at the time the choice of court agreement is concluded or at the time the court is seised. The jurisdiction conferred by such an agreement is exclusive unless the parties have agreed otherwise (Art.4(1). For cases in which the chosen court is in a State party to the Lugano Convention which is not also a Member State, see Art.4(4)). An agreement of this sort may not be made in the case of a dispute relating to a maintenance obligation towards a child under the age of 18 (Art.4(3)).

Apart from jurisdiction derived from other provisions of the Regulation, a court of a Member State before which a defendant enters an appearance has jurisdiction. This rule does not apply where appearance was entered to contest the jurisdiction (Art.5).

Where no court of a Member State has jurisdiction under the above rules, and no court of a State party to the Lugano Convention which is not a Member State has jurisdiction pursuant to the provisions of that Convention, the courts of the Member State of the common nationality of the parties have jurisdiction. In the case of the United Kingdom and Ireland, common domicile is substituted for common nationality; and a case in which the parties are domiciled in different territorial units of the same Member State amounts to common domicile in that Member State (Art.2(3)).

Where no court of a Member State has jurisdiction pursuant to any of the above rules, the courts of a Member State may, on an exceptional basis, hear the case if proceedings cannot reasonably be brought or conducted or would be impossible in a third State with which the dispute is closely connected. The dispute must have a "sufficient connection", not further defined, with the Member State of the court seised (Art.8).

Where a decision is given in a Member State or a Contracting State to the Hague Convention of 2007 in which the creditor is habitually resident, proceedings to modify the decision or to have a new decision given cannot be brought by the debtor in any other Member State as long as the creditor remains habitually resident in the State in which the decision was given. This prohibition does not apply in certain cases: (a) where the parties have agreed (in accordance with Art.4) to the jurisdiction of the courts of that other Member State; (b) where the creditor submits to the jurisdiction of the courts of that other Member State; (c) where the competent authority in the Hague Convention Contracting State of origin cannot, or refuses to, exercise jurisdiction to modify the decision or give a new decision; or (d) where the decision given in the Hague Convention Contracting State of origin cannot be recognised or declared enforceable in the Member State where proceedings to modify the decision or to have a new decision given are contemplated (Art.8).

Special rules apply where a defendant habitually resident in a State other than the Member State where the action was brought does not enter an appearance. In such a case, the court with jurisdiction must stay the proceedings so long as it is not shown that the defendant has been able to receive the document instituting the proceedings or an equivalent document in sufficient time to enable him to arrange for his defence, or that all necessary steps have been taken to this end (Art. 11(1)). If the document instituting the proceedings or an equivalent document had to be transmitted from one Member State to another pursuant to the Service Regulation, Art.19 of that Regulation (as to which see para.8–053) applies instead of this rule (Art.11(2)). Where the Service Regulation does not apply, and the document instituting the proceedings or an equivalent document had to be transmitted abroad pursuant to the Hague Convention of November 15, 1965 on the service abroad of judicial and extrajudicial documents in civil or commercial matters (as to which see para.8–045), Art.15 of that Convention applies (Art.11(3)).

The Maintenance Regulation adopts the same approach to lis pendens and related actions as is found in the Judgments Regulation, Arts 12 and 13 of the Maintenance Regulation corresponding to Arts 27 and 28 of the Judgments Regulation (as to which see Rule 31(4)). The date of seisin is addressed in Maintenance Regulation, Art.9, corresponding to Art.30 of the Judgments Regulation (see para.12–060).

*Administrative co-operation*

The Maintenance Regulation contains in Chapter VII (Arts. 49 to 63) detailed provisions, largely modelled on those in the Hague Convention of 2007, establishing a network of Central Authorities to facilitate the obtaining and enforcement of decisions as to maintenance. They have extensive duties, principally listed in Art.51.

Many types of application may be made through the Central Authority of the Member State in which the applicant resides to the Central Authority of the requested Member State. So, a creditor seeking to recover maintenance under the Regulation may make apply by that route for: (a) recognition or recognition and declaration of enforceability of a decision; (b) enforcement of a decision given or recognised in the requested Member State; (c) establishment of a decision in the requested Member State where there is no existing decision, including where necessary the establishment of parentage; (d) establishment of a decision in the requested Member State where the recognition and declaration of enforceability of a decision given in a State other than the requested Member State is not possible; (e) modification of a decision given in the requested Member State; and (f) modification of a decision given in a State other than the requested Member State. A debtor against whom there is an existing maintenance decision may make applications for: (a) recognition of a decision leading to the suspension, or limiting the enforcement, of a previous decision in the requested Member State; (b) modification of a decision given in the requested Member State; (c) modification of a decision given in a State other than the requested Member State (Arts 55 and 56; Art.57 prescribes the content of applications and requires the use of forms set out in the Annexes to the Regulation; Art.59 contains language requirements).

### *Access to justice*

Chapter IV (Arts 44 to 47) of the Regulation contain provisions as to legal aid. Article 44 gives parties who are involved in a dispute covered by this Regulation a qualified right to effective access to justice in another Member State, including enforcement and appeal or review procedures. Where the case is dealt with through the Central Authorities system, a Member State is not obliged to provide legal aid if and to the extent that the procedures of that Member State enable the parties to make the case without the need for legal aid, and the Central Authority provides such services as are necessary free of charge.

Entitlements to legal aid are not to be less than those available in equivalent domestic cases. It is to cover: (a) pre-litigation advice with a view to reaching a settlement prior to bringing judicial proceedings; (b) legal assistance in bringing a case before an authority or a court and representation in court; (c) exemption from or assistance with the costs of proceedings and the fees to persons mandated to perform acts during the proceedings; (d) in Member States in which an unsuccessful party is liable for the costs of the opposing party, if the recipient of legal aid loses the case, the costs incurred by the opposing party, if such costs would have been covered had the recipient been habitually resident in the Member State of the court seised; (e) interpretation; (f) translation of the documents required by the court or by the competent authority and presented by the recipient of legal aid which are necessary for the resolution of the case; and (g) travel costs to be borne by the recipient of legal aid where the physical presence of the persons concerned with the presentation of the recipient's case is required in court by the law or by the court of the Member State concerned and the court decides that the persons concerned cannot be heard to the satisfaction of the court by any other means (Art.45).

The requested Member State must provide free legal aid in respect of all applications by a creditor through the Central Authorities concerning maintenance obligations arising from a parent–child relationship towards a person under the age of 21. Except in the case of applications for recognition or recognition and declaration of enforceability of a decision, or for enforcement of a decision given or recognised in the requested Member State, legal aid may however be refused if the competent authority of the requested Member State considers that, on the merits, the application or any appeal or review is manifestly unfounded (Art.46). In other types of case, legal aid may be granted in accordance with national law, particularly as regards the conditions for the means test or the merits test (Art.47).

Council Regulation (EC) 664/2009 [2009] O.J. L200/46 establishes a procedure for the negotiation and conclusion of agreements between Member States and third countries concerning jurisdiction, recognition and enforcement of judgments and decisions in matrimonial matters, matters of parental responsibility and matters relating to maintenance obligations, and the law applicable to matters relating to maintenance obligations.

References in this Rule and the Comment thereon to the Lugano Convention apply equally to the revised Lugano Convention. See SI 2009/3131.

NOTE 75. The cited provisions of the Constitutional Reform Act 2005 are now in force.

NOTE 78. Matrimonial and Family Proceedings Act 1984, s.15 is further amended by SI 2007/1655, Sch., Pt 1, paras 12 and 13 (to refer to Council Regulation No.44/2001 as amended from time to time and as applied by the EC-Denmark Agreement of October 19, 2005).

NOTES 84, 85 and 86. The cited provision of the Courts Act 2003 is now in force.

NOTE 87. Civil Jurisdiction and Judgments Act 1982, Sch.3C is repealed by SI 2009/3131. See now revised Lugano Convention, Art.2.

NOTES 88 to 90. See also the similarly numbered Articles of the revised Lugano Convention.

The power to order maintenance pending suit under s.22 of the Matrimonial Causes Act 1973 is exercisable even when the jurisdiction of the court in the suit itself is subject to challenge: *Moses-Taiga v Taiga* [2005] EWCA Civ 1013, [2006] 1 F.L.R. 1074; *L-K v K (Brussels II Revised: Maintenance Pending Suit)* [2006] EWCA Civ 498. **18–171**

If the English court finds that it has no jurisdiction in the divorce proceedings, anything paid under an order for maintenance pending suit is irrecoverable, and the party entitled to maintenance under such an order can enforce it so as to recover any arrears which have accumulated up to the date on which the English divorce proceedings are terminated: *M v M (Maintenance Pending Suit: Enforcement on Dismissal of Suit)* [2008] EWHC 2153 (Fam,), [2009] 1 F.L.R. 790.

NOTE 3. Matrimonial Proceedings Act 1973, s.31 is further amended by Pensions Act 2008, Sch.6 para.8. **18–172**

The purpose of Part III is to remit hardship in the exceptional case where serious injustice would otherwise be done: *Agbaje v Agbaje* [2009] EWCA **18–174**

Civ 1, [2009] 1 F.L.R. 987 at [39]. The Court of Appeal held that comity, the respect and deference due to another Commonwealth jurisdiction (in the instant case, Nigeria), was a significant factor; it was not correct to focus on a comparison between what was awarded by the foreign court and what might have been awarded in England. (Leave has been given to appeal to the Supreme Court.)

NOTE 6. Add: and by Child Maintenance and Other Payments Act 2008, Sch.3, Pt 1, para.6 and Sch.8.

NOTE 8. Matrimonial and Family Proceedings Act 1984, s.17 is further amended by Pensions Act 2008, Sch.6 para.11.

**18–175** *Holmes v Holmes* [1989] Fam. 47 was followed in *MR v PR* [2005] 2 I.R. 618 and in *PWY v PC* [2007] IEHC 400, [2008] 2 I.R. 261 (where a material non-disclosure of a serious nature led to leave already given being set aside).

The principal object of the filter mechanism is to prevent wholly unmeritorious claims being pursued to oppress or blackmail a former spouse. The threshold is not high, but is higher than "serious issue to be tried" or "good arguable case" found in other contexts, and is best expressed by saying that in this context "substantial" means "solid": *Agbaje v Agbaje* [2010] UKSC 13, [2010] 1 A.C. 628 at [33]. If the threshold is judged to have been passed on an ex parte application, an application to set that decision aside should only be exercised if there is a compelling reason to do so: ibid.

NOTE 12. Where the proceedings in the foreign court have concluded, there is no choice between jurisdictions as in a *forum non conveniens* context: *Agbaje v Agbaje* [2010] UKSC 13, [2010] 1 A.C. 628 at [46]–[50].

**18–177** Civil Jurisdiction and Judgments Act 1982, s.41 is amended by SI 2009/3131. The domicile of individuals for the purposes of the revised Lugano Convention is governed by Civil Jurisdiction and Judgments Act 1982, s.41A as inserted by SI 2009/3131.

In *Agbaje v Agbaje* [2010] UKSC 13, [2010] 1 A.C. 628 at [55]–[57] Lord Collins of Mapesbury raised, but did not resolve, the issue whether a decision as to maintenance in another EU Member State (or in a State party to the Lugano Convention) would preclude an application in England under Part III of the 1984 Act.

NOTE 22. Matrimonial and Family Proceedings Act 1984, s.15(2) is further amended by SI 2007/1655, Sch, Pt 1, paras 12 and 13 (to refer to Council Regulation No 44/2001 as amended from time to time and as applied by the EC-Denmark Agreement of October 19, 2005).

NOTE 23. Civil Jurisdiction and Judgments Act 1982, Sch.3C is repealed by SI 2009/3131. See now revised Lugano Convention, Art.2.

NOTE 24. Civil Jurisdiction and Judgments Act 1982, Sch.3C is repealed by SI 2009/3131. See now revised Lugano Convention, Art.5(2).

NOTE 25. Civil Jurisdiction and Judgments Act 1982, Sch.3C is repealed by SI 2009/3131. See now revised Lugano Convention, Art.22(1). Add: *Moore v Moore* [2007] EWCA Civ 361, [2007] 2 F.L.R. 339.

NOTE 26. Civil Jurisdiction and Judgments Act 1982, Sch.3C is repealed by SI 2009/3131. See now revised Lugano Convention, Art.23.

NOTE 27. Civil Jurisdiction and Judgments Act 1982, Sch.3C is repealed by SI 2009/3131. See now revised Lugano Convention, Art.24.

The issue under s.16 is whether England is the appropriate venue, and it is **18–178**
wrong to characterise it as a question whether an order under Part III should be made: *Agbaje v Agbaje* [2010] UKSC 13, [2010] 1 A.C. 628 at [41]. Little assistance can be obtained from the *forum non conveniens* cases in applying s.16. There the question is whether England would be an appropriate venue for an order to be made, notwithstanding that the divorce proceedings were in a foreign country which may well have been the more appropriate forum for the divorce: *Agbaje v Agbaje* at [46]–[50]. See also *Traversa v Freddi* [2009] EWHC 3346 (Fam.), [2010] 1 F.L.R. 324.

The criteria for deciding whether a court should make an order under s.17, and if so in what manner, are specified in s.18 (as amended by the Welfare Reform and Pensions Act 1999, s.22, the Pensions Act 2004, Sch.12, para.4 and by Sch.6, Pt 2, paras 10, 12 (not yet in force)). The Supreme Court set out the principles to be applied in determining what order to make in *Agbaje v Agbaje* at [60]–[73].

NOTE 31. Add: *PWY v PC* [2007] IEHC 400, [2008] 2 I.R. 261.

NOTE 34. The fact that the party seeking relief might have claimed in the foreign proceedings, though significant, is not to be treated as determinative: *Moore v Moore* [2007] EWCA Civ 361, [2007] 2 F.L.R. 339; see Hudson, [2007] Fam. L. 611; *PWY v PC* [2007] IEHC 400, [2008] 2 I.R. 261.

NOTE 52. SI 1959/377 is further amended by SI 2008/1203. **18–182**

NOTE 67. The references to the 1920 Act, ss.6, 6A should be to s.4(6), **18–185**
(6A).

NOTE 74. Add to the list in the first sentence: SI 2008/1202. **18–188**

NOTE 76. The cited provision of the Courts Act 2003 is now in force.

NOTE 18. The cited provision of the Courts Act 2003 is now in force. **18–194**

**18–195** NOTES 25, 26 and 27. The cited provisions of the Courts Act 2003 are now in force.

**18–198** For the Hague Convention on the International Recovery of Child Support and Other Forms of Family Maintenance, signed in 2007 and designed to replace the 1973 Convention, see entry at para.18–232.

NOTE 35. The Reciprocal Enforcement of Maintenance Orders (United States of America) Order 2007, SI 2007/2005, now applies a modified version of Pt I of the 1972 Act to the United States as a whole. It adopts the approach, favoured by the United States, of vesting power to vary an order solely in the court which made it. The previous Order remains in force only in respect of applications made to a court in the United Kingdom and United States maintenance orders received by the Lord Chancellor before October 1, 2007. The procedural rules for magistrates' courts (SI 1995/2802) are amended by SI 2007/2267. The relevant Family Proceedings Rules are r.7.37 (Republic of Ireland), r.7.38 (Hague Convention countries) and r.7.39 (United States); the last mentioned is amended by SI 2007/2268 to reflect the new Order mentioned above.

NOTE 36. The Recovery of Maintenance (United States of America) Order 2007, SI 2007/2006, now applies a modified version of Pt II of the 1972 Act to the United States as a whole. The previous Order remains in force only in respect of applications made to a court in the United Kingdom and United States maintenance orders received by the Lord Chancellor before October 1, 2007. The relevant provision in the procedural rules for magistrates' courts (SI 1975/488, r.5A as inserted by SI 1979/1561 and amended by SI 2001/615 and SI 2005/617) is further amended by SI 2007/2267.

**18–202** NOTE 45. The cited provision of the Courts Act 2003 is now in force.

**18–203** See *Moore v Moore* [2007] EWCA Civ 361, [2007] 2 F.L.R. 339 where the categorisation of Spanish proceedings was relevant to the possible staying of English proceedings and *RGHR v LG* [2007] IEHC 253, [2008] 1 I.R. 369 (maintenance aspects subject to stay under the Judgments Regulation in Irish court as court second seised) and *JKN v JCN* [2010] EWHC 843 (Fam.) (entry at para.18–245, below).

NOTE 49. Civil Jurisdiction and Judgments Act 1982, Sch.3C is repealed by SI 2009/3131. See now revised Lugano Convention, Art.5(2).

NOTE 50. Civil Jurisdiction and Judgments Act 1982, Sch.3C is repealed by SI 2009/3131. See now revised Lugano Convention, Art.1(1).

**18–205** NOTE 56. Civil Jurisdiction and Judgments Act 1982, Sch.3C is repealed by SI 2009/3131. See now revised Lugano Convention, Art.17.

The correctness of the proposition in the first sentence of the text was accepted in *NG v KR (Pre-nuptial Contract)* [2008] EWHC 1532 (Fam.), [2009] 1 F.L.R. 1478 at [87]. The court noted, however, that account could be taken of foreign factors as part of the general duty placed on the court in the context of ancillary orders to consider all the circumstances of the case (Matrimonial Causes Act 1973, s.25), citing *Otobo v Otobo* [2002] EWCA Civ 949, [2003] 1 F.L.R. 102; *A v T (Ancillary Relief: Cultural Factors)* [2004] EWHC 471 (Fam.), [2004] 1 F.L.R. 977; and *C v C (Ancillary Relief: Nuptial Settlement)* [2004] EWHC 742 (Fam.), [2005] Fam. 250, where the court spoke of "a sideways look at foreign law as part of the discretionary analysis required by [English] substantive law". **18–207**

The position was more fully examined by the Court of Appeal in the same case: *Radmacher v Granatino* [2009] EWCA Civ 649, [2009] 2 F.C.R. 645. The court took into account the European context in which civil law jurisdictions generally employ notarised marital property regimes to regulate the property consequences of both marriage and divorce, while the common law attaches no property consequences to marriage and relies on a very wide judicial discretion to fix the property consequences of divorce; and in which the English courts apply the *lex fori* and their previous use of the notion of forum non conveniens is precluded. In the instant case, the husband had been awarded some £6 million by the English court despite a pre-nuptial contract under which he would have received nothing for himself.

The court also noted the developments in English domestic law as to the weight that might be given to pre-nuptial contracts. These had been reviewed by Baron J. in her judgment at first instance (*NG v KR (Pre-nuptial Contract)* [2008] EWHC 1532 (Fam.), [2009] 1 F.L.R. 1478 at [111]–[129] and had since been the subject of observations by the Judicial Committee of the Privy Council in *MacLeod v MacLeod* [2008] UKPC 64, [2009] 1 All E.R. 851. In that case, Baroness Hale of Richmond explained that the Board did not feel that the courts could now reverse "the long standing rule that ante-nuptial agreements are contrary to public policy and thus not valid or binding in the contractual sense"; any change had to come via legislation.

In the Court of Appeal in *Radmacher v Granatino* at [51] to [53], Thorpe L.J. made clear his view that considerable weight should be given to a foreign pre-nuptial contract. He considered such an approach necessary to give proper weight to the parties' agreement and to alleviate the injustice that could otherwise result from the jurisdictional rules introduced by Brussels II and the widely divergent legal and social traditions of the civil and common law. He said at [53]: "This is not to apply foreign law, nor is it to give effect to a contract foreign to English tradition. It is, in my judgment, a legitimate exercise of the very wide discretion that is conferred on the judges to achieve fairness between the parties to the ancillary relief proceedings".

Wilson L.J. suggested at [119] that considerations of public policy no longer applied. Rix L.J. noted at [64] that it was anomalous that on the one hand a pre-nuptial agreement is invalid as being contrary to public policy, and on the other hand it may be and is taken into account by the court.

The husband was of French nationality but now based in London. The wife was German and had moved, since the hearing at first instance, from Germany to Monaco. The parties had lived together before and during their marriage in London and in New York. The pre-nuptial contract, in the German language, was entered into in Germany. Although there was evidence at first instance as to the validity of the contract in French and German law and as to the content of German domestic law, the Court of Appeal was not enforcing the contract as such; there was no examination of what law might govern it. Its existence did however persuade the court to make provision for the husband only indirectly, in his capacity as a home-maker for the children of the marriage. See also *Granatino v Radmacher* [2010] UKSC 42, [2010] 3 W.L.R. 1367, at [103]–[108].

The Hague Conference on Private International Law adopted in November 2007 a Protocol on the Law Applicable to Maintenance Obligations. For commentary by the principal architect of the Protocol, see Bonomi (2008) 10 Yb. P.I.L. 333. The Protocol is essentially a revision of earlier Hague Conventions of 1956 and 1973, which had attracted support entirely from States in the civil law tradition. The European Community was considering the inclusion of provisions on applicable law in what later became the Maintenance Regulation. The eventual text of the Maintenance Regulation contains in Chapter III a single Art.15 providing that the law applicable to maintenance obligations is to be determined in accordance with the Hague Protocol. The United Kingdom is not, and will not be, so bound, but Ireland will be.

The Protocol contains a "general rule" to which there are certain exceptions or glosses. The general rule is the application of the law of the habitual residence of the creditor for the time being (Art.3). In most cases (cases of child support, by parents or others, and the support of a parent by its child), the creditor may rely on other laws if that identified by the general rule does not entitle him or her to maintenance. There is what is known as a "cascade" of potentially applicable laws set out in Art.4. These are, after the general rule of the law of the creditor's habitual residence, the *lex fori* and then the law of the common nationality of the parties if there is one. If, however, the creditor chooses to bring his or her claim in the country of the debtor's habitual residence, the order is reversed, so that the law first applied is the *lex fori* and only if no maintenance is available under that law does the law of the creditor's habitual residence apply. A Contracting State may substitute in cases coming before its own courts the notion of common domicile for that of common nationality (Art.9, a provision included at the request of Ireland).

In spousal support cases, those between spouses, ex-spouses or parties to a marriage which has been annulled, the general rule of applying the law of the creditor's habitual residence is excluded if one of the parties objects and the law of another State, in particular the State of their last common habitual residence, has a closer connection with the marriage. In such a case the law of that other State is to apply (Art.5).

In cases other than child support by parents and spousal support, the debtor may contest a claim from the creditor on the ground that there is no such obligation under *both* the law of the habitual residence of the debtor *and* the law of the common nationality of the parties, if there is one (Art. 6).

Alongside these complex rules, the Protocol also recognises party autonomy, the freedom of the parties to agree on the law which shall apply. This may be done in respect of a particular proceeding, where the parties may agree that the *lex fori* is to apply (Art.7). But the parties may also agree more generally, for example in a pre-nuptial contract, which law is to govern maintenance issues between them (Art.8). Here, there is a closed list of laws which the parties may designate, and their choice is qualified by a provision which states that "unless at the time of the designation the parties were fully informed and aware of the consequences of their designation, the law designated by the parties shall not apply where the application of that law would lead to manifestly unfair or unreasonable consequences for any of the parties" (Art 8(5)).

Civil Jurisdiction and Judgments Act 1982, s.41 is amended by SI 2009/3131. The domicile of individuals for the purposes of the revised Lugano Convention is governed by Civil Jurisdiction and Judgments Act 1982, s.41A as inserted by SI 2009/3131. **18–209**

NOTE 70. Civil Jurisdiction and Judgments Act 1982, Sch.3C is repealed by SI 2009/3131. See now revised Lugano Convention, Arts 3 and 18. **18–212**

NOTE 71. Civil Jurisdiction and Judgments Act 1982, Sch.3C is repealed by SI 2009/3131. See now revised Lugano Convention, Art.5(2). **18–213**

NOTE 91. Civil Jurisdiction and Judgments Act 1982, Sch.3C is repealed by SI 2009/3131. See now revised Lugano Convention, Art.38. **18R–220**

NOTE 1. National Assistance Act 1948, s.43 is repealed and Maintenance Orders Act 1950, s.16(2) consequentially amended by Health and Social Care Act 2008, Sch.15 Pt 5. Social Security Administration Act 1992, s.106, is repealed by Welfare Reform Act 2009, Sch.7, Pt.1. **18–224**

C. *Enforcement of Foreign Maintenance Orders*

NOTE 12. Family Proceedings Rules 1991, r.7.28, was revoked by SI 2009/636. **18–225**

NOTE 13. Maintenance Orders Act 1958, s.4, is further amended by SI 2009/871, Art.2.

Add: For these purposes, a maintenance order registered in a magistrates' court under Pt I of the Maintenance Orders (Reciprocal Enforcement) Act 1972 or Pt I of the Civil Jurisdiction and Judgments Act 1982 or Council Regulation No.44/2001 (as amended from time to time and as applied by the

EC-Denmark Agreement of October 19, 2005) is deemed to be a maintenance order made by that court: 1958 Act, s.1(4) as inserted by the Maintenance Orders (Reciprocal Enforcement) Act 1972, Sch., para.4 and amended by the Civil Jurisdiction and Judgments Act 1982, Sch.12, Part I, by SI 2001/3929, Sch.3, para.5, and by SI 2007/1655, Sch., Pt 1, para.5.

**18–232** The 21st Session of the Hague Conference on Private International Law held in November 2007 adopted a Convention on the International Recovery of Child Support and Other Forms of Family Maintenance and a Protocol on the Law Applicable to Maintenance Obligations. (For commentary on the Convention, see Spector (2005) 7 Yb. P.I.L. 63; Duncan [2008] I.F.L. 13; Doogue (2008) 17 (3) Cwth. Jud. Jo. 23; Duncan (2008) 10 Yb. P.I.L. 313; Lortie (2008) 10 Yb. P.I.L. 359. For the Protocol, see the entry at para.18–207). Within the European Community, the Maintenance Regulation covers similar ground but also deals, as the Hague Convention does not, with jurisdiction. There is a close similarity between many provisions of the two instruments, which reflects the active participation of the European Commission and many of the Member States in the negotiations at The Hague and co-operation between the two organisations. The Convention was designed to take account of important developments in the field (notably the move in countries such as Australia and the United Kingdom from court-based to administrative, formula-driven maintenance systems), to meet the specific needs of the United States which has a very large amount of "traffic" in this area, and to replace the United Nations Convention on the Recovery Abroad of Maintenance of 1956 (see para.18–198), the provisions of which have proved unsatisfactorily vague. See further the entry at para.19–141.

Text to note 40. The Maintenance Regulation takes precedence, in relations between Member States, over conventions and agreements which concern matters governed by the Regulation (such as the Hague Convention of 1973) and to which Member States are party, but does not affect such conventions and agreements as they apply between a Member State and a third State (Maintenance Regulation, Art.69).

Note 40. Civil Jurisdiction and Judgments Act 1982, Sch.3C is repealed by SI 2009/3131. See now revised Lugano Convention, Art.67.

**18–233** Text at note 41. Civil Jurisdiction and Judgments (Authentic Instruments and Court Settlements) Order 1993 does not apply in relation to the revised Lugano Convention: SI 2009/3131, reg.46. Fresh provision is made in that context, applying certain provisions of the Civil Jurisdiction and Judgments Act 1982 with modifications: SI 2009/3131, reg.47.

Council Regulation (EC) 4/2009 of December 18, 2008 on jurisdiction, applicable law, recognition and enforcement of decisions and cooperation in matters relating to maintenance obligations ([2009] O.J. L7) ("the Maintenance Regulation") replaces the provisions of the Judgments Regulation applicable to maintenance obligations and contains fresh provisions as to recognition and enforcement. It also replaces in matters relating to maintenance obligations, Regulation 405/2004, which introduced the European Enforcement Order (see para.14–229) except with regard to European Enforcement Orders on maintenance obligations issued in a Member State not bound by the Hague Protocol (Art.68(2)).

Different rules as to recognition and enforcement apply depending on the source of the decision, those in s.1 (Arts 17 to 22) of Ch.IV of the Regulation applying to decisions given in a Member State bound by the Hague Protocol of November 23, 2007 on the law applicable to maintenance obligations; and s.2 (Arts 23 to 38) to decisions given in a Member State not bound by that Protocol. Section 3 (Arts 39 to 43) contains provisions applying in all cases. Recital (20) asserts that "the 2007 Hague Protocol will be concluded by the Community in time to enable this Regulation to apply".

Some provisions of the Maintenance Regulation apply whatever the origin of a decision. So, the procedure for the enforcement of decisions given in another Member State is to be governed by the law of the Member State of enforcement. A decision given in a Member State which is enforceable in the Member State of enforcement must be enforced there under the same conditions as a decision given in that Member State of enforcement (Art.41(1)). The party seeking the enforcement of a decision given in another Member State is not required to have a postal address or an authorised representative in the Member State of enforcement (Art.41(2)). Under no circumstances may a decision given in a Member State be reviewed as to its substance in the Member State in which recognition, enforceability or enforcement is sought (Art.42). Recovery of any costs incurred in the application of the Regulation is not to take precedence over the recovery of maintenance (Art.43).

### *Decisions given in a Member State bound by the Hague Protocol*

A decision given in a Member State bound by the Hague Protocol is to be recognised in another Member State without any special procedure being required and without any possibility of opposing its recognition (Art.17(1)) and such a decision which is enforceable in the Member State of origin is to be enforceable in another Member State without the need for a declaration of enforceability (Art.17(2)). An enforceable decision carries with it by operation of law the power to proceed to any protective measures which exist under the law of the Member State of enforcement (Art.18).

A defendant who did not enter an appearance in the Member State of origin has the right to apply for a review of the decision before the competent court of that Member State where: (a) he was not served with the document instituting the proceedings or an equivalent document in sufficient time and in such a way as to enable him to arrange for his defence; or (b) he was prevented from contesting the maintenance claim by reason of force majeure or due to extraordinary circumstances without any fault on his part; unless (in either case) he failed to challenge the decision when it was possible for him to do so (Art.19(1)). There is a strict time-limit for applying for a review (Art.19(2)). It runs from the day the defendant was effectively acquainted with the contents of the decision and was able to react, at the latest from the date of the first enforcement measure having the effect of making his property non-disposable in whole or in part. The defendant must react promptly, in any event within 45 days. No extension may be granted on account of distance. If the court decides that a review is justified for one of the stated reasons, the decision is null and void. However, the creditor does not lose the benefits of the interruption of prescription or limitation periods, or the right to claim retroactive maintenance acquired in the initial proceedings (Art.19(3)).

For the purposes of enforcement of a decision in another Member State, the claimant must provide the competent enforcement authorities with: (a) a copy of the decision which satisfies the conditions necessary to establish its authenticity; (b) what is referred to as an "extract from the decision" (actually a detailed form prescribed in Annex I to the Regulation setting out all relevant details) completed by the court of origin; (c) where appropriate, a document showing the amount of any arrears and the date such amount was calculated; (d) where necessary, a transliteration or a translation of the "extract of the decision" into the official language of the Member State of enforcement or into another language that the Member State concerned has indicated it can accept. The competent authorities of the Member State of enforcement may require the claimant to provide a translation of the decision itself if, but only if, the enforcement of the decision is challenged (Art.20).

The competent authority in the Member State of enforcement must, on application by the debtor:

(a) refuse, either wholly or in part, the enforcement of the decision of the court of origin:
   (i) if the right to enforce the decision of the court of origin is extinguished by the effect of prescription or the limitation of action, either under the law of the Member State of origin or under the law of the Member State of enforcement, whichever provides for the longer limitation period;
   (ii) if the decision is irreconcilable with a decision given in the Member State of enforcement or with a decision given in another Member State or in a third State which fulfils the conditions necessary for its recognition in the Member State of enforcement. A decision which has the effect of modifying an earlier decision on maintenance on the basis of changed circumstances is not to be considered an irreconcilable decision for this purpose.

(b) suspend, either wholly or in part, the enforcement of the decision of the court of origin if the competent court of the Member State of origin has been seised of an application for a review of the decision of the court of origin under Art.19.

(c) suspend the enforcement of the decision of the court of origin where the enforceability of that decision is suspended in the Member State of origin (Art.21(2)(3)).

Grounds of refusal or suspension of enforcement under the law of the Member State of enforcement also apply in so far as they are not incompatible with the application of these rules (Art.21(1)).

Art.22 makes it clear that the recognition and enforcement of a decision on maintenance under the Maintenance Regulation does not in any way imply the recognition of the family relationship, parentage, marriage or affinity underlying the maintenance obligation which gave rise to the decision.

*Decisions given in a Member State not bound by the Hague Protocol*

A decision given in a Member State not bound by the Hague Protocol is to be recognised in the other Member States without any special procedure being required (Art.23(1)). There may, however, in certain circumstances be recognition proceedings. Any interested party who raises the recognition of a decision as the principal issue in a dispute may, in accordance with the procedures provided for in the Regulation for use primarily in the enforcement context, apply for a decision that the decision be recognised (Art.23(2)). If the outcome of proceedings in a court of a Member State depends on the determination of an incidental question of recognition, that court has jurisdiction over that question (Art.23(3)). A court of a Member State in which recognition is sought must stay the proceedings if the enforceability of the decision is suspended in the Member State of origin by reason of an appeal (Art.25).

A decision is not to be recognised:

(a) if such recognition is manifestly contrary to public policy in the Member State in which recognition is sought, but the test of public policy may not be applied to the rules relating to jurisdiction;
(b) where the decision was given in default of appearance, if the defendant was not served with the document which instituted the proceedings or with an equivalent document in sufficient time and in such a way as to enable him to arrange for his defence, unless the defendant failed to commence proceedings to challenge the decision when it was possible for him to do so;
(c) if it is irreconcilable with a decision given in a dispute between the same parties in the Member State in which recognition is sought;
(d) if it is irreconcilable with an earlier decision given in another Member State or in a third State in a dispute involving the same cause of action and between the same parties, provided that the earlier decision fulfils the conditions necessary for its recognition in the Member State in which recognition is sought.

A decision which has the effect of modifying an earlier decision on maintenance on the basis of changed circumstances is not considered an irreconcilable decision for these purposes (Art.24).

A decision given in a Member State not bound by the Hague Protocol and enforceable in that State is to be enforceable in another Member State when, on the application of any interested party, it has been declared enforceable there (Art.26). An application for a declaration of enforceability must be submitted to the court or competent authority of the Member State of enforcement notified by that Member State to the Commission, local jurisdiction being determined by reference to the place of habitual residence of the party against whom enforcement is sought, or to the place of enforcement (Art.27).

The application for a declaration of enforceability must be accompanied by: (a) a copy of the decision which satisfies the conditions necessary to establish its authenticity; (b) an "extract from the decision" issued by the court of origin using the form set out in Annex II; (c) where necessary, a transliteration or a translation of the "extract of the decision" into the official language of the Member State of enforcement or into another language that the Member State concerned has indicated it can accept. The court or competent authority seised of the application may require the claimant to provide a translation of the decision but only in connection with an appeal against a declaration of enforceability or a contest to such an appeal decision (Art.28). If the "extract from the decision" is not produced, the competent court or authority may specify a time for its production or accept an equivalent document or, if it considers that it has sufficient information before it, dispense with its production. It may require the production of a translation of the documents (Art.29).

The decision is to be declared enforceable without any review immediately on the completion of the submission of the necessary documents and at the latest within 30 days of that completion, except where exceptional circumstances make this impossible. The party against whom enforcement is sought is not at this stage of the proceedings entitled to make any submissions on the application (Art.30). Where a decision has been given in respect of several matters and the declaration of enforceability cannot be given for all of them, the competent court or authority must give it for one or more of them (Art.37).

Notice of the decision on the application for a declaration is to be given forthwith to the applicant in accordance with the procedure laid down by the law of the Member State of enforcement. The declaration of enforceability must be served on the party against whom enforcement is sought, accompanied by the decision, if that has not already been served on that party (Art.30). Either party may appeal, and the decision on appeal may be the subject of a further contest; in each case the Member States must notify details to the Commission (see Arts 32, 33, 34 and 71; for the possible staying of enforcement pending an appeal, see Art.35). During the time specified for an appeal against the declaration of enforceability and until any such appeal has been determined, no measures of enforcement may be taken other than protective measures against the property of the party against whom enforcement is sought (Art.36(3)).

When a decision must be recognised, nothing is to prevent the applicant from availing himself of provisional, including protective, measures in accordance with the law of the Member State of enforcement without a declaration of enforceability being required. A declaration of enforceability carries with it by operation of law the power to proceed to any protective measures (Art.36(1)(2)).

Although the making of Regulation 4/2009 gives the European Union exclusive competence in certain areas, Council Regulation No 664/2009 of 7 July 2009 ([2009] L 200/46) establishes a procedure for the negotiation and conclusion of agreements between Member States and third countries concerning jurisdiction, recognition and enforcement of judgments and decisions in matrimonial matters, matters of parental responsibility and matters relating to maintenance obligations, and the law applicable to matters relating to maintenance obligations.

See *T v L* [2008] IESC 48, [2009] I.L.Pr. 5 where the transitional provisions in Art.66 of the Judgments Regulation are closely examined. **18–234**

NOTE 43. Civil Jurisdiction and Judgments Act 1982, Sch.3C is repealed by SI 2009/3131. See now revised Lugano Convention, Arts 38, 39 and Annex II and Civil Jurisdiction and Judgments Act 1982, s.5A as inserted by SI 2009/3131, reg.6. **18–235**

NOTE 44. Civil Jurisdiction and Judgments Act 1982, Sch.3C is repealed by SI 2009/3131. See now revised Lugano Convention, Art.48.

NOTE 45. This note should read: Judgments Regulation, Art.40; Civil Jurisdiction and Judgments Act 1982, Sch.1, Art.33; revised Lugano Convention, Art.40.

The single appeal on a point of law is now to the county court: Civil Jurisdiction and Judgments Act 1982, ss.6 (as amended by SI 2009/871) and 6A (as inserted by SI 2009/3131). **18–237**

NOTE 50. Civil Jurisdiction and Judgments Act 1982, Sch.3C is repealed by SI 2009/3131. See now revised Lugano Convention, Arts 43, 45.

NOTE 51. Civil Jurisdiction and Judgments Act 1982, Sch.3C is repealed by SI 2009/3131. See now revised Lugano Convention, Art.47(3).

NOTE 52. Civil Jurisdiction and Judgments Act 1982, Sch.3C is repealed by SI 2009/3131. See now revised Lugano Convention, Art.46.

NOTE 53. Civil Jurisdiction and Judgments Act 1982, Sch.3C is repealed by SI 2009/3131. See now revised Lugano Convention, Art.44 and Annex IV.

**18–238** The single appeal on a point of law is now to the county court: Civil Jurisdiction and Judgments Act 1982, ss.6 (as amended by SI 2009/871) and 6A (as inserted by SI 2009/3131).

NOTE 54. Civil Jurisdiction and Judgments Act 1982, Sch.3C is repealed by SI 2009/3131. See now revised Lugano Convention, Arts 43 and 44.

## 5. STAYING OF MATRIMONIAL PROCEEDINGS

**18–244** *cf. Bentinck v Bentinck* [2007] EWCA Civ 175, [2007] 2 F.L.R. 1, decided under the Lugano Convention. In *Prazic v Prazic* [2006] EWCA Civ 497, [2006] 2 F.L.R. 1128, where Art.19 was applied, the court stayed proceedings under the Trusts of Land and Appointment of Trustees Act 1996 as related proceedings under Art.28 of the Judgments Regulation. For the temporal scope of the Regulation see *DT v FL* [2006] IEHC 98, [2007] I.L.Pr. 763.

In *L-K v L-K (No.3)* [2006] EWHC 3281 (Fam.), [2007] 2 F.L.R. 741, Singer J. described the "first past the post" regime as arbitrary and as having the potential be unfair to one party or the other.

In that case, the English petition was not accompanied by the marriage certificate, but the French courts had, at first instance and in the cour d'appel, held that the English court was first seised. Singer J. accepted the interpretation of Art.16 of Regulation 2201/2003 suggested by counsel: that it meant that the relevant document was lodged in England when it was filed in a manner accepted by the court, leading to the issue of a petition by the court. Given the practice of the registry, the absence of the marriage certificate at that stage did not prevent the requirements of Art.16 being met.

A decree absolute was pronounced in the same case despite the pendency of an appeal to the Cour de cassation. On appeal, this was held to have been, in all the circumstances, a proper exercise of the judge's discretion: *Leman-Klemmers v Klemmers* [2007] EWCA Civ 919, [2008] 1 F.L.R. 692.

In *Re N (Jurisdiction)* [2007] EWHC 1274 (Fam.), [2007] 2 F.L.R. 1196, it was held that the French court was first seised, the *requête* having been filed before the issue of the petition.

**18–245** NOTE 65. Art.16(a) does not postpone seisin until the applicant has effected (or taken a required step to effect) service. The court is seised when the document is lodged, subject to the proviso (which may only be assessed from some later perspective of hindsight) that there has not been a subsequent failure to take the required steps: *Weiner v Weiner* [2010] EWHC 1843 (Fam.). Although the applicable rules prohibit service of process in matrimonial cases on a Sunday, such service is not invalid. There is power to set it aside under CCR Ord 37 r 5(1) but such "a minor, unintentioned, completely harmless infraction of a now archaic, anomalous, pointless and technical rule" should be ignored, and the fact that the issue arose in the international context of the Brussels II *bis* Regulation makes no difference: *ibid*.

Proceedings are continuing in another jurisdiction for the purposes of Domicile and Matrimonial Proceedings Act 1973, Sch.1, para.9, when they have been commenced there and have not been dismissed. It is immaterial that a motion to dismiss them would probably succeed in the foreign court: *JKN v JCN* [2010] EWHC 843 (Fam.) at [54]–[56].

The English courts have been reluctant to decide the question of the application in this context of the decision in Case 281/02 *Owusu v Jackson* [2005] E.C.R. I–1383, [2005] Q.B. 801. The Court of Appeal refused an application for leave to appeal on the point in *Cook v Plummer* [2008] EWCA Civ 484, [2008] 2 F.L.R. 989. Thorpe LJ noted at para.[10] that the decision in *Owusu v Jackson* was "deeply unpopular in this jurisdiction" and that the United Kingdom was seeking "to mitigate its unattractive effect" by submissions in the review of the operation of the Judgments Regulation. To admit the point for consideration by the full court would have "unpredictable consequences". The issue was squarely faced for the first time in *JKN v JCN* [2010] EWHC 843 (Fam.). The respondent husband was habitually resident in England, and this was sufficient to give the English court jurisdiction under Art.3 of Brussels II *bis*; he was also domiciled in England in the sense of the Judgments Regulation. The husband applied for a stay on forum non conveniens grounds, arguing that New York was the more appropriate forum.

The wife argued that her claims for financial relief were within the Judgments Regulation, and that the court therefore had jurisdiction under Art.2 of that Regulation, and *Owusu v Jackson* plainly applied. She submitted that "maintenance" in the Judgments Regulation was to be defined autonomously and was an umbrella term for any financial award which was made in order to provide for the respective needs and resources of the parties, and that on the instant facts any award would come within that definition. It was pointed out for the husband that as only certain types of financial relief (maintenance as opposed to issues concerning rights in property) are governed by the Judgments Regulation, the effect of the wife's argument on divorce cases generally would be that the applicability of that Regulation would not be clear at the outset of proceedings, and the respondent would have no means of knowing whether it prevented an application for a stay. The court accepted the husband's argument that as financial relief is an ancillary matter, the question of jurisdiction in divorce was the prior question, and one which fell to be determined by Brussels II *bis*. By implication, the court seems to have accepted the husband's further argument that jurisdiction over ancillary relief was conferred not by either of the Regulations but by national legislation.

Insofar as the court's jurisdiction rested on Brussels II *bis*, the wife argued that *Owusu v Jackson* applied to cases governed by Brussels II *bis* as well as those under the Judgments Regulation (though not to cases within the residual jurisdiction referred to in Art.7 of Brussels II *bis*). The court held that *Owusu v Jackson* did not apply to cases governed by Brussels II *bis*, broadly accepting the arguments advanced by the husband: (a) *Owusu v Jackson* did not address the position which arises under the Domicile and Matrimonial Proceedings Act 1973 where by definition there are concurrent proceedings. To extend the *Owusu* principle would create a real risk of irreconcilable judgments and could lead to an undesirable lacuna in the law: where Art.2 of the Judgments Regulation was engaged, and there were competing proceedings in a non-Member State, there would be no mechanism for resolving the situation; (b) *Owusu v Jackson* should be limited to cases under the Judgments Regulation and not extended so as to apply to Brussels II *bis*. It was argued *inter alia* that that Regulation was essentially a commercial Regulation, not one dealing with family law. Art.2 of the Judgments Regulation had been described as "mandatory" by the European Court, but under Art.3 of Brussels II *bis* there was no corresponding obligation: Art.3 envisaged a multiplicity of Member States having concurrent jurisdiction, Art.2 of the Judgments Regulation envisaged only one; (c) were *Owusu v Jackson* to be held to apply to Brussels II *bis*, that would include cases under Art.8. In such cases Art.15 permits in certain circumstances a court of a Member State to transfer the case to another court where that is in the best interests of the child. There is no corresponding provision to deal with the situation as between a Member State and a non-Member State, and there was no justification for depriving courts of that power.

The court also considered the meaning of "other than proceedings governed by the Council Regulation" in Domicile and Matrimonial Proceedings Act 1973, Sch.1, para.9(1), words inserted to give effect to Brussels II and before the decision in *Owusu v Jackson.* The wife argued that the only proceedings not "governed by the Council Regulation" were the "residual jurisdiction" cases under s.5(2)(b) and Art.7 of Brussels II *bis*. Except in the small number of cases to which these provisions applied, the amendment to the Act removed the power to grant a stay. The court held that Parliament could not have intended such a major change in practice, and that the natural and preferable construction of "proceedings governed by the Council Regulation" is that it refers to the position where there are competing proceedings in another Member State, to which Art.19 of Brussels II *bis* applies. It is difficult to accept this convenient interpretation: the phrase defines the "matrimonial proceedings" to which the provision applies rather than the circumstances (here, the existence of proceedings in another Member State) in which those proceedings find themselves.

**18–246** NOTE 75. Add after *R v R*: *Wang v Yin* [2008] 3 N.Z.L.R. 136 (N.Z. High Ct.)

## Chapter 19

# CHILDREN

## 1. PARENTAL RESPONSIBILITY IN GENERAL

NOTE 11. Add: In *Re J (A Child) (Custody Rights: Jurisdiction)* [2005] UKHL 40, [2006] 1 A.C. 80 Baroness Hale affirmed: "If our courts have jurisdiction, then the welfare principle applies, unless it is excluded, and our law has no concept of the 'proper law of the child' ". [19] **19–005**

In the light of the overlap in the material scope of the instrument with Council Regulation (EC) 2201/2003 of November 27, 2003 concerning jurisdiction and the recognition and enforcement of judgments in matrimonial matters and the matters of parental responsibility, there is shared competence between the Community and Member States in respect of the Convention, see: Opinion 1/03 *Competence of the Community to conclude the new Lugano Convention on jurisdiction and the recognition and enforcement of judgments (opinion pursuant ot Article 300 EC)* [2006] ECR I–1145. By virtue of Council Decision 2008/431/EC of June 5, 2008, [2008] O.J. L151/36, Member States which had not already done so were authorised to ratify, or accede to the Convention in the interests of the European Community. Art.3 of the Decision provided that relevant Member States, which include the United Kingdom, should take the necessary steps to deposit simultaneously their instruments of ratification or accession with the Netherlands Ministry of Foreign Affairs "if possible before 5 June 2010." This date was not met. Under Art.61(2) of the Convention the instrument will enter into force for each State ratifying or accepting it, on the first day of the month following the expiration of three months after the deposit of its instrument of ratification or accession. See Parental Responsibility and Measures for the Protection of Children (International Obligations) (England and Wales and Northern Ireland) Regulations 2010 (SI 2010/1898). **19–006**

This new tier of private international law rules will co-exist with those found in Council Regulation 2201/2003 as well as in domestic law, in a relationship of no little complexity. Assistance as to the geographical scope of the regimes is found in the disconnection clauses, in particular Art.61 of the Regulation which provides that that instrument shall apply in preference to the 1996 Convention where a child is habitually resident in a Member State (see also Art.52, 1996 Convention). See generally McEleavy (2010) 59 I.C.L.Q. 505. A practice guide to clarify the inter-relationship of the Convention with Council Regulation 2201/2003 and the relevant rules of the Family Law Act 1986 is being prepared by the Ministry of Justice.

Where a child is not so habitually resident in a Member State but is habitually resident in a 1996 Convention Contracting State, then the latter instrument will govern jurisdiction. From a United Kingdom perspective the practical impact of the Convention jurisdiction rules applying will be limited, but it means that there will be no place for a prorogation agreement in the absence of matrimonial proceedings, even if all the agreements are present, (*cf.* Art.12(3) Council Regulation) and that prorogation in favour of the matrimonial forum would not need to be restricted to instances where those matrimonial proceedings are brought on the basis of Art.3 of Council Regulation 2201/2003 (see Convention, Art.10). Furthermore, if a child habitually resident in a non-EU Contracting State were wrongfully removed to or retained in the United Kingdom, Art.7 would apply to the jurisdictional consequences, whilst any potential conflicts of jurisdiction would otherwise be determined in accordance with Art.13.

Where a child is a refugee, internationally displaced because of disturbances in the child's home country, or the child's habitual residence cannot be established, then both the Council Regulation and the Convention would seek to assert jurisdiction over the child and neither explicitly claims priority. In such cases, which will be rare, a choice will have to be made as to which regime to be applied.

Notwithstanding the terms of Art.61 there is one situation where the Convention should be operable as regards children habitually resident in a Member State, namely where such a child has been wrongfully removed to or retained in a non-Member State Contracting State. In such a situation the benefit of Art.7 of the Convention should be available to protect the jurisdiction of the State of habitual residence. Art.61 should be regarded as inapplicable to such cases on the basis that abductions to non-Member States fall outside the scope of the Regulation.

The same reasoning can be applied to the rules on applicable law which are found within the Convention but not the Council Regulation. Consequently there should be no exclusion of these rules simply because a child is habitually resident within a Member State. However, the application of the Regulation rules of jurisdiction whenever a child is so habitually resident gives rise to a separate issue, for in accordance with Art.15 of the Convention the operation of the choice of law rules depends on jurisdiction being exercised in accordance with the provisions of the Convention. Those provisions resemble, but do not mirror the grounds contained within the Council Regulation. Therefore were jurisdiction to be taken on a Regulation basis for which there was no Convention equivalent, for example Art.12(3), then there would be no obligation under the Convention to apply Art.15. The legislator has now proceeded on the basis that the reference to Chapter II of the Convention in Art.15(1) of the Convention is to be read as including a reference to Chapter II of the Council Regulation: SI 2010/ 1898, r.7.

The impact of the general choice of law rule in Art.15 will be limited since when exercising jurisdiction in relevant cases, the authorities of Contracting

States shall continue to apply their own law (Art.15(1)). It is only in exceptional cases that the law of another State, (whether or not a Contracting State) with which the situation has a substantial connection, may be applied or taken into consideration (Art.15(2)). Potential situations can be envisaged, such as where a dispute arises as between parents who have only recently arrived from a foreign jurisdiction with which the entire family has strong and long held connections. Whilst the discretion is wide it must be doubted whether it would be applied where the foreign law were to provide for an outcome which would be considered unacceptable from a domestic perspective, for example the automatic transfer of custody from one parent to another upon the child reaching a certain age (*cf. EM (Lebanon)* v *Secretary of State for the Home Department* [2008] UKHL 64, [2009] 1 A.C. 1198). In any event there is the additional safeguard for the application of the law to be refused on the basis of public policy, taking into account the best interests of the child, (Art.22). Greater difficulty as regards the exercise of the Art.15(2) discretion may arise where the foreign law is not objectively discriminatory but simply applies a different interpretation to that adopted in England and Wales, for example in the case of leave to remove applications (*cf.* the more restrictive position adopted in New Zealand: *D v S* [2002] NZFLR 116).

Art.16 establishes a choice of law rule as regards the attribution or extinction of parental responsibility. It is not restricted to situations where jurisdiction has been taken to protect the person or property of the child, but is of general application, where there is an international element. The general rule is that the attribution or extinction of parental responsibility by operation of law, without the intervention of a judicial or administrative authority, is governed by the law of the child's current State of habitual residence (Art.16(1)). Art.16(4) confirms that where a change in habitual residence leads to a person acquiring parental responsibility, who previously had none, it is the law of the new State of habitual residence which applies. However, where a change in habitual residence leads to a loss of parental responsibility attributed by operation of law, the parental responsibility existing under the law of the former State of habitual residence will subsist (Art.16(3)). Furthermore, parental responsibility arising (or extinguished) by an agreement or a unilateral act without judicial intervention, is to be governed by the law of the child's State of habitual residence at the time the agreement was made ( Art.16(2)). By way of protection, Art.17 provides that the exercise of parental responsibility is governed by the law of the child's actual State of habitual residence, therefore where rights are held by virtue of Art.16(2) or (3) regard must be paid to any effects imposed by the primary governing law, which will often, but will not necessarily be, the *lex fori*. The public policy exception (Art.22) is also potentially applicable.

Fewer difficulties apply to the rules on recognition and enforcement. Art.61 provides that the Regulation will apply where the recognition is sought in one Member State of any judgment rendered in another Member State, even if the child concerned is habitually resident in a Contracting State. The Convention rules will therefore apply in the United Kingdom where the recognition is sought of a measure rendered in a non-Member State, Contracting State. Where the United Kingdom is the Contracting State of origin and jurisdiction has been taken under the Regulation, the child having been habitually resident in a Member State, if that jurisdiction has been taken on the basis of Art.12(3) the resultant judgment may be refused recognition in a Contracting State for the very reason that there is no Convention equivalent to this ground, (Art.23(2)(a)).

## 2. GUARDIANSHIP AND CUSTODY

### A. *Jurisdiction of the English courts*

**19R–011** NOTE 28. Supreme Court Act 1981 is now renamed Senior Courts Act 1981: Constitutional Reform Act 2005, s.59 and Sch.11, in force October 1, 2009.

NOTE 47. The court may remove a stay granted under Art.15 of the Regulation only in accordance with that Article: Family Law Act 1986, s.5(3A) as inserted by SI 2005/265, reg.11(1),(6). The mechanism operates solely between Member States and not internally between territorial units of a single Member State: *Re ESJ (A Minor: Residence Order)* [2008] N.I. Fam. 6.

NOTE 48. Family Law Act 1986, s.5(2) is further amended by SI 2005/265, reg.11(1),(3).

**19–016** NOTE 58. Supreme Court Act 1981 is now renamed Senior Courts Act 1981: Constitutional Reform Act 2005, s.59 and Sch.11, in force October 1, 2009.

**19–017** There is jurisdiction, to be exercised very sparingly, where a child was resident in England but has been taken abroad by one parent with the recent consent of the other parent: *M v M (Stay of proceedings)* [2005] EWHC 1159 (Fam.), [2006] 1 F.L.R. 138; *Re L (Residence: Jurisdiction)* [2006] EWHC 3374 (Fam.), [2007] 1 F.L.R. 1686.

**19–018** Jurisdiction over a child resident abroad was taken on nationality grounds in *Loubani v Yassin* (2006) 277 D.L.R. (4th) 79 (BCCA) having regard to the fact that the law of Saudi Arabia, in which the children were living, did not treat men and women equally; the father, having taken Canadian citizenship, had to accept the basic principle that men and women were created equal.

**19–020** Following *Al Habtour v Fotheringham* [2001] EWCA Civ 186, [2001] 1 F.L.R. 951, Sir Mark Potter P. held in *Re A (A Child) (Wardship: Habitual Residence)* [2006] EWHC 3338 (Fam.), [2007] 1 F.C.R. 390 that in wardship proceedings, it was not the function of the court to make declarations of unlawful detention abroad based upon the nationality or domicile of the child concerned. Similarly in *ES v AJ* [2010] EWHC 1113 (Fam.), [2010] Fam. Law 786 Sir Nicholas Wall P. refused to entertain an application for wardship proceedings where the children were neither habitually resident nor present in the jurisdiction, notwithstanding that they had British nationality and both parents were so habitually resident.

Add: *cf. B v D (Abduction: Inherent Jurisdiction)* [2008] EWHC 1246 (Fam.), [2009] 1 F.L.R. 1015 in which the application of the inherent jurisdiction and the Council Regulation were conflated.

Supreme Court Act 1981 is now renamed Senior Courts Act 1981: Constitutional Reform Act 2005, s.59 and Sch.11, in force October 1, 2009. **19–022**

Note 91. Add: *cf. B* v *B*, 2009 S.C. 58 in which the Inner House of the Court of Session upheld the jurisdiction of the matrimonial forum and refused to grant a stay, notwithstanding several years of litigation in England where the child had been present for almost eight years. **19–026**

Note 2. Add: *Surowiak v Dennehy*, 2006 S.C.L.R. 805, *sub nom. S v D*, 2007 S.L.T. (Sh. Ct.) 37, noted Maher, 2007 S.L.T. 117. **19–030**

Note 3. Add: Case C–435/06 *C* [2007] ECR I–10141; Case C–523/07 *Proceedings Brought by A* [2009] E.C.R. I–2805; *Re S (Care: Jurisdiction)* [2008] EWHC 3013 (Fam.), [2009] 2 F.L.R. 550.

Note 4. Add: The naming of children has separately been the subject of consideration by the European Court: Case C–148/02 *Garcia Avello v Belgium* [2003] ECR I–11613; Case C–353/06 *Grunkin and Paul* [2008] E.C.R. I–7639.

The principle of mutual trust implies that a Member State court seised of an application relating to parental responsibility must determine not only whether it has jurisdiction having regard to Arts 8 to 14 of the Regulation, but demonstrate unquestionably that it intended to respect those rules and to indicate the substantive basis of jurisdiction relied upon. Where doubt exists, a court in a Member State of recognition may ascertain the basis on which jurisdiction was exercised: Case C–256/09 *Purrucker* v *Pérez*, July 15, 2010. **19–031**

Note 5. Add: The autonomous Community definition of habitual residence to be applied in respect of matters of parental responsibility differs from that applied to other areas of Community law, including, it would appear, matrimonial actions under Council Regulation 2201/2003: Case C–523/07 *Proceedings Brought by A* [2009] 2 E.C.R. I–2805; see entries above at paras 6–127 and 18–003. For children, regard must be paid to their actual centre of interests. Moreover their presence in a Member State must not in any way be temporary or intermittent. There must be some degree of integration in a social and family environment. In this the duration, regularity, conditions and reasons for the stay on the territory of a Member State as well as the family's move to that State, the child's nationality, the place and conditions of attendance at school, linguistic knowledge and the family and social relationships of the child in that State must all be taken into consideration.

Regard may equally be paid to parental intentions to settle permanently with the child in another Member State, and in this tangible steps such as the purchase or lease of a residence in the host Member State, or an application for social housing may constitute an indicator of the transfer of the habitual residence. Conversely a short period of residence, during which there has been a peripatetic existence, would more likely indicate an absence of habitual residence in the State in question. In *Re S (A Child)(Habitual Residence)* [2009] EWCA Civ 1021, [2010] 1 F.L.R. 1146 a temporary relocation from Belgium to England, because of the father's work commitments, led to his one and a half year old daughter acquiring an English habitual residence after eight weeks. In this Thorpe L.J. drew attention to the European Union dimension of the case and the fact the family had been pursuing its right of free movement: at [15].

Note 6. Add: The effectiveness of this mechanism depends on an immediate change in habitual residence in favour of the destination State, for the three-month period of continuing jurisdiction runs from the time of the move and not the acquisition of habitual residence. See McEleavy (2004) 53 I.C.L.Q. 503.

**19–032** "In an unequivocal manner" is to be judged objectively on the basis of the relevant party's litigation conduct. Full participation in proceedings will demonstrate such acceptance, even if the possibility of challenging the jurisdiction was never raised with that party (in the absence of fraud or misrepresentation): *C v C* [2006] EWHC 3247 (Fam.). Where a party seeks particular relief from the court, that may not amount to an acceptance of jurisdiction more generally: *Surowiak v Dennehy*, 2006 S.C.L.R. 805, *sub nom S v D*, 2007 S.L.T. (Sh. Ct.) 37.

Text to note 9. The filing in the English court exercising jurisdiction in a matrimonial matter of a statement of proposed arrangements for the children is not an acceptance of the court's jurisdiction in matters of parental responsibility: *Bush v Bush* [2008] EWCA Civ 865, [2008] 2 F.L.R. 1437.

Note 9. Once a party accepts jurisdiction he should not be able to withdraw it any time before the conclusion of the case: *Re I (A Child) (Contact Application: Jurisdiction) (Centre for Family Law and Practice and another intervening)* [2009] UKSC 10, [2010] 1 A.C. 319; *Re S-R (Jurisdiction: Contact)* [2008] 2 F.L.R. 1741. Parties who subsequently join proceedings cannot upset an agreement which the original parties have made: *Re I* at [32].

Detailed consideration was given by the Supreme Court in *Re I* to the modalities of acceptance for the purposes of Art.12(3), in particular whether acceptance was required at the time the court was seised, or could follow at any time by those who had been parties at the time the court was seised. No agreement was reached but had the matter been decisive a preliminary ruling would have been required from the European Court.

There has been judicial approval of the interpretation advanced in note 9 that nothing turns on the difference between "the best interests of the child" in Art.12(3) and "the superior interests of the child" in Art.12(1): *Re I (A Child) (Contact Application: Jurisdiction) (Centre for Family Law and Practice and another intervening)* [2009] UKSC 10, [2010] 1 AC 319; *Bush* v *Bush* [2008] EWCA Civ 865, [2008] 2 F.L.R. 1437. In *Re I* it was confirmed that the requirement will not depend on a profound investigation of the child's situation but on considerations relevant to ascertaining the most appropriate forum: at [36]; see also *Bush* at [44].

NOTE 10. Add: *Re L (Residence: Jurisdiction)* [2006] EWHC 3374 (Fam.), [2007] 1 F.L.R. 1686 (jurisdiction until decree absolute, even though stage past at which proceedings concerned children).

Although Art.12(3) refers to substantial connection with a Member State, it is **19–033**
necessary (assuming that the Regulation applies as between the component units of the United Kingdom) to interpret it as requiring substantial connection with the relevant unit: *Surowiak v Dennehy*, 2006 S.C.L.R. 805, *sub nom S v D*, 2007 S.L.T. (Sh. Ct.) 37. For the meaning of "in an unequivocal manner" see entry at para.19–032 above.

In urgent cases Regulation State courts are entitled by virtue of Art.20 to take **19–034**
such provisional, including protective, measures in respect of persons or assets in that State as may be available under the law of that State, even if the court of another Regulation State has jurisdiction under the Regulation as to the substance of the matter. This is an exception to the otherwise strict *lis pendens* rule which otherwise applies to parental responsibility proceedings under the Regulation (Art.19(2)) as it does to matrimonial actions (Art.19(1) *cf.* 18R–240). In Case C–523/07 *Proceedings Brought by A* [2009] 2 E.C.R. I–2805, the European Court indicated that the standard for such intervention was high, holding that where children were temporarily outside the Member State of their habitual residence such measures could be taken where a situation arose which was likely seriously to endanger their welfare, including their health or development. The court further noted that there was no obligation on a court so acting to transfer the case to the court having jurisdiction, but it did not rule out this requirement entirely. It did hold, as was the case with Art.17, that in cases of urgency the competent judicial authorities should be advised of the steps taken. In *Re S (Care: Jurisdiction)* [2008]

EWHC 3013 (Fam.), [2009] 2 F.L.R. 550, where protective measures were required in respect of a suspected trafficked child who was habitually resident in Romania, the court held that the primary focus under Art.20 should be the identification of possible issues and risks for decision by the foreign court and the putting in place of appropriate interim measures to minimise harm arising from the materialisation of such risks and to enable the foreign court to take such advantage, as it so wished, of the steps taken in the United Kingdom. Ordinarily, fact-finding hearings would not be undertaken, unless a relevant incident had taken place in the jurisdiction and involved residents of the State who did not speak the language of the other Regulation State. In Case C–403/09 PPU *Detiček* v *Sgueglia* [2010] 3 W.L.R. 1098 the European Court reconfirmed that as an exception to the Regulation's system of jurisdiction, Art.20 must be interpreted strictly. In a case of wrongful removal between Member States it may not be used by the authorities in the Member State of refuge as a means by which to grant custody to the abducting parent. The European Court also clarified that the requirement of urgency in Art.20 related both to the situation of the child, as well as to the practical impossibility of bringing the parental responsibility application before the court with jurisdiction as to the substance of the matter. A change of circumstances deriving from the child becoming settled in the State of refuge did not suffice to render a case "urgent" for the purposes of Art.20; to find otherwise would undermine the Regulation by encouraging delay in enforcement procedures and would strengthen the position of abductors. The Court further noted that whilst Art.20 applied to persons or assets in the State in question, in the present case the applicant father, who was affected by the ruling of the Slovenian court ruling, continued to reside in Italy. Art.20 must also be interpreted in a manner which respects the fundamental rights of the child, including Art.24(3) of the Charter of Fundamental Rights of the European Union, the right to maintain on a regular basis a personal relationship and direct contact with both parents.

Provisional measures made under Art.20 may, in the Member State in which they have been made, prevail over an earlier judgment adopted by a court of another Member State which has substantive jurisdiction. However, such measures do not qualify for recognition in other Member States under the provisions of the Council Regulation (*cf.* Art.11, 1996 Hague Convention). Recourse may nevertheless be had to other international instruments or national legislation, insofar as compatible with the Regulation. This could include the Luxembourg Convention 1980 (European Convention on Recognition and Enforcement of Decisions concerning Custody of Children and on Restoration of Custody of Children), but would not extend to the 1996 Hague Convention (*cf.* Council Regulation 2201/2003, Art.61(b)): Case C–256/09 *Purrucker* v *Pérez*, July 15, 2010.

**19–035** A measure of confusion has though arisen in both Scotland and Northern Ireland as to the precise impact of the Council Regulation on the applicability of the Family Law Act rules in cases perceived to have a purely intra-United Kingdom dimension. See *S v D*, 2007 S.L.T. (Sh. Ct.) 37, noted Maher, 2007 S.L.T. 117; *B v B*, 2009 S.L.T. (Sh. Ct.) 24; *Re ESJ (A Minor: Residence Order)* [2008] N.I. Fam. 6, noted Maher, 2008 Jur. Rev. 315.

Whilst there may be an expectation that the Community rules only extend to disputes as between Member States (*cf.* Art.65 EC Treaty; Maher 2007 S.L.T. 117) the reality of the drafting of the Council Regulation is quite different. Art.14 makes clear that recourse may only be had to non-Regulation bases of jurisdiction where no court of a Member State has jurisdiction pursuant to Arts 8–13. Art.8 (habitual residence of the child) will be applicable and activate the Regulation in the vast majority of cases, including those with no ostensible international dimension. Even if a child is not habitually resident in a Regulation State, Art.12 may be applicable. Neither of these grounds is in any way limited to international cases, nor is there an over-riding provision so limiting the operation of the instrument (*cf.* Art.46, 1996 Hague Convention) so they must therefore take priority over the jurisdictional hierarchy contained within the Family Law Act 1986.

NOTE 19. Add: and further proceedings between the parties in Scotland, first *RB v RB* [2005] CSIH 60, 2005 Fam. L.R. 49, then *B v B* 2009 S.C. 58.

NOTE 22. Add: *B* v *B*, 2009 S.C. 58.

NOTE 49. Add: *B* v *B*, 2009 S.C. 58. **19–042**

This jurisdiction was exercised in *H v D* [2007] EWHC 802 (Fam.). See *Carroll v Carroll* [2005] Fam. L.R. 99 (Sh. Ct), where it was held that the Scottish courts had no "emergency" jurisdiction when the case was being actively addressed by a competent English court. Cf. Article 20, Council Regulation 2201/2003; Case C–523/07 *Proceedings Brought by A* [2009] E.C.R. I–2805. **19–045**

The competent foreign court should ordinarily be seised of proceedings, or at least the applicant must be prepared to seise that court to enable it to adjudicate on the issue of possible transfer: *Re EC (Child Abduction: Stayed Proceedings)* [2006] EWCA Civ 1115, [2007] 1 F.L.R. 57. **19–047**

Even if the qualifying criteria are satisfied and no matter how strong the claim might be, the requesting court cannot intervene or otherwise pre-empt the cession of jurisdiction: *Re S-R (Jurisdiction: Contact)* [2008] 2 F.L.R. 1741. It has though been suggested that where all the relevant conditions are met it would be difficult to envisage circumstances where a transfer would not be appropriate: *AB v JLB (Brussels II Revised: Article 15)* [2008] EWHC 2965, [2009] 1 F.L.R. 517. See also *Re RD (Child Abduction) (Brussels II Revised: Articles 11(7) and 19)* [2009] 1 F.L.R. 586. **19–048**

**19–049** Transfer requests made in the face of a pending return order made under the Hague Convention have ordinarily been rejected: *F v M and N (Abduction: Acquiescence: Settlement)* [2008] EWHC 1525, [2008] 2 F.L.R. 1270; *NJC v NPC* [2008] CSIH 34, 2008 S.C. 571. However, where a non-return order has been made following a finding of settlement, albeit within the context of Art.13(1)(b), this has been supplemented by a request that jurisdiction be transferred: *JPC v SLW and SMW (Abduction)* [2007] EWHC 1349 (Fam.); [2007] 2 F.L.R. 900. See also *RS v KS (Abduction: Wrongful Retention)* [2009] EWHC 1494 (Fam.), [2009] 2 F.L.R. 1231 (a finding of settlement within the 12-month period, led to a finding that a grave risk of harm existed). A transfer request has also been made upon a finding that two siblings would each face a grave risk of harm if returned, the elder being a suicide risk: *Re H (Abduction)* [2009] EWHC 1735 (Fam.), [2009] 2 FLR 1513. Whilst an application for transfer may be re-issued, the applicant would be required to show that it would be highly probable the court seised would relinquish the case: *AB v JLB (Brussels II Revised: Article 15)* [2008] EWHC 2965 (Fam.), [2009] 1 F.L.R. 517.

NOTE 61. Add: *Re S-R (Jurisdiction: Contact)* [2008] 2 F.L.R. 1741.

**19–050** NOTE 62. Family Law Act 1986, s.5(2) is further amended by SI 2005/265, reg.11(1),(3). See also *B v B*, 2009 S.C. 58.

**19–051** Under the 1996 Hague Convention choice of law rules will be applicable, see above, entry at para.19–006.

NOTE 66. Add: *M v M (Stay of Proceedings: Return of Children)* [2005] EWHC 1159 (Fam.), [2006] 1 F.L.R. 138; *V v V* [2006] EWHC 3374 (Fam.), *sub nom Re L (Residence: Jurisdiction)* [2007] 1 F.L.R. 1686.

**19–052** No leave of the court is required for the permanent removal of a child from England to Northern Ireland: *Re B (A Child) (Prohibited Steps Order)* [2007] EWCA Civ 1055 (Fam.), [2008] 1 F.L.R. 613.

A move may lead to a reappraisal of contact arrangements: *Re X and Y (Temporary Relocation within the United Kingdom: Appeal from Master; Interim Maintenance)* [2005] N.I. Fam. 8.

**19–055** In *Re A (Leave to Remove: Cultural and Religious Considerations)* [2006] EWHC 421 (Fam.), [2006] 2 F.L.R. 572 reference was made to criticisms of the Court of Appeal's approach and to current debate on that matter in family law circles. See Hayes (2006) 18 C.F.L.Q. 351. It was argued in *Re G (Leave to Remove)* [2007] EWCA Civ 1497, [2008] 1 F.L.R. 1587 that the approach in *Payne v Payne* [2001] EWCA Civ 166, [2002] Fam. 473 was out of date, placing too much emphasis on the effect a refusal might have on the child's primary carer. The court held that it was bound by *Payne v Payne* and there had been no major shift in society such as would justify changes in the governing principles. Criticism of the position adopted in *Payne v Payne* [2001] EWCA Civ 166, [2002] Fam. 473, in that it pays too much attention to the views of the relocating parent and too little attention to the damage caused to children by the loss of their relationship with the left behind parent, has received judicial acknowledgment: *Re D (A Child)* [2010] EWCA Civ 593. Wall L.J. noted however that the decision would remain binding until such time as it was overtaken by legislation or a decision of the Supreme Court. See also: *Re H (A Child)* [2010] EWCA Civ 915; *Re AR (A Child: Relocation)* [2010] EWHC 1346 (Fam.).

NOTE 77. Add: *Re B (Leave to Remove)* [2006] EWHC 1783 (Fam.), [2007] 1 F.L.R. 333 (removal by primary carer; motivation and practicality tests satisfied); *Re J (Children) (Residence Order: Removal Outside Jurisdiction)* [2006] EWHC Civ 1897, *sub nom. Re J (Leave to Remove; Urgent Case)* [2007] 1 F.L.R. 2033 (removal by bankrupt who saw only hope of re-establishing himself in move to Bulgaria; proposals "inchoate" but practical; leave given); *H v F (Refusal of Leave to Remove a Child from the Jurisdiction)* [2005] EWHC 2705 (Fam.), [2006] 1 F.L.R. 776 (removal to Jamaica refused on practicality grounds); *Re W (Children) (Leave to Remove)* [2008] EWCA Civ 538; [2008] 2 F.L.R. 1170 (in granting leave primary emphasis was placed on the financial consequences and drop in standard of living of mother and children being required to remain in London, post-divorce).

NOTE 78. Add: *Re B (Children) (Leave to Remove)* [2008] EWCA Civ 1034; [2008] 2 F.L.R. 2059. As to whether older children should be heard directly by the judge see: *Re W (Children) (Leave to Remove)* [2008] EWCA Civ 538; [2008] 2 F.L.R. 1170.

NOTE 79. Add: *Re A (Leave to Remove: Cultural and Religious Considerations)* [2006] EWHC 421 (Fam.), [2006] 2 F.L.R. 572 (mother's new husband working in the Netherlands; all parties Iraqi and father opposing removal relied on the child's consequential loss of the right to succeed as "mantle head" of a group of families; on facts leave given); *Re H (A Child)* [2007] EWCA Civ 222, [2007] 2 F.L.R. 317 (relocation in mother's home country with new husband).

NOTE 80. Add: *DS v RS* [2009] EWHC 1594 (Fam.), [2010] 1 F.L.R. 576 (extensive undertakings from applicant mother and a signed statement from the maternal grandparents).

NOTE 81. On the issue of costs see *Re S. (Leave to Remove: Costs)* [2010] 1 F.L.R. 834.

NOTE 82. In *Re N (Leave to Remove: Holiday)* [2006] EWCA Civ 357, [2006] 2 F.L.R. 1124, the court took into account, in giving leave for a child to travel unaccompanied to Slovakia to visit relations, the fact that Slovakia is a party to the Hague Child Abduction Convention. Even where the motives of the applicant parent are not under suspicion, regard must be paid to the consequences should the child not be returned: *Re K (Removal from Jurisdiction)* [1999] 2 F.L.R. 1084 (CA). Where a non-1980 Hague Convention State is involved expert evidence on the practicalities of the foreign legal system will ordinarily be required: *Re M (A Child)* [2010] EWCA Civ 888. See also *Re Sabina and Tamim (Temporary Removal from the Jurisdiction to Bangladesh)* [2009] NIFam 20 (expert report from Bangladeshi advocate appended to judgment permitting vacation). In *Re L (Removal from the Jurisdiction: Holiday)* [2009] NIFam 21, in addition to stringent undertakings, the applicant father was only permitted to take one of his three children abroad, in order to minimize the risk of non-return. Stephens J. noted that this arrangement could potentially be extended to each sibling in turn.

Note 83. Add: As regards a relocation solely within the jurisdiction see: *Re L (Shared Residence Order)* [2009] EWCA Civ 20, [2009] 1 F.L.R. 1157.

B. *Effect of foreign guardianship and custody orders*

**19–068** Note 20. Family Law Act 1986, s.29 is further amended by the Children and Adoption Act 2006, Sch.2, paras 2, 4.

Note 23. Family Law Act 1986, s.29(1) is further amended by the Children and Adoption Act 2006, Sch.2, paras 2, 4.

Note 25. The power under s.30 is qualified by s.30(1A) inserted by the Children and Adoption Act 2006, Sch.2, paras 2, 5.

**19–070** For the difficulties sometimes encountered in securing the recognition and enforcement in other Member States of orders made in England, see *Re ML and AL (children) (Contact Order: Brussels II Regulation)* [2006] EWHC 2385 (Fam.), [2007] 1 F.C.R. 475 and *Re ML and AL (children) (Contact Order: Brussels II Regulation) (No.2)* [2006] EWHC 3631 (Fam.), [2007] 1 F.C.R. 496.

On the difficulty of operating this part of Regulation 2201/2003 in terms of the current Family Proceedings Rules, see *Re D (Brussels II Revised: Contact)* [2007] EWHC 822 (Fam.), [2008] 1 F.L.R. 516.

A public law decision to take a child into care is a "civil matter" for the purposes of Regulation 2201/2003: Case C–435/06 *Re C* [2007] ECR I–1014.

For the interpretation of the transitional provisions in Regulation 2201/2003, Art.64 in the case of new Member States, see *D v D* [2007] EWCA Civ 1277, [2008] 1 F.L.R. 1003.

In furtherance of the Community policy of mutual recognition, the Regulation provides that certain orders may benefit from automatic enforceability in Member States. Access orders (Art.41) and orders for return made pursuant to Art.11(8), (Art.42) which are certified as having satisfied certain procedural requirements, shall be recognised and enforceable in another Member State without the need for a declaration of enforceability and without any possibility of opposing their recognition (*cf.* Art.47(2)—irreconcilability with a subsequent enforceable judgment is dealt with at the enforcement stage), see Case C–195/08 PPU *Inga Rinau* [2008] E.C.R. I–5271, [2009] Fam. 51; Case C–211/10 PPU *Povse* v *Alpago*, July 1, 2010.

Text to note 29. See Case C–195/08 PPU *Inga Rinau* [2008] E.C.R. I–5271, [2009] Fam. 51.

Without finally deciding the point, Black J. in *Re D (Brussels II Revised: Contact)* [2007] EWHC 822 (Fam.), [2008] 1 F.L.R. 516 inclined to the view that the approach of Holman J. in *Re S (Brussels II: Recognition: Best Interests of Child) (No.2)* [2003] EWHC 2974 (Fam.), [2004] 1 F.L.R. 582 remained correct under Brussels II Revised, and that the welfare of the child was not a paramount or even a primary consideration. **19–072**

NOTE 30. Add: *Re T and J (Abduction: Recognition of Foreign Judgment)* [2006] EWHC 1472 (Fam.), [2006] 2 F.L.R. 1290.

*cf. Re S (Brussels II (Revised): Enforcement of Contact Order)* [2008] 2 F.L.R. 1358 in which enforcement was refused of an outdated, fast-track compliant contact order. In *Re Jakub and Dawid (Brussels II Revised: Recognition and Enforcement of Foreign Order)* [2009] NIFam 23, the Northern Ireland High Court took into consideration the views of the children (eight and six) where the registration of a Polish residence order was appealed (appeal dismissed and residence order enforced). See generally Case C–211/10 PPU *Povse* v *Alpago*, July 1, 2010, (entry at para.19–131, above).

NOTE 37. Add: *Re G (Contact)* [2006] EWCA Civ 1507, [2007] 1 F.L.R. 1663. **19–074**

See *Da Silva v Pitts* (2007) 289 D.L.R. (4th) 540 (Ont. C.A.) where the foreign order was in fact a non-return order under the Hague Convention. **19–077**

The test for deciding whether a child should be separately represented in an international case not falling within the Hague Convention is that in *Mabon v Mabon* [2005] EWCA Civ 634, [2005] 2 F.L.R. 1011, whether or not it is the best interests of the child: *C v C* [2008] EWHC 517 (Fam.), [2008] 2 F.L.R. 6. **19–079**

Immigration issues may become relevant in considering the welfare of the child, including the question to which country a child should be returned. It is **19–081** desirable that there should be communication and co-operation between the court and the Secretary of State in such cases: *Re F (Children) (Abduction: Removal Outside Jurisdiction)* [2008] EWCA Civ 854, [2008] 2 F.L.R. 1649. Where children have no realistic prospect of being allowed to remain in the jurisdiction, the abducting parent having failed to secure asylum, this will be a relevant factor militating in favour of a return order and one which can take precedence over the settlement of the children after three years of residence: *Re F (Abduction: Removal Outside Jurisdiction)* [2008] EWCA Civ 842, [2008] 2 F.L.R. 1649.

**19–082** A majority in *EM (Lebanon) v Secretary of State for the Home Department* [2008] UKHL 64, [2009] 1 A.C. 1198 (Baroness Hale of Richmond dissenting) held in the context of an abduction case, albeit one dealt with under immigration and asylum law, that the arbitrary and discriminatory nature of Lebanese custody law was not of itself sufficient to activate a breach of Art.8 ECHR where a national of a State not party to the European Convention was concerned. However, there was unanimity that on the facts of the case Art.8 would have been breached were a return order to have been enforced.

**19–083** There is no obligation to invoke the Hague Convention in the event of an abduction and within the European Union the recognition mechanisms of Council Regulation may prove equally effective: *B v D (Abduction: Inherent Jurisdiction)* [2008] EWHC 1246 (Fam.), [2009] 1 F.L.R. 1015.

**19–084** NOTE 69. Add: A return may still be made on welfare grounds even if a non-return order is rendered in Hague Convention proceedings: *D v S (Abduction: Acquiescence)* [2008] EWHC 363 (Fam.), [2008] 2 F.L.R. 293.

**19–091** NOTE 91. Add: *S v S*, 2005 S.C.L.R. 587 (where the issue concerned the alleged concealment of the defendant's whereabouts).

NOTE 97. Add: *S v S*, 2005 S.C.L.R. 587.

NOTE 2. Add the neutral citation of *Re HE (A Child); EH v SH* [2004] IEHC 193, [2004] 2 I.R. 564.

**19–096** It was argued in *Re F (Abduction: Unborn Child)* [2006] EWHC 2199 (Fam.), [2007] 1 F.L.R. 627 that events before the birth of a child could constitute its wrongful removal or retention; the argument was rejected.

NOTE 20. The Central Authority for England and Wales is technically the Lord Chancellor but its duties are now carried out by the International Child Abduction and Contact Unit which remains under the administrative control of the Official Solicitor.

**19–097** For the autonomous meaning of habitual residence for the purposes of Council Regulation 2201/2003 (Brussels II *bis*), see the entry at para.18–003.

In the United States there is a difference of opinion between the Circuit Courts of Appeals as to whether the subjective intent of the parents is to be given weight (the view of the Third and Ninth Circuits: *Feder v Feder-Evans*, 63 F 3d 217 (3d Cir. 1995); *Mozes v Mozes*, 239 F. 3d 1067 (9th Cir 2001)) or whether the focus is upon the past experience of the child, especially on the question whether at the relevant date the child had been in a country long enough to be acclimatised there (the view of the Sixth Circuit: *Robert v Tesson*, 507 F. 3d 981 (6th Cir. 2007); *Simcox v Simcox*, 511 F. 3d 594 (6th Cir. 2007)).

Text to note 27. Article 10 of Council Regulation (EC) 2201/2003 (as to which see paras 19–128 *et seq.* of the main work) presupposes that a child may become habitually resident in a new country without the consent of both parents: *Re A; HA v MB (Brussels II Revised: Article 11(7) Application)* [2007] EWHC 2016 (Fam.), [2008] 1 F.L.R. 289, at [84].

Text to note 30. If the facts of a Hague Convention case so require, a child may be held to have no habitual residence: *Re A (Abduction: Habitual Residence)* [2007] EWHC 779 (Fam.), [2007] 2 F.L.R. 129; *Jackson v Graczyk* (2007) 86 O.R. (3d) 183 (Ont. C.A.).

Note 27. Add: *E v E* [2007] EWHC 276 (Fam.), [2007] 1 F.L.R. 1977.

Note 28. *Punter v Punter* was affirmed on appeal: [2004] 2 N.Z.L.R. 28 (NZCA). In later proceedings involving the same family and retention at the end of a two-year "shuttle custody" period, it was held that the child's habitual residence had changed during that period: *Punter v Secretary of Justice* [2007] 1 N.Z.L.R. 40 (N.Z.C.A.), citing *Watson v Jamieson*, 1998 S.L.T. 180 (O.H.).

Note 32. Add: The majority international position has moreover been **19–098**
accepted by the European Court of Human Rights: *Neulinger & Shuruk v Switzerland* [2009] E.C.H.R. 41615/07. This was accepted by the Grand Chamber: *Neulinger and Shuruk v Switzerland* [2010] ECHR 41615/07 [G.C.].

In *T Petitioner* [2007] CSOH 43, 2007 SLT 543 a right of co-decision making as to choice of school, profession and treatment in the case of serious illness in a Polish divorce decree was held to amount to rights relating to the care of the person of the child. On very similar facts it was concluded that the applicant Polish father had a right of veto: *Re F (Abduction: Rights of Custody)* [2008] EWHC 272 (Fam.), [2008] Fam. 75.

The United States Supreme Court, in a majority ruling (5), has now endorsed the standard international interpretation of custody rights, finding that the Convention's protection of a parent's custodial right 'to determine the child's place of residence' included a *ne exeat* right. The Court did not pronounce on the status of *ne exeat* orders which did not incorporate parental consent provisions: *Abbott v Abbott*, 130 S. Ct. 1983 (2010).

The word "place" in the phrase "the child's place of residence" includes the country of the child's residence; and a right to object to the child's removal to another country is as much a right of custody as a right to determine where the child is to live within the country of its residence: *Re D (A Child) (Abduction: Rights of Custody)* [2006] UKHL 51, [2007] 1 A.C. 619 (*per* Lord Hope of Craighead at [10]).

Rights of access and rights of custody are not mutually exclusive concepts; a person may have both: *Re D (A Child) (Abduction: Rights of Custody)* [2006] UKHL 51, [2007] 1 A.C. 619 (*per* Baroness Hale of Richmond at [26]).

The Irish High Court has held that a parent, even one without custody and only access rights, has, as the child's natural guardian, "rights of custody" for the purposes of the Convention: *Re JC (a minor); RC v IS* [2003] 4 I.R. 431.

It is now settled law, so far as the United Kingdom is concerned, that a right to determine the place of the child's residence, or to veto a proposed change of residence, whether it arises by court order, agreement or operation of law, is a right of custody: *Re D (A Child) (Abduction: Rights of Custody)* [2006] UKHL 51, [2007] 1 A.C. 619 (*per* Lord Hope of Craighead at [11]–[14], *per* Baroness Hale of Richmond at [31]–[37], preferring the view taken in *C v C (Abduction: Rights of Custody)* [1989] 1 W.L.R. 654; *Re P (A Child) (Abduction: Custody Rights)* [2005] Fam. 293; *Re W (Minors) (Abduction: Father's Rights)* [1999] Fam. 1, 9; and *AJ v FJ*, 2005 S.C. 428 I.H.) to that advanced by Anton (1981) 30 I.C.L.Q. 537, at p.546; *Re F (Children) (Abduction; Rights of Custody)* [2008] EWHC 272 (Fam.), [2008] 3 W.L.R. 527. See to the same effect *T, Ptr* [2007] CSOH 43, 2007 S.L.T. 543 (right of co-decision as to choice of school and treatment in case of serious illness held to amount to "rights of custody"), *JR v MR* (Fam. Ct. Australia, May 22, 1991, unreported), and *Foxman v Foxman* (Israel High Ct., October 28, 1992, unreported); and see *G v B* [1995] N.Z.F.L.R. 49; *D v C* [1999] N.Z.F.L.R. 97. Lord Carswell (at [74]) preferred to reserve the question whether a *ne exeat* clause gave rights of custody until it fell directly for decision in a case before the House. A mere right to apply to a court for a ne exeat order does not amount to a right of custody: *MW v Director-General of the Department of Community Services* [2008] HCA 1285, (2008) 244 A.L.R. 205.

To the United States cases cited add *Bader v Kramer*, 445 F 3d 346 (4th Cir. 2006) and see Silberman (2005) 38 U.C. Davis L.Rev. 1049.

**19–099** NOTE 38. Add: *A v B (Abduction: Declaration)* [2008] EWHC 2524 (Fam.), [2009] 1 F.L.R. 1253.

NOTE 42. In the latter decision it was suggested that a court would be vested with custody rights even before the respondent has been served, where a judge has exercised a judicial function as to the future conduct of the proceedings. This was applied in *X County Council v B. (Abduction: Rights of Custody in the Court)* [2009] EWHC 2635 (Fam.), [2010] 1 F.L.R. 1197 and extended to a quasi-judicial act of a legal adviser (effective adjournment by transfer to a County Court), in accordance with the Justices' Clerks Rules 2005. Whilst the Irish High Court subsequently accepted that rights of custody were vested in the English courts by virtue of service, no mention was made of the latter point: *Nottingham County Council v KB* [2010] IEHC 9.

Expert evidence on foreign law may be desirable, but in some cases the **19–101**
English court may have to form its own view of its meaning: *Re F (Children) (Abduction; Rights of Custody)* [2008] EWHC 272 (Fam.), [2008] 3 W.L.R. 527.

NOTE 49. See Beevers and Peréz Milla (2007) 3 J. Priv.Int.L. 201 and, for an account of Spanish decisions in breach of the Convention, *Carrascosa v McGuire*, 520 F. 3d 249 (3d Cir. 2008). *cf. Re K (Rights of Custody Spain)* [2009] EWHC 1066 (Fam.), [2010] 1 F.L.R. 57 in which an unmarried father was deemed to have rights of custody pursuant to the application of Spanish private international law rules. Notwithstanding the renvoi to English law, the President accepted expert evidence that a Spanish court would be likely to consider the very application of English law to be contrary to the Spanish Constitution for it would challenge the equality of rights between matrimonial and non-matrimonial children. This interpretation was upheld by the Court of Appeal: *Kennedy v Kennedy* [2009] EWCA Civ 986, [2010] 1 F.L.R. 782.

NOTE 53. Add: *Re A (Abduction: Rights of Custody: Imprisonment)* [2004] 1 F.L.R. 1; *Re L (A Child)* [2005] EWHC 1237 (Fam.), [2006] 1 F.L.R. 843.

Text to note 58. See the entry at para.19–106, below. **19–102**

NOTE 55. Add: *B v H (Habitual Residence: Wardship)* [2002] 1 F.L.R. 388; *Re D (A Child) (Abduction: Rights of Custody)* [2006] UKHL 51, [2007] 1 A.C. 619 (*per* Lord Hope of Craighead at [7]: "it is for the court to which the application is made, not the authorities of the requesting State, to decide whether the removal was wrongful within the meaning of article 3").

The correctness of the decision in *Re J (A Minor) (Custody Rights)* was **19–103**
asserted (*obiter*) by Baroness Hale of Richmond in *Re D (A Child) (Abduction: Rights of Custody)* [2006] UKHL 51, [2007] 1 A.C. 619, at [38]; she refused to recognise a parent's potential right of veto (such as a right to go to court and ask for an order about some aspect of the child's upbringing) as a right of custody. See Beevers (2006) 18 C.F.L.Q. 499.

NOTE 63. *Cf. obiter* comments of Thorpe L.J. in *Kennedy v Kennedy* [2009] EWCA Civ 986, [2010] 1 F.L.R. 782, [20] *et seq.*, espousing a broad interpretation of custody rights.

NOTE 67. Add: *AAA v ASH (Registrar General for England and Wales and the Secretary of State)* [2009] EWHC 636 (Fam.), [2010] 1 F.L.R. 1.

NOTE 68. *Cf. JMcB v LE* [2010] IESC 48 (Art.15 application; unmarried father had contacted solicitors with a view to applying to be appointed guardian, but the children were removed to England prior to the issue of proceedings. He argued that he had reached the threshold of family life for the purposes of Art.7 of the Charter of Fundamental Rights of the European Union and consequently should be considered as possessing rights of custody. The Irish Supreme Court did not support this interpretation, and the European Court also ruled against the father: Case C–400/10 PPU *JMcB v LE*, October 5, 2010.

**19–104** For perceived disadvantages in this understanding, see *Re T and J (Abduction: Recognition of Foreign Judgment)* [2006] EWHC 1472 (Fam.), [2006] 2 F.L.R. 1290, at [57]–[58].

NOTE 72. Add: *cf. RS v KS (Abduction, Wrongful Retention)* [2009] EWHC 1494 (Fam.), [2009] 2 F.L.R. 1231 in which the position adopted in *Re S (Minors) (Abduction: Wrongful Retention)* [1994] Fam. 70, that an intention to retain a child wrongfully did not have to be communicated to a left behind custodian in word or deed for the purpose of Art.12, was expressly rejected. Macur J. accepted that such an approach would threaten certainty and penalise an applicant by commencing the limitation period before he could or should have been aware that his rights had been breached.

NOTE 73. Add: *Re G (Abduction: Withdrawal of Proceedings: Acquiescence: Habitual Residence)* [2007] EWHC 2807 (Fam.), [2008] 2 F.L.R. 351.

NOTE 74. A retention will not become wrongful on the agreed date of return where the parent having care of the child has done everything to facilitate the child going home, only to be frustrated by a lack of travel documentation and the absence of co-operation on the part of the primary carer: *De L v H* [2009] EWHC 3074 (Fam.), [2010] 1 F.L.R. 1229.

**19–105** *cf. Best v Hesketh* [2005] EWCA Civ 1380, [2006] 1 F.L.R. 593, where a child abducted from Spain by its mother was re-abducted by the father back to Spain, and the Spanish court ordered that it be returned to England: in effect this meant that the child was no longer in England as a result of a wrongful removal but in accordance with a lawful order of a competent court, and the father's application under the Hague Convention, made at the time of the initial abduction, was struck out. In *Re T and J (Abduction: Recognition of*

*Foreign Judgment)* [2006] EWHC 1472 (Fam.), [2006] 2 F.L.R. 1290, a child was abducted to Spain and the left behind parent began proceedings there which resulted in custody being awarded to the abductor. It was held that the Spanish judgment was to be recognised under Council Regulation (EC) 2201/2003 and took priority over the Hague Convention; the application under the Convention also failed for other reasons.

NOTE 78. Add: *Coventry City Council v S.* [2010] IEHC 303.

A ruling under Art.15 must be from a court or other authority having power within the requesting State to make authoritative decisions relating to rights over children; an opinion of its central authority would not suffice: *Re D (A Child) (Abduction: Rights of Custody)* [2006] UKHL 51, [2007] 1 A.C. 619 (*per* Baroness Hale of Richmond at [39]). Once obtained, and save in exceptional circumstances, for example where the ruling had been obtained by fraud or in breach of the rules of natural justice, it must be conclusive as to the parties' rights under the law of the requesting State (*ibid.*, at [43]). *Hunter v Murrow (Abduction: Rights of Custody)* [2005] 2 F.L.R. 1119 concerned not the question of what were the parties' rights under the law of New Zealand but the distinct question, on which an English court was free to take its own view, as to whether those rights were properly characterised as "rights of custody" for Convention purposes. On the latter issue the court in the requested State must attach considerable weight to the authoritative decision of the requesting State and should only decline to follow it if its characterisation of the parent's rights was clearly out of line with the international understanding of the Convention's terms (*ibid.*, at [43]–[45]). Lord Carswell (at [83]) considered that on the rare occasions on which a determination under Art.15 might be expected to be sought, it should be treated almost invariably as conclusive on both limbs of the issue "whether the removal or return was wrongful within the meaning of article 3 of the Convention". **19–106**

In a majority ruling the New Zealand Court of Appeal declined to follow this interpretation, inclining instead towards the approach of the Court of Appeal in *Re D (A Child) (Abduction: Rights of Custody)* [2006] UKHL 51, [2007] 1 A.C. 61. Faced with an Art.15 request, answers should only be provided to domestic law questions, the characterisation of rights of custody as Convention rights and the determination of wrongfulness, were matters solely for the court seised of the return petition: *Fairfax v Ireton* [2009] NZCA 100, [2009] 3 N.Z.L.R. 289 (CA).

It was held in *Re D (A Child) (Abduction: Rights of Custody)* [2006] UKHL 51, [2007] 1 A.C. 619 (per Lord Hope of Craighead at [6]) that the delay inevitable if a foreign court is asked for a ruling under Art.15 meant that its use must be kept to the absolute minimum. This case led to an application to the European Court of Human Rights alleging that the delays amounted to a violation of Art.6(1) of the European Convention: *Deak v Romania and the*

*United Kingdom* [2008] E.C.H.R. 19055/05, [2008] 2 F.C.R. 303. On the facts the court held that there had been no violation of Art.6(1) in respect of the United Kingdom but there was a breach of that provision in respect of Romania.

In the light of the delays and difficulties inherent in the application of Art.15, as well as in instructing expert evidence as to the custody law of other Contracting States, Thorpe L.J. in *Re F (A Child) (Abduction: Refusal to Order Summary Return)* [2009] EWCA Civ 416, [2009] 2 F.L.R. 1023 called for greater use to be made of the European network of specialist family judges attached to the European judicial network.

Text to notes 84–86. It was said in *Re D (A Child) (Abduction: Rights of Custody)* [2006] UKHL 51, [2007] 1 A.C. 619 (*per* Lord Carswell at [79]–[80]) that no Art.15 determination has ever been requested from a United Kingdom court. The courts had made declarations purportedly under s.8; if such declarations could properly be made, they should carry altogether less weight than true Art.15 determinations. The interpretation of s.8 of the 1985 Act, allowing declarations to be made even if no request had been received under Art.15 of the Convention, in *Re P (Abduction: Declaration)* [1995] 1 F.L.R. 831 was followed in Scotland in *AJ v FJ* [2005] CSIH 36, 2005 S.C. 428.

**19–107** The Convention does not prevent a person seeking the return of a child from making a direct application to the courts of the country to which the child has been abducted: Art.29. In the case of such a direct application to the English courts there are severe disadvantages as public funding is not automatically available as it is when application is made via the Central Authority. See *Re A; HA v MB (Brussels II Revised: Article 11(7) Application)* [2007] EWHC 2016 (Fam.), at [21], [2008] 1 F.L.R. 289.

**19–108** An order may be suspended pending fulfilment of conditions: *F v M and N (Abduction: Acquiescence: Settlement)* [2008] EWHC 1525 (Fam.), [2008] 2 F.L.R. 1270; *RS v KS (Abduction: Wrongful Retention)* [2009] EWHC 1494 (Fam.), [2009] 2 F.L.R. 1231. A return order will not ordinarily be stayed pending the resolution of substantive proceedings in the State of the child's habitual residence: *K v K (Abduction: Return Order)* [2009] EWHC 132 (Fam.), [2010] 1 F.L.R. 1456.

**19–109** The House of Lords in *Re M (Children) (Abduction: Rights of Custody)* [2007] UKHL 55, [2008] 1 A.C. 1288 confirmed the approach adopted by the Court of Appeal in *Cannon v Cannon* [2004] EWCA Civ 133, [2005] 1 W.L.R. 32, that when one of the grounds for refusing to order return had been made out, the discretion to be exercised by the court in considering whether nonetheless to order return was a discretion which arose within the Convention and which had therefore to be informed by the policy of the Convention. Baroness Hale of Richmond held that when the discretion arose from the terms of the Convention itself, the discretion was at large. The court was entitled to take into account the various aspects of the Convention policy, alongside the circumstances which gave the court a discretion in the first place and the wider considerations of the child's rights and welfare. (See to the same effect *Secretary for Justice (New Zealand Central Authority) v HJ* [2007] 2 N.Z.L.R. 289 (N.Z. Sup. Ct).)

The House noted a tendency in some judgments to introduce a test or requirement of "exceptionality" into the exercise of discretion under the Convention. This was neither necessary nor desirable: the circumstances in which return may be refused were themselves exceptions to the general rule, and that in itself was sufficient exceptionality. Statements about exceptionality in *Zaffino v Zaffino (Abduction: Children's Views)* [2006] 1 F.L.R. 410, *Vigreux v Michel* [2006] EWCA Civ 630, [2006] 2 F.L.R. 1180 and *Klentzeris v Klentzeris* [2007] EWCA Civ 533, [2007] 2 F.L.R. 997 were disapproved.

NOTE 94. Add: *C v B (Abduction: Grave Risk)* [2005] EWHC 2988 (Fam.), [2006] 1 F.L.R. 1095 (strong reasons for child being in England where primary carer had family network; returned to Australia with suggestion that Australian court reconsider its earlier refusal to allow removal to England); *C v W* [2007] EWHC 1349 (Fam.), [2007] 3 F.C.R. 243 (welfare considerations favoured child remaining in England, but return to Ireland ordered).

In weighing the evidence of an abductor seeking to justify or explain the abduction, the judge must subject the evidence to rigorous and perhaps sceptical scrutiny: *Re D (Article 13b: Non-return)* [2006] EWCA Civ 146, [2006] 2 F.L.R. 305. **19–110**

Text to note 99. Practice in some other countries is much less expeditious. In *Robert v Tesson*, 507 F. 3d 981 (6th Cir. 2007), abduction in October 2003 led to a nine-day hearing before a US magistrate judge in July 2005, whose recommendations were adopted by the court in May 2006. The Circuit Court of Appeals delivered judgment on an appeal in November 2007.

NOTE 97. A report from the (London) Metropolitan Police was considered by the Irish High Court under Art.13 in *Re HE (A Child); EH v SH* [2004] IEHC 193, [2004] 2 I.R. 564.

NOTE 99. Oral evidence from a CAFCASS officer will often be heard when a child's objections to return are in issue: *Re M (A Child) (abduction: child's objections to return)* [2007] EWCA Civ 260, [2007] 2 F.L.R. 72.

In *Z v S-S* [2008] EWHC 490 (Fam.), Sumner J. held that a proposed or actual removal which starts off as consensual might turn into an unlawful removal or retention where the terms on which the consent was given radically changed; **19–113** but that was not so in the instant case. What had been an open-ended consent to future relocation of the child and its mother was ended or suspended when the mother misrepresented her trip abroad as a holiday trip and the father agreed to it on those terms: *Re L (Abduction: Future Consent)* [2007] EWHC 2181 (Fam.), [2008] 1 F.L.R. 914. Where consent is given to a removal and the children are subsequently brought back for the purposes of an agreed holiday, this will not by itself vitiate the earlier consent: *K v K (Abduction) (No 1)* [2009] EWHC 2721 (Fam.), [2010] 1 F.L.R. 1295 (*cf. K v K (Abduction)(No 2)* [2009] EWHC 3378 (Fam.), [2010] 1 F.L.R. 1310, fresh evidence admitted and additional hearing scheduled).

Reliance may be placed on consent which has been given significantly in advance of a removal, for example as a measure of reassurance where one parent has reservations about a proposed move abroad, or in pursuit of a reconciliation. The standards applied in such situations have evolved; a permissive approach was adopted in *Zenel v Haddow*, 1993 S.C. 612, whilst in *Re L (Abduction: Future Consent)* [2007] EWHC 2181 (Fam.), [2008] 1 F.L.R. 915 it was held that a future event which would activate a permitted removal must be of reasonable ascertainability and there must not have been a material change in the circumstances since the consent was given. However, in *Re P-J (Children) (Abduction, Habitual Residence: Consent)* [2009] EWCA Civ 588, [2010] 1 W.L.R. 1237, where the decision in *Zenel* was criticised, it was affirmed that such consent could be withdrawn at any time before the actual removal. The essential issue was whether "in reality" consent subsisted at the time of removal and in this a clandestine removal would ordinarily be indicative of the consent no longer existing. See also *C v H (Abduction: Consent)* [2009] EWHC 2660 (Fam.), [2010] 1 F.L.R. 225.

Note 8. The suggestion made in *Re W (Abduction: Procedure)* was advanced in *WT, Ptr* [2007] CSOH 72, and rejected.

Note 9. *T v T* is also reported *sub nom. KT v JT*, 2002 S.C. 323 (I.H.).

Note 10. Words must be evaluated in the context in which they have been used, in the light of the parties' relationship at that time and in the light of their contemporary understanding of where things stood and how they might develop: *C v H (Abduction: Consent)* [2009] EWHC 2660 (Fam.), [2010] 1 F.L.R. 225.

Note 11. Add: *C v H (Abduction: Consent)* [2009] EWHC 2660 (Fam.), [2010] 1 F.L.R. 225 (consent cannot be given by grandparents, even where the left behind parent is himself a minor).

Note 12. Add: *M v T (Abduction)* [2008] EWHC 1383 (Fam.), [2009] 1 F.L.R. 1309.

NOTE 13. Add: In *Re P-J (Children) (Abduction: Habitual Residence: Consent)* [2009] EWCA Civ 588, [2010] 1 W.L.R. 1237 both members of the panel reflected on the inter-relationship of the consent exception with Art.3, although they cautioned that they did not wish to re-open the issue.

NOTE 16. Add. The refusal of a custodial parent to assist the non-custodial parent in bringing about the return of the child is unlikely to amount to acquiescence: *De L v H* [2009] EWHC 3074 (Fam.), [2010] 1 F.L.R. 1229. **19–114**

NOTE 17. Add: *M v M* [2007] EWHC 1404 (Fam.), [2007] 2 F.L.R. 1010; *Re G (Abduction: Withdrawal of Proceedings: Acquiescence: Habitual Residence)* [2007] EWHC 2807 (Fam.), [2008] 2 F.L.R. 351 (withdrawal of Convention proceedings to seek reconciliation did not on facts amount to acquiescence so as to prejudice renewed application for return).

NOTE 18. Add: *B-G* v *B-G (Abduction: Acquiescence)* [2008] EWHC 688 (Fam.), [2008] 2 F.L.R. 965 (expressing an intention to move to the State of refuge).

NOTE 19. Add: *BT v SRT (A Child) (Abduction: Conditional Acquiesence and Consent)* [2008] EWHC 1169 (Fam.), [2008] 2 F.L.R. 972 (clear agreement by father that child could remain with mother in England for five years purportedly withdrawn ten days later as a result of mother's unenthusiastic response to father's plan to spend time in England; acquiescence established and withdrawal ineffective).

NOTE 24. Add: *C v W (Abduction)* [2007] EWHC 1349 (Fam.), [2007] 2 F.L.R. 900 (words spoken in anger).

NOTE 25. Inactivity is not in itself sufficient evidence of acquiescence: *Re F (Children) (Abduction: Rights of Custody)* [2008] EWHC 272 (Fam.), [2008] Fam. 75. Delay may be evidence of acquiescence, but delay is not in itself a basis for refusing the return of the child: *PL v EC* [2008] IESC 1, [2009] 1 I.R. 1.

NOTE 26. Add: *M v M* [2007] EWHC 1820 (Fam.) (incorrect legal advice led to 18 months inactivity, but as soon as left behind parent knew of Hague Convention he took steps the very next day; no acquiescence). *cf. D v S (Abduction: Acquiescence)* [2008] EWHC 363 (Fam.), [2008] 2 F.L.R. 293 (legal advice was not correct but nevertheless considered adequate; acquiescence established); *B-G* v *B-G (Abduction: Acquiescence)* [2008] EWHC 688 (Fam.), [2008] 2 F.L.R. 965 (applicant did not have correct advice about or detailed knowledge of his Convention rights and as a consequence expressed an intention to move to the State of refuge; acquiescence established).

The European Court of Human Rights initially endorsed this approach: *Maumousseau and Washington v France*, [2007] ECHR 39388/05; *Neulinger and* **19–115**

*Shuruk v Switzerland* [2009] ECHR 41615/07. However, in *Neulinger and Shuruk* v *Switzerland* [2010] ECHR 41615/07 [GC] the Grand Chamber concluded that the abductor would sustain a disproportionate interference with her right to respect for her family life if she were forced to return with the child to Israel (see below, entry at para.19–122).

Text to note 32. See para.19–129 for the specific rule in Regulation 2201/2003, under which a court may not refuse to order the return of the child if it is established that adequate arrangements have been made to secure the protection of the child after his or her return.

NOTE 28. Add: *Re HE (A Child); EH v SH* [2004] IEHC 193, [2004] 2 I.R. 564 (domestic violence between parents not sufficient to create grave risk to child).

NOTE 30. Add: *M, Ptr* [2007] CSOH 66, 2007 S.L.T. 433 (that child might find return stressful and previous medical symptoms might return not a grave risk); *AL, Ptr* [2007] CSOH 55 (left behind parent's lifestyle less than ideal, including cannabis use and drink-driving convictions, but grave risk to child not made out; return ordered); *Re TM and DM (minors); Minister for Justice (EM) v JM* [2003] IESC 40, [2003] 3 I.R. 178 (severely autistic child; possible delay in re-assessing needs on return to England not a grave risk); *Klentzeris v Klentzeris* [2007] EWCA Civ 533, [2007] 2 F.L.R. 997 (very strong CAFCASS report; child had panic attacks at thought of return), but note the disapproval of certain dicta in this case by the House of Lords in *Re M (Children) (Abduction: Rights of Custody)* [2007] UKHL 55, [2008] 1 A.C. 1288.

NOTE 31. Add: *Zaphiropoulos v Secretary of the Dept of Human Services* (2006) F.L.C. 93–264; *Re Z (Abduction)* [2008] EWHC 3473 (Fam.), [2009] 2 F.L.R. 298 (any concerns about domestic violence would be dealt with if the parties lived separately and protection could be provided by the local authorities); Bates [2007] I.F.L. 24.

NOTE 32. Add: *PL v EC* [2008] IESC 19, [2009] 1 I.R. 1.

NOTE 34. Add: *M v T (Abduction)* [2008] EWHC 1383 (Fam.), [2009] 1 F.L.R. 1309 (an abductor could not rely upon the emotional difficulties experienced by a child when they largely resulted from her actions); *Re H (Abduction)* [2009] EWHC 1735 (Fam.), [2009] 2 F.L.R. 1513 (older child was a suicide risk, younger brother's relationship with both parents would face "irreparable damage" if returned).

NOTE 37. Add: *Re D (Article 13b: Non-return)* [2006] EWCA Civ 146, [2006] 2 F.L.R. 305 (abducting mother, and possibly also father, shot and wounded in Venezuela, perhaps for political reasons: real risk of harm to children). In *M v M* [2007] EWHC 1820 (Fam.), it was argued that return should not be ordered to Zimbabwe which was described as a "failed State"; Roderic Wood J. rejected the notion of a "failed State", but also held that Zimbabwe was not such a State.

NOTE 37. Add: This particular point was accepted on appeal by the House of Lords: *Re M (Children) (Abduction: Rights of Custody)* [2007] UKHL 55, [2008] 1 A.C. 1288.

"Intolerable" is a strong word, but when applied to a child must mean "a situation which this particular child in these particular circumstances should not be expected to tolerate": *Re D (A Child) (Abduction: Rights of Custody)* [2006] UKHL 51, [2007] 1 A.C. 619 (*per* Baroness Hale of Richmond at [52]). **19–116**

This level was met in *Re E (Abduction: Intolerable Situation)* [2008] EWHC 2112 (Fam.), [2009] 2 F.L.R. 485 where a return would have led to a child of 11 being separated from his mother, or if the mother was to accompany him, requiring her to leave the boy's half-sibling and the father of that child with whom the boy had been living for three years. Similarly, in *RS v KS (Abduction: Wrongful Retention)* [2009] EWHC 1494 (Fam.), [2009] 2 F.L.R. 1231 it was held that undue delay and settlement could lead to a child facing an intolerable situation if summarily returned to the country of habitual residence. Adopting the formulation accepted by Baroness Hale of Richmond in *Re D (A Child) (Abduction: Rights of Custody)* [2006] UKHL 51, [2007] 1 A.C. 61 at [52], Macur J. noted that intolerable in this context should be taken to mean a situation which this particular child in these particular circumstances should not be expected to tolerate: at [45].

Text to note 39. The fact that the return of a child to a foreign country would lead to its immediate return to England was held in *Re T and J (Abduction: Recognition of Foreign Judgment)* [2006] EWHC 1472 (Fam.), [2006] 2 F.L.R. 1290 to be "nowhere near" creating an intolerable situation; but the case was complicated by the effect of Council Regulation (EC) 2201/2003.

Undertakings are accepted in the Irish courts: *Re TM and DM (minors); Minister for Justice (EM) v JM* [2003] IESC 40, [2003] 3 I.R. 178; *Re HE (a child); EH v SH* [2004] IEHC 193, [2004] 2 I.R. 564. See also *M v M* [2007] EWHC 1820 (Fam.). **19–117**

The United States actively encourages the use of undertakings: see the letter from a State Department officer cited in *Danaipour v McLarey*, 386 F. 3d 289 (1st Cir. 2004).

It was held (*obiter*) in *Re D (A Child) (Abduction: Rights of Custody)* [2006] UKHL 51, [2007] 1 A.C. 619 (*per* Baroness Hale of Richmond at [57]–[61]) **19–119** that the growing understanding of the importance of listening to the children involved in children's cases led to the conclusion that the new practice required by Art.11(2) of Council Regulation (EC) 2201/2003 ("Brussels II Revised" or "Brussels II*bis*"), of giving the child the opportunity to be heard during the proceedings unless this appeared inappropriate having regard to his or her age or degree of maturity, should be followed in all Hague Convention cases, whether or not the specific Art.13 issue had been raised. In most cases this could be through the report of an independent CAFCASS officer or other professional; in some, and especially where the child has asked to see the judge, it might also be necessary for the judge to hear the child. Whenever it seemed likely that the child's views and interests might not be properly presented to the court, and in particular where there were legal arguments which the adult parties were not putting forward, then the child should be separately represented. The restrictive view on this matter in *Re H (Abduction)* [2006] EWCA Civ 1247, [2007] 1 F.L.R. 242 was not to be followed. In *De L v H* [2009] EWHC 3074 (Fam.), [2010] 1 F.L.R. 1229, the child, at his own request, had a lengthy conversation with the trial judge, in the presence of a Cafcass officer.

In *Re F (Abduction: Joinder of Child as Party)* [2007] EWCA Civ 393, [2007] 2 F.L.R. 313, the court nonetheless re-asserted the rule that a child should only be made a party in exceptional circumstances. However, in *Re M (Children) (Abduction: Rights of Custody)* [2007] UKHL 55, [2008] 1 A.C. 1288, Baroness Hale of Richmond returned to the issue. In her view, to order separate representation in all cases, even in all child's objections cases, might be to send them the wrong messages. But it would not send the wrong messages in the very small number of cases where settlement is argued under the second paragraph of Art.12. These were the cases in which the separate point of view of the children was particularly important and should not be lost in the competing claims of the adults. In all other cases, the question was whether separate representation of the child would add enough to the court's understanding of the issues that arise under the convention to justify the intrusion, the expense and the delay that might result. In the general run of cases it would not, but she would hesitate to use the word "exceptional". In *C v C* [2008] EWHC 517 (Fam.), [2008] 2 F.L.R. 6, Ryder J. held that the question as formulated by Baroness Hale in *Re M (Children) (Abduction: Rights of Custody)* was now the test in Convention cases and counsel should not seek to rely on authorities dating from before that re-formulation.

The factors to be borne in mind in exercising the court's discretion as to the future of the child who objected to return were examined by Baroness Hale of Richmond in *Re M (Children) (Abduction: Rights of Custody)* [2007] UKHL 55, [2008] 1 A.C. 1288. The court may have to consider the nature and strength of the child's objections, the extent to which they are authentically its own or the product of the influence of the abducting parent, and the extent to which they coincide or are at odds with other considerations which are relevant to her welfare, as well as the general Convention policy. The older the child, the greater the weight that her objections are likely to carry. In settlement cases, the major objective of the Convention, of securing a swift return to the country of origin, cannot be met. It cannot any longer be assumed that that country is the better forum for the resolution of the parental dispute. So the policy of the Convention does not necessarily point towards a return in such cases.

It was said in *M, Ptr* [2007] CSOH 66, 2007 S.L.T. 433 that even a relatively mature abducted child "does not have a right of veto on return". The court set an unusually high hurdle in adding that a child's objections were to be upheld "only in exceptional circumstances"; this seems out of line with the English authorities.

The French Cour de cassation appears to have held (incorrectly) that the child's objections are not in themselves a ground for refusing the return of the child, and can only be considered as creating a grave risk of harm or an intolerable situation: *Gettlife v Grant* (February 14, 2006), 2007 *Rev. Crit.* 96, note Gallant.

Text after note 52. In recent years the age at which a child's objections might be taken into account has reduced. This is a result not only of domestic case law (*Re M (Children) (Abduction: Rights of Custody)* [2007] UKHL 55, [2008] 1 A.C. 1288), but of Art.11(2) of Council Regulation 2201/2003. Nevertheless a minimum age has still not been set. In *Re W (Minors)* [2010] EWCA Civ 520 the Court of Appeal held that at almost 6, the age of the child did not by itself foreclose the possibility that she had objections for the purpose of Art.13(2) (those objections were upheld). *Cf. A Bu* v *J Be* [2010] IESC 38 (5 year old too young to have views ascertained).

Text to note 53. The nature and content of the child's views are not relevant in assessing the child's age and maturity: *M, Ptr*, 2005 S.C.L.R. 396 (OH), not following a suggestion to the contrary in *W v W*, 2003 S.C.L.R. 685 (IH).

Note 53. Add: *Re M (A Child) (abduction: child's objections to return)* [2007] EWCA Civ 260, [2007] 2 F.L.R. 72 (bright 8-year-old, with cogent reasons for not returning to Serbia where malicious attempts had been made to implicate mother in drug offences; return refused); *M, Ptr*, 2005 S.C.L.R. 396 (OH) (objection of child aged 12 based on substantial and not capricious reasons and not result of coaching; return refused); *C v W (Abduction)* [2007] EWHC 1349 (Fam.), [2007] 2 F.L.R. 900 (views of intelligent 14-year-old did not prevail; child had not given enough weight to mother's medical condition); *C v C* [2008] CSOH 42, 2008 S.C.L.R. 329 (affirmed on appeal *sub nom. NJC v NPC* [2008] CSIH 34, 2008 S.C. 571) (the objections of three children, aged 15, 11 and 9 were not regarded as sufficient to prevent an order for the return of the children); *Re F (Children) (Abduction; Rights of Custody)* [2008] EWHC 272 (Fam.), [2008] 3 W.L.R. 527 (objections of boys aged 13 and almost 12 upheld; delay of 11 months in seeking return added force to their views).

Note 53. The "take account" threshold now represents a fairly low requirement: *Re W (Minors)* [2010] EWCA Civ 520 (objections of children aged 8 and almost 6 at the time of the interview prevailed. The case was finely balanced but the applicant father, whilst he had not acquiesced in the wrongful removal, had nevertheless permitted a situation to come about whereby the children had been settling into life in London for 9 months by the time of the trial.)

**19–120** Note 56. Add: *W* v *W (Abduction: Joinder as Party)* [2009] EWHC 3288 (Fam.), [2010] 1 F.L.R. 1342 (17 year old sibling joined as a party, because she was directly concerned in the abducted child's welfare).

Note 59. Add: *C v C* [2008] CSOH 42, 2008 S.C.L.R. 329, affirmed on appeal *sub nom. NJC v NPC* [2008] CSIH 34, 2008 S.C. 571.

Note 60. For comments by Wall L.J. qualifying his remarks in *Zaffino v Zaffino* (now reported at [2006] 1 F.L.R. 410), see *Vigreux v Michel* [2006] EWCA Civ 630, [2006] 2 F.L.R. 1180, at [63]. See the disapproval of certain dicta in *Zaffino v Zaffino* and in *Vigreux v Michel* by the House of Lords in *Re M (Children) (Abduction: Rights of Custody)* [2007] UKHL 55, [2008] 1 A.C. 1288. *Cf. Re W (Minors)* [2010] EWCA Civ 520, where the Court of Appeal was prepared to countenance the non-return of two younger siblings on the basis of Art.13(1)(b) were an older brother aged 8 deemed to have valid objections for the purposes of Art.13(2). On the facts the objections of the eldest and middle sibling were upheld and only the return of the youngest sibling was refused on the basis he would be at a grave risk of psychological harm or of facing an intolerable situation.

**19–121** Text to note 61. Delay after the date of application, for example due to the fault of the courts or other authorities in dealing with the case, has no direct relevance, but could be a factor in deciding that to return the child would place it in an intolerable situation: *Re D (A Child) (Abduction: Rights of Custody)* [2006] UKHL 51, [2007] 1 A.C. 619 (*per* Baroness Hale of Richmond at [48]–[55]).

Text after note 61. Where 12 months have not elapsed, settlement may be raised within the context of Art.13(1)(b): *RS v KS (Abduction: Wrongful Retention)* [2009] EWHC 1494 (Fam.), [2009] 2 F.L.R. 1231.

Text to note 64. It is not correct, in calculating the one-year period, to deduct the period of deliberate concealment of the child's whereabouts from the total period since abduction: *Re C (Child Abduction: Settlement)* [2006] EWHC 1229 (Fam.), [2006] 2 F.L.R. 797. *cf. Re F (Abduction: Removal Outside Jurisdiction)* [2008] EWCA Civ 842, [2008] 2 F.L.R. 1649.

Text to note 65. So the child of a parent whose immigration status is insecure, but who does not face imminent deportation, can be regarded as settled in the country concerned: *Re C (Child Abduction: Settlement)* [2006] EWHC 1229 (Fam.), [2006] 2 F.L.R. 797.

Notes 63 and 64. Add: *C v C*, 2008 S.C.L.R. 329, affirmed on appeal *sub nom. NJC v NPC* [2008] CSIH 34, 2008 S.C. 571; *F v M* [2008] EWHC 1525 (Fam.); *Secretary for Justice (New Zealand Central Authority) v HJ* [2007] 2 N.Z.L.R. 289 (N.Z. Sup. Ct.).

Note 65. See *P v S (Child Abduction: Wrongful Removal)* 2002 Fam.L.R. 2, where the Inner House of the Court of Session said (at [45]) that:

> "a situation which is stable is one which can reasonably be relied upon to last, as matters stand, and which does not contain indications that it is likely to change radically or fall apart. Equally, if the circumstances do not afford a basis for such reliance, and contain elements indicating that change is liable to occur, it will be less acceptable to describe them as stable, or to hold that a child in these uncertain circumstances can properly be described as settled in his new environment. . . . Even if, like all the other terms, the expression 'long-term' is not ideal we are in no doubt that in judging the present situation, and asking whether a child is settled at the present time, projection as to what is liable to happen into the future is an inherent element in the word 'settled', and reference to the intention of others, and in particular the abducting parent, very likely to be essential".

This was followed in *C v C* [2008] CSOH 42, 2008 S.C.L.R. 329, affirmed on appeal *sub nom. NJC v NPC* [2008] CSIH 34, 2008 S.C. 571.

Note 66. Add: *PL v EC* [2008] IESC 19, [2009] 1 I.R. 1.

Text after note 68: That a finding of settlement leads to an exercise of discretion whether or not to make a return order was confirmed by a majority in *Re M (Children) (Abduction: Rights of Custody)* [2007] UKHL 55, [2008] 1 A.C. 1288. This power was implied from the provision itself rather than deriving from Art.18 as had previously been concluded by the Court of Appeal. Art.18 was held merely to acknowledge residual powers existing under domestic law, rather than attributing any new Convention power.

Where the Art.12(2) discretion does come into play the guidance provided by Baroness Hale of Richmond is cognisant of the peculiar circumstances, namely that the major objective of the Convention, an expeditious restoration of the status quo ante, cannot be achieved. Consequently, "the policy of the Convention would not necessarily point towards a return in such cases, quite apart from the comparative strength of the countervailing factors . . . " at [47]. Equally it is clear from *Re M* that a child-centric approach must be taken and on the facts of that case it was concluded that the children "should not be made to suffer for the sake of general deterrence of the evil of child abduction world wide" (at [54]). In *F v M and N (Abduction: Acquiescence: Settlement)* [2008] EWHC 1525 (Fam.), [2008] 2 F.L.R. 1270 a return order was made following a finding of settlement, after the child had lived openly in England for almost two years, the core issue was the acknowledgement that the original State of habitual residence remained the more appropriate forum since custody proceedings had been on going there from a time prior to the removal.

**19–122** A breach of Art.20 has been upheld by the Irish High Court, where a return would have led to the child being put up for adoption, a situation deemed contrary to the rights of the family under Arts 41 and 42 of the Irish Constitution: *Foyle Health and Social Services Trust v EC, NC* [2007] 4 I.R. 528. *Cf. Nottingham County Council v KB* [2010] IEHC 9.

In *Re D (A Child) (Abduction: Rights of Custody)* [2006] UKHL 51, [2007] 1 A.C. 619, at [65], Baroness Hale of Richmond noted that s.6 of the Human Rights Act 1998, making it unlawful for the court, as a public authority, to act in a way which is incompatible with a person's Convention rights, had given Art.20 of the Hague Convention domestic effect by a different route. Baroness Hale later recognised that, as all parties to a Hague Convention case had the right to respect for their homes and family lives, Art.20 might not take matters any further: *Re M (Children) (Abduction: Rights of Custody)* [2007] UKHL 55, [2008] 1 A.C. 1288.

In a decision of potentially very great significance, *Neulinger and Shuruk v Switzerland* [2010] ECHR 41615/07 [G.C.], the Grand Chamber of the European Court of Human Rights effectively reversed the previous position of the Chamber, which had sought to align the interpretation of the European Convention on Human Rights with the policy goals of the 1980 Hague Convention: *Maumousseau and Washington v France*, [2007] ECHR 39388/05; *Neulinger and Shuruk v Switzerland* [2009] ECHR 41615/07.

The facts in *Neulinger* may have given rise to concerns (the child had been living in the State of refuge for 5 years; the father had only limited, supervised access and the mother was at risk of criminal prosecution if she accompanied the child back to Israel), but the majority decision (16:1, the dissenting judge was of the opinion that a breach of Art.8 had already occurred), is constructed in rather general terms, with an emphasis on the best interests of the abducted child.

The Court affirmed that the child's best interests, from a personal development perspective, would depend on a variety of individual circumstances, in particular his age and level of maturity, the presence or absence of his parents and his environment and experiences. In clear contrast to the established position in England and Wales and other common law Contracting States, the Court noted that those best interests had to be assessed in each individual case. In a further departure, the Court held that to ensure the domestic decision-making process was fair and allowed those concerned to present their case fully, it was required to ascertain whether the domestic courts had conducted an in-depth examination of the entire family situation and made a balanced and reasonable assessment of the respective interests of each person, with a constant concern for determining what the best solution would be for the abducted child.

The Court further held that guidance could be sought in its case law on the expulsion of aliens (*Maslov v Austria* [2008] ECHR 1638/03, [GC], [2009] I.N.L.R. 47; *Emre v Switzerland* [2008] ECHR 42034/04), according to which, in order to assess the proportionality of an expulsion measure concerning a child who had settled in the host country, it was necessary to take into account the child's best interests and well-being, and in particular the seriousness of the difficulties which he would be likely to encounter in the country of destination and the solidity of social, cultural and family ties both with the host country and with the country of destination. Account was also to be taken of the seriousness of any difficulties which might be encountered in the destination country by accompanying family members. This final point was of particular relevance to the facts of the case since the decision being challenged, that of the Swiss Federal Court, had, in common with established practice in England and Wales, made a return order on the basis that the mother could reasonably be expected to return with the child, even though she did not wish to do so. In contrast to the position of the majority in the Chamber (4:3), the Court did not emphasize the benefits of the pro-return policy of the Hague Convention. Applying its interpretation to the facts, the Court concluded that the abducting mother would sustain a disproportionate interference with her right to respect for her family life if she were forced to return with the child to Israel. And there would be a violation of Art.8 of the Convention in respect of both mother and child if the decision ordering the child's return to Israel were to be enforced.

*cf. EM (Lebanon) v Secretary of State for the Home Department* [2008] UKHL 64, [2009] 1 A.C. 1198: entry at para.19–082, above.

The European Court of Human Rights has held that the making of a custody decision while Hague Convention proceedings were pending (a practice forbidden by Art.16 of the Hague Convention; see para.19–125, main work) was a breach of Art.8 of the European Convention, as was inordinate delay (of 18 months in the instant case) in dealing with an application for the return of the child: *Caras v Romania* [2006] ECHR 7198/04, [2007] 1 F.L.R. 661. See also *Carlson v Switzerland* [2008] E.C.H.R. 49492/06.

NOTE 75. Add: *Karadzic v Croatia* [2006] ECHR 35030/04, [2006] 1 F.L.R. 36; *Bajrami v Albania* [2006] ECHR 35853/04, [2007] 1 F.L.R. 1629; and see *Monory v Romania* [2005] ECHR 71099/01 (where strained interpretation of the Hague Convention and four years delay in related divorce and custody proceedings breached Art.8 of the European Convention on Human Rights); *P v Poland* [2008] E.C.H.R. 8677/03.

Note 75. Add: *Carlson v Switzerland* [2008] E.C.H.R. 49492/06 (the passage of three-and-a-half months between the issue of the return proceedings and the decision of the trial court was held to be a contributing factor in finding a breach of Art.8).

**19–123** A Convention on Contact concerning Children (CETS No. 192) negotiated under the aegis of the Council of Europe in 2003 came into force in September 2005. The United Kingdom has not signed the Convention.

Note 78. Add: *State Central Authority & Peddar* [2008] FamCA 519; *State Central Authority & Quang* [2010] FamCA 231.

**19–125** If an order is made for the return of a child to another country, any English proceedings for a residence order should be dismissed: *Re EC (Child Abduction: Stayed Proceedings)* [2006] EWCA Civ 1115, [2007] 1 F.L.R. 57.

Article 16 does not rule out dealing with contact and rights of access. In *Re D (A Child) (Abduction: Rights of Custody)* [2006] UKHL 51, [2007] 1 A.C. 619, at [67], Baroness Hale of Richmond, citing a suggestion by Thorpe L.J. in *Hunter v Murrow (Abduction: Rights of Custody)* [2005] 2 F.L.R. 1119 at para.31, said that it should not be beyond the wit of man to devise a procedure whereby the facilitation of rights of access under Art.21 was in contemplation at the same time as the return of the child under Art.12.

Section 86 of the Children (Scotland) Act 1995 is repealed by the Adoption and Children (Scotland) Act 2007, Sch.3.

Note 81. Add: See also Case C–403/09 PPU *Detiček v Sgueglia* [2010] 3 W.L.R. 1098 (entry at para.19–034, above).

Note 82. The cited provisions of the Adoption and Children Act 2002 are now in force.

**19–126** Note 85. *cf. Best v Hesketh* [2005] EWCA Civ 1380, [2006] 1 F.L.R. 593, as to which see entry at para.19–105 above.

**19–128** The European Commission has issued a *Practice Guide* on the Regulation, a revised edition appearing in June 2005. Article 60(e) of the Regulation States that it takes precedence over the Hague Convention: see *Re T and J (Abduction: Recognition of Foreign Judgment)* [2006] EWHC 1472 (Fam.), [2006] 2 F.L.R. 1290, where the Regulation and the Convention suggested different outcomes, and *Vigreux v Michel* [2006] EWCA Civ 630, [2006] 2 F.L.R. 1180, where the two instruments worked in harmony. See the disapproval of certain dicta in *Vigreux v Michel* by the House of Lords in *Re M (Children) (Abduction: Rights of Custody)* [2007] UKHL 55, [2008] 1 A.C. 1288.

Text to note 89. There are expedited procedures for cases under the Regulation and under the Hague Convention in the Supreme Court of the United Kingdom Practice, at paras 3.4.4 *et seq*.

NOTE 89. Add: In *Re K (Rights of Custody: Spain)* [2009] EWHC 1066 (Fam.), [2010] 1 F.L.R. 57 the President acknowledged that the deadline was not always attainable, and not simply because of crowded court lists, but because of practical and legal complications for which a summary procedure was not adapted.

NOTE 90. For procedure to ensure that the obligation to hear the child is observed, see *Re F (A Child) (abduction: obligation to hear child)* [2007] EWCA Civ 468, [2007] 2 F.L.R. 697. See also *MN v RN* [2008] IEHC 382, [2009] 1 I.R. 388. **19–129**

NOTE 91. Failure to hear the child as required by Art.11(2) is a fundamental defect; a case in which this occurs will be remitted for retrial.

NOTE 92. Add: *Klentzeris v Klentzeris* [2007] EWCA Civ 533, [2007] 2 F.L.R. 997 (but note the disapproval of certain dicta in this case by the House of Lords in *Re M (Children) (Abduction: Rights of Custody)* [2007] UKHL 55, [2008] 1 A.C. 1288); *RS v KS (Abduction: Wrongful Retention)* [2009] EWHC 1494 (Fam.), [2009] 2 F.L.R. 1231.

The implications of this new power given to the courts of the habitual residence of the child were considered by Sir Mark Potter P. in *Re F (Children) (Abduction; Rights of Custody)* [2008] EWHC 272 (Fam.), [2008] Fam. 75. He held that the general approach to the exercise of the English court's discretion when grounds for refusing return were established set out by the House of Lords in *Re M (Children) (Abduction: Rights of Custody)* [2007] UKHL 55, [2008] 1 A.C. 1288 was applicable in cases falling under Regulation 2201/2003. In a Regulation case, however, the English court should bear in mind that, to the extent that the court of the requesting State might reverse its decision if it saw fit, a decision for non-return made in the immediate welfare interest of the child, unless solidly based, might well prove counterproductive so far as the child's overall, i.e. longer-term, welfare interests were concerned. **19–130**

When an English court is asked to exercise the jurisdiction given by Art.11(7) after a non-return order by the court of another Member State, the matter should be heard by a judge of the Family Division: *Re A; HA v MB (Brussels II Revised; Article 11(7) Application)* [2007] EWHC 2016 (Fam.), [2008] 1 F.L.R. 289. That point is not yet dealt with in the Family Proceedings Rules and is controversial. The application is *sui generis* and should not take the form of an application for a s.8 order (as a conciliation appointment is inappropriate in this type of case): *ibid*. In dealing with an application under Art.11(7), the court is not limited to a decision as to return or non-return; the term "the question of custody" covers all issues relating to the future of the child: *ibid.* The decision made need not be a final ruling on the issue of custody, indeed it would be difficult to reconcile the objective of expedition inherent in Arts 11(8), 40 and 42 with an obligation that there be a final custody decision: Case C–211/10 PPU *Povse v Alpago*, July 1, 2010.

Statistics in an annex to the judgment in *Re A; HA v MB (Brussels II Revised: Article 11(7) Application)* [2007] EWHC 2016 (Fam.), [2008] 1 F.L.R. 289 show that 17 per cent of applications for return under the Hague Convention sent from England to other Member States in 2004 to 2006 led to a decision by the foreign court not to return the child.

NOTE 93. Add: The mechanism does not apply where a non-return order is made on the basis of Art.12(2): *Re RD (Child Abduction) (Brussels II Revised: Arts 11(7) and 19)* [2009] 1 F.L.R. 586; or where there has not been a wrongful removal or retention: *Re RC and BC (Child Abduction) (Brussels II Revised: Article 11(7))* [2009] 1 F.L.R. 574.

Text to note 94. "The question of custody" was interpreted in *Re A; HA v MB (Brussels II Revised: Article 11(7) Application)* [2007] EWHC 2016 (Fam.), at [94], [2008] 1 F.L.R. 289 to cover all issues relating to the future of the child.

NOTE 94. There has yet to be full provision in the Family Proceedings Rules for the consideration of a matter under Art.11(7), but guidance was given by Sumner J. in *Re A; HA v MB (Brussels II Revised: Article 11(7) Application)* [2007] EWHC 2016 (Fam.), [2008] 1 F.L.R. 289. The matter should be referred to the Family Division.

The European Court has held that Art.10 must be interpreted restrictively since an abduction should not in principle lead to a transfer of jurisdiction between the Member States concerned. A "judgment on custody that does not entail the return of the child" for the purposes of Art.10(4), refers to a final order, one adopted on the basis of an examination of all the facts. Consequently there will not be a transfer of jurisdiction from the Member State of the child's habitual residence to the Member State of refuge where a court in the former State has awarded the abductor custody on a provisional basis, pending a final determination of the case: Case C–211/10 PPU *Povse v Alpago*, July 1, 2010.

Where a certified return order has been made under Art.11(8) (above, entry at para.19–072), its enforcement cannot be defeated by virtue of a provisional order made in the Member State of refuge. Where a change of circumstances has come about the European Court accepted that this could possibly require a modification of the return order, but it noted that this was a matter of substance and as such the competent court was that in the Member State of origin. The latter court could evaluate the best interests of the child and rule on the possible stay of the return order. The Court clarified that the principle of assimilation articulated in Art.47(2) whereby a judgment shall be enforced in the Member State of enforcement "in the same conditions" as if it had been delivered in that Member State, was to be interpreted strictly. The latter could only concern procedural matters surrounding the return and not provide a substantive basis of opposition to the decision of the competent court: Case C–211/10 PPU *Povse v Alpago*, July 1, 2010.

Text to note 96. An order of the court of habitual residence cannot be enforced under Art.11(8) unless a non-return order has been made; but once such an order has been made, it is immaterial that it has later been made the subject of an appeal, reversed or suspended: Case C–195/08 PPU *Inga Rinau* [2008] E.C.R. I–5271, [2008] Fam. 51. **19–131**

NOTE 95. On the interpretation of Art.10, see *Re A; HA v MB (Brussels II Revised: Article 11(7) Application)* [2007] EWHC 2016 (Fam.), [2008] 1 F.L.R. 289. It was held in that case, at [89] *et seq.*, that even if the English court was about to make a custody order which did not require the return of the child to England, it retained jurisdiction to consider Children Act 1898 applications previously commenced under the principle in *Leon v Leon* [1967] P. 275 that jurisdiction once established continues. This seems to fly in the face of the policy of the Regulation. However, an order providing for contact in England was not an order requiring the child to be returned to England: *Re A; HA v MB (Brussels II Revised: Article 11(7) Application)* [2007] EWHC 2016 (Fam.), [2008] 1 F.L.R. 289 at [95]. "Judgment" in this context means a written order of the court, as opposed to the full statement of reasons which would be described as a judgment in English domestic usage: *ibid.*, at [122] *et seq.* Jurisdiction will not be lost by the Member State of habitual residence simply as a result of delays in the Member State of refuge or as a consequence of the abductor evading service for Art.11(7) proceedings: *Re H (Jurisdiction)* [2009] EWHC 2280 (Fam.), [2010] 1 F.L.R. 598.

NOTE 96. An English order made in corresponding circumstances will be enforceable in the other Member State concerned: *Re A (Custody Decision after Maltese Non-return Order)* [2006] EWHC 3397 (Fam.), [2007] 1 F.L.R. 1923 (and see note at p.1948); or in a third Member State to which the child might have been removed: *Re A; HA v MB (Brussels II Revised: Article 11(7) Application)* [2007] EWHC 2016 (Fam.), [2008] 1 F.L.R. 289 at [70].

## 3. MAINTENANCE AND CONTRIBUTION ORDERS

References in this Rule and the Comment thereon to the Lugano Convention apply equally to the revised Lugano Convention (as to which see entry at para.11R–001, above). See SI 2009/3131. **19R–134**

NOTE 5. Civil Jurisdiction and Judgments Act 1982, Sch.3C is repealed by SI 2009/3131. See now revised Lugano Convention, Art.2.

NOTE 6. Civil Jurisdiction and Judgments Act 1982, Sch.3C is repealed by SI 2009/3131. See now revised Lugano Convention, Art.5(2).

NOTE 7. Civil Jurisdiction and Judgments Act 1982, Sch.3C is repealed by SI 2009/3131. See now revised Lugano Convention, Art.24.

NOTE 8. Civil Jurisdiction and Judgments Act 1982, Sch.3C is repealed by SI 2009/3131. See now revised Lugano Convention, Art.3.

**19–135** NOTE 9. Add: and by the Child Support Act 1995, s.18(3); Social Security Act 1998, Sch.7, para. 22; Child Support, Pensions and Social Security Act 2000, s.1 and Sch.3, para.11; Civil Partnership Act 2004, Schs 24 and 30; Constitutional Reform Act 2005, Sch.4, paras 218, 219; Child Maintenance and Other Payments Act 2008, Sch.3, Pt 1, para.6 and Sch.8.

NOTE 11. Add: *M v V* [2010] EWHC 1453 (Fam.).

**19–137** The rules governing service outside the jurisdiction are now contained in CPR, r.6.36 and PD6B, para.3.1

**19–139** For the prospective replacement of the Judgments Regulation in respect of maintenance obligations, see entry at para.19–141.

That applications under Children Act 1989, Sch.1, are applications for maintenance within the meaning of the Judgments Regulation was confirmed in *M v V* [2010] EWHC 1453 (Fam.). An application to vary a judgment as to maintenance obligations given in another Member State and registered in the English court is not to review the foreign judgment as to its substance (forbidden by Art.36 of the Judgments Regulation), nor would a variation be irreconcilable with the foreign judgment: *ibid.*

NOTE 17. Civil Jurisdiction and Judgments Act 1982, Sch.3C is repealed by SI 2009/3131. See now revised Lugano Convention, Art.3.

**19–140** NOTE 19. Civil Jurisdiction and Judgments Act 1982, Sch.3C is repealed by SI 2009/3131. See now revised Lugano Convention, Art.2.

NOTE 20. Civil Jurisdiction and Judgments Act 1982, Sch.3C is repealed by SI 2009/3131. See now revised Lugano Convention, Art.5(2).

NOTE 22. Civil Jurisdiction and Judgments Act 1982, Sch.3C is repealed by SI 2009/3131. See now revised Lugano Convention, Art.24.

**19–141** When it comes into force, Council Regulation (EC) 4/2009 of December 18, 2008 on jurisdiction, applicable law, recognition and enforcement of decisions and cooperation in matters relating to maintenance obligations ([2009] O.J.

L7) ("the Maintenance Regulation") will replace the provisions of the Judgments Regulation applicable to maintenance obligations, including those relating to children. For the jurisdictional rules of the Maintenance Regulation, see the entry at para.18–169; for the rules on the recognition and enforcement of decisions, that at para.18–233.

Council Regulation (EC) 664/2009 [2009] O.J. L200/46 establishes a procedure for the negotiation and conclusion of agreements between Member States and third countries concerning jurisdiction, recognition and enforcement of judgments and decisions in matrimonial matters, matters of parental responsibility and matters relating to maintenance obligations, and the law applicable to matters relating to maintenance obligations.

A Convention on the International Recovery of Child Support and Other Forms of Family Maintenance was agreed in November 2007 at the 21st Session of the Hague Conference on Private International Law; an Explanatory Report is in preparation. The Convention provides for the establishment of a system of Central Authorities to transmit applications for the establishment, variation, recognition or enforcement of orders; rules governing recognition and enforcement; and the recovery of sums paid in lieu of maintenance by public bodies. The Convention applies to maintenance obligations arising from a parent-child relationship towards a person under the age of 21; to the recognition and enforcement of an order (but not the creation of a new order) for spousal support when the application is made with a claim for child support; and to a limited extent to spousal support. The last category excludes the very important co-operation provisions in Chapters II and III. Individual Contracting States may limit the application of the child support provisions to persons who have not attained the age of 18, and may extend the application of the whole or any part of the Convention to any maintenance obligation arising from a family relationship, parentage, marriage or affinity, including in particular obligations in respect of "vulnerable persons". Article 31 protects the position of States, principally those of the Commonwealth, using the system of provisional and confirming orders. The United States signed the Convention at the conclusion of the Session. See also the entry at para.18–232, and for the accompanying Protocol on Applicable Law the entry at para.18–207.

Note 24. The Children (Allocation of Proceedings) Order 1991 is revoked by Allocation and Transfer of Proceedings Order 2008, SI 2008/2836. See now Art.5(1)(*b*) of the 2008 Order.

Children Act 1989, Sch.2, para.21 is amended by Children and Young Persons Act 2008, Sch.1, para.5. National Assistance Act 1948, s.43 is repealed and Maintenance Orders Act 1950 ss. 4 and 16(2) consequentially amended by Health and Social Care Act 2008, Sch.15, Pt 5. **19–142**

Notes 27 and 28. Maintenance Orders Act 1950, s.4(1) and (2), are amended by Welfare Reform Act 2009, Sch 9, Pt I.

**19–143** Note 31. Civil Jurisdiction and Judgments Act 1982, Sch.3C is repealed by SI 2009/3131. See now revised Lugano Convention, Arts 2 and 24.

Note 32. Civil Jurisdiction and Judgments Act 1982, Sch.3C is repealed by SI 2009/3131. See now revised Lugano Convention, Art.3.

**19–145** Chapter VIII of the Maintenance Regulation (see entry at para.19–141) contains a single Art.64 of particular relevance to the enforcement of contribution orders. For the purposes of an application for recognition and declaration of enforceability of decisions or for the purposes of enforcement of decisions, the term "creditor" in the Regulation includes a public body acting in place of an individual to whom maintenance is owed or one to which reimbursement is owed for benefits provided in place of maintenance (Art.64(1)). A public body may seek recognition and a declaration of enforceability or claim enforcement of: (a) a decision given against a debtor on the application of a public body which claims payment of benefits provided in place of maintenance; or (b) a decision given between a creditor and a debtor to the extent of the benefits provided to the creditor in place of maintenance (Art.64(3); for procedure, see Art.64(4)). The Regulation also contains a choice of law rule, that the right of a public body to act in place of an individual to whom maintenance is owed or to seek reimbursement of benefits provided to the creditor in place of maintenance is governed by the law to which the body is subject (Art.64(2)).

**19–147** Text to note 45. This non-recognition rule is not included in the revised Lugano Convention.

**19–149** Note 57. Civil Jurisdiction and Judgments Act 1982, Sch.3C is repealed by SI 2009/3131. See now revised Lugano Convention, Arts 2 and 24.

Note 58. Civil Jurisdiction and Judgments Act 1982, Sch.3C is repealed by SI 2009/3131. See now revised Lugano Convention, Art.5(2).

## CHAPTER 20

# LEGITIMACY, LEGITIMATION AND ADOPTION

## 1. LEGITIMACY

### A. *Jurisdiction of the English Court*

The definition in s.10 of the Legitimacy Act 1976 now also includes persons legitimated under s.2A of the Act (see entry at para.20–042): Human Fertilisation and Embryology Act 2008, Sch.6, para.19. See entry at para.20–027. **20–003**

NOTE 9. Family Law Reform Act 1987, s.1(3) is amended by Human Fertilisation and Embryology Act 2008, Sch.6, para.24(2).

For use of the power to grant a declaration of parentage, see *M v W (Declaration of Parentage)* [2006] EWHC 2341 (Fam.), [2007] 2 F.L.R. 270. **20–007**

The special provision relating to applications by the Secretary of State will apply instead to applications by the Child Maintenance and Enforcement Commission when the Child Maintenance and Other Payments Act 2008, Sch.3, para.19 is brought into force.

### B. *Recognition of the status of legitimacy*

NOTE 40. Children Act 1989, s.2 is amended and a new s.4ZA inserted, in each case to deal with parenthood in cases involving assisted reproduction by Human Fertilisation and Embryology Act 2008, Sch.6, paras 26 and 27. **20–011**

The belief must be that the marriage was valid under English law rather than under any other system of law: *Azad v Entry Clearance Officer (Dhaka)* [2001] Imm. A.R. 318 (C.A.); *A v H* [2009] EWHC 636 (Fam.), [2010] 1 F.L.R. 1. **20–027**

Provision is now made in respect of the children of void civil partnerships. Although they are not treated as legitimate, the general principle in s.1 of the Family Law Reform Act 1987 (see para.20–003) is extended (by the insertion of new s.1(5)-(8) by Human Fertilisation and Embryology Act 2008, Sch.6, para.24(3)) to cases in which a child's parents are parties to a void civil partnership if at the time when the parties registered as civil partners of each other both or either of the parties reasonably believed that the civil partnership was valid. This applies even though the belief that the civil partnership was valid was due to a mistake as to law, but only where the woman who is a parent by virtue of s.43 of the 2008 Act was domiciled in England and Wales at the time of the birth or, if she died before the birth, was so domiciled immediately before her death. There is a rebuttable presumption that one of the parties to a void civil partnership reasonably believed at the time of the formation of the civil partnership that the civil partnership was valid.

**20–029** The citation in the text of s.27 of the Family Law Act 1987 should be of s.27 of the Family Law Reform Act 1987. The reference in s.27 to parties to a marriage can only refer to a union of a man and a woman, and not to a (void) marriage between two females: *J v C* [2006] EWCA Civ 551, [2007] Fam. 1.

Section 30 of the Human Fertilisation and Embryology Act 1990 provides for the making of parental orders, providing for a child to be treated in law as the child of the parties to a marriage if the child has been carried by a woman other than the wife as the result of the placing in her of an embryo or sperm and eggs or her artificial insemination, and the gametes of the husband or the wife, or both, were used to bring about the creation of the embryo. This is subject to certain conditions, including a requirement that the husband or the wife, or both of them, must be domiciled in a part of the United Kingdom or in the Channel Islands or the Isle of Man (s.30(3)(b)). This prevented an order being made in *Re G (Surrogacy: Foreign Domicile)* [2007] EWHC 2814 (Fam.), [2008] 1 F.L.R. 1047.

It was held in *Re X (Children) (Parental Order)* [2008] EWHC 3030 (Fam.), [2009] Fam. 71 that the law of the domicile of the applicants applies to all aspects of an application for the making of a parental order under s.30 of the Human Fertilisation and Embryology Act 1990. In that case, children were born in Ukraine to a married Ukrainian surrogate mother using sperm from the male applicant and an egg from an anonymous donor. The Ukrainian mother was to be treated as the sole mother (Human Fertilisation and Embryology Act 1990, s.27(1)) despite being outside the United Kingdom throughout (s.27(3)). As the surrogate mother was married, s.28 required her husband to be treated as the sole father; had she been unmarried, the male applicant, as the biological father, would be the father under English law. The court rejected the argument that s.28 could not be applied extra-territorially. It did so apply, and the consent of the surrogate mother's husband was required. The fact that he was not the father under the law of his domicile (Ukraine) was immaterial; the intention of Parliament had been to recognise the particular relevance of marriage in surrogacy arrangements, and there was no reason why that should be affected by questions of domicile. It followed also that the male applicant had no right to apply for any order under Pt II of the Children Act 1989 without the leave of the court under s.10 of that Act. (In fact the necessary consent and leave had been obtained.)

C. *Succession by and to legitimate persons*

NOTE 35. Law Reform (Parent and Child) (Scotland) Act 1986, s.1 is amended by the Family Law (Scotland) Act 2006, Schs 2 and 3. **20–037**

Family Law Reform Act 1987, s.18(2) is applied with modifications to the case of a person who has a parent by virtue of s.43 of the Human Fertilisation and Embryology Act 2008: a new s.18(2A) is inserted by the 2008 Act, Sch.6, para.25. **20–038**

## 2. LEGITIMATION

A. *Jurisdiction of the English courts*

NOTE 53. Family Law Act 1986, s.56(5) is amended by Human Fertilisation and Embryology Act 2008, Sch.6, para.23. **20R–041**

Legitimation by subsequent civil partnership of the parents, that is the child's mother and a person deemed to be the female parent by virtue of Human Fertilisation and Embryology Act 2008, s.43, was introduced into English law by the 2008 Act, Sch.6, para.16, which inserted a new s.2A in the legitimacy Act 1976. It applies only where the female parent is domiciled in England at the date of formation of the civil partnership. The jurisdiction to make declarations in respect of legitimations extends to legitimations under s.2A, Family Law Act 1986, s.56 being amended to this effect by Human Fertilisation and Embryology Act 2008, Sch.6, para.23. **20–042**

NOTE 61. Family Law Act 1986, s.56(5) is amended by Human Fertilisation and Embryology Act 2008, Sch.6, para.23. **20–043**

B. *Recognition of Foreign Legitimations*

(1) AT COMMON LAW

NOTE 18. Family Law Act 1986, s.56(5) is amended by Human Fertilisation and Embryology Act 2008, Sch.6, para.23. **20–062**

(2) UNDER THE LEGITIMACY ACT 1976

NOTE 50. The status of illegitimacy was abolished in Scotland by the Family Law (Scotland) Act 2006, s.21. Any question arising as to the effect on a person's status of the person's parents being, or having been, married to each other (or not being, or not having been, married to each other) is determined in Scotland by the law of the country in which the person is domiciled at the time at which the question arises: *ibid.*, s.41. **20R–072**

Provision is now made for the recognition in England of legitimation by virtue of legitimation by subsequent civil partnership under foreign law. What was s.3 of the Legitimacy Act 1976 is renumbered s.3(1), and a new s.3(2) inserted by Human Fertilisation and Embryology Act 2008, Sch.6, para.17. This provides that where a person ("the child") has a female parent by virtue of s.43 of the 2008 Act, at the time of the child's birth, the female parent and the child's mother are not civil partners of each other but subsequently enter into a civil partnership, and the female parent is not at the time of the formation of the civil partnership domiciled in England and Wales but is domiciled in a country by the law of which the child became legitimated by virtue of the civil partnership, the child, if living, shall in England and Wales be recognised as having been so legitimated from the date of the formation of the civil partnership notwithstanding that, at the time of the child's birth, the female parent was domiciled in a country the law of which did not permit legitimation by subsequent civil partnership.

## 3. ADOPTION

### A. *Jurisdiction of the English courts*

**20R–092** The Children (Allocation of Proceedings) Order 1991 is revoked by Allocation and Transfer of Proceedings Order 2008, SI 2008/2836. Under the 2008 Order, an application for an adoption order under s.50 or 51 of the 2002 Act must be commenced in a magistrates' court unless any local authority will be a party to the proceedings (Art.5(1)(*e*)) but proceedings for a Convention adoption order or for an adoption order where s.83 of the 2002 Act (restriction on bringing children in) applies must be commenced in a county court which is an intercountry adoption centre (Arts 6(*c*)(*d*), 11),

**20–094** For procedure, see the Family Procedure (Adoption) Rules 2005, SI 2005/2795. For Scotland, see Adoption and Children (Scotland) Act 2007; for Northern Ireland, see Adoption (Intercountry Aspects) (Northern Ireland) Act 2001.

**20–103** After difficulties over inter-country adoptions from China (a large proportion of the whole), the Adoptions with a Foreign Element Regulations 2005 were amended by SI 2009/2563 so as to remove the requirement in reg.19 that the potential adopters visit the child in its country of origin before the Central Authority in the United Kingdom can indicate agreement to the adoption.

**20–105** NOTE 28. See *Greenwich London Borough Council v S* [2007] EWHC 820 (Fam.), [2007] 2 F.L.R. 154 (test for habitual residence in this context; see entry at para.6–129 above).

**20–111** Text to note 45. In the case of children adopted abroad, s.83 is amended to increase the relevant period from six to twelve months: Children and Adoption Act 2006, s.14(1).

The provisions set out in the text became law as ss.9–11 of the Children and Adoption Act 2006. Section 12 contains a further power enabling extra conditions to be imposed in particular types of case. Special restrictions have been imposed in respect of adoptions from Cambodia (SI 2008/1808) and Guatemala (SI 2008/1809). See also the Adoptions with a Foreign Element (Special Restrictions on Adoptions from Abroad) Regulations 2008, SI 2008/1807, which set out the exceptional circumstances in which an adoption can be considered despite the restrictions. **20–113**

Adoption and Children Act 2002, s.67, provides that "an adopted person (a) if adopted by one of a couple under s.51(2) is to be treated in law as not being the child of any person other than the adopter and the other one of the couple, and (b) in any other case, is to be treated in law . . . as not being the child of any person other than the adopters or adopter . . . ". It was held in *Re N (Recognition of Foreign Adoption Order)* [2009] EWHC 29 (Fam.), [2010] 1 F.L.R. 1102 that, in order to respect the rights given by Art.8 of the European Convention on Human Rights, this provision had to be read as if there were inserted after the reference to s.51(2) the words "or its equivalent under the foreign law of an adoption order made abroad which is recognised in England and Wales pursuant to s.66". Without this adjustment, the effect of s.67(3) where a stepfather adopted his stepchild abroad would be to deprive his wife, the mother of the child, of parental responsibility. **20–114**

Many provisions of the Adoption and Children Act 2002 as to the making and effect of an adoption order, including ss.46 and 67, are applied, with modifications, to a parental order, an order made by a court providing for a child to be treated as the lawful child of the applicants for the order following the birth of a child by a surrogate: Human Fertilisation and Embryology (Parental Orders) Regulations 2010, SI 2010/985.

Notes 51 and 52. The reference is to the Adoption and Children Act 2002.

The provisions cited in this paragraph have been much criticised as operating as a significant disincentive to prospective adopters from abroad, few of whom can spend ten weeks in England. In *Re G (Adoption: Placement Outside the Jurisdiction)* [2008] EWCA Civ 105, [2008] Fam. 97, the Court of Appeal noted these criticisms and the fact that no regulations had been made under Adoption and Children Act 2002, s.86(2) to provide an exception to the 10 week requirement in the case of proposed adoptions by family members. In the instant case, the adoptive mother could spend 10 weeks in England and the father three of those weeks and this was regarded as sufficient to enable the adoption authorities to form a judgment on the relationships between the child and the proposed adopters. See *Re G (Adoption: Placement Outside the Jurisdiction) (No.2)* [2008] EWCA Civ 105 2, [2008] 1 F.L.R. 1497. **20–115**

In *Re A (A Child) (Adoption: Assessment outside Jurisdiction)* [2009] EWCA Civ 41, [2010] Fam. 9, the local authority considered that the best future for a child was adoption by relatives who lived in the United States. They proposed a programme which would involve assessments in both the USA and England. A number of issues arose.

Under Children Act 1989, Sch.2, para.19(1), a local authority may only arrange for a child in its care to live outside England with the leave of the court. Where a child is the subject of an arrangement of that sort with the leave of the court, s.85 of the Adoption and Children Act 2002 (which creates offences where children are removed from the jurisdiction "for the purposes of adoption") is disapplied (para.19(6)). However, para.19 as a whole does not apply to a local authority placing a child for adoption with prospective adopters (para.19(9)). The court held that the phrase "for the purposes of adoption" in s.85(1) covers any case in which the purpose of removal is to render the child amenable to the jurisdiction of a foreign country to enable adoption proceedings to be taken there. "Placement for adoption" was a narrower concept than "removal for the purpose of adoption" (approving on this point *ECC v M* [2008] EWHC 332 (Fam.) and *Plymouth City Council v CR* (unreported, June 13, 2006)). Where the decision to send a child abroad was part of an inchoate care plan, in which adoption was but one of the possible options, the child was not being "removed for the purposes of adoption" contrary to s.85(1) nor was the child being placed for adoption. Such a case did not fall within para.19(9) and the local authority could properly be given leave to arrange for the child to travel to the USA. Arranging for a child to live outside England and Wales did not mean to live abroad permanently.

The local authority's plan also involved at a later stage the making of an order giving parental responsibility to the potential adopters under s.84, which requires that "at all times during the preceding ten weeks the child's home was with the applicant(s)". Noting that the purpose of this provision is to enable the court to ascertain how the child and the applicants relate to each other in what, if an adoption were to take place, would be the normal home environment, the court held that it required that the child must have had its home with the applicants in their normal place of residence, wherever that may be. The period of 10 weeks immediately preceding the application for an order need not follow the placement for adoption; it can include a period both before and after the placement itself is made. On this issue the Court of Appeal held that *Re G (A Child)* [2008] EWCA Civ 105, [2008] Fam. 97 was of no assistance and declined to approve *H County Council v B* [2005] EWHC 3437 (Fam.), where the issues had not been fully argued. The court noted with apparent approval the decision in *Re SL (Adoption: Home in Jurisdiction)* [2005] 1 F.L.R. 118 that the home referred to in the requirement for ten weeks' residence need not be the same as the home referred to in the statutory provisions requiring opportunities for inspection.

At first instance in the same case (*Haringey London Borough Council v MA* [2008] EWHC 1722 (Fam.), [2008] 2 F.L.R. 1857), Charles J. held that "entrusted to prospective adopters" in Art.17 of the Hague Convention on Protection of Children and Co-operation in respect of Intercountry Adoption had a meaning that related the placement much more closely to the proposed adoption than giving or entrusting day-to-day care to potential adopters for the purpose of an assessment, and thus in English terms the concept equated to the making of a parental responsibility order under s.84 of the Adoption and Children Act 2002, or a placement for adoption, with their respective consequences. No comment was made on this matter on appeal.

### B. *Recognition of foreign adoptions*

Note 69. Add: *Re C (Foreign Adoption: Natural Mother's Consent: Service)* [2006] 1 F.L.R. 318. **20R–117**

Two adoptions in India were recognised under the common law rule in *D v D (Foreign Adoptions)* [2008] EWHC 403 (Fam.), [2008] 1 F.L.R. 1475. **20–126**

This paragraph was cited with approval in *D v D (Foreign Adoptions)* [2008] EWHC 403 (Fam.), [2008] 1 F.L.R. 1475. The two sentences in the text from the words "If the foreign adoption . . . " were cited with approval in *Re N (Recognition of Foreign Adoption Order)* [2009] EWHC 29 (Fam.), [2010] 1 FLR 1102. **20–133**

Note 41. For s.67(3), see *Re N (Recognition of Foreign Adoption Order)* [2009] EWHC 29 (Fam.), [2010] 1 FLR 1102 (entry at para.20–133, above). **20R–139**

Note 50. For s.67(3), see *Re N (Recognition of Foreign Adoption Order)* [2009] EWHC 29 (Fam.), [2010] 1 FLR 1102 (entry at para.20–133, above). **20–141**

Note 58. It would be otherwise if X were C's stepfather: *Re N (Recognition of Foreign Adoption Order)* [2009] EWHC 29 (Fam.), [2010] 1 FLR 1102 (entry at para.20–133, above). **20–146**

## CHAPTER 21

# MENTAL INCAPACITY

**Note: All the provisions of the Mental Capacity Act 2005 came into force (insofar as they were not already in force) on October 1, 2007. Procedural rules are contained in the Court of Protection Rules 2007, SI 2007/1745. Service out of the jurisdiction is dealt with in r.39 (applying, with adaptations, provisions in the Family Proceedings (Adoption) Rules 2005, SI 2005/275) and taking evidence outside the jurisdiction in rr.114 to 116.**

### 1. JURISDICTION

**21–002** The Hague Convention on the International Protection of Adults enters into force on January 1, 2009.

The inherent jurisdiction of the High Court to protect the mentally afflicted (as to which see *Re F (Adult: Court's Jurisdiction)* [2001] Fam. 38) is not extinguished by the Mental Capacity Act 2005: *St Helens Borough Council v PE* [2006] EWHC 3460 (Fam.); *Re PS, City of Sunderland v PS* [2007] EWHC 623 (Fam.); *Local Authority X v MM* [2007] EWHC 2003 (Fam.), [2009] 1 F.L.R. 443; *Westminster City Council v C* [2008] EWCA Civ 198, [2009] Fam. 11. The exercise of that jurisdiction must take into account Art.8 of the European Convention on Human Rights: *Local Authority X v MM* [2007] EWHC 2003 (Fam.), [2009] 1 F.L.R. 443 where Munby J. held that a local authority caring for a person who lacked capacity to enter into a marriage but who did have capacity to consent to sexual relations must facilitate her continuing sexual relationship with her long-term partner. See also *Ealing LBC v S* [2008] EWHC 636 (Fam.), [2008] 2 F.L.R. 720.

### 3. RECOGNITION AND ENFORCEMENT

**21–029** The effect of the Mental Capacity Act 2005, Sch.2, para.4, which deals with the effect on property of a statutory will made by the Court of Protection, is the same as is stated by reference to the earlier law in the text to note 71: *Re P (Statutory Will)* [2009] EWHC 163 (Ch), [2010] Ch 33 (CP).

### 4. REMOVAL FROM THE JURISDICTION

**21–035** In appropriate cases the court may intervene to prevent the removal of a vulnerable adult from the jurisdiction. In *Re SA (Vulnerable Adult with Capacity: Marriage)* [2005] EWHC 2942 (Fam.), [2006] 1 F.L.R. 867 the court ordered that an adult who was profoundly deaf and mute, but who had capacity to marry, should not be taken abroad to marry until he had been given full information in terms he could understand of the significance of marrying an individual, and that no actual removal occur until he had given express consent which was notarised. *cf. X City Council v MB* [2006] EWHC 168 (Fam.), [2006] 2 F.L.R. 968 where the adult concerned lacked capacity to marry; the court would have granted an injunction against his proposed removal with a view to marriage abroad, but accepted undertakings to the same effect.

In *Re ST (Adult Patient)* [2006] EWHC 3458 (Fam.), [2008] 1 F.L.R. 111, **21–037**
Munby J. authorised the removal of a patient, who had HIV/AIDS, to Germany, saying that he was acting under the inherent jurisdiction of the High Court.

Note 86. The Mental Health Act 1983, s.86 is further amended by the Mental Health Act 2007, Sch.1, para.15 and by SI 2008/2833, Sch.3, para.62.

Note 87. Substitute: See, for removal from England to Scotland: Mental Health Act 1983, ss.80 (as amended by the Mental Health (Scotland) Act 1983, Sch.2, para.1, SI 2005/2078, and the Mental Health Act 2007, Sch.5, para.2 and Sch.11, Pt 7), 80ZA (as inserted by the Mental Health Act 2007, Sch.5, para.3) and 80A (as inserted by the Crime (Sentences) Act 1997, Sch.3, para.1 and as amended by SI 2005/2078); for removal from Scotland to England: the Mental Health Act 1983, ss.80B, 80C and 80D (all as inserted by the Mental Health Act 2007, Sch.5, para.4); for removal from England to Northern Ireland: the Mental Health Act 1983, ss.81 (as amended by SI 1986/596 and the Mental Health Act 2007, Sch.5, para.5 and Sch.11, Pt 8), 81ZA (as inserted by the Mental Health Act 2007, Sch.5, para.6) and 81A (as inserted by the Crime (Sentences) Act 1997, Sch.3, para.2 and as amended by the Mental Health Act 2007, Sch.5, para.7 and Sch.11, Pt 8); for removal from Northern Ireland to England, the Mental Health Act 1983, ss.82 (as amended by SI 1986/596 and the Mental Health Act 2007, Sch.5, para.8) and 82A (as inserted by the Crime (Sentences) Act 1997, Sch.3, para.3 and as amended by the Mental Health Act 2007, Sch.5, para.9); for removal from England to the Channel Islands or the Isle of Man: the Mental Health Act 1983, ss.83, 83ZA (as inserted by the Mental Health Act 2007, Sch.5, para.10) and 83A (as inserted by the Crime (Sentences) Act 1997, Sch.3, para.4); and for removal from the Channel Islands or the Isle of Man to England: the Mental Health Act 1983, ss.84 (as amended by the Domestic Violence, Crime and Victims Act 2004, Sch.10, para.22 and by the Mental Health Act 2007, Sch.11, Pt 8), 85 (as amended by the Mental Health Act 2007, Sch.5, para.11), 85ZA (as inserted by the Mental Health Act 2007, Sch.5, para.12) and 85A (as inserted by the Crime (Sentences) Act 1997, Sch.3, para.5 and as amended by the Mental Health Act 2007, Sch.5, para.13).

Note 88. The Mental Health Act 1983, ss.87 and 88 are both further amended by the Mental Health Act 2007, Sch.2, para.7.

## CHAPTER 22

# NATURE AND SITUS OF PROPERTY

**22R–023** Rule 120 was cited with approval in *Blue Sky One Ltd v Mahan Air* [2010] EWHC 631 (Comm.), at [154].

**22–025** Add *Jose v Riz* 2009 BCSC 1075.

**22–026** Text and note 63. Part 6 of the CPR has been substituted by SI 2008/2178, Sch.1. CPR, r.6.19 is now CPR, r.6.33. The provisions on service out of the jurisdiction in CPR r.6.20 are substituted by CPR PD6B, para.3.1.

**22–046** See entry at para.22–026, above.

**22–051** NOTE 37. See also Case C–539/03 *Roche Nederland v Primus* [2006] E.C.R. I–6535 and Case C–4/03 *Gesellschaft für Antriebstechnik mbH & CO.KG v Lamellen und Kupplungsbau Beteiligungs KG* [2006] E.C.R. I–6509.

NOTE 39. See also *TC Production LLC v Drew Pictures Pty Ltd* [2008] FCA 1110, (2008) 250 A.L.R. 97.

**22–058** In *Dornoch Ltd v Westminster International BV* [2009] EWHC 889 (Admlty), [2009] 2 Lloyd's Rep. 191, Tomlinson J. considered this paragraph of the main work. He pointed out that the question is often moot, as ships will frequently be transferred by judicial sale in proceedings *in rem.* Nevertheless, he noted the slenderness of the authority for the proposition in the main work that the law of the place of registration is displaced by the actual *situs* of the ship. Tomlinson J. considered that the decision in *Trustees Executors and Agency Co Ltd v IRC* [1973] Ch. 254, which concerned liability for estate duty, was of a different nature from the question of which law should govern the transfer of title to a ship. He considered that the decision in *Hooper v Gumm* (1867) L.R. 2 Ch. App. 282 was authority for the application of the law of the place where the vessel is physically situated at the time of sale or transfer. However, this did not preclude the law of the physical *situs* from referring to the law of the registry to determine questions of pre-existing title, especially where legal title depended upon registration.

Tomlinson J. went on to determine the related but distinct issue which arose in the instant case as to the law applicable to proprietary interests short of registered legal title. He examined the decision of the Full Federal Court of Australia in *Tisand Pty Ltd v Owners of the Ship MV Cape Moreton* [2005] FCAFC 68, which favoured the application of the law of the place of registration. However, he concluded that the register would normally be uninformative in respect of interests other than legal title and may have little connection with the ownership and management of the vehicle. Accordingly, he ruled that the law of the physical *situs* should apply. See also the subsequent decision in the same litigation: [2009] EWHC 1782 (Admlty). Compare the decision of the Federal Court of Australia in *Thor Shipping A/S v The Ship "Al Duhail"* [2008] FCA 1842, considered at para.13–016, above.

In *Blue Sky One Ltd v Mahan Air* [2010] EWHC 631 (Comm.) (noted Knight [2010] Conv. 331), Beatson J. cited this paragraph of the main work with approval (at [154]) and ruled that the validity of a mortgage of aircraft was governed by the law of its physical *situs* and not by the law of the place of registration of the aircraft (save where the aircraft was in flight over the high seas or a *territorium nullius*). He went on to reject the application of the doctrine of *renvoi* in respect of aircraft. **22–061**

This paragraph was also considered *obiter* by Tomlinson J. in *Dornoch Ltd v Westminster International BV* [2009] EWHC 889 (Admlty), [2009] 2 Lloyd's Rep. 191. He pointed to the absence of a clearly articulated justification for rejection of the law of registration. He noted that the issue was not seriously argued in *Air Foyle Ltd v Center Capital Ltd* [2002] EWHC 2535 (Comm.), [2003] 2 Lloyd's Rep. 753. See also entry at para.22–058, above.

NOTE 69. The Protocol on Matters Specific to Aircraft Equipment entered into force March 1, 2006 but not in respect of the United Kingdom.

NOTE 70. As amended by SI 2006/2316; SI 2007/274.

## Chapter 23

# IMMOVABLES

### 1. JURISDICTION OF THE ENGLISH COURT: LAND IN ENGLAND

**23R–001** The revised Lugano Convention ([2007] O.J. L339/1) entered into force on January 1, 2010 between the Member States of the European Union (including Denmark) and Norway on January 1, 2010. It will be ratified by Switzerland with effect from January 1, 2011. The text of the previous Lugano Convention contained in Sch.3C of the Civil Jurisdiction and Judgments Act 1982 was repealed by Reg. 25 of the Civil Jurisdiction and Judgments Regulations (SI 2009/3131). See entry at para.11R–001, above.

Add: *Pagliotti v Hartner* [2009] Fam. CAFC 18, (2009) 41 Fam. L.R. 41.

Note 8. The provisions on service out of the jurisdiction formerly contained in CPR, r.6.20 are now found in CPR PD6B, para.3.1. In particular, CPR, r.6.20(10) is now CPR PD6B, para.3.1(11), and CPR, r.6.20(13) is now CPR PD6B, para.3.1(14).

**23–004** The provisions on service out of the jurisdiction formerly contained in CPR, r.6.20 are now found in CPR PD6B, para.3.1.

**23–006** The revised Lugano Convention ([2007] O.J. L339/1), para.23R–001 above, restates the prior position in Art.64(2)(a). It stipulates that the revised Lugano Convention shall be applied:

> "in matters of jurisdiction, where the defendant is domiciled in the territory of a State where this Convention but not . . . [the Judgments Regulation, the 1968 Convention or the Parallel Agreement with Denmark] applies, or where Articles 22 or 23 of this Convention confer jurisdiction on the courts of such a State."

Note 11. Second sentence. The reference should be to the Civil Jurisdiction and Judgments Act 1982.

**23–008** See entry at para.23–004, above.

**23–009** See entry at para.23–004, above.

Note 17. CPR, r.6.19 is now CPR, r.6.33.

Note 18. See entry at para.23–004, above.

In Case C–420/07 *Apostolides v Orams* [2009] E.C.R. I–3571, the European Court ruled that the suspension of the application of the *acquis communautaire* in those areas of the Republic of Cyprus in which the Government of that Member State did not exercise effective control did not preclude the application of the Judgments Regulation to a judgment given by a Cypriot court sitting in the area of the island effectively controlled by the Cypriot Government concerning land situated in areas not so controlled. The European Court ruled (at [47]–[52]) that the provisions of Art.22(1) of the Regulation were not infringed by the Cypriot judgment, since that Article merely determines which Member State's courts have jurisdiction and does not allocate jurisdiction within that Member State. See also the further English proceedings holding that enforcement of such a judgment would not be manifestly contrary to English public policy: [2010] EWCA Civ 9, [2010] I.L.Pr. 360. **23–010**

In *JP Morgan Chase Bank NA v Berliner Verkehrsbetriebe (BVG) Anstalt des Offentlichen Rechts* [2010] EWCA Civ 390, [2010] I.L.Pr. 529, the Court of Appeal considered the meaning of the phrase "proceedings having as their object . . . " in the context of Art.22(2) of the Judgments Regulation and held that proceedings must be principally concerned with the matters specified in that Article. In making that assessment, the court should form an overall judgment of all the issues arising in the case.

NOTE 24. Add: Case C–343/04 *Land Oberösterreich v ČEZ a.s.* [2006] E.C.R. I–4557, at [26]. See also Case C–372/07 *Hassett v South Eastern Health Board* [2008] E.C.R. I–7403, at [19] and [22]; *JP Morgan Chase Bank NA v Berliner Verkehrsbetriebe (BVG) Anstalt des Offentlichen Rechts* [2010] EWCA Civ 390, [2010] Q.B. 276.

In *Prazic v Prazic* [2006] EWCA Civ 497, [2006] 2 F.L.R. 1128, [2007] 1 F.C.R. 503, a husband had instigated divorce proceedings in France. The wife then commenced proceedings in England claiming rights under the Trusts of Land and Appointment of Trustees Act 1996 ("TOLATA") as an equal beneficial owner of two properties in England and the proceeds of sale of a third English property. The Court of Appeal ruled that, on the authority of *Webb v Webb,* the English court did not have exclusive jurisdiction under Art.22(1), since the wife's claim raised the issue of whether the dealings between the parties gave rise to an equitable interest in the properties. The Court of Appeal then granted a stay of its proceedings pursuant to Art.28 of the Judgments Regulation. In doing so, both Thorpe L.J. (at [25]) and Laws L.J. (at [30]) noted that financial issues between spouses should be determined under the Matrimonial Causes Act 1973 and should not be circumvented by strategic reliance on TOLATA. **23–012**

NOTE 36. In Case C–343/04 *Land Oberösterreich v ČEZ a.s.* [2006] E.C.R. I–4557 the European Court was asked to determine whether Art.16(1)(a) of the 1968 Convention must be interpreted as meaning that an action which seeks to prevent a nuisance affecting, or threatening to affect, land belonging to the applicant, caused by ionising radiation emanating from a nuclear power station situated on the territory of a neighbouring State to that in which the land is situated, fell within the category of "proceedings which have as their object rights *in rem* in immovable property". The European Court ruled that Art.16(a) of the 1968 Convention was inapplicable, since the proceedings did not seek to determine the extent, content, ownership or possession of immovable property. The European Court also noted that actions for damages based on infringement of rights *in rem* or damage to property do not fall within the scope of Art.16(1)(a). See further *JP Morgan Chase Bank NA v Berliner Verkehrsbetriebe (BVG) Anstalt des Offentlichen Rechts* [2010] EWCA Civ 390, [2010] I.L.Pr. 529, at [74]–[81].

**23–013** In *J v P* [2007] EWHC 704 (Fam.), the applicant father applied for a stay of proceedings in which the respondent mother sought financial provision for their child. One ground on which the mother opposed the stay application was that the English courts had exclusive jurisdiction pursuant to Art.22(1) of the Judgments Regulation, as she was about to take out a tenancy of immovable property located in England. The court rejected this argument, in part because the tenancy had not been entered into at the time of the hearing; but it left open the question whether Art.22(1) might apply on different facts if a tenancy has been entered into between the date of issue of the claim form and the hearing.

**23–014** The *Klein* case is noted by Downes (2007) 15 E.R.P.L. 157.

See also Directive 2008/122/EC of the European Parliament and of the Council of January 14, 2009, on the protection of consumers in respect of certain aspects of timeshare, long-term holiday product, resale and exchange contracts: [2009] O.J. L33/10. Recital (18) indicates that the rules of the Judgments Regulation should continue to determine the jurisdiction of Member States in respect of such contracts. See also entry at para.11–013, above.

**23–017** The provisions on service out of the jurisdiction formerly contained in CPR, r.6.20 are now found in CPR PD6B, para.3.1. In particular, CPR, r.6.20(10) is now CPR PD6B, para.3.1(11).

**23–018** Text and notes 58 and 62. The provisions on service out of the jurisdiction formerly contained in CPR, r.6.20 are now found in CPR PD6B, para.3.1. In particular, CPR, rr.6.20(11)–(15) is now CPR PD6B, para.3.1(12)–(16).

**23–020** Note 71. See entry at para.23–018, above.

## 2. JURISDICTION OF THE ENGLISH COURT: FOREIGN LAND

Rule 122(3) was cited with approval in *Pattni v Ali* [2006] UKPC 51, [2007] 2 A.C. 85, at [26] (noted Briggs (2006) 77 B.Y.I.L. 575; Chee Ho Tham [2007] L.M.C.L.Q. 129). **23R–021**

NOTE 72. SI 2007/1655 gives the force of law to the Agreement for the application of the Judgments Regulation to Denmark.

NOTE 76. The Judgments Regulation now applies by agreement to Denmark: see entry at para.23R–021, n.72 above.

NOTE 79. *Tezcan v Tezcan* (1992) 87 D.L.R. (4th) 503 (B.C.C.A.) was cited with approval in *Jose v Riz*, 2009 BCSC 1075, at [46].

The *Moçambique* rule was abolished in New South Wales by Jurisdiction of Courts (Foreign Land) Act 1989 (NSW), s.3. The court should instead decline jurisdiction if it considers that it is not the appropriate court to hear the proceedings (s.4). In *Du Bray v McIlwraith* [2009] NSWSC 888, the court considered that it could not issue an effective judgment in respect of land in New Zealand and granted a stay of proceedings. **23–023**

In *Lucasfilm Ltd v Ainsworth* [2009] EWCA Civ 1328, [2010] 3 W.L.R. 333 (noted Dickinson [2010] L.M.C.L.Q. 181; Rogerson (2010) 62 C.L.J. 245; Roy (2010) 21 Ent. L.R. 105), the Court of Appeal held that the *Moçambique* rule precluded the English courts from asserting jurisdiction in relation to questions as to the validity of copyright in a non-EU State; and that it also extended to alleged infringements of such rights. This was the case even though the defendant was domiciled in England and the proceedings fell within the ambit of the Judgments Regulation. It concluded that the Regulation could not have been intended to extend to extra-EU subject-matter. In this respect, it reasoned that the decision in *Owusu v Jackson* was confined to the preclusion of the *forum non conveniens* doctrine where an English court had jurisdiction by virtue of the Regulation. An appeal to the Supreme Court is pending. **23–027**

On the relationship between the *Moçambique* rule and the act of state doctrine, see the decision of the Federal Court of Australia in *Habib v Commonwealth of Australia* [2010] FCAFC 12. **23–034**

See also *Luxe Holding Ltd v Midland Resources Holding Ltd* [2010] EWHC 1908 (Ch.), at [37]. **23–041**

For a Canadian perspective on this exception, see Pribetic (2009) 35 Adv. Q. 230.

In *Minera Aquiline Argentina SA v IMA Exploration Inc. and Inversiones Mineras Argentinas S.A.* [2007] 10 W.W.R. 648 (B.C.C.A.) jurisdiction was **23–042** taken in relation to a dispute over mining rights in Argentina, on the basis that there had been a misuse of confidential information and that the mining rights were held on constructive trust for the claimant.

In *Precious Metal Capital Corp v Smith* 2008 ONCA 577, the plaintiff brought a claim for breach of fiduciary duty against the defendants. The plaintiff alleged that the parties had sought to pursue a joint venture in respect of mining rights in Peru and that the defendants, in breach of duty, instead took the mining opportunities for themselves. The plaintiff contended that the defendants should hold the Peruvian properties on constructive trust. The Ontario Court of Appeal did not consider separately the application of the *Moçambique* rule and its exceptions. Rather, it ruled that the remedy sought was one relevant factor to be considered in applying the real and substantial connection test to determine whether it should take jurisdiction. In the event, the court dismissed the defendant's motion for an order dismissing or staying the action. The decision in *Precious Metal* was applied in *Galustian v The Sky Link Group of Companies, Inc.*, 2010 ONSC 292.

On the personal obligation exception, see *Victoria Oil & Gas Plc v Alhambra Resources Ltd*, 2009 ABCA 64. See also *Talacko & Ors v Talacko & Ors* [2009] VSC 349.

**23–044** In *Murakami v Wiryadi* [2008] SGCA 44, the Singapore Court of Appeal ruled that it had jurisdiction to entertain a claim that immovable property in Indonesia and New South Wales, and the proceeds of sale of such properties, were held on trust. However, it held that as Indonesian law governed these issues, the proceedings should be stayed on *forum non conveniens* grounds.

In related proceedings in New South Wales concerning ownership of immovables located in Australia ([2010] NSWCA 7), it was argued in an application for a stay of proceedings that the property was held on a resulting or constructive trust because the first respondent did not disclose the existence of the property as common matrimonial property in Indonesian divorce proceedings. Having found that Indonesian law governed the relevant matrimonial property issues, the New South Wales Court of Appeal went on to suggest that the resulting or constructive trust would also be governed by Indonesian law; but since there was no dispute as to the relevant principles of Indonesian law, the stay application was refused.

**23–047** But the analysis in *Griggs (R) Group Ltd v Evans (No.2)* [2004] EWHC (Ch.) 1088, [2005] Ch. 153 on this point was in turn doubted by the Singapore Court of Appeal in *Murakami v Wiryadi* [2008] SGCA 44, at [19].

**23–049** In *Singh v Singh* [2006] WASC 182 the claimant sought, *inter alia*, a declaration that land in Malaysia was held on trust for the claimant; and an order that the defendant should transfer the property to the claimant absolutely. The defendant applied for a judgment given in his absence to be set aside. The Supreme Court of Western Australia ruled that the defendant's failure to object to the jurisdiction within the prescribed period did not prevent it from subsequently raising the issue of non-justiciability. It noted that there were two bases on which the trust was said to exist: either that the transfer of the land from the claimant's mother to the defendant in 1991 gave rise to a trust; or that there was a subsequent declaration in 2001 in which the defendant acknowledged that, since 1991, the claimant had remained at all times the beneficial owner and declared that he held the property on trust for the claimant. The court noted that it was unclear whether the 2001 declaration evidenced the original trust or constituted a new one. If the former, then the trust was likely to be governed by Malaysian law. In such circumstances, the court held that the exception could not be triggered, since the claimant would be relying upon the law of the *situs*. The claim would instead fall within the scope of the *Moçambique* rule. If the latter, the trust might be governed by a law other than the *lex situs* and the exception might then be engaged. The court went on to note that although registration of the declaration of trust in Malaysia might not be possible, an *in personam* order to require the defendant to provide the claimant with documents that might enable him to procure the transfer of the Malaysian property to himself would be effective. Since, in the event, the defendant had also adduced evidence to the requisite standard on which the court might decline jurisdiction on *forum non conveniens* grounds, the question of the engagement of the *Moçambique* rule did not need to be determined.

In subsequent proceedings, the defendant applied unsuccessfully for summary dismissal: [2008] WASC 62. The Court of Appeal for Western Australia upheld this decision: (2009) 253 A.L.R. 575. It was alleged that the defendant had transferred immovable property in Malaysia to his wife and daughter with intent to defraud creditors. The Court of Appeal reviewed the exceptions to the *Moçambique* rule and noted that prior authorities had established that a court with *in personam* jurisdiction over the defendant could grant remedies to reverse the effects of fraud. It also noted that any review of the *Moçambique* rule and its exceptions should be conducted by the High Court of Australia. In the event, the Supreme Court of Western Australia gave summary judgment in favour of the plaintiff on this issue (*Singh v Kaur Bal* (*No.2*) [2010] WASC 69); and also held that the defendant held the property on trust for the plaintiff (*Singh v Singh* (*No.3*) [2010] WASC 64).

A challenge to the testamentary capacity of a deceased person to make a codicil to her will in respect of land overseas is not precluded by the *Moçambique* rule: *Armour v Fuller*, 2009 BCSC 409. **23–051**

NOTE 58. See now the Commission Proposal for a Regulation of the European Parliament and of the Council on jurisdiction, applicable law, recognition and enforcement of decisions and authentic instruments in matters of succession and the creation of a European Certificate of Succession COM(2009)154 final (considered at para.27R–001, below). **23–052**

**23–062** See also *Murakami v Wiryadi* [2010] NSWCA 7, at [93]–[94].

**23–064** See also *Singh v Singh* (2009) 253 A.L.R. 575, at [33]–[35].

**23E–079** See also Opinion of Bot A-G in Case C–133/08 *Intercontainer Interfrigo SC (ICF) v Balkenende Oosthuizen BV* [2010] 3 W.L.R. 24, at [49]–[51]; and the judgment of the Court at [27].

## Chapter 24

# PARTICULAR TRANSFERS OF MOVABLES

## 1. TRANSFER OF TANGIBLE THINGS

Note 3. On the relationship between Rule 124 and the recognition of foreign judgments *in rem*, see *Pattni v Ali* [2006] UKPC 51, [2007] 2 A.C. 85. **24R–001**

In *Dornoch Ltd v Westminster International BV* [2009] EWHC 889 (Admlty), [2009] 2 Lloyd's Rep. 191 a contention that the choice of law rule to determine the proprietary consequences of dealings with a ship should be the *lex loci actus* was regarded by the judge at [17] as "unlikely to be fruitful". At first instance, at any rate, the application of the *lex situs* is clear. As to whether that means the domestic *lex situs*, or allows reference to the choice of law rules of the *lex situs*, see above, entry at para.4–025; and as to whether the *situs* of a ship for these purposes is the physical place of the vessel of the port of registry, see entry at para.23–058, above. **24–005**

Note 15. Also *T Comedy (UK) Ltd v Easy Managed Transport Ltd* [2007] EWHC 611 (Comm.), [2007] 2 All E.R. (Comm.) 242.

The distinction drawn in this paragraph was applied in *Dornoch Ltd v Westminster International BV* [2009] EWHC 1782 (Admlty), [5], with approval of the approach in *Glencore International AG v Metro Trading International Inc* [2001] 1 Lloyd's Rep. 284, [14]–[32]. To the same effect, see also *Blue Sky One Ltd v Mahan Air* [2010] EWHC 631 (Comm.). Similarly, in *Luxe Holding Ltd v Midland Resources Holding Ltd* [2010] EWHC 1908 (Ch.) the court accepted that where shares in various foreign companies were disposed of in breach of a contract of sale which contained an English law and jurisdiction clause, the vendor could be considered, in accordance with English domestic law, and dealt with, as though he were a trustee of the proceeds of the disposal for the contractual purchaser, regardless of whether the *lex situs* of the shares would recognise a beneficial interest (*Lightning v Lightning* 1998, in (2009) 23 Trusts L. Int. 35 applied) in the shares or the money. **24–006**

Note 23. For the question whether the *lex situs* means the domestic law of the place of the thing, or includes a reference (where its content is proved) the doctrine of renvoi, see entry at para.4–025, above. **24–008**

In *Islamic Republic of Iran v Barakat Galleries Ltd* [2007] EWCA Civ 1374, [2009] Q.B. 22 (on which see Rushworth [2008] L.M.C.L.Q. 123; Briggs **24–012**

(2007) 78 B.Y.I.L. 628), the Iranian State had acquired what English private international law would recognise as title to the chattel while it was physically located in Iran and could, for this reason, maintain a claim in conversion for its recovery from an English defendant. Iranian law did not require the chattel to be reduced into its possession in order to acquire title, and English private international law did not do so either. The State was not precluded from making its claim as owner by the principle that the public laws of a foreign State could not be enforced in England, as the claim was patrimonial, not sovereign, in nature. But had the claim of the State been characterised as sovereign, or uniquely governmental, in nature, (for example, by its being based on legislative confiscation of a previous owner), the State would not have been entitled to succeed unless it had previously reduced the property into its possession.

**24–026** But Pt 6 of the Tribunals Courts and Enforcement Act 2007 prevents the making of orders for the handing over of protected cultural objects on loan (that is, brought into the country for temporary display at a public exhibition at an approved museum or gallery) unless the order is required to be made by a Community obligation or an international treaty: ss.134–138.

**24–042** Note 79. Companies Act 1985, ss.395–409 are replaced by Companies Act 2006, ss.860–877.

## 2. ASSIGNMENT OF INTANGIBLE THINGS

**24R–050** Regulation (EC) 593/2008 of the European Parliament and of the Council of June 17, 2008 on the law applicable to contractual obligations (Rome I) ("the Rome I Regulation") (reproduced in Appendix 2 to this Supplement) will, since its coming into force on December 17, 2009: [2008] O.J. L177/6, gradually supersede the Rome Convention. The Rome I Regulation, by Art.14, re-enacts the substance of the existing Art.12 of the Rome Convention, which governs voluntary assignment, though four points should be noted. First, Art.14 extends the scope of the rule to include contractual subrogation alongside voluntary assignment. Second, "assignment" is defined by Art.14(3) to include "outright transfers of claims, transfers of claims by way of security, and pledges or other security rights over claims". Third, recital (38) to the Regulation makes it express that Art.14 applies to the proprietary aspects of an assignment, as between assignor and assignee, in those systems (of which English law is in some respects one) which separate the contractual from the proprietary aspects of the assignment, as well as to the contractual ones. Fourth, Art.27(2) calls for a review of Art.14 to be completed by June 2010, with the possibility that this review will include proposals for reform. This reflects the fact that there was a divergence of view among the Member States, or even within individual Member States, on the question of whether Art.12 of the Rome Convention represented the correct approach to the complex issues which can arise when a right is the subject of voluntary assignment. However, at the time of writing the review had not been published. See also, on Art.14 and possible revisions which might be made, Bridge (2009) 125 L.Q.R. 671; Verhagen & Van Dongen (2010) 6 J. Priv. Int. L. 1.

NOTE 95. See Flessner and Verhagen, *Assignment in European Private International Law* (2006).

NOTE 5. On the location of a debt for the purpose of insolvency legislation referring to "a liability . . . in Australia" see *AssetInsure Pty Ltd v New Cap Reinsurance Corp Ltd* (2006) 225 C.L.R. 331, at [58]. **24–053**

The inherent logic in making this distinction was accepted, though not further discussed, in *Pacific Brands Sport & Leisure Pty Ltd v Underworks Pty Ltd* (2006) 149 F.C.R. 395, [30] (Full Ct.). **24–054**

See also *Salfinger v Niugini Mining (Australia) Pty Ltd (No.3)* [2007] FCA 1532, at [108]–[113] (as a matter of common law, the assignability of cause of action in tort or equity determined by law under which the right arises or is created). **24–066**

The Hague Securities Convention has been signed by three States (Switzerland, United States of American, Mauritius), but ratified by none. In a "Reflection Paper" dated July 22, 2007, the European Commission (Internal Market and Services Directorate General) expressed the view that it is improbable that the European Council and Parliament would adopt the Hague Convention in its final form, and that European legislation to build on the two existing Directives is more appropriate. **24–071**

For further analysis of the Hague Convention, and of a proposed UNIDROIT Convention (there will be a final diplomatic meeting to settle its terms in October 2009), and on choice of law for indirectly-held securities generally, see Ooi in Gullifer and Payne (eds.), *Intermediated Securities: Legal Problems and Practical Issues* (2010).

NOTE 53. The Explanatory Report is an HCCH Publication.

## 3. GARNISHMENT

NOTE 83. A European Commission Green Paper on Improving the Efficiency of the Enforcement of Judgments in the European Union: The Attachment of Bank Accounts, COM (2006) 618 Final was published on October 24, 2006. **24R–078**

For a French perspective on the English mechanism of enforcement of judgments by third party debt order, see Cuniberti [2009] *Clunet* 963. **24–082**

24–086 **Relationship between third party debt orders and other orders for enforcement.** Though there may be some superficial similarities between the third party debt order and other orders which a court may make in aid of the enforcement of an English judgment, the differences between them are much more important. In *Masri v Consolidated Contractors International Co Ltd (No.2)* [2008] EWCA Civ 303, [2009] Q.B. 450 the Court of Appeal approved the appointment of a receiver by way of equitable execution in order to assist the claimant to enforce an English judgment in his favour. It was explained that the court's power to make the order was unaffected by the principle in *Soc Eram Shipping Co Ltd v Hong Kong and Shanghai Banking Corp Ltd* [2003] UKHL 30, [2004] 1 A.C. 260, as the order was not proprietary in nature and, by contrast with the third party debt order, did not purport to seize an overseas debt. Neither was there any objection to the appointment to be found in the Judgments Regulation, since (i) the order was in any event made in the course of proceedings over which the English court had substantive jurisdiction, and order made in that ancillary jurisdiction did not require separate jurisdictional justification (ii) the measure was provisional or protective and in any event within the scope of Art.31 of the Judgments Regulation, and (iii) not being an order made by way of seizure of property, it was unaffected by Art.22(5) of the Regulation and by the decision in *Kuwait Oil Tanker Co SAK v Qabazard* [2003] UKHL 31, [2004] 1 A.C. 300. The principle under (i) above also explains why a court may order an officer of the judgment debtor to attend for examination under CPR, r.71.2, even where that officer is domiciled in another Member State: *Masri v Consolidated Contractors International Co Ltd (No.4)* [2008] EWCA Civ 876, [2009] 2 W.L.R. 699. However, the decision of the Court of Appeal was reversed, [2009] UKHL 43, [2010] 1 A.C. 90, on the ground that CPR r.71(2)(b) did not apply to persons who were not present within the jurisdiction; the impact of European law was not discussed.

Likewise, on the distinction between third party debt orders and writs of execution, see *Westacre Investments Inc v Yugoimport-SDPR* [2008] EWHC 801 (Comm.), [2009] 1 All E.R. (Comm.) 780.

## Chapter 25

# GOVERNMENTAL ACTS AFFECTING PROPERTY

NOTE 2. See also *Islamic Republic of Iran v Barakat Galleries Ltd* [2007] EWCA Civ 1374, [2009] Q.B. 22. 25R–001

In *R. (on the application of Kibris Turk Hava Yollari) v Secretary of State for Transport* [2009] EWHC 1918 (Admin.), [2010] 1 All ER (Comm.) 253 one of the claimants was a company incorporated in Turkey, which held an Air Operator Certificate issued by the Minister of Transport of the Republic of Turkey which permitted it to operate a fleet of five aircraft from a hub at Ercan International Airport in the Turkish Republic of Northern Cyprus (TRNC). It operated several scheduled flights each week between the United Kingdom and Turkey pursuant to an operating permit granted by the Secretary of State for Transport. The permit related to flights between the United Kingdom and Turkey and some of the flights used Turkey as an intermediary stop between the airport at Ercan and the United Kingdom. The claimants sought approval of direct air services to airports in Northern Cyprus, and claimed that the Secretary of State's refusal to grant permits on the ground that it would constitute recognition of the TRNC was unlawful. It was held that the grant of permits would amount to implied recognition that the Government in control of the TRNC was sovereign over the territory which it effectively controlled, and would undermine the express statements from the United Kingdom Government to the effect that it does not recognise the TRNC. The United Kingdom Government was under a treaty obligation not to recognise the TRNC, and the grant of the permits sought would render the United Kingdom Government in breach of its duty not to recognise the TRNC. The court was obliged to refuse to give effect to the validity of acts carried out in a territory which was unrecognised unless the acts in question could properly be regarded as regulating the day to day affairs of the people within the territory in question and could properly be regarded as essentially private in character. The acts of the TRNC which were relevant to international aviation were not acts which regulated the day to day affairs of the people who lived within the area controlled by the Government of the TRNC; the acts in question were essentially public in nature. 25–004

In *Empresa Nacional de Telecomunicaciones SA v Deutsche Bank AG* [2009] EWHC 2579 (QB), [2010] 1 All ER (Comm.) 649 a Dutch company, ETI, owned 50 per cent of the shares in Entel, a Bolivian telecommunications company. The shares in Entel were nationalised by the Bolivian Government. 25–009

The question was whether a bank holding Entel's funds in England was entitled to act on the instructions of the new board. It was held that the public policy exception to the act of state doctrine existed within very narrow limits. It was concerned with violations of international law or with very grave breaches of fundamental universal human rights. Where a foreign state had compulsorily acquired property there was scope for a range of views as to which rights of the expropriated party were such that they ought to be recognised in a domestic court. It had not been established that there was a rule of international law, whether in the nature of a human right or otherwise, that in no circumstances could property be compulsorily acquired by a state without compensation, at least where there was no element of racial or religious discrimination involved. The decree, on its face, provided for compensation. Whether the decree was in conformity with the domestic law of Bolivia was not a matter upon which the court could investigate or pronounce. The decree plainly did not fall within the public policy exception. The allegation that compensation had yet to be paid did not found an arguable public policy exception to the act of state doctrine.

NOTE 43. See also *Islamic Republic of Iran v Barakat Galleries Ltd* [2007] EWCA Civ 1374, [2009] Q.B. 22.

NOTE 45. See also *Islamic Republic of Iran v Barakat Galleries Ltd* [2007] EWCA Civ 1374, [2009] Q.B. 22, at [111].

**25–012** See also *Islamic Republic of Iran v Barakat Galleries Ltd* [2007] EWCA Civ 1374, [2009] Q.B. 22, at [143] *et seq.*: where the foreign State has sought to confiscate or attach private property, the State's title will only be recognised in England if it has reduced the property into its possession. The distinction between the two categories of cases, those where the foreign State will be able to claim its property in England even if it has not reduced it into its possession, and those where it may not claim unless it has reduced the property into its possession, depends on the way in which it has acquired ownership. If it has acquired title under public law by confiscation or compulsory process from the former owner then it will not be able to claim the property in England from the former owner or his successors in title unless it has had possession. If it has taken the property into its possession then its claim will be treated as depending on recognition; if it has not had possession it will be seeking to exercise its sovereign authority. See entry at para 5–040, above.

## CHAPTER 26

# ADMINISTRATION OF ESTATES

An EU Commission Proposal for a Regulation on succession and wills, COM(2009)154 final, was published on October 14, 2009. On December 16, 2009 the United Kingdom exercised its right to opt out of the proposal. **26R–001**

## 2. EFFECT OF AN ENGLISH GRANT

See *Kelemen v Alberta (Public Trustee)* [2007] 4 W.W.R. 562 (Alta.) (administration of trust rather than of will; governed by the choice of law rules for trusts). **26–028**

## 4. FOREIGN PERSONAL REPRESENTATIVES

This Rule and the accompanying comment (as Rule 127 from the 13th ed.), was applied in *Peer International Corp v Termidor Music Publishers Ltd* [2006] EWHC 2883 (Ch.), [2007] E.C.D.R. 1. **26R–036**

## Chapter 27

# SUCCESSION

### 1. JURISDICTION OF THE ENGLISH COURT

27R–001 Note 1. Final sentence. The European Commission has published its Proposal for a Regulation on succession and wills: COM(2009) 154 final, October 14, 2009 (see Frimston [2010] P.C.B. 105; Frimston (2010) 113 T.E.L. & T.J. 5; Lein (2009) 11 Yb. P.I.L. 107; Lokin (2010) 18(3) E.R.P.L. 685). The Proposal contains provisions on jurisdiction, applicable law, recognition and enforcement of judgments and of notarial acts, and on the introduction of a European Certificate of Inheritance. It excludes, *inter alia*, the "constitution, functioning and dissolving of trusts" (Art.1(3)(i)). The Regulation applies whether or not the deceased died resident in a Member State.

A number of the provisions are particularly noteworthy. The principal choice of law rule is the law of the habitual residence of the deceased at the time of death (Art.16). That law would apply both to movable and immovable property (subject to certain derogations). "Habitual residence" is not, however, defined in the Proposal. The Regulation also, at least to some degree, applies the *lex successionis* to the administration of the estate (Art.19(2)(f)–(h)); but with a limited derogation in favour of Member States requiring the appointment of an executor or administrator (Art.21(2)). Most controversially, the *lex successionis* also determines whether assets alienated by the deceased during his lifetime, whether by gift, settlement on trust or otherwise, constitute part of the estate of the deceased and may be subject to "clawback" to satisfy forced heirship claims arising by a foreign law that requires a proportion of assets to be left to one's spouse and/or children (Art.19(2)(j)). Art.17 of the Regulation permits a limited degree of testator autonomy as to the governing law (see also Jayme (2009) 11 Yb. P.I.L. 1).

The proposed rules of jurisdiction normally confer competence on the courts of the Member State where the deceased was habitually resident at the time of death (Art.4); but with the residual possibility that the courts of a Member State may be competent notwithstanding that the deceased died resident in a non-Member State (Art.6). The rules on recognition and enforcement of foreign judgments in Chapter IV of the Proposal are largely modelled on the Judgments Regulation; the Proposal would also allow for widespread recognition and enforcement of authentic instruments (Chapter V). The proposed European Certificate of Inheritance (Chapter VI) would be evidence in other Member States of the capacity of the heir or legatee and of the powers of the executors or administrators (Art.36); although the precise weight to be given to such a document is still to be determined.

The Ministry of Justice launched a public consultation CP41/09 (dated October 21, 2009) and an impact assessment (dated October 27, 2009), inviting views as to whether the UK should opt into the Regulation. In its consultation document, it expressed particular concern about the absence of a definition of "habitual residence", fearing that this would lead to considerable uncertainty (paras 21–26); and also about the proposal to permit clawback if the *lex successionis* so provides, fearing that this would be damaging to the interests both of the trusts industry and of charities (paras 13–20). The Proposal was also considered by the House of Lords European Scrutiny Committee: see HL European Union Committee, 6th Report of Session 2009–10, HL Paper 75 (March 24, 2010), *The EU's Regulation on Succession*, which identified broadly similar concerns (see p.5).

It was announced on December 16, 2009 that the UK would not be opting into the proposal. The Ministry of Justice will, however, continue to participate in negotiations towards a final Regulation text, with a view to seeking permission to opt in if the concluded Regulation favours the UK national interests. Its response to the public consultation exercise was published on August 24, 2010 (see CP(R) [41/09]), where it revealed that only 2 per cent of respondents believed that the Government should opt in on the basis of the Commission Proposal.

A detailed report on the Commission Proposal and on the next steps has been produced by the Max Planck Institute: (2010) 74 *RabelsZ* 522.

On the prior Green Paper, see further the Report by the Committee on Legal Affairs with recommendations to the Commission on succession and wills (2005/2148(INI)), calling for the Commission to draw up a comprehensive Regulation in this area of law. See further Dutta (2009) 73 *RabelsZ* 547; Frimston (2007) 3 P.C.B. 170; Harris (2008) 22(4) Tru.L.I. 181; Terner (2007) 14 Maastricht J. 147. The Green Paper was also considered by the House of Lords Select Committee: see HL European Union Committee, 2nd Report of 2007–8 Session, *Green Paper on Succession and Wills.*

See further the report of the Scottish Law Commission on Succession: Scot. Law Com., No.215 of April 2009, Pt 5 (discussed by Dawe [2009] P.C.B. 343). On the earlier Discussion Paper issued by the Scottish Law Commission, see Kerrigan [2008] S.L.T. 67.

In *Dellar v Zivy* [2007] EWHC 2266 (Ch.), [2007] I.L.Pr. 868, the court found that England was the most appropriate forum to determine a succession dispute where a will was drawn up as an English document, expressed using technical English legal and was to be interpreted in accordance with English law; albeit that three of the four defendants were French nationals resident in France and the case related to shares in a French company. **27–002**

NOTE 3. See also Briggs (2010) 126 L.Q.R. 20, 22–23, considering whether the succession exclusion from the Judgments Regulation applied in *Calyon v Michailaidis* [2009] UKPC 34. In that case, the Privy Council held that a

Greek judgment ostensibly determining ownership of art work upon the death of its prior owner had no *res judicata* effect.

Note 3. The provisions on service out of the jurisdiction formerly contained in CPR, r.6.20 are now found in CPR PD6B, para.3.1. CPR, rr.6.20(12) and (13) are now CPR PD6B, para.3.1(13) and (14) respectively.

## 3. CHOICE OF LAW

### A. *Intestate succession*

**27R–010** Note 18. Add: *Dion v Rieser* [2010] NSWSC 50, at [18]–[19].

**27–011** For a recent example of the application of the doctrine of *renvoi* to succession to movable property upon intestacy, see *Re Haji-Ioannou, Haji-Iannou v Frangos* [2009] EWHC 2310 (QB), [2010] 1 All E.R. (Comm.) 303 (noted Bunn (2010) 118 T.E.L. & T.J. 4).

Second sentence. For recent examples of the determination of domicile in a succession context, see *Cyganik v Agulian* [2006] EWCA Civ 129, [2006] 1 F.C.R. 406; *Re Haji-Ioannou, Haji-Iannou v Frangos* [2009] EWHC 2310 (QB), [2010] 1 All E.R. (Comm.) 303; *Holliday v Musa* [2010] EWCA Civ 335, [2010] Fam. Law 702.

**27–012** In *Gorjat v Gorjat* [2010] EWHC 1537 (Ch.), the deceased had instructed a bank to transfer certain Swiss bank accounts held in his own name into new accounts held in the joint names of himself and his second wife. When he died intestate some months later, the children from his first marriage challenged the validity of those transfers on the grounds of lack of capacity and undue influence. The court characterised the issue as one relating to the validity of an *inter vivos* transfer, and not as a matter of succession. It therefore went on to apply contractual choice of law rules in the Rome Convention (on the basis that the gift was to be treated as a contract for Convention purposes) and Rule 209 in relation to the deceased's capacity to make the *inter vivos* gift. On the facts, however, it was held that the same law would have been applicable even if the matter had been classified as a succession issue.

In Case C–518/08 *Fundaciŭ Gala-Salvador Dalí v Société des Auteurs dans les Arts Graphiques et Plastiques*, April 15, 2010, the European Court considered a rule of French law which stated that, upon the death of the author of a work of art, the beneficiaries of the resale right payable when that work of art changed hands were limited to the author's heirs at law, excluding any legatees specified in the deceased's will. The French Court asked the European Court whether the French rule was compatible with Directive 2001/84 of the European Parliament and the Council on the resale right for the benefit of the author of an original work of art. Art.6(1) thereof states that:

"The royalty provided for . . . shall be payable to the author of the work and, subject to Article 8(2), after his death to those entitled under him/her."

The European Court ruled that the Directive imposed a right to resale payments but did not restrict the operation of national law to determine who could benefit from that right. The European Court also declined to rule the reference inadmissible, on the alleged basis that Spanish law, not French law, governed the right of resale. It ruled that determination of the relevant applicable law was a matter for the national court seised.

### B. *Testamentary succession*

#### (1) Capacity

NOTE 38. Second sentence. See now Mental Capacity Act 2005, Sch.3, in force October 1, 2007; and above, entries to Ch.21. **27–023**

Second para. On the application of the Mental Capacity Act 2005 to the execution of a will on behalf of a party domiciled overseas owning immovable property in England, see *In the Matter of P* [2009] EWHC 163 (Ch.), [2010] Ch. 33, at [32]–[34] (noted Rees (2009) 15 T. & T. 494, Rich (2009) 105 T.E.L. & T.J. 9).

Second para. A challenge to the testamentary capacity of a deceased person to make a codicil to her will in respect of land overseas is not precluded by the *Moçambique* rule (considered in Rule 122(3) of the main work): *Armour v Fuller*, 2009 BCSC 409.

Contrast *Re Jagos*, 2007 ABQB 56 (Alta.), where the Court of Queen's Bench of Alberta refused to apply the law of the beneficiary's domicile to determine her right to take a benefit under a will. **27–026**

#### (2) Formal Validity

NOTE 51. Final sentence. For a comparative analysis of the effects of the Convention, see Neels (2007) 56 I.C.L.Q. 613. **27–029**

First sentence. Sections 23–25 (not yet in force) and s.26 (in force, SI 1983/236) of the Administration of Justice Act 1982. **27–038**

NOTE 67. SI 2006/1014 gave force of law to amendments to s.25(4) and (9) of Administration of Justice Act 1982. Other amendments by the Constitutional Reform Act 2005 are to be made from a date to be appointed.

**27–049** Add *Taylor v Farrugia* [2009] NSWSC 801.

See also the provisions on the succession rights of cohabitants in the Family Law (Scotland) Act 2006. The legislation requires, *inter alia*, that the deceased was domiciled in Scotland at the time of death: see *Chebotareva v King's Executrix*, 2008 Fam. L.R. 66 (noted Roodt (2009) Edin. L.R. 147).

### (3) Material or Essential Validity

**27–053** A number of amendments and additions to the Inheritance (Provision for Family and Dependents) Act 1975 were made by the Civil Partnership Act 2004.

In *Dellar v Zivy* [2007] EWHC 2266 (Ch.), [2007] I.L.Pr. 868, the court confirmed that questions of interpretation are determined by the law intended by the deceased. In the absence of indiciations to the contrary, this is rebuttably presumed to be the law of the testator's habitual residence at the time of making the will.

Note 6. See also *Taylor v Farrugia* [2009] NSWSC 801.

### (4) Interpretation

**27R–055** This Rule was cited with approval in *Dellar v Zivy* [2007] EWHC 2266 (Ch.), [2007] I.L.Pr. 868.

**27–056** See *Re Jagos*, 2007 ABQB 56 (Alta.).

**27–064** In *McGowan v Hamblett* [2007] 1 N.Z.L.R. 120, the testator had been resident in New Zealand at the time of his death and had executed a will in New Zealand. The estate included immovable property located in England and the will was resealed in England under the Colonial Probates Act 1892. The will evidenced an apparent intention to divide the estate equally between the testator's widow and his three children; but the issue arose as to whether the widow was entitled to an exemption from inheritance tax to the extent of her interest. The High Court ruled that the will was to be interpreted according to New Zealand law, even in respect of the English immovables, since it was a document executed in New Zealand.

### (6) Revocation

**27R–084** See Neels (2007) 56 I.C.L.Q. 613, for a comparative analysis of the law applicable to revocation.

# CHAPTER 28

# THE EFFECT OF MARRIAGE ON PROPERTY

NOTE 1. A revised version of the Green Paper was published by the Commission on July 17, 2006: COM (2006) 400 final. The European Commission announced, in COM(2010)171 final, April 20, 2010, that it intended to present a proposal for a Regulation "on the conflicts of laws in matters concerning matrimonial property rights" during the course of 2010. At the date of writing this proposal had not been presented. **28R–001**

The analysis in the main work was examined in *Murakami v Wiryadi* [2010] NSWCA 7, [93]–[127]. The NSW Court of Appeal, at [122], criticised the terminology of "fictitious" contract, both generally and as an apt description of the property rights regime contained in Indonesian law, which was the matrimonial domicile of the parties. The court, endorsing the approach of Kekewich J. in *Re De Nicols (No.2)* [1900] 2 Ch. 410 and agreeing with the analysis put forward by Goldberg (1970) 19 I.C.L.Q. 557, held that the "reasonable expectation" of the parties to an Indonesian marriage was that the Indonesian joint property regime would apply, according to its terms, to land acquired by the spouses in New South Wales. The way to achieve that result was to infer a matrimonial property contract on those terms, with the result that the property regime of Indonesian law should be regarded in Australia, and enforced, as though it were a contract to which the parties had subscribed at the outset of their marriage. **28–021**

## Chapter 29

# TRUSTS

29–002 Note 1. The Hague Trusts Convention entered into force for Liechtenstein and San Marino in 2006, for Switzerland in 2007, and for Monaco in 2008.

29–003 Note 9. See also Lupoi (2007) 21(2) Tru.L.I. 80.

29–006 The same exclusion is to be found in the Rome I Regulation (Regulation (EC) 593/2008 of the European Parliament and of the Council of June 17, 2008 on the law applicable to contractual obligations [2008] O.J. L177/6; with *corrigendum* [2009] O.J. L307/87), Art.1(2)(h).

On the relationship between choice of law rules for trusts and for assignment, see Bridge (2010) 125 L.Q.R. 671, 685.

29–007 On the impact that the Rome II Regulation (Regulation (EC) 864/2007 of the European Parliament and of the Council, on the Law Applicable to Non-Contractual Obligations: [2007] O.J. L199/40), which entered into force on January 11, 2009, will have on trusts, see entries at paras 29–063 and 34–044, below.

29–008 In *Berezovsky v Abramovich* [2010] EWHC 647 (Comm.), at [176], the court held that "the effect of the 1987 Act is to apply the provisions of the Convention to oral trusts or putative trusts which are governed by English law."

Note 31. Mental Health Act 1983, s.96(1)(d), has been repealed by Mental Capacity Act 2005, as from October 1, 2007.

29–010 The European Commission Proposal for a Regulation on succession and wills COM(2009) 154 final, October 14, 2009, Art.1(3)(i) excludes from its ambit the "constitution, functioning and dissolving of trusts." For discussion of the Proposal, see entry at para.27R–001, above. On the difficulties of delineating succession and trusts issues in the context of a proposed EU Regulation on Succession and Wills, see Harris (2008) 22(4) Trusts L. Int. 181, 201–205.

29–011 Note 49. See further Hayton (2006) 13(2) J. Int. Corp. 55.

29–012 Compare the position in Italy: Ubertazzi (2008) 14 Trusts and Trustees 111.

See *Re Jagos*, 2007 ABQB 56 (Alta.), where the court determined the law applicable to a trust in order to decide whether trust funds should be transferred from the Public Trustee of Alberta to a guardian trustee for the benefit of a beneficiary who was 16 years of age and lacked capacity by the law of Alberta. **29–015**

In *Berezovsky v Abramovich* [2010] EWHC 647 (Comm.), at [177], the court noted that although Art.6 refers to "the terms of the instrument creating or the writing evidencing the trust, interpreted, if necessary, in the light of the circumstances of the case," in the case of a trust created orally, "that provision must clearly be modified . . . and so must be read by reference to the words spoken in the course of creating the trust." The same approach would be adopted at common law. **29–016**

Note 65. Add *Dornoch Ltd v Westminster International BV* [2009] EWHC 889 (Admlty), [2009] 2 Lloyd's Rep. 191, at [85].

In *Berezovsky v Abramovich* [2010] EWHC 647 (Comm.), the court considered whether it was possible to infer that a particular law was chosen from the fact that the other competing law was that of a non-trust state (referring to Harris, *Hague Trusts Convention*, at p.209). Without deciding the point, the court appeared to consider it doubtful that any such inference could be drawn. **29–017**

On implied choice of law in Canada, see *Webster-Tweel v Royal Trust Corporation of Canada*, 2010 ABQB 139.

In *Singh v Singh* [2006] WASC 182, the claimant sought a declaration that land in Malaysia was held on trust for him; and an order that the defendant should transfer the property to the claimant absolutely. A question also arose of priorities between this trust (which was the subject of a declaration in 2001) and another declaration in favour of a different beneficiary in 1999. The court considered the four factors in Art.7, without having to reach a firm view as to the governing law of each trust. It raised but did not decide the issue of which law would determine questions of priorities between the two trusts. It appears, however, that had it been necessary to resolve matters, the court would also have applied the law applicable to the 2001 declaration to determine the effect of the 1999 trust on the validity of the 2001 trust. See also the subsequent proceedings before the Court of Appeal for Western Australia (2009) 253 A.L.R. 575, and the Supreme Court of Western Australia [2010] WASC 69 and [2010] WASC 64, considered in para.23–049, above. **29–019**

Note 94. See also Beaumont [2006] Jur. Rev. 2.

The domicile of the testatrix was considered in determining the governing law under Art.7 in *Re Jagos*, 2007 ABQB 56 (Alta.). **29–020**

This paragraph and the preceding paragraph of the main work were considered in *Webster-Tweel v Royal Trust Corporation of Canada*, 2010 ABQB 139, at [82]–[84].

**29–021** In *Martin v Secretary of State for Work and Pensions* [2009] EWCA Civ 1289, [2010] W.T.L.R. 671, the Court of Appeal ruled that French law was applicable under Art.7 of the Hague Trusts Convention and would not impose an implied trust (see entry at para.29–064, below). It did not consider Art.5 of the Convention, which states that: "The Convention does not apply to the extent that the law specified by Chapter II does not provide for trusts or the category of trusts involved." It did, however, consider that French law would equally be applicable on common law principles.

In *Berezovsky v Abramovich* [2010] EWHC 647 (Comm.), at [121] and [183], the court considered the view expressed in the von Overbeck Report, para.61, that a judge might tend to conclude that a trust is most closely connected with a State which has the institution of a trust. The court referred to the countervailing view expressed by Harris, *Hague Trusts Convention*, at pp.226–227, that the question of validity was irrelevant to the ascertainment of the law of closest connection. The court expressed the provisional view (at [183]) that the "argument that Art.7 somehow enables a court to avoid the selection of a country with no law by allowing that fact to displace what would otherwise be the result of applying the objective tests set out in that Article seems to me to be probably wrong." No express reference to Art.5 of the Convention was made (see above). See also para.29–021 of the main work.

**29–037** Final sentence. But contrast the position in Canada: *Webster-Tweel v Royal Trust Corporation of Canada*, 2010 ABQB 139, at [67]–[84].

**29–038** In *Oakley v Osiris Trustees* [2008] UKPC 2, (2007–08) 10 I.T.E.L.R. 789, the Privy Council considered the degree of evidence required to effect a change to the proper law of two trusts from the law of Jersey to the law of the Isle of Man. Both trusts contained a power for the trustees to declare by deed that the proper law should be changed. Oakley was the director of one of the two original corporate trustees, and director of the single successor trustee company, DMS. The successor company produced a signed resolution dated December 3, 1997 which stated, *inter alia*, that the proper law of the trust was, from that date, Manx Law. Oakley subsequently replaced the resolution with a deed of variation and confirmation purportedly executed in October 1998 and declaring that the proper law had changed from December 3, 1997. In July 1999, two other trustees were appointed. They commenced proceedings alleging misfeasance and breaches of duty by Oakley and DMS regarding the conduct of the trusts' affairs after December 3, 2007, while DMS was the sole trustee. They relied upon provisions of Jersey law. This raised a preliminary issue as to the governing law of one of the trusts ("the Tabatha Trust"). The Privy Council considered that the proper law of the Tabatha Trust had been the law of the Isle of Man since December 4, 1997, the date when Oakley apparently signed the resolution. Although Oakley had not considered what formalities were required and subsequently doubted the effectiveness of the document, the Privy Council found that he had the requisite legal intention at the time of acting. Lord Scott, dissenting, however, considered that a valid change of the proper law could not occur unless the following three factors were demonstrated: (a) that a document with the requisite degree of formality evidencing the change of governing law was produced; (b) the document had to be a document of the trustee, DMS; (c) the action of the trustee in bringing the document into being had to be a proper discharge of the fiduciary power.

On changing the applicable law in Canada, see *Webster-Tweel v Royal Trust Corporation of Canada*, 2010 ABQB 139, at [85]–[88].

Variation of Trusts Act 1958, ss.1 and 2 are amended by the Mental Capacity Act 2005, in force October 1, 2007.

On the recognition of trusts in continental jurisdictions, see Perrin (2008) 10 Yb. P.I.L. 629. **29–047**

See also *Dornoch Ltd v Westminster International BV* [2009] EWHC 1782 (Admlty), [2009] 2 Lloyd's Rep. 420, at [24]. **29–049**

*cf.* the position in Italy: Mazzocchi (2006) 12(6) Trusts and Trustees 21. **29–052**

Jersey has recently enacted far-reaching legislation in Art.9 of the Trusts (Amendment No.4) (Jersey) Law 2006 (replacing Art.9 of the Trusts (Jersey) Law 1984) which protects trusts governed by Jersey law from the application of any other law (see Matthams (2007) 14 J. Int. Corp. P. 109). It then provides in Art.9(4) that: **29–054**

> "No foreign judgment with respect to a trust shall be enforceable to the extent that it is inconsistent with this Article irrespective of any applicable law relating to conflicts of law [*sic*]."

In part, this legislation is a response to the tendency of English judges to vary trusts governed by Jersey law in ancillary relief proceedings and to send out a message of deterrence (See Birt (2009) 13 Jersey and Guernsey Law Review 5; Dixon (2008) 15 J. Int. Corp. P. 267; Gothard (2006) 12(3) Trusts and Trustees 8; Winfield (2006) 12(6) Trusts and Trustees 6; Hanson and Renouf [2006] (Sept) I.F.L. 135; Hanson and Renouf [2006] P.C.B. 310; Matthews (2008) 22(2) Tru.L.I. 63). The legislation has been strongly criticised: see Harris (2007) 11 Jersey and Guernsey Law Review 9; (2007) 11 Jersey and Guernsey Law Review 184; Hanson and Renouf [2007] Fam. Law 340; for an alternative view, see Hochberg (2007) 11 Jersey and Guernsey Law Review 20. For interpretation of the Jersey law, and a refusal to give it literal effect in

Jersey, see *Re the B Trust* [2006] J.R.C. 185, judgment of December 8, 2006), noted by Harris (2007) 11 Jersey and Guernsey Law Review 184); see also *Re the H Trust* [2006] J.R.C. 187, judgment of October 2, 2007, in which the reasoning in *Re the B Trust* was approved. In *Mubarak* v *Mubarak*, [2008] JRC 136, [2009] 1 F.L.R. 664, the Royal Court of Jersey held that an English order could not be enforced, and the trustees could not be directed by the Jersey courts to comply with it, if the variation in question was not one which the trustees themselves could have made without the court's intervention (albeit that, on the facts, the Jersey court found that the husband had given his consent to the Jersey courts themselves varying the trust on the terms of the English order). The Jersey Court of Appeal upheld the decision ([2008] JCA 196; noted Meiklejohn (2009) 15 Trusts & Trustees 228; Renouf (2009) 13 Jersey and Guernsey Law Review 225; Renouf and Blakemore (2009) 39 Fam. Law 226) on the basis that the approval of all relevant parties had been obtained pursuant to Art.47 of the Trusts (Jersey) Law 1984, so as to affect a variation of the trust. By contrast with *Re the B Trust*, this was ultimately a case in which *consensual* variation could be demonstrated. That being the case, there was no obligation to examine further the meaning and effect of Art.9 of the Law. The result is that the observations of the Royal Court of Jersey as to the meaning of that Article remain pertinent: see further *Barclays Private Bank & Trust Ltd v Hsu* [2010] J.R.C. 003A. However, a Green Paper on possible further reform of the Trusts (Jersey Law) 1984 so as, *inter alia*, to clarify the meaning and scope of its conflicts provisions, was issued in July 2008.

There is, however, evidence that, in the light of the Jersey legislation, English judges are becoming aware of the need to show restraint in varying trusts governed by foreign laws. In *Re the B Trust*, the Bailiff urged the English courts to show greater caution in exercising their jurisdiction to vary foreign law trusts pursuant to s.24 of the Matrimonial Causes Act 1973 (at [30]). In *Mubarak v Mubarak* [2007] EWHC 220 (Fam.), [2007] 2 F.L.R. 364, permission to appeal refused [2007] EWCA Civ 879, Holman J. varied a trust in ancillary relief proceedings to allow a wife to recover assets where the husband had, over many years, failed to pay sums due her. Nonetheless, he noted the cautionary implications of the new Jersey law and was "very respectful indeed of the sovereignty of the foreign State and of the jurisdiction of the foreign court" (at [146]). He said that he did "deeply appreciate that 'as a general rule it will be an exorbitant exercise of jurisdiction for this court to purport to vary the terms of a Jersey settlement'" (at [159]). See also *A v A* [2007] EWHC 99 (Fam.), in which Munby J. declined to rule that a trust governed by English law, but with substantial connections with Jersey, was a sham.

Guernsey has now followed the lead of Jersey and enacted legislation designed, in particular, to prevent the recognition of English ancillary relief orders varying Guernsey law trusts. Section 14(1) of the Guernsey (Trusts) Law 2007 applies to Guernsey law trusts and sets out the matters to which Guernsey law alone shall apply. Section 14(3) states that no Guernsey law trust is to be invalidated or impugned, and the officers of the trust shall be under no liability, by virtue not just that a foreign law confers a right on a person by way of personal relationship to the settlor *but also by reason of personal relationship to the beneficiary*. This goes significantly further than other offshore legislation. Guernsey's rules on the effects of foreign judgments are still more radical than those in Art.9(4) of the Jersey Law. Section 14(4) of the Guernsey Law prevents both the *recognition and* enforcement of a foreign judgment that is inconsistent with the Guernsey Law. There is still further protection in s.14(4), which provides that a foreign judgment will also be refused recognition if the Royal Court, for the purposes of protecting the interests of the beneficiaries or in the interests of the proper administration of the trust, so orders. The effect of s.14(4) is to make the protection of Guernsey law against English ancillary relief orders exceedingly wide. For discussion, see Harris (2008) 12 Jersey and Guernsey Law Review 289; Noseda (2008) 22(3) Tru.L.I. 117.

For a comparative analysis of trusts asset protection legislation, see Panico, *International Trust Laws* (2010), Ch.11; Thomas and Hudson, *The Law of Trusts* (2010), Chs 43 and 44.

NOTE 1. See also Harper, Goodman, Matthews and Hamlin, *International Trust and Divorce Litigation* (2007), esp. chaps 3 and 8.

NOTE 2. See also *Re Jagos*, 2007 ABQB 56 (Alta.). **29–055**

This paragraph was cited with approval in *Webster-Tweel v Royal Trust Corporation of Canada*, 2010 ABQB 139, at [64]. **29–058**

Part 6 of the CPR has been substituted by SI 2008/2178, Sch.1. **29–059**

Where a party agrees in a contract to hold property on trust, this is a claim "in respect of a contract" within the meaning of CPR PD6B, para.3.1(6): *Cherney v Deripaska* [2008] EWHC 1530 (Comm.), [2009] 1 All E.R. (Comm.) 333 (appeal dismissed without consideration of this point [2009] EWCA Civ 849, [2010] 2 All E.R. (Comm.) 456). See also *Elektrim SA v Vivendi Holdings* [2008] EWCA Civ 1178, [2009] 1 Lloyd's Rep. 59. See further *Cecil v Bayat* [2010] EWHC 641 (Comm.), at [141], where it was held that a trust claim premised upon an agreement in principle, not a binding contract, was not a claim "in respect of a contract".

In *Cecil v Bayat* [2010] EWHC 641 (Comm.), the court applied the CPR provisions on claims for a remedy against the defendant as constructive trustee (CPR PD6B, para.3.1(15)) and on claims for restitution (CPR PD6B, para.3.1(16)) to claims based upon: (i) liability to account for breach of fiduciary duties; (ii) liability to account as constructive trustee on the basis of knowing receipt; and (iii) dishonest assistance in breach of trust or fiduciary duty. Both CPR provisions require that the defendant's alleged liability arises from acts committed within the jurisdiction. In this respect, the court applied the test of whether substantial and efficacious acts had been committed within the jurisdiction, even if such acts had also been committed outside the jurisdiction. See also *Astrazeneca UK Limited v Albemarle International Corporation* [2010] EWHC 1028 (Comm.), [2010] 2 Lloyd's Rep. 61.

On the enforcement of foreign judgments against offshore trusts and the implications of the Privy Council's decision in *Pattni v Ali* [2006] UKPC 51, [2007] 2 A.C. 85, see Collins (2009) 15(1) Trusts & Trustees 18. Courts in both the Cayman Islands (*Miller v Gianne and Redwood Corp* [2007] C.I.L.R. 18; and *Bandone v Sol Properties Ltd*, Grand Court, June 5, 2008) and Jersey (*Re Karinska and Greencap Ltd* [2008] JRC 152, judgment of September 16, 2008) have recently sanctioned the enforcement of non-monetary judgments.

NOTE 14. The provisions on service out of the jurisdiction formerly contained in CPR, r.6.20 are now found in CPR PD6B, para.3.1. In particular, CPR, rr.6.20(11)–(15) is now CPR PD6B, para.3.1(12)–(16).

NOTE 15. CPR, r.6.20(11) is now CPR PD6B, para.3.1(12).

NOTE 16. CPR, r.6.20(12) is now CPR PD6B, para.3.1(13).

NOTE 17. CPR, r.6.20(13) is now CPR PD6B, para.3.1(14).

NOTE 18. CPR, r.6.20(14) is now CPR PD6B, para.3.1(15).

NOTE 19. CPR, r.6.20(15) is now CPR PD6B, para.3.1(16).

**29–060** The provisions of the Matrimonial Causes Act 1973 should not be circumvented by a spouse relying on the Trusts of Land and Appointment of Trustees Act 1996 to claim a beneficial interest in a matrimonial home when ancillary relief proceedings are already underway: *Prazic v Prazic* [2006] EWCA Civ 497, [2006] 2 F.L.R. 1128, [2007] 1 F.C.R. 503.

**29–061** In *Gómez* v *Gómez-Monche Vives* [2008] EWCA Civ 1065, [2009] Ch. 245; noted Hayton (2009) 23(1) Tru.L.I. 3, Briggs (2008) 79 B.Y.I.L. 533 (reversing, in part, [2008] EWHC 259 (Ch.), [2008] 3 W.L.R. 305), it was held that where the governing law of the trust had been expressly chosen by the parties, this would almost always be the system of law with which the trust had its closest and most real connection for the purposes of determining its domicile within the meaning of Art.5(6) of the Judgments Regulation.

The Court of Appeal also held that Art.5(6) applied to a claim against a beneficiary of an express trust to whom the trustees had paid capital and income to which she was allegedly not entitled. The court noted that it was alleged that the beneficiary held the assets on constructive trust and stated that Art.5(6) does not apply to such trusts. It held, however, that: "The claim of constructive trust goes to remedy and not to the question whether the first defendant is sued as a beneficiary of the written trust" (at [79]). The claim had proceeded on the basis that defendant was a beneficiary of the written trust:

> "and the claimants are suing her for sums which she received by way of overpayment of her entitlement. The relief claims an account of all monies which she has received, including those to which it is conceded she is entitled, and this is a necessary preliminary to identifying the monies to which she is entitled." (at [82]).

It was also held that the holder of a fiduciary power was not within the scope of Art.5(6) and could not be considered to be a person sued "as trustee".

At first instance, Morgan J. had stated that a resulting trust created by operation of law where the settlor had not disposed of the whole beneficial interest fell outside the terms of Art.5(6). The Court of Appeal did not need to address this point.

**29–062** Add: *Walbrook Trustees (Jersey) Ltd v Fattal Chancery Division* [2009] EWHC 1446, [2010] 1 All E.R. (Comm.) 526, at [67] (affirmed without express consideration of this point [2010] EWCA Civ 408).

**29–063** The Rome II Regulation (entry at para.29–007, above) excludes from its scope non-contractual obligations arising out of the relations between settlors, trustees and beneficiaries of a trust created voluntarily (Art.1(2)(e)). The meaning of this exclusion is considered further at the entry to para.34–044, below. To the extent that there is any conflict between the Regulation's scope and the Hague Trusts Convention, the latter prevails (Art.28(1)). Strictly speaking, this means that the Convention prevails only where the trust in question falls within the scope of Art.3 of the Convention; and not where the trust falls within the extended scope of the Convention in the United Kingdom under s.1(2) of the Recognition of Trusts Act 1987. However, a pragmatic response would be that Art.20 of the Convention allows a Contracting State to extend the scope of the Convention to "trusts declared by judicial decisions"; and so the authority to extend the scope of the Convention comes from the Convention itself, which should prevail over the Regulation. Whilst this might be a satisfactory analysis for constructive trusts imposed irrespective of the will of the parties, it does not provide an answer for the full range of trusts within the scope of s.1(2) of the 1987 Act, since the United Kingdom extended the scope of the Regulation still further and applied it to any other trusts arising under the law of any part of the United Kingdom, even though Art.20 does not expressly allow it to do so. Arguably, that further extension derives its force solely from a United Kingdom statute, not the Convention, and should not prevail over the Regulation.

In any event, the Convention does not apply to the preliminary question of when a trust arises. Hence, the question whether a constructive or resulting trust arises is a matter for the choice of law rules of the forum (see para.29–063 of the main work). It is the basis of the claim which is alleged to give rise to the trust that must be classified. This means that, for all trusts other than those expressly excluded by Art.1(2)(e) of the Rome II Regulation (i.e. trusts created voluntarily), the question whether the trust *arises* is a matter for the choice of law rules contained *within* the Regulation. Hence, if it is alleged that a constructive trust is imposed, against the will of the "trustee", to prevent unjust enrichment, then the choice of law rules applicable to unjust enrichment in the Regulation will determine if such a trust exists. The operation and effects of the trust and the obligations imposed on the trustee will thereafter be determined by the rules in the Recognition of Trusts Act 1987 (see para.29–065 of the main work).

**29–064** *Lightning v Lightning* is now reported at (2009) 23 Trusts L. Int. 35. The judgment in *Lightning v Lightning* was considered by the Singapore Court of Appeal in *Murakami v Wiryadi* [2008] SGCA 44.

In *Martin v Secretary of State for Work and Pensions* [2009] EWCA Civ 1289, [2010] W.T.L.R. 671, the appellant, who was in receipt of social security payments, had failed to disclose the existence of a property in his name in France. He alleged that the property had only been placed in his name in view of the provisions of French succession law, so that the child that he had with his former partner would inherit the property, rather than the other children of his former partner. He asserted that he held the property on trust for his former partner, who had paid the purchase price. The Court of Appeal accepted that *Lightning v Lightning Electrical Contractors Ltd* (2009) 23 Tru.L.I. 35 and *Webb v Webb* [1991] 1 W.L.R. 1410 established that the *lex situs* need not necessarily be applied to such a trust. Nonetheless, it held that as the alleged trust arose in connection with a transaction in contemplation of French succession law, French law should also apply to the trusts issue; and, there being no implied trust in French law, the appeal failed. It held that the same result would ensue both at common law and by application of Art.7 of the Hague Trusts Convention.

In *Luxe Holding Ltd v Midland Resources Holding Ltd* [2010] EWHC 1908 (Ch.), it was held that a vendor who broke his contract of sale by reselling to someone else was accountable as a "quasi-trustee" to the first intended purchaser for the proceeds of the sale. The court applied English law, which had been chosen by the original contracting parties to govern their relationship, on the basis that they had voluntarily subjected themselves to English remedies. In this respect, the court followed the rulings in *De Beers Consolidated Mines Ltd v British South Africa Co* [1910] 2 Ch. 502 and *Lightning v Lightning Electrical Contractors Ltd*, 1998, reported (2009) 23 Trusts L. Int. 35. No reference to the Hague Trusts Convention was made.

In *Murakami v Wiryadi* [2010] NSWCA 7, the New South Wales Court of Appeal had provisionally determined, for the purposes of a stay application, that Indonesian law was applicable to a matrimonial property regime. It was alleged that the first respondent had failed to disclose the existence of immovable property and bank assets located in Australia as common matrimonial property during Indonesian divorce proceedings; and that, accordingly, those assets were held by the first respondent on resulting or constructive trust for the appellant. Citing *Lightning v Lightning Electrical Contractors Ltd* (2009) 23 Tru.L.I. 35 with approval (at [133]), the court found that there was an implied marital contract governed by Indonesian law; and that the law applicable to this relationship should also determine whether an equitable interest in the property arose in favour of the appellant.

On the law applicable to resulting and constructive trusts in Canada, see *Cooper-Standard Automotive Canada Limited (Re)*, 2009 51188 (ON S.C.).

## Chapter 30

# CORPORATIONS AND CORPORATE INSOLVENCY

## 1. DOMICILE AND RESIDENCE

**30R–001** Note 1. Add in line 14: See also Regulation (EC) 1082/2006 of the European Parliament and of the Council of July 5, 2006 on a European grouping of territorial cooperation (EGTC), [2006] O.J. L210/19, and for implementation in the United Kingdom, SI 2007/1949, as amended by SI 2008/728; Directive 2005/56/EC on cross-border mergers of limited liability companies [2005] O.J. L310/1, implemented in the United Kingdom in SI 2007/2974.

Add in line 21: Case C–210/06 *Cartesio Oktató és Szolgáltató bt* [2008] E.C.R. I–9641; Enriques and Troger [2008] C.L.J. 521; Gerner-Beurle and Schillig (2010) 59 I.C.L.Q. 303.

Add at end: See also European Commission, *Communication from the Commission to the European Parliament and the Council: An area of freedom, security and justice serving the citizen* COM (2009) 262 final, para.3.4 (possibility of measures designed to implement common rules determining the law applicable to matters of company law).

**30–002—30–003** See now Companies Act 2006.

**30–002** Note 5. See also *889457 Alberta Inc v Katanga Mining Ltd* [2008] EWHC 2679 (Comm.), [2009] I.L.Pr. 175.

Note 6. As to the new Lugano Convention, see above, entry at para.11–020.

Note 8. See also *Australian Securities and Investment Commission v Medical Defence Association of Western Australia* [2005] FCAFC 173.

Notes 13 and 14. See previous entry.

## 2. STATUS

**30R–009** Note 34. *SEB Trygg Holding Aktiebolag v Manches* [2005] EWHC 35 (Comm.), [2005] 2 Lloyd's Rep. 129 was affirmed in part and reversed in part by the Court of Appeal, *sub nom. SEB Trygg Liv Holding AB v Manches*

[2005] EWCA Civ 1237, [2006] 1 W.L.R. 2276, without reference to the point.

NOTE 34. Add: *Trustees of Our Lady of the Sacred Heart v The Registrar-General* [2008] NTSC 13.

NOTES 35–38. Add: See also *Pillar Securitisation Sarl v Spicer & Shinners* [2010] EWHC 836 (Ch.) at [33]–[38]. **30–010**

NOTES 50, 51. See previous entry. Add: *Republic of Kazakhstan v Istil Group Inc* [2006] EWHC 448 (Comm.), [2006] 2 Lloyd's Rep. 370, affd. [2007] EWCA Civ 471, [2008] 1 All E.R. (Comm.) 88, but see at [36] *per* Arden L.J.; see also *Republic of Kazakhstan v Istil Group Inc (No.2)* [2007] EWHC 2729 (Comm.), [2008] 1 Lloyd's Rep. 382. **30–011**

See *R. (on the application of Kibris Turk Hava Yollari) v Secretary of State for Transport* [2009] EWHC 1918 (Admin.), [2010] 1 All E.R. (Comm.) 253. **30–014**

NOTE 74. See now Companies Act 2006, Pt 34, concerned with "overseas companies", defined (s.1044) as a company incorporated outside the United Kingdom, as opposed to Great Britain. For service of documents on overseas companies, see *ibid.*, s.1139(2). See also Overseas Companies Regulations 2009, SI 2009/1801, in force from October 1, 2009. **30–019**

## 3. CAPACITY AND INTERNAL MANAGEMENT

For detailed discussion of Rule 162, see *Haugesund Kommune v Depfa ACS Bank* [2010] EWCA Civ 579, [2010] 2 Lloyd's Rep. 323 where a majority of the Court of Appeal held that, in applying the law of the place of incorporation, the concept of "capacity" in Rule162 had to be given a broader "internationalist" meaning and must not be confined to the narrow definition accorded by English domestic law. "Capacity" should be interpreted as the legal ability of a corporation to exercise specific rights, in particular, the legal ability to enter into a contract with a third party. Thus, a lack of substantive power to conclude a contract of a particular type was equivalent to a lack of capacity. Similarly, the concept of a corporation's "constitution" had to be given a broad "internationalist" interpretation. Rather than merely looking at a charter or memorandum and articles it is necessary, for the purposes of the English conflict of laws, to examine all the sources of power of the corporation, including constitutional documents, but also relevant statutes and other rules of law of the country where the corporation was created. See at [27]–[61], [155]–[160], *per*, respectively Aikens and Pill L.JJ. *cf.* Etherton L.J., at [133]–[145] who said that "corporate capacity" should bear the meaning it had in English domestic law. **30R–020— 30–022**

NOTES 75, 76. As to Companies Act 1985, ss.36–36C, see below, entry at para.30–023. **30R–020**

NOTES 75–82. Add: *Haugesund Kommune v Depfa ACS Bank*, above, entry at paras 30R–020—30–022.

NOTE 76. Add in line 16: *Reeves v Sprecher* [2007] EWHC 117 (Ch.), [2008] B.C.C. 49; *Alberta Inc v Katanga Mining Ltd* [2008] EWHC 2679 (Comm.), [2009] I.L.Pr. 175 at [33]; *Debt Collect London Ltd v SK Slavia Praha-Fotbal AS* [2010] EWHC 57 (QB). Add in line 17: *cf. Virgtel Ltd v Zabusky* [2006] QSC 66; *Oates v Consolidated Capital Services Ltd* [2008] NSWSC 464.

Add in line 22: Civil Jurisdiction and Judgments Act 1982, Sch. 3C is repealed by Civil Jurisdiction and Judgments Regulations 2009 (SI 2009/3131), reg. 25. The relevant provision of the new Lugano Convention, above entry at para.11R–001, is Art.22(2).

**30–021** NOTE 78. Companies Act 2006, s.1046 allows the Secretary of State to make provision by regulations requiring an overseas company to deliver to the registrar for registration a return containing specified particulars and to deliver with the return specified documents. For the regulations, see Overseas Companies Regulations 2009, S1 2009/1801, in force from October 1, 2009. There are no specific provisions in the 2006 Act concerning Manx and Channel Island companies. Presumably such companies will be regarded as overseas companies.

**30–022** NOTE 79. For floating charges in Scotland, see now Bankruptcy and Diligence etc. (Scotland) Act 2007, Pt 2. And see Companies Act 2006, ss. 878–892.

**30–023** See now Overseas Companies (Execution of Documents and Registration of Charges) Regulations 2009, SI 2009/1917, in force from October 1, 2009. Part 2 of the Regulations applies ss.43, 44 and 46 of the Companies Act 2006, in a modified form, to overseas companies.

Section 43 of the 2006 Act, as modified, provides that under the law of England (and Northern Ireland) a contract may be made: (a) by an overseas company, by writing under its common seal or in any manner permitted by the laws of the territory in which the company is incorporated for the execution of documents by such a company; and (b) on behalf of any overseas company, by any person who, in accordance with the laws of the territory in which the company is incorporated, is acting under the authority (express or implied) of that company: s.43(1). Any formalities required by law in the case of a contract made by an individual also apply, unless a contrary intention appears, to a contract made by or on behalf of an overseas company: s.43(2).

Section 44 of the 2006 Act, as modified, enables a document to be executed by an overseas company under the law of England (and Northern Ireland): (a) by affixing its common seal; or (b) if it is executed in a manner permitted by the laws of the territory in which the company is incorporated for the execution of documents by such a company: s 44(1). A document which: (a) is signed by a person who, in accordance with the laws of the territory in which an overseas company is incorporated, is acting under the authority (express or implied) of the company; and (b) is expressed (in whatever form of words) to be executed by the company, has the same effect in relation to that company as it would have in relation to a company incorporated in England (or Northern Ireland) if executed under the common seal of a company so incorporated: s.44(2). In favour of a purchaser, a document is deemed to have been duly executed by an overseas company if it purports to be signed in accordance with s.44(2) and, for these purposes a "purchaser" means a purchaser in good faith for valuable consideration including a lessee, mortgagee or other person who for valuable consideration acquires an interest in property: s.44(3). Where a document is to be signed by a person on behalf of more than one overseas company, it is not duly signed for the purposes of s.44 unless he signs it separately in each capacity: s.44(4). References in s.44 to a document being (or purporting to be) signed by a person who, in accordance with the laws of a territory in which an overseas company is incorporated, is acting under the authority (express or implied) of the company are to be read, in a case where that person is a firm, as references to its being (or purporting to be) signed by an individual authorised by the firm to sign on its behalf: s.44(5). Section 44 applies to a document that is (or purports to be) executed by an overseas company in the name of or on behalf of another person whether or not that person is an overseas company: s.44(6).

Section 46 of the 2006 Act, as modified, deals with the execution of deeds. A document is validly executed by an overseas company as a deed for the purposes of s.1(2)(b) of the Law of Property (Miscellaneous Provisions) Act 1989 (and for the purposes of the law of Northern Ireland), if, and only if: (a) it is duly executed by the company; and (b) it is delivered as a deed (s.46(1)) and for the latter purpose a document is presumed to be delivered upon its being executed, unless a contrary intention is proved: s.46(2).

Section 48 of the 2006 Act, as modified, is concerned with execution of documents by overseas companies for the purposes of the law of Scotland: s.48(1). In this respect, for the purposes of any enactment: (a) providing for a document to be executed by a company by affixing its common seal; or (b) referring (in whatever terms) to a document so executed, a document signed or subscribed by or on behalf of an overseas company in accordance with the provisions of the Requirements of Writing (Scotland) Act 1995 has effect as if so executed: s.48(2).

Section 51 of the Companies Act 2006, as modified, deals with pre-incorporation contracts, deeds and obligations. A contract that purports to be made by or on behalf of an overseas company at a time when the company has not been formed has effect, subject to any agreement to the contrary, as one made by the person purporting to act for the company or as agent for it, and he is personally liable on the contract accordingly: s.51(1). Section 51(1) applies (a) to the making of a deed under the law of England (or Northern Ireland) and (b) to the undertaking of an obligation under the law of Scotland, as it applies to the making of a contract: s.51(2).

Regulation 7 of the 2009 Regulations revokes SI 1994/950 which inserted sections 36A–36C into the Companies Act 1985. For Northern Ireland, SR (NI) 2003/5 is also revoked.

NOTE 84. Add in line 3: *Rimpacific Navigation Inc v Daehan Shipbuilding Co Ltd* [2009] EWHC 2941 (QB), [2010] 2 Lloyd's Rep. 236.

**30–024** NOTE 92. Add: *Reeves v Sprecher* [2007] EWHC 117 (Ch.), [2008] B.C.C. 49; *Alberta Inc v Katanga Mining Ltd* [2008] EWHC 2679 (Comm.), [2009] I.L.Pr. 175 at [33]. *cf. Virgtel Ltd v Zabusky* [2006] QSC 66; *Oates v Consolidated Capital Services Ltd* [2008] NSWSC 464.

This paragraph was cited with approval in *Debt Collect London Ltd v SK Slavia Praha-Fotbal AS* [2010] EWHC 57 (QB).

NOTE 97. On choice of law and piercing the corporate veil, see Chee Ho Tham [2007] L.M.C.L.Q. 22.

NOTE 1. See entry at n.92, above.

**30–025** NOTE 5. The exclusion in Regulation (EC) of the European Parliament and of the Council of June 17, 2008 on the law applicable to contractual obligations (Rome I) [2008] O.J. L177/6 (reproduced in Appendix 2 to this Supplement) is to the same effect: see Art.1(2)(f) of the Rome I Regulation.

NOTE 6. Add at end: See *Haugesund Kommune v Depfa ACS Bank* [2010] EWCA Civ 579, [2010] 2 Lloyd's Rep. 323; *Debt Collect London Ltd v SK Slavia Praha-Fotbal AS* [2010] EWHC (QB).

**30–026** The scope of the exclusion in Art.1(2)(f) of the Regulation would seem to correspond with that found in Art.1(2)(e) of the Rome Convention, as discussed in this paragraph.

NOTE 14. The exclusion contained in the Rome I Regulation (entry at para. 30–025, n.5, above) is to the same effect: see Art.1(2)(g) of the Regulation.

**30–027** The matters discussed in this paragraph, will, it is suggested, also be excluded from the Rome I Regulation by virtue of Art. 1(2)(f).

NOTE 18. As to Companies Act 1985, s.36C, see entry at para.30–023.

**30–028** There is no doubt that the exclusion in Art.1(2)(f) of the Rome I Regulation will be given an autonomous interpretation.

**30–029—30–030** As regards the new Lugano Convention, the references in these paragraphs should now be to Art.22(2).

NOTE 20. See above, entry at para.30R–020, n. 76.

References to Companies Act 1985 are replaced by Companies Act 2006. **30–030**

Text at note 30. Companies Act 1985, s.212 is replaced in pertinent part by Companies Act 2006, ss.793, 820–821. Companies Act 1985, s.216(1) is replaced by Companies Act 2006, s.794(1).

Companies Act 1985, s.151 is replaced in somewhat changed form by Companies Act 2006, s.678, though the latter provision applies only to the acquisition of shares of public companies. **30–031**

## 4. WINDING UP PROCEEDINGS NOT FALLING WITHIN COUNCIL REGULATION (EC) 1346/2000 ON INSOLVENCY PROCEEDINGS

### A. *Jurisdiction of English Courts*

Note 44. As to the new Lugano Convention, see now Civil Jurisdiction and Judgments Act 1982, s.43A, inserted by SI 2009/3131, reg. 20. Sch. 3C of the 1982 Act is repealed by SI 2009/3131, reg. 25. The relevant provisions of the new Lugano Convention are Arts 1(2)(b) and 22(2). **30R–033**

Note 46. Companies Act 1985, ss.425–427 concerned with schemes of arrangement is replaced with minor amendments by Companies Act 2006, ss.895–901. On service under Insolvency Rules 1986, r.12.10, 12.11 and 12.12, in the context of company voluntary arrangements, see *Re T & N Ltd (No. 3)* [2006] EWHC 842 (Ch.), [2006] 1 W.L.R. 2831. As to CPR, r.6.8, see now CPR, r.16(15), inserted by SI 2008/2178.

Add in line 16: *Re OJSC ANK Yugraneft* [2008] EWHC 2614 (Ch.), [2009] 1 B.C.L.C. 298; *HSBC, Petitioner* [2009] CSOH 147, 2010 S.L.T. 281.

Notes 47 and 48 and accompanying text. See above, entry at para.30R–033, n.44.

Note 49. The reference to Sch. 3C, Art.23 is now a reference to Art.29 of the new Lugano Convention.

Note 50. For the UNCITRAL Model Law on Cross-Border Insolvency, see below, paras S30R–344, *et seq.* **30–034**

Note 53. Council Regulation (EC) 44/2001 now has effect in relation to Denmark in accordance with the Agreement made on October 19, 2005 between the European Community and the Kingdom of Denmark on jurisdiction and the recognition and enforcement of judgments in civil and commercial matters ([2005] O.J. L299/62): see SI 2007/1655, in force from July 1, 2007. **30–035**

Note 67 and accompanying text. For the purposes of the new Lugano Convention, the references are to Arts 22(2) and 60. SI 2009/3131, reg. 20 **30–037** inserts a new s. 43A into Civil Jurisdiction and Judgments Act 1982 defining the seat of a company for the purposes of the new Convention. Sch. 3C of the 1982 Act is repealed by SI 2009/3131, reg. 25.

**30–041** NOTE 79. See previous entry.

**30–042** NOTE 81. Add in line 3: See generally *Re OJSC ANK Yugraneft* [2008] EWHC 2614 (Ch.), [2009] 1 B.C.L.C. 298.

Text to notes 82, 84 and note 86. As to Companies Act 1985, s.425, see entry at para.30R–033.

NOTE 84. In *Re OJSC ANK Yugraneft* [2008] EWHC 2614 (Ch.), [2009] 1 B.C.L.C. 298 the view was expressed that the core principles went to the discretion of the court. And see *HSBC, Petitioner*, above. See, further, on jurisdiction to sanction schemes of arrangement, *Re La Mutuelles du Mans Assurances IARD* [2005] EWHC 1599 (Ch.), [2006] B.C.C. 11; *Re DAP Holding NV* [2005] EWHC 2092 (Ch.), [2006] B.C.C. 48; *Re The Home Insurance Co* [2005] EWHC 2485 (Ch.), [2006] B.C.L.C. 476; *Re Sovereign Marine & General Insurance Co* [2006] EWHC 1335 (Ch.), [2006] B.C.C. 774; Look Chan Ho (2006) 22 Insolvency L. & Pr. 145.

**30–044** NOTE 93. Add: And see Third Parties (Rights against Insurers) Act 2010, s.18 (not yet in force).

**30–045** NOTE 95. Add: *Re OJSC ANK Yugraneft* [2008] EWHC 2614 (Ch.), [2009] 1 B.C.L.C. 298.

**30–048** Fourth sentence. On the duty of overseas companies to register particulars, see now Companies Act 2006, s.1046; SI 2009/1801.

**30–073** NOTES 9 and 10. See above, entry at para.30R–033, n. 44.

**30–074** NOTE 11. See *Liquidator of Bank of Credit and Commerce SA, Noter* [2007] CSOH 165, 2007 S.L.T. 1149. See too Cross-Border Insolvency Regulations 2006 (SI 2006/1030), which implement in Great Britain the UNCITRAL Model Law on Cross-Border Insolvency. According to reg.7 of the Regulations an order made by a court in either part of Great Britain in the exercise of jurisdiction in relation to the subject matter of the Regulations shall be enforced in the other part of Great Britain as if it were made by a court exercising the corresponding jurisdiction in that other part (reg.7(1)). Nothing in reg.7(1), however, requires a court in either part of Great Britain to enforce, in relation to property situated in that part, any order made by a court in the other part of Great Britain (reg.7(2)). By virtue of reg.7(3), the courts having jurisdiction in relation to the subject matter of the Regulations in either part of Great Britain shall assist the courts having the corresponding jurisdiction in the other part of Great Britain. See *Hynd's Trustee, Petitioner* [2009] CSOH 76, 2009 S.C. 593 (a case of bankruptcy: Model Law applies to assistance given by British courts to foreign insolvency proceedings and by foreign courts to British insolvency proceedings, but does not apply to recognition or enforcement of insolvency orders made in another British court. This is dealt with by Insolvency Act 1986, s.426(1)).

For further discussion of the Model Law, see below, paras S30R–344, *et seq.*

B. *Effect of an English Winding Up Order*

Note 22. Add: *Bloom v Harms Offshore AHT* [2009] EWCA Civ 632, [2010] Ch. 187. **30R–076**

Note 23. *Re HIH Casualty and General Insurance Ltd* [2005] EWHC 2125 (Ch.), [2006] 2 All E.R. 671 was affirmed [2006] EWCA Civ 732, [2007] 1 All E.R. 177 by the Court of Appeal whose decision has been reversed by the House of Lords, [2008] UKHL 21, [2008] 1 W.L.R. 852, below, entry at para.30–081, nn.57–65. For comment, see Smart (2008) 124 L.Q.R. 554; Rogerson [2008] C.L.J. 476; Townsend (2008) 71 M.L.R. 811; Briggs (2008) 79 B.Y.I.L. 501; Meng Seng Wee [2009] L.M.C.L.Q. 18; Chee Ho Tam [2009] L.M.C.L.Q. 113.

Add in line 3: *Bloom v Harms Offshore AHT* [2009] EWCA Civ 632, [2010] Ch. 187; *Re Swissair Schweizerische Luftverkehr-Aktiengesellschaft* [2009] EWHC 2099 (Ch.), [2009] B.P.I.R. 1505.

Note 29. Add in line 3: *Bloom v Harms Offshore AHT,* above; *cf. Federal Commissioner of Taxation v Linter Textiles Australia Ltd* [2005] HCA 20, (2005) 220 C.L.R. 592; *International Transportation Service Inc v The Owners and/or Demise Charterers of the Ship or Vessel "Convenience Container"* [2006] HKCFI 465, [2006] 2 Lloyd's Rep. 556. **30–078**

Add in line 6: *Bloom v Harms Offshore AHT,* above.

Notes 29, 30, 32–37 and 39. See above, entry at para.30R–076.

Notes 29, 32–37. Add: *Re Swissair Schweizerische Luftverkehr-Aktiengesellschaft* [2009] EWHC 2099 (Ch.), [2009] B.P.I.R. 1505.

Note 38. Add: See *ML Ubase Holdings Co Ltd v Trigem Computer Inc* [2007] NSWSC 859.

**30–079** NOTE 42. Add at end: *Bloom v Harms Offshore AHT*, above. See also *AWB Geneva SA v North America Steamships Ltd* [2007] EWCA Civ 739, [2007] 2 Lloyd's Rep. 315.

NOTE 43. Add in line 3: *Bloom v Harms Offshore AHT*, above.

**30–080—30–081** NOTES 54, 56, 57 62, 64. See above, entry at para.30R–076.

**30–081** NOTE 47. Add: *Bloom v Harms Offshore AHT*, above.

NOTES 57–65 and accompanying text. In *Re HIH Casualty and General Insurance Ltd* [2005] EWHC 125 (Ch.), [2006] 2 All E.R. 671 David Richards J. held, in respect of a request for assistance from the Supreme Court of New South Wales pursuant to s.426 of the Insolvency Act 1986, that where an Australian company was in liquidation in Australia and in England (the English liquidation being ancillary to the principal liquidation in Australia) the court had no power to direct the English liquidator to transfer funds for distribution in the principal liquidation, if the scheme for *pari passu* distribution in the principal liquidation is not substantially the same as under English law. In so holding, David Richards J. followed the approach of Sir Richard Scott V.C. in *Re Bank of Credit and Commerce International SA (No.10)* [1997] Ch. 213, referred to in this paragraph of the main work. This decision was affirmed by the Court of Appeal, [2006] EWCA Civ 732, [2007] 1 All E.R. 177, but on somewhat different grounds. In the view of the court, there might be circumstances where the remission of assets for distribution in the foreign liquidation would be for the overall benefit of the creditors, notwithstanding that their interests in the liquidation in England, when viewed in isolation, would be adversely affected. Thus, for example, the savings in cost by avoiding duplication may offset any reduction in prospective dividend: or a loss of priority may be sufficiently offset by an increase in the pool available to those whose priority was changed: or the admission of further creditors might be offset by an increase in the assets available to that class of creditor (*ibid.*, at [41]). Where there was such a countervailing advantage to creditors it may be that an order for transfer may properly be made (*ibid.*) but in the circumstances of the case no such countervailing advantages were evident. More generally "all the cases and all the academic commentators demonstrate clearly that the court will not order the transfer of assets by liquidators in an ancillary winding up in England to the liquidators in the principal liquidation abroad if rights of creditors would be prejudiced and they would obtain no countervailing advantage in the principal liquidation. They do not show, because the situation has not arisen, that if there is sufficient countervailing advantage the court will not order a transfer pursuant to s.426 because it would disturb the implementation of the statutory scheme arising under English law in consequence of the order or resolution to wind up the company" (*ibid.*, at [42]). In *Re Bank of Credit and Commerce International SA*

*(No.10)*, above, the question of countervailing advantage had not arisen and in that case the court was not considering a request by the foreign liquidator under s.426 (*ibid.*, at [46]). The decision of the Court of Appeal was reversed by the House of Lords, [2008] UKHL 21, [2008] 1 W.L.R. 852, which decided unanimously that there was power to order direct remittal of the English assets to Australia for distribution in the Australian liquidation. According to Lord Hoffmann, with whom Lord Walker of Gestingthorpe concurred, a discretion to order remission of assets to a country whose insolvency scheme is not in accordance with English law arises not only under s.426 of the 1986 Act, but also under the inherent power of the court at common law which reflects, subject to pragmatic limitations, the principle of the universality of bankruptcy. Applying this principle (which is reflected in judicial decisions) an English court should, so far as is consistent with justice and United Kingdom public policy, co-operate with the courts in the country where the principal liquidation is being conducted so as to ensure that all of a company's assets are distributed to its creditors under a single system of distribution: at [10], [11], [18]–[21], [24], [26], [27], [30], [63]. In contrast, Lord Scott of Foscote, with whom Lord Neuberger of Abbotsbury concurred, held that a discretion to order remission of assets to a liquidator in a country whose insolvency scheme is not in accordance with English law only arises under s.426(4) and (5) of the 1986 Act and thus could only operate in relation to countries to which s.426 has been applied: at [59]–[62], [66], [69], [74]–[77]. Lord Phillips of Worth Matravers appears to have agreed with the latter view (*ibid.* at [37], [42], [44] though at [43] he also stated that "it is in accordance with international comity and with the principle of universalism, as explained by . . . Lord Hoffmann that the English court should accede to the request of the Australian liquidators."

With agreement on the outcome, if not on the reasoning, it was held, unanimously, that the mere fact that under the insolvency law of Australia there would be a significant class of preferential creditors whose debts would not have priority under English law was not a significant reason to refuse to remit the English assets. There was nothing unacceptably discriminatory or unfair in relation to the Australian insolvency law as regards preferential creditors which would justify an English court in refusing to exercise its discretion to remit. Therefore, it was appropriate, in all the circumstances of the case, to order remission of the English assets to Australia for distribution by the Australian liquidators in accordance with Australian law.

See further, *Re Swissair Schweizerische Luftverkehr-Aktiengesellschaft* [2009] EWHC 2099 (Ch.), [2009] B.P.I.R. 1505 at [4]–[12] (court has general power to order remittal of assets where there would be a *pari passu* distribution in the foreign liquidation without necessitating resort to Insolvency Act 1986, s.426); *Rubin v Eurofinance SA* [2010] EWCA Civ 895; and see *New Cap Reinsurance Corp Ltd v Grant* [2009] NSWSC 662, (2009) 257 A.L.R. 740.

See also *Daewoo Motor Co Ltd v Stormglaze UK Ltd* [2005] EWHC 2799 (Ch.), [2006] B.P.I.R. 415; *Re Collins & Aikman Europe SA* [2006] EWHC

1343 (Ch.), [2007] I.L.Pr. 11; Smart (2008) 124 L.Q.R. 554; Rogerson [2008] C.L.J. 476; Townsend (2008) 71 M.L.R. 811; McCormack [2009] C.L.J. 169; Meng Seng Wee [2009] L.M.C.L.Q. 18; Chee Ho Tham [2009] L.M.C.L.Q. 113.

Note 59. On *Re Bank of Credit and Commerce International SA (No.10)* [1997] Ch. 213, see *Re HIH Casualty and General Insurance Ltd* [2008] UKHL 21, [2008] 1 W.L.R. 852 at [15]–[25], [56], [59]–[60], [72]; *Re Swissair Schweizerische Luftverkehr- Aktiengesselschaft* [2009] EWHC 2099 (Ch.) at [4]–[12], [2009] B.P.I.R. 1505. *Cf. Liquidator of Bank of Credit and Commerce International SA, Noter* [2007] CSOH 165, 2007 S.L.T. 1149. See Look Chan Ho (2007) 23 Insolvency L. & Pr. 174; Chee Ho Tham [2009] L.M.C.L.Q. 113.

Note 61. Add: *Perpetual Trustee Co Ltd v BNY Corporate Trustee Services Ltd* [2009] EWHC 2953 (Ch.), [2009] 2 B.C.L.C. 400, affd. [2009] EWCA Civ 1160, [2010] 3 W.L.R. 87.

**30–082** Note 66. *Cf.* Chee Ho Tam [2007] L.M.C.L.Q. 23, 36–41.

**30–084** Note 70. *Cf. Masri v Consolidated Contractors International Company SAL (No.4)* [2009] UKHL 43, [2010] 1 A.C. 90 (court has no jurisdiction under CPR r.71.2 to order examination of a foreign director of a foreign company in connection with proceedings to enforce a judgment debt).

Note 74. Add: See also *Re Bernard L Madoff Investment Securities LLC* [2009] EWHC 442 (Ch.), [2009] 2 B.C.L.C. 78.

**30–087** Note 82. On choice of law in insolvency transaction avoidance see Look Chan Ho (2008) 20 Sing. Acad. L.J. 343; Look Chan Ho (2009) 24 B.J.I.B. & F.L. 86, 132.

**30–090** Note 91. See now CPR, r.6.30 *et seq.*, inserted by SI 2008/2178.

**30–093** Note 96. As to the position under the UNCITRAL Model Law on Cross-Border Insolvency, implemented in Great Britain in the Cross-Border Insolvency Regulations 2006, see above, entry at para.30–074, n.11 and below, paras S30R–344 *et seq.*

Note 98. See *Liquidator of Bank of Credit and Commerce International SA, Noter* [2007] CSOH 165, 2007 S.L.T. 1149; *Hynd's Trustee, Petitioner* [2009] CSOH 76, 2009 S.C. 593.

**30–094** Note 3. Add: *Rubin v Eurofinance SA* [2010] EWCA Civ 895; *New Cap Reinsurance Corp Ltd v Grant* [2009] NSWSC 662, (2009) 257 A.L.R. 740. See also *Perpetual Trustee Co Ltd v BNY Corporate Trustee Services Ltd*

[2009] EWHC 2953 (Ch.), [2010] 2 B.C.L.C. 237. And see entry at para.30–093, n.96.

NOTE 10. *cf. Re HIH Casualty and General Insurance Ltd* [2008] UKHL 21, [2008] 1 W.L.R. 852, above, entry at para.30–081, nn.57–65.; *Re Swissair Schweizerische Luftverkehr-Aktiengesellschaft* [2009] EWHC 2099 (Ch.), [2009] B.P.I.R. 1505. **30–095**

C. *Effect of a Foreign Winding up Order*

NOTE 24. Add at end: *Cambridge Gas Transportation Corp v Official Committee of Unsecured Creditors of Navigator Holdings Plc* [2006] UKPC 26, [2007] 1 A.C. 508; *Re OJSC ANK Yugraneft* [2008] EWHC 2614 (Ch.), [2009] 1 B.C.L.C. 298; *Jefferies International Ltd v Landsbanki Islands HF* [2009] EWHC 894 (Comm.); *Perpetual Trustee Co Ltd v BNY Corporate Services Ltd* [2009] EWHC 1912 (Ch.), [2009] 2 B.C.L.C. 400, at [48], [62]–[63], affd., without reference to these points, [2009] EWCA Civ 1160, [2010] Ch. 347; see also *Perpetual Trustee Co Ltd v BNY Corporate Trustee Services Ltd* [2009] EWHC 2593 (Ch.), [2010] 2 B.C.L.C. 237; *Rubin v Eurofinance SA* [2010] EWCA Civ 895; see also *Re HIH Casualty and General Insurance Ltd* [2008] UKHL 21, [2008] 1 W.L.R. 852; *Re Phoenix Kapitaldienst GmbH* [2008] B.P.I.R. 1082 (Mr Registrar Jacques); *Re Cavell Insurance Co Ltd* (2006) 269 D.L.R. (4th) 679 (Ont. CA) (solvent scheme of arrangement under Companies Act 1985, s.425, in respect of an English company, recognised in Ontario on the basis of the "real and substantial connection" principle established in *Morguard Investments Ltd v De Savoye* [1990] 3 S.C.R. 1077, main work, paras 14–083–14–084). *cf. Re Flightlease Ireland Ltd* [2006] IEHC 193, [2008] 1 I.L.R.M. 53 (real and substantial connection principle rejected in Ireland). See also *AssetInsure Pty Ltd v New Cap Reinsurance Corp Ltd* [2006] HCA 13, (2006) 225 C.L.R. 331. **30–099**

NOTE 44. *cf. ML Ubase Holdings Co Ltd v Trigem Computer Inc* [2007] NSWSC 859 at [65]. **33–103**

NOTE 51. For the implementation in Great Britain of the UNCITRAL Model Law on Cross Border Insolvency in the Cross-Border Insolvency Regulations 2006, see below, paras S30R–344 *et seq.* **30–104**

NOTES 52 and 53. Add: *Cambridge Gas Transportation Corp v Official Committee of Unsecured Creditors of Navigator Holdings Plc* [2006] UKPC 26, [2007] 1 A.C. 508; *Re HIH Casualty and General Insurance Ltd* [2008] UKHL 21, [2008] 1 W.L.R. 852; *Re OJSC ANK Yugraneft* [2008] EWHC 2614 (Ch.), [2009] 1 B.C.L.C. 298; *Jefferies International Ltd v Landsbanki Islands HF* [2009] EWHC 894 (Comm.); *Perpetual Trustee Co Ltd v BNY Corporate Trustee Services Ltd* [2009] EWHC 1912 (Ch.), [2009] 2 B.C.L.C. 400, at [48], [62]–[63], affd., without reference to these points, [2009] EWCA

Civ 1160, [2010] Ch. 347; see also *Perpetual Trustee Co Ltd v BNY Corporate Trustee Services Ltd* [2009] EWHC 2593 (Ch.), [2010] 2 B.C.L.C. 237; *Rubin v Eurofinance SA* [2010] EWCA Civ 895. See Moss (2006) 19 Insolvency Intelligence 123; Chee Ho Tham [2007] L.M.C.L.Q. 129.

**30–105** NOTE 54. See above, entry at para.30–104, n.51. The Cross-Border Insolvency Regulations 2006 do not amend the Insolvency Act 1986, s.426. See below, para.S30–345. See generally on s.426, *Re HIH Casualty and General Insurance Ltd*, above.

**30–107** NOTE 57. *Fourie v Le Roux* [2005] EWCA Civ 204, [2006] 2 B.C.L.C. 531, was affirmed, in part [2007] UKHL 1, [2007] 1 W.L.R. 320.

**30–108** NOTE 60. It has been doubted whether assistance, at common law, can take the form of applying provisions of foreign insolvency law which form no part of the domestic insolvency law of the forum: see *Cambridge Gas Transportation Corp v Official Committee of Unsecured Creditors of Navigator Holdings Plc* [2006] UKPC 26, [2007] 1 A.C. 508, at [22]; *Perpetual Trustee Co Ltd v BNY Corporate Trustee Services Ltd* [2009] EWHC 1912 (Ch.), [2009] 2 B.C.L.C. 400, at [48], [62]–[63], affd., without reference to these points, [2009] EWCA Civ 1160, [2010] Ch. 347; and see *Perpetual Trustee Co Ltd v BNY Corporate Trustee Services Ltd* [2009] EWHC 2593 (Ch.), [2010] 2 B.C.L.C. 237; see also *Re Phoenix Kapitaldienst GmbH* [2008] B.P.I.R. 1082 (Mr Registrar Jacques); *cf. Re HIH Casualty and General Insurance Ltd* [2008] UKHL 21, [2008] 1 W.L.R. 852, as to which see entry at para.30–081, nn.57–65, above; *Re Swissair Schweizerische Luftwerkehr-Aktiengesellschaft* [2009] EWHC 2099 (Ch.), [2009] B.P.I.R. 1505.

In *Rubin v Eurofinance SA* [2010] EWCA Civ 895 it was held, however, that orders made by a United States court conducting bankruptcy proceedings under Chapter 11 of the United States Bankruptcy Code, recognised as foreign main proceedings, could be recognised and enforced in England in exercise of the common law power to assist a foreign court in insolvency proceedings even though the orders would not be recognised and enforced under the common law rules relating to the recognition and enforcement of foreign judgments *in personam* (Rule 36, main work, paras 14R–048 *et seq.*). And see *New Cap Reinsurance Corp Ltd v Grant* [2009] NSWSC 662, (2009) 257 A.L.R. 740.

NOTE 63. See also *Re HIH Casualty and General Insurance Ltd*, above.

NOTE 67. In line 1 add: *Re HIH Casualty and General Insurance Ltd*, above.

**30–109** NOTE 72. See also *Re HIH Casualty and General Insurance Ltd*, above.

NOTE 81. As to Companies Act 1985, s.425, see entry at para.30R–033, n.46. **30–111**

NOTE 83. Companies Act 1989, s.183(3) was amended by SI 2001/3929 to include a judgment required to be recognised or enforced under Council Regulation (EC) 44/2001 on jurisdiction and the recognition and enforcement of judgments in civil and commercial matters (the Judgments Regulation). Section 183(3) is further amended by SI 2007/1655 to take account of the application of the Agreement made between the European Community and Denmark whereby the Regulation is to have effect, as regards Denmark, in accordance with the terms of that Agreement: see reg.5 and Sch., Pt I. **30–112**

NOTES 84–86 and 88. See *Re HIH Casualty and General Insurance Ltd* [2008] UKHL 21, [2008] 1 W.L.R. 852 and above, entry at para.30–081, nn.57–65. **30–113**

NOTE 88. Add at end: *Daewoo Motor Co Ltd v Stormglaze UK Ltd* [2005] EWHC 2799 (Ch.), [2006] B.P.I.R. 415.

NOTE 89. And see *Re HIH Casualty and General Insurance Ltd*, above. **30–114**

NOTE 96. In line 2 add: *Re HIH Casualty and General Insurance Ltd*, above.

NOTE 1. See *Re HIH Casualty and General Insurance Ltd*, above at [28].

NOTE 5. As to *Re HIH Casualty and General Insurance Ltd* [2005] EWHC 2125 (Ch.), [2006] 2 All E.R. 671, affirmed by the Court of Appeal, [2006] EWCA Civ 732, [2007] 1 All E.R. 177, whose decision was reversed by the House of Lords, [2008] UKHL 21, [2008] 1 W.L.R. 852, see above, entry at para.30–081, nn.57–65. **30–115**

Add at end: See also *Daewoo Motor Co Ltd v Stormglaze Ltd*, above.

NOTE 12. *Fourie v Le Roux* [2005] EWCA Civ 204, [2006] B.C.L.C. 531, was affirmed, in part [2007] UKHL 1, [2007] 1 W.L.R. 320.

NOTE 13. See entry at para.30–115, n.5. **30–116**

NOTES 16–18. See *Re HIH Casualty and General Insurance Ltd* [2008] UKHL 21, [2008] 1 W.L.R. 852.

## D. *Receivers*

NOTE 32. See now Companies Act 2006, s.867. The recommendations of the Law Commission have not been implemented in Companies Act 2006, but **30–121** s.894 of the 2006 Act gives the Secretary of State a general power to amend the provisions of the Act which relate to company charges.

Note 33. See now Companies Act 2006, ss.878–892. These provisions are thought to be inconsistent with the registration requirements under Scots law contained in the Bankruptcy and Diligence etc. (Scotland) Act 2007, ss.37–49. The Department of Trade and Industry has issued a Consultative Document containing proposals for amending the relevant sections of the Companies Act 2006, pursuant to s.894 of the 2006 Act: see Department of Trade and Industry, *Companies Act 2006, Registration of Floating Charges in Scotland, A Consultative Document* (May, 2007).

**30–122** Note 35. Companies Act 1985, s.424 is not re-enacted in Companies Act 2006 but the position seems to be the same as under the 1985 Act: Companies Act 2006, ss.861(5), 879(6).

Note 36. See now Companies Act 2006, ss.860–865, 869–877.

**30–123** Note 37. Companies (Northern Ireland) Order 1986 is repealed by Companies Act 2006, s.1284(2). For the relevant legislation, see Companies Act 2006, Pt 25, Ch.1 and next entry.

**30–125** Notes 46–50 and accompanying text. For the English registration provisions, see Companies Act 2006, Pt 25, Ch.1. The provisions apply to companies registered in England or Northern Ireland (s.861(5)), but the Secretary of State may, by regulations, make provision about the registration of charges over property in the United Kingdom of a registered overseas company: s.1052. For the regulations, see Overseas Companies (Execution of Documents and Registration of Charges) Regulations 2009, SI 2009/1917, Pt 3, in force from October 1, 2009. As to charges created in, or over property in, jurisdictions outside the United Kingdom, see s.866. As to charges created in, or over property in, another United Kingdom jurisdiction, see s.867.

**30–127** Notes 53 and 55. Add: *Daewoo Motor Co Ltd v Stormglaze UK Ltd* [2005] EWHC 2799 (Ch.), [2006] B.P.I.R. 415 (appointment of English provisional liquidators to assist Korean receivers of a company incorporated in Korea in order to realise assets of the company within England and to transmit them to the receivers in Korea); *Re Stanford International Bank Ltd* [2010] EWCA Civ 137, [2010] B.P.I.R. 679.

**30–129** See previous entry. A receiver is not a "foreign representative" for the purposes of the UNCITRAL Model Law on Cross-Border Insolvency, as implemented in Great Britain in the Cross-Border Insolvency Regulations 2006 if the powers conferred on and the duties imposed on the receiver are duties to gather in and preserve assets and not to liquidate or distribute them: *Re Stanford International Bank Ltd*, above (United States receiver appointed in proceedings brought by United States Securities and Exchange Commission). This does not necessarily preclude recognition at common law, see below, para.S30–362.

NOTE 72. As to Companies Act 1985, s.398(3), see now Companies Act 2006, s.866(2). **30–133**

Text after note 82. See now Companies Act 2006. **30–135**

NOTE 82. Administrative receivership does not fall within the UNCITRAL Model Law on Cross-Border Insolvency, as implemented in Great Britain in the Cross-Border Insolvency Regulations 2006: see below, para.S30–362.

NOTE 93. Administration falls within the UNCITRAL Model Law on Cross-Border Insolvency, as implemented in Great Britain in the Cross-Border Insolvency Regulations 2006: see below, para.S30–362. **30–138**

NOTE 13. As to Companies Act 1985, s.735(1), see now Companies Act 2006, s.1(1). **30–141**

### E. *UNCITRAL Model Law on Cross-Border Insolvency*

The provisions of the UNCITRAL Model Law on Cross-Border Insolvency, as implemented in Great Britain in the Cross-Border Insolvency Regulations 2006 are discussed below, paras S30R–344 *et seq.* **30–144—30–148**

## 5. COUNCIL REGULATION (EC) 1346/2000 ON INSOLVENCY PROCEEDINGS

### A. *Introduction and Scope*

NOTE 45. As to Art.16, see paras 30R–283 *et seq.*

NOTE 47. Add in line 3: Fletcher, *Insolvency in Private International Law* 2nd edn (2005), *Supplement* (2007), paras 7.37–7.141 (hereafter Fletcher, Supplement). **30–150**

Add in line 5: McCormack [2009] C.L.J. 169; McCormack (2010) 30 L.S. 126; Mevorach (2010) 6 J. Priv. Int. L. 327.

Add at end: See also European Commission, *Communication from the Commission to the European Parliament and the Council, An area of freedom, security and justice serving the citizen* COM (2009) 262 final, para.3.4 (possibility of measures designed to implement common measures to ensure convergence of national rules on insolvency procedures for banks).

**30–151** Notes 57 and 58 and text thereto. Further amendments are contained in: Council Regulation (EC) 694/2006 amending the lists of insolvency proceedings, winding-up proceedings and liquidators in Annexes A, B and C to Regulation (EC) 1346/2000 ([2006] O.J. L121/1) and replacing the original lists with new lists in Annexes A, B and C; Council Regulation (EC) 1791/2006 adapting certain Regulations and Decisions in the fields of free movement of goods, freedom of movement of persons, company law, competition policy, agriculture (including veterinary and phytosanitary legislation), transport policy, taxation, statistics, energy, environment, cooperation in the fields of justice and home affairs, customs union, external relations, common foreign and security policy and institutions, by reason of the accession of Bulgaria and Romania ([2006] O.J. L363/1), Annex, Part II; Council Regulation (EC) 681/2007 amending the lists of insolvency proceedings, winding-up proceedings and liquidators in Annexes A, B and C to Regulation (EC) 1346/2000 on insolvency proceedings ([2007] O.J. L159/1) and replacing the earlier version of the lists with new lists in Annexes A, B and C: the latter Regulation entered into force on June 14, 2007, except in relation to the Czech Republic where the relevant date is January 1, 2008; Council Regulation (EC) 788/2008 of July 24, 2008 amending the lists of insolvency proceedings and winding-up proceedings in Annexes A and B to Regulation (EC) 1346/2000 on insolvency proceedings and codifying Annexes A, B and C to that Regulation ([2008] O.J. L213/1).

**30–154** Note 79. Add: Case C–1/04 *Staubitz-Schreiber* [2006] E.C.R. I–701 at [21]; Case C–111/08 *SCT Industri AB i likvidation v Alpenblume AB* [2009] I.L.Pr. 743.

**30–158** Note 93. To the extent that the UNCITRAL Model Law on Cross-Border Insolvency, as implemented in Great Britain in the Cross-Border Insolvency Regulations 2006, conflicts with an obligation of the United Kingdom under the EC Insolvency Regulation, the requirements of the Regulation prevail: Cross-Border Insolvency Regulations 2006, Sch.1, Art.3. See below, para.S30–363. On the relationship between the Regulation and the Model Law, see *Re Bud-Bank Leasing SP. Z0. 0* [2010] B.C.C. 255 (Mr Registrar Baister).

**30–160** Notes 96 and 97 and text thereto. See Case C–341/04 *Eurofood IFSC Ltd* [2006] E.C.R. I–3813, [2006] Ch. 508, at [31] ("the concept of the centre of main interests is peculiar to the Regulation. Therefore, it has an autonomous meaning and must be interpreted in a uniform way, independently of national legislation"); *Hans Brochier Holdings Ltd v Exner* [2006] EWHC 2594 (Ch.), [2007] B.C.C. 127; *Stojevic v Komercni Banka AS* [2006] EWHC 3447 (Ch.), [2007] B.P.I.R. 141; *Re Lennox Holdings plc* [2009] B.C.C. 155. And see *Re Stanford International Bank Ltd* [2010] EWCA Civ 137, [2010] B.P.I.R. 679; *Pillar Securitisation Sarl v Spicer & Shinners* [2010] EWHC 836 (Ch.)

An Italian court has referred these questions to the European Court. First, is the concept of "the centre of the debtor's main interests" in Art.3(1) of the Insolvency Regulation to be interpreted in accordance with Community law or national law, and, if the former, how is the concept to be defined and what are the decisive factors or considerations for the purpose of identifying the "centre of main interests"? Secondly, can the presumption laid down in Art.3(1) of the Insolvency Regulation, according to which

> "[I]n the case of a company, the place of the registered office shall be presumed to be the centre of its main interests in the absence of proof to the contrary",

be rebutted if it is established that the company carries on genuine business activity in a State other than that in which it has its registered office, or is it necessary, in order for the presumption to be deemed rebutted, to establish that the company has not carried on any business activity in the State in which it has its registered office? Thirdly, if a company has, in a Member State other than that in which it has its registered office, immovable property, a lease agreement concluded by the debtor company with another company in respect of two hotel complexes, and a contract with a banking institution, are these sufficient to rebut the presumption laid down in Art.3(1) of the Insolvency Regulation that the place of the company's "registered office" is the centre of its main interests and are such circumstances sufficient for the company to be regarded as having an "establishment" within the meaning of Art.3(2) of that Regulation? Fourthly, if a ruling on jurisdiction by the Corte di Cassazione is based on an interpretation of Art.3 of the Insolvency Regulation which is at variance with that of the European Court, is the application of that provision of Community law, as interpreted by the European Court, precluded by Art.382 of the Code of Civil Procedure, according to which rulings on jurisdiction by the Corte di Cassazione are final and binding?: Case C–396/09 *Interedil Srl, in liquidation* (pending).

NOTE 98 and text thereto. See Case C–1/04 *Staubitz-Schreiber* [2006] E.C.R. I–701; Case C–341/04 *Eurofood IFSC Ltd*, above; Case C–339/07 *Seagon v Deko Marty Belgium NV* [2009] 1 W.L.R. 2168; Case C–292/08 *German Graphics Graphische Maschinen GmbH v van der Schee* [2009] E.C.R. I–8421.

NOTE 3. In line 7 add: *Re Parkside Flexibles SA* [2006] B.C.C. 589; *Re Sendo Ltd* [2005] EWHC 1604 (Ch.), [2006] 1 B.C.L.C. 395; *Re Collins & Aikman Corp Group* [2005] EWHC 1754 (Ch.), [2006] B.C.C. 606; *Cross Construction Sussex Ltd v Tseliki* [2006] EWHC 1056 (Ch.), [2006] B.P.I.R. 888; *Syska v Vivendi Universal SA* [2008] EWHC 2155 (Comm.), [2008] 2 Lloyd's Rep. 646, appeal dismissed [2009] EWCA Civ 677, [2009] 2 All E.R. (Comm.) 891.

In line 10 add: *MPOTEC GmbH* [2006] B.C.C. 681 (Trib. Gde. Inst, Nanterre).

Add at end: The European Court referred to the Recitals in Case C–1/04 *Staubitz-Schreiber* [2006] E.C.R. I–701, Case C–341/04 *Eurofood IFSC Ltd* [2006] E.C.R. I–3813, [2006] Ch. 508 and Case C–339/07 *Seagon v Deko Marty Belgium NV* [2009] 1 W.L.R. 2168.

Note 5. Add: *Re Parkside Flexibles SA* [2006] B.C.C. 589; *Re Collins & Aikman Corp Group* [2005] EWHC 1754 (Ch.), [2006] B.C.C. 606; *Syska v Vivendi Universal SA* [2008] EWHC 2155 (Comm.), [2008] 2 Lloyd's Rep. 646, appeal dismissed [2009] EWCA Civ 677, [2009] 2 All E.R. (Comm.) 891.

**30–162** Note 12. See entry at para.30–151, nn.57, 58.

Note 14. Add at end: See *Re Stanford International Bank Ltd* [2010] EWCA Civ 137, [2010] B.P.I.R. 679.

**30–164** Note 29. For discussion of the meaning of "investment undertaking", see *Byers v Yacht Bull Corp* [2010] EWHC 133 (Ch.), [2010] B.C.C. 368.

Note 31. The Insurers (Reorganisation and Winding-Up) Regulations 2004 (SI 2004/353) are further amended by SI 2007/851, SI 2007/108 and SI 2007/126. Insurers (Reorganisation and Winding-Up) (Lloyd's) Regulations 2005 (SI 2005/1998) are also amended by SI 2007/851.

Note 32. Add at end: See also *Re DAP Holding NV* [2005] EWHC 2092 (Ch.), [2006] B.C.C. 48; *Re HIH Casualty and General Insurance Ltd* [2008] UKHL 21, [2008] 1 W.L.R. 852 at [32], [40].

Note 33. Financial Markets and Insolvency (Settlement Finality) Regulations 1999 (SI 1999/2979) are amended by SI 2006/50, SI 2007/108, SI 2007/126, SI 2007/832 and SI 2009/1972.

Note 34. Credit Institutions (Reorganisation and Winding-Up) Regulations 2004 (SI 2004/1045) are amended by SI 2007/830, SI 2007/108 and SI 2007/126.

Notes 34 and 35. Add: See *Jefferies International Ltd v Landsbanki Islands HF* [2009] EWHC 894 (Comm.); *Winding-Up Board of Landsbanki Islands HF v Mills* [2010] CSOH 100 (discussing the Credit Institutions (Reorganisation and Winding Up) Regulations 2004 (SI 2004/1045), as amended, in some detail).

B. *International Jurisdiction*

NOTE 41. Add: Fletcher, Supplement, paras 7.37–7.69. **30R–165**

NOTE 44. See entry at para.30–151, nn.57, 58. **30–167**

NOTE 46. See previous entry. Add: *Re Parkside Flexibles SA* [2006] B.C.C. 589; *Re MG Rover Espana SA* [2006] EWHC 3426 (Ch.), [2006] B.C.C. 599; *Re Sendo Ltd* [2005] EWHC 1604 (Ch.), [2006] 1 B.C.L.C. 395; *Re Collins & Aikman Corp Group* [2005] EWHC 1754 (Ch.), [2006] B.C.C. 606; *Re MG Rover Belux SA/NV* [2006] EWHC 1296 (Ch.); *Re Collins & Aikman Europe SA* [2006] EWHC 1343 (Ch.), [2007] I.L.Pr. 11; *Hans Brochier Holdings Ltd v Exner* [2006] EWHC 2594 (Ch.), [2007] B.C.C. 127; *Re Lennox Holdings plc* [2009] B.C.C. 155.

NOTE 50. See entry at para.30–151, nn.57, 58.

NOTES 61–75 and text thereto. The meaning of "time of opening" has not been clearly resolved by the European Court. In Case C–1/04 *Staubitz-Schreiber* [2006] E.C.R. I–701, a case of bankruptcy, the individual debtor filed an initial application for a German court to open bankruptcy proceedings. Before the German appellate court could give a judgment opening the proceedings, the debtor moved her centre of main interests from Germany to Spain. Did the (German) court originally seised retain jurisdiction or was jurisdiction "transferred" to the (Spanish) court of the new centre of main interests? The European Court held that the court of the Regulation State which is originally seised in these circumstances retains jurisdiction and that to allow a "transfer" of jurisdiction would be contrary to the objectives of the Regulation: Recital (4). It was the intention of the Community legislature to avoid incentives for the parties to transfer assets or judicial proceedings from one Regulation State to another in order to obtain a more favourable legal position. That objective would not be achieved if the debtor could move the centre of his main interests to another Regulation State between the time when the request to open insolvency proceedings was lodged and the time when the judgment opening the proceedings was delivered and thus determine the court having jurisdiction and the applicable law (*ibid.*, at [25]). Such a "transfer" of jurisdiction would also be contrary to the objective, stated in Recitals (2) and (8) to the Regulation, of efficient and effective cross-border proceedings, as it would oblige creditors to be in continual pursuit of the debtor wherever he chose to establish himself more or less permanently and would often mean in practice that the proceedings would be prolonged (*ibid.*, at [26]). Finally, retaining the jurisdiction of the court first seised ensures greater legal certainty for creditors who have assessed the risks to be assumed in the event of the debtor's insolvency with regard to the place where the centre of his main interests was situated when they entered into a legal relationship with him (*ibid.*, at [27]). Although the facts of the case involved a request by the debtor **30–169—30–170** to open proceedings the reasoning would seem to be equally applicable where the request to open proceedings is that of a creditor.

In Case C–341/04 *Eurofood IFSC Ltd* [2006] E.C.R. I–3813, [2006] Ch. 108, a company incorporated and registered in Ireland was a wholly owned subsidiary of a company incorporated in Italy which was also the parent company of a corporate group. The Italian company and many of its subsidiaries became insolvent and entered "extraordinary administration" in Italy by virtue of a decree of the Italian Parliament. Subsequently, a creditor of the Irish company presented a petition for the winding up of the Irish company to the Irish High Court and sought and obtained the appointment of a provisional liquidator. After that process an Italian court gave a judgment opening insolvency proceedings against the Irish company in Italy. The Irish Supreme Court referred a number of questions to the European Court, one of which concerned the time at which insolvency proceedings are opened for the purposes of the Regulation. The European Court noted (*ibid.*, at [49]) that the Regulation does not define sufficiently precisely what is meant by a "decision to open insolvency proceedings" and that the appropriate interpretation of the expression should be sought in the light of the objective of ensuring the effectiveness of the system established by the Regulation and, in particular the avoidance of claims to concurrent jurisdiction (*ibid.*, at [52]–[53]). "In those circumstances, a 'decision to open insolvency proceedings' for the purposes of the Regulation must be regarded as including not only a decision which is formally described as an opening decision by the legislation of the Member State of the court which handed it down, but also a decision handed down following an application, based on the debtor's insolvency, seeking the opening of proceedings referred to in Annex A to the Regulation, where that decision involves divestment of the debtor and the appointment of a liquidator referred to in Annex C to the Regulation. Such divestment involves the debtor losing the powers of management which he has over his assets. In such a case, the two characteristic consequences of insolvency proceedings, namely the appointment of a liquidator referred to in Annex C and the divestment of the debtor, have taken effect, and thus all the elements constituting the definition of such proceedings, given in Article 1(1) of the Regulation, are present" (*ibid.*, at [54]). The decision of the Irish court to appoint a provisional liquidator to the Irish company clearly, according to this principle, constituted a decision to open insolvency proceedings since a provisional liquidator is listed in the Irish list in Annex C, so that the Irish proceedings were first to open, and the same result would ensue in respect of the United Kingdom since a provisional liquidator appears in the United Kingdom's list in Annex C. For vigorous criticism of this aspect of the case, see Moss (2006) 19 Insolvency Intelligence 97; Moss (2008) 21 Insolvency Intelligence 33. In applying the European Court's answer to this question, the Irish Supreme Court held that a decision to appoint a provisional liquidator by an Irish court constituted a decision to open main proceedings within the meaning of the Regulation: see *Re Eurofood IFSC Ltd (No.2)* [2006] IESC 41, [2006] 4 I.R. 307.

A second question which was referred by the Irish court but not answered by the European Court (and see *Re Eurofood IFSC Ltd (No.2)*, above at [24]) was whether the Irish doctrine of relation back, whereby the commencement of a liquidation is deemed to take place at the date of presentation of the winding-up petition, would be a second ground for deciding that the Irish proceedings were first to open. The point (which could arise under United Kingdom insolvency law, see Insolvency Act 1986, s.129) is, therefore, unresolved though it may be pointed out that Jacobs A-G, without reaching a definite conclusion on the issue, inclined to the view that the national law doctrine of relation back should prevail: see [2006] E.C.R. I–8813, at [89]–[95]. Contrast Art.23(4) of the UNCITRAL Model Law on Cross-Border Insolvency, as implemented in Great Britain in the Cross-Border Insolvency Regulations 2006, which stipulates that the date of opening of a foreign proceeding shall be determined in accordance with the law of the State in which the foreign proceeding is taking place, including any rule by virtue of which the foreign proceeding is deemed to have opened at an earlier time: see below, para.S30–403.

For other aspects of these cases, see below, entries at paras 30–172–30–173; 30–328; 31–107; 31–108.

Note 62. *Re Collins & Aikman Corp Group* [2005] EWHC 1754 (Ch.) is now reported at [2006] B.C.C. 606.

Note 79. Add: Fletcher, Supplement, paras 7.42–7.69. **30–171**

Note 81. Add: *Re Parkside Flexibles SA* [2006] B.C.C. 589; *Re Sendo Ltd* [2005] EWHC 1604 (Ch.), [2006] 1 B.C.L.C. 395; *Re Lennox Holdings plc* [2009] B.C.C. 155. See *Re Stanford International Bank Ltd* [2010] EWCA Civ 137, [2010] B.P.I.R. 679 (meaning of "centre of main interests" in UNCITRAL Model Law to be interpreted in the same way as it is under the Regulation).
*Re Collins & Aikman Corp Group* [2005] EWHC 1754 (Ch.) is now reported at [2006] B.C.C. 606.

Note 83. Add: *Re Parkside Flexibles SA*, above; *Re Sendo Ltd*, above; *Re Lennox Holdings plc*, above.

Note 85. See previous entry.

Notes 89–92 and accompanying text. The Opinion of Jacobs A-G in Case C–341/04 *Eurofood IFSC Ltd* [2006] E.C.R. I–3813, [2006] Ch. 508, discussed in these paragraphs, appeared to offer some, if limited, support to the "head office function" test (see main work, para.30–171, but see *Re Eurofood IFSC Ltd (No.2)* [2006] IEHC 41, [2006] 4 I.R. 307 at [25]–[29]) in locating the centre of the debtor's main interests. The European Court reflected some **30–172—30–173** of the views of the Advocate General but perhaps did not, at least explicitly, support that test to the same degree. The Court pointed out that under the jurisdictional regime established by the Regulation each debtor constituting a distinct legal entity is subject to its own court jurisdiction, i.e. there is no specific rule for corporate groups as such (*ibid.*, at [30]) but, further, the concept of centre of main interests, which is peculiar to the Regulation must be given an autonomous meaning and be interpreted in a uniform way, independently of national law (*ibid.*, at [31]). Referring to Recital (13) to the Regulation and in agreement with the Advocate General, the Court emphasised that the centre of main interests should correspond to the place where the debtor conducts the administration of his interests on a regular basis and is therefore ascertainable by third parties, a principle which indicates identification of the centre of main interests by reference to criteria that are both objective and ascertainable by third parties. That objectivity and that possibility of ascertainment by third parties are necessary to ensure legal certainty and foreseeability concerning the determination of the court with jurisdiction to open main insolvency proceedings. That legal certainty and that foreseeability are all the more important because, as a result of Art.4(1) of the Regulation, determination of the court with jurisdiction entails determination of the law to be applied (*ibid.*, at [32]–[33]). Thus where a debtor is a subsidiary company whose registered office and that of its parent company are situated in two different Regulation States, the presumption laid down in the second sentence of Art.3(1) of the Regulation, whereby the centre of main interests of that subsidiary is situated in the Regulation State where its registered office is situated, can be rebutted only if factors which are both objective and ascertainable by third parties enable it to be established that an actual situation exists which is different from that which locating it at that registered office is deemed to reflect. That could be so in particular in the case of a company not carrying on any business in the Regulation State in which its registered office is situated (the so called "letterbox" company, *ibid.*, at [35]). In contrast, where a company carries on its business in the territory of the Regulation State where its registered office is situated, the mere fact that its economic choices are or can be controlled by a parent company in another Regulation State is not enough to rebut the presumption laid down by the Regulation (*ibid.*, at [37]).

These observations may lend greater weight to the presumption than is given in the English case law, but such is not an inevitable conclusion. The "letterbox" company is an easy case (as to which, see *Pillar Securitisation Sarl v Spicer & Shinners* [2010] EWHC 836 (Ch.); see also *HSBC, Petitioner* [2009] CSOH 147, 2010 S.L.T. 281). But as to other possible cases the Court merely indicates that the *mere* fact that the subsidiary's economic choices are or can be controlled by the parent in another Regulation State is *not enough* to rebut the presumption. There is no indication in the judgment of relevant factors which might be *enough* to rebut the presumption. This prompts three comments. First, it would seem that this lack of clarity or guidance will lead to further references to the European Court, an outcome which does not conduce to the speedy and efficient disposition of the court which has jurisdiction to open main insolvency proceedings, or, one might add, reflect the requirements of legal certainty which the Court was so anxious to protect. Secondly, this lack of guidance leaves a degree of latitude to national courts. Thirdly, as regards the English case law, it is fair to say that the *mere fact* that the economic choices of the subsidiary are or can be controlled by a parent in another Regulation State has not been enough to justify displacing the presumption in Art.3(1): much more has been required. Since the decision of the European Court in *Eurofood IFSC Ltd*, an English court has held that the presumption was rebutted, in the case of a company incorporated, and with its registered office, in England, where the company's entire business operations were run out of Germany, Germany also being the State in which most of its employees were located, where its principal bank accounts were kept and where the vast majority of the documents (in the German language) were situated and the law of which governed most of the legal and contractual relationships of the company: see *Hans Brochier Holdings Ltd v Exner* [2006] EWHC 2594 (Ch.), [2007] B.C.C. 127; see also *Re Lennox Holdings plc* [2009] B.C.C. 155; *Re Stanford International Bank Ltd* [2010] EWCA Civ 137, [2010] B.P.I.R. 679; *MPOTEC* [2006] B.C.C. 681 (Trib. Gde. Inst., Nanterre); *cf. Pillar Securitisation Sarl v Spicer & Shinners* [2010] EWHC 836 (Ch.). For discussion of *Eurofood IFSC Ltd*, see Moss (2006) 19 Insolvency Intelligence 97; Armour [2006] C.L.J. 505; Moss and Haravon (2007) 20 Insolvency Intelligence 20; Paulus (2007) 20 Insolvency Intelligence 85; Wessels (2007) 20 Insolvency Intelligence 103; Moss (2008) 21 Insolvency Intelligence 333; Winkler (2008) 26 Berkeley J. Int. L. 352.

NOTE 88. See also *MPOTEC GmbH* [2006] B.C.C. 681 (Trib. Gde. Inst., Nanterre); Moss and Haravon (2007) 20 Insolvency Intelligence 20. For the *Daisytek* case in the French Cour de Cassation, see *French Republic v Klempka* [2006] B.C.C. 841. **30–172**

As to Companies Act 1985, s.735(1), see Companies Act 2006, s.1(1). **30–175**

NOTES 5 and 9. As to the meaning of "EEA State", see now Interpretation Act 1978, Sch.1, inserted by Legislative and Regulatory Reform Act 2006, s.26(1). See below, entry at para.30–189, n.86.

NOTE 10. Add: Case C–341/04 *Eurofood IFSC Ltd* [2006] E.C.R. I–3813, [2006] Ch. 508, at [52]. See also *Hans Brochier Holdings Ltd v Exner* [2006] EWHC 2594 (Ch.), [2007] B.C.C. 127. **30–176**

NOTE 11. Add: Case C–341/04 *Eurofood IFSC Ltd*, above.

NOTE 12. Add: Case C–1/04 *Staubitz-Schreiber* [2006] E.C.R. I–701, at [25].

NOTE 15. Add: Case C–341/04 *Eurofood IFSC Ltd*, above at [40]–[41].

Note 16. Add: Case C–341/04 *Eurofood IFSC Ltd*, above at [40]–[42]. See also *Public Prosecutor v Segard (As Administrator for Rover France SAS)* [2006] I.L.Pr. 681 (CA, Versailles).

Note 17. Case 294/02 *Commission v AMI Semiconductor Belgium BVJA* is now reported at [2005] E.C.R. 1–2175.

**30–177** Note 19. Add in line 1: Case C–339/07 *Seagon v Deko Marty Belgium NV* [2009] 1 W.L.R. 2168; Case C–111/08 *SCT Industri AB i likvidation v Alpenblume AB* [2009] I.L.Pr. 743; Case C–292/08 *German Graphics Graphische Maschinen GmbH v van der Schee* [2009] E.C.R. I–8421. Add at end: *Re La Mutuelles du Mans Assurances IARD* [2005] EWHC 1599 (Ch.), [2006] B.C.C. 11; *Re DAP Holding NV* [2005] EWHC 2092 (Ch.), [2006] B.C.C. 48; *Citigate Dewe Rogerson Ltd v Artaban Public Affairs SPRL* [2009] EWHC 1689 (Ch.), [2009] B.P.I.R. 1355; *Byers v Yacht Bull Corp* [2010] EWHC 133 (Ch.), [2010] B.C.C. 368.

Note 20. Add in line 3: Case C–339/07 *Seagon v Deko Marty Belgium NV* [2009] E.C.R. I–767, [2009] 1 W.L.R. 2168 (court of Regulation State in territory of which insolvency proceedings have been opened has jurisdiction to decide an action to set a transaction aside by virtue of insolvency that is brought against a person whose registered office is in another Regulation State); Case C–111/08 *SCT Industri AB i likvidation v Alpenblume AB* [2009] E.C.R. I–5655 (exception in Art.1(2)(b) of Judgments Regulation applied to judgment of a court in Regulation State A regarding registration of ownership of shares in a company having its registered office in regulation State A according to which transfer of shares was to be regarded as invalid on the ground that the court of Regulation State A did not recognise the powers of a liquidator from Regulation State B in the context of insolvency proceedings conducted and closed in Regulation State B); Case C–292/08 *German Graphics Graphische Maschinen GmbH v van der Schee* [2009] E.C.R. I–8421 (exception in Art.1(2)(b) of Judgments Regulation, read in conjunction with Art.7(1) of Insolvency Regulation, must be interpreted, account being taken of Art.4(2)(b) of the Insolvency Regulation, as meaning that it does not apply to an action based on a reservation of title against a purchaser who is insolvent, where the asset covered by the reservation of title is situated in the Regulation State of the opening of those proceedings at the time of opening of those proceedings against that purchaser); *Byers v Yacht Bull Corp* [2020] EWHC 133 (Ch.), [2010] B.C.C. 368 (claim for a declaration as to beneficial ownership of an asset, brought by a liquidator arose under the general law and did not fall within the exception in Art.1(2)(b) of the Judgments Regulation). See also *Citigate Dewe Rogerson Ltd v Artaban Public Affairs SARL* [2009] EWHC 1689 (Ch.), [2009] B.P.I.R. 1355.

Note 22. In Case C–339/07 *Seagon v Deko Marty Belgium NV* [2009] 1 W.L.R. 2168, the German Bundesgerichtshof referred the following questions to the European Court. First, on interpreting Art.3(1) of the Insolvency Regulation and Art.1(2)(b) of the Judgments Regulation, do the courts of the Member State within the territory of which insolvency proceedings regarding the debtor's assets have been opened have international jurisdiction under the Insolvency Regulation in respect of an action in the context of the insolvency to set a transaction aside that is brought against a person whose registered office is in another Member State? Secondly, if that question is to be answered in the negative, does an action in the context of the insolvency to set aside a transaction fall within Art.1(2)(b) of the Judgments Regulation? The European Court held that Art.3(1) of the Insolvency Regulation must be interpreted as meaning that the courts of the Regulation State within the territory of which insolvency proceedings have been opened have jurisdiction to decide an action to set aside a transaction by virtue of insolvency that is brought against a person whose registered office is in another Regulation State. Accordingly there was no need to decide the second question. See above, entry at para.30–177, n.20. For comment, as to the questions referred, see Dutta [2008] L.M.C.L.Q. 88. And see below, entry at para.30R–197.

NOTE 25. Add: See Case C–1/04 *Staubitz-Schreiber* [2006] E.C.R. I–701, at [28]; Case C–341/04 *Eurofood IFSC Ltd* [2006] E.C.R. I–3813, [2006] Ch. 508 at [57]; Case C–292/08 *German Graphics Graphische Maschinen GmbH v van der Schee* [2009] E.C.R. I–8421. **30–178**

NOTES 30 and 33. See previous entry.

NOTES 43 and 44. Contrast the definition of "establishment" in the UNCITRAL Model Law on Cross-Border Insolvency, as implemented in Great Britain in the Cross-Border Insolvency Regulations 2006, Sch.1, Art.2(e): see below, para.S30–378. And see above, entry at para.30–160, nn. 96 and 97. **30–179**

NOTE 46. Add in line 1: See *Eco Jet Ltd v Selafa MJA* [2005] B.C.C. 979 (CA, Paris). **30–180**

NOTES 47 and 49. Add: *Cross Construction Sussex Ltd v Tseliki* [2006] EWHC 1056 (Ch.), [2006] B.P.I.R. 888. *cf.* Case–1/04 *Staubitz-Schreiber* [2006] E.C.R. I–701, at [24]–[27]. **30–181**

NOTES 50 and 51. Add: Case C–1/04 *Staubitz-Schreiber*, above.

NOTE 60. See entry at para.30–151, nn.57 and 58. **30–185**

NOTE 65. Add: See *Hans Brochier Holdings Ltd v Exner* [2006] EWHC 2594 (Ch.), [2007] B.C.C. 127, at [17]. **30–186**

NOTE 83. Insurers (Reorganisation and Winding-Up) Regulations 2004 are further amended by SI 2007/108, SI 2007/126 and SI 2007/851. Insurers **30–188**

(Reorganisation and Winding-Up) (Lloyd's) Regulations 2005 are amended by SI 2007/851. And see *Re HIH Casualty and General Insurance Ltd* [2008] UKHL 21, [2008] 1 W.L.R. 852 at [32], [40]–[41].

**30–189** Note 86. The definition of "EEA State" is now to be found in Interpretation Act 1978, Sch.1, inserted by Legislative and Regulatory Reform Act 2006, s.26: see SI 2007/108, reg.8. Such a State is defined as a State which is a Member State or any other State which is a party to the EEA Agreement.

Note 88. Add: *Re DAP Holding NV* [2005] EWHC 2092 (Ch.), [2006] B.C.C. 48; *Re Sovereign Marine and General Insurance Co Ltd* [2006] EWHC 1335 (Ch.), [2006] B.C.C. 774.

**30–191—30–193** For a detailed judicial discussion of the Credit Institutions Insolvency Regulations, see *Winding-Up Board of Landsbanki Islands HF v Mills* [2010] CSOH 100.

**30–191** Note 98. Add: Wessels (2006) 21 J. Int. Banking L. and Reg. 301.

Note 99. Credit Institutions (Reorganisation and Winding-Up) Regulations 2004 are amended by SI 2007/108, SI 2007/126 and SI 2007/830.

Add at end: See *Jefferies International Ltd v Landsbanki Islands HF* [2009] EWHC 894 (Comm.); *Winding-Up Board of Landsbanki Islands HF v Mills* [2010] CSOH 100.

**30–192** Note 6. See entry at para.30–189, n.86.

**30–194** Note 26. Illustration 6 must be read in the light of the decision of the European Court in Case C–341/04 *Eurofood IFSC Ltd* [2006] E.C.R. I–3813, [2006] Ch. 508, above, entry at paras 30–172—30–173, nn.89–92.

### C. *Choice of Law*

**30R–197** In Case C–444/07 *MG Probud Gdynia Sp. Z 0.0. v Hauptzollamt Saarbrucken* (pending) the Sąd Rejonowy Gdansk (Poland) referred two questions to the European Court. First, in the light of Arts 3, 4, 16, 17 and 25 of the Insolvency Regulation, i.e. in the light of the rules governing jurisdiction of the courts of the State in which insolvency proceedings are opened, the law applicable to those proceedings and the conditions governing, and the effects of recognition of, those proceedings, do the public administrative authorities of a Member State have the power to seize funds held in the bank account of an economic subject following a declaration of insolvency made in another EU Member State (application of so-called seizure of assets), thereby contravening the national legal rules of the Member State which opened such proceedings (Art.4 of the Regulation), where the conditions for the application of the provisions of Arts 5 and 10 of the Regulation do not exist? Second, in the light of Art.25 *et seq.* of the Regulation, may the administrative authorities of the Member State in which secondary proceedings have not been opened and which must recognise the insolvency proceedings pursuant to Art.16 of the Regulation refuse, on the basis of domestic legal rules, to recognise the decisions made by the State of the opening of insolvency proceedings relating to the conduct and closure of insolvency proceedings pursuant to Arts 31 to 51 of the 1968 Convention on jurisdiction and the enforcement of judgments in civil and commercial matters? The reference was subsequently withdrawn by order of the European Court.

See generally on Art.4 of the Regulation, *Syska v Vivendi Universal SA* [2008] EWHC 2155 (Comm.), [2008] 2 Lloyd's Rep. 646, appeal dismissed [2009] EWCA Civ 677, [2009] 2 All E.R. (Comm.) 891.

See *Syska v Vivendi Universal SA* [2009] EWCA Civ 677, [2009] 2 All E.R. (Comm.) 891 at [16]. **30–202**

See Case C–292/08 *German Graphics Graphische Maschinen GmbH v van der Schee*, above, entry at para.30–177, n. 20 and below, entry at para.30R–317, n.33. **30–204**

Note 53. Add in line 2: Case C–341/04 *Eurofood IFSC Ltd* [2006] E.C.R. I–3813, [2006] Ch. 508, at [60]–[68]. **30–206**

In *Syska v Vivendi Universal SA*, above, it was held that the term "current contracts" in Art.4(2)(e) included arbitration clauses. **30–208**

In *Syska v Vivendi Universal SA*, above, it was held that a pending arbitration claim falls within the expression "lawsuit pending" and is thus governed by Art.15 of the Regulation: see below, entry at paras 30R 279–30-281. **30–209**

Notes 76 to 78. On Arts 40 and 42 of the Insolvency Regulation, see *R Jung GmbH v SIFA SA* [2006] B.C.C. 678 (CA, Orléans). **30–214**

Note 84. On the flexibility of English law in this respect in the context of administration, see *Re MG Rover Belux SA/NV* [2006] EWHC 1296 (Ch.); *Re Collins & Aikman Europe SA* [2006] EWHC 1343 (Ch.), [2007] I.L.Pr. 11. **30–215**

Note 94. See Look Chan Ho (2008) 20 Sing. Acad. L.J. 343. See Case C–339/07 *Seagon v Deko Marty Belgium NV* [2009] 1 W.L.R. 2168; Case C–111/08 *SCT Industri AB i likvidation v Alpenblume Ltd* [2009] E.C.R. I–5655; *Byers v Yacht Bull Corp* [2010] EWHC 133 (Ch.), [2010] B.C.C. 368, above entry at para.30–177, n. 20. **30–219**

**30R–240** See Case C–292/08) *German Graphics Graphische Maschinen GmbH v van der Schee*, above, entry at para.30–177, n. 20 and below, entry at para.301–317.

**30R–249** NOTE 83. Add in line 3: Omar (2006) Conv. 353.

**30–256** NOTES 98 and 99. Financial Markets and Insolvency (Settlement Finality) Regulations 1999 (SI 1999/2979) are amended by SI 2006/50, SI 2007/108, SI 2007/832 and SI 2009/1972.

**30R–279— 30–281** A number of issues concerning Art.4(2)(e), 4(2)(f) and Art.15 were considered in *Syska v Vivendi Universal SA* [2008] EWHC 2155 (Comm.), [2008] 2 Lloyd's Rep. 646, appeal dismissed [2009] EWCA Civ 677, [2009] 2 All E.R. (Comm.) 891. At first instance it was held that Art.4(2)(f) covers every type of proceeding brought by individual creditors but the exception for "lawsuits pending" in Art.4(2)(f) and in Art.15 is restricted: it does not cover executions, namely proceedings before or after judgment on the merits which are aimed at seizure of assets which are part of the debtor's estate. Secondly, it was held that "lawsuits" for these purposes include arbitrations. Thirdly, it was held that Art.15 was not limited to proprietary claims (not following the decision of the Irish High Court in *Re Flightlease Ireland Ltd* [2005] IEHC 274). Fourthly, it was held there was, in the circumstances of the case, a conflict between Art.4(2)(e) and the exception for "lawsuits pending" in Art.4(2)(f) and the specific rule for "lawsuits pending" in Art.15. This was because Polish law, the law of the State of opening, applicable under Art.4(2)(e), rendered the arbitration agreement ineffective as a "current contract" and terminated the reference to arbitration whereas the effect of English law, as the law applicable to the arbitration, was to allow the arbitration to continue.

On appeal, the principal issue was the alleged conflict between Art.4(2)(e) and Art.15. It was held by the Court of Appeal that in reality there was no such conflict. Once it was accepted that an existing arbitration was a "lawsuit pending" within the meaning of Arts 4(2)(f) and 15, the only relevant provision was Art.15 which expressly states that the effects of insolvency proceedings on that lawsuit "shall be governed solely by the law of the Member State in which the lawsuit is pending". Articles 4(2)(e) and 4(2)(f) would, of course, apply to determine the effects of insolvency proceedings on lawsuits commenced after the date on which the insolvency proceedings are commenced.

**30–280** NOTE 50. Add in line 2: See *Syska v Vivendi Universal SA*, above, at [62].

**30–281** NOTES 51 and 54. *Re Flightlease Ireland Ltd* [2005] IEHC 274 (Irish High Court) was not followed in *Syska v Vivendi Universal SA*, above. See entry at paras 30R 279–30-281.

D. *Recognition of Insolvency Proceedings*

NOTE 57. Add: Fletcher, Supplement, paras 7.44–7.69. **30R–283**

NOTE 58. Add: Case C–341/04 *Eurofood IFSC Ltd* [2006] E.C.R. I–3813, [2006] Ch. 508; *French Republic v Klempka* [2006] B.C.C. 841 (French Cour de cassation). And see Case C–393/07 *Seagon v Deko Marty Belgium NV* [2009] 1 W.L.R. 2168.

NOTES 61 and 62. See previous entry. **30–285**

NOTE 68. Add: See *Public Prosecutor v Segard (As Administrator for Rover France SAS)* [2006] I.L.Pr. 681 (CA, Versailles). **30R–287**

NOTE 80. Add: Case C–341/04 *Eurofood IFSC Ltd*, above. **30–295**

NOTE 83. See above, entry at para.30–151, nn.57, 58. **30–298**

NOTE 33. Add: Case C–353/07 *Seagon v Deko Marty Belgium NV* [2009] 1 W.L.R. 2168 at [26]–[27]. And see Case C–111/08 *SCT Industri AB i likvidation v Alpenblume AB* [2009] I.L.Pr. 743; Case C–292/08 *German Graphics Graphische Maschinen GmbH v van der Schee* [2009] E.C.R. I–8421; *Byers v Yacht Bull Corp* [2010] EWHC 133 (Ch.), [2010] B.C.C. 368. **30R–317**

In Case C–292/08 *German Graphics Graphische Maschinen GmbH v van der Schee* (above), the Dutch Hoge Raad referred three questions to the European Court. First, must Art.25(2) of the Insolvency Regulation be interpreted as meaning that the words "provided that Convention (that is to say the Judgments Regulation) is applicable" featuring in that provision imply that, before it can be concluded that the provisions on recognition and enforcement of the Judgments Regulation are applicable to judgments other than those referred to in Art 25(1) of the Insolvency Regulation, it is first necessary to examine whether, pursuant to Art.1(2)(b) of the Judgments Regulation, such judgments fall outside the scope of that Regulation? Secondly, must Art.1(2)(b) of the Judgments Regulation, in conjunction with Art.7(1) of the Insolvency Regulation, be interpreted as meaning that it follows from the fact that an asset to which a reservation of title applies is situated, at the time of the opening of insolvency proceedings against the purchaser, in the Member State in which those insolvency proceedings are opened, that a claim of the seller based on that reservation of title, such as that of German Graphics, must be regarded as a claim which relates to bankruptcy or the winding-up of an insolvent company, within the meaning of Art.1(2)(b) of the Judgments Regulation, and which is therefore outside the material scope of that Regulation? Thirdly, is it relevant in the context of Question 2 that, pursuant to Art.4(2)(b) of the Insolvency Regulation, the law of the Member State in which the insolvency proceedings are opened is to determine the assets which form part of the estate? The European Court held that, in respect of the first question,

Art.25(2) of the Insolvency Regulation must be interpreted as meaning that the words "provided the Convention is applicable" imply that, before it can be concluded that the recognition and enforcement provisions of the Judgments Regulation are applicable to judgments other than those referred to in Art.25(1) of the Insolvency Regulation, it is necessary to determine whether such judgments fall outside the material scope of the Judgments Regulation. As regards the second and third questions, the exception in Art.1(2)(b) of the Judgments Regulation, read in conjunction with Art.7(1) of the Insolvency Regulation, must be interpreted, account being taken of Art.4(2)(b) of the Insolvency Regulation, as meaning that it does not apply to an action brought by a seller based on a reservation of title against a purchaser who is insolvent, where the asset covered by the reservation of title is situated in the Regulation State of the opening of those proceedings at the time of the opening of those proceedings against that purchaser. And see *Byers v Yacht Bull Corp* [2010] EWHC 133 (Ch.), [2010] B.C.C. 368.

**30–323** NOTE 49. Delete *Klempka v ISA Daisytek SAS* [2004] I.L.Pr. 111. Add: Case C–341/04 *Eurofood IFSC Ltd*, above; *French Republic v Klempka* [2006] B.C.C. 841 (French Cour de cassation).

NOTE 50. Add: Case C–341/04 *Eurofood IFSC Ltd*, above.

**30R–325** NOTE 54. Add: Case C–341/04 *Eurofood IFSC Ltd* [2006] E.C.R. I–3813, [2006] Ch. 508, at [60]–[68].

**30–327** NOTE 57. See previous entry.

NOTE 58. Add: Case C–341/04 *Eurofood IFSC Ltd*, above; *French Republic v Klempka* [2006] B.C.C. 841 (French Cour de cassation). See also *Public Prosecutor v Segard (As Administrator for Rover France SAS)* [2006] I.L.Pr. 681 (CA, Versailles).

NOTE 59. Add: Case C–341/04 *Eurofood IFSC Ltd*, above.

NOTE 60. Add: Case C–341/04 *Eurofood IFSC Ltd*, above, at [63].

NOTE 61. Add: Case C–341/04 *Eurofood IFSC Ltd*, above, at [62]–[64].

**30–328** NOTE 62. Add: Case C–341/04 *Eurofood IFSC Ltd*, above, at [66].

NOTE 63. Add: Case C–341/04 *Eurofood IFSC Ltd*, above, at [66]–[67] where the European Court observed that a Member State may refuse to recognise insolvency proceedings opened in another Member State where the decision to open the proceedings was taken "in flagrant breach of the fundamental right to be heard". In the particular context of the *Eurofood* case the Irish court could not confine itself to "transposing its own conception of an oral hearing and of how fundamental that requirement is in its legal order, but must assess, having regard to the whole of the circumstances, whether or not the provisional liquidator appointed by the High Court was given sufficient opportunity to be heard" in the Italian court. See also *Public Prosecutor v Segard (As Administrator for Rover France SAS)* [2006] I.L.Pr. 681 (CA, Versailles); *French Republic v Klempka* [2006] B.C.C. 841 (French Cour de cassation).

NOTE 64. Add: Case C–341/04 *Eurofood IFSC Ltd*, above, at [66].

NOTE 65. Add: Case C–341/04, *Eurofood IFSC Ltd*, above, at [66] ("equality of arms principle is of particular importance").

NOTE 66. Add: Case C–341/04 *Eurofood IFSC Ltd*, above, at [66] (though "the specific detailed rules concerning the right to be heard may vary according to the urgency of the ruling to be given, any restriction on the exercise of that right must be duly justified and surrounded by procedural guarantees ensuring that persons concerned by such proceedings actually have the opportunity to challenge the measures adopted in urgency").

### E. *Co-operation and Co-ordination*

NOTE 70. Although Art.31 of the Insolvency Regulation, reproduced in Rule 189, refers to a duty to co-operate between liquidators, and is silent as to co-operation between courts and judges, it has been reported that in a case proceeding in Germany and the Netherlands, the German judge telephoned the Dutch judge in order to co-ordinate further developments: see Paulus (2007) 20 Insolvency Intelligence 85. For the position under the UNCITRAL Model Law, as implemented in Great Britain in the Cross-Border Insolvency Regulations 2006, Sch.1, Art.25, see below, para.S30–411; and see Fletcher, Supplement, para.8.98. **30R–330—30–334**

See *Re Nortel Networks SA* [2009] EWHC 206 (Ch.), [2009] B.C.C. 343 (High Court has inherent jurisdiction to issue letter of request to foreign court under Insolvency Regulation, and, in the particular circumstances of this case, with a view to enabling administrators to be heard prior to the opening of secondary proceedings in other Regulation States: this reflects a duty under Art.31(2) which extends to courts as well as office-holders). See further, *Re Nortel Networks SA (No. 2)* [2009] EWHC 1482 (Ch.), [2010] B.C.C. 21.

After this paragraph insert material set out below. **30–343**

## 6. UNCITRAL MODEL LAW ON CROSS-BORDER INSOLVENCY

### A. *Introduction and Principles*

S30R–344 **Rule 189A—The UNCITRAL Model Law on Cross-Border Insolvency,[1] as implemented in Great Britain in the Cross-Border Insolvency Regulations 2006,[2] applies where—**

**(1) assistance is sought in Great Britain by a foreign court[3] or a foreign representative[4] in connection with a foreign proceeding[5]; or**

**(2) assistance is sought in a foreign State in connection with a proceeding under British insolvency law[6]; or**

**(3) a foreign proceeding and a proceeding under British insolvency law in respect of the same debtor are taking place concurrently; or**

**(4) creditors or other interested persons in a foreign State have an interest in requesting the commencement of, or participating in, a proceeding under British insolvency law.[7]**

Comment

S30–345 **Background.** As pointed out in the main work,[8] the Insolvency Act 2000 provided[9] that the Secretary of State may, by regulations made with the agreement of the Lord Chancellor,[10] make any provision which he considers necessary or expedient for the purpose of implementing the UNCITRAL Model Law on Cross-Border Insolvency, i.e. the Model Law contained in Annex I of the report of the 30th Session of UNCITRAL.[11] Such regulations

[1] See main work, paras 30–144 *et seq.*

[2] SI 2006/1030, reg.2(1) and Sch.1, which sets out the text of the Model Law, as implemented in Great Britain. In what follows references to the Model Law and to specific articles of that Law are to the version set out in Sch.1, unless otherwise indicated. The Model Law can apply to cases of bankruptcy.

[3] Defined in Art.2(f): see below, para.S30–362.

[4] Defined in Art.2(j): see below, para.S30–362.

[5] Defined in Art.2(i): see below, para.S30–362.

[6] Defined in reg.3 and Art.2(a): see below, para.S30–362.

[7] Art.1(1). See generally, *Re OJSC ANK Yugraneft* [2008] EWHC 2614 (Ch.), [2009] 1 B.C.L.C. 298; *Re Bud-Bank Leasing SP. Z0. 0* [2010] B.C.C. 255 (Mr Registrar Baister); *Re Swissair Schweizerische Luftverker-Aktiengesellschaft* [2009] EWHC 2099 (Ch.), [2009] B.P.I.R. 1505; *Perpetual Trustee Co Ltd v BNY Corporate Trustee Services Ltd* [2009] EWHC 1912 (Ch.), [2009] 2 B.C.L.C. 400, at [48], [57]–[64], affd., without reference to these points, [2009] EWCA Civ 1160, [2010] Ch. 347; *Re Stanford International Bank Ltd* [2010] EWCA Civ 137, [2010] B.P.I.R. 679; *Rubin v Eurofinance SA* [2010] EWCA Civ 895.

[8] Main work, para.30–144.

[9] Insolvency Act 2000, s.14(1).

[10] Insolvency Act 2000, s.14(6)(a).

[11] Insolvency Act 2000, s.14(4). See Report of the 30th session of UNCITRAL, 12–30 May 1997, Official Records of the General Assembly of the United Nations, 52nd session, Supplement No.17, Annex 1, pp.68–78. The original text of the Model Law can also be found in Fletcher, *Insolvency in Private International Law* 2nd edn (2005), Appendix IV with commentary, Ch.8.

may, in particular, (a) apply any provision of insolvency law[12] in relation to foreign proceedings[13] whether begun before or after the regulations enter into force, (b) modify the application of insolvency law, whether in relation to foreign proceedings or otherwise, and (c) amend any provision of s.426 of the Insolvency Act 1986.[14]

The Cross-Border Insolvency Regulations 2006[15] represent the implementation of the UNCITRAL Model Law in Great Britain,[16] with amendments to the "original" Model Law which are regarded as appropriate in the British context.[17] The Regulations entered into force on April 4, 2006.[18] **S30–346**

The main work identified the principal features of the Model Law.[19] Rules 189A to 189F and Comment thereto discuss those features in more detail, focussing on the Model Law as it is implemented in the Regulations. **S30–347**

**UNCITRAL Model Law[20] to have force of law.** Regulation 2(1) of the Cross-Border Insolvency Regulations 2006 provides that the UNCITRAL Model Law shall have the force of Law in Great Britain in the form set out in Sch.1 to the Regulations (which contains the UNCITRAL Model Law with certain modifications to adapt it for application in Great Britain). It follows that the Model Law, as modified by the Schedule, has the force of law in England and Scotland and references to the Model Law or to articles thereof in what follows are references to the text, or to articles, of the Schedule.[21] The 2006 Regulations do not apply to Northern Ireland where separate regulations have been enacted, in very similar, but not identical, form to the 2006 Regulations.[22] **S30–348**

**Interpretation.** Regulation 2(2) makes specific reference to certain documents which may be considered in ascertaining the meaning and effect of any provision of the Model Law, as set out in Sch.1. These are: (a) the UNCITRAL Model Law[23] (in its unmodified form)[24]; (b) any documents of the **S30–349**

---

[12] "Insolvency law" has the same meaning as in Insolvency Act 1986, s.426(10)(a) and (b) (as amended by Insolvency Act 2000, Sch.4, Pt II: Insolvency Act 2000. s.14(4). See below, para.S30–362.

[13] "Foreign proceedings" has the same meaning as in the original Model Law, Art.2(a): Insolvency Act 2000, s.14(4). See below, para.S30–362.

[14] Insolvency Act 2000, s.14(2). The Regulations implementing the Model Law in Great Britain contain no such amendments.

[15] SI 2006/1030.

[16] i.e. England and Scotland: see below, para.S30–348.

[17] For Northern Ireland, see below, para.S30–348.

[18] Reg.1(1).

[19] Main work, paras 30–145 *et seq.*

[20] Defined in reg.1(2) as "the Model Law on Cross-Border Insolvency as adopted by the United Nations Commission on International Trade Law on 30th May 1997".

[21] Discussion of the Schedule is generally limited to its application in England.

[22] See Cross-Border Insolvency Regulations (Northern Ireland) 2007, SR 2007/115, in force from April 12, 2007. For some of the differences, see below, paras S30–364, S30–368.

[23] Reg.2(2)(a).

[24] Above, n.11.

United Nations Commission on International Trade Law and its working group relating to the preparation of the UNCITRAL Model Law[25]; and (c) the Guide to Enactment of the UNCITRAL Model Law[26] prepared at the request of the United Nations Commission on International Trade Law made in May 1997.[27] Doubtless these various documents may be of assistance in resolving interpretative difficulties which may arise. It should be noted, however, that reference to these documents is without prejudice to any practice of the courts as to other matters which the courts may consider in interpreting a legislative text[28] so that reference to these specific documents is apt to include them in the interpretative process but not apt to exclude from consideration other material customarily referred to in that process.[29] More generally, the Model Law itself contains a legislative canon of interpretation since Art.8 provides that in "the interpretation of this law, regard is to be had to its international origin and to the need to promote uniformity in its application and the observance of good faith". The injunction in this canon is tolerably clear, but how British courts will react to it must be more speculative.[30]

**S30–350** **Structure of Cross-Border Insolvency Regulations 2006.** The Regulations, themselves, deal with certain general, but important, matters some of which are referred to above[31] and others of which are mentioned below.[32] Then follow five schedules.

**S30–351** *Schedule 1.* This contains the text of the Model Law, as modified to adapt it for application in Great Britain.[33] This Schedule consists of five Chapters. Chapter 1, entitled "General Provisions", contains eight Articles concerned with: scope of application[34]; key definitions[35]; relationship with other insolvency regimes[36]; allocation of jurisdiction within Great Britain[37]; public

---

[25] Reg.2(2)(b). For these documents, see: *http://www.uncitral.org/uncitral/en/uncitral_texts/insolvency.html.*

[26] UNCITRAL document CAN.9/442 (hereafter "Guide to Enactment"). See *Re Bud-Bank Leasing SP. Z0. 0* [2010] B.C.C. 255 (Mr Registrar Baister); *Re Stanford International Bank Ltd* [2010] EWCA Civ 137, [2010] B.P.I.R. 679; *Rubin v Eurofinance SA* [2010] EWCA Civ 895; and see UNCITRAL Practice Guide on Cross-Border Insolvency Cooperation (Doc. V.09–89284) adopted on July 1, 2009, and adopted by the General Assembly on December 16, 2009, in Resolution 64/112.

[27] Reg.2(2)(c).

[28] Reg.2(2).

[29] See Fletcher, Supplement, paras 8.84 *et seq*. Some assistance may be derived from Insolvency Service, *Implementation of UNCITRAL Model Law on Cross-Border Insolvency in Great Britain* (August, 2005); Insolvency Service, *Implementation of UNCITRAL Model Law on Cross-Border Insolvency in Great Britain: Summary of Responses and Government Reply* (March, 2006).

[30] See Fletcher, Supplement, para.8.84. See also, Guide to Enactment, Art.8. See *Re Stanford International Bank Ltd*, above; *Rubin v Eurofinance SA*, above.

[31] Above, paras S30–348—S30–349.

[32] Below, paras S30–362 *et seq.*

[33] Above, para.S30–348.

[34] Art.1.

[35] Art.2.

[36] Arts 3 and 7.

[37] Art.4.

policy[38]; and interpretation.[39] These provisions form the general subject matter of Rule 189A and this Comment. A further article, Art.5, is concerned with the authorisation of British insolvency officeholders to act in a foreign State.[40] This article forms the basis of Rule 189F and the Comment thereto, Chapter II, entitled "Access of Foreign Representatives and Creditors to Courts in Great Britain", contains six articles dealing with various matters concerning rights of access to British courts.[41] These articles form the substance of Rule 189B and the Comment thereto. Chapter III, entitled "Recognition of a Foreign Proceeding and Relief", consists of ten substantial articles concerned with recognition of foreign insolvency proceedings,[42] and with the relief that may be granted by British courts consequent on such recognition.[43] These articles form the subject matter of Rule 189C and Comment thereto. Chapter IV, entitled "Cooperation with Foreign Courts and Foreign Representatives", consists of only three articles but deals with the important matters of cooperation and direct communication between a court of Great Britain and foreign courts or foreign representatives,[44] cooperation and direct communication between the British insolvency officeholder and foreign courts or foreign representatives,[45] and with the forms that cooperation may take.[46] These provisions form the basis for Rule 189D and Comment thereto. Finally, Chapter V, entitled "Concurrent Proceedings" contains five articles setting out provisions which may be resorted to in situations where there are concurrent proceedings involving the same debtor in Great Britain and in a foreign State.[47] These provisions are addressed in connection with Rule 189E and the Comment thereto.

*Schedule 2.* This Schedule, consisting of 12 Parts and 79 paragraphs makes very detailed provision about procedural matters in England in connection with the application of the Model Law.[48] **S30–352**

*Schedule 3.* This Schedule makes provision about miscellaneous procedural matters in relation to proceedings under the Model Law in Scotland.[49] **S30–353**

*Schedule 4.* This Schedule makes provision in relation to notices delivered to the registrar of companies under the Regulations.[50] **S30–354**

---

[38] Art.6
[39] Art.8 above, para.S30–349.
[40] See also Art.26.
[41] Arts 9–14.
[42] Arts 15–18, 20.
[43] Arts 19, 21–23.
[44] Art.25.
[45] Art.26.
[46] Art.27.
[47] Arts 28–32.
[48] This Schedule is given effect by reg.4.
[49] This Schedule is given effect by reg.5.
[50] This Schedule is given effect by reg.6.

S30–355 *Schedule 5*. This Schedule contains the forms prescribed for use in connection with proceedings under the Regulations.[51]

S30–356 **Scope of application.** Rule 189A reproduces para.1 of Art.1 of the Model Law, Art.1 being headed, generally, "Scope of Application". Article 1(1) thus, firstly, delimits the situations in which resort may be had to the Model Law, albeit in rather general terms which are worked out in more detail in subsequent chapters of the Model Law. Despite delimiting material scope in this sense, clauses (1)–(4) of Rule 189A (Art.1(1)(a)–(d)) also summarise what may be called the basic principles to which it is the intention of the Model Law to give effect.

S30–357 **Clause (1) of the Rule (Article 1(1)(a)).** This clause provides that the Model Law applies where assistance is sought in Great Britain by a foreign court or a foreign representative in connection with a foreign proceeding. The principle covers several issues falling within Chapter II[52] concerned with access to courts in Great Britain, issues falling within Chapter III concerned with recognition of a foreign proceeding and relief[53] and issues falling within Chapter IV concerned with cooperation with foreign courts and foreign representatives.[54]

S30–358 **Clause (2) of the Rule (Article 1(1)(b)).** Clause (2) provides that the Model Law applies where assistance is sought in a foreign State in connection with a proceeding under British insolvency law. In one sense this cannot depend on the Model Law as implemented in Great Britain because any assistance which can be sought in a foreign State in connection with a proceeding under British insolvency law will ultimately depend on the law of that foreign State and in particular on whether the foreign State has enacted the Model Law and on the form in which it has been enacted in that foreign State.[55] This much is recognised as a general principle in Chapter I where Art.5 provides that a "British insolvency officeholder" is authorised to act in a foreign State on behalf of a proceeding under British insolvency law, *as permitted by the applicable foreign law*.[56] In a somewhat different sense, however, this principle embraces the provisions concerned with cooperation with foreign courts and representatives set out in Chapter IV[57] and the

---

[51] See Sch.2, para.73; Sch.3, para.15.

[52] Arts 9–12. See Rule 189B.

[53] Arts 15–17, 19, 21. See Rule 189C. See *Perpetual Trustee Co Ltd v BNY Corporate Trustee Services Ltd* [2009] EWHC 1912 (Ch.), [2009] 2 B.C.L.C. 400, affd., without reference to these points, [2010] EWCA Civ 1160, [2010] Ch. 347; *Re Stanford International Bank Ltd* [2010] EWCA Civ 137, [2010] B.P.I.R. 679; *Rubin v Eurofinance SA* [2010] EWCA Civ 895 and see *Re OJSC ANK Yugraneft* [2008] EWHC 2614 (Ch.), [2009] 1 B.C.L.C. 298.

[54] Arts 25–27. See Rule 189D.

[55] See Fletcher, Supplement, para.8.103. Legislation based on the Model Law has been enacted in Colombia (2006); Eritrea (1998); Japan (2000); Mexico (2000); New Zealand (2006); Poland (2003); Romania (2003); Montenegro (2002); Serbia (2004); South Africa (2000); British Virgin Islands (2005); United States (2005): See *http://www.uncitral.org/uncitral/en/uncitral_texts/insolvency/1997Model_status.html*.

[56] Emphasis added. See Rule 189F.

[57] Arts 25–27. See Rule 189D.

provisions concerned with the coordination of concurrent proceedings set out in Chapter V.[58]

**Clause (3) of the Rule (Article 1(1)(c).** This clause stipulates that the Model Law applies where a foreign proceeding and a proceeding under British insolvency law in respect of the same debtor are taking place concurrently. This principle implicates issues covered, in particular, by Chapters IV[59] and V[60] of the Model Law, and also, by necessary implication, issues involving access to British courts which fall within Chapter II.[61] **S30–359**

**Clause (4) of the Rule (Article 1(1)(d)).** Clause (4) provides that the Model Law applies where creditors or other interested persons in a foreign State have an interest in requesting the commencement of, or participating in, a proceeding under British insolvency law. This clause emphasises that the right to commence or participate in a proceeding under British insolvency law is not confined to foreign representatives but extends also, in particular, to creditors in a foreign State or to other persons in a foreign State who have a relevant interest. The principle embodied in the clause is reflected particularly in Chapter II.[62] **S30–360**

**Excluded entities.** Article 1(2) of the Model Law, as originally promulgated by UNCITRAL, permits a State which enacts the Law to exclude certain entities from the scope of the Law where such an entity is subject to a special insolvency regime. In the Model Law, as implemented in Great Britain, a lengthy list of entities is excluded.[63] The list includes: certain utility companies[64]; certain transport undertakings[65]; certain public private partnership companies[66]; building societies[67]; credit institutions[68]; insurance and re-insurance companies.[69] The provisions of the Model Law may not, accordingly, be invoked in respect of an insolvency proceeding involving such an entity. **S30–361**

**Definitions.** It is necessary to draw attention to the definition of certain expressions which are referred to in this Rule.[70] "Foreign court"[71] means a judicial or other authority competent to control or supervise a foreign proceeding.[72] It follows from this that the Model Law may be invoked irrespective of whether the foreign proceeding has been commenced before a judicial body or **S30–362**

---

[58] Arts 29–30. See Rule 189E.
[59] Art.27(e). See Rules 189D.
[60] Arts 29–30. See Rule 189E.
[61] Art.9. See Rule 189B.
[62] Arts 13–14. See Rule 189B.
[63] Art.1(2) and (3). Contrast the position in respect of implementation in Northern Ireland, S.R. 2007/115, Art.1(2) and (3) where a smaller number of entities are excluded.
[64] Art.1(2)(a) and (b).
[65] Art.1(2)(b) and (c).
[66] Art.1(2)(e).
[67] Art.1(2)(g).
[68] Art.1(2)(h) and (i).
[69] Art.1(2)(j)–(l).
[70] Other definitions will be referred to where relevant.
[71] Art.2(f).
[72] Art.2(g).

administrative body. "Foreign representative"[73] means a person or body, including one appointed on an interim basis, authorised in a foreign proceeding to administer the reorganisation or the liquidation of the debtor's assets or affairs or to act as a representative of the foreign proceeding.[74] "Foreign proceeding"[75] means a collective judicial or administrative proceeding in a foreign State, including an interim proceeding, pursuant to a law relating to insolvency in which proceeding the assets and affairs of the debtor are subject to control and supervision by a foreign court, for the purpose of reorganisation or liquidation.[76] Two points may be made in relation to this definition. First, it would not seem to include a foreign equivalent to English administrative receivership since that process is not collective. Conversely,[77] it would appear to include the foreign equivalents of English administration, creditors' voluntary liquidation and voluntary arrangements between corporate or individual debtors and creditors, since these procedures are collective and involve control by the court (or at least the possibility of control by the court).[78] Secondly, the relevant proceeding must be a proceeding "pursuant to a law relating to insolvency", which raises an issue as to whether a proceeding involved in an insolvency context but which is not found in legislation relating to insolvency is covered.[79] It is suggested that a functional rather than formal interpretation should be adopted and that a proceeding found outside a State's insolvency legislation but which can be transposed into the insolvency context should be covered.[80] A further important definition is that of "British insolvency law".[81] This expression is stated to mean, in relation to England,[82] provision extending to England and made by or under the Insolvency Act 1986 (with the exception of Pt 3 of that Act which deals with receiverships) or by or under that Act as extended or applied by or under any other enactment (excluding the Cross-Border Insolvency Regulations 2006).[83] More generally, reg.3 of the Regulations allows for the "modification of British insolvency law" by providing in reg.3(1) that British insolvency law as defined above and Pt 3 of the Insolvency Act 1986 shall apply with such modifications as the context

---

[73] Art.2(j). The rules relating to restrictions on unqualified persons acting as liquidators, etc. contained in Insolvency Act 1986, s.388 do not apply to foreign representatives since the section is disapplied in relation to such representatives: see reg.8.

[74] Rule 189A(1) and (3). See *Rubin v Eurofinance SA* [2010] EWCA Civ 895. "Foreign representative" does not include a receiver appointed by a foreign court if the powers conferred on and duties imposed on the receiver are duties to gather in and preserve assets, not to liquidate or distribute them: *Re Stanford International Bank Ltd* [2010] EWCA Civ 137, [2010] B.P.I.R. 679.

[75] Art.2(i).

[76] *ibid.* See Fletcher, pp.455–456; *Re Stanford International Bank Ltd* [2010] EWCA Civ 137, [2010] B.P.I.R. 679; *Rubin v Eurofinance SA* [2010] EWCA Civ 895 (meaning of "foreign representative" and "debtor"). See also *Re Bud-Bank Leasing SP.ZO. 0* [2010] B.C.C. 255 (Mr Registrar Baister).

[77] See Fletcher, pp.455–456.

[78] See e.g. Companies Act 1985, s.425, now Companies Act 2006, s.895 (in force).

[79] Fletcher, Supplement, para.8.89.

[80] *ibid.* See *Re Stanford International Bank Ltd,* above; *Rubin v Eurofinance SA*, above. See also *Re Bud-Bank Leasing SP. ZO. 0.*, above.

[81] Rule 189A(2)–(4). See *Hynd's Trustee, Petitioner* [2009] CSOH 76, 2009 S.C. 593 (a case of bankruptcy).

[82] Art.2(a)(i).

[83] For Scotland, see Art.2(a) (ii).

requires for the purpose of giving effect to the provisions contained in the Regulations.[84] That notwithstanding, in the case of any conflict between any provision of British insolvency law or of Pt 3 of the Insolvency Act 1986 and the provisions of the Regulations, the latter shall prevail.[85]

**Relationship with other procedures for assistance.** The application of the Model Law appears to be without prejudice to the availability of other forms of cross-border assistance.[86] Thus, in principle, common law principles of assistance,[87] the statutory procedure under s.426 of the Insolvency Act 1986[88] and the EC Insolvency Regulation[89] co-exist alongside the Model Law subject to two caveats. The first, referred to above,[90] is that where there is a conflict between British insolvency law and the Regulations, the Regulations prevail.[91] The second is to be found in Art.3 of the Model Law which provides that to "the extent that this Law conflicts with an obligation of the United Kingdom under the EC Insolvency Regulation, the requirements of the EC Insolvency Regulation prevail." Further, Art.7 of the Model Law provides that nothing in the Model Law limits the power of a court[92] or a British insolvency officeholder to provide additional assistance to a foreign representative under other laws of Great Britain. For these and other purposes "British insolvency officeholder" means the official receiver within the meaning of s.399 of the Insolvency Act 1986 when acting as liquidator, provisional liquidator, trustee, interim receiver or nominee or supervisor of a voluntary arrangement[93] and a person acting as an insolvency practitioner within the meaning of s.388 of the Insolvency Act 1986 other than a person acting as an administrative receiver.[94] **S30–363**

For the sake of completeness, it is also worth noting that when the Model Law makes reference to the "law of Great Britain"[95] that reference includes a reference to the law of either part of Great Britain (including its rules of private international law).[96] **S30–364**

---

[84] Reg.3(1).

[85] Reg.3(2).

[86] See *Re Swissair Schweizerische Luftverkehr-Aktiengesellschaft* [2009] EWHC 2099 (Ch.), [2009] B.P.I.R. 1505; *Perpetual Trustee Co Ltd v BNY Corporate Trustee Services Ltd* [2009] EWHC 1912 (Ch.), [2009] 2 B.C.L.C. 400, affd., without reference to these points, [2009] EWCA Civ 1160, [2010] Ch. 347; *Rubin v Eurofinance SA* [2010] EWCA Civ 895. See also Art.7.

[87] See main work, para.30–104 and above, entries at para.30–081, nn.57–65, para.30–104, nn.52, 53 and para.30–108, n.60.

[88] See main work, paras 30–105 *et seq.*

[89] See main work, Rules 168 *et seq.*

[90] Above, para.S30–362.

[91] Reg.3(2).

[92] See below, paras S30–365 *et seq.*

[93] Art.2(b)(i).

[94] Art.2(b)(ii). See also for Scotland, Art.2(b)(iii).

[95] See, e.g. Arts 21(3), 23(5).

[96] Art.2(q). The Model Law, as implemented in Northern Ireland (S.R. 2007/115), does not contain any provisions indicating that a reference to the law of Northern Ireland includes a reference to its rules of private international law. *cf.* Insolvency Act 1986, s.426(5); main work, paras 30–113—30–114 and above, entry at para.30–114, n.89.

S30–365 **Competent court.** The Model Law contains no rules concerned directly with the international jurisdiction of courts. It is, however, first necessary to determine which court in England or Scotland, as the case may be, is the appropriate court to exercise the functions which have to be performed under the Model Law and secondly, because the Model Law applies in Great Britain, it may be necessary to determine whether the English court or the Scottish court should assume jurisdiction.

S30–366 As to the first issue, Art.4(1) of the Model Law provides that the functions referred to in the Law which relate to recognition of foreign proceedings and cooperation with foreign courts shall, as regards England, be performed by the Chancery Division of the High Court[97] and, as regards Scotland, shall be performed by the Court of Session.[98]

S30–367 As regards allocation of jurisdiction as between England and Scotland, Art.4(2) provides that the court in either part of Great Britain shall have jurisdiction in respect of the functions of recognition of foreign proceedings and cooperation with foreign courts if (a) the debtor has (i) a place of business; or (ii) in the case of an individual, a place of residence; or (iii) assets, situated in that part of Great Britain; or (b) the court in that part of Great Britain considers for any other reason that it is the appropriate forum to consider the question or provide the assistance requested. The grounds at (a) are clear enough, but ground (b) appears to give a court a complete discretion as to whether it takes jurisdiction to hear an application under the Model Law.[99] Article 4(3), however, gives some guidance in relation to factors of which account may be taken in applying ground (b). It provides that in "considering whether it is an appropriate forum to hear an application for recognition of a foreign proceeding in relation to a debtor, the court shall take into account the location of any court in which a proceeding under British insolvency law is taking place in relation to the debtor and the likely location of any future proceedings under British insolvency law in relation to the debtor".[1] This would appear to allow account to be taken, in deciding which forum is appropriate, of the relative convenience and efficiency of proceedings in either forum.

S30–368 **Cooperation between courts within Great Britain.** Regulation 7 of the 2006 Regulations contains special provision (which does not originate in the Model Law) concerned with cooperation between courts exercising jurisdiction in relation to cross-border insolvency within Great Britain. Thus it is

---

[97] Including Chancery District Registries.

[98] See *Hynd's Trustee, Petitioner* [2009] CSOH 76, 2009 S.C. 593.

[99] See The Insolvency Service, *Implementation of UNCITRAL Model Law on Cross-Border Insolvency in Great Britain: Summary of Responses and Government Reply* (March 2006), para.64.

[1] In the Model Law the expression "the court", except as otherwise provided in Arts 14(4) and 23(6)(b) means in relation to any matter the court which in accordance with the provisions of Art.4 has jurisdiction in relation to that matter: Art.2(c).

provided that an order made by a court in either part of Great Britain in the exercise of jurisdiction in relation to the subject matter of the Regulations shall be enforced in the other part of Great Britain as if it were made by a court exercising the corresponding jurisdiction in that other part.[2] The foregoing obligation, however, does not require a court in either part of Great Britain to enforce, in relation to property situated in that part, any order made by a court in the other part of Great Britain.[3] More generally, the courts having jurisdiction in relation to the subject matter of the Regulations in either part of Great Britain have a duty to assist the courts having the corresponding jurisdiction in the other part.[4] It will be obviously noted that these provisions only apply as between England and Scotland and do not include Northern Ireland. Perhaps somewhat surprisingly, there is no equivalent provision in the Regulations which implement the Model Law in that jurisdiction.[5] Thus it would seem that as between England and Scotland on the one hand and Northern Ireland on the other, cooperation between courts exercising jurisdiction in relation to matters which are the subject of the Regulations appears to depend on the Model Law, as implemented in the respective jurisdictions.[6]

**Public policy exception.** By way of general provision, Art.6 of the Model Law stipulates that nothing in the Model Law prevents the court from refusing to take an action governed by the Model Law if the action would be manifestly contrary to the public policy of Great Britain or any part of it[7]. While enactment of a public policy exception is unsurprising, it is most unclear what the content of "the public policy of Great Britain" precisely is and how, if at all, it differs from the public policy of, respectively, England and Scotland. **S30–369**

**Procedural matters.** Schedule 2 to the Regulations contains detailed procedural rules in relation to proceedings under the Model Law in England.[8] The detail of these procedural rules is beyond the scope of a work on the conflict of laws, but it may be helpful to identify the various groups of rules contained in the 12 parts of that Schedule. These are as follows: introductory provisions (Pt 1); applications for recognition (Pt 2); applications for relief (Pt 3); replacement of foreign representative (Pt 4); reviews of court orders (Pt 5); court procedure and practice in relation to principal applications and orders (Pt 6); applications to the Chief Land Registrar (Pt 7); misfeasance by foreign representative (Pt 8); general provision as to court procedure and practice (Pt 9); costs (Pt 10); appeals (Pt 11); and general matters (Pt 12). **S30–370**

---

[2] reg.7(1). See, on this provision, *Hynd's Trustee, Petitioner* [2009] CSOH 76, 2009 S.C. 593. See above, entry at para.30–074, n.11. *cf.* Insolvency Act 1986, s.426 (1); main work, para.30–093.

[3] reg.7(2). *cf.* Insolvency Act 1986, s.426(2).

[4] reg.7(3). *cf.* Insolvency Act 1986, s.426(4).

[5] SR 2007/115. *cf.* Insolvency Act 1986, s.426 (1), (2) and (4) which refer to the United Kingdom.

[6] Above, para.S30–348.

[7] See *Re Bud-Bank Leasing SP. ZO. O.* [2010] B.C.C. 1505 (Mr Registrar Baister), at [27].

[8] Above para.S30–352. For procedural guidance in connection with a recognition and relief application, see *Re Rajapakse* [2007] B.P.I.R. 99 (Mr Registrar Nicholls) arising out of *Re Rajapakse* (2005) 346 B.R. 233. See Fletcher (2007) 20 Insolvency Intelligence 138. See also *Re Bud-Bank Leasing SP. ZO. O.* [2010] B.C.C. 1505 (Mr Registrar Baister) at [32]–[33].

## B. *Access of Foreign Representatives or Creditors to Courts in Great Britain*

S30R–371 **Rule 189B—A foreign representative is entitled to apply directly to a court in Great Britain[9] and a foreign creditor has the same rights regarding the commencement of, and participation in, a proceeding under British insolvency law as creditors in Great Britain,[10] in accordance with Chapter II of the UNCITRAL Model Law, as implemented in Great Britain in the Cross-Border Insolvency Regulations 2006.[11]**

### Comment

S30–372 **Introduction.** Rule 189B states the basic principles which inform Chapter II of the Model Law, the detail of which is set out in Arts 9–14. Essentially there are two such principles: the right of direct access of a foreign representative to a court in Great Britain; and the rights of foreign creditors to commence and participate in, a proceeding under British insolvency law.

S30–373 **Right of direct access.** Article 9 of the Model Law provides that a foreign representative[12] is entitled to apply directly to a court in Great Britain[13] This provision is designed to indicate that the foreign representative does not have to comply with "formal requirements such as licences or consular action"[14] before access to the relevant court can be gained. It is for this reason that the Regulations disapply s.388 of the Insolvency Act 1986 in respect of anything done by a foreign representative under or by virtue of the Regulations or in relation to relief granted or cooperation or coordination provided under them.[15] In effect, therefore, a foreign representative does not have to hold the status of a licensed insolvency practitioner in order to gain access to a court in England or Scotland.

S30–374 **Limited jurisdiction.** Article 10 stipulates that the sole fact that an application is made to a court in Great Britain under the Model Law by a foreign representative does not subject that representative or the foreign assets and affairs of the debtor to the jurisdiction of the courts of Great Britain or any part of it for any purpose other than the application. Article 10 constitutes what has been described as a "safe conduct" rule,[16] designed to ensure that the court to which an application is made does not thereby assume jurisdiction over all the

---

[9] Model Law, Arts 2(c), 2(j), 4, 9. See *Re OJSC ANK Yugraneft* [2008] EWHC 2614 (Ch.), [2009] 1 B.C.L.C. 298 at [26], [51]; *Rubin v Eurofinance SA* [2010] EWCA Civ 895.

[10] Reg.3(1); Model Law, Arts 2(a), 12(1).

[11] Model Law, Arts 9–14. See *Re OJSC ANK Yugraneft,* above, at [53]; *Perpetual Trustee Co v BNY Corporate Trustee Services Ltd* [2009] EWHC 1912 (Ch.), [2009] 2 B.C.L.C. 400, affd., without reference to these points, [2010] EWCA Civ 1160, [2010] Ch. 347; *Rubin v Eurofinance SA*, above.

[12] As defined in Art.2(j), above, para.S30–362. *Re OJSC ANK Yugraneft*, above, at [26], [51]; *Rubin v Eurofinance SA*, above.

[13] i.e. the relevant court under Art.4 of the Model Law, above, paras S30–364 *et seq.*

[14] Guide to Enactment, para.93.

[15] Reg.8.

[16] Guide to Enactment, para.94.

assets of the debtor merely because the application for recognition of a foreign proceeding[17] has been made. The Article also makes it clear that the application alone is not a ground for the relevant court to assume jurisdiction over the foreign representative in respect of matters unrelated to insolvency.[18]

**Application to commence a proceeding under British insolvency law.** A foreign representative appointed in a foreign main proceeding[19] or foreign non-main proceeding[20] is entitled to apply to commence a proceeding under British insolvency law if the conditions for commencing such a proceeding are otherwise met.[21] This provision is aimed at ensuring that the foreign representative appointed in the proceedings indicated has standing to commence a proceeding under British insolvency law in the relevant court.[22] But the Article makes clear that, insofar as it is necessary that the conditions for commencing such a proceeding are otherwise met, the provision does not modify in any respect the conditions under which an insolvency proceeding may be commenced in England or Scotland, as the case may be.[23] The right conferred by Art.11 is available without prior recognition of the relevant foreign proceeding not least because the commencement of an insolvency proceeding without prior recognition may be "crucial in cases of urgent need for preserving the assets of the debtor".[24] **S30–375**

It will be noted that Art.11 refers to the right of a foreign representative appointed in a "foreign main proceeding" or "foreign non-main proceeding". It is therefore necessary to draw attention to the meaning of these important terms. **S30–376**

**"Foreign main proceeding."** A "foreign main proceeding" means a foreign proceeding taking place in the State where the debtor has the centre of its main interests.[25] The concept of the "centre of main interests" of the debtor is not defined in the Model Law and, in this respect, the concept is as problematical as it is in the context of its use in the EC Insolvency Regulation.[26] It is possible, though far from clear, that some uniformity will be developed by the courts along with the principles developed in decisions dealing with the EC Insolvency Regulation[27] but the extent of this is purely speculative, not least because of the obvious fact that States which implement the Model Law are far from identical with those which are required to implement the EC Regulation. In any event, the meaning of "centre of main interests" is something of an evolving concept in the context of the EC **S30–377**

---

[17] As defined in Art.2(i), above, para.S30–362.

[18] Guide to Enactment, paras 94–95. This does not preclude the court from asserting jurisdiction over the representative or assets on other grounds, e.g. in respect of a tort: *ibid.*

[19] As defined in Art.2(g). See below, para.S30–377.

[20] As defined in Art.2(h). See below, para.S30–378.

[21] Art.11.

[22] Guide to Enactment, para.98.

[23] *ibid.*

[24] *ibid.*, para.99.

[25] Art.2(g). See *Rubin v Eurofinannce SA* [2010] EWCA Civ 896.

[26] See main work, para.30–021 *et seq.* and above, entries at paras 30–169—30–173.

[27] *ibid.* But see the presumption in Art.16(3), below para.S30–387.

Insolvency Regulation.[28] The expression receives no detailed explanation in the Guide to Enactment, although certain paragraphs in that document have been interpreted as meaning that "the standing to commence a proceeding under British insolvency law is a significant right and should only be given to a representative from a jurisdiction where the debtor has a substantial presence".[29] This observation begs many questions and does not take the point much further, although regard must be had to the injunction in Art.8, in relation to interpretation, of the regard which is to be had to the international origin of the Model Law and to the need to promote uniformity in its application and the observance of good faith.[30] In principle, it would seem highly unlikely that English courts will depart from their approach to the concept in the context of the EC Regulation.[31]

S30–378 **"Foreign non-main proceeding".** Article 2(h) of the Model Law defines a "foreign non-main proceeding" as "a foreign proceeding, other than a foreign main proceeding taking place in a State where the debtor has an establishment within the meaning of sub-paragraph (e)" of Art.2. For these purposes "establishment" means "any place of operations where the debtor carries out a non-transitory economic activity with human means and assets or services".[32] This definition has a superficial resemblance to (a) the text of the original Model Law (then contained in Art.2(f)) and (b) the equivalent definition contained in Art.2(h) of the EC Insolvency Regulation.[33] However, there are two important differences. First, the original Model Law prescribed the relevant non-transitory activity as one carried out with human means and goods or services.[34] Secondly, the EC Insolvency Regulation prescribed the non-transitory activity as one carried out with "human means and goods.[35] The difference between these formulations and that in the Model Law, as implemented in Great Britain, is that the latter (in the case of the original Model Law) replaces "goods" with "assets" and (in the case of the EC Regulation) "goods" is replaced by "assets or services". The reference to "assets" expands the original Model Law to include, for example, intangible movable property and probably, immovables as well (the EC Regulation does not even include a reference to services[36]). The outcome is a more flexible

---

[28] *ibid.* See *Re Stanford International Bank Ltd* [2010] EWCA Civ 137, [2010] B.P.I.R. 679 (meaning of "centre of main interests" under Model Law to be interpreted in the same manner as under the EC Insolvency Regulation and in the light of Case C–341/04 *Eurofood IFSC Ltd* [2006] E.C.R. I–3812, [2006] Ch. 580: and see above, entry at paras 30–172–30–173).

[29] Insolvency Service, *Implementation of UNCITRAL Model Law on Cross-Border Insolvency in Great Britain: Summary of Responses and Government Reply* (March, 2006), para.81.

[30] Above, para.S30–349.

[31] *Re Stanford International Bank Ltd* [2010] EWCA Civ 137, [2010] B.P.I.R. 679, following the approach of the European Court in Case C–341/04 *Eurofood IFSC Ltd*, above, including, it would seem, at [56], the inflexible approach of the European Court to corporate groups; see above, entry at paras 30–172—30–173, nn.89–92.

[32] Art.2(e). See *Re Stanford International Bank Ltd* [2009] EWHC 1441 (Ch.) at [96]–[99], affd. [2010] EWCA Civ 137, [2010] B.P.I.R. 679.

[33] Main work, para.30–180.

[34] Art.2(f) of the original Model Law.

[35] Art.2(h), main work, para.30–180.

[36] *ibid.*

definition of establishment as regards the implementation of the Model Law in Great Britain.

**Participation in proceeding under British insolvency law.** Article 12 of the Model Law provides that the foreign representative is, *upon recognition of a foreign proceeding*, entitled to participate in a proceeding regarding the debtor under British insolvency law. The emphasised expression in this passage indicates that one of the benefits of recognition is the opportunity afforded to the foreign representative to "participate" in a proceeding regarding the debtor. "Participate" is not defined in the Model Law. However, the purpose of Art.12 is to confer procedural standing on the foreign representative[37] so that he may "make petitions, requests or submissions concerning issues such as protection, realisation or distribution of assets of the debtor or cooperation with the foreign proceeding"[38] which has been recognised. Article 12 is designed to permit the foreign representative to play a full part in the insolvency process and the term "participate" has the breadth and flexibility to convey this.[39] The precise requests or submissions etc. which the foreign representative may make in any particular proceeding will, of course, be determined by British insolvency law.[40] **S30–379**

**Access of foreign creditors.** Article 13(1) of the Model Law states the important principle that "foreign creditors have the same rights regarding the commencement of, and participation in, a proceeding under British insolvency law as creditors in Great Britain", thus confirming the principle of equality of treatment as regards foreign and other creditors.[41] Article 13(2), however, makes it clear that the general principle does not affect the ranking of claims under British insolvency law, except that the claim of a foreign creditor shall not be given a lower priority than that of general unsecured claims solely because the holder of such a claim is a foreign creditor. Further provision is made in respect of claims by foreign tax or social security authorities.[42] **S30–380**

**Foreign tax, etc. claims.** There is a long-standing rule whereby foreign claims which are characterised as revenue or penal claims are denied enforcement in Great Britain.[43] Article 13(3) of the Model Law, in part, overturns this rule in proceedings to which the Model Law applies. Specifically, Art.13(3) provides that a "claim may not be challenged solely on the grounds that it is a claim by a foreign tax or social security authority but such a claim may be challenged—(a) on the ground that it is in whole or in part a penalty, or (b) on any other ground that a claim may be rejected in a proceeding under British insolvency law." Sub-rule (a) makes it clear that a foreign revenue or social **S30–381**

---

[37] Guide to Enactment, paras 100–101.
[38] *ibid.*, para.100.
[39] Insolvency Service, *Implementation of the UNCITRAL Model Law on Cross-Border Insolvency in Great Britain* (August, 2005), para.46.
[40] Guide to Enactment, para.101.
[41] *ibid.*, paras 103–104.
[42] Art.13(3).
[43] See e.g. *Government of India v Taylor* [1955] A.C. 491; main work, Rule 3.

security claim can be challenged on the grounds that it is penal in character.[44] This brings proceedings under the Model Law into line with the position under the EC Insolvency Regulation.[45] Sub-rule (b), however, makes it clear that a foreign revenue or social security claim may be challenged on any general grounds which may be available under British insolvency law.

**S30–382** **Notification to foreign creditors.** Article 14 of the Model Law emphasises the principle of equality of treatment between creditors by setting out provisions relating to notification to foreign creditors of a proceeding under British insolvency law. Thus, whenever under British insolvency law notification is to be given to creditors in Great Britain, such notification shall also be given to the known creditors that do not have addresses in Great Britain.[46] The court[47] may order that appropriate steps be taken with a view to notifying any creditor whose address is not yet known.[48] The required notification shall be made to the foreign creditors individually unless (a) the court considers that under the circumstances some other form of notification would be more appropriate or (b) the notification to creditors in Great Britain is to be by advertisement[49] only, in which case the notification to the known foreign creditors may be by advertisement in such foreign newspapers as the British insolvency office-holder[50] considers most appropriate for ensuring that the content of the notification comes to the notice of the known foreign creditors.[51] These provisions enable notification to take place expeditiously.[52]

**S30–383** When notification of a right to file a claim is to be given to foreign creditors the notification must: (a) indicate a reasonable time period for filing claims and specify the place for their filing; (b) indicate whether secured creditors[53] need to file their secured claims; and (c) contain any other information required to be included in such a notification to creditors pursuant to the law of Great Britain and the orders of the court.[54]

### C. *Recognition of a Foreign Proceeding and Relief*

**S30R–384** **RULE 189C—A foreign representative may apply to a court in Great Britain for recognition of the foreign proceeding in which the foreign**

---

[44] Main work, Rule 3.

[45] Main work, para.30–213. NOTE 43. For a claim by a foreign revenue authority under the Model Law, see *Re Rivkin* [2008] EWHC 2609 (Ch.), [2009] B.P.I.R. 153 (a case of bankruptcy).

[46] Art.14(1). See Guide to Enactment, para.106.

[47] For these purposes, "court" means the court which has jurisdiction in relation to the particular proceeding under British insolvency law under which notification is to be given to creditors: Art.14(4).

[48] Art.14(1).

[49] Which may be in the London Gazette: see Sch.2, para.48.

[50] Defined in Art.2(b). See above, para.S30–363.

[51] Art.14(2).

[52] See Guide to Enactment, para.108. The original Model Law specifically provided in Art.14(2) that in respect of notification no letters rogatory or other similar formalities are required.

[53] Defined in Art.2(m) as a creditor of the debtor who holds in respect of his debt a security over property of the debtor.

[54] Art.14(3).

**representative has been appointed[55] and such proceeding shall be recognised[56] and, where appropriate, relief granted,[57] in accordance with Chapter III of the UNCITRAL Model Law, as implemented in Great Britain in the Cross-Border Insolvency Regulations 2006.[58]**

COMMENT

**Introduction.** Rule 189C identifies what is essentially the core principle of the Model law, namely the recognition of a foreign proceeding and the relief which may be granted by the recognising court consequent upon such recognition. The detail concerning the principle is contained in Chapter III of the Model Law which contains nine elaborate articles which govern this matter. **S30–385**

**Application for recognition.** Article 15 defines the "core procedural requirements"[59] for an application by a foreign representative for recognition of a foreign proceeding.[60] To this end, it is first provided that a foreign representative[61] may apply to the court[62] for recognition of the foreign proceeding[63] in which the foreign representative has been appointed.[64] An application for recognition must be accompanied by appropriate evidentiary material. Such material may be: (a) a certified copy of the decision commencing the foreign proceeding and appointing the foreign representative; or (b) a certificate from the foreign court affirming the existence of the foreign proceeding and of the appointment of the foreign representative; or (c) in the absence of evidence referred to at (a) and (b), above, any other evidence acceptable to the court of the existence of the foreign proceeding and of the appointment of the foreign representative.[65] Additionally, an application for recognition must also be accompanied by a statement identifying all foreign proceedings,[66] proceedings under British insolvency law[67] and s.426 **S30–386**

---

[55] Model Law, Arts 2(c), 2(i), 2(j), 4, 15.

[56] *ibid*, Art.17. See [2009] B.P.I.R. 1505; *Re Stanford International Bank Ltd* [2010] EWCA Civ 137, [2010] B.P.I.R. 679; *Rubin v Eurofinance SA* [2010] EWCA Civ 895; *Samsun Logix Corp v DEF* [2009] EWHC 576 (Ch.); *D/S Norden A/S v Samsun Logix Corp.* [2009] EWHC 2304 (Ch.), [2009] B.P.I.R. 1367; *Re Swissair Schweizerische Luftverkehr-Aktiengesellschaft* [2009] EWHC 2099 (Ch.), [2009] B.P.I.R. 1505 at [13]; and see *Re Bud-Bank Leasing SP. ZO. 0* [2010] B.C.C. 255 (Mr Registrar Baister); *Re Rivkin* [2008] EWHC 2609 (Ch.), [2009] B.P.I.R. 153 (a case of bankruptcy); *Perpetual Trustee Co Ltd v BNY Corporate Trustee Services Ltd* [2009] EWHC 1912, [2009] 2 B.C.L.C. 400, at [48], [61]–[63], affd., without reference to these points, [2010] EWCA Civ 1160, [2010] Ch. 347.

[57] *ibid*, Arts 19, 21. See cases cited in preceding note.

[58] *ibid*, Arts 15–24.

[59] Guide to Enactment, para.112.

[60] As to procedural matters in England, see 2006 Regulations, Sch.2, paras 2–6.

[61] As defined in Art.2(j), above, para.S30–362.

[62] Which means the relevant court as determined by Art.4, above, paras S30–365 *et seq*.

[63] As defined in Art.2(i), above, para.S30–362.

[64] Art.15(1).

[65] Art.15(2).

[66] As defined in Art.2(i), above, para.S30–362.

[67] As defined in Art.2(a), above, para.S30–362.

requests[68] that are known to the foreign representative.[69] The foreign representative is required to provide the court with a translation into English of documents supplied in support of the application for recognition.[70]

S30–387 **Presumptions concerning recognition.** Article 16 establishes certain presumptions which are intended to assist in expediting the process of recognition. First, if the decision or certificate referred to at points (a) and (b), set out in the previous paragraph, indicates that the foreign proceeding is a proceeding within the meaning of the Model Law[71] and that the foreign representative is a person or body so defined in the Model Law,[72] the court is entitled to so presume.[73] Secondly, the court is entitled to presume that documents submitted in support of the application are authentic whether or not they have been legalised.[74] This presumption applies to documents submitted in evidence on the basis of point (c) set out in the previous paragraph.[75] Thirdly, and most importantly, in the absence of proof to the contrary, the debtor's registered office, or habitual residence in the case of an individual, is presumed to be the centre of the debtor's main interests.[76] The third presumption leaves open the critical question of the strength to be attributed to it and also that of the quantum of proof to the contrary that will suffice to rebut it. This may well he likely to give rise to problems, at least in the context of companies, analogous to those which have already been experienced in relation to the EC Insolvency Regulation.[77]

S30–388 **Decision to recognise foreign proceeding.** Article 17(1) of the Model Law states, as a general principle, subject only to the public policy exception in Art.6 of the Model Law,[78] that a foreign proceeding shall be recognised if: (a) it is a foreign proceeding within the meaning of the Model Law[79]; (b) the foreign representative applying for recognition is a person or body so defined in the Model Law[80]; (c) the application meets the requirements of Art.15(2) and (3)[81]; and (d) the application has been submitted to the court referred to

[68] Defined as "a request for assistance in accordance with s.426 of the Insolvency Act 1986 made to a court in any part of the United Kingdom:" Art.2(l).

[69] Art.15(3). See *Rubin v Eurofinance SA* [2010] EWCA Civ 895; *Re Bud-Bank Leasing SP. ZO. 0.* [2010] B.C.C. 255 (Mr Registrar Baister) at [33].

[70] Art.15(4).

[71] Art.2(i), above, para.S30–362.

[72] Art.2(j), above, para.S30–362.

[73] Art.16(1).

[74] Art.16(2).

[75] Guide to Enactment, paras 114–116.

[76] Art.16(3). See *Re Stanford International Bank Ltd* [2010] EWCA Civ 137, [2010] B.P.I.R. 679. See also *Re Bud-Bank Leasing SP. ZO. 0.* [2010] B.C.C. 255 (Mr Registrar Baister).

[77] See main work, paras 30–171 *et seq;* Case C–341/04 *Eurofood IFSC Ltd.* [2006] E.C.R. I-3813, [2006] Ch. 508; above, entry at paras 30–172—30–173.

[78] Above, para.S30–362. See *Re Bud-Bank Leasing SP. ZO. 0.,* above; *Re Stanford International Bank Ltd,* above; *Rubin v Eurofinance SA* [2010] EWCA Civ 895; *Samsun Logix Corp v DEF* [2009] EWHC 576 (Ch.); *D/S Norden A/S v Samsun Logix Corp* [2009] EWHC 2304 (Ch.), [2009] B.P.I.R. 1367.

[79] Art.2(i), above, para.S30–362.

[80] Art 2(j), above para.S30–362.

[81] Above, para.S30–386.

in Art.4.[82] It will be noted that, apart from the public policy exception, the conditions for recognition do not permit the court to evaluate the merits of the foreign court's decision by which the proceeding has been commenced or the foreign representative appointed.[83] The foreign representative's ability to obtain early recognition and the consequential ability to invoke, in particular, Arts 20–24 of the Model Law[84] may be essential to protect the assets of the debtor from dissipation or concealment.[85] Thus, Art.17(3) of the Model Law places an obligation on the court to decide upon an application for recognition of a foreign proceeding "at the earliest possible time".

Article 17(2) draws an important distinction in respect of the nature of the foreign proceeding for which recognition is sought. The foreign proceeding shall be recognised (a) as a foreign main proceeding if it is taking place in the State where the debtor has the centre of its main interests,[86] or (b) as a foreign non-main proceeding if the debtor has an establishment, within the meaning of the Model Law,[87] in the foreign State.[88] This distinction is important, as pointed out below,[89] because the relief which follows from recognition may depend upon the category into which a foreign proceeding falls. Thus, for example, recognition of a foreign main proceeding brings about an automatic stay of individual actions concerning the assets of the debtor[90] and the suspension of the right to transfer, encumber or otherwise dispose of any assets of the debtor.[91] Where, in contrast, a foreign proceeding is recognised as a non-main proceeding relief available depends, in general, on the discretion of the court.[92]

**Modification or termination of recognition.** Article 17(4) opens up the possibility of "revisiting"[93] the decision on recognition. It provides that the provisions of Arts 15, 16, 17[94] and 18[95] do not prevent the modification or termination of recognition if it is shown that the grounds for granting it were fully or partially lacking or have fully or partially ceased to exist and in such a case, the court may, on the application of the foreign representative or a person affected by recognition, or of its own motion, modify or terminate recognition, either altogether or for a limited time, on such terms and conditions as the court thinks fit. This provision is designed to take account, for example, of a change in circumstances after the decision on recognition was **S30–389**

---

[82] Above, paras S30–365 *et seq.*
[83] Guide to Enactment, para.125.
[84] See below, paras S30–391 *et seq.*
[85] Guide to Enactment, para.125.
[86] Art.17(2)(a). And see Art.2(g). See above, para.S30–377.
[87] Art.2(e). See above, para.S30–378.
[88] Art.17(2)(b).
[89] Below, paras S30–391 *et seq.*
[90] Art.20(1)(a),(b).
[91] Art.20(1)(c), below, para.S30–393, subject to exceptions in Art.20(2).
[92] Art.21, below paras S30–398 *et seq.*
[93] Guide to Enactment, para.129
[94] Above, paras S30–386 *et seq.*
[95] Below, para.S30–390. See *D/S Norden A/S v Samsun Logix Corp* [2009] EWHC 2304 (Ch.), [2009] B.P.I.R. 1367.

originally taken. Such may be the case where the recognised foreign proceeding has been terminated or its nature has changed, as where a reorganisation proceeding has been changed to a liquidation procedure.[96] Additionally, new facts may occur which require or justify a change of the court's original decision, as where, for example, the foreign representative disregards conditions imposed by the court when it granted relief.[97]

S30–390 **Subsequent information.** From the time of filing an application for recognition of the foreign proceeding the foreign representative is obliged to inform the court promptly of, first "any substantial change in the status of the recognised foreign proceeding or the status of the foreign representative's appointment".[98] Thus, it is possible that after an application for recognition or after recognition itself, changes occur in the foreign proceeding that would have affected the decision on recognition, e.g. the foreign proceeding may be terminated or changed from a liquidation proceeding into a reorganisation proceeding, or the terms of appointment of the foreign representative may be modified or the appointment terminated.[99] The foreign representative is under a duty to inform the court of such matters promptly and of any other matters that might amount to substantial changes. Secondly, the foreign representative is, from the time of filing an application for recognition, obliged to inform the court promptly of "any other foreign proceeding,[1] proceeding under British insolvency law[2] or section 426 request[3] regarding the same debtor that becomes known to the foreign representative".[4] This provision in effect extends the duty to identify all proceedings in respect of the debtor which exist when an application for recognition is made[5] to the time after the application for recognition has been filed.[6] Such information permits the court to consider whether relief which has been granted should be coordinated with the existence of the insolvency proceedings that have been commenced after the decision on recognition.[7]

S30–391 **Application for recognition and relief.** Article 19 concerns relief which may be granted, in the discretion of the court, when an application for recognition is made. From the time of filing an application for recognition until the application is decided upon, the court may, at the request of the foreign representative, where relief is urgently needed to protect the assets of the debtor or the interests of creditors, grant relief of a provisional nature including: (a) staying execution against the debtor's assets; (b) entrusting the administration or realisation of all or part of the debtor's assets located in Great Britain to the foreign representative or another person designated by the

---

[96] Guide to Enactment, para.130.
[97] *ibid.*
[98] Art.18(a). As to procedural matters in England, see 2006 Regulations, Sch.2, para.6.
[99] Guide to Enactment, para.133.
[1] Art.2(i), above, para.S30–362.
[2] Art.2(a), above, para.S30–362.
[3] Art.2(l), above, para.S30–386.
[4] Art.18(b).
[5] Art.15(3), above, para.S30–387.
[6] Guide to Enactment, para.134.
[7] Art.30. See Rule 189D; Guide to Enactment, para.134.

court, in order to protect and preserve the value of assets that, by their nature or because of other circumstances, are perishable, susceptible to devaluation or otherwise in jeopardy; and (c) any relief mentioned in Art.21(1)(c),(d), or (g).[8] The relief available under this provision is of somewhat limited form since it is available at the moment from which the application for recognition is made and before recognition is granted.[9] First, the relief must be "urgently needed" to protect the assets of the debtor and the interests of creditors. Secondly, such relief includes staying execution against the debtor's assets or entrusting the administration or realisation of these assets (which must be assets located in Great Britain) to the foreign representative or another person designated by the court but only to protect and preserve assets which by their nature or by virtue of other circumstances are perishable, susceptible to devaluation or otherwise in jeopardy, a limited category of assets. Thirdly, while the relief identified at point (c) above, includes some of the forms of relief, available in the discretion of the court, upon recognition being granted, under Art.21, such relief is limited to three forms: suspension of the right to transfer, encumber or otherwise dispose of any assets of the debtor[10]; relief providing for the examination of witnesses, the taking of evidence or the delivery of information concerning the debtor's assets, affairs, rights, obligations or liabilities[11]; and such additional relief that would be available to a British insolvency officeholder under the law of Great Britain (which includes any relief that may be available under para.43 of Sch.B1 to the Insolvency Act 1986).[12]

The limited character of relief available under Art.19 is further emphasised in two ways. First, the relief granted under the Article terminates when the application for recognition is decided upon, unless the relief is extended under Art.21(1)(f).[13] Secondly, the court may refuse to grant relief under Art.19 if such relief would interfere with the administration of a foreign main proceeding.[14] This means that if there is a foreign main proceeding pending, any relief granted in favour of a foreign non-main proceeding, must be consistent, or should not interfere, with the foreign main proceeding.[15] In effect, therefore, there is an obligation to coordinate pre-recognition relief in respect of a foreign non-main proceeding with the foreign main proceeding.[16] S30–392

**Effects of recognition of a foreign main proceeding.** Article 20 attributes, subject to the terms set forth in the provision, certain automatic effects to the recognition of a foreign main proceeding. By way of general principle, Art.20 first provides that upon recognition of a foreign proceeding that is a foreign main proceeding, subject to Art.20(2): (a) commencement or continuation of S30–393

[8] Art.19(1). As to procedural matters in England, see 2006 Regulations, Sch.2, paras 7–9.
[9] See Guide to Enactment, paras 135–137.
[10] Art.21(1) (c). See below, para.S30–398.
[11] Art.21(1)(d). See below, para.S30–398.
[12] Art.21.
[13] Art.19(2). As to Art.21 (1)(f), see below para.S30–398.
[14] Art.19(3).
[15] Guide to Enactment, para.140.
[16] *ibid* See also Art.30, below, para.S30–419.

individual actions or individual proceedings concerning the debtor's assets, rights, obligations or liabilities is stayed; (b) execution against the debtor's assets is stayed; and (c) the right to transfer, encumber or otherwise dispose of any assets of the debtor is suspended.[17] The consequences of these automatic effects are expanded in Art.20(2) of the Model Law. The stay and suspension is to be (a) the same in scope and effect as if the debtor, in the case of an individual, had been adjudged bankrupt under the Insolvency Act 1986,[18] or, in the case of a debtor other than an individual, had been made the subject of a winding-up order under the Insolvency Act 1986; and (b) subject to the same powers of the court and the same prohibitions, limitations, exceptions and conditions as would apply under the law of Great Britain in such a case; the automatic stay and suspension provisions, referred to above are to be interpreted in the light of Art.20(2).[19] The latter article thus means that, in relation to England, the stay and suspension is subject to the provisions of the insolvency law of England.[20]

S30–394 **Exceptions.** Particular issues are excluded from the effect of the automatic stay and/or suspension. Thus, without prejudice to Art.20(2) the stay and suspension referred to in Art.20(1), *in particular*, does not affect any right: (a) to take any steps to enforce security[21] over the debtor's property; (b) to take any steps to repossess goods in the debtor's possession under a hire-purchase agreement[22]; (c) exercisable under or by virtue or in connection with the provisions referred to in Art.1(4)[23]; or (d) of a creditor to set off its claim against the claim of the debtor, provided that, in relation to English law, the right is one which would have been exercisable if an individual debtor had been adjudged bankrupt under the Insolvency Act 1986[24] or, in the case of a debtor other than an individual, had been made the subject of a winding-up order under the Insolvency Act 1986.[25]

S30–395 **Limitation on commencement of actions etc.** The automatic stay on commencement of actions etc., in respect of the debtor, does not affect the right to: (a) commence individual actions or proceedings to the extent necessary to preserve a claim against the debtor; or (b) commence or continue any criminal proceedings or any action or proceedings by a person or body having

---

[17] Art.20(1).

[18] In the case of Scotland, a person who has had his estate sequestrated under the Bankruptcy (Scotland) Act 1985: Art.20(1). And see Art.2(o).

[19] Art.20(2)(a) and (b).

[20] Or Scotland, as the case may be.

[21] Emphasis added. This would seem to emphasise the generality of Art.20(2) and the particularity, but not exclusivity, of the exceptions in Art.20(3). "Security" is defined, in relation to England, as any mortgage, charge, lien or other security: see Art.2(n)(i). For Scotland, see Art.2(n)(ii).

[22] Defined in Art.2(k), to include "a conditional sale agreement, a chattel leasing agreement and a retention of title agreement".

[23] Concerned with rights arising under financial market contracts.

[24] Or in the case of Scotland, an individual debtor (Art.2(o)) who has had his estate sequestrated under the Bankruptcy (Scotland) Act 1985: Art.20(3).

[25] Art.20(3).

regulatory, supervisory or investigative functions of a public nature, being an action or proceedings brought in the exercise of those functions.[26] This provision, where applicable, again overrides the effect on the automatic stay imposed by Art.20(1)(a).[27]

**Proceeding under British insolvency law.** The consequences of automatic recognition, as stipulated by Art.20(1), are expressly stated not to affect the right to request or otherwise initiate the commencement of a proceeding under British insolvency law or the right to file claims in such a proceeding.[28] S30–396

**Modification or termination of stay or suspension.** Without prejudice to any powers of the court under Art.20(2)[29] and in addition to those powers, the court may, on the application of the foreign representative or a person affected by the stay and suspension indicated by Art.20(1), or of its own motion, modify or terminate such stay or suspension or any part of it, either altogether or for a limited time, on such terms and conditions as the court thinks fit.[30] This provision thus gives full power to change the terms of, or even eliminate, the stay or suspension in an appropriate case. S30–397

**Recognition of a foreign proceeding and discretionary relief.** The relief available in respect of recognition of a foreign main proceeding under Art.20 is, in principle, as pointed out above,[31] automatic. By contrast the relief available under Art.21 is afforded in respect of a foreign main proceeding or a foreign non-main proceeding, but whether such relief will be granted lies in the discretion of the court. Article 21(1) provides that upon recognition of a foreign proceeding, whether main or non-main, where necessary to protect the assets of the debtor or the interests of creditors, the court may, at the request of the foreign representative grant any appropriate relief. Such relief includes, but is not limited to, the following: (a) staying the commencement or continuation of individual actions or individual proceedings concerning the debtor's assets, rights, obligations or liabilities to the extent that they have not been stayed under Art.20[32]; (b) staying execution against the debtor's assets to the extent that execution has not been stayed under Art.20[33]; (c) suspending the right to transfer, encumber or otherwise dispose of the assets of the debtor to the extent that this right has not been suspended under Art.20[34]; (d) providing for the examination of witnesses, the taking of evidence or the S30–398

---

[26] Art.20(4).
[27] Above, para.S30–393.
[28] Art.20(5).
[29] Above, para.S30–393.
[30] Art.20(6).
[31] Para.S30–393.
[32] i.e. Art.20(1)(a), above, para.S30–393. See *Perpetual Trustee Co Ltd v BNY Corporate Trustee Services Ltd* [2009] EWHC 1912 (Ch.), [2009] 2 B.C.L.C. 400, affd., without reference to these points, [2009] EWCA Civ 1160, [2010] Ch. 347.
[33] i.e. Art.20(1)(b), above, para.S30–393.
[34] i.e. Art.20(1)(c), above, para.S30–393.

delivery of information concerning the debtor's assets, affairs, rights, obligations or liabilities[35]; (e) entrusting the administration or realisation of all or part of the debtor's assets located in Great Britain to the foreign representative or another person designated by the court; (f) extending relief granted under Art.19[36]; and (g) granting any additional relief that may be available to a British insolvency officeholder under the law of Great Britain, including any relief provided under para.43 of Sch.B1 to the Insolvency Act 1986.[37]

S30–399 **Assets in Great Britain.** The relief declared available at (e), above, enables assets located in Great Britain to be "turned over" to the foreign representative for distribution in a foreign proceeding. This is taken further in Art.21(2). There it is provided that upon recognition of a foreign proceeding, whether main or non-main, the court may, at the request of the foreign representative, entrust the distribution of all or part of the debtor's assets located in Great Britain to the foreign representative or another person designated by the court, subject to the important proviso that the court is satisfied that the interests of creditors in Great Britain are adequately protected.[38] Further, and more generally, in granting relief under Art.21 to a representative of a foreign non-main proceeding, the court must be satisfied that the relief relates to assets that, under the law of Great Britain, should be administered in the foreign non-main proceeding or concerns information required in that proceeding.[39]

S30–400 **Limitation on stay.** By way of limitation, Art.20(4) provides that no stay under Art.21(1)(a)[40] shall affect the right to commence individual actions or proceedings to the extent necessary to preserve a claim against the debtor or the right to commence or continue any criminal proceedings or any action or proceedings by a person or body having regulatory, supervisory or investigative functions of a public nature, being an action or proceedings brought in the exercise of those functions.

---

35 See *Re Rivkin* [2008] EWHC 2609 (Ch.), [2009] B.P.I.R. 153; see also *Re Bernard L Madoff Investment Securities LLC* [2009] EWHC 442 (Ch.), [2009] 2 B.C.L.C. 78, at [15]. In *Rubin v Eurofinance SA* [2010] EWCA Civ 895 it was held that the English court could recognise and enforce a judgment given in adversarial proceedings by an American bankruptcy court in bankruptcy proceedings, applying common law rules as to assistance to the foreign court, even though the judgment would not be entitled to recognition and enforcement as a judgment *in personam*, at common law, under Rule 36 of the main work. No concluded view was expressed as to the position under the Model Law, but see Art.27. And see above, entry at para.30–108, n. 60 and below, entry at para.S30R 409, n. 80.

36 i.e. Art.19(1), above, para.S30–391.

37 This provision would enable the court, if it considered it appropriate, to override the rights which would otherwise be exercisable by secured and other creditors under Arts 20(2) and 20(3) (above, para.S30–394) so that they are exercisable only with the consent of the officeholder or the consent of the court. See also *Perpetual Trustee Co Ltd v BNY Corporate Services Ltd* [2009] EWCA Civ 1160, [2010] Ch. 347.

38 See *Re Swissair Schweizerische Luftverkehr-Aktiengesellschaft* [2009] EWHC 2099 (Ch.), at [13]–[18], [2009] B.P.I.R. 1505; and see *Re Stanford International Bank Ltd* [2010] EWCA Civ 137, [2010] B.P.I.R. 679. See also Art.22, below, para.S30–401.

39 Art.21(3). See *Re Swissair Schweizerische Luftverkehr-Aktiengesellschaft*, above, at [15].

40 Above, para.S30–395.

**Protection of creditors.** Article 21(2) introduces the principle of adequate protection of the interests of creditors, albeit creditors in Great Britain.[41] Article 22 gives the principle of adequate protection a more general role in the process of determining whether relief shall be granted. First, in granting or denying relief under Arts 19[42] or 21[43] or in modifying or terminating relief under Art.22(3)[44] or Art.20(6),[45] the court must be satisfied that the interests of the creditors (including any secured creditors[46] or parties to hire-purchase agreements[47]) and other interested persons, including if appropriate the debtor, are adequately protected.[48] Secondly, the court may subject relief granted under Arts 19[49] or 21[50] to conditions it considers appropriate, including the provision by the foreign representative of security or caution for the proper performance of his functions.[51] Thirdly, the court may, at the request of the foreign representative or a person affected by relief granted under Arts 19[52] or 21,[53] or of its own motion, modify or terminate that relief.[54] **S30–401**

**Actions to avoid acts detrimental to creditors.** Article 23 is an important provision concerned with the avoidance of certain transactions which prejudice creditors.[55] The purpose of the provision is to give the foreign representative, upon recognition of a foreign proceeding, standing to make an application to the court for an order under or in connection with certain specified sections of the Insolvency Act 1986 whereby transactions entered into by the debtor to the detriment of creditors may be set aside.[56] The relevant sections may be invoked to avoid: transactions at an undervalue[57]; preferences[58]; extortionate credit transactions[59]; floating charges to secure past indebtedness[60]; transactions defrauding creditors[61]; and actions to facilitate the recovery of excessive pension contributions made by individual debtors.[62] By virtue of Art.23(2), where the foreign representative makes an application **S30–402**

---

[41] Above, para.S30–399. See *Re Swissair Schweizerische Luftverkehr-Aktiengesellschaft*, above.

[42] Above, paras S30–391 *et seq.*

[43] Above, paras S30–398 *et seq.*

[44] Below, text at n.54.

[45] Above, para.S30–397.

[46] As defined in Art.2(m), above, paras S30–383 *et seq.*

[47] As defined in Art.2(k), above, para.S30–394.

[48] Art.22(1). *Re Swissair Schweizerische Luftverkehr-Aktiengesellschaft*, above, at [14] (interests of creditors); *Re Rivkin* [2008] EWHC 2609 (Ch), [2009] B.P.I.R. 153 (interests of "other interested persons" in a case of bankruptcy).

[49] Above, paras S30–391 *et seq.*

[50] Above, paras S30–398 *et seq.*

[51] Art.22(2).

[52] Above, paras S30–391 *et seq.*

[53] Above, paras S30–398 *et seq.*

[54] Art.22(3).

[55] See Fletcher, Supplement, paras 8.96–8.97; Look Chan Ho (2008) 20 Sing. Acad. L.J. 343.

[56] Art.23(1). The specified sections are ss.238, 239, 242, 243, 244, 245, 339, 340, 342A, 343 and 423 (and, for Scotland, ss.34–36A and s.61).

[57] *ibid.*, ss.238, 339.

[58] *ibid.*, ss.239, 340.

[59] *ibid.*, ss.244, 343.

[60] *ibid.*, s.245.

[61] *ibid.*, s.423.

[62] *ibid.*, s.342A.

(described as "an article 23 application") under the foregoing sections and other listed sections of the 1986 Act,[63] such sections are made applicable whether or not the debtor has been adjudged bankrupt, or in the case of a company is being wound up or is in administration, with the modifications described below.[64]

S30–403 **Modifications.** Article 23(3) provides a modified test for determining the time which is to be regarded as the "relevant time" in relation to the avoidance provisions as applicable in respect of the relevant foreign proceeding: that time is stated to be "the date of opening of the relevant foreign proceeding".[65] For these purposes the "date of the opening of the foreign proceeding" shall be determined in accordance with the law of the State in which the foreign proceeding is taking place, including any rule of law by virtue of which the foreign proceeding is deemed to have opened at an earlier time.[66] It will be noted that this formulation is apt to include the foreign State's rule, if such there be, concerning "relation back", as regards the relevant time.[67]

S30–404 **Foreign non-main proceeding.** When the foreign proceeding is a foreign non-main proceeding, the court[68] must be satisfied that the Article 23 application relates to assets that, under the law of Great Britain, should be administered in the foreign non-main proceeding.[69]

S30–405 **Proceeding under British insolvency law.** At any time when a proceeding under British insolvency law is taking place regarding the debtor, the foreign representative may not make an Article 23 application except with the permission of the High Court in the case of a proceeding under British insolvency law taking place in England.[70] Further, nothing in Art.23 affects the right of a British insolvency officeholder to make an application under or in connection with any of the provisions which are made applicable by Art.23(1).[71]

S30–406 **Adequate protection of creditors.** On making an order on an Article 23 application, the court[72] may give such directions regarding the distribution of any proceeds of the claim by the foreign representative, as it thinks fit to ensure that the interests of creditors in Great Britain are adequately protected.[73]

---

[63] The listed sections in Art.23(2) are: ss.240, 241, 341, 342, 342B–342F, 424 and 425 (and, for Scotland ss.36B and 36C of the Bankruptcy (Scotland) Act 1985).

[64] Art.23(2)(a) and (b).

[65] Art.23(3)(a)–(l).

[66] Art.23(4).

[67] *cf.* Case C–341/04 *Eurofood IFSC Ltd* [2006] E.C.R. I–3813, [2006] Ch. 508; above, entry at paras 30–169—30–170.

[68] Which means the court in which the Article 23 application is taking place: Art.23(6) (b).

[69] Art.23(5).

[70] Art.23(b)(a)(i). In relation to a proceeding in Scotland, permission must be obtained from the Court of Session: Art.23(b)(a)(ii).

[71] Art.23(8). See above, para.S30–402.

[72] Which means the court in which the Article 23 application is taking place: Art.23(6)(b).

[73] Art.23(7).

**No retrospective effect.** Nothing in Art.23(1) applies in respect of transactions entered into before April 4, 2006, the date on which the Cross-Border Insolvency Regulations 2006 entered into force.[74] **S30–407**

**Intervention by foreign representative in proceedings in Great Britain.** Article 24 provides that upon recognition of a foreign proceeding, the foreign representative may, provided the requirements of the law of Great Britain are met, intervene in any proceedings in which the debtor is a party. The article applies to foreign representatives of both main and non-main proceedings.[75] The right to intervene extends to individual court actions or other proceedings instituted by the debtor against a third party or proceedings instituted by a third party against the debtor.[76] **S30–408**

### D. *Cooperation with Foreign Courts and Foreign Representatives*

**RULE 189D—In respect of the matters referred to in Rule 189A, a court in Great Britain may cooperate to the maximum extent possible with foreign courts[77] or foreign representatives,[78] either directly or through a British insolvency officeholder,[79] in accordance with Chapter IV of the UNCITRAL Model Law, as implemented in Great Britain in the Cross-Border Insolvency Regulations 2006.[80]** **S30R–409**

#### COMMENT

**General principles.** Chapter IV of the Model Law makes general provision for cooperation and direct communication between a court of Great Britain and foreign courts or foreign representatives,[81] for cooperation and direct communication between the British insolvency officeholder and foreign courts or foreign representatives,[82] and for the forms which such cooperation may **S30–410**

---

[74] Art.23(9).

[75] Guide to Enactment, para.168.

[76] *ibid.*, para.169.

[77] Model Law, Art.2(f).

[78] *ibid.*, Art.2(j).

[79] *ibid.*, Arts 2(b), 2(c), 25(1).

[80] *ibid.*, Arts 25–27. In *Rubin v Eurofinance SA* [2010] EWCA Civ 895 it was held that a judgment given in adversarial proceedings by a United States bankruptcy court could be enforced in England at common law, in the exercise of the power to give assistance to the foreign court, even though the judgment did not satisfy the requirements for enforcing a judgment *in personam* at common law (main work, Rule 36). No concluded view was expressed as to the position under the Model Law. It was said, however, (at [63]) that although Art.27 did not refer to enforcement as a form of co-operation which could be offered, Art.25 Permitted cooperation with the foreign court or foreign representative to "the maximum extent possible" and that should "surely include enforcement, especially since enforcement is available under the common law".

See also *Perpetual Trustee Co Ltd v BNY Corporate Trustee Services Ltd* [2009] EWHC 1912 (Ch.), [2009] 2 B.C.L.C. 400, at [62]–[63], affd. [2009] EWCA Civ 1160, [2010] Ch. 347.

[81] Art.25.

[82] Art.26.

take,[83] in respect of the matters referred to in Rule 189A.[84] The three articles which comprise Chapter IV are framed in very broad and general terms. As a consequence, the court will have the opportunity to develop its own practices in relation to cooperation and coordination[85] with the objective of achieving efficient and optimal outcomes in cross-border cases.[86]

S30–411 **British courts, foreign courts and foreign representatives.** Article 25(1) provides that in relation to the matters referred to in Art.1(1), (i.e. Rule 189A), "the court *may* cooperate to the maximum extent possible with foreign courts or foreign representatives either directly or through a British insolvency officeholder". The emphasised word in this provision, *"may"*, indicates that ultimately such cooperation is discretionary. This is a departure from the text of the provision in the original Model Law where the word used is the mandatory "shall". This change was introduced in the Model Law, as implemented in Great Britain, because it was believed that some discretion as to whether to cooperate was preferable, although it is also believed that the court will only refuse cooperation in response to an actual request where it has good reasons for doing so.[87] Further, and importantly, Art.25(2) states that the "court is entitled to communicate directly with, or to request information or assistance directly from, foreign courts or foreign representatives". The provision gives legislative legitimacy to a practice which has gained some, albeit uncertain, support from English courts.[88] It avoids time-consuming procedures traditionally in use such as letters of request.[89]

S30–412 **British insolvency officeholder, foreign courts and foreign representatives.** Article 26 deals with cooperation and direct communication between the British insolvency officeholder and foreign courts or foreign representatives. In relation to the matters dealt with in Art.1(1) of the Model Law (Rule 189A), a British insolvency officeholder "*shall to the extent consistent with his other duties under the law of Great Britain*, in the exercise of his functions and subject to the supervision of the court, cooperate to the maximum extent possible with foreign courts or foreign representatives".[90] It will be noted, first, that the obligation of the British insolvency officeholder to cooperate is expressed in mandatory terms ("shall", as emphasised, above), but secondly that the obligation is imposed (as in the following words, emphasised above) to the extent consistent with his "other duties under the law of Great Britain". The latter expression thus reduces, somewhat, the mandatory nature of the principal obligation. The limitation was introduced, apparently, to avoid a

---

[83] Art.27.

[84] Model Law, Art.1(1).

[85] Insolvency Service, *Implementation of UNCITRAL Model Law on Cross-Border Insolvency in Great Britain: Summary of Responses and Government Reply* (March, 2006), para.157.

[86] Guide to Enactment, para.173.

[87] Insolvency Service, *Implementation of UNCITRAL Model Law on Cross-Border Insolvency in Great Britain: Summary of Responses and Government Reply* (March, 2006), paras 148–153.

[88] See Fletcher, Supplement, para.8.98. See also Kawaley (2007) 20 Insolvency Intelligence 113.

[89] Guide to Enactment, para.179.

[90] Art.26(1).

potential situation in which a British insolvency officeholder perceived a conflict of interest between his position and that of the foreign representative, so that the British insolvency officeholder would not be forced to seek directions from the court before he considered it safe to refuse to exercise his functions in a particular manner (if so requested by the foreign representative or court) or give less than maximum cooperation.[91] It will, secondly, be noted that the cooperation of the British insolvency officeholder is "subject to the supervision of the court" which, in the exercise of that function, may further limit the power of the British insolvency officeholder. Additionally, the British insolvency officeholder is entitled to communicate directly with foreign courts and foreign representatives, in the exercise of his functions, but, again, subject to the supervision of the court.[92]

**Forms of cooperation.** Article 27 provides that cooperation "referred to in Article 25 and 26 may be implemented by any appropriate means including" (but, therefore, not limited to) the following: (a) appointment of a person to act at the direction of the court[93]; (b) communication of information by any means considered appropriate by the court[94]; (c) coordination of the administration and supervision of the debtor's assets and affairs[95]; (d) approval or implementation by courts of agreements concerning the coordination of proceedings[96]; (e) coordination of concurrent proceedings regarding the same debtor.[97] Given that these are only examples of the forms of cooperation that may be appropriate,[98] the court is given a considerable degree of latitude, in particular, because the examples themselves are in somewhat general terms. **S30–413**

## E. *Concurrent Proceedings*

**RULE 189E—The effect of commencement of a proceeding under British insolvency law after recognition of a foreign main proceeding, in respect of the same debtor[99] and the coordination of a proceeding, in respect of the same debtor,[1] are determined in accordance with Chapter V of the UNCITRAL Model Law, as implemented in Great Britain in the Cross-Border Insolvency Regulations 2006.[2]** **S30R–414**

---

[91] Insolvency Service, *Implementation of UNCITRAL Model Law on Cross-Border Insolvency in Great Britain: Summary of Responses and Government Reply* (March, 2006), paras 150–151.

[92] Art.26(2).

[93] Art.27(a).

[94] Art.27(b).

[95] Art.27(c); and see below, Rule 189E.

[96] Art.27(d); and see below, Rule 189E.

[97] Art.27(e); and see below, Rule 189E.

[98] See generally *Rubin v Eurofinance SA* [2010] EWCA Civ 895, above, para.S30–411, n. 80. See Insolvency Service, *Implementation of UNCITRAL Model Law on Cross-Border Insolvency in Great Britain: Summary of Responses and Government Reply* (March 2006), paras 154, 157.

[99] reg.3(1); Model Law, Arts 2(a), 2(g), 28.

[1] Model Law, Arts 2(a), 2(i), 29.

[2] *ibid.*, Arts 28–32.

COMMENT

S30–415 **Introduction.** Rule 189E states the principle of the Model Law as regards concurrent proceedings in respect of the same debtor. The relevant provisions are contained in Chapter V of the Model Law which consists of five articles dealing respectively, with: the commencement of a proceeding under British insolvency law after recognition of a foreign main proceeding[3]; the coordination of a proceeding under British insolvency law and a foreign proceeding[4]; coordination of more than one foreign proceeding[5]; the presumption of insolvency based on recognition of a foreign main proceeding[6]; and a rule concerned with payment in concurrent proceedings.[7]

S30–416 **Commencement of proceeding under British insolvency law after recognition of foreign main proceeding.** Article 28 provides that after recognition of a foreign main proceeding, "the effects of a proceeding under British insolvency law in relation to the same debtor shall, insofar as the assets of that debtor are concerned, be restricted to assets that are located in Great Britain and, to the extent necessary to implement cooperation and coordination under Arts 25, 26 and 27, to other assets of the debtor that, under the law of Great Britain, should be administered in that proceeding". The original version of the Model Law provided that after recognition of a foreign main proceeding, a proceeding under the law of an enacting State could only be commenced if the debtor had assets in the enacting State.[8] The Model Law, as implemented in Great Britain, contains no such requirement, nor is there any jurisdictional requirement that the debtor has an establishment in Great Britain.[9] The consequence of this is that, in England, the normal jurisdictional rules applicable in insolvency cases not falling within the EC Regulation will be applied to determine whether the English court has jurisdiction.[10] In general, these rules do not require the presence of assets as a necessity but rather that there be a sufficient connection between the debtor and England and that there are persons who would benefit from the making of an order declaring the debtor insolvent.[11] Nonetheless, the proceeding in Great Britain is territorial in scope in that it is confined to assets of the debtor that are located there (or will be located there if an order is made) and only extends to other assets of the debtor that under the law of Great Britain should be administered in that proceeding to the extent necessary to implement cooperation and coordination under Arts 25–27.[12]

---

[3] Art.28.
[4] Art.29.
[5] Art.30.
[6] Art.31.
[7] Art.32.
[8] Art.28 of the original Model Law. See Guide to Enactment, paras 125, 185–186.
[9] *cf.* the EC Insolvency Regulation, Art.3(2), main work Rule 169(2).
[10] These rules were principally developed in the context of the winding up of companies. See main work, paras 30–034 *et seq.*
[11] See main work, Rule 163(2).
[12] See above, Rule 189D.

**Coordination of proceeding under British insolvency law and foreign proceeding.** Article 29 provides that where a foreign proceeding and a proceeding under British insolvency law are taking place concurrently, the court may seek cooperation and coordination under Arts 25–27.[13] More specifically, firstly, when the proceeding in Great Britain is taking place at the time the application for recognition of the foreign proceeding is filed, (i) any relief granted under Arts 19 or 21[14] must be consistent with the proceeding in Great Britain and (ii) if the foreign proceeding is recognised in Great Britain as a foreign main proceeding, Art.20 (providing for an automatic stay etc.)[15] does not apply.[16] The disapplication of Art.20 is obviously necessary if appropriate cooperation and coordination is to be achieved. Secondly, when the proceeding in Great Britain commences after the filing of the application for recognition of the foreign proceedings: (i) any relief in effect under Arts 19 or 21[17] shall be reviewed by the court and shall be modified or terminated if inconsistent with the proceeding in Great Britain; (ii) if the foreign proceeding is a foreign main proceeding, the stay and suspension referred to in Art.20(1) shall be modified or terminated pursuant to Art.20(6),[18] if inconsistent with the proceeding in Great Britain; and (iii) any proceedings brought by the foreign representative by virtue of Art.23(1)[19] before the proceeding in Great Britain commenced shall be reviewed by the court and the court may give such directions as it thinks fit regarding the continuance of those proceedings.[20] Thirdly, in granting, extending or modifying relief granted to a representative of a foreign non-main proceeding, the court must be satisfied that the relief relates to assets that, under the law of Great Britain, should be administered in the foreign non-main proceeding or concerns information required in that proceeding.[21] S30–417

Essentially, the principle of Art.29 is that the commencement of a proceeding in Great Britain does not prevent or terminate the recognition of a foreign proceeding: this allows a court in Great Britain, taking account of all the circumstances, to provide relief in favour of the foreign proceeding.[22] Nonetheless, Art.29 maintains a degree of pre-eminence of the proceeding in Great Britain through the provisions in Art.29(a) and (b), described above,[23] without establishing a rigid hierarchy between the proceedings: such a hierarchy would "unnecessarily hinder the ability of the court to cooperate and exercise its discretion under articles 19 and 20".[24] Article 29(c) emphasises the S30–418

---

[13] *ibid.*

[14] Above, paras S30–391 *et seq.* See *Re Swissair Schweizerische Luftverkehr-Aktiengesellschaft* [2009] EWHC 2099 (Ch.), [2009] B.P.I.R. 1505 at [14] (Art.29(a)(i)).

[15] Above, paras S30–398 *et seq.*

[16] Art.29(a).

[17] Above, paras S30–391 *et seq.*

[18] Above, paras S30–393 *et seq.*

[19] Above, para.S30–402.

[20] Art.29(b).

[21] Art.29(c).

[22] Guide to Enactment, para.189.

[23] *ibid.*, para.190.

[24] *ibid.*

principle that relief granted in respect of a foreign non-main proceeding should be limited to assets that are to be administered in that proceeding or must concern information required in that proceeding.[25]

S30–419 **Coordination of more than one foreign proceeding.** In relation to matters referred to in Art.1(1),[26] in respect of more than one foreign proceeding regarding the same debtor, the general principle is that the court may seek cooperation and coordination under Arts 25–27.[27] Specifically, first, any relief granted under Arts 19 or 21[28] to a representative of a foreign non-main proceeding after recognition of a foreign main proceeding must be consistent with the foreign main proceeding.[29] Secondly, if a foreign main proceeding is recognised after the filing of an application for recognition of a foreign non-main proceeding, any relief in effect under Arts 19 and 21[30] shall be reviewed by the court and shall be modified or terminated if inconsistent with the foreign main proceeding.[31] Thirdly, if, after recognition of a foreign non-main proceeding, another foreign non-main proceeding is recognised, the court shall grant, modify or terminate relief for the purpose of facilitating coordination of the proceedings.[32]

S30–420 Article 30 deals with cases where the debtor is subject to insolvency proceedings in more than one foreign State and foreign representatives of more than one foreign proceeding seek recognition or relief in Great Britain. The provision applies whether or not an insolvency proceeding is pending in Great Britain. If, in addition to two or more foreign proceedings, there is a proceeding in Great Britain, the court will have to act pursuant to both Art.29 and Art.30.[33] The objective of the article is similar to that of Art.29 in that the core issue in relation to concurrent proceedings is the promotion of cooperation, coordination and consistency of relief granted in respect of the different proceedings, achieved by "appropriate tailoring of relief to be granted or by modifying or terminating relief already granted".[34] In contrast to Art.29 (which, in principle, gives pre-eminence to the proceeding in Great Britain), Art.30 gives preference to the foreign main proceeding, if there is one. This is reflected in the requirement that any relief in favour of a foreign non-main proceeding (whether already granted or to be granted) must be consistent with the foreign main proceeding.[35] In the case of more than one foreign non-main

---

[25] *ibid.*, para.191. See also Art.19(4), above, para.S30–391 and Art.30, below, para.S30–420.
[26] Rule 189A.
[27] Art.30. See Rule 189D.
[28] Above, paras S30–391 *et seq.*
[29] Art.30(a).
[30] Above, paras S30–391 *et seq.*
[31] Art.30(b).
[32] Art.30(c).
[33] Guide to Enactment, para.192.
[34] *ibid.*, para.193.
[35] *ibid.*

proceeding, the provision does not treat any foreign proceeding preferentially.[36]

**Presumption of insolvency.** In the absence of evidence to the contrary, recognition of a foreign main proceeding is, for the purpose of commencing a proceeding under British insolvency law, proof that the debtor is unable to pay its debts or, in relation to Scotland, is apparently insolvent within the meaning given to those expressions under British insolvency law.[37] This provision may be of particular importance when the need to prove insolvency would be "a time consuming exercise and of little additional benefit bearing in mind that the debtor is already in an insolvency proceeding in the State where it has its centre of main interests and the commencement of a local proceeding may be urgently needed for the protection of local creditors".[38] **S30–421**

**Payment in concurrent proceedings.** Without prejudice to secured claims[39] or rights *in rem*,[40] a creditor who has received part payment in respect of its claim in a proceeding pursuant to a law relating to insolvency in a foreign State may not receive a payment for the same claim in a proceeding under British insolvency law regarding the same debtor, so long as the payment to other creditors of the same class is proportionately less than the payment the creditor has already received.[41] This rule restates the hotchpot principle, which is designed to avoid situations in which a creditor might obtain more favourable treatment than other creditors of the same class by obtaining payment of the same claim in insolvency proceedings in other jurisdictions.[42] **S30–422**

### F. *British Insolvency Officeholder Acting in Foreign State*

**RULE 189F—A British insolvency officeholder is authorised to act in a foreign State on behalf of a proceeding under British insolvency law, as permitted by the applicable foreign law.**[43] **S30R–423**

### COMMENT

Article 1(1) of the Model Law provides that the Law applies where assistance is sought in a foreign State in connection with a proceeding under British **S30–424**

[36] *ibid.*

[37] Art.31

[38] Guide to Enactment, para.197.

[39] Described in the Guide to Enactment, para.200, as "claims guaranteed by particular assets".

[40] Described in the Guide to Enactment, *ibid.*, as "rights relating to a particular property that are enforceable also against third parties".

[41] Art.32.

[42] Guide to Enactment, para.198. "For example, an unsecured creditor has received 5 per cent of its claim in a foreign proceeding; that creditor also participates in the insolvency proceeding in the enacting State, where the rate of distribution is 15 per cent; in order to put the creditor in the equal position as the other creditors in the enacting State, the creditor would receive 10 per cent of its claim in the enacting State". *ibid.* Art.32 does not affect the ranking of claims as established by British insolvency law: *ibid.*, para.199.

[43] Reg.3(1); Model Law, Arts 2(a), 2(b), 5.

insolvency law.[44] Rule 189F reproduces Art.5 of the Model Law whereby a British insolvency officeholder is authorised to act in a foreign State on behalf of a proceeding under British insolvency law, as permitted by the applicable foreign law. Article 5 thus confers, as a matter of the law of Great Britain, capacity on the British officeholder to act in a foreign State. The extent to which the officeholder will be permitted so to act, what actions he may take and the assistance he may obtain will, however, obviously depend, ultimately, on the law of the relevant foreign State and this is made clear in Art.5 by providing that the authority of the officeholder to act is "as permitted by the foreign applicable law".

**S30–425** Where the foreign State has itself enacted the Model Law the assistance, etc. available to the British officeholder will depend on the version of the Model Law as enacted in that foreign State. This may not be identical with the original version of the Model Law (as the Cross-Border Insolvency Regulations 2006 illustrate) or with the version of the Model Law, as implemented in Great Britain in the 2006 Regulations. Further, some foreign States, in implementing the Model Law, have imposed a condition of reciprocity whereby the foreign court or officeholder seeking assistance may only engage with the Model Law in the foreign State if the State from which the foreign court or officeholder comes has itself implemented the Model Law.[45] This is not problematic as far as a British court or officeholder is concerned since the 2006 Regulations provide clear proof of implementation. It should be noted, however, that there is no condition of reciprocity attached to the Model Law, as implemented in Great Britain.

It is also possible that the British officeholder will be permitted to act in a foreign State even if that State has not implemented the Model Law, either because the insolvency law of that State so permits or because other cooperative procedures may be available under the law of the foreign State.[46]

---

[44] Above, Rule 189A.

[45] See Fletcher, Supplement, paras 8.101, 8.103. For discussion of enactment of the Model Law in other States, see Look Chan Ho (ed.), *Cross-Border Insolvency: A Commentary on the UNCITRAL Model Law* (2006); Wessels, *International Insolvency Law* 2nd edn (2006).

[46] See Guide to Enactment, para.85. *cf. Bloom v Harms Offshore AHT* [2009] EWCA Civ 632, [2010] Ch. 187.

## CHAPTER 31

# BANKRUPTCY

### 1. ENGLISH BANKRUPTCIES NOT FALLING WITHIN COUNCIL REGULATION (EC) 1346/2000 ON INSOLVENCY PROCEEDINGS

#### A. *Jurisdiction of the English Courts*

NOTE 2. Civil Jurisdiction and Judgments Act 1982 Sch. 3C is repealed by SI 2009/3131, reg. 25. The revised Lugano Convention does not apply to bankruptcy: Art.1(2)(b). **31R–001**

The UNCITRAL Model Law on Cross-Border Insolvency, as implemented in Great Britain in the Cross-Border Insolvency Regulations 2006, applies to bankruptcy. It is discussed in detail in Ch.30 of this Supplement: see above, paras S30R–344 *et seq.* For particular cases on bankruptcy and the Model Law, see *Thurmond v Rajapakse* [2008] B.P.I.R 283 (Mr Registrar Nicholls); *Re Rivkin* [2008] EWHC 2609 (Ch.), [2009] B.P.I.R. 153; *Hynd's Trustee, Petitioner* [2009] CSOH 76, 2009 S.C. 593.

NOTE 3. For further amendments to the lists contained in Annexes A, B and C to Council Regulation (EC) on Insolvency Proceedings, see above, entry at para.30–151, nn.57 and 58.

NOTE 4. In relation to the functions of recognition of foreign proceedings and co-operation with foreign courts pursuant to the UNCITRAL Model Law, jurisdiction is assigned to the Chancery Division of the High Court: see Cross-Border Insolvency Regulations 2006 Sch.1 (hereafter Model Law), Art.4.

NOTES 17 and 18. For a recent case on domicile in the context of bankruptcy, see *Henwood v Barlow Clowes International Ltd* [2008] EWCA Civ 577, [2008] B.P.I.R. 778. **31–005**

NOTE 23. Add at end: *Cross Construction Sussex Ltd v Tseliki* [2006] EWHC 1056 (Ch.), [2006] B.P.I.R. 888; *Stojevic v Komercni Banka AS* [2006] EWHC 3447 (Ch.), [2007] B.P.I.R. 141. **31–008**

NOTE 42. See now, CPR Pt 6, rr.6.36 *et seq.* and PD6B, inserted by SI 2008/2178. **31–013**

NOTE 48. Add: See *Buchler v Al-Midani (No.2)* [2005] EWHC 3183 (Ch.), [2006] B.P.I.R. 867. **31–014**

**31–019** Note 66. *Cf. Re HIH Casualty and General Insurance Ltd.* [2008] UKHL 21, [2008] 1 W.L.R. 852 above, entry at para.30–081, nn.57–65; *Rubin v Eurofinance SA* [2010] EWCA Civ 895 at [43] *et seq.*

**31–025** Note 66. Add: See *Bloom v Harms Offshore AHT* [2009] EWCA Civ 632, [2010] Ch. 187 at [22]–[23].

**31–027** Note 3. See *Rubin v Eurofinance SA* [2010] EWCA Civ 895 at [43] *et seq.* And see previous entry.

B. *Effect of an English Bankruptcy as an Assignment of Property*

**31–030** Note 8. Add: *cf.* UNCITRAL Model Law, Art.13(3), above, para.S30–381.

**31–032** Note 9. Add: *cf. R v R (Bankruptcy Jurisdiction Concerning Real Property Abroad*) [2007] EWHC 2589 (Fam.), [2008] 2 F.L.R. 474.

**31–034** Note 13. As to the position under the UNCITRAL Model Law see above, para.S30–368. See *Hynd's Trustee, Petitioner,* [2009] CSOH 76, 2009 S.C. 593.

Note 14. *Re HIH Casualty and General Insurance Ltd* [2005] EWHC 2125 (Ch.), [2006] 2 All E.R. 671 was affirmed [2006] EWCA Civ 732, [2007] 1 All E.R. 177 by the Court of Appeal whose decision has been reversed by the House of Lords, [2008] UKHL 21, [2008] 1 W.L.R. 852.

**31–035** Note 18. See previous entry.

**31–036** Note 20. See entry at para.31–034, n.14, above.

Add: *ML Ubase Holdings Co Ltd v Trigem Computer Inc* [2007] NSWSC 859.

**31–038** Notes 25 and 26. Add: *ML Ubase Holdings Ltd v Trigem Computer Inc*, above.

Note 32. Add at end: But *cf. Bloom v Harms Offshore AHT* [2009] EWCA Civ 632, [2010] Ch. 187.

**31–040** Note 33. See entry at para.31–034, n.14, above.

Add: *ML Ubase Holdings Co Ltd v Trigem Computer Inc*, above.

**31–041** Note 35. Add at end: *cf.* UNCITRAL Model Law, Art.32, above, para.S30–422.

C. *Choice of Law*

NOTE 44. *Re HIH Casualty and General Insurance Ltd* [2005] EWHC 2125 (Ch.), [2006] 2 All E.R. 671 was affirmed [2006] EWCA Civ 732, [2007] 1 All E.R. 177 by the Court of Appeal, whose decision was reversed by the House of Lords, [2008] UKHL 21, [2008]1 W.L.R. 852. **31R–044**

Add: See generally *Re HIH Casualty and General Insurance Ltd* [2008] UKHL 21, [2008] 1 W.L.R. 852.

NOTE 57. But see now *Re HIH Casualty and General Insurance Ltd* [2008] UKHL 21, [2008] 1 W.L.R. 852, entry at para.30–081, nn.59–65. **31–048**

NOTE 60. Add: Look Chan Ho (2008) 20 Sing. Acad. L.J. 343. **31–049**

NOTE 62. On "Article 23 applications" under the UNCITRAL Model Law, see above, paras S30–402 *et seq.* As to relief under Arts 21 and 22 of the Model Law see *Re Rivkin* [2008] EWHC 2009 (Ch.), [2009] B.P.I.R. 153, and above, para. S30–391.

2. FOREIGN BANKRUPTCIES NOT FALLING WITHIN COUNCIL REGULATION (EC) 1346/2000 ON INSOLVENCY PROCEEDINGS

A. *Jurisdiction of Foreign Courts*

See generally, *Rubin v Eurofinance SA* [2010] EWCA Civ 632. **31R–059**

NOTE 89. For the position under the UNCITRAL Model Law, see above, para.S30–368; *Hynd's Trustee, Petitioner* [2009] CSOH 76, 2009 S.C. 593. **31–060**

NOTE 95. See also *Re HIH Casualty and General Insurance Ltd* [2008] UKHL 21, [2008] 1 W.L.R. 852 at [6]. And above, entry at para.31R–059. **31–064**

B. *Effect in England of Foreign Bankruptcy as an Assignment of Property*

(1) BANKRUPTCY IN SCOTLAND OR NORTHERN IRELAND

NOTE 16. For the position under the UNCITRAL Model Law, see above, para.S30–368; *Hynd's Trustee, Petitioner* [2009] CSOH 76, 2009 S.C. 593. **31–071**

(2) BANKRUPTCY IN ANY OTHER COUNTRY

NOTES 29–32. Add: *ML Ubase Holdings Co Ltd v Trigem Computer Inc* [2007] NSWSC 859. **31–076**

C. *Effect in England of Foreign Bankruptcy as a Discharge of Debts*

NOTE 78. Add: See also *AWB (Geneva) SA v North American Steamships Ltd* [2007] EWCA Civ 739, [2007] 2 Lloyd's Rep. 315. **31–093**

## 3. BANKRUPTCIES FALLING WITHIN COUNCIL REGULATION (EC) 1346/2000 ON INSOLVENCY PROCEEDINGS

### B. *International Jurisdiction*

**31–107** NOTE 10. Add: *Stojevic v Komercni Banka* [2006] EWHC 1056 (Ch.), [2007] B.P.I.R. 141; *Official Receiver v Eichler* [2007] B.P.I.R. 1636.

NOTE 13 and accompanying text. In Case C–1/04 *Staubitz-Schreiber* [2006] E.C.R. I–701, the European Court came to the same conclusion as that of Colomer A–G. which is set out in the text: see above, entry at paras 30–169—30–170, nn.61–75 and text thereto.

NOTE 14. The need to determine the debtor's centre of main interests did not arise in Case C–1/04 *Staubitz-Schreiber*, above.

NOTE 16. Add: *Cross Construction Sussex Ltd v Tseliki* [2006] EWHC 1056 (Ch.), [2006] B.P.I.R. 888; *Stojevic v Komercni Banka AS* [2006] EWHC 3447 (Ch.), [2007] B.P.I.R. 141. In the latter case it was emphasised that it would be wrong to equate an individual debtor's indirect economic interests in a company, as such, with his own interests. See also *Official Receiver v Eichler* [2007] B.P.I.R. 1636.

NOTE 18. Add in line 1: *Cross Construction Sussex Ltd v Tseliki,* above; *Stojevic v Komercni Banka AS,* above; *Official Receiver v Eichler*, above.

NOTE 19. See previous entry.

NOTE 20. Add: Case C–341/04 *Eurofood IFSC Ltd* [2006] E.C.R. I–3813, [2006] Ch. 508.

**31–108** NOTES 24, 25 and 26. In Case C–1/04 *Staubitz-Schreiber*, above, the European Court held, in relation to Art.3(1) of the Regulation, that where the debtor changes his centre of main interests between the time of a request to open proceedings and the time of the opening of those proceedings, jurisdiction is retained by the court to which the request is made. In this respect, the decision of the Court of Appeal in *Shierson v Vlieland-Boddy* [2005] EWCA Civ 974, [2005] 1 W.L.R. 3966, discussed in the text, can no longer stand. See also *Official Receiver v Eichler* above.

**31–109** NOTE 30. The conclusion that the debtor in *Shierson v Vlieland-Boddy*, above, had an "establishment" in England because he was carrying on the activity of managing and letting a business property in England, held in the name of a "front", in the form of a company incorporated in the British Virgin Islands, so that the debtor had a "place of operations where the debtor carries out a non-transitory economic activity with human means and goods" in England, is criticised by Moss (2006) 19 Insolvency Intelligence 20. In such a case it is difficult to conclude that the business property is a "place of operations" *of the debtor* and, further, difficult to conclude that mere activity of the debtor alone constitutes "human means".

### C. *Choice of Law*

NOTE 40. See entry at para. 30R–197, above. **31–112**

### D. *Recognition of Insolvency Proceedings*

NOTE 51. See above, entries at paras 30R–197 and 30–285. **31–116**

NOTES 54 and 55. See above, entries at paras 30–327 and 30–328.

## CHAPTER 32

# CONTRACTS. GENERAL RULES

**The Rome I Regulation applies to contracts concluded as from December 17, 2009.**

### 1. THE LAW GOVERNING A CONTRACT

32–002 By Contracts (Applicable Law) Act 1990, s.4A (added by SI 2009/3064, reg.2), the 1990 Act is disapplied where the Rome I Regulation applies.

32–013 Regulation (EC) 593/2008 of the European Parliament and of the Council of June 17, 2008 on the law applicable to contractual obligations (Rome I) ("the Rome I Regulation") replaced the Rome Convention when it came into force on December 17, 2009: [2008] O.J. L177/6. It applies to contracts concluded as from December 17, 2009 (Art.28, as amended by a corrigendum [2009] O.J. L307/87). The Rome I Regulation is reproduced in Appendix 2 to this Supplement. See Plender and Wilderspin, *The European Private International Law of Obligations* (3rd ed 2009), Chaps. 4–15; *Rome I Regulation: the Law Applicable to Contractual Relations in Europe* (ed. Leible and Ferrari, 2009); Bonomi (2008) 10 Yb. P.I.L. 165; Lein, *ibid.* 177; Lagarde and Tenenbaum, 2008 *Rev. Crit.* 727; Crawford, 2010 S.L.T. 17.

By the Law Applicable to Contractual Obligations (England and Wales and Northern Ireland) Regulations 2009 (SI 2009/3064), Reg.5, the Rome I Regulation applies as between the different parts of the United Kingdom (except as regards insurance contracts falling within Art.7 of the Rome I Regulation). For Scotland see SSI 2009/410.

In May 2006 the United Kingdom Government decided that it would not opt in to the Rome I proposal. One of the main reasons was that in its original proposal, the Commission proposed a provision in similar terms to that of Art. 7(1) of the Rome Convention which would not have been subject to any right of reservation by any Member State. The prospect of applying this provision gave rise to widespread concern in commercial circles, particularly in the City of London. These concerns turned on the likelihood of significant legal uncertainty and the extent to which the provision would undermine the key principle of party autonomy: see See Ministry of Justice, *Rome I—Should the UK Opt in?* Consultation Paper CP05/08, April 2, 2008, especially paras 79–81.

But after further negotiations on the text of the draft Regulation (and in particular on what became Art.9), in July 2008 the United Kingdom Government announced its intention to opt into the Regulation, and notified the European Commission, which decided that the Rome I Regulation would apply to the United Kingdom: Decision 2009/26/EC [2009] O.J. L10/22.

In the Rome I Regulation, the term "Member State" normally means Member States to which the Regulation applies. But in Art.3(4) (entry at para.32–132, below) and Art.7 (entries at 33R–136, 33R–158, and 33R–189, below) the term means all the Member States: Art.1(4). Article 22(1) provides that in States comprising several territorial units with their own rules on contractual obligations, each unit is to be considered as a country for the purposes of identifying the applicable law, but by Art.22(2) a Member State is not obliged to apply the Regulation to conflicts solely between the laws of such units.

Regulation (EC) 662/2009 of the European Parliament and of the Council establishes a procedure for the negotiation and conclusion of agreements between Member States and third countries on particular matters concerning the law applicable to contractual and non-contractual obligations: [2009] O.J. L200/25.

Recital (7) of the Rome I Regulation states that the substantive scope and the provisions of the Regulation should be consistent with the Judgments Regulation and the Rome II Regulation. **32–023**

Recital (10) of the Regulation states that obligations arising out of dealings prior to the conclusion of the contract are covered by Art.12 of the Rome II Regulation (below, entry at paras S35–242 *et seq.*), and that such obligations should therefore be excluded from the scope of the Rome I Regulation.

Final sentence. CPR, r.6.20(5)(c) has been replaced by CPR PD6B, para.3.1(6)(c). **32–027**

Article 1(1) of the Rome I Regulation provides that it is to apply, in situations involving a conflict of laws, to contractual obligations in civil and commercial matters, and that it does not apply, in particular, to revenue, customs or administrative matters. The equivalent provision in the Rome Convention (Art.1(1)) refers to "any situation involving a choice between the laws of different countries" and does not contain any specific exclusion of revenue, customs or administrative matters.

By Art.1(2) the following are excluded from the scope of the Regulation:

(a) Questions involving the status or legal capacity of natural persons, without prejudice to Art.13 (which deals with incapacity). This is in the same terms as Art.1(2)(a) of the Rome Convention.

(b) Obligations arising out of family relationships and relationships deemed by the law applicable to such relationships to have comparable effects, including maintenance obligations. Recital (8) states that family relationships should cover parentage, marriage, affinity and collateral relatives, and that the reference in Art.1(2) to relationships having comparable effects to marriage and other family relationships should be interpreted in accordance with the law of the Member State in which the court is seised. This is an expanded version of part of Art.1(2)(b) of the Rome Convention, which excluded "rights and duties arising out of a family relationship, parentage, marriage or affinity, including maintenance obligations in respect of children who are not legitimate".

(c) Obligations arising out of matrimonial property regimes, property relationships deemed by the law applicable to such relationships to have comparable effects to marriage, and wills and succession. This replaces the Rome Convention exclusion in Art.1(2)(b) of "wills and succession, rights in property arising out of a matrimonial relationship . . . ".

(d) Obligations arising under bills of exchange, cheques and promissory notes and other negotiable instruments to the extent that the obligations under such other negotiable instruments arise out of their negotiable character. This is the same as the Rome Convention, Art.1(2)(c).

(e) Arbitration agreements and agreements on the choice of court. This is the same as the Rome Convention, Art.1(2)(d).

(f) Questions governed by the law of companies and other bodies, corporate or unincorporated, such as the creation, by registration or otherwise, legal capacity, internal organisation or winding-up of companies and other bodies, corporate or unincorporated, and the personal liability of officers and members as such for the obligations of the company or body. This is the same as the Rome Convention, Art.1(2)(e).

(g) The question whether an agent is able to bind a principal, or an organ to bind a company or other body corporate or unincorporated, in relation to a third party. This is the same as the Rome Convention, Art.1(2)(f).

(h) The constitution of trusts and the relationship between settlors, trustees and beneficiaries. This is the same as the Rome Convention, Art.1(2)(g).

(i) Obligations arising out of dealings prior to the conclusion of a contract. This is new. As Recital (10) to the Rome I Regulation states, obligations arising out of dealings prior to the conclusion of the contract are covered by Art.12 of the Rome II Regulation (below, paras S35–242 *et seq.*) and should therefore be excluded from the scope of the Rome I Regulation.

(j) Insurance contracts arising out of operations carried out by organisations other than undertakings referred to in Art.2 of Directive 2002/83/EC of the European Parliament and of the Council of November 5, 2002 concerning life assurance the object of which is to provide benefits for employed or self-employed persons belonging to an undertaking or group of undertakings, or to a trade or group of trades, in the event of death or survival or of discontinuance or curtailment of activity, or of sickness related to work or accidents at work.

**Determination of habitual residence.** Recital (39) of the Rome I Regulation states that for the sake of legal certainty there should be a clear definition of habitual residence, in particular for companies and other bodies, corporate or unincorporated; and that unlike Art.60(1) of the Judgments Regulation the conflict of laws rule in the Rome I Regulation should proceed on the basis of a single criterion; otherwise, the parties would be unable to foresee the law applicable to their situation.

Accordingly Art.19 (which has no counterpart in the Rome Convention) provides that for the purposes of the Regulation, the habitual residence of companies and other bodies, corporate or unincorporated, shall be the place of central administration. The habitual residence of a natural person acting in the course of his business activity shall be his principal place of business. Where the contract is concluded in the course of the operations of a branch, agency or any other establishment, or if, under the contract, performance is the responsibility of such a branch, agency or establishment, the place where the branch, agency or any other establishment is located shall be treated as the place of habitual residence.

By Art.19(3) for the purposes of determining the habitual residence, the relevant point in time shall be the time of the conclusion of the contract.

*Particular Contracts.* Recital (23) of the Rome I Regulation states that as regards contracts concluded with parties regarded as being weaker, those parties should be protected by conflict of laws rules that are more favourable to their interests than the general rules, and special provision is made for contracts of carriage (Art.5), consumer contracts (Art.6), insurance contracts (Art.7), and individual employment contracts (Art.8). See the entries in Chap.33 below in relation to such contracts.

Article 2 of the Rome I Regulation provides that any law specified by the Regulation shall be applied whether or not it is the law of a Member State. This is in substance the same as Rome Convention, Art.2. **32–028**

Article 1(3) of the Rome I Regulation provides that it shall not apply to evidence and procedure, without prejudice to Art.18. This is the same as the Rome Convention, Art.1(2))h). **32–041**

See Art.1(2)(j) of the Rome I Regulation. **32–042**

Article 20 of the Rome I Regulation provides that the application of the law of any country specified by the Regulation means the application of the rules of law in force in that country other than its rules of private international law, unless provided otherwise in the Regulation. This is substantially similar to the Rome Convention, Art.15. **32–043**

32–047— 32–053 In Case C–133/08 *Intercontainer Interfrigo SC (ICF) v Balkenende Oosthuizen BV* [2010] 3 W.L.R. 24 the European Court emphasised that the rule providing for the severance of a contract was of an exceptional nature. The objective of the Rome Convention to raise the level of legal certainty by fortifying confidence in the stability of the relationships between the parties to the contract could not be attained if the system for determining the applicable law was unclear and that law could not be predicted with some degree of certainty. The possibility of separating a contract into a number of parts in order to make it subject to a number of laws ran counter to the objectives of the Convention and must be allowed only where there were a number of parts to the contract which may be regarded as independent of each other. In order to determine whether a part of a contract might be made subject to a different law it was necessary to ascertain whether the object of that part was independent in relation to the purpose of the rest of the contract. If that was the case, each part of a contract must be made subject to one single law. In particular, therefore, the rules relating to the prescription of a right must fall under the same legal system as that applied to the corresponding obligation. In that regard, it must be borne in mind that, under Art.10(1)(d) of the Convention, the law applicable to a contract governed in particular the prescription of obligations. Consequently, a part of a contract may be governed by a law other than that applied to the rest of the contract only where the object of that part was independent.

32–055 Article 18(1) of the Rome I Regulation provides that the law governing a contractual obligation under the Regulation shall apply to the extent that, in matters of contractual obligations, it contains rules which raise presumptions of law or determine the burden of proof. This is substantially similar to the Rome Convention, Art.14(1).

A contract or an act intended to have legal effect may be proved by any mode of proof recognised by the law of the forum or by any of the laws referred to in Art.11 under which that contract or act is formally valid, provided that such mode of proof can be administered by the forum: Art.18(2). This is substantially similar to the Rome Convention, Art.14(2).

## 2. DETERMINATION OF THE APPLICABLE LAW

32R–061 A choice of law is not a contractual promise that such law will be applied: *Ace Insurance Ltd v Moose Enterprise Pty Ltd* [2009] NSWSC 724 (noted Yeo [2010] L.M.C.L.Q. 194), not adopting the suggestion by Briggs, *Agreements On Jurisdiction and Choice of Law* (2008), para.11.52 that if a party to an agreement brings proceedings before a court or tribunal which will not apply the law which was promised, so far as the parties were concerned, to govern, and was agreed by them to be applicable in the resolution of disputes, he will have incapacitated himself from performing that which was undertaken to be done, and be in breach of contract. The court confirmed that there was a well-established distinction between a choice of jurisdiction clause, which imposed contractual obligations on the parties, and a choice of law clause, which was merely declaratory of their intent as to the applicable legal system. Not being promissory in effect, a choice of law clause did not found implied negative stipulations.

Recital (11) of the Rome I Regulation states that the parties' freedom to choose the applicable law should be one of the cornerstones of the system of conflict of laws rules in matters of contractual obligations. **32–062**

By Art.3(1) a contract shall be governed by the law chosen by the parties. The choice shall be made expressly or clearly demonstrated by the terms of the contract or the circumstances of the case.

The terms of this provision are substantially the same as those in Art.3 of the Rome Convention. But Recital (12) contains the useful clarification (which reflects the position under English law) that an agreement between the parties to confer on one or more courts or tribunals of a Member State exclusive jurisdiction to determine disputes under the contract should be one of the factors to be taken into account in determining whether a choice of law has been clearly demonstrated.

By Art.3(5) the existence and validity of the consent of the parties as to the choice of the applicable law shall be determined in accordance with the provisions of Arts 10, 11 and 13.

See entry at para.32–132, below. **32–070**

This paragraph was approved in *Halpern v Halpern (Nos 1 and 2)* [2007] EWCA Civ 291, [2008] Q.B. 195 (on which see Briggs (2007) 78 B.Y.I.L. 624), where the issue was whether a compromise agreement to settle disputes in an arbitration could be governed by Jewish law (Halacha). Consequently as a matter of English conflict of laws principles there could be no question of Jewish law being agreed either expressly or by implication as the applicable law of the contract. The applicable law was English law. But Jewish law might be relied on as part of the contractual framework, where there was distinct body of Jewish law. Points which arose outside questions of interpretation, such as duress, mistake, frustration and the consequences thereof would be a matter of English law as the applicable law of the contract. But as an aid to interpretation, the context of the compromise, including the fact that it was settling disputes, the subject of an arbitration, which was applying Jewish law, could make Jewish law material. *Cf. Investment Dar Company KSCC v Blom Developments Bank Sal* [2009] EWHC 3545 (Ch.) (Sharia law). **32–081**

Recital (13) of the Rome I Regulation states that the Regulation does not preclude parties from incorporating by reference into their contract a non-State body of law or an international convention. This is a reference to incorporation and not choice of law.

NOTE 98. The Rome I Regulation contains no such provision.

**32–083** Article 3(1) of the Rome I Regulation provides that by their choice the parties can select the law applicable to the whole or to part only of the contract.

**32–084** By Art.3(2) of the Rome I Regulation the parties may at any time agree to subject the contract to a law other than that which previously governed it, whether as a result of an earlier choice made under this Article or of other provisions of this Regulation. Any change in the law to be applied that is made after the conclusion of the contract shall not prejudice its formal validity under Art.11 or adversely affect the rights of third parties.

**32–086** CPR, r.6.20 has been replaced by CPR PD6B, para.3.1.

**32–088** Recital (13) of the Rome I Regulation states that the Regulation does not preclude parties from incorporating by reference into their contract a non-State body of law or an international convention.

**32–089** NOTE 21. See *Halpern v Halpern* (*Nos 1 and 2*), above, entry at para.32–081.

**32–093** NOTE 38. See *FR Lurssen Werft GmbH & Co KG v Halle* [2010] EWCA Civ. 587, [2010] 2 Lloyd's Rep. 20; *Emeraldian LP v Wellmix Shipping Ltd* [2010] EWHC 1411 (Comm.).

**32R–107** Recital (16) of the Rome I Regulation states that to contribute to the general objective of the Regulation, legal certainty in the European judicial area, the conflict of laws rules should be highly foreseeable; but the courts should, however, retain a degree of discretion to determine the law that is most closely connected to the situation.

Article 4(1) (on which see Ferrari, 2009 *Rev. Crit.* 459) provides that to the extent that the law applicable to the contract has not been chosen in accordance with Art.3, the law governing the contract shall be determined as follows: (a) a contract for the sale of goods shall be governed by the law of the country where the seller has his habitual residence; (b) a contract for the provision of services shall be governed by the law of the country where the service provider has his habitual residence; (c)/(d) a contract relating to a right *in rem* in immovable property or to a tenancy of immovable property shall be governed by the law of the country where the property is situated; but a tenancy of immovable property concluded for temporary private use for a period of no more than six consecutive months shall be governed by the law of the country where the landlord has his habitual residence, provided that the tenant is a natural person and has his habitual residence in the same country; (e) a franchise contract shall be governed by the law of the country where the franchisee has his habitual residence; (f) a distribution contract shall be governed by the law of the country where the distributor has his habitual residence; (g) a contract for the sale of goods by auction shall be governed by the law of the country where the auction takes place, if such a place can be determined; (h) a contract concluded within a multilateral system which brings together or facilitates the bringing together of multiple third-party buying and selling interests in financial instruments, as defined by Art.4(1), point (17) of Directive 2004/39/EC, in accordance with non-discretionary rules and governed by a single law, shall be governed by that law. See Ancel (2008) 10 Yb. P.I.L. 221 (and also 2008 *Rev. Crit.* 561) (Rome I Regulation and distribution agreements); Garcia Gutierrez, *ibid.* 233 (Rome I Regulation and franchise agreements); Garcimartin Alferez (2008) 10 Yb. P.I.L. 245 (Rome I Regulation and financial market contracts).

Where the contract is not covered by Art.4(1) or where the elements of the contract would be covered by more than one of Art.4(1)(a)–(h) the contract shall be governed by the law of the country where the party required to effect the characteristic performance of the contract has his habitual residence: Art.4(2).

Where it is clear from all the circumstances of the case that the contract is manifestly more closely connected with a country other than that indicated in Arts 4(1) or 4(2), the law of that other country shall apply: Art.4(3).

Where the law applicable cannot be determined pursuant to Arts 4(1) or 4(2), the contract shall be governed by the law of the country with which it is most closely connected: Art.4(4).

Recital (1) restates or elaborates upon some of these provisions. It states that where there has been no choice of law, the applicable law should be determined in accordance with the rule specified for the particular type of contract. Where the contract cannot be categorised as being one of the specified types or where its elements fall within more than one of the specified types, it should be governed by the law of the country where the party required to effect the characteristic performance of the contract has his habitual residence. In the case of a contract consisting of a bundle of rights and obligations capable of being categorised as falling within more than one of the specified types of contract, the characteristic performance of the contract should be determined having regard to its centre of gravity. Recital (20) states that where the contract is manifestly more closely connected with a country other than that indicated in Art.4(1) or (2), an escape clause should provide that the law of that other country is to apply. In order to determine that country, account should be taken, *inter alia*, of whether the contract in question has a very close relationship with another contract or contracts. Recital (21) says that in the absence of choice, where the applicable law cannot be determined either on the basis of the fact that the contract can be categorised as one of the specified types or as being the law of the country of habitual residence of the party required to effect the characteristic performance of the contract, the contract should be governed by the law of the country with which it is most closely connected. In order to determine that country, account should be taken, *inter alia*, of whether the contract in question has a very close relationship with another contract or contracts.

See entry at paras 32–047—32–053, above. **32–111**

**32–113** NOTE 91. Add: *Habib Bank Ltd v Central Bank of Sudan* [2006] EWHC 1767 (Comm.), [2006] 2 Lloyd's Rep. 412; see also *Albon v Naza Motor Trading Sdn Bhd* [2007] EWHC 9 (Ch.), [2007] 1 W.L.R. 2489 (presumption not displaced); *Gorjat v Gorjat* [2010] EWHC 1537 (Ch.) (*inter vivos* assignment by way of gift).

**32–116** Second sentence. See, e.g. *Ark Therapeutics plc v True North Capital Ltd* [2005] EWHC 1585 (Comm.), [2006] 1 All E.R. (Comm.) 138.

NOTE 4. See Garcimartin Alferez (2008) 10 Yb. P.I.L. 245 (Rome I Regulation and financial market contracts).

**32–117** NOTE 9. See also Ancel (2008) 10 Yb. P.I.L. 221 (and also 2008 *Rev. Crit.* 561) (Rome I Regulation and distribution agreements); Garcia Gutierrez, *ibid.* 233 (Rome I Regulation and franchise agreements).

**32–121—32–123** Articles 5 to 8 of the Rome I Regulation contain specific rules for the determination of the applicable law of particular types of contract: contracts for the carriage of goods and passengers (Art.5); consumer contracts (Art.6); insurance contracts (Art.7); and individual employment contracts (Art.8). These are dealt with in the entries to Chap.33, below.

**32–122** See Case C–133/08 *Intercontainer Interfrigo (ICF) SC v Balkenende Oosthuizen BV* [2010] 3 W.L.R. 24, entry at para.32–125, below.

**32–124** NOTE 22. See also *Emeraldian LP v Wellmix Shipping Ltd* [2010] EWHC 1411 (Comm.).

**32–125** Case C–133/08 *Intercontainer Interfrigo SC (ICF) v Balkenende Oosthuizen BV* [2010] 3 W.L.R. 24 concerned Arts 4(4) and 4(5) of the Rome Convention (see now Arts 5 and 4(4) of the Rome I Regulation). A contract was made in the context of a project for a train connection for freight traffic between Amsterdam and Frankfurt am Main (Germany). A Belgian company (ICF) entered into a charterparty with two Dutch companies (Balkenende and MIC) The contract provided, inter alia, that ICF was to make train wagons available to MIC and would ensure their transport via the rail network. MIC, which had hired out the load capacity to third parties, was responsible for all operational aspects of the transport of the goods concerned. The parties did not enter into any written contract, but they gave effect, during a limited period, to what had been agreed between them. ICF sent to MIC a written draft contract, which contained a clause stating that Belgian law had been chosen as the law applicable. That draft was never signed by any of the parties to the agreement. ICF sued Balkenende and MIC in the Netherlands for unpaid invoices. Balkenende and MIC claimed that the action was time-barred under Dutch law, which they said was the law applicable to the contract. ICF claimed that the applicable law was Belgian law, under which the claim was not time-barred.

The Hoge Raad asked (among other questions) whether the presumptions in Art.4 would be disregarded under Art.4(5), on the basis that it appeared from the circumstances as a whole that the contract was more closely connected with another country, only if it was evident from the circumstances in their totality that the connecting criteria indicated therein did not have any genuine connecting value, or if it was clear therefrom that there was a stronger connection with some other country. The Court's answer was that Art.4(5) must be construed as meaning that, where it is clear from the circumstances as a whole that the contract is more closely connected with a country other than that determined on the basis of one of the criteria set out in Arts 4(2) to (4), it is for the court to disregard those criteria and apply the law of the country with which the contract is most closely connected.

NOTE 22. See also *Pablo Star Ltd v Emirates Integrated Telecommunications Co PJSC* [2009] EWCA Civ 1044; *Commercial Marine Piling Ltd v Pierse Contracting Ltd* [2009] EWHC 2241 (TCC), [2009] 2 Lloyd's Rep. 659. **32–126**

## 3. MANDATORY RULES

See generally Chong (2006) 2 J. Priv. Int. L. 27; Dickinson (2007) 3 J. Priv. Int. L. 53; Bonomi (2008) 10 Yb. P.I.L. 285; Hellner (2009) 5 J Priv. Int. L. 447. **32R–131**

Article 3(3) of the Rome I Regulation provides that where all other elements relevant to the situation at the time of the choice are located in a country other than the country whose law has been chosen, the choice of the parties shall not prejudice the application of provisions of the law of that other country which cannot be derogated from by agreement. Recital (15) states that this rule should apply whether or not the choice of law was accompanied by a choice of court or tribunal; and that whereas no substantial change was intended as compared with Art. 3(3) of the Rome Convention, the wording of the Rome I Regulation was aligned as far as possible with Art.14 of the Rome II Regulation. **32–132**

Article 3(4) provides that where all other elements relevant to the situation at the time of the choice are located in one or more Member States, the parties' choice of applicable law other than that of a Member State shall not prejudice the application of provisions of Community law, where appropriate as implemented in the Member State of the forum, which cannot be derogated from by agreement. For this purpose Member State includes not only Member States to which the Regulation applies, but means all the Member States of the European Union, and thus will apply where the elements are located in, e.g. Denmark: see Art.1(4).

Recital (37) states that considerations of public interest justify giving the courts of the Member States the possibility, in exceptional circumstances, of applying exceptions based on public policy and overriding mandatory provisions. The concept of "overriding mandatory provisions" should be distinguished from the expression "provisions which cannot be derogated from by agreement" and should be construed more restrictively.

Article 9 deals with "overriding mandatory provisions", by which is meant (Art.9(1)) provisions the respect for which is regarded as crucial by a country for safeguarding its public interests, such as its political, social or economic organisation, to such an extent that they are applicable to any situation falling within their scope, irrespective of the law otherwise applicable to the contract under this Regulation.

By Art.9(2) nothing in the Regulation is to restrict the application of the overriding mandatory provisions of the law of the forum.

By Art.9(3) effect may be given to the overriding mandatory provisions of the law of the country where the obligations arising out of the contract have to be or have been performed, in so far as those overriding mandatory provisions render the performance of the contract unlawful. In considering whether to give effect to those provisions, regard shall be had to their nature and purpose and to the consequences of their application or non-application.

In its original proposal, the Commission proposed a provision in similar terms to that of Art.7(1) of the Rome Convention which, given the required uniform application of Council Regulations, would not have been subject to any right of reservation by any Member State. The prospect of applying this provision gave rise to widespread concern in commercial circles, particularly in the City of London. These concerns turned on the likelihood of significant legal uncertainty and the extent to which the provision would undermine the key principle of party autonomy.

This issue subsequently became a key factor in the United Kingdom Government's decision not to opt in to the Rome I proposal. The Government sought deletion of this proposal, but during the course of negotiations it became clear that it would not be possible to secure sufficient agreement on this amongst Member States as the majority already applied Art.7(1) of the Rome Convention. Discussions then focussed on finding a generally acceptable compromise that would be narrower in scope than the Commission's original proposal and would keep any legal uncertainty to a minimum. The final result of these negotiations was Art.9(3). The focus of Art.9(3) is on the application of certain rules of the country where the contract is to be or has been performed, which render the contractual performance unlawful. The United Kingdom Government took the view that Art.9(3) represented a satisfactory outcome to the negotiations on this provision. It reflected the English law position in the light of *Ralli Bros v Compania Naviera Sota y Aznar* [1920] 2 K.B. 287, and to that extent should not introduce any significant additional uncertainty into the law, and also constituted an improvement in terms of legal certainty over the existing law. It would remove the current uncertainty as to whether the European Court would consider that the old English jurisprudence could continue to be applied under the Convention in the light of the United Kingdom's reservation in respect of Art.7(1). In particular, it is unclear whether the *Ralli Bros* decision is consistent with that reservation and therefore properly remains available to our courts. It was also unclear whether *Foster v Driscoll* [1929] 1 K.B. 470 properly fell within the scope of the public policy rule and whether on that basis it remained available to United Kingdom courts in light of the reservation. Article 9(3) was formulated in terms which were sufficiently broad to cover situations of unlawful contractual performance where the applicable law was foreign. There was no such clarity under English law (see main work, para.32–146): see Ministry of Justice, *Rome I—Should the UK Opt in?* Consultation Paper CP05/08, April 2, 2008, paras 79–81.

See *Emeraldian LP v Wellmix Shipping Ltd* [2010] EWHC 1411 (Comm.) (Art.3(3) did not apply to letter issued by Chinese company guaranteeing charterparty governed by English law: not a case where all elements connected with China). **32–133**

NOTE 56. See *Lilly Icos Llc v 8pm Chemists Ltd* [2009] EWHC 1905 (Ch.), [2010] F.S.R. 95, [261]–[266] (principle not applicable to undertaking to court to pay damages). **32–144**

## 4. MATERIAL VALIDITY

By Art.10(1) of the Rome I Regulation the existence and validity of a contract, or of any term of a contract, shall be determined by the law which would govern it under the Regulation if the contract or term were valid. Nevertheless, a party, in order to establish that he did not consent, may rely upon the law of the country in which he has his habitual residence if it appears from the circumstances that it would not be reasonable to determine the effect of his conduct in accordance with the law specified in Art.10(1): see Art.10(2). *Cf.* Rome Convention, Art.8. **32R–154**

CPR, r.6.20(5)(c) has been replaced by CPR PD6B, para.3.1(6)(c). **32–159**

NOTE 95. See also *The Hornbay* [2006] EWHC 373 (Comm.), [2006] 2 Lloyd's Rep. 44. **32–163**

## 5. FORMAL VALIDITY

By Art.11(1) of the Rome I Regulation a contract concluded between persons who, or whose agents, are in the same country at the time of its conclusion is formally valid if it satisfies the formal requirements of the law which governs it in substance under the Regulation or of the law of the country where it is concluded. **32R–175**

Article 11(2) provides that a contract concluded between persons who, or whose agents, are in different countries at the time of its conclusion is formally valid if it satisfies the formal requirements of the law which governs it in substance under the Regulation, or of the law of either of the countries where either of the parties or their agent is present at the time of conclusion, or of the law of the country where either of the parties had his habitual residence at that time.

A unilateral act intended to have legal effect relating to an existing or contemplated contract is formally valid if it satisfies the formal requirements of the law which governs or would govern the contract in substance under this Regulation, or of the law of the country where the act was done, or of the law of the country where the person by whom it was done had his habitual residence at that time: Art.11(3).

By Art.11(5) a contract the subject matter of which is a right *in rem* in immovable property or a tenancy of immovable property shall be subject to the requirements of form of the law of the country where the property is situated if by that law: (a) those requirements are imposed irrespective of the country where the contract is concluded and irrespective of the law governing the contract; and (b) those requirements cannot be derogated from by agreement.

## 6. SCOPE OF THE APPLICABLE LAW

**32R–188** Article 12 of the Rome I Regulation provides that the applicable law governs in particular: (a) interpretation; (b) performance; (c) within the limits of the powers conferred on the court by its procedural law, the consequences of a total or partial breach of obligations, including the assessment of damages in so far as it is governed by rules of law; (d) the various ways of extinguishing obligations, and prescription and limitation of actions; (e) the consequences of nullity of the contract. This is the same as Art.10 of the Rome Convention, including the reference to the consequences of nullity of the contract, which had been the subject of a reservation to the Rome Convention by the United Kingdom.

Article 12(2) provides that in relation to the manner of performance and the steps to be taken in the event of defective performance, regard shall be had to the law of the country in which performance takes place.

By Art.16 (multiple liability) if a creditor has a claim against several debtors who are liable for the same claim, and one of the debtors has already satisfied the claim in whole or in part, the law governing the debtor's obligation towards the creditor also governs the debtor's right to claim recourse from the other debtors. The other debtors may rely on the defences they had against the creditor to the extent allowed by the law governing their obligations towards the creditor.

**32–198** Note 60. See also *Catalyst Recycling Ltd v Nickelhütte Aue GmbH* [2008] EWCA Civ 541, at [57].

Note 96. Companies Act 1985, s.427 is replaced by Companies Act 2006, s.900. **32–207**

Article 17 of the Rome I Regulation provides that where the right to set-off is not agreed by the parties, set-off shall be governed by the law applicable to the claim against which the right to set-off is asserted. **32–208**

By Art.14 of the Rome I Regulation the relationship between assignor and assignee under a voluntary assignment or contractual subrogation of a claim against another person (the debtor) shall be governed by the law that applies to the contract between the assignor and assignee under the Regulation. The law governing the assigned or subrogated claim shall determine its assignability, the relationship between the assignee and the debtor, the conditions under which the assignment or subrogation can be invoked against the debtor and whether the debtor's obligations have been discharged. The concept of assignment includes outright transfers of claims, transfers of claims by way of security and pledges or other security rights over claims: see also entry at para.24–050, above. **32–211**

Article 15 provides that where a person (the creditor) has a contractual claim against another (the debtor) and a third person has a duty to satisfy the creditor, or has in fact satisfied the creditor in discharge of that duty, the law which governs the third person's duty to satisfy the creditor shall determine whether and to what extent the third person is entitled to exercise against the debtor the rights which the creditor had against the debtor under the law governing their relationship.

## 7. CAPACITY

Article 13 of the Rome I Regulation provides that in a contract concluded between persons who are in the same country, a natural person who would have capacity under the law of that country may invoke his incapacity resulting from the law of another country, only if the other party to the contract was aware of that incapacity at the time of the conclusion of the contract or was not aware thereof as a result of negligence. *Cf.* Rome Convention, Art.11. See *Gorjat v Gorjat* [2010] EWHC 1537 (Ch.) (capacity to make an *inter vivos* assignment by way of gift). **32R–216**

Note 22. See also *Haugesund Kommune v Depfa ACS Bank* [2010] EWCA Civ. 579 on capacity of corporations.

## 8. PUBLIC POLICY

See *Duarte v Black and Decker Corp* [2007] EWHC 2720 (QB), [2008] 1 All E.R. (Comm.) 401, at [56]–[63] on Art.16 of the Rome Convention. **32–232**

Article 21 of the Rome I Regulation provides (in substantially the same terms as the Rome Convention, Art.16) that the application of a provision of the law of any country specified by the Regulation may be refused only if such application is manifestly incompatible with the public policy (ordre public) of the forum.

**32–239** Note 80. See *Lilly Icos Llc v 8pm Chemists Ltd* [2009] EWHC 1905 (Ch.), [2010] F.S.R. 95, [261]–[266] (principle not applicable to undertaking to court to pay damages).

## Chapter 33

# PARTICULAR CONTRACTS

## 1. CERTAIN CONSUMER CONTRACTS

Regulation (EC) 593/2008 of the European Parliament and of the Council of June 17, 2008 on the law applicable to contractual obligations (Rome I) ([2008] O.J. L177/6), hereafter the "Rome I Regulation" or "the Regulation", reproduced in Appendix 2 to this Supplement, makes fresh provision for the determination of the law applicable to certain consumer contracts which are concluded after December 17, 2009 (Arts 28, 29). These new provisions are contained in Art.6 of the Regulation, the main features of which are identified in what follows. See generally, Tang, *Electronic Consumer Contracts in the Conflict of Laws* (2009); Hill, *Cross-Border Consumer Contracts* (2008), especially Ch.12; *Chitty on Contracts* (30th edn 2008) Vol. 1, paras 30–231 *et seq.*; Ragno in *Rome I Regulation: The Law Applicable to Contractual Obligations in Europe* (ed. Leible and Ferrari, 2009), p.129; see also European Commission, *Proposal for a Directive of the European Parliament and of the Council on consumer rights,* COM (2008) 614. **33R–001**

Article 6(1) of the Regulation provides (subject to the exclusion of contracts of carriage (Art.5, below entries at paras 33R–263–33–278 and certain specific exclusions in Art.6(4)) that a contract concluded by a natural person for a purpose which can be regarded as being outside his trade or profession (the consumer) with another person acting in the exercise of his trade or profession (the professional) shall be governed by the law of the country where the consumer has his habitual residence, provided that the professional: (a) pursues his commercial or professional activities in the country where the consumer has his habitual residence, or (b) by any means, directs such activities to that country or to several countries including that country, and the contract falls within the scope of such activities. Notwithstanding this provision the parties may (Art.6(2) of the Regulation) choose the law applicable to a contract which fulfils the requirements of Art.6(1) in accordance with the general rule of freedom of choice contained in Art.3 of the Regulation (entry at para.32–062, above). The effect of such a choice is, however, limited by the second sentence of Art.6(2) where it is provided that a choice of law may not have the result of depriving the consumer of the protection afforded to him by provisions that cannot be derogated from by agreement by virtue of the law which, in the absence of choice, would have been applicable on the basis of Art.6(1). Art.6(3) stipulates that if the requirements in Art.6(1)(a) or (b) are not fulfilled, the law applicable to a contract between a consumer and a professional shall be determined pursuant to the general choice of law rules contained in Arts 3 and 4 of the Regulation (entries at paras 32–062 and 32R–107, above).

Apart from the exclusion of contracts of carriage and insurance contracts referred to in Art.6(1), (though see Financial Services and Markets Act 2000 (Law Applicable to Contracts of Insurance) Regulations 2009 (SI 2009/3075), reg.4), Art.6(4) of the Regulation provides that Art.6(1) and (2) shall not apply to a series of more specific contracts. First, Art.6(1) and (2) do not apply to a contract for the supply of services where the services are to be supplied to the consumer exclusively in a country other than that in which he has his habitual residence (Art.6(4)(a), reproducing the exclusion found in Art. 5(4)(b) of the Rome Convention, Rule 211(4)(b)). Secondly, Art.6(1) and (2) will not apply to a contract of carriage other than a contract relating to package travel within the meaning of Council Directive 90/314/EEC of June 13, 1990 on package travel, package holidays and package tours ([1990] O.J. L158/59, implemented in the United Kingdom by SI 1992/3288) (Art.6(4)(b), *cf.* Art.5(4)(a) of the Rome Convention, Rule 211(4)(a)). Thirdly, Art.6(1) and (2) will not apply to a contract relating to a right *in rem* in immovable property other than a contract relating to the right to use immovable properties on a timeshare basis within the meaning of Directive 94/47/EC of October 26, 1994 ([1994] O.J. L280/83, implemented in the United Kingdom in Timeshare Regulations 1997, SI 1997/1081, amending Timeshare Act 1992) (Art.6(4)(c), *cf.* main work, paras 33–233, 33–243, 33–247; and see Directive 2008/122/EC of the European Parliament and of the Council of January 14, 2009 on the protection of consumers in respect of certain aspects of timeshare, long-term holiday product, resale and exchange contracts, [2009] O.J. L33/10). A more complicated exclusion is, fourthly, to be found in Art.6(4)(d). This provides that Art.6(1) and (2) are not to apply to rights and obligations which constitute a financial instrument and rights and obligations constituting the terms and conditions governing the issuance or offer to the public and public take-over bids of transferable securities, and the subscription and redemption of units in collective investment undertakings, in so far as these activities do not constitute provision of a financial service. The scope of this exclusion is explained in Recitals (26) and (28)–(30) to the Regulation. For comment see Lehmann in *Rome I Regulation: The Law Applicable to Contractual Obligations in Europe* (ed. Leible and Ferrari, 2009), p.85; Garcimartin Alfarez (2008) 10 Yb. P.I.L. 245. Fifthly, Art.6(4)(d) excludes the application of Art.6(1) and (2) in relation to a contract concluded within the type of system falling within the scope of Art.4 (1)(h). Such a system is a multilateral system which brings together or facilitates the bringing together of multiple third-party buying and selling interests in financial instruments, as defined in Art.4(1) (17) of Directive 2004/39/EC (the Market in Financial Instruments Directive, MiFID [2004] O.J. L145/1). See Lehmann in *Rome I Regulation: The Law Applicable to Contractual Obligations in Europe* (ed. Leible and Ferrari, 2009), p.85; Garcimartin Alfarez, above. Such contracts are, in the absence of a choice of law, subject to a specific choice of law rule contained in Art.4(1)(h) (above, entry at para.32R–107). See generally, Lehmann in *Rome I Regulation: The*

*Law Applicable to Contractual Obligations in Europe* (ed. Leible and Ferrari, 2009), p.85; Garcimartin Alfarez (2009) 5 J. Priv. Int. L.85; (2008) 10 Yb. P.I.L. 245.

As explained in the previous entry, in cases falling within Art. 6 of the Rome I Regulation, Rule 211(1) and (2) will be replaced by Art.6(1) and (2) of the Regulation. Thus, pursuant to Art.6(1), the contract will be governed by the law of the consumer's habitual residence if the professional pursues his commercial or professional activities in that country (Art.6(1)(a)) or if the professional by any means directs such activities to that country or to several countries including that country (Art.6(1)(b)) and the contract falls within the scope of such activities. Article 6(1) is derived from Art.15(1)(c) of the Judgments Regulation (see main work, paras 11–368 *et seq.*; and see Gillies (2008) 16 International Journal of Law and Information Technology 242) and should, so far as possible, be interpreted consistently with the latter provision (see Recitals (7) and (24) to the Rome I Regulation) particularly by attributing autonomous meanings to the various terms used in Art.6(1). Further, although Art.19 of the Regulation contains a specific definition of the habitual residence of companies and other bodies corporate or unincorporated, no such definition is provided of the habitual residence of a natural person which, inevitably, a consumer will be. Accordingly, an autonomous meaning of the habitual residence of a consumer will have to be sought in general principles (see main work, paras 6–125 *et seq.*) **33–004— 33–026**

As regards Art.6(1)(a), the provision would appear to cover cases where the professional pursues his commercial or professional activities directly in the country of the consumer's habitual residence by carrying out those activities there, at a place of business there. It would also appear to cover cases where the professional pursues the relevant activities in the country where the consumer is habitually resident through a branch, agency or other establishment which is situated in that country (*cf.* Art.19 (3) of the Regulation and Art.5(2), second indent, of the Rome Convention, main work, para.33–012). It is also necessary that the contract falls within the scope of relevant activities pursued in the country where the consumer is habitually resident.

Article 6(1)(b) is designed to take account of the development of distance selling techniques, particularly techniques involving electronic commerce which, as is pointed out in the main work, paras 33–017 *et seq.* were difficult to accommodate realistically within the provisions of Art.5 of the Rome Convention. Traditional distance selling techniques would include: specific invitations to a consumer to purchase which invitation is received in the country where he is habitually resident, e.g. by mail order or door-step selling; advertising in the country of the consumer's habitual residence, e.g. through general dissemination in the press or by radio or television. It is also likely that the notion of directing activities by advertising involves some specific intent to advertise in the country of the consumer's habitual residence, an intention, the existence of which, may be derived from the nature of the publication in an appropriate case (*c.f.* Art.5(2), first indent, of the Rome Convention, main work, paras 33–009–33–010). It should be noted that, unlike the position in the Rome Convention, Art.5(2), first indent, there is no requirement in Art.6(1)(b) of the Regulation that the consumer take in the country of his habitual residence all the steps necessary on his part for the conclusion of the contract (see main work, para.33–011).

As is pointed out in the main work, paras 33–017 *et seq.*, it is very difficult to accommodate techniques involving electronic commerce within Art.5 of the Rome Convention. Article 6(1)(b) of the Regulation is, at least in part, designed to address these difficulties through reference to the notion that the professional by any means directs such activities to the country of the consumer's habitual residence or to several countries including that country. Applying this formula, where a professional sends specific invitations or advertisements to a particular consumer or group of consumers by electronic mail to the country of habitual residence, there seems little doubt that Art.6 may be invoked provided a contract is concluded in consequence (by whatever means). Further, it would seem clear that promotional material on a professional's website may amount, in principle, to advertising. A more difficult question, however, is when the availability of this material in the country of the consumer's habitual residence will be a consequence of the professional directing activities to that country. Some guidance is provided in Recital (24) which refers to a joint declaration by the Council and Commission on Art.15(1)(c) of the Judgments Regulation. According to this, for Art.15(1)(c) to be applicable it is, first, not sufficient for an undertaking to target its activities at the Member State of the consumer's habitual residence or at a number of Member States including that Member State: a contract must also be concluded within the framework of its activities. Secondly, the declaration states that the mere fact that an internet site is accessible is not sufficient for Art.15 to be applicable although a factor will be that the internet site solicits the conclusion of distance contracts and that a contract has actually been concluded at a distance, by whatever means: in this respect, the language or currency which a website uses is said not to constitute a relevant factor. From these observations one may conclude, first, that the concept of targeted activity only becomes relevant where a contract is concluded at a distance by whatever means, as a result of that activity. Secondly, the website need not necessarily be an interactive one. If the site invites consumers to mail or fax orders, then it aims to conclude contracts at a distance. Thirdly, however, a site which offers information to potential consumers all over the world but, for example, refers them to a local agent for the purposes of concluding the actual contract does not aim to conclude distance contracts. Finally, it will be noted that Art.6(1)(b) is not subject to any condition that the consumer has taken, in the country of his habitual residence, all the steps necessary on his part for the conclusion of the contract: this will reduce the difficulties seen, in this respect, in the application of Art.5(2), first indent, of the Rome Convention (see main work, para.33–018).

Article 6(2) recognises the principle of party autonomy in relation to consumer contracts, in accordance with Art.3 of the Regulation. Article 6(2) also provides that the choice cannot have the result of depriving the consumer of the protection afforded to him by provisions that cannot be derogated from by agreement by virtue of the law, which, in the absence of choice, would have been applicable on the basis of Art.6(1). This in effect, permits the limited party autonomy recognised in Art.5 of the Rome Convention (main work, paras 33–008 *et seq.*) but is not restricted by the conditions set out in Art.5(2) of the Convention. Article 6 (2) thus prevents avoidance of compulsory provisions of the law of the country in which the consumer is habitually resident by the choice of another country's law. It is likely that the various provisions discussed in main work, paras 33–032 *et seq.*, will be regarded as provisions bearing this character.

Article 27 of the Regulation contains a review clause requiring the Commission to submit to the European Parliament, the Council and the European Economic and Social Committee a report on the application of the Rome I Regulation, that Report to be accompanied, if appropriate, by proposals to amend the Regulation. Article 27(1)(b) requires the report to include an evaluation of Art.6, in particular as regards the coherence of Community law in the field of consumer protection. And see European Commission, *Proposal for a Directive of the European Parliament and of the Council on consumer rights*, COM (2008) 614.

NOTE 46. Add: Tang, *Electronic Consumer Contracts in the Conflict of Laws* (2009); Gillies (2007) 3 J. Priv. Int. L. 89; Tang (2007) 3 J. Priv. Int. L. 113; Gillies (2008) 16 International Journal of Law and Information Technology 242. **33–017**

NOTE 52. Add in line 17: Hill, *Cross-Border Consumer Contracts* (2008), paras 12.26–12.31. **33–019**

The general rules on the law governing the formal validity of a contract which are contained in Art.11 of the Rome I Regulation do not apply to consumer contracts which fall within the scope of Art.6 of the Regulation. The form of such contracts is governed by the law of the country where the consumer has his habitual residence (Art.11(4)). Article 1(3) of the Regulation provides that the Regulation does not apply to evidence and procedure. See generally Illmer [2009] C.J.Q. 237. It is suggested that the observations in these paragraphs are applicable to cases falling within Art. 6 of the Regulation. **33–027—33–029**

*cf.* Art.9(1) and (2) of the Rome I Regulation (above, entry at para.32–132). **33–030**

*cf.* Art.6(3) of the Regulation (above, entry at para.33R–001). **33–031**

NOTE 10. Add at end: Consumer Credit Act 1974 is amended by Consumer Credit (EU Directive) Regulations 2010, SI 2010/1010), largely implementing

Directive 2008/48/EC of the European Parliament and of the Council on credit agreements for consumers ([2008] O.J. L133/66).

**33–039** NOTE 18. *Office of Fair Trading v Lloyds TSB Bank plc* [2004] EWHC 2600 (Comm.), [2005] 1 All E.R. 843 has been reversed, in part, by the Court of Appeal, [2006] EWCA Civ 268, [2007] Q.B.1. The Court of Appeal held that "connected lender" liability under s.75 of the Consumer Credit Act 1974 attaches to all transactions entered into using credit cards issued under consumer credit agreements regulated by the 1974 Act whether they are entered into in the United Kingdom or elsewhere. The decision of the Court of Appeal was affirmed by the House of Lords: [2007] UKHL 48, [2008] 1 A.C. 316.

**33–043** NOTE 31. Add in line 5: See Enterprise Act 2002 (Amendment) Regulations 2006, SI 2006/3363.

Add at end: Directive 2009/22/EC of the European Parliament and of the Council of April 23, 2009 on injunctions for the protection of consumers' interests (codified version), [2009] O.J. L110/30. See generally Hill, *Cross-Border Consumer Contracts* (2008), Ch.8.

On the Unfair Commercial Practices Directive, see De Groote and De Vulder [2007] J.B.L. 16. The Unfair Commercial Practices Directive is implemented in the United Kingdom in the Business Protection from Misleading Marketing Regulations 2008, SI 2008/1276 and the Consumer Protection from Unfair Trading Regulations 2008, SI 2008/1277, in force from May 26, 2008.

The European Commission published a Green Paper on the Review of the Consumer *Acquis* (2007/C 61/01): see [2007] O.J. C61/1. For the results of the review, see European Commission, *Proposal for a Directive of the European Parliament and of the Council on consumer rights*, COM (2008) 614.

**33–044— 33–054** On the material in these paragraphs, see European Commission, *Proposal for a Directive of the European Parliament and of the Council on consumer rights*, above.

**33–044** NOTE 41. Add: See also Case C–168/05 *Mostaza Claro v Centro Móvil Milenium SL* [2006] E.C.R. I–10421.

**33–045** NOTE 44. As to the meaning of "EEA Agreement" see now Interpretation Act 1978, Sch.1, inserted by Legislative and Regulatory Reform Act 2006, s.26; Enterprise Act 2002, s.212(5), as substituted by SI 2007/528.

**33–049** NOTE 55. The role of the Director General of Fair Trading, which was abolished by Enterprise Act 2002, s.3, has passed to the Office of Fair Trading: *ibid*. See, further, Enterprise Act 2002, Pt 8 and SI 2007/528.

NOTE 56. Add in line 3: See generally Case C–205/07 *Gysbrechts and Santurel Inter BVBA* [2008] E.C.R. I–9947. **33–050**

NOTE 65. See above, entry at para.33–045, n.44. **33–051**

NOTE 66. See also Directive 2008/48/EC of the European Parliament and of the Council of April 23, 2008 on credit agreements for consumers and repealing Council Directive 87/102/EEC ([2008] O.J. L133/66 Art.22(4)). See entry at para.33–031, n.10.

## 2. CONTRACTS OF EMPLOYMENT

Article 6 of the Rome Convention, as reproduced in Rule 212, is essentially reproduced in Art.8 of the Rome I Regulation, although Art.8 of the Regulation contains some clarification of, and different terminology to, Art.6 of the Convention. Article 8 will apply to contracts concluded after December 17, 2009 (Arts 28, 29). **33R–058— 33–079**

Article 8(1) provides that an individual employment contract shall be governed by the law chosen by the parties in accordance with Art.3 of the Regulation (above, entry at para.32–062). Such a choice of law may not, however, have the result of depriving the employee of the protection afforded him by provisions that cannot be derogated from by agreement under the law that, in the absence of choice, would have been applicable under Art.8(2), (3) and (4). This essentially reproduces Art.6(1) of the Rome Convention (Rule 212(1)), as discussed in the main work, paras 33–067 *et seq.*

Article 8(2) states that to the extent that the law applicable to the contract has not been chosen by the parties, the contract shall be governed by the law of the country in which or, failing that, from which, the employee habitually carries out his work in performance of the contract. Additionally, it is provided that the country where the work is habitually carried out shall not be deemed to have changed if the employee is temporarily employed in another country (Art.8(2), second sentence).

It should first be noted that whereas Art.6(2)(a) of the Rome Convention (Rule 212(2)(a), main work, para.33–075) refers to the law of the country *in* which the employee carries out his work, as does Art.8(2) of the Regulation, the Convention, in contrast to the Regulation, does not refer to the law of the country *from* which the employee habitually carries out his work in performance of the contract. The effect of Art.8(2) would seem to be as follows. If the employee habitually carries out his work in performance of the contract in one country, then that country's law will be the applicable law (*cf.* main work, para.33–075). If the employee habitually carries out his work in more than one country, or in no particular country, or in a place which is not a country then one must ask whether there is one country *from* which the employee habitually carries out his work in performance of the contract. An example of the latter situation might be the case of an airline pilot, based in one particular country, who is required to fly aircraft to several different countries (*cf.* main work, paras 33–076–33–077). The second sentence of Art.8(2) is designed to ensure that the place where work is habitually carried out is not to be regarded as having changed if the employee is temporarily employed in another country. Recital (36) to the Regulation explains that:

> "work carried out in another country should be regarded as temporary if the employee is expected to resume working in the country of origin after carrying out his tasks abroad. The conclusion of a new contract of employment with the original employer or an employer belonging to the same group of companies should not preclude the employee from being regarded as carrying out his work in another country temporarily".

Article 8(3) provides that where the applicable law cannot be determined according to Art.8(2), the contract shall be governed by the law of the country where the place of business through which the employee was engaged is situated. This rule will apply where the employee carries out his work in more than one country, or in no particular country, or in a place which is not a country *and* there is no one country *from* which he habitually carries out his work (*cf.* main work, para.33–077). Article 8(4) contains a rule of displacement modelled on the proviso to Art.6(2) of the Rome Convention, to the effect that if it appears from the circumstances as a whole that the contract is more closely connected with a country other than that indicated in Art.8(2) or (3), the law of that other country shall apply (*cf.* Art.4 (3) of the Rome I Regulation, above entry at para.32R–107, main work, para.33–078).

**33R–058** NOTE 96. Add: *Chitty on Contracts* (30th ed. 2008), paras 30–276 *et seq*; Mankowski in *Rome I Regulation: The Law Applicable to Contracts in Europe* (ed. Leible and Ferrari, 2009), p.171; Hoey and McArdie, 2008 Jur. Rev. 291; Barnard (2009) 38 I.L.J. 122.

**33–061** The policy of protecting the employee also informs Art.8 of the Rome I Regulation: see Recitals (23) and (35) to the Regulation.

**33–063—**
**33–066** Whatever the position may be under the Rome Convention, there can be no doubt that the expression "individual employment contract" in Art.8 of the Rome I Regulation will be given an autonomous meaning (*cf.* cases cited at para.33–064, n.17 (next entry). Further, that meaning should correspond, so far as possible, with the meaning given to the expression in the context of Art.18 of the Judgments Regulation (see Recital (7) to the Rome I Regulation; main work, para.11–379 *et seq.*; and *cf.* cases cited in next entry). The following criteria may form the broad contours of an autonomous meaning. The first criterion identifying a contract of employment is the provision of services by one party over a period of time for which remuneration is paid; the second criterion is the existence of control and direction over the provision of the services by the counterparty; and the third criterion is the integration to some extent of the provider of services within the organisational framework of the counterparty (see *Benatti v WPP Holdings Italy Srl* [2007] EWCA Civ

263, [2007] 1 W.L.R. 2316 at [46]). These criteria are not, however, "hard edged" criteria which can be mechanically applied, since there may, for example, be degrees of control and degrees of integration within the relevant organisational framework (*ibid.* at [47]). And in applying these broad criteria regard must be had, particularly, to the terms of the contract (*ibid.*). Article 8 would not seem to apply to collective agreements but only to contracts entered into by individual employees.

NOTE 17. Add at end: *Benatti v WPP Holdings Italy Srl* [2007] EWCA Civ 263, [2007] 1 W.L.R. 2316; *Samengo-Turner v J & H Marsh & McLennan (Services) Ltd* [2007] EWCA Civ 723, [2008] I.C.R. 18; *Duarte v Black & Decker Corp* [2007] EWHC 2720 (QB), [2008] 1 All E.R. (Comm.) 401. Cavalier and Upex (2006) 55 I.C.L.Q. 587. **33–064**

NOTE 22. Add: *Chunilal v Merrill Lynch International Inc* [2010] EWHC 1467 (Comm.). **33–067**

The expression "mandatory rules" as used in Art.6(1) of the Rome Convention, is replaced in Art.8(1) of the Rome I Regulation by the expression "provisions that cannot be derogated from by agreement". The change of terminology appears to have no substantive effect. The submissions made in these paragraphs appear to hold good under Art.8(1) of the Regulation. **33–069—33–071**

NOTE 27 and text thereto. *Cf. Duarte v Black & Decker Corp* [2007] EWHC 2720 (QB), [2008] 1 All E.R. (Comm.) 401 (mandatory rules in Art.6(1) of the Rome Convention are specific provisions such as those in the Employment Rights Act 1996 and the Factories Acts whose overriding purpose is to protect employees: they do not include rules governing the enforceability of restrictive covenants in employment contracts: such covenants if valid under a foreign governing law, but which are void under English law may be denied application on public policy grounds (Art.16 of the Convention), if the employee is working in England). **33–069**

NOTE 28. *Lawson v Serco Ltd* [2006] UKHL 3, [2006] 1 All E.R. 823 is now reported at [2006] I.C.R. 250.

*cf.* Art.9 (1) and (2) of the Rome I Regulation, above, entry at para.32–132. **33–072—33–073**

For the position under the Rome I Regulation see above, entry at para.33R–058. **33–074—33–078**

NOTE 38. Add: In Case C–29/10 *Koelzsch v Etat de Grand-Duche de Luxembourg* (pending) the Cour d'appel of Luxembourg referred the following question to the European Court: Is the rule of conflict in Art.6(2)(a) of the Rome Convention, which states that an employment contract is governed by **33–075** the law of the country in which the employee habitually carries out his work in performance of the contract, to be interpreted as meaning that, in the situation where the employee works in more than one country, but returns systematically to one of them, that country must be regarded as that in which the employee habitually carries out his work?

For a view from an English court, see *Chunilal v Merrill Lynch International Inc* [2010] EWHC 1467 (Comm.).

NOTE 40. See above entry at para.33–069, n.28.

**33–076** NOTE 42. See *Chunilal v Merrill Lynch International Inc,* above.

**33–077** NOTE 49. Add at end: See also *Diggins v Condor Marine Crewing Services Ltd* [2009] EWCA Civ 1133, [2010] I.C.R. 213.

NOTE 50. Add at beginning: *cf. Chunilal v Merrill Lynch International Inc* [2010] EWHC 1467 (Comm.).

**33–079** The Rome I Regulation makes no special provision for determining the law applicable to the formal validity of an employment contract. The relevant choice of law rules are those contained in Art.11(1) and (2) of the Regulation, above entry at para.32R–175.

**33–080** *cf.* Art.21 of the Rome I Regulation, above, entry at para.32–232.

**33–081** NOTE 71. See above, entry at para.33–069, n.28. See *Diggins v Condor Marine Crewing Services Ltd* [2009] EWCA Civ 1133, [2010] I.C.R. 213.

**33–082** NOTE 73. Add: See also Council Directive 2000/78/EC of November 27, 2000 establishing a general framework for equal treatment in employment ([2000] O.J. L303/16), implemented in the United Kingdom, in so far as it relates to discrimination on grounds of age, in the Employment Equality (Age) Regulations 2006, SI 2006/1031.

Add in line 6: Case C–346/06 *Ruffert v Land Niedersaschen* [2008] E.C.R. I–1489; Case C–310/07 *Svenska Staten v Holmquist* [2008] E.C.R. I–7871, [2009] I.C.R. 675; Barnard [2009] 38 I.L.J. 122.

NOTES 73–78 and text thereto. Recital (34) to the Rome I Regulation states that the rule on individual employment contracts in Art.8 should not prejudice the application of overriding mandatory provisions of the country to which a worker is posted in accordance with the Posted Workers Directive.

**33–083—33–085** See Dickinson, *The Rome II Regulation* (2008), paras 3–124–3–145.

NOTE 80 and text thereto. See now CPR r.6.36 and PD6B, para.3.1(6)(c), inserted by SI 2008/2178, in force from October 1, 2008. **33–083**

NOTE 86. As to the position under Regulation (EC) 864/2007 of the European Parliament and of the Council on the Law Applicable to Non-Contractual Obligations ("Rome II"), see below, para.S35–177. **33–084**

The various statutes referred to in these paragraphs will doubtless be regarded as provisions of English law which cannot be derogated from by agreement for the purposes of Art.8(1) of the Rome I Regulation. But see Barnard (2009) 38 I.L.J. 122. **33–086— 33–103**

NOTES 7, 9, 11, 17, 21, 24 and 31. See above, entry at para.33–069, n.28. **33–090— 33–095**

NOTE 11. Add: See also *Williams v University of Nottingham* [2007] I.R.L.R. 660 (EAT) and next entry. **33–091**

NOTES 16–20. See *Bleuse v MBT Transport Ltd* [2008] I.C.R. 488 (E.A.T.) (*Lawson v Serco Ltd* [2006] UKHL 3, [2006] I.C.R. 250 applied to exclude claims for unfair dismissal and unlawful deductions from wages under Employment Rights Act 1996); *Hunt v United Airlines Inc* [2008] I.C.R. 934; (claim for unfair dismissal: *Lawson v Serco Ltd,* above, applied): *Dolphin Drilling PTE Ltd v Winks* (UKEATS/0049/08/B1, April 21, 2009) (E.A.T.); *Duncombe v Secretary of State for Children, Schools and Families* [2009] EWCA Civ 1355, [2010] I.C.R.815; *Ministry of Defence v Wallis* (UKEAT/0546/06/ZT) July 30, 2010 (E.A.T.); *Ravat v Halliburton Manufacturing & Services Ltd* [2010] CSIH 52 (all concerned with unfair dismissal: *Lawson v Serco Ltd,* above, applied; *Tradition Securities and Futures SA v X* [2009] I.C.R. 88; *Ministry of Defence v Wallis*, above (sex discrimination). And see *Diggins v Condor Marine Crewing Services Ltd* [2009] EWCA Civ 1133, [2010] I.C.R. 213. **33–092**

NOTE 26 and text thereto. Different principles apply where the relevant right in the Employment Rights Act 1996 derives from European law. Here there is an obligation to give direct effect to the European right through interpretation of the relevant English law. In consequence *Lawson v Serco Ltd*, above, will not apply and the scope of the right may depend, instead, on whether the contract of employment is governed by English law or by the law of another Member State: *Duncombe v Secretary of State for Children, Schools & Families* [2009] EWCA Civ 1355, [2010] I.C.R.815 (application of Fixed-Term Employees (Prevention of Less Favourable Treatment) Regulations 2002); *Ministry of Defence v Wallis* (UKEAT/0546/08/ZT) July 30, 2010 (EAT) (sex discrimination); *Bleuse v MBT Transport Ltd*, above (right to paid annual leave under Working Time Regulations 1998 applied where English law was the law applicable to the contract). See also *Holis Industries Ltd v* **33–094**

*GMB* [2008] I.C.R. 464 (EAT) (Transfer of Undertakings (Protection of Employment) Regulations 2006 and collective redundancy consultation obligations in Trade Union and Labour Relations (Consolidation) Act 1992, s.188, apply to transfer of a business which after transfer is based outside the United Kingdom). *cf. Williams v University of Nottingham*, above.

**33–098** The Sex Discrimination Act 1975 is amended by the Sex Discrimination Act 1975 (Amendment) Regulations 2008, SI 2008/656 and the Sex Discrimination (Amendment of Legislation) Regulations 2008, SI 2008/963.

NOTE 38. Add: See *Tradition Securities and Futures SA v X* [2009] I.C.R. 88.

**33–100** NOTE 43. See also *Holis Industries Ltd* v GMB, above, entry at para.33–094, n.26.

**33–101** NOTE 48. See on Disability Discrimination Act 1995, s.68(2), *Williams v University of Nottingham*, above. A virtually identical provision is contained in the Employment Equality (Age) Regulations 2006 (SI 2006/1031), reg.10.

**33–103** NOTE 60. See above, entry at para.33–069, n.28.

**33–105** NOTE 71. See above, entry at para.33–069, n.28.

## 3. CONTRACTS FOR THE SALE, PLEDGE AND HIRE OF MOVABLES

**33R–106** In relation to the Rome I Regulation, the law applicable to a contract for the sale, pledge or hire of a movable, which is not a consumer contract for the purposes of Art.6 of the Regulation, will be determined in accordance with Arts 3 or 4 of the Regulation (see above, entries at paras 32–062 and 32R–107). These provisions will apply to contracts concluded after December 17, 2009 (Arts 28, 29).

Pursuant to Art.3 of the Regulation, the contract will be governed by the law chosen by the parties which choice must be made expressly or clearly demonstrated by the terms of the contract or the circumstances of the case (Art.3(1)). The effect of a choice of law may be limited by reference to Art.3(3) or (4); and see also Art.9(1) and (2) (above, entry at para.32–132).

To the extent that the law applicable to the contract has not been chosen in accordance with Art.3, Art.4 (1) first provides that the law governing the contract shall be determined by reference to the following rules.

A contract for the sale of goods shall be governed by the law of the country where the seller has his habitual residence (Art.4(1)(a)). For these purposes, the concept of "sale of goods" should be interpreted in the same way as when applying Art.5(1)(a) of the Judgments Regulation: see Recital (17) to the Rome I Regulation. See also Case C–381/08 *Car Trim GmbH v KeySafety*

*Systems SRL* [2010] 2 All E.R. (Comm.) 770 (Art.5(1)(a) and (b) must be interpreted as meaning that where the purpose of the contract is the supply of goods to be manufactured or produced and, even though the purchaser has specified certain requirements with regard to the provision, fabrication and delivery of the components to be produced, the purchaser has not supplied the materials and the supplier is responsible for the quality of the goods and their compliance with the contract, the contract must be considered as a contract for the "sale of goods", rather than a contract for the "supply of services"). The habitual residence of the seller will be determined in accordance with Art.19 of the Rome I Regulation. Thus the habitual residence of companies and other bodies, corporate or unincorporated, shall be the place of central administration and the habitual residence of a natural person acting in the course of his business activity shall be the principal place of business (Art.19(1)). Where the contract is concluded in the course of the operations of a branch, agency or any other establishment, or if, under the contract, performance is the responsibility of such a branch, agency or other establishment, the place where the branch, agency or any other establishment is located shall be treated as the place of habitual residence (Art.19(2)). The relevant point of time for determining habitual residence shall be the time of the conclusion of the contract (Art.19(3)).

Article 4(1)(g) supplies a special choice of law rule for a contract for the sale of goods by auction. Such a contract shall be governed by the law of the country where the auction takes place, if such a place can be determined. It may not be possible to determine where an auction takes place, in some situations, where the auction is conducted over the internet.

Rule 213 is principally concerned with sale of goods. It is worth drawing attention, however, to another rule contained in Art.4(1), Art.4(1)(h) which provides that a contract concluded within a multilateral system which brings together or facilitates the bringing together of multiple third-party buying and selling interests in financial instruments as defined in the Markets in Financial Instruments Directive 2004, Art.4(1)(17) ([2004] O.J. L145/1), in accordance with non-discretionary rules and governed by a single law, shall be governed by that law. See Recitals (18) and (31) to the Regulation.

Article 4(1)(b) of the Regulation provides a rule for determining the law applicable to "a contract for the provision of services" which expression should be interpreted in the same way as when applying Art.5(1)(b) of the Judgments Regulation: Recital (17) to the Regulation; Case C–533/07 *Falco Privatstiftung v Weller-Lindhorst* [2010] Bus. L.R. 210; see also Case C–381/08 *Car Trim GmbH v KeySafety Systems SRL*, above. Such a contract shall be governed by the law of the country where the service provider has his habitual residence. A contract for the hire of a movable will almost certainly be regarded as such a contract and will be governed by the law of the country where the hirer is habitually resident, as defined in Art.19, referred to above.

In relation to sale of goods and contracts for the hire of movables, Art.4(1)(a) and 4(1)(b) reproduce, in effect, the outcomes reached by applying

Art.4(2) of the Rome Convention (Rule 213 (3); main work, paras 33–113 *et seq*.

A contract for the pledge of a movable may also be construed to be a contract for the provision of services for the purposes of Art.4(1)(b). Here, however, it is less clear who is to be regarded as the "service provider". In the main work it is suggested that the characteristic performance of a contract of pledge is that of the pledgor since he is the person who provides the security for a loan: see main work, para.33–115. Whether the same outcome will be reached under Art.4(1)(b) of the Regulation is far from clear. It is also possible that a contract for the pledge of a movable may not fall within Art.4(1)(b), so that pursuant to Art.4(2), the contract may be governed by the law of the country where the party required to effect the characteristic performance of the contract has his habitual residence. It is, however, suggested that it is most unlikely that a contract for the pledge of a movable will be regarded as a contract where the applicable law cannot be determined on the basis of Art.4(1)(b) or 4(2) so that, pursuant to Art.4(4), the contract will be governed by the law of the country with which it is most closely connected. On pledge see Art.14(3) of the Regulation, above, entry at para.24–050.

The rules in Art.4 (1)(a), (b), (g) and (h) and in Art.4(2) may be displaced where it is clear from all the circumstances of the case that the contract is manifestly more closely connected with a country other than the one indicated in those provisions. In such a case the applicable law will be the law of that other country: Art.4(3).

Articles 4(1)(e) and (f) supply special choice of law rules for determining the law applicable to, respectively, franchise contracts and distribution contracts. As regards franchise contracts, the general rule is that the applicable law is the law of the country where the franchisee has his habitual residence (Art.4(1)(e)). As regards distribution contracts, the general rule is that the applicable law is the law of the country where the distributor has his habitual residence (Art.4(1)(f)). See above, entry at para.32R–107.

It is possible that a particular contractual arrangement contains elements that would be covered by more than one of the points in Art. 4(1), referred to above. An example might be a sale and distribution arrangement covered by both Art.4(1)(a) and Art.4(1)(f) (*cf. Print Concept GmbH v GEW (EC) Ltd* [2001] EWCA Civ 352, [2002] C.L.C. 352; main work, para.33–411). In such cases Art.4(2) of the Regulation provides that the contract shall be governed by the law of the country where the party required to effect the characteristic performance of the contract has his habitual residence. Application of the concept of characteristic performance in such situations may not, however, be without difficulty since the characteristic performance of each contract covered may be different. Recital (19) to the Regulation states that in such situations "the characteristic performance of the contract should be determined having regard to its centre of gravity". But this begs the question of how the centre of gravity is to be determined. It is possible that the centre of gravity will be taken to be the performance of the substantial or principal obligations under the contract, but even if this view is accepted, it may not necessarily be easy to determine, in a particular case, what these obligations are to be taken to be. Furthermore, as regards "mixed" and complex contracts, it may not be possible to determine the characteristic performance (*cf.* main work, para.32–117, n.9) in which case Art.4(4) may come into play so that the contract will be governed by the law of the country with which it is most closely connected. Where a mixed contract does fall within Art.4(2) the applicable law may be displaced by reference to Art.4(3) of the Regulation.

*cf.* Art.6 of the Rome I Regulation, above, entry at para.33R–001. **33–109**

*cf.* Arts 3 and 4 of the Rome I Regulation, above, entry at para.33R–106. **33–110—33–112**

*cf.* Art.4(1) and 4(2) of the Rome I Regulation, above, entry at para.33R–106. **33–113—33–116**

*cf.* Art.4(3) and 4(4) of the Rome I Regulation. **33–117—33—119**

NOTE 12. Add at beginning: Case C–133/08 *Intercontainer Interfrigo SC (ICF) v Balkenende Oosthuizen BV* [2010] 3 W.L.R. 24. Add in line 6: *Pablo Star Ltd v Emirates Integrated Telecommunications Co PJSC* [2009] EWCA Civ 1044. **33–117**

*cf* Art.4(1)(a) and 4(3) of the Rome I Regulation. **33–120**

Article 25(1) of the Rome I Regulation provides that the Regulation shall not prejudice the application of international conventions to which one or more Member States are parties at the time the Regulation is adopted and which lay down "conflict-of-law" rules relating to contractual obligations. According to Art.25(2), however, the Regulation shall, as between Member States, take precedence over conventions concluded exclusively between two or more of them in so far as such conventions concern matters governed by the Regulation. See also Art.26; and *cf.* Recital (13) to the Regulation. **33–121—33–123**

The provisions of the Unfair Contract Terms Act 1977, as discussed in these paragraphs, would seem to be overriding mandatory provisions of the law of the forum, applicable under Art.9(1) and 9(2) of the Rome I Regulation. **33–125—33–126**

Additionally, in the context of a contract for the sale of goods or for the provision of services, for example, effect may be given to the overriding mandatory provisions of the law of the country where the obligations arising out of the contract have to be or have been performed, in so far as those overriding mandatory provisions render performance of the contract unlawful. In considering whether to give effect to those provisions, regard shall be had to their nature and purpose and to the consequences of their application or non-application (Art.9(3) of the Regulation). See above, entry at para.32–132; *cf.* main work, paras 32–141 *et seq.*

NOTE 51. Add in line 3: *Trident Turboprop (Dublin) Ltd v First Flight Couriers Ltd* [2009] EWCA Civ 290, [2010] Q.B. 86.

**33–127— 33–128** The same outcomes seem to be reached under Art.3(3) of the Rome I Regulation which provides that where all other elements relevant to the situation at the time of the choice of law are located in a country other than the country whose law has been chosen, the choice of the parties shall not prejudice application of the law of that other country which cannot be derogated from by agreement. See above, entry at para.32–132.

There is a further limitation on the effect of a choice of law which is contained in Art.3(4) of the Regulation. According to this, where all other elements relevant to the situation at the time of the choice of law are located in one or more Member States the parties' choice of applicable law other than that of a Member State shall not prejudice the application of provisions of Community law, where appropriate as implemented in the Member State of the forum, which cannot be derogated from by agreement. For these purposes "Member State" includes Denmark: Art.1(4). See above, entry at para.32–013.

**33–129— 33–134** The principles discussed in these paragraphs are unaffected by the Rome I Regulation which does not apply to the proprietary effects of, for example, a sale of goods.

**33–132** NOTES 69 to 71 and text thereto. For English law on registration of company charges, see now Companies Act 2006, Pt 25, Ch.1; Overseas Companies (Execution of Documents and Registration of Charges) Regulations 2009, S1 2009/1917, Pt 3.

## 4. CONTRACTS OF INSURANCE AND RE-INSURANCE

**33R–136** Rules 214, 215 and 216 state the relevant principles for determining the law applicable to contracts of insurance derived from the Rome Convention, where the contract covers risks situated outside the territories of the European Communities, and from the various Insurance Directives, where the contract covers risks situated in an EEA State: see, respectively for discussion, paras 33–137–33–140, 33–144 *et seq.*, 33–159 *et seq.* and paras 33–190 *et seq.* of the main work. Article 7 of Regulation (EC) 593/2008 of the European Parliament and of the Council of June 17, 2008 on the law applicable to contractual obligations (Rome I), ([2008] O.J. L177/6, Appendix 2 to this Supplement) contains, however, discrete choice of law rules for the identification of the law applicable to insurance contracts which will largely replace the existing rules. The new provisions will apply to contracts concluded after December 17, 2009 (Arts 28, 29). Broadly, Art.7 is a consolidation of the current rules, retaining the substance of the current law and is intended to ensure that all the relevant rules are situated in one instrument: see Ministry of Justice, *Rome I—Should the UK Opt In?* Consultation Paper CP05/08, April 2, 2008. Given these objectives and outcomes it is appropriate to draw attention to the main features of the article as a whole so as to avoid confusion with the existing rules. For discussion, see *Chitty on Contracts* (30th edn 2008), paras 30–252 *et seq.*; Gruber in *Rome I Regulation: The Law Applicable to Contractual Obligations in Europe* (ed. Leible and Ferrari, 2009), p.109; Heiss (2008) 10 Yb.P.I.L. 261; Merrett (2009) 5 J. Priv. Int. L. 49. See also European Commission, *Communication from the Commission to the European Parliament and the Council: An area of freedom, security and justice serving the citizen* COM (2009) 262 final, para.3.4 (possibility of measures implementing common rules for determining law applicable to insurance contracts).

Article 7 consists of six paragraphs and several sub-paragraphs dealing, respectively, with: scope (Art.7(1)); the law applicable to a contract covering a "large risk" within the meaning of the article (Art.7(2)); the law applicable to an insurance contract other than a contract covering a large risk (Art.7(3)); additional rules to determine the law applicable to insurance contracts for which a Member State imposes an obligation to take out insurance (Art.7(4); a provision clarifying, for the purpose of Art.7(3) and Art.7(4), the position where the insurance contract covers risks situated in more than one Member State (Art.7(5)); and a provision indicating how the country in which the risk is situated is to be identified when it is necessary to do so for the purpose of the article (Art.7(6)). It is specifically provided that Art.7 does not apply to re-insurance contracts (Art.7(1), second sentence). It is further provided that an insurance contract cannot be a consumer contract for the purposes of Art.6 (Art.6(1); Recital (32) to the Regulation; but see below on SI 2009/3075, reg.4). Article 1(2)(j) excludes from the scope of the Regulation altogether insurance contracts arising out of operations carried out by organisations other than undertakings referred to in Art.2 of Directive 2002/83/EC of the European Parliament and of the Council of November 5, 2002 concerning life assurance ([2002] O.J. L345/1), the object of which is to provide benefits for employed or self-employed persons belonging to an undertaking or group of undertakings, or to a trade or group of trades, in the event of death or survival or of discontinuance or curtailment of activity, or of sickness related to work or accidents at work.

As regards the scope of Art.7 (which does not apply to re-insurance contracts, as pointed out above), Art.7(1) provides that the article applies to contracts referred to in Art.7(2), whether or not the risk covered by the contract is situated in a Member State, and to all other insurance contracts covering risks situated inside the territory of the Member States. For the purposes of Art.7 "Member State" means all the Member States so that Denmark is included (Art.1(4)). Article 7 will thus apply where the risk covered by the contract is situated in Denmark. Notwithstanding Art.22(2) of the Regulation, Art.7 applies in the case of conflicts between, (a) the laws of different parts of the United Kingdom, or (b) the laws of one or more parts of the United Kingdom and Gibraltar, in relation to contracts of insurance described in Art.7 as it applies in the case of conflicts between the laws of different countries: Financial Services and Markets Act 2000 (Law Applicable to Contracts of Insurance) Regulations 2009, reg.3 (SI 2009/3075).

Since the relevant choice of law rules may depend on where the risk is situated, Art.7(6) supplies the necessary rules for making this determination. As regards non-life insurance, the country in which the risk is situated is to be determined in accordance with Art.2(d) of the Second Council Directive 88/357 on the coordination of laws, regulations and administrative provisions relating to direct insurance other than life insurance and laying down provisions to facilitate the exercise of freedom to provide services ([1988] O.J. L172/1). According to Art.2(d), the Member State where the risk is situated means: the Member State in which the property is situated where the insurance relates either to buildings or to buildings and their contents, in so far as the contents are covered by the same policy; the Member State of registration, where the insurance relates to vehicles of any type; the Member State where the policy holder took out the policy in the case of policies of a duration of four months or less covering travel or holiday risks, whatever the class concerned; and in all cases not explicitly covered by the foregoing provisions, the Member State where the policy holder has his habitual residence or if the policy holder is a legal person the Member State where the latter's establishment to which the contract relates is situated. As regards life assurance, Art.7(6) provides that the country in which the risk is situated shall be the country of commitment within the meaning of Art.1(1)(g) of Directive 2002/83/EC concerning life assurance ([2002] O.J. L345/1). Article 1(1)(g) of that Directive defines Member Sate of the commitment as the Member State where the policy holder has his/her habitual residence or, if the policy holder is a legal person, the Member State where the latter's establishment to which the contract relates is situated.

Article 7(2) of the Regulation sets out the choice of law rules in respect of contracts covering "large risks". The first sub-paragraph provides that a contract covering a large risk, as defined in Art.5(d) of the First Council Directive 73/239 EEC of July 24, 1973 on the coordination of laws, regulations and administrative provisions relating to the taking-up and pursuit of the business of direct insurance other than life insurance ([1973] O.J. L228/3), shall be governed by the law chosen by the parties in accordance with Art.3 of the Rome I Regulation (above, entry at para.32–062). In this respect, the provision permits the choice of any law, irrespective of whether it is the law of a Member State and irrespective of whether the law chosen is that of a country in which the risk is situated. According to Art.5(d) of the Directive a large risk is defined as a risk which is classified as a risk relating to: damage to or loss of, railway stock, aircraft, ships (sea, lake, river and canal vessels), goods in transit, aircraft liability, liability for ships (as above); credit (covering general insolvency, export credit, instalment credit, mortgages and agricultural credit), suretyship (covering direct and indirect suretyship); damage and loss to vehicles; certain events involving fire and natural forces; other damage to property; motor vehicle liability; general liability; and miscellaneous financial loss.

The second sub-paragraph of Art.7(2) stipulates that in the absence of a choice of law satisfying Art.3 of the Regulation, the contract will be governed, as a general rule, by the law of the country (which need not be a Member State) in which the insurer has his habitual residence (as defined in Art.19). This sub-paragraph also provides that where it is clear from all the circumstances of the case that the contract is manifestly more closely connected with another country, the law of that other country shall apply (*cf.* Art.4(1)(b) and 4(3) of the Regulation, above entry at para.32R–107).

Where the insurance contract does not fall within Art.7(2), the relevant choice of law rules are found in Art.7(3). These choice of law rules only apply to contracts covering risks situated inside the territory of the Member States. Unlike Art.7(2) which only applies to non-life insurance, Art.7(3) is capable of applying to life assurance. Non-life risks which are the subject of Art.7(3) include: accident insurance; sickness insurance; legal expenses insurance; insurance for assistance; credit and suretyship insurance where the risks do not relate to a business carried on by the policy holder; and where the policy holder does not carry on a business which satisfies certain detailed requirements of the First Life Directive (above), land vehicle insurance, fire insurance, insurance against damage to property, motor vehicle liability, general liability (other than aircraft liability and liability for ships) and insurance against miscellaneous financial loss (Art.5(d)(iii) of the First Life Directive). Article 7(3) of the Regulation establishes a more limited form of party autonomy for these classes of insurance by specifying the laws that may be chosen to govern the contract under Art.3 of the Regulation.

First, Art.7(3)(a) permits a choice of the law of any Member State where the risk is situated at the time of the conclusion of the contract and this seems to mean that where the risk is situated in more than one Member State, the law of any such State may be chosen. Secondly, Art.7(3)(b) allows the parties to choose the law of the country (which need not be a Member State) where the policy holder has his habitual residence. Thirdly, Art.7(3)(c) provides that, in the case of life assurance, the parties may choose the law of the Member State of which the policy holder is a national. Where the policy holder is a national of a non-unitary State, this gives rise to the difficulty referred to in the main work, para.33–202 and to the difficulty referred to in the main work, para.33–203 where the policy holder has dual nationality. Fourthly, Art.7(3)(d) establishes that where the contract covers risks limited to events occurring in a Member State other than the Member State where the risk is situated, the parties may choose the law of the former Member State. Fifthly, Art.7(3)(e) provides that where a policy holder of a contract to which Art.7(3) applies pursues a commercial or industrial activity and the contract covers two or more risks which relate to these activities which are situated in different Member States, the parties may choose the law of any of the Member States concerned or the law of the country of habitual residence of the policy holder.

The second sub-paragraph of Art.7(3) provides that where, in the cases set out in Art.7(3)(a), Art.7(3)(b) and Art.7(3)(e), the Member States referred to grant greater freedom of choice of the law applicable to the contract, the parties may take advantage of that freedom. This is a somewhat obscure provision which introduces a species of the doctrine of renvoi into the Regulation (*cf.* Art.20, above entry at para.32–043). For these purposes, it has been provided that where the law referred to in Art.7(3)(a) or 7(3)(b), or one of the laws referred to in Art.7(3)(e) is a law of any part of the United Kingdom, the parties to the contract may choose as the law applicable to the contract, (a) the law of another country; or (b) the law of another part of the United Kingdom, if that choice complies with Arts 3, 6 and 9–22 of the Regulation: see Financial Services and Markets Act 2000 (Law Applicable to Contracts of Insurance) Regulations 2009 (SI 2009/3075), reg.4. These Regulations also provide (reg.5) that where the parties may choose the applicable law under the Rome I Regulation or under reg.4 of the Regulations, and where the risk to which the contract relates is covered by Community co-insurance (within the meaning of Council Directive 78/473/EEC on the coordination of laws, regulations and administrative provisions relating to Community insurance ([1978] O.J. L151/25)), co-insurers other than the leading insurer (within the meaning of the foregoing Directive) are not to be treated as parties to the contract. Expressions used in regs 4 and 5 and in the Rome I Regulation have the same meaning as in the Rome I Regulation unless the context requires otherwise: reg.1(3).

Article 7(3), third sub-paragraph, provides that to the extent that the law applicable to the contract has not been chosen in accordance with Art.7(3), the contract shall be governed by the law of the Member State in which the risk is situated at the time of the conclusion of the contract. For the purposes of this provision, Art.7(5) stipulates that where the contract covers risks situated in more than one Member State, "the contract shall be considered as several contracts each relating to only one Member State". There is no "escape clause" allowing application of the law of another Member State if it is clear from the circumstances of the case that the contract is manifestly more closely connected with the law of another country.

Article 7(3) only applies if the risk is situated in a Member State and also, together with Art.7(5), provides for the situation where the risk is situated in more than one Member State. Where the risk is situated in a non-Member State, it would appear that the law applicable to the contract will be generally determined by reference to Arts 3 and 4 of the Regulation. Financial Services and Markets Act 2000 (Law Applicable to Contracts of Insurance) Regulations 2001, as reproduced in Rules 215 and 216 of the main work, do not apply to contracts of insurance entered into on or after December 17, 2009: Financial Services and Markets Act 2000 (Law Applicable to Contracts of Insurance) Regulations 2009, reg.2.

Article 7(4) of the Regulation provides additional rules for contracts covering risks for which a Member State imposes an obligation to take out insurance. According to Art.7(4)(a), the insurance contract will not satisfy the obligation to take out insurance unless it complies with the specific provisions relating to that insurance laid down by the Member State that imposes the obligation. Where the law of the Member State in which the risk is situated and the law of the Member State imposing the obligation to take out insurance contradict each other, the latter shall prevail. For these purposes, where the contract covers risks situated in more than one Member State, Art.7(5) provides that the contract shall be considered as constituting several contracts each relating to only one Member State. Article 7(4)(b), by way of derogation from Art.7(2) and (3), permits a Member State to lay down that the insurance contract shall be governed by the law of the Member State that imposes the obligation to take out insurance.

Insurance contracts are subject to the review clause in Art.27 of the Regulation. By June 17, 2013, the Commission is required to submit to the European Parliament, the Council and the European Economic and Social Committee a report on the application of the Regulation, the report to be accompanied if appropriate, by proposals to amend the Regulation. The report is to include a study on the law applicable to insurance contracts and an assessment of the provisions to be introduced, if any (Art.27(1)(a)). See European Commission, *Communication from the Commission to the European Parliament and the Council: An area of freedom, security and justice serving the citizen*, COM (2009) 262 final, para.3.4 (above, entry at paras 33R–136, 33R–158, 33R–189).

*cf* Art.7(1), (2) and (6) of the Rome I Regulation. See previous entry. **33–137—33–155**

NOTE 8. For the meaning of "EEA State", see Interpretation Act 1978, Sch.1: Financial Services and Markets Act 2000, Sch.3, para.8, as substituted by SI 2007/108. **33–138**

NOTE 19. Add at beginning: But *cf. Wasa International Insurance Co Ltd v Lexington Insurance Co* [2009] UKHL 40, [2010] 1 A.C. 180. **33–141**

NOTE 24. Add: *Commercial Union Assurance Co of Canada v National Union Fire Insurance Co of Pittsburgh* [2007] 1 W.W.R. 167 (Man.): *American Home Insurance Co v Temple Insurance Co* (2009) 94 O.R. (3d) 534. **33–142**

NOTE 26. Add in line 1: See also *Commercial Union Assurance Co of Canada v National Union Fire Insurance Co of Pittsburgh*, above; *American Home Insurance Co v Temple Insurance Co* (2009) 94 O.R. (3d) 534.

NOTE 28. See generally *Wasa International Insurance Co Ltd v Lexington Insurance Co*, above. **33–143**

NOTES 53 and 54. Add: *Travelers Casualty and Surety Co of Canada v Sun Life Assurance Co of Canada (UK) Ltd* [2006] EWHC 2716 (Comm.), [2007] Lloyd's Rep. I.R. 619, where the point was also left open. **33–146**

NOTE 57. Add at end: *Travelers Casualty and Surety Co of Canada v Sun Life Assurance Co of Canada (UK) Ltd*, above; *CGU International Insurance plc v Astrazeneca Insurance Co* [2005] EWHC 2755 (Comm.), [2006] 1 C.L.C. 162.

**33–148** NOTE 70. In line 12 add: *Travelers Casualty and Surety Co of Canada v Sun Life Assurance Co of Canada (UK) Ltd*, above, at [23]–[25].

NOTE 72. Add in line 2: But see Third Parties (Rights against Insurers) Act 2010, s.18.

**33–150** NOTE 76. See also *Travelers Casualty and Surety Co of Canada v Sun Life Assurance Co of Canada (UK) Ltd,* above.

**33–151— 33–152** NOTES 82 and 83. See previous entry.

**33–155** NOTE 3. Add: *Travelers Casualty and Surety Co of Canada v Sun Life Assurance Co of Canada (UK) Ltd,* above.

**33R–158** See entry at para.33R–136, above.

NOTE 19. Add: Merrett (2006) 2 J. Priv. Int. L. 409.

**33–159— 33–185** *cf.* Rome I Regulation, Art.7(1), (3), (5) and (6), above entry at paras 33R–136, 33R–158, 33R–189.

NOTE 27. Add in line 2. *Travelers Casualty and Surety Co of Canada v Sun Life Assurance Co of Canada (UK) Ltd,* above.

NOTE 30. See previous entry.

**33–163** NOTE 56. Add: See also *Travelers Casualty and Surety Co of Canada v Sun Life Assurance Co of Canada (UK) Ltd,* above at [19].

**33–182** NOTES 12, 13 and 14. Add at end: *Travelers Casualty and Surety Co of Canada v Sun Life Assurance Co of Canada (UK) Ltd,* above.

**33–189** See entry at para.33R–136, above.

**33–190— 33–207** *cf.* Rome I Regulation, Art.7(1), (3), (5) and (6), above entry at paras 33R–136, 33R–158, 33R–189.

**33R–209** Article 7 of the Rome I Regulation does not apply to re-insurance contracts (Art.7(1), second sentence). The law applicable to such contracts will therefore be determined by Art.3 of the Regulation if the parties have made a choice of law satisfying that provision, or, in the absence of a choice of law, by Art.4 of the Regulation. For the purposes of Art.4(1), a contract of re-insurance would appear to be a contract for the provision of services and would thus be governed under the general rule by the law of the country where the re-insurer, as service provider, has his habitual residence, as determined by Art.19 of the Regulation (Art.4(1)(b)). Application of that law may be displaced under Art.4(3) of the Regulation. It is most unlikely that Art.4(2) will be relevant to contracts of re-insurance. For comment see Merkin (2009) 5 J. Priv. Int. L. 69.

NOTE 31. Add: *CGU International Insurance plc v Astrazeneca Insurance Co* [2005] EWHC 2755 (Comm), [2006] 1 C.L.C. 162; *Dornoch Ltd v Mauritius Union Insurance Co Ltd* [2006] EWCA Civ 389, [2006] 2 Lloyd's Rep. 475; *Wasa International Insurance Co Ltd v Lexington Insurance Co* [2009] UKHL 40, [2010] 1 A.C. 180. **33–211**

NOTES 32 and 33. See previous entry. **33–212—33–213**

This paragraph was cited with approval in *CGU International Insurance plc v Astrazeneca Insurance Co*, above. In *Wasa International Insurance Co Ltd v Lexington Insurance Co*, above, the House of Lords applied the narrower view, in the circumstances of the case, that the question involved one of construction of the reinsurance contract. **33–212**

*cf.* Art.3 of the Rome I Regulation, above entry at para.32–132. **33–214—33–216**

NOTES 39, 45 and 46. Add: See *Dornoch Ltd v Mauritius Union Insurance Co Ltd* [2006] EWCA Civ 389, [2006] 2 Lloyd's Rep. 475; *Gard Marine & Energy Ltd v Lloyd Tunnicliffe* [2009] EWHC 2388 (Comm.).

*cf.* Art.4(1)(b) and 4(3) of the Rome I Regulation, above entry at para.33R–209. **33–217—33–220**

NOTE 58: Add: *Dornoch Ltd v Mauritius Union Insurance Co Ltd,* above.

## 5. CONTRACTS WITH REGARD TO IMMOVABLES

Under the Rome I Regulation, the parties may choose the law to govern a contract with regard to an immovable in accordance with Art.3 of the Regulation. To the extent that the law applicable to the contract has not been so chosen, Art.4(1) supplies particular choice of law rules for some classes of contracts with regard to immovables. These rules will apply to contracts concluded after December 17, 2009 (Arts 28, 29). **33R–223—33–239**

By Art.4(1)(c), in the absence of a choice of law, a contract relating to a right *in rem* in immovable property or to a tenancy of immovable property shall be governed by the law of the country where the property is situated. This is subject to an exception in Art.4(1)(d) where it is provided that a tenancy of immovable property concluded for a temporary period of no more than six consecutive months shall be governed by the law of the country where the landlord has his habitual residence, provided that the tenant is a natural person and has his habitual residence in the same country.

Taken together, Art.4(1)(c) and 4(1)(d) appear to be based on Art.22(1) of the Judgments Regulation (see main work paras 23–010 *et seq.*), which is in very similar terms, though there is no requirement that the immovable be situated in a Member State. In this respect, therefore Art.4(1)(c) and Art.4(1)(d) are likely to be interpreted consistently with Art.22(1) of the Judgments Regulation (see also Recitals (7) and (17) to the Regulation). The formulation in Art.4(1)(c) is rather different from, and possibly narrower than, that employed in Art.4(3) of the Rome Convention, as reproduced, in part, in Rule 218 (2) since the latter provision refers to a "right to use immovable property" rather than a tenancy of immovable property. It would seem, therefore, that a contract conferring a right to use immovable property which does not amount to a tenancy of that property will not fall within Art.4(1)(c). Article 4(1)(d) has no counterpart in the Rome Convention.

The law applicable under Art.4(1)(c) or Art.4(1)(d), as the case may be, may be displaced under Art.4(3) of the Regulation where it is clear from all the circumstances of the case that the contract is manifestly more closely connected with a country other than that indicated by those provisions, in which case, the law of that other country shall apply.

Where the contract involves a right to use immovable property not amounting to a tenancy, it is possible that the contract may be governed by Art.4(1)(b) (provision of services) or Art.4(4) (because the applicable law cannot be determined pursuant to Art.4(1)).

Article 6(4)(c) generally excludes from the provisions on consumer contracts a contract relating to a right *in rem* in immovable property or a tenancy of immovable property subject to one exception, namely a contract relating to a right to use immovable properties on a timeshare basis within the meaning of Directive 94/47/EC of the European Parliament and of the Council of October 26, 1994 on the protection of purchasers in respect of certain aspects of contracts relating to the purchase of the right to use immovable properties on a timeshare basis ([1994] O.J. L280/83). Broadly speaking, under Art.2 of the Directive, such a contract means any contract or group of contracts concluded for at least three years under which, directly or indirectly, on payment of a certain global price, a real property right or any other right relating to the use of one or more immovable properties for a specified or specifiable period of the year, which may not be less than one week, is established or is the subject of a transfer or an undertaking to transfer (*cf.* main work, paras 33–233, 33–244 *et seq.*). See now, Directive 2008/122/EC of the European Parliament and of the Council of January 14, 2009 on the protection of consumers in respect of timeshare, long-term holiday product, resale and exchange contracts, [2009] O.J. L33/10, which must be implemented in the United Kingdom by February 23, 2011.

See Case C–133/08 *Intercontainer Interfrigo SC (ICF) v Balkenende Oosthuizen BV* [2010] 3 W.L.R. 24, *per* Bot A.G., at [50]–[51], [78], [110]–[116] of the Opinion. See also *Chalbury McCouat International Ltd v PG Foils Ltd* [2010] EWHC 2050 (T.C.C.). **33–228—33–230**

NOTE 40. See Directive 2008/122/EC, entry at paras 33R–223—33–239. **33–233**

NOTE 41. *Office of Fair Trading v Lloyds TSB Bank Plc* [2004] EWHC 2600 (Comm.), [2005] 1 All E.R. 843 was reversed, in part, by the Court of Appeal, [2006] EWCA Civ 268, [2007] Q.B. 1. The decision of the Court of Appeal was affirmed by the House of Lords: [2007] UKHL 48, [2008] 1 A.C. 316.

In general, the formal validity of a contract with regard to an immovable is governed, under the Rome I Regulation, by the general rules on formal validity in Art.11(1)–(3). Article 11(5), however, establishes an additional rule, in this respect, in relation to a contract the subject matter of which is a right *in rem* in immovable property or a tenancy of immovable property. Where the contract falls within Art.11(5), its formal validity shall be governed by the requirements of form of the country where the property is situated if by that law: (a) those requirements of form are imposed irrespective of the country where the contract is concluded and irrespective of the law governing the contract, and (b) those requirements cannot be derogated from by agreement. Notwithstanding the different terminology used in Art.9(6) of the Rome Convention, as discussed in paras 33–240 *et seq.* of the main work, the effect of Art.11(5) of the Regulation would appear to be the same as that reached under Art.9(6) of the Convention. **33–240—33–243**

If the contract is a timeshare arrangement which falls within Art.6(4)(c) of the Regulation, described above, then pursuant to Art.11(4) its formal validity will be governed, subject to Art.11(5), by the law of the country where the consumer has his habitual residence.

*cf.* above, entry at paras 33R–223—33–239. See Directive 2008/122/EC of the European Parliament and of the Council of January 14, 2009 on the protection of consumers in respect of certain aspects of timeshare, long-term holiday product, resale and exchange contracts, [2009] O.J. L33/10, which must be implemented in the United Kingdom by February 23, 2011. **33–244—33–247**

NOTE 5. For the meaning of "EEA State", see Interpretation Act 1978, Sch.1, inserted by Legislative and Regulatory Reform Act 2006, s.26; Enterprise Act **33–247**

2002, s.212(5), as substituted by SI 2007/528. See above, entry at para. 33–037, n.18.

## 6. CONTRACTS FOR THE CARRIAGE OF PERSONS OR GOODS GENERALLY

**33R–249** The Rome I Regulation makes fresh provision as to the law applicable to contracts of carriage concluded after December 17, 2009 (Art.28). For the purposes of the Regulation, the term "carrier" refers to the party who undertakes to carry the goods, whether or not he performs the carriage himself (Recital 22; *cf.* main work, para.33–271).

In the case of a contract for the carriage of goods and to the extent that the law applicable to the contract has not been chosen in accordance with Art.3 of the Regulation, the law applicable is the law of the country of habitual residence of the carrier (habitual residence being defined in Art.19), provided that the place of receipt or the place of delivery or the habitual residence of the consignor is also situated in that country (Art.5(1)). The term "consignor" refers to any person who enters into a contract of carriage with the carrier (Recital 22). The reference to "the place of receipt" (replacing "place of loading" in the Rome Convention) seems to mean the place where the carrier or his agent took possession of the goods which may not be where the goods are loaded on whatever vehicle is to effect the carriage (*cf.* main work, para.33–275). If the requirements for the application of the law of the carrier's habitual residence are not met, the law of the country where the place of delivery as agreed by the parties is situated applies (Art.5(1)).

In the case of the carriage of passengers, the choice of the applicable law under Art.3 of the Regulation is restricted. The parties may choose only the law of the country where (a) the passenger has his habitual residence (defined, but only in the case of a passenger acting in the course of his business activity, in Art.19); or (b) the carrier has his habitual residence; or (c) the carrier has his place of central administration; or (d) the place of departure is situated; or (e) the place of destination is situated. To the extent that the applicable law has not been chosen by the parties in accordance with these rules, the applicable law is the law of the country where the passenger has his habitual residence, provided that either the place of departure or the place of destination is situated in that country. If these requirements are not met, the law of the country where the carrier has his habitual residence applies (Art.5(2)).

In the case of all contracts of carriage, whether of goods or of passengers, where it is clear from all the circumstances of the case that the contract, in the absence of a choice of law, is manifestly more closely connected with a country other than that indicated in Art.5(1) and (2), the law of that other country applies (Art.5(3); *cf.* main work, paras 33–277–33–278).

**33–252** Where the Rome I Regulation applies, a contract for the carriage of passengers which is a contract relating to package travel within the meaning of Council Directive 90/314/EEC of June 13, 1990 on package travel, package holidays and package tours is governed by the rules applicable to consumer contracts (see entry at para.33R–001) and not those applying to contracts of carriage (Rome I Regulation, Art.6(4)(b)).

The Rome I Regulation does not prejudice the application of international transport conventions to which one or more Member States are parties at the time when the Regulation was adopted (June 17, 2008) and which lay down conflict-of-law rules relating to contractual obligations (Regulation, Art.25(1); the exception in Art.25(2), which applies only to conventions concluded exclusively between two or more Member States, seems to have no relevance to the international transport conventions). **33–253**

## 7. CONTRACTS OF AFFREIGHTMENT

Article 5 of the Rome I Regulation provides a discrete set of choice of law rules for determining the law applicable to a contract of carriage. Article 5 applies to contracts for the carriage of goods (by whatever means of transport) and to the carriage of passengers. The provision will apply to contracts entered into after December 17, 2009 (Arts 28, 29). See Nielsen in *Rome I Regulation: The Law Applicable to Contractual Obligations in Europe* (ed. Leible and Ferrari, 2009), p.99. The following comments are confined to the application of the provision in the context of the carriage of goods by water. For other forms of carriage of goods and for the carriage of passengers, see above, entry at para.33R–249. **33R–263— 33–278**

Contracts for the carriage of goods are dealt with in Art.5(1) and 5(3), the substance of which is broadly similar to Art.4(4) and 4(5) of the Rome Convention as reproduced in Rule 220 of the main work. Article 5(1) provides that to:

> "the extent that the law applicable to a contract for the carriage of goods has not been chosen in accordance with Art.3 of the Regulation, the law applicable shall be the law of the country of habitual residence of the carrier, provided that the place of receipt or the place of delivery or the habitual residence of the consignor is also situated in that country. If those requirements are not met, the law of the country where the place of delivery as agreed by the parties is situated shall apply".

As pointed out below, the law applicable in the absence of choice under Art.5(1) may be displaced by reference to the rule of displacement contained in Art.5(3).

The meaning of "contract for the carriage of goods" (whatever the means of transport) is not defined in the text of the Regulation. However, Recital (22) to the Regulation explains that, in this respect, no "change is intended with respect to Art.4(4), third sentence, of the Rome Convention. Consequently, single voyage charter parties and other contracts the main purpose of which is the carriage of goods should be treated as contracts for the carriage of goods". One may possibly deduce from this that "contract for the carriage of goods" by water has the same meaning under the Regulation as it has under the Convention: see main work, paras 33–265 *et seq.*, though see below, entry at para.33–266. It is clear that the meaning given to contract for the carriage of goods and other concepts in Art.5 must be an autonomous one.

The parties are free to choose the law applicable to a contract for the carriage of goods in accordance with Art.3(1) of the Regulation, such choice being either express or clearly demonstrated by the terms of the contract or the circumstances of the case. The factors referred to in main work, paras 33–268–33–269 may well demonstrate such a choice in particular cases, as may an exclusive jurisdiction clause, or, perhaps a non-exclusive jurisdiction clause, in the relevant contract (see Recital (12) to the Regulation).

To the extent that the applicable law has not been chosen in accordance with Art.3, Art.5(1) will become relevant. The provision is made up of what one might call the general rule, contained in the first sentence, and a residual rule, contained in the second sentence.

Generally, the applicable law will be the law of the country of the habitual residence of the carrier, provided that the place of receipt or the place of delivery or the habitual residence of the consignor is also situated in that country. "Place of receipt" would seem to mean the place where the carrier receives the goods from the consignor (*cf.* main work, para.33–273). "Place of delivery" would seem to mean the place where the carrier is required to deliver the goods (*cf.* main work, para.33–273). Although it is not explicitly stated in the Regulation, it would also seem that the place of receipt and place of delivery are those agreed at the time of conclusion of the contract (*cf.* main work, para.33–273).

The meaning of "carrier" is not defined in the text of the Regulation but Recital (22) states that the term "should refer to the party to the contract who undertakes to carry the goods, whether or not he performs the carriage itself". This reflects the position under the Rome Convention: see main work, para.33–271. Further, there is no definition of "consignor" in the text of the Regulation but Recital (22) explains that the term should refer to any person who enters into a contract of carriage with the carrier (*cf.* main work, para.33–275).

If the requirements of the first sentence of Art.5(1) are not met, then the residual rule contained in the second sentence provides that "the law of the country where the place of delivery as agreed by the parties shall apply". It is not clear, in relation to this provision, whether the relevant place of delivery is that agreed by the parties at the time the contract is concluded or whether, if the parties subsequently agree on a different place of delivery, that different place may be the relevant place. Consistency with the general rule might indicate the place originally agreed upon, but this might be thought to be unrealistic. A different view could suggest that a subsequent agreement to change the place of delivery is a relevant factor in determining whether either rule in Art.5(1) may be displaced by reference to Art.5(3) of the Regulation.

Article 5(3) provides a rule of displacement to the effect that where it is clear from all the circumstances of the case that the contract, in the absence of a choice of law, is manifestly more closely connected with a country other than that indicated in Art.5(1), the law of that other country shall apply (*cf.* main work, paras 33–277–33–278).

A contract of carriage is not, with one limited exception (package tours), a consumer contract for the purposes of the Regulation: see Art.6(4)(b), above, entry at para.33R–001. Where the contract is a mixed contract for the carriage of goods and passengers, it is conceivable that, in the absence of a choice of law governing the contract as a whole, that application of Art.5(1) and (2) might result in the contract having two different applicable laws (*cf.* main work, para.33–251).

NOTE 84 and text thereto. In Case C–133/08 *Intercontainer Interfrigo (ICF) SC v Balkenende Oosthuizen BV* [2010] 3 W.L.R. 24 (a case on carriage by rail) the European Court considered a number of issues arising under Art.4(1), 4(2), 4(4) and 4(5) of the Rome Convention. First it was held that the wording of Art.4(4) equated with contracts of carriage not only single voyage charter-parties but also other contracts, in so far as the main purpose of those contracts was the carriage of goods. In a charterparty, the owner, who effected performance, undertook as a matter of course to make a means of transport available to the charterer. It was conceivable, however, that the owner's obligations related not merely to making available the means of transport but also the carriage of goods proper. In such circumstances, the contract in question came within the scope of Art.4(4) where its main purpose was the carriage of goods. However, the presumption set out in the second sentence of Art.4(4) applied only where the owner, assuming that he was regarded as the carrier, had his principal place of business, at the time the contract was concluded, in the country in which the place of loading or the principal place of business of the consignor was situated. The second sentence of Art.4(4) thus applied to a charterparty, other than a single voyage charterparty, only where the main purpose of the contract was not merely to make available a means of transport, but the actual carriage of goods. See [2010] 3 W.L.R. 24 at [33], [35]–[37]. **33–266**

Under the second sentence of Art.4(1) a part of the contract could, by way of exception, be made subject to a law other than that applied to the rest of the contract, where it had a closer connection with a country other than that with which the other parts of the contract were connected. This rule, providing for "severance" of a contract, was, however, of an exceptional nature, and only applied where there were a number of parts of the contract which could be regarded as independent of each other, having regard to the purpose of the rest of the contract. Where Art.4(4) applied to the charterparty, the law applicable by virtue of that provision applied to the whole of the contract, unless the part of the contract relating to carriage was independent of the rest of the contract. See [2010] 3 W.L.R. 24 at [42]–[49].

The objective of Art.4(5) of the Convention was to counterbalance the presumptions in Art.4(2)–(4) by reconciling the requirements of legal certainty, as achieved by those presumptions, with the necessity of providing for a certain flexibility in determining the law which was actually most closely connected with the contract in question. As was apparent from the wording and objective of Art.4, the court always had to determine, initially, the applicable law on the basis of Art.4(2)–(4). However, where it was clear from the circumstances as a whole that the contract was more closely connected with a country other than that identified on the basis of Art.4(2)–(4), the court should disregard the law the law indicated by the relevant presumption and apply the law of the country with which the contract was most closely connected. See [2010] 3 W.L.R. 24 at [54]–[59], [62]–[64]. *cf.* Rome I Regulation, entry at paras 33R–263—33–278.

**33–268** *cf.* Art.5(1) of the Rome I Regulation, entry at paras 33R–263—33–278.

NOTE 3. CPR, r.6.20(5)(c) has been replaced by PD6B, para.3.1(6)(c).

NOTE 96. Add: *Horne Linie GmbH & Co v Panamericana Formas e Impresos SA* [2006] EWHC 373 (Comm.), [2006] 2 Lloyd's Rep. 44.

**33–270—33–278** See above, entry at para.33–266. *cf.* Art.5(1) of the Rome I Regulation, entry at paras 33R–263—33–278.

**33–270** See generally Case C–133/08 *Intercontainer Interfrigo SC (ICF) v Balkenende Oosthuizen BV* [2010] 3 W.L.R. 24, above entry at para.33–266.

**33–271** See above, entry at para.33–266.

**33–277** NOTE 40. See above, entry at para.33–266. *cf.* Art.5(3) of the Rome I Regulation, above entry at paras 33R–263—33–278.

**33–279** NOTE 42. Art. 12(2) of the Rome I Regulation is to the same effect as Art.10(2) of the Rome Convention, discussed in this paragraph.

**33–280** NOTE 50. The Rome I Regulation contains no specific rules relating to agency. Article 1(2)(g) of the Regulation specifically excludes the question whether an agent is able to bind a principal, in relation to a third party, from the scope of the Regulation.

**33–286** NOTE 69. *cf.* Art.25 of the Rome I Regulation.

NOTE 71. *cf.* Art.9(1) and (2) of the Rome I Regulation, above, entry at para.32–132.

NOTE 72. Add in penultimate line: *Mediterranean Shipping Co SA v Trafigura Beheer BV* [2007] EWCA Civ 794, [2007] 2 Lloyd's Rep. 622. **33–287**

NOTE 84. See now CPR PD6B, para.3.1(6)(c). **33–292**

## 8. CONTRACTS BETWEEN BANKER AND CUSTOMER

The Rome I Regulation contains no specific rule concerning contracts between banker and customer. In general terms, at least, some types of contract between banker and customer will be regarded as contracts for the provision of services which, absent a choice of law satisfying Art.3(1) of the Regulation, will be governed by the law of the habitual residence of the bank as service provider: Art.4(1)(b). For these purposes, the law of the habitual residence of the bank will be either its place of central administration (Art.19(1)) or where the banking contract is concluded through the operations of a branch of the bank, the place where the branch is located (Art.19(2)). The law applicable under this general rule may be displaced by reference to Art.4(3) of the Regulation. It appears to be possible that a contract between banker and customer may be a consumer contract in an appropriate case, for the purposes of Art.6 of the Regulation. Any relevant provisions will apply to contracts entered into after December 17, 2009 (Arts 28, 29). **33R–297**

The general principle may, however, as explained below, require considerable modification in relation to particular banking transactions.

NOTES 10 and 11. *Marconi Communications International Ltd v PT Pan Indonesia Bank Ltd TBK* [2005] EWCA Civ 422 is now reported at [2007] 2 Lloyd's Rep. 72.

NOTE 10. Add in line 6: *Walsh v National Irish Bank Ltd* [2008] 2 I.L.R.M. 56.

NOTE 14. See previous entry. **33–298**

*cf.* Art.3(1) of the Rome I Regulation. **33–299—33–302**

NOTE 20. *cf.* Art.1(2)(d) of the Rome I Regulation. **33–299**

NOTE 22. Add: See also *Halpern v Halpern (Nos 1 and 2)* [2007] EWCA Civ 291, [2008] Q.B. 195; *Musawi v R E International (UK) Ltd* [2007] EWHC 2981 (Ch.), [2008] 1 Lloyd's Rep. 326 (Jewish law).

NOTE 30. See entry at para.33R–297, nn.10 and 11. Add in last line: See also *Trafigura Beheer BV v Kookmin Bank Co* [2005] EWHC 2350 (Comm.), at [15]. **33–300**

**33–302** NOTE 35. *cf.* Art.3(1) of, and Recital (12) to, the Rome I Regulation.

NOTE 40. Add: See *Emeraldian Limited Partnership v Wellmix Shipping Ltd* [2010] EWHC 1411 (Comm.); *Commercial Marine Piling Ltd v Pierse Contracting Ltd* [2009] EWHC 2241 (TCC), [2009] 2 Lloyd's Rep. 659.

NOTE 47. See entry at para.33R–297, nn.10 and 11.

**33–304** NOTE 58. The equivalent passage in the 13th edition of this work was approved in *Walsh v National Irish Bank Ltd* [2008] 2 I.L.R.M. 56 at [26].

NOTES 59 and 60: Add: *Walsh v National Irish Bank Ltd*, above.

**33–305** NOTE 61. See entry at para.33R–297, nn.10 and 11.

NOTE 61. Add at end: *Walsh v National Irish Bank Ltd*, above.

NOTE 62. Under Art.4(1)(b) of the Rome I Regulation, the law governing a bank account will normally be that of the country in which the account is kept since that country will be the habitual residence of the bank.

NOTE 64. This might be a situation where it is not possible to determine the applicable law under Art.4(1) or 4(2) of the Regulation, so that the applicable law will be the law of the country with which the contract is most closely connected pursuant to Art.4(4) of the Regulation : and see Recital (21) to the Regulation.

Add at end: *Walsh v National Irish Bank,* above.

**33–306** The position would appear to be the same in relation to Art.4(3) of the Rome I Regulation.

**33–307** NOTE 75. The granting of a loan would appear to be the provision of a service for the purposes of Art.4(1)(b) of the Regulation. The applicable law will thus normally be the law of the country where the bank (or branch thereof) is habitually resident.

**33–308** NOTE 80. This may be a situation in which the applicable law cannot be determined on the basis of Art.4(1) or 4(2) of the Regulation so that under Art. 4(3) the applicable law will be that of the country with which the contract is most closely connected.

**33–309— 33–314** The component contracts making up a letter of credit could be regarded as contracts for the provision of services (Art.4(1)(b) of the Regulation) and if such a characterisation was adopted this would lead to the possibility that each contract would be governed by a different law. In such circumstances, Art.4(3) could be invoked to secure the application of one law, the law of the country where payment is to be made against presentation of documents, at least in respect of the contract between issuing and correspondent bank (main work, para.33–311), that between the beneficiary and confirming bank (main work, para.33–312) and that between the beneficiary and the issuing bank (main work, para.33–313). See Recital (20) to the Regulation. Alternatively, a letter of credit may be a transaction which is not covered by Art.4(1) at all since it involves a congeries of contracts so that Art.4(2) applies. If this characterisation is adopted, then the law of the habitual residence of the party who is to effect the performance which is characteristic of each of the component contracts will be the applicable law, subject to displacement under Art.4(3), which might then lead to the application of a single law to all the contracts : and see Recital (20) to the Regulation; Ministry of Justice, *Rome 1—Should the UK Opt In?,* Consultation Paper CP05/08, April 2008, para.4.3. Finally, it is possible that resort may be made to Art.4(4).

NOTE 85. Add: *Habib Bank Ltd v Central Bank of Sudan* [2006] EWHC 1767 (Comm.), [2007] 1 W.L.R. 470. **33–309**

NOTE 94. See entry at para.33R–297, nn.10 and 11. Add at end: *Trafigura Beheer BV v Kookmin Bank Co* [2005] EWHC 2350 (Comm.); *Trafigura Beheer BV v Kookmin Bank Co* [2006] EWHC 1450 (Comm.), [2006] 2 Lloyd's Rep. 455, at [107]. **33–311**

NOTE 2. Add: See also *Trafigura Beheer BV v Kookmin Bank Co*, above. **33–312**

NOTE 6. See entry at para.33R–297, nn.10 and 11.

NOTE 9. Add: See also *Trafigura Beheer BV v Kookmin Bank Co* [2005] EWHC 2350 (Comm.); *Trafigura Beheer BV v Kookmin Bank Co* [2006] EWHC 1450 (Comm.), [2006] 2 Lloyd's Rep. 455, at [106]. **33–313**

The provision by a bank of a performance bond would appear to be the provision of a service by the bank for the purposes of Art.4(1)(b) of the Regulation. Thus the applicable law will normally be the habitual residence of the bank (or branch thereof), usually the place at which payment under the bond is due. **33–314**

NOTE 29. The provision of a counter-guarantee by a bank is likely to be regarded as the provision of a service for the purposes of Art.4(1)(b) of the Regulation and thus governed, normally, by the law of the habitual residence of the bank (or branch thereof) at which the counter-guarantee was issued. **33–317**

NOTES 30–32. Article 4(3) could be invoked in these circumstances to displace the application of Art.4(1)(b): see Recital (20)) to the Regulation.

NOTE 31. Add in line 2: *Commercial Marine Piling Ltd v Pierse Contracting Ltd* [2009] EWHC 2241 (TCC), [2009] 2 Lloyd's Rep. 659.

**33–318** NOTE 33. It is likely that a contract of bailment will be treated as a contract for the provision of a service within Art.4(1)(b) of the Rome I Regulation. The applicable law will, thus, normally be the law of the habitual residence of the bank (or branch thereof) at which the items are deposited.

**33–320** *cf.* Art.9(1) and (2) of the Rome I Regulation.

**33–321** NOTE 50. See entry at para.33R–297, nn.10 and 11.

## 9. NEGOTIABLE INSTRUMENTS GENERALLY

**33–329—33–332** The same exclusion as that contained in Art.1(2)(c) of the Rome Convention is found in the Rome I Regulation, Art.1(2)(d).

**33–332** NOTE 71. See *Standard Bank plc v. Agrinvest International Inc* [2007] EWHC 2595 (Comm.), [2008] 1 Lloyd's Rep. 532.

## 10. BILLS OF EXCHANGE AND PROMISSORY NOTES

**33R–334** NOTE 77. Add in line 3: *Karafarin Bank v Dara* [2009] EWHC 3265 (Comm.), [2010] 1 Lloyd's Rep. 236.

**33–337** NOTE 95. Add at end: *Karafarin Bank v Dara*, above.

**33–338** NOTE 98. The same exclusion as that continued in Art.1(2)(c) of the Rome Convention is found in the Rome I Regulation, Art.1(2)(d). An option contract to purchase promissory notes does fall within the Rome Convention: *Standard Bank plc v Agrinvest International Inc* [2007] EWHC 2595 (Comm.), [2008] 1 Lloyd's Rep. 532.

NOTES 7 and 8. Add: See also *Karafarin Bank v Dara*, above.

**33–340** NOTE 23. See previous entry. In line 8 add: See also *Trafigura Beheer BV v Kookmin Bank Co* [2005] EWHC 2350 (Comm.); *Trafigura Beheer BV v Kookmin Bank Co* [2006] EWHC 1450 (Comm.), [2006] 2 Lloyd's Rep. 455.

**33R–342** NOTE 31. Add at beginning: *Karafarin Bank v Dara*, above, at [10].

**33–374—33–375** See *Karafarin Bank v Dara*, above, at [25]–[27].

**33–376** NOTES 31–33: Add: *cf. Karafarin Bank v Dara*, above, at [25]–[26].

## 11. INTEREST

As regards the Rome I Regulation, it seems that the position in respect of claims in contract is the same as that stated in Rule 226 of the main work, as discussed in these paragraphs: see Arts 1(3), 12(1)(b) and 12 (1)(c) of the Regulation. As regards claims in tort (main work, paras 33–395–33–396) see Regulation (EC) 864/2007 of the European Parliament and of the Council of July 11, 2007 on the law applicable to non-contractual obligations (Rome II) ([2007] O.J. L199/40), Arts 1(3) and 15(h), below, entries at paras S35–186 and S35–257. The Rome II Regulation is reproduced in Appendix 1 to this Supplement. **33R–379— 33–401**

NOTE 41. Add in last line: See now, *Maher v Groupama Grand Est* [2009] EWCA Civ 1191, [2010] 1 W.L.R. 1564 (a case on tort). **33R–379**

NOTE 42. See previous entry.

NOTE 43 and text thereto. Supreme Court Act 1981 is now renamed Senior Courts Act 1981: Constitutional Reform Act 2005, s.59 and Sch.11, in force from October 1, 2009.

Add: *cf. Maher v Groupama Grand Est*, above.

In *Maher v Groupama Grand Est*, above, the Court of Appeal reviewed the authorities referred to in these paragraphs and in the accompanying notes in a case of tort, under Private International Law (Miscellaneous Provisions) Act 1995, according to which liability was governed by French law. The court concluded that Senior Courts Act 1981, s.35A created a remedy exercised at the court's discretion rather than a substantive right to interest and that therefore, although the existence of a legal right to claim interest was to be determined by French law as the *lex causae,* whether or not such a substantive right existed or not, an award of interest under s.35A was to be classified as a procedural matter, governed by English law as the *lex fori* (expressing a preference for the view of Hobhouse J. in *Midland International Trade Services v Sudairy, Financial Times*, May 2, 1990 to the dicta in *Kuwait Oil Tanker SAK v Al Bader* [2000] 2 All E.R. (Comm.) 271 (C.A.)) although in exercising its discretion the court might well take into account any relevant provisions of French law relating to the recovery of interest. See at [33], [37], [40]–[43]. The court made no reference to the position under the Rome Convention or the Rome II Regulation, so the case is not conclusive on the proper approach to interest under those instruments. Equally, it is not conclusive as to the correct approach to interest under the Rome I Regulation. *cf. Al Qatani & Sons Beverage Industry Co v Antliff* [2010] EWHC 1735 (Comm.) at 59. Presumably, this case will also mean that the rate of interest is a matter for the *lex fori* taking into account provisions of the applicable law on this matter. **33–392— 33–393**

**33–392** Note 86. *Harding v Wealands* [2004] EWCA Civ 1735, [2005] 1 W.L.R. 1735 was reversed by the House of Lords, [2006] UKHL 32, [2007] 2 A.C. 1, but this does not affect the point made in the text.

**33–393** Note 87. The Supreme Court Act 1981 is now the Senior Courts Act 1981: see above, entry at para.33R–379, n.43 and text thereto.

**33–394** Note 3. Add in line 1: *Karafarin Bank v Dara* [2009] EWHC 3265 (Comm.), [2010] 1 Lloyd's Rep. 236.

**33–395— 33–396** See now *Maher v Groupama Grand Est* [2009] EWCA Civ 1191, [2010] 1 W.L.R. 1564, above, entry at paras 33–392—33–393.

**33–395** Notes 5–8 and text thereto. The Supreme Court Act 1981 is now the Senior Courts Act 1981: see above, entry at 33–379, n.43.

Note 12. Add: *cf. Harding v Wealands* [2006] UKHL 32, [2007] 2 A.C. 1. See below, entry at para.35–058.

**33–397— 33–399** See on these paragraphs, *Maher v Groupama Grand Est* [2009] EWCA Civ 1191, [2010] 1 W.L.R. 1564, above, entry at paras 33–392—33–393.

**33–397** Note 23. See entry at para.33–392, n.86.

**33–398— 33–399** The Supreme Court Act 1981 is now the Senior Courts Act 1981: see above, entry at paras 33R–379, n.43 and text thereto.

**33–400** This paragraph was cited with approval in *Gater Assets Ltd v Nak Naftogaz Ukrainiy (No.3)* [2008] EWHC 1108 (Comm.), [2008] 2 Lloyd's Rep. 295 at [19].

**33–401** The Supreme Court Act 1981 is now the Senior Courts Act 1981: see above, entry at paras 33R–379, n.43 and text thereto.

## 12. CONTRACTS THROUGH AGENTS

### A. *Contract of Agency*

**33R–404** The Rome I Regulation contains no explicit rules for the determination of the law applicable to agency contracts. Reference must thus be made to the general rules in the Regulation which will apply to contracts concluded after December 17, 2009 (Arts 28, 29).

As regards a contract between principal and agent, in general, in the absence of a choice of law, it would appear that the contract is one for the provision of services for the purposes of Art.4(1)(b) of the Regulation and that for those purposes the service provider is the agent (*cf.* Case C–19/09 *Wood Floor Solutions Andreas Domberger GmbH v Silva Trade SA* [2010] 1 W.L.R. 1900, [34] (Judgments Regulation, Art.5(1)(b))). Accordingly the applicable law will be the law of the country in which the agent is habitually resident, as determined by Art.19 of the Regulation, subject to possible displacement under Art.4(3) of the Regulation.

A contract between principal and agent, in general, must be distinguished from a distribution contract. According to Art.4(1)(f) a distribution contract shall be governed, in the absence of a choice of law, by the law of the country in which the distributor has his habitual residence. This law may be displaced, in an appropriate case, by reference to Art.4(3) of the Regulation. It is possible that a distribution contract may be accompanied, as part of the whole transaction, by another contract or contract, so that the elements of the contract may be covered by more than one of points (a) to (h) of Art.4(1), thereby bringing Art.4(2) into play. An example might be an arrangement whereby the distributor agrees to distribute products manufactured by a "principal" which the latter supplies and sells to the former for distribution as agreed. Here the contract will be governed by the law of the country where the party required to effect the characteristic performance of the contract has his habitual residence and it is possible that this party will be the principal (see main work, para.33–411). On the other hand, Art.4(1)(f) might be regarded as a free standing provision which should apply to all contracts where a distributor is a party (see main work, para.33–411, text at nn.73–74).

A contract of agency, in general must also be distinguished from a franchise contract. In the absence of a choice of law, a franchise contract, according to Art.4(1)(e) shall be governed by the law of the country where the franchisee has his habitual residence. This law may be displaced by reference to Art.4(3) of the Regulation.

If the contract between principal and agent is a consumer or employment contract, the law applicable must be determined in accordance with Arts 6 and 8 respectively of the Rome I Regulation.

For the purposes of the foregoing, the expressions "agent", "distribution contract" and "franchise contract" will undoubtedly be given an autonomous meaning.

NOTE 48. Add in line 4: Bowstead & Reynolds, *Agency* (19th ed., 2010), ch.12. **33–407**

NOTE 49. Add: *Dan Gamache Trucking Inc v Encore Metals Inc* (2008) BCSC 343 at [62] (whether a party is an agent is determined by the proper law of the contract by which the alleged agency relationship was created).

NOTE 57 and text thereto. The Rome I Regulation does not apply to the question of whether an agent is able to bind a principal to a third party: Art.1(2)(g). **33–408**

NOTE 64. Add in line 1: *Cf.* Bowstead & Reynolds, *Agency* (19th ed., 2010), paras 12–004, 12–010.

**33–410—33–412** *cf.* above, entry at para.33R–404.

**33–410** NOTE 69. Add: *Albon v Naza Motor Trading SDN BHD* [2007] EWHC 9 (Ch.), [2007] 1 Lloyd's Rep. 297.

**33–412** *cf.* Article 4(3) of the Rome I Regulation.

NOTE 77. Add: *Albon v Naza Motor Trading SDN BHD,* above.

**33–413** *cf.* Article 3(3) and (4) of the Rome I Regulation, above, entry at para.32–132.

NOTE 80. Add in line 1: Bowstead & Reynolds, *Agency* (19th ed., 2010), paras 12–009 and 12–017—12–018, arguing that the principal-agent contract must be considered as separate from the act of conferring authority on the agent.

**33–414** *cf.* Article 11(1) and (2) of the Rome I Regulation, above, entry at para.32R–175.

**33–415** It would seem that the consumer contract provisions in Art.6 of the Rome I Regulation are capable of applying to certain contracts of agency: main work, paras 33–07, 33–415; above, entry at para.33R–001.

**33–416** NOTE 95 Add: Agents with authority to contract (as opposed to mere authority to negotiate) only constitute "commercial agents" if they have authority to contract in the principal's name as well as on his behalf: *Sagal v Atelier Bunk GmbH* [2009] EWCA Civ 700.

NOTE 97. On the interpretation of the Commercial Agents Directive and implementing Regulations in the United Kingdom, see *Lonsdale v Howard & Hallam Ltd* [2007] UKHL 32, [2007] 1 W.L.R. 2055. See also *Jacobs & Turner Ltd v Celsius Sarl,* 2007 S.L.T 722.

NOTE 98. Add at end: See now Art.8 of the Rome I Regulation (above, entry at paras 33R–058—33–079).

**33–421** NOTE 15. See previous entry.

**33–423** NOTE 21. See also *Accentuate Ltd v Asigra Inc* [2009] EWHC 2655 (QB), [2009] 2 Lloyd's Rep. 599.

B. *Relation of Principal and Third Party*

The Rome I Regulation does not apply to the question whether an agent is able to bind a principal, or an organ to bind a company or other body corporate or unincorporated, in relation to a third party: see Art.1(2)(g) of the Regulation. **33R–428**

NOTE 39. *SEB Trygg Holding Aktiebolag v Manches* [2005] EWHC 35 (Comm.), [2005] 2 Lloyd's Rep. 129 was affirmed, in part, and reversed, in part, by the Court of Appeal, *sub nom. SEB Trygg Liv Holding AB v Manches* [2005] EWCA Civ 1237, [2006] 1 W.L.R. 2276. No explicit consideration is given to issues of conflict of laws. It appears, however, to have been assumed (a) that issues of actual authority are to be referred to the law governing the relationship between principal and agent and (b) that issues of ostensible or apparent authority are governed by the law applicable to the transaction between agent and third party: for comment, see Reynolds [2006] J.B.L. 537.

Add at end: *Sea Trade Maritime Corp v Hellenic Mutual War Risks Association (Bermuda) Ltd (No.2)* [2006] EWHC 2530 (Comm.), [2007] 1 Lloyd's Rep. 280; *Donegal International Ltd v Zambia* [2007] EWHC 197 (Comm.), [2007] 1 Lloyd's Rep. 397, at [435]; *Dan Gamache Trucking Inc v Encore Metals Inc* (2008) BCSC 343 at [62]; *Sea Emerald SA v Prominvestbank Joint Stockpoint Commercial Industrial and Investment Bank* [2008] EWHC 1979 (Comm.); *Novus Aviation Ltd v Onur Air Tacimacilik AS* [2009] EWCA Civ 122, [2009] 1 Lloyd's Rep. 576, at [40]; *Calyon v Wytwornia Sprzetu Komunikacynego Pzl Swidnik SA* [2009] EWHC 1914 (Comm.), at [95]; *Rimpacific Navigation Inc v Daehan Shipbuilding Co Ltd* [2009] EWHC 2941 (Comm.), [2010] 2 Lloyd's Rep. 236, at [32]–[34]. Note, however, the criticism of the text of Rule 228 in Bowstead & Reynolds, *Agency* (19th ed., 2010), para.12–015.

NOTE 40. Add: Bowstead & Reynolds, *Agency* (19th ed., 2010), ch.12. **33–429**

See Art.1(2)(g) of the Rome I Regulation. For discussion of the scope and effect of the exclusion in Art.1(2)(g), see Bowstead & Reynolds, *Agency* (19th ed., 2010), paras 12–011 to 12–015. **33–430**

NOTE 44. See Art.1(2)(f) of the Rome I Regulation.

See also Bowstead & Reynolds, *Agency* (19th ed., 2010), para.12–030. **33–433**

NOTES 52, 53 and 54. See above, entry at para.33R–428, n.39 in relation to the decision in *SEB Trygg v Manches*. Add: *Sea Emerald SA v Prominvestbank Joint Stockpoint Commercial Industrial and Investment Bank* [2008] EWHC 1979 (Comm.).

NOTE 52. Add in line 4: *Novus Aviation Ltd v Onur Air Tacimacilik AS* [2009] EWCA Civ 122, [2009] 1 Lloyd's Rep. 576, at [40]; *Calyon v Wytwornia Sprzetu Komunikacynego Pzl Swidnik SA* [2009] EWHC 1914 (Comm.), at [95]; *Rimpacific Navigation Inc v Daehan Shipbuilding Co Ltd* [2009] EWHC 2941 (Comm.), [2010] 2 Lloyd's Rep 236, at [32]–[34]. In *Rimpacific*, David Steel J. (at [29]–[31]) rejected the submission that Companies Act 1985, s.36, as modified by Regs 3 and 4 of the Foreign Companies (Execution of Documents) Regulations (SI 1994/950) (now Companies Act 2006, s.43, as modified by Reg.3 of the Overseas Companies (Execution of Documents and Registration of Charges Regulations (SI 2009/1917)) required that, for contracts entered into by overseas companies, the law of the company's place of incorporation be applied instead. On this last point, see also *Azov Shipping Co v Baltic Shipping Co* [1999] 2 Lloyd's Rep. 159, 172.

**33–434** NOTE 58. Add: *Cf.* Bowstead & Reynolds, *Agency* (19th ed., 2010), paras 12–017 to 12–018.

NOTES 59 and 60. See above, entry at para.33R–428, n.39 in relation to the decision in *SEB Trygg v Manches*.

**33–436** NOTE 64. See above, entry at para.33R–428, n.39 in relation to the decision in *SEB Trygg v Manches*.

**33–437** NOTE 70. Add: For a similar view, see Bowstead & Reynolds, *Agency* (19th ed., 2010), para.12–018.

**33–439** NOTE 76. For the view that the rules of the Rome I Regulation can nevertheless be imported for this purpose, see Bowstead & Reynolds, *Agency* (19th ed., 2010), paras 12–014 to 12–015.

NOTES 79–80. *Cf.* Bowstead & Reynolds, *Agency* (19th ed., 2010), paras 12–013, 12–016.

**33–443** NOTE 88. The law applicable to any contract concluded between an agent and third party will, in cases falling within the Rome I Regulation, be determined by the relevant choice of law rules contained in the Regulation.

NOTE 91. Following the coming into force of the Rome II Regulation (below, paras S35–165 *et seq.*), the agent's liability may, depending on its character, fall to be characterised as "contractual" (within the Rome Convention or Rome I Regulation) or "non-contractual" (within the Rome II Regulation). See Dickinson, *The Rome II Regulation: The Law Applicable to Non-Contractual Obligations* (2008), pp.530–531.

**33–444** *cf.* Art.11(1) and (2) of the Rome I Regulation.

## 13. WAGERING CONTRACTS

A wagering contract would appear to be a contract for the provision of services within the meaning of Art.4(1)(b) of the Rome I Regulation. Thus in the absence of a choice of law, the law applicable to the contract will be the law of the country in which the service provider, i.e. the party who offers the facility for placing the wager, is habitually resident. This law may be displaced by reference to Art.4(3) of the Regulation (*cf.* main work, para.33–454). **33R–466**

Some wagering contracts may fall within the consumer contract provisions found in Art. 6 of the Rome I Regulation, as could some loans made for the purpose of gaming (*cf.* main work, para.33–407).

NOTE 6. All provisions of the Gambling Act 2005, which are referred to in the Comment to Rule 229, are in force from September 1, 2007: see SI 2006/3272. **33–447**

NOTE 13. Add at end: *Paradise Enterprises v Kakavas* [2010] VSC 25.

NOTE 19. The Rome I Regulation does not apply to obligations arising under cheques: Art.1(2)(d). **33–453**

## CHAPTER 34

# RESTITUTION

34R–001 This Rule should now be read in the light of the amendments introduced by (1) Regulation (EC) 864/2007 of the European Parliament and of the Council of July 11, 2007 on the law applicable to non-contractual obligations (Rome II): [2007] O.J. L199/40, which entered into force on January 11, 2009, and is reproduced in Appendix 1 to this Supplement and (2) Regulation (EC) 593/2008 of the European Parliament and of the Council of June 17, 2008 on the law applicable to contractual obligations (Rome I): [2008] O.J. L177/6 (with *corrigendum* [2009] O.J. L307/87), which applies to contracts concluded on or after December 17, 2009, and is reproduced in Appendix 2 to this Supplement. In particular, the Rome II Regulation rules described in the entry to para.34–014 below apply in the English courts from January 11, 2009 and introduce new choice of law rules in this area.

34–005 The Rome II Regulation introduces a European autonomous definition of non-contractual obligations (See Recital (11) and Art.1) and of unjust enrichment (Art.10). See also below, paras 34–014, 34–033 and 34–044.

On the conflict of laws issues raised by misappropriated and misapplied assets, see Briggs, in Degeling and Edelman (eds.), *Unjust Enrichment in Commercial Law* (2008), Ch.4.

On the application of the choice of law rules for unjust enrichment, restitution for wrongs and equitable claims to commercial fraud, see McGrath, *Commercial Fraud in Civil Practice* (2009), Ch.20.

34–008 This position has been affected by Art.1(2)(e) of the Rome II Regulation which provides that "non-contractual obligations arising out of the relations between the settlors, trustees and beneficiaries of a trust created voluntarily" are excluded from the scope of the Regulation. This is discussed further below, para.34–044; see also para.29–063 of this supplement.

34–011 But see entry below, para.34–051.

34–014 The Rome II Regulation introduces new choice of law rules for non-contractual obligations, including obligations arising out of unjust enrichment (see Chong (2008) 57 I.C.L.Q. 863; Dickinson, *The Rome II Regulation* (2008), Ch.10 (2nd supplement, 2010); Pitel in Ahern and Binchy, *The Rome II Regulation on the Law Applicable to Non-Contractual Obligations* (2009)

231; Pitel [2008] Nederlands Internationaal Privaatrecht 456; Rushworth and Scott [2008] L.M.C.L.Q. 274). The Regulation applies whether or not the governing law is that of a Member State (Art.3). It applies to civil and commercial maters (Art.1(1)). It is suggested that, by analogy to the case law on Art.1 of the Judgments Regulation (on which, see para.11–024 of the main work), causes of action involving public bodies acting in the exercise of their peculiarly public powers and duties should fall outside the scope of the Regulation. However, Art.1(1) also states that the Regulation will not apply to "administrative matters or the liability of the State for acts and omissions in the exercise of State authority". In view of this, it is uncertain whether a claim such as that arising in *Kleinwort Benson Ltd v Glasgow City Council* [1999] 1 A.C. 153 (considered at para.11–286 of the main work) would fall within the scope of the Regulation. In that case, the interest rate swap agreement had been declared *ultra vires* the local authority and void *ab initio* and the alleged obligation to make restitution flowed from that finding. Impractical as the result may seem, it may be that such a cause of action would, if raising choice of law issues, be held to be excluded from the ambit of the Rome II Regulation. Although the "contract" in *Kleinwort Benson* had already been declared *ultra vires*, and the litigation did not raise public law specific issues, the obligation to make restitution arose from an absence of State authority to conclude the agreement. The applicability of the Regulation is determined by the nature of the obligation itself rather than by the particular issue in dispute between the parties to the litigation.

The Regulation also contains a series of exclusions in Art.1(2), discussed in Ch.35 of this supplement. The exclusion of "non-contractual obligations arising out of the relations between the settlors, trustees and beneficiaries of a trust created voluntarily" in Art.1(2)(e), which is of particular relevance to the law of restitution, is considered below, entry at para.34–044 (see also above, entry at para.29–063).

The term "unjust enrichment" will almost certainly be subject to a common European meaning (see Dickinson, *The Rome II Regulation* (2008), pp.491–500). No positive definition is provided in the Regulation. However, some guidance might be drawn from Case C–47/07P *Masdar (UK) Ltd v Commission of the European Communities* [2008] E.C.R. I–9761, where the European Court examined the potential non-contractual liability of the Commission under the EC Treaty. The Court observed (at [44]) that:

> "According to the principles common to the laws of the Member States, a person who has suffered a loss which increases the wealth of another person without there being any legal basis for that enrichment has the right, as a general rule, to restitution from the person enriched, up to the amount of the loss".

It went on to note that unlawfulness or fault were not essential elements of an action for unjust enrichment. See also the earlier decision in Case C–446/04

*FII Group Litigation v Commissioners of Inland Revenue* [2006] E.C.R. I–11753. Both cases are noted by Williams (2010) 47 C.M.L. Rev. 555.

Where a non-contractual obligation arises out of unjust enrichment, including payments of amounts wrongly received, and this concerns an existing relationship between the parties, such as one arising by contract or from a tort closely connected with the unjust enrichment, then it is to be governed by the law applicable to that relationship (Art.10(1)). This means that, for example, a claim for recovery of payments on the basis that there has been a failure of consideration after termination for breach of contract will be governed by the law applicable to the contract.

Where the applicable law cannot be determined on this basis, as where there is no underlying relationship from which the claim arises, and if the parties have a common habitual residence when the event giving rise to the enrichment occurs, then the law of that State will apply (Art.10(2)). Hence, a claim by X, a German resident, for recovery of a mistaken payment made to Y, another German resident, will be governed by German law.

If there is no underlying relationship and the parties do not have a common habitual residence, then the law of the place where the unjust enrichment took place will apply (Art.10(3)).

The rules in Arts 10(1)–(3) may be displaced if it is clear from all the circumstances of the case that the non-contractual obligation arising out of unjust enrichment is manifestly more closely connected with another country (Art.10(4)).

Article 14(1) then provides that the parties may choose the law applicable to a non-contractual obligation, either by agreement entered into after the event giving rise to the damage occurred or, where all parties are pursuing a commercial activity, such a choice may also be concluded by an agreement freely negotiated before that event occurred. An implied choice of law is possible provided that it is demonstrated with reasonable certainty by the circumstances of the case. (See further Recital (31)). The choice will not prejudice the rights of third parties. Where, but for the choice, all elements of the situation at the time when the event giving rise to the damage occurred point to a single State other than that whose law was chosen, the choice of the parties is upheld but is subject to the mandatory rules of the country of objective connection (Art.14(2)). This provision is likely to be applied by analogy to Art.3(3) of the Rome Convention (on which, see Rule 205(1) of the main work). Where all the relevant elements are located in one or more Member States, the choice of law is upheld but is subject to provisions of Community law (where appropriate, as implemented in the Member State of the forum) which cannot be derogated from by agreement (Art.14(3)).

Article 13 states that, where a claim for restitution arises in the context of an infringement of an intellectual property right, then the special intellectual property rules laid down in Art.8 for tort claims shall apply. These will usually point to the law of the country for which protection is claimed. No agreement on choice of law under Art.14 is permitted.

There are special rules on *negotiorum gestio,* considered below, entry at para.34–053.

Article 15 contains provisions, common to tortious and other non-contractual obligations, on the scope of the governing law. The *lex causae* applies to: the basis and extent of liability and the determination of persons who may be liable for acts performed by them; the grounds for exemption or limitation of liability and any division of liability; the existence, nature and assessment of damages or remedies; within the limits of the procedural powers conferred on the court, the measures to prevent or terminate injury or damage or to ensure the provision of compensation; whether a right to claim damages or a remedy may be transferred, either *inter vivos* or on death; the persons entitled to compensation for damage sustained personally; liability for acts of another person; and the manner in which an obligation may be extinguished and rules of prescription and limitation, including rules relating to the commencement, interruption and suspension of such a period.

There are also rules on subrogation in Art.19, which are modelled on Art.13 of the Rome Convention (on which see para.32–211 of the main work). These apply where a creditor has a non-contractual claim upon the debtor and a third person has a duty to satisfy the creditor or has done so in discharge of that duty. The law which governs the third party's duty to satisfy the creditor will determine whether and to what extent the third party may exercise against the debtor the rights which the creditor had against the debtor under the law governing their relationship.

All the provisions of the Regulation are subject to the overriding mandatory rules of the forum (Art.16) and should be disapplied to the extent that their application is manifestly incompatible with the public policy of the forum (Art.26). It is envisaged that application of the *lex causae* where it would have the effect of causing non-compensatory, exemplary or punitive damages of an excessive nature to be awarded may, depending on the circumstances and the legal order of the forum, be regarded as contrary to public policy (Recital (32)).

The rules of the Rome II Regulation will also apply to conflicts between the laws of different parts of the United Kingdom (or between the laws of one or more parts of the United Kingdom and Gibraltar) by virtue of the Law Applicable to Non-Contractual Obligations (England and Wales and Northern Ireland) Regulations 2008 (SI 2008/2986), Reg. 6.

A further modification is introduced by the Rome I Regulation (see entry at para.32–013, above). One important consequence for the United Kingdom of participating in the Rome I Regulation is that it is bound by Art.12(1)(e), which states that the law applicable to a contract by virtue of the Regulation shall govern the consequences of nullity of the contract. Contracting States were permitted to reserve the right not to apply the equivalent provision of the Rome Convention (Art.10(1)(e)), and the United Kingdom availed itself of this right pursuant to s.2(2) of the Contracts (Applicable Law) Act 1990 (see para.34–027 of the main work). In contrast, no reservation is permitted under the Regulation.

**34–017** See also *Berezovsky v Abramovich* [2010] EWHC 647 (Comm.).

**34–019** See also *Dornoch Ltd v Westminster International BV* [2009] EWHC 889 (Admlty), [2009] 2 Lloyd's Rep. 191, at [87].

The doctrine will be excluded under the Rome II Regulation, Art.24.

**34–020** See *OJSC Oil Co Yugraneft v Abramovich* [2008] EWHC 2613 (Comm.), at [247].

On the application of the rules on service out of the jurisdiction to a *quantum meruit* claim, see *Cecil v Bayat* [2010] EWHC 641 (Comm.), at [116]–[118].

**34–020—34–028** The Rome I Regulation effects a partial change to the law for contracts concluded on or after December 17, 2009. Article 12(1)(e) stipulates that the law applicable to a contract by virtue of the Regulation's rules shall govern the consequences of nullity of the contract (see further entry at para.34–014, above). Nonetheless, Art.12(1)(e) is itself subject to any mandatory rules of the forum (Art.9(2)) and to the public policy derogation (Art.21); as well as to other relevant provisions in the Regulation preserving the application of mandatory rules. These provisions are described further at paras 32–132 and 32–232, above.

It is not entirely clear what would happen if it were alleged that the contract, including the choice of law clause contained in it, were the product of duress or otherwise not the subject of agreement between the parties. It may be that such arguments should be made pursuant to Art.10(2) of the Regulation, which allows a party to demonstrate lack of consent to the choice of law clause by relying upon the law of his habitual residence if it would not be reasonable to determine the effects entirely according to the law applicable to the contract.

It is important to note that Art.12(1)(e) deals only with the consequences of nullity and does not deal with other restitutionary claims arising in connection with a contract, as where, for instance, the contract is rescinded. Many of these situations will now be subject to the choice of law rules in the Rome II Regulation, described in para.34–014, above. Hence, the rules in the Rome I Regulation apply to determine the consequences of nullity of a contract. In respect of all other restitutionary claims in relation to a contract, the rules in the Rome II Regulation apply (at least insofar as the issue falls within the material scope of each Regulation pursuant to Art.1).

**34–024** In *Astrazeneca UK Limited v Albemarle International Corporation* [2010] EWHC 1028 (Comm.), [2010] 2 Lloyd's Rep. 61 the claimant asserted that the defendant had wrongly breached a 2005 agreement governed by English law and containing an English jurisdiction clause; and had forced the claimant by duress to enter into a subsequent agreement with the defendant in 2008, which contained a jurisdiction and choice of law clause in favour of South Carolina. It sought, *inter alia*, restitution of the sums paid under the 2008 agreement. The court held that the duress claim fell within CPR PD6B, para.3.1(16), on the basis that it was a claim for restitution in the context of a voidable contract, arising out of substantial and efficacious acts committed within the jurisdiction. Since there was insufficient evidence specifically to impugn the jurisdiction clause in the 2008 agreement, however, the court held that the duress claim should be stayed in favour of the courts of South Carolina.

In *CIMB Bank Bhd v Dresdner Kleinwort Ltd* [2008] SGCA 36, [2008] 4 S.L.R. 543, the Singapore Court of Appeal held that Rule 230(2)(a) was inapplicable to a claim for recovery of payments made pursuant to a contract that both parties accepted to be void. An employee had fraudulently exceeded his authority to conclude a contract on behalf of one of the parties. The court ruled that this fraud was perpetrated on both of the intended contracting parties and, on the facts, had the effect of rendering the entire agreement, including an English choice of law clause, void. In the event, the court applied Rule 230(2)(c) and held that Singaporean law applied to the claim, being both the law of the place of enrichment and where the enriched party had changed its position.

See also *Focus Energy Ltd v Aye Aye Soe* [2008] SGHC 206.

On the choice of law issues raised by void contracts, see further Chong, in Giliker (ed.), *Re-examining Contract and Unjust Enrichment: Anglo-Canadian Perspectives*, (2007), Ch.9.

In *Haugesund Kommune v Depfa ACS Bank* [2010] EWCA Civ 579, [2010] 2 Lloyd's Rep. 323 Haugesund was found to have no capacity according to Norwegian law to conclude banking swap contracts containing English jurisdiction and choice of law clauses; with the effect that the "contracts" were void according to English law. The Court of Appeal held that the availability of a claim for restitution against Haugesund was governed by English law, being the law that would have governed the "contracts." The court could, however, refer to the relevant Norwegian legislation in deciding whether and to what extent a restitutionary remedy was available. This was explained (at [100]) on the basis that "it seems logical and consistent with comity to take account of the same foreign statute [that led to the incapacity] to see whether, as a matter of English public policy, the right to a restitutionary claim should be restricted in some way." On the facts, there was, however, no evidence of a relevant restriction in the Norwegian legislation. **34–026**

In *OJSC Oil Co Yugraneft v Abramovich* [2008] EWHC 2613 (Comm.), Christopher Clarke J. agreed that Rule 230(2)(c) was an indicator of the proper law of an unjust enrichment claim but that it could not replace the **34–030** principle itself, which was that the proper law of the obligation applied. Hence "In the case of [Rule 230(2)](c) the place of enrichment may, depending on the facts, be of the greatest importance or very little importance at all" (at [247]).

In *CIMB Bank Bhd v Dresdner Kleinwort Ltd* [2008] SGCA 36, [2008] 4 S.L.R. 543, both parties accepted that the "contract" was void. The Singapore Court of Appeal applied Rule 230(2)(c), rather than Rule 230(2)(a). See further entry at para.34–024, above. See also *Focus Energy Ltd v Aye Aye Soe* [2008] SGHC 206.

**34–032** It is very likely that such claims will be subjected to the choice of law rules in tort under the Rome II Regulation. Even if they are classified as restitutionary, however, the effect will be the same, since Art.10(1) of the Regulation will subject the claim to the law of the tortious relationship.

**34–033** Sixth sentence. This sentence was cited with approval in *OJSC Oil Co Yugraneft v Abramovich* [2008] EWHC 2613 (Comm.), at [179]–[181]. See also *Murakami v Wiryadi* [2008] SGCA 44.

The Rome II Regulation delineates torts and delicts from obligations arising out of unjust enrichment. There is a European autonomous definition of torts and delicts, and of unjust enrichment (Recital (11)), which affects the classification of such obligations in English courts. In particular, non-contractual equitable obligations generally fall within the scope of the Regulation (subject to the exclusion in Art.1(2)(e), considered below, entry at para.34–044).

Non-contractual obligations for which the remedy is compensation for loss are likely to fall within the definition of torts and delict. For this reason, a claim for dishonest assistance in breach of trust is likely to be classified as tortious for Regulation purposes.

The classification of a claim for dishonest receipt of trust property is less certain. The claim does depend upon showing an element of wrongdoing by the defendant. However, the obligation arises where misapplied trust property has been received and dealt with by a defendant for his own benefit. The measure of damages is usually restitutionary. This suggests that the claim may better be classified as arising out of unjust enrichment (but contrast Dickinson, *The Rome II Regulation* (2008), pp.350–354). Such claims will not be caught by the exclusion in Art.1(2)(e) of claims arising out of the relations between the settlors, trustees and beneficiaries of a trust created voluntarily, since they involve third parties to the trust. Nor will the law applicable to the trust necessarily govern a claim for dishonest receipt of trust property, since Art.10(1) of the Regulation applies the law of the underlying relationship only where that relationship exists between the parties to the claim.

Article 1(2)(g) of the Regulation excludes non-contractual obligations arising out of violations of privacy and rights relating to personality, including defamation. It is suggested that an action for breach of confidence would nonetheless fall within the scope of the Regulation, since it is based upon the misuse of confidential information, rather than upon invasion of the privacy, personality or reputation of the claimant. The claimant may seek compensatory or restitutionary damages for breach of confidence. The former claim is very likely to be classified as tortious for the purposes of the Regulation. The latter claim may be classified either as tortious for Regulation purposes; or as a claim in unjust enrichment, albeit based upon non-contractual wrongdoing. Even if the latter classification were adopted, Art.10(1) would, in any event, have the result that the law applicable to the "tort" of breach of confidence would govern the claim for restitution.

NOTE 8. See also Stevens, in Degeling and Edelman (eds.), *Equity in Commercial Law* (2005), Ch.8.

NOTE 11. See also *Wilson and Partners Ltd v Nicholls* [2009] NSWSC 1033, at [308]–[311].

This approach is supported by the decision of the New South Wales Court of Appeal in *Murakami v Wiryadi* [2010] NSWCA 7. After reviewing the relevant authorities, the court concluded that, where Indonesian law governed the parties' matrimonial property by virtue of a marital contract, that same law should determine whether the first respondent held property located in Australia (that had allegedly not been disclosed in Indonesian divorce proceedings) on resulting or constructive trust for the appellant. **34–034**

The choice of law rules for dishonest assistance in breach of trust were analysed at length in *OJSC Oil Co Yugraneft v Abramovich* [2008] EWHC 2613 (Comm.), at [169]–[236]. In particular, Christopher Clarke J. did not consider that the decision in *Grupo Torras SA v Al Sabah* [2001] C.L.C. 221 (CA) represented a departure from the rule of double actionability. Although the Court of Appeal's decision in *Grupo Torras* did not require that Spanish law recognised a liability consisting of the same elements and basis of liability, it did require the defendant "to be civilly liable under Spanish law to the same extent as in English law" (*Yugraneft*, at [212]). In particular, "The Court of Appeal [in *Grupo Torras*] did not hold that all the Court needed to do, in a case of dishonest assistance, was to make its assessment of '*dishonesty*' against the '*background*' of the local law of custom. . . . It proceeded to consider causation under Spanish law because the claimant needed to establish civil liability '*to a similar extent*'." (At [214], emphasis in original.) **34–035**

Christopher Clarke J. went on to consider the impact of the Private International Law (Miscellaneous Provisions Act) 1995 and indicated that he "would strongly incline to holding that a claim in dishonest assistance was, for the purposes of the 1995 Act a 'tort'" (at [223]). However, since the claim would not succeed under the relevant foreign law, Russian law, in any event, he did not need to express a definitive view as to whether the 1995 Act applied.

**34–036** The decision in *Base Metal Trading Ltd v Shamurin* [2004] EWCA Civ 1316, [2005] 1 W.L.R. 1157 was applied by the Singapore High Court in *Focus Energy Ltd v Aye Aye Soe* [2008] SGHC 206, at [31]–[33].

**34–038** In *OJSC Oil Co Yugraneft v Abramovich* [2008] EWHC 2613 (Comm.), the court accepted that a claim in knowing receipt was subject to Rule 230 and went on to apply the proper law of the obligation to make restoration.

**34–040** On the treatment of breach of confidence under the Rome II Regulation, see Wadlow (2008) 30 E.I.P.R. 309.

**34–041** On the application of the CPR provisions on claims for a remedy against the defendant as constructive trustee (CPR PD6B, para.3.1(15)) and on claims for restitution (CPR PD6B, para.3.1(16)) to causes of action based upon: (i) liability to account for breach of fiduciary duties; (ii) liability to account as constructive trustee on the basis of knowing receipt; and (iii) dishonest assistance in breach of trust or fiduciary duty, see *Cecil v Bayat* [2010] EWHC 641 (Comm.); and entry at para.29–059, above.

**34–042** The ambit of the decision in *Paramasivam v Flynn* (1998–99) 160 A.L.R. 203 was considered by the New South Wales Court of Appeal in *Murakami v Wiryadi* [2010] NSWCA 7, at [128]–[149]. See also *Wilson and Partners Ltd v Nicholls* [2009] NSWSC 1033.

**34–043** See *OJSC Oil Co Yugraneft v Abramovich* [2008] EWHC 2613 (Comm.), at [215]–[217], where the court held that the four stage test approved in *Kuwait Oil Tanker SAK v Al Bader* [2000] 2 All E.R. (Comm.) 271 (CA) had no application to a claim in knowing receipt or knowing assistance.

Penultimate sentence. In *Rickshaw Investments Ltd and Another v Nicolai Baron von Uexkull* [2007] 1 S.L.R. 377 (noted Briggs (2007) 11 Sing Yb. I.L. 123), the Singapore Court of Appeal applied the law applicable to a contract of employment to claims for breach of fiduciary duty and breach of confidence arising from the contractual relationship. See also *Focus Energy Ltd v Aye Aye Soe* [2008] SGHC 206. The decision in *Rickshaw* was considered by the New South Wales Court of Appeal in *Murakami v Wiryadi & Ors* [2010] NSWCA 7, at [137].

Add at end: Pursuant to Art.10(1) of the Rome II Regulation (entry at para. 34–005, above), the law applicable to the underlying relationship determines whether a fiduciary relationship exists and whether the fiduciary is under an obligation to make restitution. This means that the law applicable to the contract applies where the parties are in a contractual relationship. The remedies to be awarded are, in principle, a matter for the *lex causae* under the Regulation (Art.15(c)). This suggests that if, by the *lex causae*, a fiduciary relationship exists, the English courts will recognise it even if such a relationship would not have arisen on the facts in English domestic law. In cases where the *lex causae* does not know the concept of the fiduciary relationship, it is likely that the English courts will still adopt the approach described in para.34–043 of the main work and determine the nature of the duties under the governing law and ask whether they have the characteristics of a fiduciary relationship.

If, however, the fiduciary relationship arises pursuant to a trust created voluntarily, and the claim for breach of fiduciary duty arises between settlor, trustee or beneficiary, then the claim will fall outside the Regulation (Art.1(2)(e)). Indeed, any claim arising in the trust context that falls within the scope of the Hague Trusts Convention will be governed by that Convention, rather than the Regulation (Art.28(1)).

On the law applicable to constructive trusts, see entries at para.29–064, above. **34–044**

The ability to trace was examined solely according to the rules of English law in *OJSC Oil Co Yugraneft v Abramovich* [2008] EWHC 2613 (Comm.), although without the question of the law applicable to tracing arising directly.

Article 1(2)(e) of the Rome II Regulation excludes from the Regulation's scope non-contractual obligations arising out of the relations between settlors, trustees and beneficiaries of a trust created voluntarily. The term "trust created voluntarily", which also appears in Art.3 of the Hague Trusts Convention, is not a term of art in trust law. Its meaning is considered at para.29–007 of the main work (See also *Underhill and Hayton on Trusts and Trustees* 17th edn (Hayton, 2006), pp.1249–1250). Clearly, the exclusion covers express trusts and, unlike Art.3 of the Hague Trusts Convention, does not require such trusts to be evidenced in writing. Some constructive trusts are also created voluntarily, such as where duly executed mutual wills are made, or where a specifically enforceable contract exists. Such trusts will fall outside the scope of the Regulation. Resulting trusts arising upon the failure of express trusts should also fall within the exclusion (*cf.* the Explanatory Report on the Hague Trusts Convention by von Overbeck, *Actes et Documents de la 15e Session*, p.370, at [51]). Equally, some trusts clearly *will* fall within the ambit of the Regulation, since they are in no sense created voluntarily. This includes a constructive trust imposed where a trustee renews a lease for himself, or purchases for himself the freehold reversion to a lease held by him as trustee, or obtains for himself assets which he should have acquired for the trust.

It might be suggested that the Regulation should apply only to the *personal* obligation to account as constructive trustee, since any obligation to hold *property* on constructive trust is not concerned with the law of obligations.

However, the scope of the Regulation should be defined by whether the *cause of action* is based on a non-contractual obligation; and it is suggested that it should apply even if the remedy awarded is proprietary in nature. The cause of action will still be a breach of a non-contractual obligation; and Art.15(c) suggests that the remedy to be awarded for breach of that obligation is a matter for the *lex causae.* If the *lex causae* provides for the imposition of a constructive trust or for the tracing of assets, this should be given effect.

Although an English court should give effect to the remedy of the *lex causae* under Art.15(c), it will not be feasible for it to award remedies unknown in English law, or which are unduly burdensome for it to grant. It may be regarded as outside the procedural competence of the English courts (Art.1(3)), or contrary to English public policy (Art.26) to grant such remedies. In such circumstances, an English court is likely to continue to determine the nature of the rights awarded by the *lex causae* and impose a suitable English remedy to protect those rights. The English courts may do so by imposing a constructive trust, where the English court cannot directly award the foreign remedy and where the trust gives suitable effect to the rights and remedy of the claimant according to the *lex causae.*

**34–050** Notwithstanding the Rome II Regulation, once a constructive trust is deemed to exist, its operation will continue to be governed by the Hague Trusts Convention (Art.28(1)). See further para.29–065 of the main work.

**34–051** Article 20 of the Rome II Regulation provides: "If a creditor has a claim against several debtors who are liable for the same claim, and one of the debtors has already satisfied the claim in whole or in part, the question of that debtor's right to demand compensation from the other debtors shall be governed by the law applicable to that debtor's non-contractual obligation towards the creditor". This means that where the non-contractual obligation owed by the debtor to the creditor is tortious, his right to claim a contribution from other debtors will be governed by the law applicable to the tort. Only where the non-contractual obligation owed to the creditor is restitutionary will the restitution choice of law rules determine the debtor's right to a contribution. See further Dornis (2008) 4 J. Priv. Int. L. 237.

Note 71. But see *Hewden Tower Cranes Ltd v Wolffkran GmbH* [2007] EWHC 857 (TCC), [2007] 2 Lloyd's Rep. 138, where the court classified a claim for contribution as a matter relating to tort for the purposes of the Judgments Regulation. Moreover, in *Greene Wood & McClean v Templeton Insurance Ltd* [2009] EWCA Civ 65, [2009] 1 W.L.R. 2013 it was held that a claim pursuant to the Civil Liability (Contribution) Act 1978 was one "in respect of" a contract within the meaning of what was CPR, r.6.20(5) (now (CPR PD6B, para.3.1(6)), even though the claimant was not party to the contract in question and the claim was not brought under that contract. However, the decision is confined to the wording of what is now CPR PD6B, para.3.1(6), which refers to a claim that "is made in respect of a contract" and does not require the claim to arise under the contract itself (see further *Albon v Naza Motor Trading* [2007] EWHC 9 (Ch.), [2007] 1 Lloyd's Rep. 297; *Sharab v Prince Al-Waleed Bin Tala Bin Abdal-Aziz-Al-Saud* [2009] EWCA Civ 353, [2009] 2 Lloyd's Rep. 160, affirming [2008] EWHC 1893 (Ch.)); *Cecil v Bayat* [2010] EWHC 641 (Comm.), at [43]–[49]).

Note 74. Contrast the approach taken by the Supreme Court of Victoria in *Fluor Australia v ASC Engineering* [2005] VSC 423 and [2007] VSC 262, where the court refused to apply the relevant Victorian contribution statute, Part IV of the Wrongs Act 1958 (Vic), (which is in very similar terms to the to the Civil Liability (Contribution) Act 1978). The court did not need to determine whether the choice of law rules for tort or restitution were applicable, since in neither case would this have lead to the application of the Victorian statute.

Second paragraph. The Rome II Regulation (entry at para.34–005, above) **34–053** contains rules on *negotiorum gestio* (see Dickinson, *The Rome II Regulation* (2008), Ch.11). Where a non-contractual obligation arising out of an act performed without due authority in connection with the affairs of another person concerns a relationship between the parties, such as one arising in contract or tort, and that relationship is closely connected with the non-contractual obligation, then the law applicable to the relationship will apply (Art.11(1)). Where the law cannot be determined on this basis, then if the parties have their habitual residence in the same State when the event giving rise to the damage occurs, the law of that country will apply (Art.11(2)). If they do not share a common habitual residence, the applicable law is that of the country in which the act was performed (Art.11(3)). These various provisions can each be displaced where it is clear from all the circumstances of the case that the obligation is manifestly more closely connected with another country (Art.11(4)). Furthermore, the parties may agree to submit their obligations to the law of their choice pursuant to Art.14 (considered above, para.34–014).

# Chapter 35

# TORTS

## 1. THE LAW APPLICABLE TO ISSUES IN TORT

**35R–001** Note 1. The Rome II Regulation applies from January 11, 2009: see Regulation (EC) 864/2007 of the European Parliament and of the Council of July 11, 2007 on the Law Applicable to Non-Contractual Obligations (Rome II), [2007] O.J. L199/40 and below, paras S35–165 *et seq*. The Rome II Regulation is reproduced in Appendix 1 to this Supplement. Add: Mortensen (2006) 55 I.C.L.Q. 839.

**35–002** Note 2. In cases falling within the scope of the Rome II Regulation (see previous entry), the 1995 Act has been disapplied, with effect from January 11, 2009, by the Law Applicable to Non-Contractual Obligations (England and Wales and Northern Ireland) Regulations 2008 (SI 2008/2986). See below, entry at para.S35–169.

Note 5. Defamation is also excluded from the scope of the Rome II Regulation. See below, entry at para.S35–185.

**35–004** Note 13. Add: Dickinson, *The Rome II Regulation, The Law Applicable to Non-Contractual Obligations* (2008), paras 1.15–1.43.

Note 14. Add: Symeonides (2007) 32 So. Ill. Univ. L. J. 39.

Note 26. Add: Symeonides, *The American Choice-of-Law Revolution: Past, Present and Future* (2006). See also the Annual Surveys of American Choice of Laws Cases, most recently Symeonides (2009) 57 Am.J. Comp L. 269.

**35–005** Note 28. Add: See Handford (2008) 32 Melbourne Univ. L.R. 822.

Notes 33 and 34. *Re T & N Ltd* [2005] EWHC 2990 (Ch.) is now reported, *sub nom. Re T & N Ltd (No.2)*, at [2006] 1 W.L.R. 1792. Add at end: *Bank of Credit and Commerce SA v Ali* [2006] EWHC 2135 (Ch.).

**35–006** Note 37. *Re T & N Ltd* [2005] EWHC 2990 (Ch.) is now reported, *sub nom. Re T & N Ltd (No.2)*, at [2006] 1 W.L.R. 1792.

**35–007** Note 46. See previous entry.

NOTE 53. See entry at para.35–006, n.37. **35–009**

NOTE 54. In *Lucasfilm Ltd v Ainsworth* [2009] EWCA Civ 1328, [2010] 3 W.L.R. 333, an action involving a claim for breach of U.S. copyright, the Court of Appeal gave a restrictive interpretation to its earlier decision in *Pearce*: see below, entry at 35–030—35–032. An appeal to the Supreme Court is pending. **35–010**

NOTE 59. The Rome II Regulation, above, entry at para.35R–001, n.1, will apply in Scotland. See the Law Applicable to Non-Contractual Obligations (Scotland) Regulations (SSI 2008/404). **35–011**

NOTE 60. See also *British Columbia v Imperial Tobacco Canada Ltd* (2006) 274 D.L.R. (4th) 711 (BCCA). *Yeung v Au* (2004) B.C.S.C. 1648 has been affirmed: (2006) 269 D.L.R. (4th) 727 (BCCA). *Castillo v Castillo* 2005 SCC 83 is now reported at (2005) 260 D.L.R. (4th) 439 (Sup. Ct. Can.) and noted by Walker (2006) 43 C.B.L.J. 487.

Add: *Vogler v Szenderoi* (2008) 290 D.L.R. (4th) 642 (N.S.C.A.).

NOTE 61. See *Vogler v Szenderoi*, above.

NOTE 64. See also *Sweedman v Transport Accident Commission* [2006] HCA 8, (2006) 226 C.L.R. 362; *Puttick v Tenon Ltd* [2008] HCA 54, (2008) 238 C.L.R. 265. *Neilson v Overseas Projects Corp of Victoria Ltd* [2005] HCA 54 is now reported at (2005) 223 C.L.R. 331. *BHP Bilton Ltd v Schultz* [2004] HCA 61 is now reported at (2004) 221 C.L.R. 30.

NOTE 65. See *Puttick v Tenon Ltd*, above, in which it was not possible to determine the *lex loci delicti* on the material before the Court.

NOTE 67. Add: On the decision in *Neilson v Overseas Projects Corp of Victoria Ltd*, above, see *O'Driscoll v J Ray Mcdermott SA* [2006] WASCA 25; Dickinson (2006) 122 L.Q.R. 183; Mortensen (2006) 2 J. Priv. Int. L. 1; Mills [2006] C.L.J. 37; Davies [2006] Melbourne Univ. L.R. 8. In *Dornoch Ltd v Westminster International BV* [2008] EWHC 889 (Admlty), [2009] 2 Lloyd's Rep. 191, at [85], Tomlinson J. (in considering the application of the doctrine of *renvoi* to an issue concerning title to movable property) commented that there was "great force" in the observation of Heydon J. in *Neilson v Overseas Projects Corp of Victoria Ltd* [2005] HCA 54, (2005) 221 A.L.R. 213, at [271], that it would be absurd if the applicable law regime which the Chinese Government had enacted for incidents causing injuries of the type suffered by the claimant should be set at naught by reason of Australian law, as it would be if the supposed "no renvoi" principle existed. See also *Blue Sky One Ltd v Mahan Air* [2010] EWHC 631 (Comm.), esp. at [164]–[166], [180], [182]; Hughes (2010) 6 J. Priv. Int. L. 195.

**35–015** Note 90. As to the temporal application and general scope of the Rome II Regulation, see below, paras. S35–168, S35–175 *et seq.*

Note 91. See entry at para.35–006, n.37.

**35–018** Note 97. See previous entry.

Note 99. As to *Harding v Wealands* [2004] EWCA Civ 1735, [2005] 1 W.L.R. 1539, see now [2006] UKHL 32, [2007] 2 A.C. 1.

**35–021** Note 11. For the position under the Rome II Regulation, see below, para. S35–193. Add: *Dornoch Limited v Westminster International BV* [2008] EWHC (Admlty) 889, [2009] 2 Lloyd's Rep. 191, at [85].

Note 13. See above, entry at para.35–11, nn.64 and 67.

**35–022— 35–024** These passages were cited with approval in *Trafigura Beheer BV v Kookmin Bank Co* [2006] EWHC 1450 (Comm.), [2006] 2 Lloyd's Rep. 455, at [64]–[75]. In particular, it was said that the words "for the purposes of private international law" in s.9(2) of the Private International Law (Miscellaneous Provisions) Act 1995 indicated that Parliament intended that the court should examine relevant issues to decide whether they should be characterised as relating to tort not only by reference to English legal concepts and classifications but by taking a broad internationalist view of legal concepts: *ibid.*, at [68]; see also Morse (1996) 45 I.C.L.Q. 888; *Harding v Wealands* [2006] UKHL 32, [2007] 2 A.C. 1, at [65].

**35–022** Notes 15 and 16. For the position under the Rome II Regulation, see below, paras S35–170, S35–175 *et seq.*

**35–023** In *OJSC Oil Company Yugraneft v Abramovich* [2008] EWHC 2613 (Comm.), at [221]–[223], Christopher Clarke J. admitted (without it being necessary to decide the point) a strong inclination to hold that a claim in dishonest assistance (classified as equitable under English law) should be characterised as a claim in "tort" for the purposes of the 1995 Act. On this view, a claim for damages or an injunction to restrain breach of confidence outside contract may also be argued to fall within the 1995 Act. *cf. Douglas v Hello! Ltd (No.3)* [2005] EWCA Civ 595, [2006] Q.B. 125, [97], citing the 13th edition of this work (decision revd. in part on other grounds [2007] UKHL 21; [2008] 1 A.C. 1). See also main work, para.34–040.

Text after note 21. See also *Congentra AG v Sixteen Thirteen Marine SA* [2008] EWHC 1615 (Comm.), [2008] 2 C.L.C. 51.

**35–024** Note 24. See previous entry.

**35–025** For an issue oriented approach to characterisation in this area, see *Maher v Groupama Grand Est* [2009] EWHC 38 (QB), [2009] 1 W.L.R. 1752, at

[17]–[18] (QB), [2009] EWCA Civ 1191, [2010] 1 W.L.R. 1564, at [8]–[11], and *Knight v AXA Assurance* [2009] EWHC 1900 (QB), at [24]–[25].

NOTE 25. For the position under the Rome II Regulation, see below, para.S35–255. **35–026**

Add: See *Congentra AG v Sixteen Thirteen Marine SA* [2008] EWHC 1615 (Comm.), [2008] 2 C.L.C. 51.

NOTE 28. Add: *Government of the Islamic Republic of Iran v Barakat Galleries Ltd* [2008] EWCA Civ 1374, [2009] Q.B. 22; *Blue Sky One Ltd v Mahan Air* [2010] EWHC 631 (Comm.). **35–027**

NOTE 29. For the position under the Rome II Regulation, see below, para.S35–177.

NOTE 30. Add: Lipstein [2005] C.L.J. 593. For the position under the Rome II Regulation, see below, paras S35–288 *et seq*. **35–028**

NOTES 31–35. See *Lucasfilm Ltd v Ainsworth* [2009] EWCA Civ 1328, [2010] 3 All E.R. 329. **35–029**

In *Lucasfilm Ltd v Ainsworth* [2009] EWCA Civ 1328, [2010] 3 W.L.R. 333 (noted Dickinson [2010] L.M.C.L.Q. 181; Rogerson [2010] C.L.J. 245), the Court of Appeal, while not referring to the 1995 Act or specifically addressing choice of law issues, appeared to suggest (at [100]) that a foreign intellectual property right was in principle capable of being infringed by an act in England. Ultimately, however, the court determined (at [174]–[183]) that claims for infringement of a foreign, non-EU or Lugano Convention State's intellectual property rights (in *Ainsworth*, US copyright) are not justiciable before an English court. The court reasoned (at [103]–[156]) that neither the terms of the Judgments Regulation, nor the European Court's decision in Case C–281/02 *Owusu v Jackson* [2005] ECR I–1383, [2005] Q.B. 801, nor the Court of Appeal's own decision in *Pearce v Ove Arup Partnernship Ltd* [2000] Ch. 403 (a case concerning infringement of copyright under the laws of an EU Member State) prevented it from reaching this conclusion. Referring with approval to the decisions of Laddie J. in *Coin Controls v Suzo International* [1999] Ch. 43, of the New Zealand High Court in *Atkinson Footwear v Hodgskin International Services* (1994) 31 I.P.R. 186, and of the US Court of Appeals for the Federal Circuit in *Voda v Cordis Corporation*, 476 F. 3d 887 (F. Cir. 2007), the court rejected (at [181]) the suggested distinction (main work, para.35–032) between questions of subsistence or registration of an intellectual property right and questions of its infringement: all those questions were, in the Court of Appeal's view, non-justiciable under the "local actions" principle established by *British South Africa Co v Companhia de Moçambique* [1893] A.C. 602. An appeal to the Supreme Court is pending. **35–030—35–032**

For the position under the Rome II Regulation, see below, entry at para.35–231.

**35–033** Note 65. Add in line 7: *Amaca Pty Ltd v Frost* [2006] NSWCA 173; *Puttick v Tenon Ltd*, above, entry at para.35–011, n.64.

**35–034—35–038** Notes 66, 68, 71, 86 and 87. For the position under the Rome II Regulation, see below, paras S35–259 *et seq.*

Note 86. Add: During discussions leading to the adoption of the Rome II Regulation, it was suggested that Art.12 of the Rome Convention applies to assignments of non-contractual obligations: see below, para.S35–259.

Note 87. Add in line 3: See also *Yeung v Au* (2006) 269 D.L.R. (4th) 727 (BCCA).

**35–039—35–044** Notes 89, 96, 1, 14 and 17. For the position under the Rome II Regulation, see below, paras S35–255, S35–261, S35–265.

Note 89. Add: See also *Garsec Pty Ltd v His Majesty Sultan of Brunei* [2008] NSWCA 211, (2008) 250 A.L.R. 682, concerning the personal immunity of a foreign sovereign, but compare *Al Jedda v Secretary of State for Defence* [2010] EWCA Civ 758, at [91] (Arden L.J.), [166]–[169] (Elias L.J.), where a rule of Iraqi law conferring immunity on multinational forces in Iraq was held to apply only to proceedings before local Iraqi courts and not to exclude liability in proceedings before an English court.

Note 92. *Yeung v Au* (2004) B.C.S.C. 1648 has been affirmed: (2006) 269 D.L.R. (4th) 727 (BCCA). Add after reference to *Yeung v Au*: *Smith v Skanska Construction Services Ltd* [2008] EWHC 1776 (QB) (vicarious liability of agent).

**35–043** The Third Parties (Rights Against Insurers) Act 1930 will be repealed and replaced by the provisions of the Third Parties (Rights Against Insurers) Act 2010 (not yet in force) conferring more extensive rights against the insurer of a person subject to UK insolvency events to which the Act applies. Under section 18 of the 2010 Act, save as expressly provided, the application of the Act does not depend on whether there is a connection with a part of the United Kingdom, and in particular it does not depend on (a) whether or not the liability (or the alleged liability) of the insured to the third party was incurred in, or under the law of, England and Wales, Scotland or Northern Ireland, (b) the place of residence or domicile of any of the parties, (c) whether or not the contract of insurance (or a part of it) is governed by the law of England and Wales, Scotland or Northern Ireland, or (d) the place where sums due under the contract of insurance are payable.

NOTE 18. See, more recently, *Gerling Australia Insurance Company Pty* v *Ludgater Holdings Ltd* [2009] NZCA 397, at [23]–[50] where the view taken in this paragraph was considered, but rejected in favour of a tortious classification. The ultimate decision in this case, that the court did not have subject matter jurisdiction, was affirmed by the New Zealand Supreme Court, without addressing this issue of characterisation (see *Ludgater Holdings Ltd v Gerling Australia Insurance Company Pty* [2010] NZSC 49, [2010] 3 N.Z.L.R. 713, at [9]–[10], [34]).

NOTE 20. Add: See *Markel International Co Ltd v Craft* [2006] EWHC 3150 (QB), [2007] Lloyd's Rep. I.R. 403. In *Maher v Groupama Grand Est* [2009] EWHC 38 (QB), [2009] 1 W.L.R. 1752 and *Knight v AXA Assurance* [2009] EWHC 1900 (QB), the proposition in the text was accepted as the "correct starting point", with the result that the law applicable to the insurance contract should determine: (a) the injured party's right to proceed directly against the wrongdoer's insurers; and (b) any question concerning the insurer's liability under the policy. That law was not, however, to be applied to questions concerning the assessment of damages, for which purposes the insurer's liability should be seen as tortious. This division of the issues was approved by the Court of Appeal in *Maher v Groupama Grand Est* [2009] EWCA Civ 1191, [2010] 1 W.L.R. 1564. See below, entry at para.35–044.

A different approach was, however, taken by Blair J. and the Court of Appeal in *Maher v Groupama Grand Est* [2009] EWHC 38 (QB), [2009] 1 W.L.R. 1752, [2009] EWCA Civ 1191, [2010] 1 W.L.R. 1564 and by Sharp J. in *Knight v AXA Assurance* [2009] EWHC 1900 (QB). While the judges in these cases were prepared to accept that questions as to the existence of the insurer's liability should be viewed as contractual and determined by the law applicable to the contract of insurance (see above, entry at para.35–043, n.20), questions concerning the assessment of damages were characterised as raising an issue that "falls to be decided primarily in the context of a claim against the person responsible to the accident" and "arises in, tort not contract" (*Maher* (C.A.), at [22]) and such questions were therefore, to be governed as a matter of procedure by the *lex fori*, consistently with the 1995 Act (*Harding v Wealands* [2006] UKHL 32, [2007] 2 A.C. 1). **35–044**

NOTES 25, 32, 33 and 42. For the position under the Rome II Regulation, see below, paras S35–256 *et seq.* **35–046—35–049**

NOTES 26, 27 and 28. In *Dawson v Broughton* (2007) 151 So.J. 1167 it was held in the Manchester County Court that the defence of contributory negligence to a claim in tort should be classified as substantive and not procedural and that this included the question of whether contributory negligence results in any reduction in damages. **35–046**

NOTE 30. Add: See also *Bank of Credit and Commerce International SA v Ali* [2006] EWHC 2135 (Ch.). **35–047**

Final sentence. See *Hornsby v James Fisher Rumic Ltd* [2008] EWHC 1944 (QB).

Note 32. Add: *OJSC Oil Company Yugraneft v Abramovich* [2008] EWHC 2613 (Comm.). *Cf. Harley v Smith* [2010] EWCA Civ 78.

**35–048** Notes 39 and 41. See above, entry at para.35–039, n.92.

Note 39. Add: *BP plc v AON Ltd* [2006] EWHC 424 (Comm.), [2006] 1 All E.R. (Comm) 789.

**35–050— 33–058** Notes 46, 49, 51, 52, 59, 60, 62–66, 69–72, 75, 77–79. *Harding v Wealands* [2004] EWCA Civ 1735, [2005] 1 W.L.R. 1539 was reversed by the House of Lords, [2006] UKHL 32, [2007] 2 A.C. 1. For comment, see Rogerson [2006] C.L.J. 515; Scott [2007] L.M.C.L.Q. 44; Dougherty and Wyles (2007) 56 I.C.L.Q. 443; Weintraub (2007) 42 Texas Int. L.J. 311; Briggs (2006) 77 B.Y.I.L. 565; Beaumont and Tang (2008) 12 Edin L.R. 131. See generally, Gray (2008) 4 J. Priv. Int. L. 279. And see above, entry at paras 7–043 *et seq.*

Notes 46, 59, 64, 65, 78. *Re T & N Ltd* [2005] EWHC 2990 (Ch.) is now reported, *sub nom. Re T & N Ltd (No.2)*, at [2006] 1 W.L.R. 1792.

Notes 45, 46, 50, 54, 66, 69 and 75. As to the position under the Rome II Regulation, see below, paras S35–186, S35–268 *et seq.*

**35–050** Note 46. Add: *Maher v Groupama Grand Est* [2009] EWHC 38 (QB), [2009] 1 W.L.R. 1752, affd. [2009] EWCA Civ 1191, [2010] 1 W.L.R. 1564, and *Knight v AXA Assurance* [2009] EWHC 1900 (QB). See generally on substance and procedure, *Harding v Wealands* [2006] UKHL 32, [2007] 2 A.C. 1; Gray (2008) 4 J. Priv. Int. L. 279.

**35–051** Note 49. Add: See also *Hamilton v Merck & Co Inc* [2006] NSWCA 55, (2006) 230 A.L.R. 156 (although the law applicable to the tort was the law of Queensland, the provisions of Queensland law requiring notice before action and a compulsory conference before representative proceedings were commenced were procedural in nature and thus inapplicable).

**35–052** Notes 51 and 52 and text thereto. In *Harding v Wealands* [2006] UKHL 32, [2007] 2 A.C. 1, it was said (at [24]) that whether the claimant is awarded money damages or, for example, restitution in kind is a matter of remedy governed by the law of the forum: see also, *ibid.,* at [55], [66], [77].

**35–053** Note 54. In line 3 add: Briggs (2006) 77 B.Y.I.L. 565; Beaumont and Tang (2008) 12 Edin. L.R. 131; Gray (2008) 4 J. Priv. Int. L. 279. Add at end: For the treatment of claims to interest, see main work, paras 33–396—33–400;

*Maher v Groupama Grand Est* [2009] EWCA Civ 1191, [2010] 1 W.L.R. 1564 (entry at paras 33–392—33–393, above).

NOTE 60. See *Harding v Wealands*, above. **35–055**

NOTES 62 to 65 and text thereto. Although the House of Lords expressed no specific views on these issues in *Harding v Wealands,* above, the general approach taken in the case indicates that that they would be regarded as procedural for the purposes of Private International Law (Miscellaneous Provisions) Act 1995, s.14(3)(b).

NOTE 65. Add in line 2 after reference to *Re T&N Ltd*: *Maher v Groupama Grand Est* [2009] EWHC 38 (QB), [2009] 1 W.L.R. 1752 affd. [2009] EWCA Civ 1191, [2010] 1 W.L.R. 1564, and *Knight v AXA Assurance* [2009] EWHC 1900 (QB). Add at end: *Goh Suan Hee v Ter Cher Teck* [2009] SGCA 52, [2010] L.R.C. 480 (Sing. C.A.).

NOTE 66 and text thereto. This question did not arise and was not referred to **35–056**
in *Harding v Wealands*, above.

NOTES 69 and 71. In *Harding v Wealands,* above, the distinction between **35–057**
heads of recoverable damage, governed by the applicable law of the tort and questions of the assessment or quantification of damage so recoverable, governed by the law of the forum, was accepted. See next entry.

The decision of the Court of Appeal in *Harding v Wealands* [2004] EWCA **35–058**
Civ 1735, [2005] 1 W.L.R. 1539 was reversed by the House of Lords, [2006] UKHL 32, [2007] 2 A.C. 1. The House of Lords held that all the relevant provisions of Ch.5 of the New South Wales Motor Accidents Compensation Act 1999, referred to in this paragraph, including, in particular the financial ceiling on damages for pain and suffering and the discount rate, were procedural in nature and thus inapplicable even though the law applicable to the tort was the law of New South Wales. Such questions were to be determined by English law as the law of the forum pursuant to Private International Law (Miscellaneous Provisions) Act 1995, s.14(3)(b). The latter provision preserved the common law and at common law such questions were classified as procedural.

NOTE 76. In *Harding v Wealands*, above, at [39], the House of Lords appeared to approve explicitly the decision of the High Court of Australia in *Stevens v Head* (1993) 176 C.L.R. 433. The subsequent change of view by the High Court in *John Pfeiffer Pty Ltd v Rogerson* (2000) 203 C.L.R. 503, to the effect that financial limits on recoverable damages for pain and suffering were substantive, was said to be required by constitutional imperatives of Australian federalism and did not affect the position of the traditional distinction between substance and procedure at common law. See also *Amaca Pty Ltd v*

*Frost* [2006] NSWCA 173; *McNeilly v Imbree* [2007] NSWCA 156. *Cf. Goh Suan Hee v Ter Cher Teck* [2009] SGCA 52, [2010] L.R.C. 480 (Sing. C.A.) suggesting that the Singaporean courts would likely favour the approach taken in *Pfeiffer v Rogerson* and in the Rome II Regulation (see below, entry at para.S35–257) over that adopted by the House of Lords in *Harding v Wealands*.

**35–059** NOTE 80. For the position under the Rome II Regulation, see above, entry at para.34–051 and below, para.S35–267.

NOTE 81. Add: *Sweedman v Transport Accident Commission* [2006] HCA 8, (2006) 226 C.L.R. 362; *Fluor Australia Pty Ltd v ASC Engineering Pty Ltd* [2005] VSC 423; [2007] VSC 262. *cf. Hewden Tower Cranes Ltd v Wolffkran GmbH* [2007] EWHC 857 (TCC), [2007] 2 Lloyd's Rep. 138 (claim for contribution classified as a matter of tort for the purposes of Art.5(3) of the Judgments Regulation). See generally, Dornis (2008) 4 J. Priv. Int. L. 237.

NOTE 83. *cf. Fluor Australia Pty Ltd v ASC Engineering Pty Ltd*, above.

NOTE 84. See entry at n.81, above.

NOTES 85 and 86. *cf.* cases cited at n.81, above.

**35–061** NOTE 87. For the position under the Rome II Regulation, see below, paras S35–186, S35–268 *et seq.*

NOTE 88 and text thereto. See entries at paras 35–050–35–058. In *Harding v Wealands* [2006] UKHL 32, [2007] 2 A.C. 1 Lord Woolf, at [8], expressed the view that the use of "procedure" in conjunction with "rules of evidence, pleading and practice" in Private International Law (Miscellaneous Provisions) Act 1995, s.14(3)(b) made it natural to regard the assessment of damages as a matter of procedure rather than substance.

**35–063** NOTE 93. See, e.g., *Parker v TUI UK Ltd* [2009] EWCA Civ 1261, at [22]–[23]. For the position under the Rome II Regulation, see below, entry at para.S35–186.

NOTE 94. Add: *Global Multimedia International Ltd v ARA Media Services* [2006] EWHC 3612 (Ch.); *Sharp v Ministry of Defence* [2007] EWHC 224 (QB).

NOTE 96. Add: Where such facts, or the application of a foreign law, are specifically pleaded, CPR, r.16(1) and the overriding objective may require the pleading party also to plead the applicable foreign law or risk having the relevant part of its case excluded on case management grounds: *cf. Global Multimedia International Ltd v Ara Media Service* [2006] EWHC 3107 (Ch.),

[2007] 1 All E.R. (Comm.) 1160; *Tamil Nadu Electricity Board v St CMS Electricity Co Ltd* [2007] EWHC 1713 (Comm.), [2008] 2 Lloyd's Rep. 484, discussed above, entry at para.9.025.

NOTE 1. Add: *Cf. Crosstown Music Company LLC v Rive Droite Music Limited* [2009] EWHC 600 (Ch.), at [85]–[90], affd. [2010] EWCA Civ 1222. Note also the decision of the Court of Appeal in *Lucasfilm Ltd v Ainsworth* [2009] EWCA Civ 1328; [2010] 3 W.L.R. 333 (above, entry at paras 35–030—35–032) concerning the justiciability of claims for infringement of foreign intellectual property rights. **35–065**

NOTES 4 and 11. For the position under the Rome II Regulation, see below, para.S35–171. **35–066—35–067**

NOTE 9 Add at end: *O'Driscoll v J Ray McDermott* [2006] WASCA 25. **35–066**

NOTE 13. Add: George (2007) 3 J. Priv. Int. L. 137. For the position under the Rome II Regulation, see below, para.S35–196. **35–068**

NOTE 67. Add: *Hornsby v James Fisher Rumic Ltd* [2008] EWHC 1944 (QB). **35–076**

NOTE 68. For the position under the Rome II Regulation, see below, para.S35–199. **35–077**

## 2. DETERMINATION OF THE APPLICABLE LAW

### A. *The General Rule*

For the position under the Rome II Regulation, see below, paras S35–194 *et seq.* **35R–081**

NOTE 87. Add in line 3: *Trafigura Beheer BV v Kookmin Bank Co* [2006] EWHC 1450 (Comm.), [2006] 2 Lloyd's Rep. 455; *Congentra AG v Sixteen Thirteen Marine SA* [2008] EWHC 1615 (Comm.), [2008] 2 C.L.C. 51. Delete "Rule 204" and substitute "Rule 234". **35–082**

NOTE 95. Add after principal reference: See also *Hornsby v James Fisher Rumic Ltd* [2008] EWHC 1944 (QB). **35–083**

NOTE 96. Add: *R. (on the application of Al-Jedda) v Secretary of State for Defence* [2007] UKHL 58, [2008] 1 A.C. 332 (for later proceedings, see [2009] EWHC 397 (QB) and [2010] EWCA Civ 758); *cf. Bici v Ministry of Defence* [2004] EWHC 786 (QB); *Sharp v Ministry of Defence* [2007] EWHC 224 (QB) (English law applied by agreement between parties).

NOTE 96. *Harding v Wealands* [2004] EWCA Civ 1735, [2005] 1 W.L.R. 1539 was reversed by the House of Lords, but not on this point which the House found it unnecessary to consider in view of the determination that matters of assessment of damages were procedural and thus governed by English law as the law of the forum.

**35–084** NOTE 97. See now CPR r.6.36 and PD6B, para.3.1(9), inserted by SI 2008/2178.

**35–085** NOTE 2. As to *Harding v Wealands*, see entry at para.35–083, n.96. Add: *Hornsby v James Fisher Rumic Ltd* [2008] EWHC 1944 (QB).

Text following note 2. For a different approach to the problems raised by trans-boundary torts causing personal injury and property damage, in the context of the Rome II Regulation, see Dickinson, paras 4.47–4.58 and 5.31–5.33.

**35–086** Text to note 5. See previous entry.

NOTE 6. Add: The failure to transfer money resulting in the liquidation of a company in which the claimant was a shareholder did not constitute "damage" to the shares for the purposes of s.11(2)(b): *Middle Eastern Oil LLC v National Bank of Abu Dhabi* [2009] EWHC 2895 (Comm.), [2009] 1 Lloyd's Rep. 251.

**35–087** NOTE 7. See also Case C–343/04 *Land Oberösterreich v CEZ a.s.* [2006] E.C.R. I–4557, and see Betlem and Bernasconi (2006) 122 L.Q.R. 124. For the position under the Rome II Regulation, see paras S35–222 below *et seq*.

**35–088** NOTE 12. Add: *Ark Therapeutics plc v True North Capital Ltd* [2005] EWHC 1585 (Comm.), [2006] 1 All E.R. (Comm.) 138; *Equitas Ltd v Wave City Shipping Co Ltd* [2005] EWHC 923 (Comm.), [2005] 2 All E.R. (Comm.) 301; *Dornoch Ltd v Mauritius Union Assurance Co Ltd* [2006] EWCA Civ 389, [2006] 2 Lloyd's Rep. 475; *Trafigura Beheer BV v Kookmin Bank Co* [2006] EWHC 1450 (Comm.), [2006] 2 Lloyd's Rep. 455; *Middle Eastern Oil LLC v National Bank of Abu Dhabi* [2009] EWHC 2895 (Comm.), [2009] 1 Lloyd's Rep. 251; and see *Ashton Investments Ltd v Rusal* [2006] EWHC 2545 (Comm.), [2007] 1 Lloyd's Rep. 311.

NOTES 13 and 14. See previous entry.

NOTE 18. Add: See also *Ashton Investments Ltd v Rusal*, above. In *OJSC Oil Company Yugraneft v Abramovich* [2008] EWHC 2613 (Comm.), in considering the law applicable to a dishonest assistance claim, Christopher Clarke J. referred (at [224] and [234]) to Russia as the place where "in substance" the wrong took place. In that case, however, it was not necessary to reach a concluded view as to whether the claim fell within the scope of the 1995 Act (see above, entry at para.35–023).

NOTE 23. Add: *Trafigura Beheer BV v Kookmin Bank Co*, above, at [87]. **35–089**

NOTES 25 and 26. Add *Trafigura Beheer BV v Kookmin Bank Co*, above. See also *Dornoch Ltd v Mauritius Union Assurance Co Ltd*, above.

NOTE 27. Add: See also *Ark Therapeutics v True North Capital Ltd*, above; *Dornoch Ltd v Mauritius Union Assurance Co Ltd*, above; and see *Trafigura Beheer BV v Kookmin Bank Co*, above; *Congentra AG v Sixteen Thirteen Marine SA* [2008] EWHC 1615 (Comm.), [2008] 2 C.L.C. 51.

NOTE 30. Add: *Ark Therapeutics Ltd v True North Capital Ltd*, above; *Dornoch Ltd v Mauritius Union Assurance Co Ltd*, above.

NOTE 34. Add at end: See also *Equitas Ltd v Wave City Shipping Co Ltd*, above (inducing breach of contract); *Ashton Investments Ltd v Rusal*, above (breach of confidence, interference with business by unlawful means and conspiracy).

NOTE 41. As to *Harding v Wealands,* see above, entry at para.35–083, n.96. In Illustration 4, although the law applicable to the tort is the law of New South Wales, that will not include provisions of that law placing a financial limit on the amount of damages that can be recovered for non-economic loss since such questions are procedural and thus governed by English law as the law of the forum: *Harding v Wealands* [2006] UKHL 32, [2007] 2 A.C. 1. **35–091**

B. *Rule of Displacement*

For the position under the Rome II Regulation, see below, paras S35–196 *et seq.* **35R–094**

NOTE 56. Add: See also *Hornsby v James Fisher Rumic Ltd* [2008] EWHC 1944 (QB). **35–096**

NOTE 57. *Harding v Wealands* [2004] EWCA Civ 1735, [2005] 1 W.L.R. 1539 has been reversed by the House of Lords, [2006] UKHL 32, [2007] 2 A.C. 1. It was not found necessary to determine whether the Court of Appeal was correct in holding that the law of New South Wales, applicable under Private International Law (Miscellaneous Provisions) Act 1995, s.11(1), could not be displaced under s.12 of the Act.

NOTE 58 and text thereto. For an example of a case where the law applicable under the general rule of s.11(2)(c) of the 1995 Act was displaced under s.12, see *Trafigura Beheer BV v Kookmin Bank Co* [2006] EWHC 1450 (Comm.), [2006] 2 Lloyd's Rep. 455. See also *Middle Eastern Oil LLC v National Bank of Abu Dhabi* [2009] EWHC 2895 (Comm.); [2009] 1 Lloyd's Rep. 251. Contrast *Ark Therapeutics Ltd v True North Capital Ltd* [2005] EWHC 1585 **35–097**

(Comm.), [2006] 1 All E.R. (Comm.) 138; *Dornoch Ltd v Mauritius Union Assurance Co Ltd* [2006] EWCA Civ 389, [2006] 2 Lloyd's Rep. 475; *cf. Congentra AG v Sixteen Thirteen Marine SA* [2008] EWHC 1615 (Comm.), [2008] 2 C.L.C. 51.

**35–098** NOTE 59. See *Harding v Wealands* [2006] UKHL 32, [2007] 2 A.C. 1, at [59] and above, entry at para.35–096, n.57.

**35–101** NOTE 68. Add: See *Trafigura Beheer BV v Kookmin Bank Co*, above, at [97] (clear from the terms of s.12(2) that the factors that the court can take into account as connecting a tort with a country under s.12 are broadly stated).

**35–102— 35–104** The commentary in these paragraphs was approved in *Hornsby v James Fisher Rumic Ltd* [2008] EWHC 1944 (QB), at [47].

**35–102** NOTE 69. Add before reference to *MacKinnon v Iberia Shipping Co*: *Hornsby v James Fisher Rumic Ltd*, above, entry at 35–102–35–104.

NOTE 70. See above, entry at para.35–097, n.57. Add: *Hornsby v James Fisher Rumic Ltd*, above.

NOTE 71. See also *Sharp v Ministry of Defence* [2007] EWHC 224 (QB). *cf. R. (on the application of Al-Jedda) v Secretary of State for Defence* [2007] UKHL 58, [2008] 1 A.C. 332; *Hornsby v James Fisher Rumic Ltd*, above.

NOTE 72. Add after first reference: *Smith v Skanska Construction Services Ltd* [2008] EWHC 1776 (QB); *Hornsby v James Fisher Rumic Ltd*, above.

NOTE 73. Add in line 2: *Trafigura Beheer BV v Kookmin Bank Co*, above (if the governing law of a contract or a chosen jurisdiction provision in a contract is the law of country A, that may be a factor that connects the alleged tort under consideration with country A: the contractual "matrix" in which it is said the alleged tort occurred is a "factor" for consideration under s.12). See also *Middle Eastern Oil LLC v National Bank of Abu Dhabi* [2009] EWHC 2895 (Comm.), [2009] 1 Lloyd's Rep. 251. *Cf. Congentra AG v Sixteen Thirteen Marine SA* [2008] EWHC 1615 (Comm.), [2008] 2 C.L.C. 51.

NOTE 74. Add: *Baines v Baines* (2009) unreported, July 29, 2009 (Judge Platts, QBD, Preston District Registry).

NOTE 75. Add after reference to *Hulse v Chambers*: *Smith v Skanska Construction Services Ltd* [2008] EWHC 1776 (QB), at [148].

**35–104** NOTE 79. See above, entry at para.35–097, n.57.

**35–105** NOTE 82. Add: *Ark Therapeutics plc v True North Capital Ltd* [2005] EWHC 1585 (Comm.), [2006] 1 All E.R. (Comm.) 138; *R. (on the application of*

*Al-Jedda) v Secretary of State for Defence* [2007] UKHL 58, [2008] 1 A.C. 332; *Dornoch Ltd v Mauritius Union Assurance Co Ltd* [2006] EWCA Civ 389, [2006] 2 Lloyd's Rep. 475; *Trafigura Beheer BV v Kookmin Bank Co* [2006] EWHC 1450 (Comm.), [2006] 2 Lloyd's Rep. 455; *Congentra AG v Sixteen Thirteen Marine SA* [2008] EWHC 1615 (Comm.), [2008] 2 C.L.C. 51; *Hornsby v James Fisher Rumic Ltd* [2008] EWHC 1944 (QB); *Middle Eastern Oil LLC v National Bank of Abu Dhabi* [2009] EWHC 2895 (Comm.), [2009] 1 Lloyd's Rep. 251. As to *Harding v Wealands*, see entry at para.35–097, n.57.

NOTE 84. Add: *R. (on the application of Al-Jedda) v Secretary of State for Defence* [2006] EWCA Civ 327, [2007] Q.B. 621 at [104]–[106], affd. [2008] UKHL 58, [2008] 1 A.C. 332.

NOTE 85. See previous entry.

NOTE 86. See entry at n.84, above.

NOTE 87. Add: *Trafigura Beheer BV v Kookmin Bank Co*, above at [119]. **35–106**

NOTE 88. Add: *Hornsby v James Fisher Rumic Ltd* [2008] EWHC 1944 (QB), at [50].

NOTE 92. Add: See also *Smith v Skanska Construction Services Ltd* [2008] EWHC 1776 (QB), at [148] (vicarious liability). **35–107**

In *R. (on the application of Al-Jedda) v Secretary of State for Defence* [2006] EWCA Civ 327, [2007] Q.B. 621 the Court of Appeal held that Iraqi law governed a claim by the claimant, who held dual British and Iraqi nationality, that he had been wrongfully arrested and detained by British forces in Iraq. Under Iraqi law the multi-national force of which the British forces were part was entitled to intern and detain people where it was necessary for imperative reasons of security. It was contended that Iraqi law should be displaced under s.12 of the 1995 Act in favour of English law, given that the claim was a claim by a British citizen against the British Government in respect of activities on a base operated according to British law (and inviolable from Iraqi process) by British troops governed by British law (and immune from Iraqi law). This contention was rejected. The law of Iraq had been adapted in line with resolutions of the Security Council to give the multi-national force all the authority to take all necessary measures to contribute to the maintenance of security and stability in Iraq, including internment where this was necessary for imperative reasons of security. "Given that the laws of Iraq have been adapted to give the multi-national force the requisite powers, it would be very odd if the legality of [the claimant's] detention was to be governed by the law of England and not the law of Iraq." (*ibid.*, at [106]). Accordingly, it was not substantially more appropriate for the applicable law to be English law. The **35–108** decision of the Court of Appeal on this aspect of the case was unanimously upheld by the House of Lords, [2008] UKHL 58, [2008] 1 A.C. 332. See especially at [40]–[43], *per* Lord Bingham and at [153], *per* Lord Brown of Eaton-under-Heywood. For later proceedings, see *Al-Jedda v Secretary of State for Defence* [2010] EWCA Civ 758.

By contrast, in *Trafigura Beheer BV v Kookmin Bank Co* [2006] EWHC 1450 (Comm.), [2006] 2 Lloyd's Rep. 455 (on which see Briggs (2007) 123 L.Q.R. 18) it was held that the general rule applicable under s.11(2)(c) of the 1995 Act was displaced, pursuant to s.12. Here the Dutch claimant sought a declaration of non-liability in England in respect of a claim brought against it in Korea by a Korean bank which had issued a letter of credit to the claimant. The claim alleged that the claimant had failed to pass on bills of lading to the bank, thereby depriving the bank of its security. This, it was alleged, constituted a breach of duty by the claimant amounting to a tort under Korean law, but not under English law. It was first held that the claim was a claim in tort for the purposes of s.9(1) of the 1995 Act (see above, entry at paras 35–022—35–024), so that it then became necessary to determine the law applicable to the tort under the Act. It was then held that the most significant element or elements of the events alleged to constitute the tort under s.11(2)(c) occurred in Singapore. However, this notwithstanding, it was substantially more appropriate that the applicable law for determining the claim should be English law because the contracts (including the letter of credit) which constituted the contractual matrix between the parties in which the alleged tort occurred were governed by English law: "it would seem bizarre for all those parties' contractual relations to be governed by one applicable law, yet to hold that the law of another country is to determine non-contractual rights and obligations": [2006] EWHC 1450 (Comm.), [2006] 2 Lloyd's Rep. 455, at [118]. See also *Middle Eastern Oil LLC v National Bank of Abu Dhabi* [2009] EWHC 2895 (Comm.), [2009] 1 Lloyd's Rep. 251. *cf. Congentra AG v Sixteen Thirteen Marine SA* [2008] EWHC 1615 (Comm.), [2008] 2 C.L.C. 51, at [13]–[18].

NOTES 1 to 6 and text thereto. In *Harding v Wealands* [2006] UKHL 32, [2007] 2 A.C. 1 the House of Lords reversed that part of the Court of Appeal's decision ([2004] EWCA Civ 1735, [2005] 1 W.L.R. 1539) which treated the various issues of damages as substantive and held them to be procedural. The House found it unnecessary to deal with the other aspect of the decision of the Court of Appeal to the effect that the law applicable under the general rule, the law of New South Wales, could not be displaced in favour of English law under s.12 of the 1995 Act.

NOTE 1. Add: *Cf. Hornsby v James Fisher Rumic Ltd* [2008] EWHC 1944 (QB), where the law (English law) held to be applicable under s.12 was neither the place of injury nor the place of registration of the vessel on board which the injury occurred.

Note 6. Add: *cf. R. (on the application of Al-Jedda) v Secretary of State for Defence*, above.

Notes 7 to 11. *cf.* Art.17 of the Rome II Regulation, below, para.S35–264. **35–109**

Note 7. Add: *Gouldbourn v Balkan Holidays Ltd* [2010] EWCA Civ 372 (standards for ski instructors).

Notes 34, 36, 37. As to *Harding v Wealands* [2004] EWCA Civ 1735, [2005] 1 W.L.R. 1539, see above, entry at para.35–108, nn.3 to 6. **35–111**

## 3. PUBLIC POLICY AND RELATED QUESTIONS

For the position under the Rome II Regulation, see below, paras S35–175 *et seq.*, S35–217 *et seq.* **35R–112**

Note 44. Add: *Al Jedda v Secretary of State for Defence* [2010] EWCA Civ 758.

Note 45. Add in line 4: See also Case C–341/04 *Eurofood IFSC Ltd* [2006] E.C.R. I–3613, [2006] Ch. 508. **35–116**

Note 49. Add: See also *R. (on the application of Al-Jedda) v Secretary of State for Defence* [2006] EWCA Civ 327, [2007] Q.B. 621, at [97], affd. [2008] UKHL 58, [2008] 1 A.C. 332. *Cf. Al-Jedda v Secretary of State for Defence* [2010] EWCA Civ 758, [76]–[86]; [171]–[183].

In *Al Jedda v Secretary of State for Defence* [2010] EWCA Civ 758, however, the Court of Appeal rejected the submission that Iraqi law, if it had imposed tortious liability on the UK government with respect to the claimant's detention by British troops, would have contravened English public policy for the reason that an applicable resolution of the UN Security Council required the UK as a matter of international law to detain individuals for imperative reasons of security. For Arden L.J. (at [86]) the requirements of the UN Resolution were a relevant, but not sufficient, factor: it being necessary to show that the Iraqi rule imposing liability was in itself "offensive or unobjectionable". The availability of a remedy under the applicable foreign law which would not be available under English law was not, therefore, a sufficient basis for invoking public policy. By contrast, Elias L.J. rejected (at [176]–[178]) the submission that international law should be given priority over national law. In his view (at [174]), the purpose of relevant provision of Iraqi law, requiring judicial oversight of detention, was to ensure that basic liberties were properly protected and it was not possible to contend that a rule of this kind was "an affront to fundamental principles of fairness and justice". The third member of the court, Sir John Dyson, did not address this issue in his judgment.

**35–119** Note 56. Add: See also *Mbasogo v Logo Ltd* [2006] EWCA Civ 1370, [2007] Q.B. 846.

**35–120** Note 57. *cf.* Rome II Regulation, Art.16, below para.535–272. For the possible impact on the law applicable of the act of state doctrine (in the form recognised in *Nissan v Attorney-General* [1970] A.C. 179), see *Al Jedda v Secretary of State for Defence* [2010] EWCA Civ 758, at [218]–[224] (Elias L.J.); *cf.* Arden L.J, at [108]–[110].

Note 59. *cf.* Regulation (EC) 593/2008 of the European Parliament and of the Council of June 17, 2008 on the law applicable to contractual obligations (Rome I) ([2008] O.J. L177/6), Art.9. Above, entry at para.32–132.

**35–121** Note 66. No reference was made to this point in *Harding v Wealands* [2006] UKHL 32, [2007] 2 A.C. 1.

**35–122** Notes 71 and 72. Add: *cf. Mbasogo v Logo Ltd*, above.

## 4. LAW APPLICABLE TO DEFAMATION AND RELATED CLAIMS

**35R–123** Note 80. The Rome II Regulation does not apply to non-contractual obligations arising out of violations of privacy and rights relating to personality, including defamation: Art.2(g). However, not later than December 31, 2008, the European Commission is required to submit to the European Parliament, the Council and the European Economic and Social Committee a study on the situation in the field of the law applicable to non-contractual obligations arising out of violations of privacy and rights relating to personality, taking into account rules relating to freedom of the press and freedom of expression in the media, and conflict-of-law issues related to Directive 95/46/EC of the European Parliament and of the Council of October 24, 1995 on the protection of individuals with regard to the processing of personal data and on the free movement of such data ([1995] O.J. L281/31): Art.30(2). A comparative study was commissioned and submitted in February 2009, but the study and reaction by the Commission has not yet been officially published: see JLS/2007/C4 208, Final Report. The European Parliament's JURI committee has launched an own initiative procedure (INI/2009/2170), and prepared a working document on this topic (see http://conflictoflaws.net/2010/rome-ii-and-defamation-online-symposium [Accessed October 14, 2010]). See below, paras S35–172, S35–185.

**35–128** Note 97. In line 14 add: *Ehrenfeld v Bin Mahfouz* 9 N.Y. 3d 501, 88 N.E. 2d 830 (2007); *Ehrenfeld v Bin Mahfouz* 518 F. 3d 102 (2d Cir. 2008) arising out of *Bin Mahfouz v Ehrenfeld* [2005] EWHC 1156 (QB); Libel Terrorism Protection Act 2008 (New York); Securing the Protection of our Enduring and Established Constitutional Heritage Act 2010 (also known as The Speech Act) amending Title 28, United States Code, to prohibit recognition and enforcement of foreign defamation judgments and certain foreign judgments against the providers of interactive computer services; see Balin, Handman and Reid [2009] E.H.R.L.R. 303.

NOTE 11. Add in penultimate line: *Al Amoudi v Brisard* [2006] EWHC 1062, [2007] 1 W.L.R. 113; *Atlantis World Group of Cos NV v Gruppo Editoriale L'Espresso SpA* [2008] EWHC 1323 (QB), [2009] E.M.L.R. 270; *Mardas v New York Times Co* [2008] EWHC 3135 (QB), [2009] E.M.L.R. 152; See also *Carrie v Tolkien* [2009] EWHC 1765 (QB), [2009] E.M.L.R. 164. On the phenomenon of "libel tourism", see Garnett and Richardson (2009) 5 J. Priv. Int. L. 471; Hartley (2010) 59 I.C.L.Q. 25. And see Defamation Bill [H.L.], introduced in Session 2010–2011, especially clauses 10 and 13. **35–131**

NOTE 13. See previous entry.

NOTE 11. *Re T & N Ltd* [2005] EWHC 2990 (Ch.) is now reported, *sub nom. Re T & N Ltd (No.2)*, at [2006] 1 W.L.R. 1792. **35–136**

NOTE 36. See previous entry. **35–137**

NOTE 49. Add in line 8: *Al Amoudi v Brisard*, above. Add in line 11: *Burke v NYP Holdings Inc* (2005) 48 B.C.L.R. (4th) 363. Add in line 16: *Nationwide News Pty Ltd v University of Newlands* [2005] NZCA 317. **35–141**

NOTE 54. Add : See also *Nationwide News Pty Ltd v University of Newlands*, above. **35–142**

NOTE 55. Add in line 2: *Al Amoudi v Brisard*, above, where it was held that there is no rebuttable presumption of law that an article placed on an internet website that is open to general access has been published to a substantial number of people within the jurisdiction and that the claimant bears the burden of proving that the material in question has been accessed and downloaded. And see *Atlantis World Group of Cos NV v Gruppo Editoriale L'Espresso SpA* [2008] EWHC 1323 (QB), [2009] E.M.L.R. 269; *Times Newspapers Ltd v United Kingdom* [2009] E.M.L.R. 254 (European Court of Human Rights) (rule of English law whereby a new cause of action in defamation accrues whenever defamatory material is downloaded from the internet not a violation of Art.10 (right of freedom of expression) of European Convention on Human Rights). *Cf.* Ministry of Justice, *Defamation and the Internet: the Multiple Publication Rule*, Consultation Paper CP 20/09, September 16, 2009; Defamation Bill [H.L.], above, clause 10.

NOTE 59. Add: *Atlantis World Group of Cos NV v Gruppo Editoriale L'Espresso SpA* [2008] EWHC 1323 (QB), [2009] E.M.L.R. 269. See also Edwards (2004) 8 Edin. L.R. 99; *Desjean v Intermix Media Inc* (2006) FC 1395, (2006) 28 B.L.R. (4th) 315.

NOTE 60. See above, entry at para.35–131, n.11.

NOTES 61 and 62. Add: *Lucasfilm Ltd v Ainsworth* [2009] EWCA Civ 1328, [2010] 3 W.L.R. 333 at [193]–[194].

**35–145** NOTE 69. Add: Fentiman (2006) 59 Curr. Leg. Prob. 391.

NOTE 72. *Neilson v Overseas Projects Corp of Victoria Ltd* [2005] HCA 54, (2005) 221 A.L.R. 213 is now reported at (2005) 223 C.L.R. 331.

**35–147** NOTE 74. See previous entry.

**35–151** NOTE 80. See entry at para.35–145, n.72.

**35–154** NOTE 85. Add in line 3: *Bank of Credit and Commerce International SA v Ali* [2006] EWHC 2135 (Ch.).

NOTE 86. Add: *Bank of Credit and Commerce International SA v Ali*, above.

**35–158** NOTE 96. Add: See *Metropolitan International Schools Ltd v Designtechnica Corp.* [2009] EWHC 1765 (QB), [2010] 3 All E.R. 548 at [81]–[114].

After paragraph 35–164 add the following material.

## 5. REGULATION (EC) 864/2007 OF THE EUROPEAN PARLIAMENT AND OF THE COUNCIL OF JULY 11, 2007 ON THE LAW APPLICABLE TO NON-CONTRACTUAL OBLIGATIONS (THE ROME II REGULATION)[1]

### A. *Introduction, Scope and General Matters*

**S35–165** **Background.** In July 2003 the European Commission presented a proposal for a Regulation of the European Parliament and of the Council on the Law Applicable to Non-Contractual Obligations (Rome II).[2] The proposal, which was aimed at introducing uniform choice of law rules in respect of non-

[1] On the Rome II Regulation see generally Dickinson, *The Rome II Regulation: The Law Applicable to Non-Contractual Obligations* (2008) and Supplement (2010) ("Dickinson") Ch.1–16; Plender and Wilderspin, *The European Private International Law of Obligations* (3rd edn 2009), Chs 16 *et seq.*; the collected papers in (2007) 9 Yb. P.I.L. and in Ahern & Binchy, *The Rome II Regulation on the Law Applicable to Non-Contractual Obligations* (2008) ("Ahern & Binchy"); Symeonides (2008) 56 Am. J. Comp. L. 173; Kozyris (2008) 56 Am. J. Comp L. 471; Rushworth and Scott [2008] L.M.C.L.Q. 274; De Boer (2009) 56 Neth.Int.L.R. 295.

[2] COM/2003/0427 final, with Explanatory Memorandum, described hereafter as "Explanatory Memorandum". See on this, House of Lords, European Union Committee, *The Rome II Regulation,* HL Paper 66 (2004); and the references in main work, para.35R-001, n.1, to which may be added Malatesta (ed.), *The Unification of Choice of Law Rules on Torts and Other Non-Contractual Obligations in Europe* (2006) (hereafter "Malatesta").

contractual obligations arising out of a tort or delict and non-contractual obligations arising out of an act other than a tort or delict, was not received with any enthusiasm in the United Kingdom.[3] Nonetheless, the United Kingdom opted into the negotiations.[4] The negotiating process involved extensive input from the European Parliament[5] and, indeed co-decision by the Council and the Parliament on the final outcome.[6] After an amended proposal was submitted by the Commission in February, 2006[7] a Council Common Position was reached in September, 2006.[8] That position was considered in the European Parliament, which proposed several amendments,[9] most of which were not accepted by the Council.[10] The matter then became subject to the conciliation procedure and a joint text was approved by the Conciliation Committee on June 25, 2007.[11] After necessary linguistic revisions, the Regulation emerged as Regulation (EC) 864/2007 of the European Parliament and of the Council of July 11, 2007 on the Law Applicable to Non-Contractual Obligations (Rome II) (referred to hereafter as the "Rome II Regulation" or the "Regulation").[12] The Rome II Regulation is reproduced in Appendix 1 to this Supplement.

**Legal basis.** The Commission's original proposal and the eventual Rome II Regulation are based on Art.61(c) of the EC Treaty, which enables the Council to adopt measures in the field of judicial cooperation in civil and commercial matters, as provided for in Art.65, which refers to "measures in the field of judicial co-operation in civil matters having cross-border implications" to be taken "in so far as necessary for the proper functioning of the internal market." Such measures may include "promoting the compatibility of the rules applicable in the Member States concerning the conflict of laws and of jurisdiction".[13] The "internal market" basis for the Regulation was received S35–166

---

3 See generally HL Paper 66 (2004).

4 Not without some confusion as to the consequences: see HL Paper 66 (2004), paras 80–83 and Minutes of Evidence, pp.86–87.

5 See European Parliament legislative resolution on the proposal for a regulation of the European Parliament and of the Council on the Law Applicable to Non-Contractual Obligations ("Rome II") COM 2003 427-C5–0338/2003–2003/0168 (COD): P6TA 2005 0284; Proposal for a Regulation of the European Parliament and of the Council on the Law Applicable to Non-Contractual Obligations ("Rome II"), Outcome of the European Parliament's second reading (Strasbourg, January 15–18, 2007) 2003/0168 (COD), CODEC 637 JUST CIV 164.

6 See Art.251 of the EC Treaty.

7 See Commission of the European Union, Amended proposal for a European Parliament and Council Regulation on the Law Applicable to Non-Contractual Obligations ("Rome II"), February 21, 2006, COM (2006) 83 final.

8 See [2006] O.J. C289/68.

9 See Outcome of European Parliament's second reading, above, n.5.

10 See COM (2007) 126.

11 PE-CONS 3619/2007–C6–0142/2007/-2003/168 (COD).

12 [2007] O.J. L199/40. Ireland is also taking part in the adoption and application of the Regulation: Recital (39). Denmark is not: Recital (40). For the purposes of the Regulation, "Member State" means any Member State other than Denmark: Art.1(4). In what follows the expression "Regulation State" will generally be used instead of "Member State".

13 Art.65(b) of the Treaty. See Recitals (1)–(7).

with considerable scepticism in the United Kingdom, as can be seen in the views of the House of Lords European Union Committee[14] and in the evidence of witnesses which was received by that Committee.[15] It would seem unlikely, however, that the European Court would be receptive to a challenge to the *vires* of the Regulation.[16]

S35–167 **Rome II Regulation in outline.** This commentary attempts to provide an account of the main features of the Rome II Regulation as it applies to non-contractual obligations arising out of tort/delict. It is helpful, however, at the outset, to identify the overall subject matter and structure of the Regulation. After the initial Preamble (and 40 Recitals), the Regulation is arranged into seven Chapters. Chapter I is concerned with scope. Chapter II sets out the principal choice of law rules for non-contractual obligations arising out of tort/delict consisting of: the general rule (Art.4); and particular choice of law rules for product liability (Art.5), unfair competition and acts restricting free competition (Art.6), environmental damage (Art.7), infringement of intellectual property rights (Art.8), and industrial action (Art.9). Chapter III deals with certain non-contractual obligations which are not regarded as arising out of tort/delict, specifically, unjust enrichment (Art.10), *negotiorum gestio* (Art.11), *culpa in contrahendo* (Art.12) and intellectual property rights (Art.13).[17] Chapter IV, containing one article (Art.14), sets forth a provision by which, in certain circumstances, the parties may choose the law to govern non-contractual obligations. Chapter V contains common rules applicable in respect of all non-contractual obligations falling within the Regulation, concerned with: the scope of the applicable law (Art.15); overriding mandatory provisions (Art.16); rules of safety and conduct (Art.17); direct actions against the insurer of the person liable (Art.18); subrogation (Art.19); multiple liability (Art.20); formal validity (Art.21); and burden of proof (Art.22). "Other Provisions" are found in Chapter VI. This consists of provisions concerned with: habitual residence (Art.23); the exclusion of renvoi (Art.24); States with more than one legal system (Art.25); public policy of the forum (Art.26); relationship with other provisions of Community law (Art.27); and relationship with existing international conventions (Art.28). Chapter VII contains "Final Provisions" concerned with: a list of conventions referred to in Art.28

---

[14] HL Paper 66 (2004), paras 50–76, 184–185. The Committee also concluded that the Commission, in making its original proposal, failed adequately to comply with the Protocol on Subsidiarity and Proportionality: *ibid.*, paras 77–78, 186. *cf.* Rome II Regulation, Recital (38).

[15] See, especially, HL Paper 66 (2004), Minutes of Evidence, pp.19, 22, 46, 54–56, 74. *cf. ibid.*, pp.1–6. Certain doubts as to the *vires* of the Regulation, insofar as it applies to all situations within its scope whether or not the subject matter of the dispute is connected with the functioning of the internal market, were also expressed by the Council Legal Service (Council document 7015/04), but amendments formulated to address this point were rejected in the Council discussions.

[16] See Dickinson, Ch.2.

[17] Unjust enrichment and *negotiorum gestio* are discussed in Ch.34. For *culpa in contrahendo*, see below, paras S35–242 *et seq.* For intellectual property, see below, paras S35–228 *et seq.*

(Art.29); a review clause (Art.30); application in time (Art.31); and date of application (Art.32).

**Temporal and spatial application.** Article 31 of the Rome II Regulation (headed "Application in time") stipulates that the Regulation "shall apply to events giving rise to damage which occur after its entry into force." Article 32 (headed "Date of application") provides that, with one exception,[18] the Regulation shall apply from January 11, 2009. As regards Article 31, however, there is no date specified for entry into force. In such circumstances, by application of general rules of EC law on the application in time of EC legislation, the date of "entry into force" is the twentieth day following that of its publication in the Official Journal, i.e. August 20, 2007.[19] As to Article 32, there is a lack of clarity as to what the Regulation is to apply to as from January 11, 2009. It is suggested that in combination, Arts 31 and 32 should be construed, on their present wording, as meaning that events giving rise to damage after August 20, 2007 are subject to the Regulation in circumstances where the law applicable to the non-contractual obligation in question is determined by the court, whether at trial or by way of a preliminary issue, on or after January 11, 2009.[20] The lack of clarity in the temporal application of the Regulation remains, however, highly unsatisfactory and in *Homawoo v GMF Assurance SA*[21] Slade J. referred several questions concerning the interpretation of Arts 31–32 to the European Court. In terms of its spatial application, the Regulation applies in all Member States of the European Community, with the exception of Denmark.[22] S35–168

**Directly applicable.** As a Regulation, the Rome II Regulation is directly applicable and no United Kingdom legislation is required to bring it into effect. Nevertheless, the Law Applicable to Non-Contractual Obligations (England and Wales and Northern Ireland) Regulations 2008 have been adopted to clarify the relationship between the Rome II Regulation and existing legislation in England and Northern Ireland and to extend its scope to conflicts solely between the laws of different parts of the United Kingdom or S35–169

---

[18] Art.28 concerned with the list of conventions which applies from July 11, 2008.

[19] EC Treaty, Art.254(1). Some commentators have, however, argued that the Regulation should be taken as applying only to events giving rise to damage on or after January 11, 2009 (i.e. on the date specified in Art.32 for its application) and this view was favourably received by Slade J. in *Homawoo v GMF Assurance SA* [2010] EWHC 1941 (QB), at [50]. It also reflects the current approach of the German Courts, apparently without detailed argument on this issue (see Bundesgerichtshof (BGH), July 9, 2009, NJW 2009, 3371, paras 17 and 22).

[20] Dickinson, paras 3.320–3.322 (rejecting the suggestion in earlier supplements to this edition that the Regulation should apply to proceedings issued on or after January 11, 2009). This view of the Regulation's temporal effect was adopted (*obiter*) by Tomlinson J. in *Bacon v Nacional Suiza Cia Seguros y Reseguros SA* [2010] EWHC 2017 (QB), referring (at [57]) to this paragraph. By contrast, in *Homawoo v GMF Assurance SA*, above, Slade J. (at [43]–[49]) inclined to the view that there was no warrant for interpreting the words "shall apply from" in Art.32 as meaning either "shall apply to proceedings commenced" or "shall apply to the determination by a court", but considered it necessary, in light of the wording of Arts 31–32, to refer the matter to the European Court (see text at n.21, below).

[21] *Homawoo*, above, at [51]–[52].

[22] Art.1(4). See n.12 above.

Gibraltar.[23] These Regulations came into force on January 11, 2009.[24] By Reg.2, a new section (s.15A) is inserted in the 1995 Act in terms that nothing in that Act applies to affect the determination of issues relating to tort which fall to be determined under the Rome II Regulation. By regulation 4, a like amendment is made to the Foreign Limitation Periods Act 1984.[25] Finally, in accordance with the option presented in Art.25(2) of the Rome II Regulation, reg.6 provides that the rules in Rome II will extend to conflicts solely between the laws of different parts of the United Kingdom (including, for these purposes, Gibraltar).

**S35–170** **Interpretation.** The Rome II Regulation will be subject to interpretation by the European Court by way of a reference to that court under Art.234 of the EC Treaty, but such a reference can only be made by a court or tribunal of a Member State against whose decisions there is no judicial remedy under national law.[26] Consequently, the task of interpreting the Regulation will largely fall on national courts.[27] There are no explicit guides to the process of interpretation in the Regulation itself. Nevertheless, the European Court and national courts will doubtless have regard to the need for uniformity in the interpretation and application of the Regulation amongst the Regulation States[28] and to this end will endeavour to attribute autonomous meanings to terms which are likely to have different meanings in the laws of the various Regulation States. Recitals to the Regulation support this conclusion: thus, because the concept of "non-contractual obligation" varies from one Regulation State to another, it "should be understood as an autonomous concept;"[29] similarly, "*culpa in contrahendo*" is, for the purposes of the Regulation, "an autonomous concept and should not necessarily be interpreted within the meaning of national law."[30] In addition, Recitals dealing with particular provisions may assist in their interpretation.[31] And, more generally, courts may take heed of the advice in Recital (7) to the effect that the "substantive scope and the provisions of this Regulation should be consistent with Council

---

[23] SI 2008/2986. Similar legislation has been adopted by the Scottish Parliament: see Law Applicable to Non-Contractual Obligations (Scotland) Regulations 2008 (SSI 2008/404).

[24] Reg.1(1).

[25] Below, para.S35–262. Reg.1(3) provided that Reg.4 extends to Northern Ireland only, but this would appear to be an error, as the 1984 Act does extends only to England and Wales (s.7(4)). But this error was corrected by a correction slip issued in September 2009. Reg.5 modifies the Foreign Limitation Periods (Northern Ireland) Order 1985 (SI 1985/754).

[26] See main work, paras 11–019, 11–058 *et seq.*

[27] According to Recital (8) the "Regulation should apply irrespective of the nature of the court or tribunal seised". It is doubtful, however, whether the Regulation is binding on private arbitration tribunals or bodies (such as the Financial Ombudsman Service) that are not required to apply rules of law in determining complaints (Dickinson, paras 3.77–3.85). *Cf. National Navigation Co v Endesa Generacion SA* [2009] EWCA Civ 1397, [2010] 1 Lloyd's Rep 193, at [118] (Brussels I Regulation).

[28] See the comments of Owen J. in *Jacobs v Motor Insurers Bureau* [2010] EWHC 231 (QB), [2010] 1 All E.R. (Comm) 1128, at [22]–[24], referring to Recital (6) of the Regulation and the Explanatory Memorandum accompanying the Commission's Proposal.

[29] Recital (11). See below, para.S35–177.

[30] Recital (30). *Cf.* Recital (27) (below, para.S35–240).

[31] See, e.g. Recitals (20)–(28).

Regulation (EC) 44/2001 of December 22, 2000 on jurisdiction and the recognition and enforcement of judgments in civil and commercial matters (Brussels 1) and the instruments dealing with the law applicable to contractual obligations" and approach interpretation, if possible, in a manner that is apt to achieve such consistency. The Recital also means that there should be consistency as between the Rome II Regulation and Regulation (EC) 593/2008 of the European Parliament and of the Council of June 17, 2008 on the law applicable to contractual obligations (Rome I) (hereafter the "Rome I Regulation").[32] Finally, in interpreting the Regulation, the courts must consider the objectives of the Regulation, as stated in the Recitals, foremost among which are the need for legal certainty and to ensure fairness between the parties.[33]

**Review clause.** Article 30 of the Rome II Regulation provides for review of certain matters arising in connection with the Regulation. Not later than August 20, 2011, the Commission is required to submit to the European Parliament, the Council and the European Economic and Social Committee a report on the application of the Regulation and if necessary the report shall be accompanied by proposals to adapt the Regulation.[34] The report is to include: (i) a study on the effects of the way in which foreign law is treated in the different jurisdictions and on the extent to which courts in Regulation States apply foreign law in practice pursuant to the Regulation; and (ii) a study of the effects of Art.28 of the Regulation with respect to the Hague Convention of May 4, 1971 on the law applicable to traffic accidents.[35] As to (i), the treatment of foreign law (whether it must be pleaded by the parties or applied by the court of its own motion, etc.) varies amongst Regulation States.[36] An amendment to the Commission's proposal, introduced by the European Parliament, sought to provide a specific rule on the determination of the content of foreign law.[37] This was not accepted: the provision for review seems to represent a compromise position. As to (ii), several Regulation States are parties to the Hague Convention on the law applicable to traffic accidents,[38] and will be able to continue to apply that instrument as a result of Art.28. This could produce a lack of uniformity in the application of the Regulation in those States compared with those Regulation States which do not apply the **S35–171**

---

32 [2008] O.J. L177/6. See Recital (7) to the Rome I Regulation.

33 See, e.g., Recitals (6), (14), (16), (19) and (34).

34 Art.30(1).

35 Art.30(1)(i), (ii).

36 For the English position, see main work, Ch.9.

37 See European Parliament legislative resolution on the proposal for a regulation of the European Parliament and of the Council on the Law Applicable to Non-Contractual Obligations ("Rome II") (COM (2003) 427-C5–338/2003—2003/168 (COD)); P6_TA (2005) 284, Art.13. In a statement (accompanying the Regulation) the Commission has indicated that it will publish at the latest four years after the entry into force of the Regulation a "horizontal study on the application of foreign law in civil and commercial matters by the courts of the Member States, having regard to the aims of the Hague Programme. It is also prepared to take appropriate measures if necessary." *Cf.* below, para.S35–186.

38 Austria, Belgium, Czech Republic, France, Latvia, Lithuania, Luxembourg, The Netherlands, Poland, Slovakia, Slovenia and Spain.

Hague Convention. Presumably, the provision for review is designed to allow any lack of uniformity to be evaluated.[39]

S35–172 A highly controversial issue in the negotiation of the Regulation was whether violations of privacy and rights relating to personality, including defamation should be included in the body of the Regulation.[40] Eventually, these matters were excluded.[41] According to Art.30(2), not later than December 31, 2008, the Commission is to submit to the European Parliament, the Council and the European Economic and Social Committee a study on the situation in the field of the law applicable to non-contractual obligations arising out of violations of privacy and rights relating to personality, taking into account rules relating to freedom of the press and freedom of expression in the media, and conflict of laws issues related to Directive 95/41/ EC of the European Parliament and of the Council of October 24, 1995 on the protection of individuals with regard to the processing of personal data and on the free movement of such data.[42] This provision for review smacks of political compromise.[43]

S35–173 **Relationship with other provisions of Community law.** The Rome II Regulation does not prejudice the application of provisions of Community law which, in relation to particular matters, lay down conflict of laws rules relating to non-contractual obligations.[44] In this connection, Recital (35) states that:

---

[39] In a statement (accompanying the Regulation) the Commission indicates that being aware of the different practices followed in Regulation States as regards the level of compensation awarded to victims of road traffic accidents, it is prepared to examine the specific problems resulting for EU residents involved in road traffic accidents in a Member State other than the Member State of their habitual residence. To that end the Commission undertook to make available to the European Parliament and to the Council, before the end of 2008, a study on all the options, including insurance aspects, for improving the position of cross-border victims which would pave the way for a Green Paper. A study, prepared for the Commission by external consultants, has been published online (*http://ec.europa.eu/internal_market/insurance/docs/motor/20090129report_en.pdf*) and formed the basis for a public consultation by DG Markt, launched on March 29, 2009 (*http://ec.europa.eu/internal_market/consultations/2009/cross-border-accidents_en.htm*). In its consultation paper, the Commission presented several options for the future development of policy in this area, including: (a) to await the results and impact of the Rome II Regulation (Option 1); and (b) to apply the law of the country of the victim's residence to claims of visiting victims of road traffic accidents (Option 6). In its response to the consultation, the United Kingdom Ministry of Justice indicated a strong preference for the first of these options.

[40] See below, para.S35–185.

[41] Art.1(2)(g).

[42] [1995] O.J. L281/31.

[43] In a statement (accompanying the Regulation) the Commission indicates that it will submit, not later than December 2008, a study on the situation in the field of the law applicable to non-contractual obligations arising out of violations of privacy and rights relating to personality and that it will take into consideration all aspects of the situation and take appropriate measures if necessary. A study, prepared by external consultants, has been delivered to the Commission, but not yet published. The European Parliament's JURI committee has launched an own initiative procedure (INI/2009/2170), and prepared a working document on this topic (see http://www.conflictoflaws.net/2010/rome-ii-and-defamation-online-symposium/).

[44] Art.27. See Recital (35).

"This Regulation should not prejudice the application of other instruments laying down provisions designed to contribute to the proper functioning of the internal market in so far as they cannot be applied in conjunction with the law designated by the rules of this Regulation. The application of provisions of the applicable law designated by the rules of this Regulation should not restrict the free movement of goods and services as regulated by Community instruments, such as Directive 2000/31/EC of the European Parliament and of the Council of 8 June 2000 on certain legal aspects of information society services, in particular electronic commerce, in the Internal Market (Directive on electronic commerce)."

These provisions are all that remains in the text of the Regulation to evidence the highly controversial nature of the discussions during the legislative process concerning the supposed "country of origin principle" in Community law.[45] Although there may, no doubt, be situations in which the free movement provisions of the EC Treaty and internal market legislation may affect the regulation of non-contractual liability within the Member States' legal systems,[46] in which case they will take effect under the Regulation as overriding mandatory provisions of the forum's legal order (Art.16[47]), the better view is that, in general, they have no direct or automatic effect upon the operation of the rules of applicable law in the Rome II Regulation. One notable exception consists of the wide-ranging rules of applicable law in Art.4 of the Insolvency Regulation, which may apply to non-contractual obligations.[48] More controversially, the United Kingdom legislation implementing the Directive on electronic commerce (to which Recital (35) specifically refers) could, on one view, be taken to require the application of United Kingdom law to regulate the (non-contractual) liability of locally established information society service providers, while excluding its application to regulate the (non-contractual liability) of service providers established in other Member States.[49]

**Relationship with existing international conventions.** The Regulation does not prejudice the application of international conventions to which one or more Regulation States are parties at the time the Regulation is adopted[50] and which lay down conflict of laws rules relating to non-contractual obligations.[51] This notwithstanding, the Regulation, as between Regulation States, S35–174

45 For background and discussion, see Vitellino in Malatesta (ed.), *The Unificaion of Choice of Law Rules on Torts and Other Non-Contractual Obligations in Europe* (2006), 271; Dickinson, paras 16.04–16.35.

46 See, e.g. Case C–115/08 *Land Oberösterreich v CEZ* [2009] E.C.R. I–10265.

47 See below, para.S35–272.

48 See, generally, main work, paras 30R–197 *et seq.*

49 Main work, paras 35–158—35–162. Several questions concerning the relationship between EU law and the Directive on electronic commerce have been referred to the European Court in Case C–509/09 *eDate Advertising GmbH v X* (pending).

50 i.e. July 11, 2007.

51 Art.28(1). Foremost among these are the Hague Conventions on traffic accidents (1971) and products liability (1973) to which several Regulation States, but not the United Kingdom, are parties.

takes precedence over conventions concluded exclusively between two or more such States in so far as such conventions concern matters governed by the Regulation.[52] Article 29(1)[53] requires Regulation States to notify the Commission of the aforementioned conventions by July 11, 2008, and after that date Regulation States are required to notify the Commission of all denunciations of such conventions. The Commission is obliged to publish in the Official Journal of the European Union, within six months of receipt, a list of the aforementioned conventions and a list of denunciations.[54]

S35–175 **Scope in general**. Article 1(1) of the Rome II Regulation provides that the Regulation "shall apply, in situations involving a conflict of laws, to non-contractual obligations in civil and commercial matters. It shall not apply, in particular, to revenue, customs or administrative matters or to the liability of the State for acts and omissions in the exercise of State authority (*acta iure imperii*)". The reference to "situations involving a conflict of laws" seems to indicate that the situation must be one which implicates the need to make a choice of law, although this requirement appears unlikely to have any real impact.[55] In the context, of the Regulation "non-contractual obligations" means "non-contractual obligations" arising out of tort/delict[56] and non-contractual obligations arising out of unjust enrichment, *negotiorum gestio* and pre-contractual dealings (*culpa in contrahendo*).[57] The meaning of "non-contractual obligations arising out of tort/delict" is examined below.[58] The exclusion of "revenue, customs and administrative matters" from the category of "civil and commercial matters" reflects the wording of the Judgments Regulation and, subject to what is said below, is a category the meaning of which is likely to be interpreted in a manner which is consistent with the

---

[52] Art.28(2). See Recital (36). According to Recital (37) the Commission will make a proposal to the European Parliament and the Council concerning the procedures and conditions under which Regulation States would be entitled to negotiate and conclude on their own behalf agreements with third countries in individual and exceptional cases, concerning sectoral matters, containing provisions on the law applicable to non-contractual obligations. Following a proposal by the Commission (COM (2008) 893 final), the Community legislature adopted a Regulation establishing a procedure for the negotiation and conclusion of agreements between Member States and third countries on particular matters concerning the law applicable to contractual and non-contractual obligations (Regulation (EC) 662/2009 of the European Parliament and the Council [2009] O.J. L200/25).

[53] Art.29 will apply from July 11, 2008: see Art.32.

[54] Art.29(2). Currently, that list has not been published, but it is understood that the United Kingdom has notified the following conventions under Art.29(1): International Convention Relating to the Arrest of Sea-going Ships (Brussels, May 10, 1952); European Patent Convention (Munich, October 5, 1973); Hague Convention on the law applicable to trusts and their recognition (July 1, 1985) (as to which, see below, para.S35–183); International Convention on salvage (London, April 28, 1989).

[55] On this point, see *Jacobs v Motor Insurers Bureau* [2010] EWHC 231 (QB), [2010] 1 All E.R. (Comm.) 1128, at [20], [31], but *cf.* [2010] EWCA Civ 1208, at [38]. *cf.* the differently worded Art.1(1) of the Rome Convention; main work, para.32–022.

[56] Arts 4–9.

[57] Arts 10–12. The Rome I Regulation does not apply to obligations arising out of dealings prior to the conclusion of a contract: Art.1(2)(i). Such obligations are covered by Art.12 of the Rome II Regulation (below, paras S35–242 *et seq.*): see Recital (10) to the Rome I Regulation.

[58] Para.S35–177. For convenience the expressions "tort/delict" will be limited to "tort" in what follows.

interpretation of the Judgments Regulation.[59] More generally, "civil and commercial matters" is also likely to be interpreted in the same manner in which it is interpreted in the context of the Judgments Regulation.[60]

**Acta iure imperii.** Unlike the position in relation to the Judgments Regulation,[61] the Rome II Regulation specifically excludes from its scope "the liability of the State for acts and omissions in the exercise of State authority". The meaning and scope of this exclusion is expanded somewhat in Recital (9) where claims arising out of *acta iure imperii* are said to include "claims against officials who act on behalf of the State and liability for acts of public authorities, including liability of publicly appointed office holders." This seems apt to exclude from the ambit of the Regulation, in England, cases such as *Sharp v Ministry of Defence*[62] and *R. (on the application of Al-Jedda) v Secretary of State for Defence*.[63] If this observation is correct, such cases will continue to be governed by Part III of the Private International Law (Miscellaneous Provisions) Act 1995.[64] S35–176

**Meaning of "non-contractual obligation" and "tort/delict".** Articles 4–9 of the Rome II Regulation apply to certain non-contractual obligations arising out of tort/delict which are not otherwise excluded from the scope of the Regulation by Art.1(1), referred to above, and Art.1(2) which is discussed below.[65] This type of "non-contractual obligation" is not, however, defined in the Regulation. That notwithstanding, it is said that the expression "non-contractual obligation" must be understood as an autonomous concept[66] and that is likely to mean that "non-contractual obligation arising out of a tort/delict" must similarly be understood as an autonomous concept, necessitating the delimitation of the scope of tort/delict for this purpose. Any observations, in this respect, must inevitably be tentative, but the following general points may be made. First, it must, obviously, not be assumed that a claim that would be characterised as tortious in English law will necessarily be characterised as a claim involving a non-contractual obligation arising out of a tort for the purposes of the Regulation.[67] Thus, for example, English domestic law treats claims for interference with property rights as belonging to the law of tort (e.g. conversion), whereas civil law systems often treat such claims as belonging to S35–177

---

59 Main work, paras 11–026 *et seq.* See also Art.1(1) of the Rome I Regulation.

60 Main work, paras 11–024 *et seq.* See also Art.1(1) of the Rome I Regulation. On this point, see *Jacobs v Motor Insurers Bureau* [2010] EWHC 231 (QB), [2010] 1 All E.R. (Comm.) 1128, at [19] revd. [2010] EWCA Civ 1208 without addressing this point. *Cf.* Dickinson, Supplement, para 3.269.

61 Though see Case C–292/05 *Lechouritou v Dimosio tis Omospondiakis Dimokratias tis Germanias* [2007] 2 All E.R. (Comm) 57.

62 [2007] EWHC 224 (QB); see also *Bici v Ministry of Defence* [2004] EWHC 786 (QB).

63 [2008] UKHL 58, [2008] 1 A.C. 332. See above, entry at para.35–108. As to the treatment of State liability under international and EC law, see Dickinson, paras 3.280–3.286.

64 Rules 231, 232, 233 and 234.

65 Paras. S35–178 *et seq.*

66 Recital (11). This is easy to say but much more difficult to achieve. See Dickinson, paras 3.86 *et seq.*; Scott in Ahern and Binchy, 57.

67 This follows from Recital (11). In many cases (e.g. negligence) there is unlikely to be any definitional problem.

the law of property (*rei vindicatio*).[68] Conversely, it must, equally, not be assumed that a claim which would not be characterised as tort for the purposes of English law cannot be characterised as tort for the purposes of the Regulation.[69] Secondly, it is advantageous, as a starting point, to distinguish between contractual obligations, governed by the Rome Convention or (when it enters into force), by the Rome I Regulation, and non-contractual obligations governed by the Rome II Regulation. Drawing this distinction may not necessarily be easy.[70] Initial guidance may (it can be put no higher than that) be found in the definition of "matters relating to tort, delict or quasi-delict" in the Brussels Convention and the Judgments Regulation as covering "all actions which seek to establish the liability of the defendant and which are not related to a 'contract'".[71] But the analogy is of limited assistance since (a) the expression thereby interpreted is different to that under consideration and (b) it is, in any event, overbroad in delimiting a non-contractual obligation arising out of tort, since "matters relating to tort, delict or quasi-delict" have been held to include some types of pre-contractual liability[72] which is dealt with as *culpa in contrahendo* under the Rome II Regulation.[73] Thirdly, it is also likely that whatever national law might say, at the European level it is unlikely to be held that a particular obligation may be treated as sounding, alternatively, say, as either contract or tort, or as tort or unjust enrichment, etc. That said, it would appear possible for a single factual scenario to generate two or more obligations with different characterisations and for there to arise from acts in the performance of a contractual obligation a concurrent liability in contract, within the Rome I Regulation, and in tort, within the Rome II Regulation.[74] Finally, it is to be hoped that the definitional exercise will not be carried out

---

[68] By referring to "obligations", the Regulation would appear to exclude matters of personal status and title to movable and immovable property: see Dickinson, paras 3.88–3.103; Scott, n.66 above, 72–76; Chong (2008) 57 I.C.L.Q. 863, 893–896. Fawcett, Harris and Bridge, *International Sale of Goods in the Conflict of Laws* (2005), pp.1012–1014. See also Nicholas, *Introduction to Roman Law* (1962), pp.226–227.

[69] *cf. Trafigura Beheer BV v Kookmin Bank Co* [2006] EWHC 1450 (Comm.), [2006] 2 Lloyd's Rep. 455; above, entry at para.35–108. Thus, in certain situations, obligations arising in equity or by reason of a bailment may fall within the scope of the Rome II Regulation. As to claims for knowing receipt and dishonest assistance, see above, entry at para.34–033. In *Jacobs v Motor Insurers Bureau* [2010] EWHC 231 (QB), [2010] 1 All E.R. (Comm.) 1128, (revd. [2010] EWCA Civ 1208 without addressing this point) a claim by the victim of a road traffic accident for statutory compensation from the MIB under the Motor Vehicles (Compulsory Insurance) (Information Centre and Compensation Body) Regulations (SI 2003/37) was characterised as one "arising out of a tort/delict" under the Regulation.

[70] See, for example, the different views expressed by commentators as to whether tortious liability in negligence based on a "voluntary assumption of responsibility" (e.g. *Hedley Byrne & Co. Ltd v Heller & Partners* [1964] A.C. 465) should be classified as "contractual" or "non-contractual": Dickinson, paras 3.130–3.133; Cheshire, North and Fawcett, *Private International Law* (14th edn Fawcett and Carruthers, 2008), pp.779–780 (non-contractual); Scott, n.66 above, pp.61–72 (contractual).

[71] Case 189/87 *Kalfelis v Schroeder* [1988] E.C.R. 5565, 5585; main work, para.11–299.

[72] See Case C–334/00 *Fonderie Officine Macchaniche SpA v HWS GmbH* [2002] E.C.R. I-7357. On its face, the formulation in *Kalfelis* is also apt to include a restitutionary claim but has been held not to do so: *Kleinwort Benson Ltd v Glasgow City Council* [1999] 1 A.C. 153.

[73] Art.12; below, paras S35–242 *et seq*. See also the Rome I Regulation, Art.1(2)(i).

[74] Dickinson, paras 3.124–3.139; Fawcett, Harris and Bridge, *International Sale of Goods in the Conflict of Laws* (2005), Ch.20. See also main work, para.35–066; Case 189/87 *Kalfelis v Schroeder*, above; but *cf. Source Ltd v TUV Rhineland Holding AG* [1998] Q.B. 54 (CA).

in too abstract a fashion but, rather will be carried out having regard to the need for appropriate practical outcomes in difficult cases.[75]

**Specific exclusions.** Article 1(2) of the Regulation contains a list of non-contractual obligations which are specifically excluded from the scope of the Regulation. Accordingly, when a non-contractual obligation arising from tort falls within one of these exclusions the Rome II Regulation will not apply. Application of these exclusions is not free of difficulties, some of which are mentioned, if not resolved, below. At the outset it may be pointed out that it has been suggested since they are exceptions, the exclusions will have to be interpreted strictly[76] and that some of them reflect those in Art.1(2) of the Rome Convention.[77] **S35–178**

**Family relationships.** Article 1(2)(a) excludes non-contractual obligations arising out of family relationships and relationships deemed by the law applicable to such relationships to have comparable effects including maintenance obligations. This formulation is apt to include, for example, civil partnerships under UK law.[78] Whether a non-contractual obligation arising out of a tort arises out of such a relationship may not necessarily be easy to decide. One example that has been given is a claim for compensation for damage caused by late payment of a maintenance obligation.[79] Another example may be a claim by a spouse for damages after divorce, against a co-respondent (if such claims still exist).[80] Conversely, a claim that a husband cannot be liable in tort to his wife because of inter-spousal immunity,[81] or a claim that a parent is vicariously liable for the torts of a child are thought to be within the scope of the Regulation.[82] Such claims are rarely, if ever, likely to arise. **S35–179**

**Matrimonial property etc.** Article 1(2)(b) excludes from the scope of the Regulation non-contractual obligations arising from a tort which arise out of matrimonial property regimes, property regimes deemed by the law applicable to such relationships to have comparable effects to marriage, and wills and succession. There are likely to be few, if any, situations which fall within this provision.[83] **S35–180**

**Bills of exchange etc.** The Regulation does not apply to non-contractual obligations arising out of a tort "arising under bills of exchange, cheques and promissory notes and other negotiable instruments to the extent that the **S35–181**

---

75 *cf.* main work, para.2–045.
76 Explanatory Memorandum, comment on Art.1.
77 Main work, paras 32–031 *et seq.* See also Art.1(2) of the Rome I Regulation.
78 See Recital (10). See, to the same effect, the Rome I Regulation, Art.1(2)(b).
79 Explanatory Memorandum, comment on Art.1.
80 *cf. Phillips v Batho* [1913] 3 K.B. 25; main work, para.18–083. But such a claim may not amount to a tort but rather may be *sui generis*.
81 *cf.* main work paras 35–039, 35–041.
82 Explanatory Memorandum, comment on Art.11(b) and 11(h) of the original proposal. See below, paras S35–256, S35–261. *cf.* main work, para.35–039.
83 The reference to "wills" would not seem apt to exclude, for example, an action against a lawyer for negligent drafting of a will. See, to the same effect, the Rome I Regulation, Art.1(2)(c).

obligations under such other negotiable instruments arise out of their negotiable character".[84] This provision is included, apparently, for the same reason as it is included in the Rome Convention,[85] in particular because the Geneva Conventions of June 7, 1930 and March 19, 1931 regulate much of this subject matter and because these obligations are not dealt with uniformly in Regulation States.[86] It would seem unlikely that this provision will exclude an action for conversion (assuming it is a tort for the purposes of the Regulation[87]) of a cheque since it cannot readily be said that such an action is one "arising under" the cheque.

**S35–182** **Companies, etc.** Article 1(2)(d) excludes non-contractual obligations arising out of a tort which arise out of the law of companies and other bodies corporate or unincorporated regarding matters such as the creation, by registration or otherwise, legal capacity, internal organisation or winding-up of companies and other bodies corporate or unincorporated, the personal liability of officers and members as such for the obligations of the company or body and the personal liability of auditors to a company or to its members in the statutory audits of accounting documents. The purpose of this provision is to exclude matters which properly belong to company law rather than to the law of torts.[88] Four points may usefully be made. First, it would seem that the reference to "legal capacity" does not include the capacity of a company or other body to commit a tort,[89] since this concerns the legal consequences which arise when a corporation or other body does something. While what a company may do does not fall within the Regulation, the consequences of what it does should be governed by the law applicable to the tort.[90] Secondly, it should be noted that the reference to the liability of auditors only excludes the liability of auditors to the company or its members. This would not exclude, for example, the liability of the vendor of a company's financial or legal advisers to the purchaser of the company.[91] Thirdly, the liability of directors under company law (e.g. Companies Act 2006, ss.170–181), although not specifically mentioned, would appear to fall within the scope of this exception and the corresponding exception in the Rome I regime.[92] Fourthly, amendments proposing a separate exception for non-contractual liability relating to transactions on stock exchanges or otherwise relating to financial instruments were proposed during negotiations in the Council, but rejected. Accordingly, the non-contractual liability of issuers, their officers

---

[84] Art.1(2)(c). See, to the same effect, the Rome I Regulation Art.1(2)(d).

[85] Rome Convention, Art.1(2)(c).

[86] Explanatory Memorandum, comment on Art.1(2)(c). It should be noted, however, that the Geneva Conventions are largely concerned with contractual obligations only.

[87] Above, para.S35–177.

[88] *cf. Base Metal Trading Ltd v Shamurin* [2004] EWCA Civ 1316, [2005] 1 W.L.R. 1157; and see main work, Rule 162. See, to the same effect, the Rome I Regulation, Art.1(2)(f).

[89] According to Recital (12) the "law applicable should also govern the question of the capacity to incur liability in tort/delict." Art.15(1)(a) provides that, *inter alia*, the applicable law governs the "determination of persons who may be held liable for acts performed by them." See below, para.S35–255.

[90] See main work, para.35–040.

[91] See HL Paper 66 (2004), para.85.

[92] *Base Metal Trading Ltd v Shamurin* [2004] EWCA Civ 1316, [2005] 1 W.L.R. 1157; Dickinson, paras 3.162–3.169.

and advisers for the contents of prospectuses and other offering documents falls within the scope of the Regulation.

**Trusts, etc.** The Regulation will not apply to non-contractual obligations arising out of a tort (if such there be) "arising out of the relations between the settlors, trustees, and beneficiaries of a trust created voluntarily".[93] The wording of Art.1(2)(e) suggests that claims by or against persons other than those listed (for example, the holders of fiduciary powers,[94] advisers, and third party holders of trust assets) are capable of being brought within the scope of the Regulation. In any event, in accordance with Art.28(1), the Regulation's application in relation to trusts remains subject to the provisions of the Recognition of Trusts Act 1987 in so far as they give effect to the United Kingdom's commitments under the 1985 Hague Convention on the law applicable to trusts and their recognition,[95] but the Regulation must take priority over the 1987 Act in so far as it is formulated more broadly than the Convention requires.[96] S35–183

**Nuclear damage.** Non-contractual obligations arising out of a tort "arising out of nuclear damage" are similarly excluded from the scope of the Regulation.[97] S35–184

**Violations of privacy, etc.** Article 1(2)(g) provides that the Regulation does not apply to non-contractual obligations arising out of violations of privacy and rights relating to personality, including defamation. Whether such matters should be included in or excluded from the scope of the Regulation gave rise to considerable controversy. Its exclusion was strongly advocated by the press and other media, the views of which eventually prevailed.[98] As pointed out above, these matters are to be reviewed under the review clause contained in Art.30.[99] Defamation and related claims will thus continue to be governed, almost exclusively by Rule 235 and most claims for invasion of privacy by Rules 231–234. The exclusion would also appear to extent to civil claims to enforce legislation concerning the protection of personal data.[1] Finally, although there is no reason in principle why claims by companies and other bodies to protect their business reputation or the privacy of their operations should not be capable of falling within the scope of the exception, the legislative history of the Regulation suggests that claims arising in the context of competition between businesses may fall within the Regulation's S35–185

---

93 Art.1(2)(e). See above, entry at para.29–063, and Dickinson, paras 3.173 *et seq.* See, to the same effect, the Rome I Regulation, Art.1(2)(h).

94 *Gomez v Gomez-Monche Vives* [2008] EWCA Civ 1065, [2009] Ch. 245.

95 Including as a result of the extension by declaration under Art.20 of the Hague Convention to trusts "declared by judicial decisions".

96 *cf.* main work, para.29–008.

97 Art.1(2)(f).

98 See HL Paper 66 (2004), paras 110–130; Minutes of Evidence, pp.31–45, 89–92.

99 Above, para.S35–172.

1 *cf.* Art.30(2).

scope even if, as a matter of national law, the claim is based on the law of defamation or privacy.[2]

S35–186 **Evidence and procedure.** Article 1(3) stipulates that the Regulation shall not apply to evidence and procedure without prejudice to Art.21 (concerned with "formal validity") and Art.22 (concerned with "burden of proof").[3] At this stage it will suffice to draw attention to two points. First, the exclusion of evidence and procedure seems to mean, that English practice in relation to the pleading and proof of foreign law continues to have effect.[4] Secondly, while characterisation of matters relating to evidence and procedure is primarily a matter for national law, it is possible that the European Court will regard itself as competent to determine the role and scope of evidence and procedure within the framework of the Regulation.[5]

S35–187 **Relationship with existing law.** Where, for whatever reason, the Rome II Regulation does not apply,[6] the law applicable to a tort or to an issue in tort will continue to be governed by Part III of the Private International Law (Miscellaneous Provisions) Act 1995, i.e. Rules 231–234, where it applies. Defamation and related claims which will be governed largely by Rule 235.[7]

S35–188 **General matters.** It will be helpful to draw attention to certain general matters at this stage so as to facilitate the subsequent discussion.

S35–189 **Universal application.** Article 3 of the Regulation provides that any "law specified by this Regulation shall be applied whether or not it is the law of a Member State". In this sense, therefore, the Regulation has "universal effect" and will apply to determine the applicable law in all cases falling within the scope of the Regulation, irrespective of whether the facts of the case exhibit any link to the European Union other than the fact that the case is being litigated in an English forum.[8]

S35–190 **States with more than one legal system.** Article 25(1) provides that where a State comprises several territorial units, each of which has its own rules of law in respect of non-contractual obligations, (e.g. the United Kingdom, the United States), each territorial unit shall be considered a country for the purposes of identifying the law applicable under the Regulation. In accordance with Art.25(2), Parliament has extended the Regulation's application to

---

[2] para.S35–215 below, text to nn.84–85; Dickinson, para.3.227.

[3] See below, paras S35–268 *et seq.* *cf.* the Rome I Regulation, Arts 1(3) and 18.

[4] See main work, Ch.9. On this point, see Dickinson, paras.14.63–14.86; Illmer (2009) 28 C.J.Q. 237, 258–259.

[5] See Dickinson, paras 14.54–14.62; Illmer (2009) 28 C.J.Q. 237; Schoeman [2010] L.M.C.L.Q. 81. *cf.* public policy in respect of recognition of judgments under the Judgments Regulation, main work, paras 14–208 *et seq.*

[6] See above, paras S35–175 *et seq.*

[7] See above, para.S35–185.

[8] See above, para.S35–166. For critical comment, see HL Paper 66 (2004), paras 87–94.

conflicts solely between the laws of different parts of the United Kingdom (including, for these purposes, Gibraltar).[9]

**Article 2: "non-contractual obligations".** Article 2 which is (perhaps curiously) headed "non-contractual obligations" contains three rules. First, for the purpose of the Regulation, "damage shall cover any consequence arising out of tort/delict, unjust enrichment, *negotiorum gestio* or *culpa in contrahendo*".[10] Secondly, the Regulation "shall apply also to non-contractual obligations that are likely to arise".[11] Thirdly, any reference in the Regulation to "(a) an event giving rise to damage shall include events giving rise to damage that are likely to occur; and (b) damage shall include damage that is likely to occur".[12] One effect of this, in general terms, is to make the Regulation applicable to threatened torts.[13] S35–191

**Meaning of "habitual residence".** The Rome II Regulation makes frequent reference to the law of a party's "habitual residence".[14] Article 23 provides some guidance as to the meaning of this expression for the purposes of the Regulation. First, the habitual residence of companies and other bodies corporate or unincorporated, shall be the place of central administration.[15] Secondly, however, where the "event giving rise to the damage occurs, or the damage arises in the course of the operation of a branch, agency or other establishment, the place where the branch, agency or any other establishment is located shall be treated as the place of habitual residence".[16] Thirdly, in the case of a natural person acting in the course of his or her business activity, the habitual residence is that person's principal place of business.[17] This leaves to general principles the determination of the habitual residence of a natural person who is not acting in the course of a business activity.[18] S35–192

**Exclusion of renvoi.** Article 24 stipulates that the application of the law of any country specified by the Regulation means the application of the rules of law in force in that country other than its rules of private international law. This, obviously, excludes the doctrine of renvoi.[19] S35–193

---

[9] See above, para.S35–169.

[10] Art.2(1).

[11] Art.2(2).

[12] Art.2(3).

[13] And, of course, to other non-contractual obligations which are likely to arise.

[14] Arts 4, 5, 10, 11, 12.

[15] Art.23(1). *cf.* the Rome I Regulation, Art .19(1). For the meaning of "central administration", see main work, paras 30–005 *et seq.*, para.32–120.

[16] Art.23(1), second paragraph. *cf.* the Rome I Regulation, Art.19(1), second paragraph. For the meaning of "branch, agency or other establishment," see main work, paras 11–310 *et seq.*

[17] Art. 23(2). *cf.* the Rome I Regulation, Art.19(2). For the meaning of "principal place of business", see main work, paras 11–115 *et seq.* and 32–120.

[18] See main work, paras 6–124 *et seq.* and Rule 204. See also Case C–523/07 *Proceedings Brought by A* [2009] ECR I–2805, concerning the concept of "habitual residence" in the Brussels II*bis* Regulation.

[19] See main work, Rule 1 and para.35–021. *Cf. Dornoch Ltd v Westminster International BV* [2009] EWHC 889 (Admlty), [2009] 2 Lloyd's Rep. 191, at [85].

## B. *The General Rule for Tort/Delict*

**S35–194** The general rule to be applied to determine the law applicable to a non-contractual obligation arising out of a tort/delict is contained in Art.4 of the Rome II Regulation which provides as follows:

> "1. Unless otherwise provided for in this Regulation, the law applicable to a non-contractual obligation arising out of a tort/delict shall be the law of the country in which the damage occurs irrespective of the country in which the event giving rise to the damage occurred and irrespective of the country or countries in which the indirect consequences of that event occurred.
> 2. However, where the person claimed to be liable and the person sustaining damage both have their habitual residence in the same country at the time when the damage occurs, the law of that country shall apply.
> 3. Where it is clear from all the circumstances of the case that the tort/delict is manifestly more closely connected with a country other than that indicated in paragraphs 1 or 2, the law of that other country shall apply. A manifestly closer connection with another country might be based in particular on a pre-existing relationship between the parties, such as a contract, that is closely connected with the tort/delict in question."[20]

**S35–195** **General Principle.** Article 4(1) requires, as a general principle, application of the law of the country in which the damage occurs. And, for these purposes, damage includes damage that is likely to occur.[21] The law of the place of damage applies irrespective of the country in which the event giving rise to the damage occurred,[22] and irrespective of the country or countries in which the indirect consequences of that event occur. The general principle therefore focusses on the place where the "direct" damage is suffered by the claimant and ignores the fact that "indirect" damage may be suffered by the claimant elsewhere. The distinction between direct and indirect damage reflects a distinction drawn in interpreting Art.5(3) of the Judgments Regulation[23] and that jurisprudence may assist in interpreting Art.4(1) of the Rome II Regulation in difficult cases.[24] Relatively little difficulty is likely to arise in the context of torts causing personal injury. The place of damage will generally be

---

[20] See generally, Recitals (13)–(18). For comment, see Hohloch (2007) 9 Yb. P.I.L. 1; Symeonides (2008) 56 Am. J. Comp. L. 173, 186 *et seq.*; Dickinson, Ch.4; Fentiman in Ahern & Binchy, 85. As to choosing the law applicable to a tort by contract, see Art.14, below, paras S35–248 *et seq.*

[21] Art.2(3)(b), above, para.S35–191.

[22] An event giving rise to damage includes events giving rise to damage which are likely to occur: Art.2(3)(a), above, para.S35–191.

[23] See main work, para. 11–301; Recital (7).

[24] *cf.* Case C–220/88 *Dumez France v Hessische Landesbank* [1990] E.C.R. I–49; Case 364/93 *Marinari v Lloyds Bank plc* [1995] E.C.R. I–2719; Case C–168/02 *Kronhofer v Maier* [2004] ECR I–6009.

the country where the victim suffered injury.[25] Where death results from personal injury the same result should ensue.[26] The fact that the victim, or his or her dependants, suffered financial loss elsewhere would seem to be irrelevant.[27] In cases where the claim involves damage to property, the general principle, it is suggested, would generally point to the place where the property was situated when it was damaged as being the place of damage.[28] Where the claim is for economic loss not consequent on personal injury, death or damage to property more difficulty will arise. First, in principle, the place of damage should, normally be the place where the direct economic loss was suffered.[29] Secondly however, a claimant may suffer direct financial loss in more than one country. In the Explanatory Memorandum, accompanying the Commission's original proposal it is suggested that in such cases "the laws of all countries concerned will have to be applied on a distributive basis, applying what is known as *Mosaikbetrachtung* in German law".[30]

**Common habitual residence.** Where the person claimed to be liable[31] and the person sustaining the damage[32] both have their habitual residence[33] in the same country at the time when the damage occurs, Art.4(2) requires that the law of that country shall apply. It is obvious that Art.4(2) constitutes an exception to Art.4(1) but four points may be noted. First, it would seem that the law of the common habitual residence applies irrespective of the degree of connection between that law and the common habitual residence (unless a case can be brought within Art.4(3)). Secondly, the mere fact of common habitual residence triggers the exception: there is no requirement of any prior relationship between the parties.[34] Thirdly the exception seems to apply **S35–196**

[25] Recital (17). See *Jacobs v Motor Insurers Bureau* [2010] EWHC 231 (QB), [2010] 1 All E.R. (Comm.) 1128, at [32]–[41] (revd. [2010] EWCA Civ 1208 without addressing this point) in which Owen J. rejected the submission that the relevant 'damage' in that case was suffered in England where the MIB had refused to compensate the claimant for his injuries suffered in a road traffic accident in Spain. Instead, the judge (at [40]) identified the relevant damage as that suffered at the hands of "the tortfeasor" in Spain. *cf.* Private International Law (Miscellaneous Provisions) Act 1995, s.11 (2) (a), Rule 232 (2) (a); main work, para.35–085.

[26] *ibid.*

[27] *Jacobs v Motor Insurers Bureau*, above. *cf. Vile v Von Wendt* (1980) 103 D.L.R (3d) 356 (Ont.).

[28] See Recital (17). *cf.* Private International Law (Miscellaneous Provisions) Act 1995, s.11 (2) (b); Rule 232(2)(b); main work, para.35–086; Case C–189/08 *Zuid-Chemie BV v Philippo's Mineralenfabriek NV/SA*, July 17, 2009 (Judgments Regulation, Art.5(3)).

[29] Case C–220/88 *Dumez France v Hessische Landesbank*, above.

[30] Explanatory Memorandum, comment on Art.3(1) of the original proposal. And see HL Paper 66 (2004), para.99; Dickinson, paras 3.298–3.301, 4.69–4.74; Mills in Ahern and Binchy, 133, 134–136.

[31] That person will generally, but not necessarily, be the defendant in the proceedings. In *Jacobs v Motor Insurers Bureau*, above, Owen J. expressed the view (at [43]) that the references to "parties" in Art.4(2) should be taken as a reference to "the injured party and the tortfeasor." The decision was reversed, [2010] EWCA Civ 1208, without this point being addressed. See also Dickinson, para 4.83.

[32] That person will generally, but not necessarily, be the claimant in the proceedings. See the materials referred to in the preceding footnote.

[33] As defined in part, in Art.23, above, para.35–192.

[34] *cf. Edmunds v Simmonds* [2001] 1 W.L.R 1003. It is conceivable that both claimant and defendant were habitually resident in England on the facts of *Harding v Wealands* [2006] UKHL 32, [2007] 2 A.C. 1.

irrespective of the issue in the case. There is thus no room for the operation of *depeçage*, so that the law of the country of damage applies, say, to the issue of the standard of liability[35] whereas the law of the common habitual residence applies to, say, the issue of heads of damage.[36] Fourthly, it is the fact of identity of habitual residence, and not the fact that the content of the laws of the parties' habitual residence is identical, that is determinative.

**S35–197** **"Escape clause".** Article 4(3) is what is described in Recital (18) as an "escape clause". Where it is clear from all the circumstances of the case that the tort/delict is manifestly more closely connected with a country other than that indicated in Art.4(1) or (2), the law of that country shall apply. A manifestly closer connection might be based, in particular on a pre-existing relationship between the parties, such as a contract, that is closely connected with the tort/delict in question. The first point to be stressed is that the provision does not in terms appear to permit assessment of whether a particular issue is manifestly more closely connected with another law.[37] It must appear from all the circumstances of the case that the *tort* is manifestly more closely connected with another law.[38] Secondly it will be for the party relying on Art.4(3) to establish that its terms are satisfied.[39] Thirdly, the requirement that the tort be *manifestly* more closely connected with the law of another country (which must be clear from the circumstances of the case) suggests that the court must be satisfied that the threshold of closer connection has been clearly demonstrated, although it should not be necessary to demonstrate the absence of any "real" or "genuine" connection with the country whose law is otherwise applicable.[40] Fourthly, while a manifestly closer connection might *in particular* be based on a pre-existing relationship between the parties, such as a contract, that is not a complete statement of the circumstances which will suffice to establish the manifestly closer connection. Circumstances other than a pre-existing relationship may be relevant: and a pre-existing relationship other than one arising out of a contract may also be relevant.[41] Thus it would seem that the event or events which give rise to damage could be circumstances relevantly considered under Art.4(3), as could factors relating to the parties, and possibly also, factors relating to the consequences of the event or events.[42] Fifthly as a matter of drafting it is not entirely clear whether it will be possible to invoke Art.4(3) so as to displace

---

[35] *cf. Boys v Chaplin* [1971] A.C 356; *Babcock v Jackson,* 42 N.Y 2d 473, 191 N.E 2d 279 (1963), [1963] 2 Lloyd's Rep. 286; Private International Law (Miscellaneous Provisions) Act 1995, s.12 (1) Rule 233 (1); *Edmunds v Simmonds,* above. See main work, paras 35–098, 35–106, 35–107.

[36] *ibid.* Add: See Dickinson, paras.4.78–4.79; Mills, n.30 above, 136–148.

[37] *cf.* 1995 Act s.12 (1), Rule 233 (1). See main work, paras 35–098, 35–106–35–107 and the materials cited in the preceding footnote.

[38] *Jacobs v Motor Insurers Bureau*, above, n.31 at [46]. See also HL Paper 66 (2004), para.96.

[39] See main work, para.35–106.

[40] A similar approach was taken by the European Court in relation to Art.4(5) of the Rome Convention in Case C–133/08 *Intercontainer Interfrigo (ICF) SC v Balkenende Oosthuizen* [2010] 3 W.L.R. 24. See Dickinson, Supplement, paras 4.95C–4.95E. *Cf.* Fentiman, n.20 above, 103–110.

[41] *cf.* 1995 Act, s.12 (2); main work, paras 35–101 *et seq.*

[42] *ibid. Cf.* Fentiman, n.20 above, 98–100.

Art.4(2) in circumstances where the tort is manifestly more closely connected with the law of the country in which the damage occurs, i.e. the law applicable under Art.4(1). This is because Art.4(3) speaks of a tort which is manifestly more closely connected with a country other than that indicated in Art.4(1) or 4(2) in which case "*the law of that other country should apply*.[43] It is suggested, however, that there is no particularly good reason for not allowing Art.4(2) to be displaced in favour of the law applicable under Art.4(1).

**Maritime torts.** The Regulation makes no special provision for "maritime torts".[44] The original Commission proposal contained a provision defining the territory of a State in the context of ships which enabled the general rule to be applied in that context.[45] Although that provision was eventually deleted, there is no suggestion in the Regulation's *travaux préparatoires* that it was intended to exclude maritime torts from the scope of the Regulation and, in the absence of a specific exclusion, the better view is that they fall within scope, governed by Art.4.[46] It is conceivable that if (as appears likely) the Regulation is to apply in this situation, the law applicable under Art.4(1) may be as indicated in the discussion in the main work,[47] i.e the law of the flag or State of registration of the ship, in respect of a tort internal to a ship on the high seas and the law of the littoral State in respect of torts in foreign territorial waters. The position is even more difficult in respect of ship collisions on the high seas which have historically been governed by general maritime law as administered in England, rather than the law of any particular country, as such, and it may be that (assuming that the Regulation applies) the country of damage under Art.4(1) would be the law of the flag or State of registration of the ship with respect to which, or to persons or cargo on board which, the collision is claimed to have had adverse consequences. S35–198

**Aerial torts.** Similarly, no special provision is made for "aerial torts".[48] It is, again, conceivable that if (as appears likely) Art.4 is to be construed to apply to such cases the law applicable under Art.4(1) may be as indicated in the discussion in the main work,[49] i.e. the law of the country in which an aircraft is registered, in respect of torts internal to an aircraft committed over the high seas or the law of the country to which the airspace belonged in respect of collisions between aircraft over-flying territory. Where there is a collision between aircraft over the high seas, the same difficulty as was identified in the previous paragraph must be addressed. S35–199

---

[43] Art.4(3) (emphasis added).

[44] See main work, paras 35–068 *et seq.*

[45] Commission Proposal, Art.18.

[46] See George (2007) 3 J. Priv. Int. L 137, 168–171; Dickinson, paras 3.311–3.314 (concluding that the Regulation applies to torts on the high seas). *Cf.* Cheshire, North and Fawcett, *Private International Law* (14th edn Fawcett and Carruthers, 2008), pp.859–860 (taking the opposite view); Basedow (2010) 74 *RabelsZ* 118, 135–137 (arguing that the Regulation does not apply to torts external to the vessel occurring on the high seas).

[47] paras 35–068 *et seq.* See Dickinson, paras 4.48–4.57.

[48] Main work, paras 35–077 *et seq.*

[49] *ibid.* See also the materials cited at nn.46–47 above.

S35–200 **General rule and special rules.** Articles 5 to 9 of the Rome II Regulation discussed below[50] provide special rules for product liability, unfair competition and acts restricting free competition, environmental damage, infringement of intellectual property rights and industrial action.[51] However, as will be seen, Art.4 remains relevant in some of these special cases.

## C. *Product Liability*

S35–201 Article 5 of the Rome II Regulation contains a special rule concerned with the determination of the law applicable to a non-contractual obligation arising out of damage caused by a product.

> "1. Without prejudice to Article 4(2), the law applicable to a non-contractual obligation arising out of damage caused by a product shall be:
> (a) The law of the country in which the person sustaining the damage had his or her habitual residence when the damage occurred, if the product was marketed in that country; or, failing that,
> (b) the law of the country in which the product was acquired, if the product was marketed in that country; or, failing that,
> (c) The law of the country in which the damage occurred, if the product was marketed in that country.
> However, the law applicable shall be the law of the country in which the person claimed to be liable is habitually resident if he or she could not reasonably foresee the marketing of the product, or a product of the same type, in the country the law of which is applicable under (a), (b) or (c).
> 2. Where it is clear from all the circumstances of the case that tort/delict is manifestly more closely connected with a country other than that indicated in paragraph 1, the law of that other country shall apply. A manifestly closer connection with another country might be based in particular on a pre-existing relationship between the parties, such as a contract, that is closely connected with the tort/delict in question."[52]

[50] Paras S35–201 *et seq.*

[51] It is said that "specific rules should be laid down for special torts/delicts where the general rule does not allow a reasonable balance to be struck between the interests at stake" Recital (19).

[52] For comment, see Huber & Illmer (2007) 9 Yb. P.I.L. 31; Symeonides (2008) 56 Am. J. Comp. L. 173, 207 *et seq.*; Kozyris (2008) 56 Am. J.Comp. L. 471, 485 *et seq.*; Dickinson, Ch.5; Illmer (2009) 73 *RabelsZ* 271; Stone, in Ahern and Binchy, 175. The parties may, by contract, choose the law applicable to a non-contractual obligation arising out of damage caused by a product: Art.14, below, paras S35–248 *et seq.*

The need for a special rule in regard to product liability was treated with some scepticism in the United Kingdom.[53] The special rule is justified in the Regulation by reference to meeting "the objectives of fairly spreading the risks inherent in a modern high technology society, protecting consumers' health, stimulating innovation, securing undistorted competition and facilitating trade. Creation of a cascade system of connecting factors together with a foreseeability clause, is a balanced solution in regard to these objectives."[54] It may well be said that the supposed justification merely states a conclusion without establishing in any convincing fashion how the choice of law rules established help to reach that conclusion.[55] S35–202

**Hierarchy of rules.** Initially, Art.5(1) establishes a hierarchy of rules for determining the law applicable in product liability cases. The primary rule is (a) that the applicable law shall be the law of the country in which the person sustaining the damage had his or her habitual residence when the damage occurred if the product was marketed in that country.[56] Failing that, i.e. if the product was not marketed in the country where the person sustaining the damage has his or her habitual residence, then (b), the applicable law shall be the law of the country in which the product was acquired, if the product was marketed in that country.[57] Failing that, i.e. if the product was not marketed where it was acquired, then (c), the applicable law shall be the law of the country in which the damage occurred, if the product was marketed in that country.[58] For the purposes of these rules, it would appear (though the matter is far from clear) that the product which is marketed in the relevant country need not be the thing that actually caused the damage but may be an identical product.[59] A further difficulty might arise if the product is not marketed in any S35–203

---

[53] HL Paper 66 (2004), paras 105–110. It was felt that such matters could be adequately dealt with under the general rule.

[54] Recital (20).

[55] It should be noted that the Hague Convention on the Law Applicable to Products Liability 1973 is in force in Finland, France, Luxembourg, the Netherlands, Slovenia and Spain. The Regulation will not prejudice the application of this Convention in those Regulation States when the Regulation becomes applicable: Art.28(1), above, para.S35–174. The relationship between the Regulation and Council Directive 85/374/EEC on the approximation of laws, regulations and administrative provisions of the Member States concerning liability for defective products, implemented in the United Kingdom in the Consumer Protection Act 1987, is unclear. The Directive imposes strict liability on producers for death, injury, loss and damage to property caused by defective products. But Member States' laws still contain differences because the Directive permits certain options and covers only certain types of damage: see HL Paper 66 (2004), para.103. And of course Art.3 of the Regulation (above, para.S35–189) provides that any law specified by the Regulation shall be applied whether or not it is the law of Regulation State.

[56] Art.5(1)(a). As to the meaning of habitual residence see Art.23, above para.S35–192.

[57] Art.5(1)(b) There appears on the face of this sub-rule to be no requirement that the victim acquired the product in that country. For the view that the sub-rule in Art.5(1)(b) has no application to claims by "bystanders", who did not themselves acquire the product, see Dickinson, para.5.40. See also Stone, n.52 above, 189 (acquisition must be connected to victim).

[58] Art.5(1)(c).

[59] Explanatory Memorandum, comment on Art.4 of the original proposal; Cheshire, North and Fawcett, *Private International Law* (14th ed. Fawcett and Carruthers, 2008), 807; Dickinson, para.5.21.

of the countries referred to in (a), (b) or (c), above and the common habitual residence rule described below is also inapplicable. In the absence of a default rule in Art.5, it might be thought necessary to fall back on Art.4, which applies "unless otherwise provided for in this Regulation". The better view, however, being more consistent with the structure and objectives of Art.5, is that the law of the country in which the person claimed to be liable is habitually resident (designated under the foreseeability clause[60]) should also apply in such cases.[61] Finally, it is unclear how Art.5(1) is intended to apply in situations where injury has resulted from the consumption of, or exposure to, a product over a period of time while the victim was habitually resident in or traveling in different countries.[62] In such situations, in order for Art.5(1)(a) or Art.5(1)(c) to apply, must it be demonstrated that the product was marketed in every country of habitual residence, or in every place where the victim consumed or was exposed to the product and "damage" was suffered? Moreover, if the product was marketed in one or more but not all of those places, should that conclusion lead to the partial application of the sub-rule in question or its wholesale rejection? Again, how should the foreseeability clause be applied? The Regulation is silent as to how these problems should be addressed, and the Commission's suggestion elsewhere that the Regulation's rules should be applied on a distributive basis where the connecting factors point to more than one country[63] seems inadequate as a solution in this particular context. Most straightforwardly, perhaps, the relevant sub-rule(s) could be treated as not applying to such cases.[64] Alternatively, the relevant country could be determined at the time when the product first produced its adverse effects.[65]

S35–204 **Article 4(2).** The foregoing rules are without prejudice to Art.4(2). This means that where the person claimed to be liable and the person sustaining damage both have their habitual residence in the same country at the time the damage occurs, the law of the common habitual residence will apply.[66] This appears to be even so in the somewhat unlikely case that the product is not marketed in that country. As Art.5(1) cross-refers only to Art.4(2) (not to Art.4(3)) and the escape clause in Art.5(2) applies only to the law "indicated in" Art.5(1), it may be (although considerable doubt remains) that the law of the parties' common habitual residence cannot itself be displaced on the grounds that the tort/delict is manifestly more closely connected with another country.[67]

S35–205 **Foreseeability clause.** A proviso within Art.5(1) provides that the law applicable shall be the law of the country in which the person claimed to be

---

[60] See below, para.S35–205.
[61] Dickinson, para.5.45; Illmer, n.52 above, 296–297. *Cf.* Cheshire, North and Fawcett, n.59 above, 807.
[62] *cf.* main work, para.35–085.
[63] See above, para.S35–195.
[64] Dickinson, paras.5.31–5.33.
[65] Cheshire, North and Fawcett, n.59 above, 838.
[66] See above, para.S35–196.
[67] Dickinson, para.5.46. *Cf.* Cheshire, North and Fawcett, n.59 above, 808; Illmer, n.52 above, 302.

liable is habitually resident if he or she could not reasonably foresee the marketing of the product, or a product of the same type in the country the law of which is applicable under (a), (b) or (c).[68] While the purpose of this clause is clear enough, problems may well arise as to whether a particular product is of the "same type" as the product which caused the damage. It is likely, but yet again not clear, that a "product of the same type" must be one produced by the same undertaking and which is substantially the same, but not identical to, the product causing the damage.[69]

**Escape clause.** Article 5(2) supplies an "escape clause" by virtue of which the application of the law declared applicable under Art.5(1) may be displaced. Article 5(2) is identical in all material respects to the parallel provision in Art.4(3) and most of the points made in relation to Art.4(3)[70] may be repeated here. Attention can be drawn, however, to a drafting difficulty similar to that which arises in the context of Art.4(3). **S35–206**

Article 5(2) provides that where it is clear from all the circumstances of the case that the tort/delict is manifestly more closely connected with a "*law other than that indicated in paragraph 1, the law of that other country shall apply*".[71] This might suggest the law to be applied through the escape clause must be of a country other than the country of habitual residence of the person sustaining the damage, the country of acquisition or in which damage occurred. It is suggested that this is an unlikely construction and that these countries can be considered as circumstances of the case in determining the country, if any, with which the tort is manifestly more closely connected. **S35–207**

**Meaning of "damage".** For the purpose of Art.5, damage would seem to mean any consequence arising out of a tort/delict falling within the scope of the Article.[72] This would include personal injury or death caused by a product, damage to property caused by a product and economic loss caused by a product.[73] **S35–208**

**Meaning of "product"**. Article 5 contains no definition of the term product. The Explanatory Memorandum to the Commission's original proposal suggested that for the definition of "product" Art.2. of Directive 85/374/EEC[74] would apply.[75] That provision states that "'product' means all movables even if incorporated into another movable or into an immovable. **S35–209**

---

[68] Art.5(1), proviso.

[69] Dickinson, paras 5.34–5.36. *Cf.* Art.7 of the Hague Product Liability Convention, referring to "his own products of the same type".

[70] Above, para.S35–197.

[71] Emphasis added. See above, para.S35–197.

[72] Art.2, above, para.S35–191.

[73] *cf.* Directive 85/374/EEC, above, n.55, Art.9 of which has a narrower definition of damage.

[74] As amended by Directive 1999/34/EC of the European Parliament and of the Council of May 10 1999: see [1985] O.J. L210/29; [1999] O.J. L141/20.

[75] Explanatory Memorandum, comment on Art.4 of the original proposal.

'Product' includes electricity." This seems a broad interpretation of the term.[76]

S35–210 **Meaning of "marketed" and "marketing".** These expressions are not defined in Art.5(1) of the Regulation. They would seem to include situations in which the product is put on to the market in a State[77] or made available through commercial channels in a State.[78] What is not clear is whether "marketed" and "marketing" includes advertising a product in a State where it is not available, which product may be acquired through a transaction concluded with a person in another State and which causes damage, say, in the former State. Internet advertising of products could be particularly problematic, but it is suggested that such modern business practice should fall within the rubric of "marketed" and "marketing". It would seem that the product does not necessarily have to be marketed by the defendant, or with his consent, since the foreseeability clause would be inconsistent with such a requirement.

S35–211 **Meaning of "person claimed to be liable".** The range of persons who may be potentially liable under Art.5 of the Regulation is not indicated in the provision itself. It would appear to include, potentially, the manufacturer of a finished product or of a component; possibly, the producer of raw material; possibly, an intermediary or retailer; possibly, an importer of a product; and possibly, a person who by putting his name, trademark or other distinguishing feature on a product presents himself as its producer.[79] Whether any particular person will be liable, however, will depend on the applicable law.[80]

### *D. Unfair Competition and Acts Restricting Free Competition*

S35–212 Article 6 of the Rome II Regulation sets out choice of law rules which are expressed to apply to "Unfair competition and acts restricting free competition" in the following terms:

> "1. The law applicable to a non-contractual obligation arising out of an act of unfair competition shall be the law of the country where competitive relations or the collective interests of consumers are, or are likely to be, affected.
> 2. Where an act of unfair competition affects exclusively the interests of a specific competitor, Article 4 shall apply.
> 3. (a) The law applicable to a non-contractual obligation arising out of a restriction of competition shall be the law of the country where the market is, or is likely to be, affected.

---

[76] As a result of Directive 1999/34/EEC, above, unprocessed primary agricultural products (crops, livestock and fish) are now included in the definition of product.
[77] *cf. Distillers Co Ltd v Thompson* [1971] A.C 458 (PC).
[78] *cf.* Hague Convention on the Law Applicable to Products Liability 1973, Art.7.
[79] See Council Directive 85/374/EEC, above n.55, Arts 2 and 3; Explanatory Memorandum, comment on Art.4 of the original proposal.
[80] See Art.15(a), (g).

(b) When the market is, or is likely to be, affected in more than one country, the person seeking compensation for damage who sues in the court of the domicile of the defendant, may instead choose to base his or her claim on the law of the court seised, provided that the market in that Member State is amongst those directly and substantially affected by the restriction of competition out of which the non-contractual obligation on which the claim is based arises; where the claimant sues, in accordance with the applicable rules on jurisdiction, more than one defendant in that court, he or she can only choose to base his or her claim on the law of that court if the restriction of competition on which the claim against each of these defendants relies directly and substantially affects also the market in the Member State of that court.

4. The law applicable under this Article may not be derogated from by an agreement pursuant to Article 14."

This provision is concerned with two distinct types of claim in tort, the first a claim for "unfair competition" and the second a claim arising out of a "restriction of competition", i.e. competition or anti-trust law, and it will be convenient to deal with these situations separately in what follows. **S35–213**

**Exclusion of Article 14.** Under Art.6(4), the opportunity afforded to the parties, in Art.14,[81] to choose the law applicable to a non-contractual obligation is excluded where the non-contractual obligation falls within Art.6. This exclusion may be justified on the ground that Art.6 embraces matters which relate to the public interest as well as to the private interests of the parties. Choice of the applicable law under Art.14 would appear to remain possible where an act of unfair competition affects exclusively the interests of a specific competitor, as Art.6(2) refers in such cases to the general rules in Art.4[82] and the law applicable is not, therefore, determined "under" Art.6. **S35–214**

**Meaning of "unfair competition".** One difficulty with Art.6, particularly from an English law perspective, is the meaning to be attributed to the expression "unfair competition", including the related expression "act of unfair competition". Presumably, "unfair competition" will have to be interpreted in an autonomous fashion so as to give it a uniform meaning in Regulation States for the purposes of the Regulation.[83] What this meaning will turn out to be must be a matter of speculation. For example, in English law there is no tort, as such, of unfair competition. Where English law protects against unfair competition, it does so through particular torts such as passing- **S35–215**

---

[81] Below, paras S35–248 *et seq*. For comment on Art.6, see Hellner (2007) 9 Yb. P.I.L. 46; Wadlow (2008) 30 E.I.P.R. 309; Dickinson, Ch.6; Rodriguez Pineau (2009) 5 J. Priv. Int. L. 311; Fitchen, *ibid.*, 337.

[82] See below, para.S35–218.

[83] There is, however, no Recital which explicitly states that this is to be the case: *cf.* Recitals (11), (30).

off, some of the economic torts (inducing breach of contract, interference with contractual relations), possibly breach of confidence, slander of goods[84] and even the general law of defamation.[85] In contrast, the concept of unfair competition in civil law legal systems may be much broader.[86] The Explanatory Memorandum to the Commission's original proposal states that the concept includes matters such as "acts calculated to influence demand (misleading advertising, forced sales, etc.), acts that impede competing suppliers (disruption of deliveries by competitors, enticing away a competitor's staff, boycotts), and acts that exploit a competitor's value (passing-off and the like)."[87] It is also possible that guidance might be sought in the Unfair Commercial Practices Directive[88] which states, generally, that a "commercial practice shall be unfair if (a) it is contrary to the requirements of professional diligence, and (b) it materially distorts or is likely to materially distort the economic behaviour with regard to the product of the average consumer whom it reaches or to whom it is addressed or of the average member of the group when a commercial practice is directed to a particular group of consumers."[89] Beyond the situation of consumers, a general definition may also be found in Art.10*bis* of the Paris Convention for the Protection of Industrial Property 1893, as subsequently revised.[90] That provision defines unfair competition as any "act of competition contrary to honest practice in industrial or commercial matters."[91] In particular Art.10 *bis* prohibits (i) all acts of such a nature as to create confusion by any means whatever with the establishment, the goods, or the industrial or commercial activities, of a competitor; (ii) false allegations in the course of a trade of such a nature as to discredit the establishment, the goods, or the industrial or commercial activities of a competitor; (iii) indications or allegations the use of which in the course of trade is liable to mislead the public as to the nature, the manufacturing process, the characteristics, the suitability for their purpose, or the quantity of

---

[84] See Fawcett and Torremans, *Intellectual Property and Private International Law* (1998), pp.678–683; Horton and Robertson (1995) 17 E.I.P.R. 568; Thunken (2002) 51 I.C.L.Q. 909; Wadlow (2006) 28 E.I.P.R. 433 at p.469.

[85] This is particularly problematic since the Regulation does not apply to defamation. It may be argued that the exclusion of defamation does not exclude slander of goods in the English sense (above, para.S35–185). Defamation was excluded because of concerns over freedom of expression in the media. Such concerns do not arise in relation to slander of goods: see Thunken, above. Indeed it may be argued that such concerns do not arise where a trader publishes a libel about a trade competitor purely to damage the latter's business. See below para.S35–219.

[86] See generally, Price (1978–1979) 53 Tulane L. Rev. 164.

[87] Explanatory Memorandum, comment on Art.5 of the original proposal. These situations are capable of giving rise to claims in English law. As to infringements of intellectual property rights, see Art.8, below, para.S35–228 *et seq.*

[88] Directive 2005/29/EC of the European Parliament and of the Council concerning unfair business-to-consumer commercial practices in the internal market and amending Council Directive 84/450/EEC, Directives 97/7/EC, 98/27/EC and 2002/65/EC of the European Parliament and of the Council and Regulation (EC) 2006/2004 of the European Parliament and of the Council (Unfair Commercial Practices Directive): [2005] O.J. L149/22.

[89] Art.5(2).

[90] The United Kingdom is a party to this Convention.

[91] Art.10*bis* (2).

the goods".[92] But this provides only very broad contours which will need much detailed supplementation by the courts.[93]

**The relevant "market".** As appears below,[94] Art.6(3) determines the law applicable to non-contractual obligations arising out of restrictions of competition by reference to the location of the market affected by the anti-competitive conduct. Further, although the connecting factor in Art.6(1) does not explicitly use the term "market", it would appear also to require the court to identify and locate the market where competitive relations or the collective interests of consumers are affected.[95] These rules, therefore, would appear to require Member State courts to undertake a process of market definition, involving both legal and economic criteria, in order to determine the applicable law. The most obvious starting point for that exercise would be the principles developed in the context of Arts 81 and 82 of the EC Treaty,[96] but these principles may be thought to be overly complex, not fit for purpose and likely to promote (unsatisfactorily) the potential application of the law of several countries on a distributive basis. Against this background, whatever the economic reality, Member State courts may prefer to identify the affected market(s) along territorial lines, as being situated within the borders of a specific country.[97] **S35–215A**

**Nature of Article 6(1) and (2).** Somewhat opaquely, Recital (21) to the Regulation states that the special rule in Art.6 "is not an exception to the general rule in Art.4(1) but rather a clarification of it. In matters of unfair competition, the conflict-of-law rule should protect competitors, consumers and the general public and ensure that the market economy functions properly. The connection to the law of the country where competitive relations are, or are likely to be, affected generally satisfies these objectives." In other words, Art.6(1), at least, is an attempt to apply Art.4(1) taking into account the particular circumstances of unfair competition. It should, however, be noted that (in contrast to Art.4(1)), Art.6(1) is not subject to rules of displacement corresponding to Arts.4(2) and 4(3).[98] Article 6(2) requires direct application of Art.4 (including the rules of displacement in Arts 4(2) and 4(3)) where an act of unfair competition affects exclusively the interests of a competitor and no adaptation of the latter provision is required. **S35–216**

**Article 6(1).** According to Art.6(1) the law applicable to an act which is characterised as an act of unfair competition is the law of the country where competitive relations or the collective interests of consumers are, or are likely **S35–217**

---

[92] Art.10*bis* (3).

[93] In its first decision concerning the Rome II Regulation, the German Bundesgerichtshof left open the question whether an action by a consumer organisation to restrain the use of unfair terms in consumer contracts falls within Art.4 or Art.6(1) of the Regulation, but accepted that the Regulation applied to cases of this kind: see Xa ZR 19/08, NJW 2009, 3371, para.19.

[94] Paras S35–220 *et seq*.

[95] Below, para.S35–217, text to n.2.

[96] Commission Notice on the definition of relevant market for the purposes of Community competition law [1997] O.J. C372/5.

[97] See Dickinson, para.6.64; Fitchen, n.81 above, 360–364.

[98] *cf.* above, paras.S35–196 and S35–197.

to be, affected. The nature of situations to which Art.6(1) is likely to apply are limited by reference to Art.6(2) which only applies to situations where the act of unfair competition affects exclusively a specific competitor. Article 6(1), therefore, concerns situations where competitive relations, in general, and the collective interests of consumers, in general, are affected. Examples might be misleading advertising and trade boycotts.[99] The provision thus appears to refer to the effects on competitors' interests in general and the effects on the public.[1] The relevant country, for these purposes, appears to be "the market where competitors are seeking to gain the customer's favour".[2] The first question which arises is whether any effect on the market is sufficient to trigger the provision or whether the effect on the market must reach a particular degree. According to the Explanatory Memorandum to the Commission's original proposal "only the direct substantial effects of an act of unfair competition should be taken into account".[3] In contrast, however, to Art.5 of the Commission's proposal, Art.6(1) does not include the words "directly and substantial". In their absence, there would appear to be no requirement of a "substantial effect", although it may be that the indirect (including spill-over) consequences of an act of unfair competition can be excluded from account by analogy with Art.4(1).[4] The second question which arises is as to the application of Art.6(1) in cases where the relevant act or acts affect more than one market in different countries or a single market whose geographical area covers two or more countries.[5] Here, the Explanatory Memorandum to the Commission's original proposal states that such situations give rise to "the distributive application of the laws involved",[6] i.e. the law applicable to the relevant act will be identified by reference to the law of each country in which the market affected is situated. This solution, however, appears highly unsatisfactory, particularly as Art.6(1) focuses on the effect of conduct on the market rather than the individual claimant, and does not contain a "escape clause" or rule corresponding to Art.6(3)(b).[7] Thirdly, it appears that the action may be brought by a competitor or competitors or a trade or consumer's association.[8] Finally, it may be noted that neither the law

---

[99] Explanatory Memorandum, comment on Art.5 of the original proposal.

[1] *ibid.*

[2] *ibid.*

[3] *ibid.*

[4] Dickinson, paras 6.53–6.55.

[5] See above, para.S35–215A.

[6] Explanatory Memorandum, comment on Art.5

[7] *cf.* below, para.S35–221.

[8] Explanatory Memorandum, comment on Art.5. In its first decision concerning the Rome II Regulation, the German Bundesgerichtshof left open the question whether an action by a consumer organisation to restrain the use of unfair terms in consumer contracts falls within Art.4 or Art.6(1) of the Regulation, but accepted that the Regulation applied to cases of this type. The Court referred to Recital (21) of the Regulation as supporting the view that both Art.4 and Art.6(1), in this context, required that consumers be protected according to the law of the place where the collective interests are affected: see Xa ZR 19/08, NJW 2009, 3371, para.19. See also Directive 98/27/EC of the European Parliament and of the Council on injunctions for the protection of consumer's interests ([1998] O.J. L166/51), implemented in the United Kingdom in Enterprise Act 2002, Pt 8; Case C–167/2000 *Verein für Konsumenteninformation v Henkel* [2002] E.C.R. I-8111. Directive 98/27/EC and the later amendments to it have been codified in Directive 2009/22/EC of the European Parliament and Council ([2009] O.J. L110/30), which entered into force on December 29, 2009.

of the common habitual residence provision in Art.4(2) nor the "escape clause" in Art.4(3) is applicable in cases falling within Art.6(1).

**Article 6(2).** Article 6(2) deals with a rather narrower form of unfair competition, where the alleged act affects "exclusively the interests of a specific competitor". Suggested examples are: enticing away a competitor's staff; corruption; industrial espionage; disclosure of business secrets; or inducing a breach of contract.[9] In the Explanatory Memorandum accompanying its original proposal, the Commission suggested that these were situations where an act of unfair competition "targets a specific competitor", and were to be regarded as "bilateral".[10] Neither test, however, fits easily with the wording of Art.6(2) or with the Commission's examples and it may, therefore, be more helpful to ask whether the act of unfair competition gives a competitive advantage to the defendant at the expense of a single competitor, without at the same time materially changing the conditions of competition in the market as a whole.[11] On this view, cases of passing off or misleading or comparative advertising would appear to fall within Art.6(1), not Art.6(2).[12] Such cases are governed by the general rule contained in Art.4 of the Regulation. Accordingly, as a general rule, the law applicable is the law of the country in which the direct damage occurs irrespective of the country in which the event giving rise to the damage occurred and irrespective of the country or countries in which the indirect consequences of that event occur.[13] Thus, if an act of unfair competition carried out in country A causes direct damage to a competitor in country B, the law of country B will apply, even if the indirect consequences of the act occur in country A or C. The application of this general rule is capable of being displaced in favour of the law of the common habitual residence of the parties pursuant to Art.4(2) or by reference to the "escape clause" contained in Art.4(3).[14] S35–218

**Content of applicable law.** Where an act, classified as an act of unfair competition for the purposes, in particular, of Art.6(2), is found to be governed by English law, the relevant substantive law will be the rules of English law concerning the tort, if any, which may have been committed on the facts. This does not preclude, as a result of the autonomous interpretation of unfair competition, the application of a the law of a country, such as England, where the claim would be for slander of goods or defamation of a competitor.[15] S35–219

**Acts restricting free competition.** Article 6(3) concerns the determination of the law applicable to non-contractual obligations arising out of a restriction of competition. In such cases the applicable law shall be the law of the country S35–220

---

[9] Explanatory Memorandum, comment on Art.5 of the original proposal.
[10] Explanatory Memorandum, comment on Art.5 of the original proposal.
[11] Dickinson, para.6.29.
[12] Dickinson, *ibid. Cf.* Cheshire, North and Fawcett, n.59, above, at 810.
[13] Art.4(1), above, para.S35–195.
[14] Above, paras S35–197. As to the parties' ability to choose the law applicable, see above, para.S35–214.
[15] See para.S35–215 above.

where the market is, or is likely to be, affected.[16] Three points, in particular, may be noted. First, it appears that the provision applies to infringements of both national and Community competition law.[17] More particularly "the concept of restrictions of competition should cover prohibitions on agreements between undertakings, decisions by associations of undertakings and concerted practices which have as their object or effect the prevention, restriction or distortion of competition within a Member State or within the internal market, as well as the abuse of a dominant position within a Member State or within the internal market, where such agreements, decisions, concerted practices or abuses are prohibited by Articles 81 and 82 of the Treaty or by the law of a Member State."[18] Secondly, the reference in Art.6(3)(a) is to the law of the country where the market is, or is likely to be, affected, without any restrictions on the country whose law is involved, while Recital (22)[19] envisages application of the competition law of any country. The possibility is thus opened up of the English courts applying United States' anti-trust law in respect of acts which are characterised as acts restricting free competition, committed in England, which affect the market in the United States, though this may be subject to the public policy exception.[20] Thirdly, the text of Art.6(3)(a) does not, in contrast to Art.6(3)(b), require that the effect on the relevant market be "direct" and "substantial". A proviso to that effect had been included in a recital to the Council Common Position, but that recital was deleted during the conciliation process.[21] It seems doubtful, therefore, whether a requirement of a "substantial effect" on the market exists as a pre-condition to the application of Art.6(3)(a), although it may be that the indirect (including spill-over) consequences of an act of unfair competition can be excluded from account by analogy with Art.4(1).[22]

S35–221 **Market affected is in more than one country.** Where the market is, or is likely to be, affected in more than one country (whether because the restriction of competition affects a market whose geographical area covers two or more countries,[23] or because it affects two or more separate markets), then, in principle, Art.6(3)(a) would lead to a distributive application of the laws involved, i.e. the law applicable to the relevant act would be the law of each country in which the market affected was situated.[24] Article 6(3)(b), however, makes further provision for such situations, being apparently intended to promote the more effective private enforcement of EC competition rules.[25] When the market is, or is likely to be, affected in more than one country, the person seeking compensation for damage who sues in the court of the

---

[16] Art.6(3)(a).
[17] Recital (22).
[18] Recital (23).
[19] Above, text at n.17.
[20] Art.26; below, para.S35–273.
[21] Council Common Position, Recital (20).
[22] Dickinson, paras 6.65–6.66. *Cf.* Hellner, n.81 above, 61–64.
[23] See above, para.S35–215A.
[24] Explanatory Memorandum, comment on Art.5. *Cf.* above, para.S36–217.
[25] On the subject of private enforcement, see the Commission's White Paper on damages actions for breach of the EC anti-trust rules (COM(2008) 165 final), the accompanying Staff Working Paper (SEC(2008) 404) and the articles by Rodriguez Pineau and Fitchen (n.81 above).

domicile of the defendant (i.e. the person from whom compensation is sought), may instead choose to base his or her claim on the law of the court seised, provided that the market in that Member State is amongst those directly and substantially affected by the restriction of competition out of which the non-contractual obligation on which the claim is based arises. The defendant has no similar option and he has no right to oppose the claimant's choice, although it appears that he may effectively preclude its exercise by bringing an action for negative declaratory relief in another court. Article 6(3)(b) also stipulates that where the claimant sues, in accordance with the applicable rules on jurisdiction, more than one defendant in the court of the domicile, he or she can only choose to base his or her claim on the law of that court if the restriction of competition on which the claim against each of the defendants relies directly and substantially affects also the market in the Member State of that court. This amplification of the general principle of Art.6(3)(b) is obviously necessary to protect the interests of co-defendants, once the general principle is accepted.

### E. *Environmental Damage*

Article 7 of the Rome II Regulation provides a choice of law rule with regard to what is generally described as "environmental damage". According to this: **S35–222**

> "The law applicable to a non-contractual obligation arising out of environmental damage or damage sustained by persons or property as a result of such damage shall be the law determined pursuant to Article 4(1), unless the person seeking compensation for damage chooses to base his or her claim on the law of the country in which the event giving rise to the damage occurred."[26]

**Scope.** An initial question arises as to the scope of Art.7. For these purposes, it is necessary to determine what is meant by "environmental damage" since the provision applies to determine the applicable law of a non-contractual obligation arising out of such damage and includes the law applicable to damage sustained by persons or property as a result of such damage. There is, of course, no definition contained in the Article itself, though it seems tolerably clear that the expression will be given an autonomous meaning.[27] Guidance is to be found in Recital (24) to the Regulation which provides that environmental damage "should be understood as meaning adverse change in a natural resource, such as water, land or air, impairment of a function performed by that resource for the benefit of another natural **S35–223**

---

[26] For comment, see Kadner Graziano (2007) 9 Yb. P.I.L. 71; Symeonides (2008) 56 Am. J. Comp. L. 173, 209 *et seq.*; Dickinson, Ch.7; Bogdan, in Ahern and Binchy, 219. The parties may agree by contract to submit such a non-contractual obligation to a law of their choice pursuant to Art.14 of the Regulation: see below, paras S35–248 *et seq.*

[27] See Recital (24).

resource or the public, or impairment of the variability among living organisms." Although broad in character, this guidance provides at least a framework in which more detailed treatment of the concept can be developed.[28] It also assists in determining whether damage to persons or property arises out of this kind of damage. It would, additionally, seem to be the case that environmental damage must be caused by an event which is a result of human activity.[29] Further, although Art.7 does not specifically refer to economic losses resulting from environmental damage, there would appear no reason to exclude claims with respect to such losses from its scope, although they should probably be treated as "indirect consequences" of the event giving rise to damage and not relevant in identifying the law applicable.[30] Finally, as the Regulation applies only to "civil and commercial matters", Art.7 will not apply to claims by public authorities to recover costs incurred in the exercise of their public powers to clean up environmental damages, although claims by public authorities as landowners will fall within scope.[31]

S35–224 **General choice of law rule.** The general rule applicable under Art.4(1) determines the law applicable to a non-contractual obligation arising out of environmental damage and that applicable where damage is sustained by persons or property as a result of environmental damage. Under Art.4(1) the applicable law will be the law of the country in which the environmental damage occurs, irrespective of the country in which the event giving rise to the damage occurred and irrespective of the country or countries in which the indirect consequences of that event occurred.[32] Where damage is sustained by persons or property as a result of environmental damage, the applicable law is likely to be the law of the country in which the person was when he or she suffered the damage or the law of the country where the property was when it was damaged. In the latter cases the damage must be "direct" and must be caused by the environmental damage. Normally, the country where the environmental damage occurred will be the same as that in which damage to persons or property occurred. Economic losses resulting from environmental damage should be treated as "indirect consequences" and left out of account in determining the law applicable under Art.4(1). It must be emphasised that Art.7 refers only to Art.4(1). Application of Art.4(2) (the common habitual residence exception)[33] and Art.4(3) (the escape clause[34]) is thus excluded.

---

[28] Further inspiration may be found in Directive 2004/35/EC of the European Parliament and of the Council on environmental liability with regard to the prevention and remedying of environmental damage ([2004] O.J. L143/56), Art.2(1), according to which environmental damage means (a) damage to protected species and natural habitats, (b) water damage, which is any damage that significantly adversely affects the ecological, chemical and/or quantitative status and/or ecological potential of waters, (c) land damage, which is any land contamination that creates a significant risk of human health being adversely affected as a result of the direct or indirect introduction, in, on or under land, of substances, preparations, organisms or micro-organisms. See HL Paper 66 (2004), para.134.

[29] See Explanatory Memorandum, comment on Art.7.

[30] Dickinson, paras 7.12–7.13.

[31] Dickinson, *ibid.*, paras 7–03–7.06. *Cf.* Kadner Graziano, n.26 above, 80–86.

[32] Above, para.S35–195.

[33] Above, para.S35–196.

[34] Above, para.S35–197.

**Law of the country in which the event occurred.** Article 7 provides for the possibility for a person seeking compensation for damage to base his or her claim on the law of the country in which the event giving rise to the damage occurred. The question of when the person seeking compensation can make the choice of the law applicable appears to be a matter to be determined in accordance with the law of the Regulation State in which the court is seised.[35] Under English procedural rules, it may be open to the claimant (with the permission of the court) to amend his pleading to make the election at any time up to judgment. The justification for making this option available to the claimant is to be found in a Recital and in the Explanatory Memorandum to the Commission's original proposal. Recital (25) refers to Art.174 of the EC Treaty which provides for a high level of protection, based on the precautionary principle and the principle that preventive action should be taken, the principle of priority for corrective action at source and the principle that the polluter pays. These principles, it is argued, fully justify the use of the principle of discriminating in favour of the person sustaining the damage. In more detail, the Commission explained that if the law of the country in which damage is suffered were the exclusive choice of law rule, that would mean that a victim suffering damage in a "low-protection" country would not enjoy the "higher-level" of protection which may be available in neighbouring countries where the event may have occurred.[36] The general objectives of the European Union in environmental matters are not only to respect the victim's legitimate interests but also to establish a legislative policy that contributes to raising the general level of environmental protection, especially as the perpetrator of environmental damage generally derives an economic advantage from the harmful activity pursued.[37] If the law of the country of damage were the exclusive rule, this would give an operator an "incentive to establish his facilities at the border so as to discharge toxic substances into a river and enjoy the benefit of the neighbouring country's laxer rules. This solution would be contrary to the underlying philosophy of the European substantive law of the environment and the 'polluter pays' principle."[38] S35–225

**Meaning of "event".** It is clear that the claimant can rely on the law of country in which the event which gave rise to the damage occurred and, normally, there will be no doubt about the country in which that event occurred. But it is possible that cases could arise in which an act in country A gives rise to an incident in country B which causes environmental damage in country C. Is the act in country A or the incident in country B the relevant event for the purposes of Art.7? This could be a point of importance if the law of country A were more favourable to the claimant than the law of country B, or *vice versa*. How such a case would be resolved were it to arise, must be speculative. One solution might be to identify the "event giving rise to S35–226

[35] Recital (25); Explanatory Memorandum, comment on Art.7.

[36] Explanatory Memorandum, *ibid. cf.* Case 21/76 *Bier BV v Mines de Potasse d'Alsace SA* [1976] E.C.R. 1735, [1978] Q.B. 708.

[37] Explanatory Memorandum, *ibid.*

[38] *ibid.*

damage" with the human activity which is the principal or substantial cause of the environmental damage.[39]

S35–227 **Rules of safety and conduct.** The Explanatory Memorandum to the Commission's original proposal refers to a further difficulty in relation to civil liability in respect of environmental damage which arises because of "the close link with the public law rules governing the operator's conduct and the safety rules with which he is required to comply".[40] As drafted, Art.7 envisages that a person acting in country A in a manner authorised by the law of country A but whose activity causes environmental damage in country B where the activity does not comply with applicable safety standards will be liable under the law of country B. Here, account needs to be taken of Art.17 of the Regulation which provides that in assessing the conduct of the person claimed to be liable account shall be taken, as a matter of fact and in so far as it is appropriate, of the rules of conduct and safety which were in force at the place and time of the event giving rise to the liability.[41] This would enable account to be taken of the fact that the operator has complied with the law of country A and the safety standards that country has imposed. But Art.17 will not relieve the operator of liability under the rule declared applicable by Art.7. As the Explanatory Memorandum puts it: "Taking account of foreign law is not the same thing as applying it: the court will apply only the law that is applicable under the conflict rule, but it must take account of another law as a point of fact, for example, when assessing the seriousness of the fault or the author's good or bad faith for the purposes of the measure of damages".[42] Accordingly, the role to be played by rules of safety and conduct will depend on the content of the law applicable under Art.7. It remains to be seen how Arts 7 and 17 will interact in practice.[43]

### F. *Infringement of Intellectual Property Rights*

S35–228 The choice of law rules applicable to a non-contractual obligation arising from an infringement of an intellectual property right are contained in Art.8 of the Rome II Regulation. According to this provision:

---

[39] It is unlikely that Art.7 will be construed to give the victim a further choice, as between the law of country A and the law of country B since Art.7 already gives the victim a choice. Yet a further complication could arise if the person responsible for the act in country A is not the same person as is responsible for the activity giving rise to the incident in country B (e.g. Case C–188/07 *Commune de Mesquer v Total France SA and Total International Ltd* [2008] E.C.R. I–4501). Here, the relevant event might depend on which of these persons is the defendant or if each of them is a defendant, the event may be different for each of them.

[40] Explanatory Memorandum, comment on Art.7.

[41] See below, para.S35–264. *cf.* main work, para.35–109.

[42] Explanatory Memorandum, comment on Art.13 of the original proposal.

[43] Note, however, that the failure to accord equivalent treatment to a licence granted by another Member State may constitute a violation of EU law, or render a rule of the applicable law objectionable on public policy grounds: Case C–115/08 *Land Oberösterreich v ČEZ*, [2009] E.C.R. I–10265.

"1. The law applicable to a non-contractual obligation arising from an infringement of an intellectual property right shall be the law of the country for which protection is claimed.
2. In the case of a non-contractual obligation arising from an infringement of a unitary Community intellectual property right, the law applicable shall, for any question that is not governed by the relevant Community instrument, be the law of the country in which the act of infringement was committed.
3. The law applicable under this Article may not be derogated from by an agreement pursuant to Article 14."[44]

**Exclusion of Article 14.** Article 8(3) does not permit the parties to depart from Art. 8(1) and 8(2) by an agreement, pursuant to Art.14,[45] by which they designate as the applicable law a law other than that which is applicable under either of those provisions.[46] **S35–229**

**Non-contractual obligations covered.** Article 8 is located in the Chapter of the Regulation dealing with non-contractual obligations arising out of tort. However, Art.13 of the Regulation additionally provides that Art.8 shall also determine the law applicable to a non-contractual obligation arising from an infringement of an intellectual property right in respect of situations falling within Chapter III of the Regulation, which will, principally, be likely to be unjust enrichment. Thus an obligation based on unjust enrichment arising from an infringement of an intellectual property right is governed by the same law as the infringement itself.[47] **S35–230**

**Meaning of "intellectual property right".** Article 8 does not define the intellectual property rights to which is applies.[48] Recital (26), however, states that the expression "should be interpreted as meaning, for instance, copyright, related rights, the *sui generis* right for the protection of databases and industrial property rights". This statement does not appear to be exhaustive. **S35–231**

---

[44] For comment, see Boschiero (2007) 9 Yb. P.I.L. 87; Symeonides (2008) 56 Am. J. Comp. L. 173, 209 *et seq.*; Dickinson, Ch.8; Schack in Leible and Ohly (eds.), *Intellectual Property and Private International Law* (2009), p.79; Leistner, *ibid.*, p.97. For discussion of Art.8 of the Commission's original proposal, which except for the absence of Art.8(3), is largely replicated in the Regulation, see Pertegas in Malatesta (ed.), *The Unification of Choice of Law Rules on Torts and Other Non-Contractual Obligations in Europe* (2006), p.221.

[45] Below, paras. S35–248 *et seq.*

[46] Some systems of law allow limited scope for party autonomy in relation to infringement of intellectual property rights: see, e.g., Swiss Private International Law Act, s.110(2).

[47] Explanatory Memorandum, comment on Art.9 of the original proposal.

[48] In *Lucasfilm Ltd v Ainsworth* [2009] EWCA Civ 1328, [2010] 3 W.L.R. 333 (see above, entry at paras 35–030—35–032), the Court of Appeal suggested (at [181]) that a right under foreign law to sue for passing off/unfair competition fell within the category of "foreign intellectual property rights" which were, potentially, non-justiciable under English law on the basis that "[c]ommercially speaking they are all the same sort of right—a right to exclude others". An appeal to the Supreme Court is pending.

Overall, however, the meaning of intellectual property rights is likely to be developed by reference to a principle of autonomous interpretation.[49]

S35–232 **Relationship with unfair competition.** The relationship between Art.8 and Art.6 (unfair competition, etc.[50]) is in need of clarification because unfair competition issues may also arise in connection with intellectual property rights and the law applicable under Art.6 may not necessarily coincide with that applicable under Art.8.[51]

S35–233 **Article 8(1).** Article 8(1) of the Regulation stipulates that the law applicable to a non-contractual obligation arising from an infringement of an intellectual property right shall be the law of the country for which protection is claimed, the *lex loci protectionis*.[52] This is described, extravagantly, as a "universally acknowledged principle."[53] Applying the rule requires application of the law of the country under whose substantive law the claimant seeks to be protected, giving the claimant a measure of discretion in the presentation of his claim. It is that law which will determine whether an infringement of the relevant intellectual property right, governed by that law, has occurred. Where the claimant claims to be protected under the law of more than one country, it will be necessary, presumably, to determine whether the alleged acts of infringement fall within the scope of protection of any of the implicated laws.[54] It would seem, however, that issues relating to the validity of the intellectual property right, and to the ownership of the intellectual property right would not fall within Art.8(1) of the Rome II Regulation: Art.8(1) is only concerned with determining the law applicable to infringement.[55]

S35–234 Article 8(1) contains no reservation in favour of applying the law of the common habitual residence of the parties such as that contained in Art.4(2) of the Regulation. Nor is there an "escape clause" corresponding to Art.4(3).

---

[49] The definition of "intellectual property rights" in Recital (26) is not limited to those subsisting under the laws of the Member States of the EU, and appears capable of encompassing (for example) a claim for breach of US copyright. However, in *Lucasfilm Ltd v Ainsworth*, above, involving such a claim (arising before the entry into force of the Rome II Regulation) the Court of Appeal held that claims based on infringement of a foreign, non-EU or Lugano Convention State's intellectual property right were non-justiciable before an English Court. The Court of Appeal took the view that it was not precluded from reaching this conclusion by the terms of the Judgments Regulation. An appeal to the Supreme Court is pending.

[50] Above, paras S35–212 *et seq*.

[51] See, HL Paper 66 (2004), para.137, Minutes of Evidence, p.81. See also Dickinson, para.6.34; *cf. Lucasfilm Ltd v Ainsworth* [2009] EWCA Civ 1328, [2010] 3 W.L.R. 333, [181].

[52] See Recital (26). For criticism, see HL Paper 66 (2004), Minutes of Evidence, pp.47, 117–118, 131–132.

[53] Recital (26). For other approaches taken in Europe, see main work, paras 35–028—35–032; Pertegas, above, n.44, pp.232–235.

[54] The *lex loci protectionis* principle extends, apparently to infringements of intellectual property rights granted under national legislation or international conventions: Explanatory Memorandum, comment on Art.8.

[55] See Pertegas, above, n.44, at p.239. It has been suggested that it may be inappropriate to legislate for infringement without considering other issues with which infringement is closely related such as ownership of intellectual property rights. See HL Paper 66 (2004), Minutes of Evidence, p.118.

**Unitary Community rights: Article 8(2).** Article 8(2) provides, that in the case of a non-contractual obligation arising from an infringement of a unitary Community intellectual property right, the law applicable shall, for any question not governed by the relevant Community instrument, be the law of the country in which the act of infringement occurred. Relevant unitary Community intellectual property rights will include: Community trademarks,[56] Community designs[57] and Community plant variety rights.[58] Initially, therefore, the law applicable to infringements of such a unitary right will normally be the Community instrument which establishes the relevant right. A default rule is needed, however, when the question at issue is not governed by the instrument. This cannot be the *lex loci protectionis* because the area for which protection would have to be sought is supranational and thus would not be capable of designating a national law. Accordingly, Art.8(2) adopts application of the law of the country[59] in which the act of infringement was committed.[60] In the usual case there may be no difficulty in determining the country in which the act of infringement was committed but there will be cases where locating the relevant country may be problematic, e.g. cases where it is alleged that a copyright has been infringed over the internet.[61] Further difficulty may arise where acts of infringement are committed in more than one country, a situation which may involve the application of each country's law to determine whether, on the basis of each of them, the unitary right has been infringed. **S35–235**

## G. *Industrial Action*

Article 9 of the Rome II Regulation provides a special choice of law rule in relation to non-contractual obligations arising out of industrial action, in the following terms: **S35–236**

> "Without prejudice to Article 4(2), the law applicable to a non-contractual obligation in respect of the liability of a person in the capacity of a worker or an employer or the organisations representing their professional interests

---

[56] Council Regulation (EC) 40/94 of December 20, 1993 on the Community Trade Mark: [1994] O.J. L11/1. This Regulation and the later amendments to it have been repealed and re-enacted in consolidated form in Council Regulation (EC) 207/2009 ([2009] O.J. L78, 1).

[57] Council Regulation (EC) 6/2002 of December 12, 2001 on Community Designs: [2002] O.J. L3/1.

[58] Council Regulation (EC) 2100/94 of July 24, on Community Plant Variety Rights: [1994] O.J. L227/1. See also Dickinson, paras 8.15–8.16.

[59] The Commission's original proposal used the expression Member State rather than country.

[60] Use of the past tense "was committed" might be thought to suggest that Art.8(2) does not apply to threatened acts of infringement, but this view seems contrary to the general approach of the Regulation and the reasons underlying the perceived need for a special rule for Community IPR infringements in Art.8(2) *cf.* Arts 2, 6, 9.

[61] For discussion in the context of Art.5(3) of the Conventions and the Judgments Regulation, see Fawcett and Torremans, *Intellectual Property and Private International Law* (1998), pp.156–162; Pertegas, *Cross-Border Enforcement of Patent Rights* (2002), pp.12–118; and see main work, para.35–089, n.29.

for damages caused by an industrial action, pending or carried out, shall be the law of the country where the action is to be, or has been, taken."[62]

S35–237 The original proposal by the Commission contained no special rule for determining the law applicable to a non-contractual obligation arising out of industrial action. Article 9 was introduced by the European Parliament's amendment of the original proposal, against the background of concerns expressed by certain Member States as to the implications of the ECJ's judgment in the *Torline* case.[63]

S35–238 **General principle.** The law applicable to a non-contractual obligation in respect of the liability of a person in the capacity of a worker or employer or the organisations representing their professional interests for damages caused by an industrial action, pending or carried out is the law of the country where the action is to be, or has been, taken. It is correct, in principle, that normally the legality of industrial action should be governed by the law of the country where the action takes place. The law relating to labour relations is a sensitive area in which the applicable rules are very much linked with the political, economic and industrial relations systems prevailing in a particular country. Thus, in principle, it is normally inappropriate to judge the legality of action taking place in one country by reference to rules prevailing in a different country. Further, as is pointed out in Recital (27) the "exact concept of industrial action such as strike action or lock-out varies from one Member State to another and is governed by each Member State's internal rules."[64] It is for this reason that Art.9 assumes as a general principle that the law applicable will be that of the country where the action is, or is to be, taken, "with the aim of protecting the rights and obligations of workers and employers."[65]

S35–239 **Application of Article 4(2).** The rule in Art.9 is without prejudice to the application of Art.4(2) of the Regulation. This means that where the parties have a common habitual residence in a country other than that in which the industrial action is taken, the law of that common habitual residence will govern any non-contractual obligation arising out of such action. It may be questioned, given the sensitivity of the context in which Art.9 operates,

---

[62] For comment, see Palao Moreno (2007) 9 Yb. P.I.L. 115; Dickinson, Ch.9. The parties may agree to submit such a non-contractual obligation to the law of their choice pursuant to Art.14 of the Regulation: see below, paras S35–248 *et seq*.

[63] Case C–18/02 *Danmarks Rederiforening, acting on behalf of DFDS Torline A/S v LO Landsorganisationen i Sverige, acting on behalf of SEKO Sjöfolk Facket för Service och Kommunikation* [2004] ECR I–1417. See also P6_ TCO CPD (2003) 168, Council document 9009/04 ADD8; Dickinson, paras 9.01–9.11.

[64] It is unclear why this observation is limited to Member States since the Regulation has universal effect (Art.3).

[65] Recital (27). Recital (28) states that Art.9 is without prejudice to the conditions relating to the exercise of industrial action in accordance with national law and without prejudice to the legal status of trade unions or of the representative organisations of workers as provided for in the "law of the Member States". It is unclear why this observation is limited to the "law of the Member States". See preceding note.

whether it is appropriate to apply Art.4(2) to non-contractual obligations arising out of industrial action. The rule, from which there is no "escape clause", is liable to produce unsatisfactory results, particularly where industrial action is organised on an international basis.

**Meaning of "industrial action".** "Industrial action" is one term in the Regulation which should not be given an autonomous interpretation, bearing in mind the sensitivity of labour relations in many countries and the different rules which may prevail in different countries as to what is permissible or impermissible industrial action.[66] Article 9 seems to accept that industrial action may be "individual" (worker and employer) or "collective" (organisations of workers such as trades unions and employer or organisations of employers). It is likely that collective industrial action will normally be involved.[67] This will obviously include strikes and lock-outs but will also extend to boycotts[68] and the like. The action may be "pending" or "carried out." The reference to "pending" action and to the "country where action is to be . . . taken" confirm that liability with respect to threatened industrial action also falls within Art.9. **S35–240**

**"Liability of a person . . . for damages".** Article 9 refers to the law applicable to a non-contractual obligation in respect of the "liability of a person . . . for damages caused by" industrial action. In the context of an industrial dispute the remedy which is sought may not be "damages" but an injunction, particularly if the industrial action is threatened but not yet carried out.[69] This raises the question of whether, in the context of Art.9, the only remedy sought can be damages since it is that word and not the word "damage" which is used in the Article.[70] Normally, the law applicable to the non-contractual obligation will determine the nature of the remedy claimed[71] and, "within the limits of powers conferred on the court by its procedural law, the measures which a court may take to prevent or terminate injury or damage . . . ".[72] It therefore seems highly unlikely that it was intended in Art.9 to impose a limit on the scope of the applicable law by restricting the available remedy to damages. That view would appear to be confirmed by the reference in Art.9 to industrial action that is "pending", as well as "carried out".[73] The natural remedy to seek in such cases is an injunction (or rather its equivalent under a foreign law provided that such a remedy is within the powers conferred on the court under its procedural law). Article 9 should not, therefore, be construed to be limited to claims for damages but rather, and **S35–241**

---

66 See the reference to "internal rules" in Recital (27) and "national law" in Recital (28).

67 Indeed the French text of Art.9 is headed "Responsabilité du fait de grève ou de lock out". Strikes or lock-outs are normally part of a collective action.

68 *cf. The Amur-2528* [2001] 1 Lloyd's Rep. 421.

69 As in *The Amur-2528*, above, an injunction may also be sought to prevent the continuance of industrial action.

70 The French text of Art.9 uses the term "dommages" rather than (*cf.* Art.2(3)) "dommage".

71 Art.15(c). See below, para.S35–257.

72 Art.15(d). See below, para.S35–258.

73 Above, para.S35–240.

subject to other provisions of the Regulation,[74] to permit the grant of injunctive or declaratory relief.

### H. *Culpa in Contrahendo*

**S35–242** Article 12 of the Rome II Regulation (headed "*culpa in contrahendo*") is to be found in Chapter III of the Regulation, along with unjust enrichment (Art.10)[75] and *negotiorum gestio* (Art.11).[76] Matters falling within Art.12, will therefore, not be regarded, as such, as being subject to the choice of law rules for tort/delict contained in Chapter II of the Regulation. Essentially, Art.12 is concerned with what may be loosely described as pre-contractual liability. Legal systems may differ as to the conceptual basis on which such liability may be based.[77] Article 12 thus provides a discrete choice of law rule on the question for the purposes of the Regulation. It is considered in the discussion of the Regulation as applied to non-contractual obligations arising out of tort/delict because the typical situations which it covers generally tend to involve tort in English law which does not subscribe to the principle of *culpa in contrahendo* (literally, "fault in the formation of contract"), as such.[78]

**S35–243** Article 12 of the Regulation provides as follows:

> "1. The law applicable to a non-contractual obligation arising out of dealings prior to the conclusion of a contract, regardless of whether the contract was actually concluded or not, shall be the law that applies to the contract or that would have been applicable to it had it been entered into.
>
> 2. Where the law applicable cannot be determined on the basis of paragraph 1, it shall be:
>
> (a) the law of the country in which the damage occurs, irrespective of the country in which the event giving rise to the damage occurred and irrespective of the country or countries in which the indirect consequences of that event occurred; or

---

[74] In particular, Art.15(d). See below para.S35–258.

[75] See above, entry at para.34–014.

[76] See above, entry at para.34–053.

[77] See generally *Chitty on Contracts* 29th edn (2004), Vol I, para.1–115; Fawcett, Harris and Bridge, *International Sale of Goods in the Conflict of Laws* (2005), pp.331–334, 1024–1030; Kessler and Fine (1964) 77 Harv. L. Rev. 401; Dietrich (2001) 21 Leg. Stud 153; see also Giliker (2003) 52 I.C.L.Q. 969. Conceptual responses to pre-contractual liability include contract, tort, restitution for unjust enrichment), a mixture of these, or as lying between contract and tort: see Zimmermann, *The Law of Obligations—Roman Foundations of the Civilian Tradition* (1996), p.245. For the position under Art.5(3) of the Judgments Regulation, see main work, paras 11–287–11–288.

[78] *Chitty on Contracts* (29th ed. 2004), Vol. I, para.1–115. *cf.* Italian Civil Code, Art.1337: "During the course of the negotiations and in the formation of the contract, the parties must act in good faith".

(b) where the parties have their habitual residence in the same country at the time when the event giving rise to the damage occurs, the law of that country; or
(c) where it is clear from all the circumstances of the case that the non-contractual obligation arising out of dealings prior to the conclusion of the contract is manifestly more closely connected with a country other than that indicated in points (a) and (b), the law of that other country."[79]

**Scope of Article 12.** According to Recital (30) to the Regulation *culpa in contrahendo* is an autonomous concept and should not necessarily be interpreted within the meaning of national law.[80] The Recital goes on to point out that it should include "the violation of the duty of disclosure and the breakdown of contractual negotiations." But Art.12 "covers only non-contractual obligations presenting a direct link with the dealings prior to the conclusion of a contract. The means that if, while a contract is being negotiated, a person suffers personal injury, Art.4 or other relevant provisions of this Regulation should apply".[81] The terminology and these various observations suggest that Art.12 will apply to fault based claims, for example, to non-disclosure, fraudulent or negligent misrepresentations and duress which occur during the negotiation of a contract. Equally, however, these observations emphasise that the "*culpa*" in whatever form must occur in the context of negotiations with a view to concluding a contract. Thus Art.12 would not, it seems, apply in a case where (for example) a misrepresentation is made outside contractual negotiations or where a third party relies on a representation made in connection with a contract concluded between the representor and a different party. Such cases will fall, normally, within Art.4. Finally, as the principal connecting factor under Art.12 is the law applicable to a contract (or putative contract), its application may be restricted to claims between the parties (or prospective parties) to that contract, and not any third party (e.g. an agent) involved in the pre-contractual dealings.[82] S35–244

**Article 12(1): applicable law.** Article 12(1), it is clear, applies regardless of whether the contract was concluded or not. Where the contract has been concluded the law applicable to the non-contractual obligation arising out of dealings prior to the conclusion of the contract is to be the law applicable to the contract.[83] The law applicable to the contract will be determined in S35–245

[79] For comment, see Volders (2007) 9 Yb. P.I.L. 127; Dickinson, Ch.12. The parties may agree to submit the non-contractual obligation to the law of their choice pursuant to Art.14 of the Regulation: see below, paras S35–248 *et seq*. See also the Rome I Regulation, Art.1(2)(i) and Recital (10) to that Regulation.

[80] This would be particularly difficult in the context of a system of law which, like English law, does not recognise the concept as such.

[81] Recital (30). The reference to the possibility or suffering personal injury during the course of negotiation of a contract might seem somewhat fanciful: but see the discussion of German law in Kessler and Fine, above, n.77, at p.403, Zimmermann, above, n.77, at pp.11 *et seq*.

[82] Dickinson, paras.12.07–12.08.

[83] *Morgan Stanley & Co International Plc v China Haisheng Juice Holdings Co Ltd* [2009] EWHC 2409 (Comm.), [2010] 1 Lloyd's Rep 265, at [35].

accordance with the relevant provisions of the Rome Convention.[84] Although Art.12(1) does not expressly provide for this, it is to be expected that the words "the law that applies to the contract" will be understood, in the case of consumer and employment contracts to which the special rules in Arts 5 and 6 of the Rome Convention[85] (and Arts 6 and 8 of the Rome I Regulation) apply, to be capable of referring not only to the law chosen by the parties to govern the contract but also to non-derogable rules of the consumer's country of habitual residence or, as the case may be, the law that would apply to the employment contract in the absence of choice. Any other interpretation would treat the consumer/employee less favourably in relation to pre-contractual obligations than in relation to contractual obligations. Where the contract is not concluded, then, subject to what is said below, the applicable law is the law that would have been applicable to the contract had it been entered into. Again the latter law will have to be determined by reference to relevant provisions of the Rome Convention.[86] There may, however, be great difficulty determining "the law that would have been applicable" to a failed contract, in circumstances where the parties' negotiations were continuing and where they may not have turned their attention to the "boilerplate" question of applicable law. But once the applicable law of the contract or putative contract has been identified (assuming that this is possible), the substantive law of that country will determine what liabilities attach to pre-contract dealings. The relevant substantive law may be found in the law of contract, tort, restitution (unjust enrichment) or in any *sui generis* rules which may be contained in the legal system of the applicable law, depending on the approach of the latter to these kinds of liabilities.[87]

S35–246 **Article 12(1): law applicable cannot be determined.** Article 12(2) provides a "default rule" to determine the applicable law where the law applicable cannot be determined on the basis of Art.12(1). Where a contract *has been* concluded it does not seem possible to say that its applicable law "*cannot be determined*". The contract must have an applicable law. However, where a contract has not been concluded, it is possible that the parties may not have reached a stage in the contractual negotiations where it would be possible, on the basis of the relevant rules of the Rome Convention, or, when relevant, the Rome I Regulation to determine the law that would be applied to it were it eventually entered into: for example, in negotiations involving a complex joint venture arrangement, the parties to the various contracts involved may not have been clearly identified. In circumstances such as these, the "default" rule in Art.12(2) will come in to play.

---

[84] Main work, Chs 32, 33, or, when it becomes relevant, those of the Rome I Regulation.

[85] Main work, paras 33R–001—33–105.

[86] *ibid.*, or, when relevant, the Rome I Regulation.

[87] Rome I Regulation, Art.1(2)(1), read together with Recital (10) would appear to preclude a contractual classification for "obligations arising out of dealings prior to the conclusion of a contract", but this leaves open the possibility that contractual obligations may relate to, but not "arise out of", pre-contract acts or omissions (see Dickinson, paras 12.09–12.10). Further, the scope of Arts 10, 11 and 12 would seem to be mutually exclusive.

**Article 12(2).** The "default" rule in Art.12(2) is framed in terms which are almost identical to the general choice of law rule for non-contractual obligations arising out of tort/delict, contained in Art.4 of the Rome II Regulation. The general principle is (a) that the applicable law is the law of the country in which the damage occurs, irrespective of the country in which the event giving rise to the damage occurred and irrespective of the country or countries in which the indirect consequences of that event occurred.[88] Where, (b) the parties have their habitual residence[89] in the same country at the time when the event giving rise to the damage occurs, the applicable law shall be the law of that country.[90] Where, (c) it is clear from all the circumstances of the case that the non-contractual obligation arising out of dealings prior to the conclusion of a contract is manifestly more closely connected with a country other than that indicated in points (a) and (b), the applicable law shall be the law of the other country.[91] Two points may be made on this "escape clause" in this context. First, the escape clause refers to "dealings prior to the *conclusion of a contract*".[92] As pointed out above,[93] it is hard to see how the "default" rule can operate at all where a contract has been concluded since a concluded contract must have an applicable law. Allied to this, the escape clause refers to dealings prior to the conclusion of a contract but does not refer to dealings prior to a contract which has not been concluded. It is suggested that the escape clause should be construed to cover this situation. Secondly, it is suggested that the escape clause (Art.12(2)(c)) may be invoked to displace the law of the common habitual residence (Art.12(2)(b)) in favour of the law of the country in which the damage occurs (Art.12(2)(a)) where it is clear that the non-contractual obligation is manifestly more closely connected with that country.[94] S35–247

## I. *Freedom of Choice*

Article 14 of the Rome II Regulation permits the parties to agree to submit non-contractual obligations to the law of their choice subject to the conditions stipulated in the article. As regards non-contractual obligations arising out of tort/delict, this option is available in respect of Art.4 (the general rule), Art.5 (product liability), Art.7 (environmental damage) and Art.9 (industrial action). The option is also available in respect of Art.12 (*culpa in contrahendo*). The option is explicitly stated not to be available in relation to Art.6 (unfair S35–248

---

88 Art.12(2)(a). See above, para.S35–195.

89 See above, para.S35–192.

90 Art.12(2)(b). See above, para.S35–196. In contrast to Art.4(2), Art.12(2)(b) refers to the common habitual residence of the "parties" (presumably, the parties to the relevant contract; cf. Art.4(2): "the person claimed to be liable and the person sustaining damage") at the time of the event giving rise to damage (*cf.* Art.4(2): "at the time when the damage occurs").

91 Art.12(2)(c). See above, para.S35–197.

92 Emphasis added.

93 Para.S35–246.

94 See above para.S35–197. Art.12(2)(c) may of course be invoked to secure the application of any other law in an appropriate case.

competition and acts restricting free competition)[95] and Art.8 (infringement of intellectual property rights).[96]

S35–249 **Time of choice.** The parties may make a choice of law by an agreement entered into after the event giving rise to the damage occurred.[97] Presumably, this is intended to protect the weaker party, i.e. normally the victim of the tort.[98] Where all the parties are pursuing a commercial activity, the choice of law may also be made by an agreement freely negotiated before the event giving rise to the damage occurred.[99] It appears that the requirement that an advance agreement be "freely negotiated" was intended, primarily at least, to exclude standard form contracts (*contrats d'adhésion*).[1]

S35–250 **Making the choice.** The choice of law shall be expressed or demonstrated with reasonable certainty by the circumstances of the case and shall not prejudice the rights of third parties.[2] An express or "implied" choice of law is thereby permitted, although an express choice appears the more likely of the two possibilities. In line with the approach taken in the Rome Convention,[3] questions concerning the existence and validity of the parties' consent to a choice of law agreement under Art.14 should principally be determined by reference to the law applicable to the agreement containing the term in question, which will normally be the same law as that which the parties have chosen to govern non-contractual obligations.[4]

S35–251 **Limitation on choice: "internal" situations.** Where all the elements relevant to the situation at the time when the event giving rise to the damage occurs are located in a country other than the country whose law has been chosen, the choice of the parties shall not prejudice the application of provisions of the law of that other country which cannot be derogated from by agreement.[5] This provision limits the effect of the choice in what is, in reality an "internal" contractual situation apart from the choice of law.

S35–252 **Limitation on choice: Community law.** Where all the elements relevant to the situation at the time when the event giving use to the damage occurs are located in one or more Regulation States, the parties' choice of the law applicable other than that of a Regulation State shall not prejudice the

---

[95] Art.6(4). See above, para.S35–214.

[96] Art.8(3). See above, para.S35–229. For comment on Art.14, see de Boer (2007) 9 Yb. P.I.L. 19; Dickinson, Ch.13; Kadner Graziano in Ahern and Binchy, 113; Bertoli (2009) 92 *Rivista di diritto internationale* 697.

[97] Art.14(1)(a).

[98] Explanatory Memorandum, comment on Art.10 of the original proposal.

[99] Art.14(1)(b).

[1] Dickinson, paras 13.38–13.41.

[2] Art.14(1), final paragraph. This formula is similar to Art.3(1) of the Rome Convention: see main work, Rule 203(1). See also Art.3(1) of the the Rome I Regulation, above, entry at para.32–062.

[3] Rome Convention, Arts 3(4) and 8. See also Rome I Regulation, Arts 3(5) and 10.

[4] Dickinson, paras 13.11–13.19

[5] Art.14(2). This formula is similar to Art.3(3) of the Rome Convention and Art.3(3) of the the Rome I Regulation: see main work Rule 205(1).

application of Community law, where appropriate as implemented in the Regulation State of the forum, which cannot be derogated from by agreement.[6] The effect of this provision is that where the tort is only linked with Regulation States (excluding, for these purposes, Denmark[7]), the English forum must apply mandatory rules of Community law, as implemented in the United Kingdom where necessary, even if the law chosen by the parties is that of a non-Regulation State and even if that law would not otherwise apply to the non-contractual obligation in question.[8]

**Limitation on choice: other mandatory rules of the law of the forum.** Article 16 (headed "overriding mandatory provisions") provides that nothing in the Regulation shall restrict the application of the provisions of the law of the forum in a situation where they are mandatory irrespective of the law otherwise applicable to the non-contractual obligation.[9] Although Art.14 does not refer to Art.16, there is no reason to suspect that Art.16 cannot apply so as to restrict the effect of a contractual choice of law under Art.14 by reference to mandatory rules of English law. **S35–253**

## J. *Scope of the Law Applicable*

Article 15 sets out the various issues that will be governed by the law applicable to a non-contractual obligation arising out of a tort or delict, as determined by Arts 4–9 of the Rome II Regulation or, where relevant, the law applicable to pre-contractual liability as determined by Art.12 of the Regulation. The preamble to the Article states that the applicable law shall govern, in particular, the issues identified in Art.15 so that it is possible that other issues not so identified will also be governed by the applicable law. **S35–254**

**Basis and extent of liability etc.** Article 15(a) provides that the applicable law will govern the "basis and extent of liability, including the determination of persons who may be held liable for acts performed by them". Thus the standard of liability (whether strict or based on fault), the meaning of fault, including the question whether an omission can amount to fault, causation, the identification of the defendant or defendants and possibly the division of liability between joint tortfeasors will be governed by the applicable law.[10] **S35–255**

---

6 Art.14(3). *cf.* the Rome I Regulation, Art.3(4), above, entry at para.32–132.

7 Above, para.S35–168. *Cf.* Rome I Regulation, Art.1(4).

8 An example might be a choice of the law of a country where the standard of liability in product liability cases was lower than that imposed by Consumer Protection Act 1987, implementing in the United Kingdom, Council Directive, 85/374/EEC on the approximation of laws, regulations and administrative provisions of the Member States concerning liability for defective products, above, para.S35–202.

9 See, further, below, para.S35–272.

10 See Explanatory Memorandum, comment on Art.11(a) of the original proposal. It is possible, however, that division of liability between joint tortfeasors properly falls within Art.15(b) ("division of liability") but this makes little difference since "division of liability" is also governed by the applicable law by virtue of Art.15(b). Contribution between persons jointly liable, where one has satisfied the claim, is dealt with separately by Art.20 (see below, para.S35–267).

S35–256 **Grounds for exemption from liability etc.** The applicable law will also govern "the grounds for exemption from liability, any limitation of liability and any division of liability".[11] Thus whether there is a defence to liability,[12] whether liability is limited and (if the matter does not fall within Art.15(a) or Art.20)[13] apportionment of liability between joint tortfeasors will be governed by the applicable law. More particularly, it has been suggested that questions such as the effect of *force majeure*, necessity, third party fault, and fault by the victim fall within Art.15(b).[14] It has also been suggested that Art.15(b) will cover the question of whether actions in tort between spouses are permitted.[15]

S35–257 **Existence, nature and extent of damage etc.** Article 15(c) provides that "the existence, the nature and the assessment of damage or the remedy claimed" are matters governed by the law applicable to the tort. This will include: the nature of the available remedy[16]; questions of remoteness of damage; the duty, if any, to mitigate damage; the available heads of damage; and matters of assessment (quantification) of damages.[17]

S35–258 **Measures . . . to prevent . . . injury or damage etc.** Article 15(d) provides that the applicable law shall, "within the limits of powers conferred on the court by its procedural law", govern "the measures which a court may take to prevent or terminate injury or damage or to ensure the provision of compensation". This provision, it has been suggested, "refers to forms of compensation, such as whether the damage can be repaired by payment of damages, and ways of preventing or halting the damage, such as an interlocutory injunction, though without actually obliging the court to order measures which are unknown in the procedural law of the forum."[18] The wording of Art.15(d)

---

[11] Art.15(b).

[12] If the defence is based on a contract between the parties, it is suggested that the contract must be valid by the law which applies to it. The law governing the tort will determine whether the contract is capable of supplying a defence: see main work, para.35–048.

[13] Above, n.10, and below para.S35–267.

[14] Explanatory Memorandum, comment on Art.10(b) of the original proposal.

[15] *ibid.*

[16] The wording of Art.15(c) appears sufficiently broad to encompass questions concerning the availability of punitive or restitutionary damages for a tort/delict (see Dickinson, paras 14.20–14.23). See also Recital (32) (below, para.S35–273).

[17] This reverses the effect of *Boys v Chaplin* [1971] A.C. 356 in so far as it was held that assessment of damages was a procedural question governed by the law of the forum and the decision in *Harding v Wealands* [2006] UKHL 32, [2007] 2 A.C. 1, to the same effect: see Beaumont and Tang (2008) 12 Edin. L.R. 131; *Maher v Groupama Grand Est* [2009] EWHC 38 (QB), [2009] 1 W.L.R. 1752, at [16]; *Goh Suan Hee v Ter Cher Teck* [2009] SGCA 52, [2010] L.R.C. 480 (Sing. C.A.), at [18], [23]. It is possible that *Harding v Wealands* provides an example of "limitation of liability" falling under Art.15(b) but this makes no difference since that question is also governed by the applicable law. On assessment of damages, see also Recital (33), the status and effect of which is extremely obscure. It states that according "to the current national rules on compensation awarded to victims of road traffic accidents, when quantifying damages for personal injury in cases in which the accident takes place in a State other than that of the habitual residence of the victim, the court seised should take into account all the relevant actual circumstances of the specific victim, including in particular the actual losses and costs of after-care and medical attention." As to Recital (33), see Dickinson, paras 14.26–14.31; Rushworth in Ahern and Binchy, 207–210.

[18] Explanatory Memorandum, comment on Art.11(d) of the original proposal.

appears sufficiently broad to cover questions concerning the currency of any damages award and the court's powers to award interest.[19]

**Transfer of right to claim damages etc.** The applicable law will govern "the question whether a right to claim damages or a remedy may be transferred, including by inheritance".[20] The law governing the tort will determine whether a right of action may be assigned, although it is unclear whether the Rome Convention or the Rome II Regulation applies to this issue.[21] It will also determine whether an action may be brought by a victim's heir to obtain compensation for damage sustained by the victim.[22] S35–259

**Persons entitled to compensation etc.** Article 15(f) provides that the law applicable to the tort will determine "the persons entitled to compensation for damage sustained personally." This means that the applicable law will determine who may be a proper claimant. More particularly, it will determine whether a person other than the "direct" victim may be compensated, including (for example) whether a relative may obtain damages for pain and suffering consequent on bereavement as a result of the death of a "direct" victim of a tort, and whether a particular person is entitled to claim as a dependant consequent on the death of a "direct" victim of a tort.[23] S35–260

**Liability for acts of another person.** The applicable law will determine whether a person may be liable "for the acts of another person."[24] This provision clearly covers cases of vicarious liability of an employer for the torts of an employee. It is also said to cover the question of the liability of a parents for their children[25] and the liability of principals for their agents.[26] S35–261

**Prescription etc.** Finally, Art.15(h) provides that the applicable law governs "the manner in which an obligation may be extinguished and rules of prescription and limitation, including rules relating to the commencement, interruption and suspension of a period of prescription or limitation." Accordingly, for matters falling within its scope, the Rome II Regulation will S35–262

---

19 *cf.* main work, paras 33–395 to 33–400 and 36–082 *et seq.*; *Maher v Groupama Grand Est* [2009] EWHC 38 (QB), [2009] 1 W.L.R. 1752, and [2009] EWCA Civ 1191, [2010] 1 W.L.R. 1564 (entry at paras 33–392—33–393, above); *Knight v AXA Assurance* [2009] EWHC 1900 (QB) (interest).

20 Art.15(e).

21 See Dickinson, paras 14.38–14.40. Whichever view is correct, the law applicable to the tort governs relations between the assignor and the debtor: Explanatory Memorandum, comment on Art.11(f) of the original proposal; Rome Convention, Art.12(2); main work, Rule 126 (1)(b). The law applicable to the tort will not govern relations between assignor and assignee which will be a matter for the law applicable to the assignment: Rome Convention, Art.12(1); main work, Rule 126(1)(a). *cf.* the Rome I Regulation, Arts 14 and 15.

22 Explanatory Memorandum, *ibid.*

23 *ibid.*

24 Art.15(g).

25 Explanatory Memorandum, comment on Art.11(h) of the original proposal.

26 *ibid.* The law applicable to the tort only determines whether vicarious liability exists in respect of a particular relationship. Whether the particular relationship exists is a matter for the law governing that relationship. *Cf.* main work, para.35–039.

supersede the Foreign Limitation Periods Act 1984.[27] Article 15(h) will also cover, for example, the question whether non-contractual liability is discharged by death of the tortfeasor.[28]

## K. *Particular Issues*

**S35–263** Apart from identifying the scope of the applicable law, in Art.15, Chapter V of the Regulation also contains "common rules" which are applicable in respect of particular issues which may arise in connection with non-contractual obligations falling within the Regulation. The following paragraphs discuss these with particular reference to non-contractual obligations arising out of tort/delict or *culpa in contrahendo*.

**S35–264** **Rules of safety and conduct.** Article 17 of the Regulation provides that in "assessing the conduct of the person claimed to be liable, account shall be taken, as a matter of fact and in so far as is appropriate, of the rules of safety and conduct which were in force at the place and time of the event giving rise to liability". Attention has already been drawn to the potential impact of this provision in the context of liability for environmental damage.[29] Here, it may be added that, in general, the provision allows the court a degree of flexibility as to the role to be played by rules of safety and conduct, having regard to the particular facts ("account shall be taken . . . *in so far as is appropriate*"[30]). Further, these rules of safety and conduct do not affect the determination of the governing law: they merely, at least potentially, affect the way in which that law may be applied to the facts underlying the claim, as for example when assessing the seriousness of fault under the applicable law or the defendant's good or bad faith for the purposes of the measure of damages under the applicable law.[31]

**S35–265** **Direct action against insurer of person liable.** Article 18 of the Regulation contains a discrete rule which provides that the person who suffers damage "may bring his or her claim against the insurer of the person liable to provide compensation if the law applicable to the non-contractual obligation or the law applicable to the insurance contract so provides." Thus, the claimant has the choice between the law applicable to the tort or that applicable to the contract of insurance,[32] in deciding whether to bring a direct action against the insurer of the defendant. Presumably, the time at which, and the

---

[27] Foreign Limitation Periods Act 1984, s.7, inserted by the Law Applicable to Non-Contractual Obligations (England and Wales and Northern Ireland) Regulations 2008 (SI 2008/2986).
[28] *cf.* main work, para.35–042.
[29] Above, para.S35–227.
[30] Emphasis added.
[31] Explanatory Memorandum, comment on Art.13 of the original proposal.
[32] For the determination of the law applicable to an insurance contract, see main work, Rules 214–215. As to the position under the Rome I Regulation, see Art.7 of that Regulation, above, entry at paras 33R–136, 33R–158, 33R–189. See also *Maher v Groupama Grand Est* [2009] EWHC 38 (QB), [2009] 1 W.L.R. 1752, at [16] (*cf.* above, entry at para.35–044).

manner in which, the claimant must make the choice are matters for the procedural law of the forum.[33]

**Subrogation.** Article 19 of the Regulation makes provision for subrogation. "Where a person (the creditor) has a non-contractual claim upon another (the debtor), and a third person has a duty to satisfy the creditor, or has in fact satisfied the creditor in discharge of that duty, the law which governs the third person's duty to satisfy the creditor shall determine whether, and the extent to which, the third person is entitled to exercise against the debtor the rights which the creditor had against the debtor under the law governing their relationship."[34] Thus, where an insurer has paid or is under an obligation to indemnify an insured, the law applicable to the contract of insurance will determine whether and to what extent, the insurer is subrogated to the rights of the insured against the tortfeasor.[35] S35–266

**Multiple liability.** According to Art.20 of the Regulation if "a creditor has a claim against several debtors who are liable for the same claim and one of the debtors has already satisfied the claim in whole or in part, the question of that debtor's right to demand compensation from the other debtors shall be governed by the law applicable to that debtor's non-contractual obligation towards the creditor." Thus the law applicable to a non-contractual obligation arising out of a tort will govern whether and the extent to which the tortfeasor (at least if he has satisfied the claim) may claim contribution from other persons responsible.[36] Article 20 does not, on its face, address the situation in which a tortfeasor claims contribution from other persons responsible before he has satisfied the claim against him. In such cases, although the case for giving priority to the law applicable to the liability of the contribution claimant over other potentially applicable laws is weaker, the rule in Art.20 might be capable of being applied by analogy. Application of the law applicable to the contribution claimant's liability could also, potentially, be justified by treating such a claim as an aspect of "division of liability" within Art.15(b).[37] Possible alternative solutions in this situation include: (a) characterising the claim as involving a "non-contractual obligation arising out of unjust enrichment" within Art.10 of the Regulation[38]; or (b) treating the claim as one in tort (Arts 4–9) and as concerning the (indirect) consequences to the contribution claimant of the contribution defendant's tortious conduct towards the claimant in the main proceedings.[39] The need to choose between these S35–267

[33] See Explanatory Memorandum, comment on Art.14 of the original proposal. See above, para.S35–225.

[34] *cf.* Rome Convention, Art.13; main work, para.32–211. *cf.* the Rome I Regulation, Arts 14 and 15. See Dornis (2008) 4 J. Priv. Int. L. 237; Dickinson, paras 14.109–14.114.

[35] *cf.* main work, para.35–038.

[36] See Dornis (2008) J. Priv. Int. L. 237; Dickinson, paras.14.115–14.120. *cf.* main work, paras 34–011, 35–059.

[37] Above, para.S35–256.

[38] Cheshire, North and Fawcett, *Private International Law* (14th edn Fawcett and Carruthers, 2008), 793. *Cf.* main work, para.35–059.

[39] *cf. Hewden Tower Cranes Ltd v Wolffkran GmbH* [2007] EWHC 857 (TCC), [2007] 2 Lloyd's Rep 138, [30]–[32] (Judgments Regulation, Art.5(3)). See also Dickinson, para.14.119.

solutions may be sidestepped in English contribution proceedings if, consistently with earlier authority,[40] the right of contribution under the Civil Liability (Contribution) Act 1978 is accorded the status of an overriding mandatory provision under Art.16 of the Regulation.[41] It may, however, be doubted whether a statute such as the 1978 Act falls within the category of "overriding" provisions to which Art.16 applies.[42]

S35–268 **Formal validity.** "A unilateral act intended to have legal effect and relating to a non-contractual obligation shall be formally valid if it satisfies the formal requirements of the law governing the non-contractual obligation in question or the law of the country in which the act is performed."[43] It is not easy to identify situations arising out of tort where this provision will be relevant. The Explanatory Memorandum to the Commission's original proposal states that "although the concept of formal validity plays a minor role in the creation of non-contractual obligations, an obligation can well arise as a result of a unilateral act by one or other of the parties."[44] It is notable that no examples are given. Article 21 may be more likely, therefore, to apply in connection with formal requirements concerning the release of non-contractual liability.

S35–269 **Burden of proof.** Although the Regulation is expressed not to apply to "Evidence and procedure",[45] this is without prejudice to Art.22, headed "Burden of proof". According to Art.22(1), the law governing a non-contractual obligation "shall apply to the extent that, in matters of non-contractual obligations, it contains rules which raise presumptions of law or determine the burden of proof." Thus, if the applicable law contains, say, a presumption of contributory negligence which the claimant has to disprove, that presumption should be given effect.[46] Similarly, if the applicable law places the burden of disproving negligence on the defendant, as opposed to the position in English law where the burden of proving negligence lies on the claimant, then effect should be given to the rule concerning burden of proof contained in the applicable law.[47]

S35–270 **Acts intended to have legal effect.** Article 12(2) provides that acts "intended to have legal effect may be proved by any mode of proof recognised by the law of the forum or by any of the laws referred to in Art.21 under which

---

[40] Main work, para.35–059.
[41] Below, para.S35–272.
[42] *Ibid.*
[43] Art.21.
[44] Comment on Art.16 of the original proposal. Art.21 takes precedence over Art.1(3). See above, para.S35–186.
[45] See above, para.S35–186.
[46] See main work, para.35–062. *cf.* Rome Convention, Art.14(1); Rome I Regulation, Art.18 (1).
[47] *ibid.*

that act is formally valid, provided that such mode of proof can be administered by the forum".[48]

## L. *Overriding Mandatory Provisions and Public Policy*

Articles 16 and 26, respectively, make application of the law which governs the particular non-contractual obligation subject to overriding mandatory provisions of the law of the forum and to the operation of the public policy of the forum. **S35–271**

**Overriding mandatory provisions.** Article 16 provides that nothing in the Regulation "shall restrict the application of the provisions of the law of the forum in a situation where they are mandatory irrespective of the law otherwise applicable to the non-contractual obligation."[49] It will be noted that Art.16 does not refer to all rules which cannot be derogated from but only to rules which apply irrespective of the law applicable to the non-contractual obligation, i.e. "overriding" provisions.[50] Further, it may be that in the context of the Regulation, the European Court will seek to police the outer limits of this category of rules, and the circumstances in which they may be deployed by Member State courts.[51] Finally, in contrast to the Commission's original proposal,[52] Art.16 makes no provision for account to be taken of the mandatory rules of a third country with which the situation is closely connected. **S35–272**

**Public policy.** The potential application of the public policy of the forum is secured by Art.26 which stipulates that "application of a provision of the law of any country specified by this Regulation may be refused only if such application is manifestly incompatible with the public policy (*ordre public*) of the forum".[53] It is clear from this formulation that public policy is only to be invoked in exceptional cases.[54] Normally, the content of public policy will depend on English law,[55] but it may be that in the context of the Regulation, the European Court will seek to police the outer limits of the concept.[56] Although there is no explicit reference in the text of the Regulation[57] Recital (32) to the Regulation envisages the possibility that a law designated by the **S35–273**

---

[48] *cf.* Rome Convention, Art.14(2); main work, para.32–179; Rome I Regulation, Art.18(2).

[49] *cf.* Rome Convention, Art.7(2); main work, Rule 205(2). See Recital (32). *cf.* the Rome I Regulation, Art.9, above, entry at para.32–132.

[50] *cf.* main work, paras 1–053 *et seq.*; para.35–121.

[51] See Dickinson, paras 15.15–15.21.

[52] *cf.* Art.12(1) of the Commission's original proposal.

[53] *cf.* Rome Convention, Art.16; main work, Rule 210. See, to the same effect, the Rome I Regulation, Art.21.

[54] Recital (32). See also Recital (37) to the Rome I Regulation.

[55] See main work, Rule 2, and para.35–116.

[56] *cf.* Case C–7/98 *Krombach v Bamberski* [2000] E.C.R. I–1935, [2001] Q.B. 709; Case C–341/04 *Eurofood IFSC Ltd* [2006] E.C.R. I–3813, [2006] Ch. 508; Case C–394/07, *Gambazzi v DaimlerChrysler Canada Inc.* [2009] E.C.R. I–2563; Case C–420/07 *Apostolides v Orams* [2009] E.C.R. I–3571.

[57] *cf.* Art.24 of the Commission's original proposal, criticised in HL Paper 66 (2004), paras 164–170.

Regulation "which would have the effect of causing non-compensatory damages of an excessive nature to be awarded may, depending on the circumstances of the case and the legal order of the Member State of the court seised, be regarded as being contrary to the public policy (*ordre public*) of the forum". Whether this observation is likely to influence English courts must be speculative.[58]

[58] It seems likely that English courts will give effect to foreign laws permitting non-compensatory damages where such an award would be available in a domestic case: see HL Paper 66 (2004), para.168; main work, para.35–117. See, more generally, Symeonides (2003) 5 Yb. P.I.L. 1; Rodriguez Pineau (2009) 5 J. Priv. Int. L. 311, 330–334.

# CHAPTER 36

# FOREIGN CURRENCY OBLIGATIONS

## 1. THE MONEY OF ACCOUNT

NOTE 1. Add: Black, *Foreign Currency Claims in the Conflict of Laws* (2010). **36R–001**

NOTE 2. Add: *Addax Bank BSC v Wellesley Partners LLP* [2010] EWHC 1904 (QB).

NOTE 28. Slovenia, Cyprus, Malta and Slovakia are the latest Member States of the European Union to adopt the Euro as their *lex monetae*: Council Decision (EC) 495/06 ([2006] O.J. L195/25) (Slovenia); Council Decision (EC) 503/07 ([2007] O.J. L186/29) (Cyprus); Council Decision (EC) 504/07 ([2007] O.J. L186/32) (Malta); Council Decision (EC) 608/08 ([2008] O.J. L195/24) (Slovakia). **36–011**

Council Regulation (EC) 974/98 is further amended by Council Regulation (EC) 2169/05 ([2005] O.J. L346/1).

NOTE 29. The effective date as regards Slovenia is January 1, 2007: Council Decision (EC) 495/06 ([2006] O.J. L195/25). The effective date as regards Cyprus and Malta is January 1, 2008: Council Decision (EC) 503/07 ([2007] O.J. L186/29); Council Decision (EC) 504/07 ([2007] O.J. L186/32). The effective date as regards Slovakia is January 1, 2009: Council Decision (EC) 608/08 ([2008] O.J. L195/24). **36–012**

NOTE 30. The rate of exchange between the Slovenian tolar and the Euro was fixed irrevocably with effect from January 1, 2007: Council Regulation (EC) 1086/06 ([2006] O.J. L195/1). The rate of exchange between the Maltese lira and the Euro was fixed irrevocably with effect from January 1, 2008: Council Regulation (EC) 1134/07 ([2007] O.J. L256/1). The rate of exchange between the Cyprus pound and the Euro was fixed irrevocably with effect from January 1, 2008: Council Regulation (EC) 1135/07 ([2007] O.J. L256/2). The rate of exchange between the Slovak koruna and the Euro was fixed irrevocably with effect from January 1, 2009: Council Regulation (EC) 694/08 ([2008] O.J. L195/3).

NOTE 32. The cash changeover date (the date by which the previous currencies ceased to be legal tender) was subsequently fixed at January 1, 2002 for all

Member States participating in the Euro (except as set out below): Council Regulation (EC) 2169/05 ([2005] O.J. L346/1). The cash changeover date for Slovenia was fixed at January 1, 2007: Council Regulation (EC) 1647/06 ([2006] O.J. L309/2). The cash changeover date for Cyprus and Malta was fixed at January 1, 2008: Council Regulation (EC) 835/07 ([2007] O.J. L186/1); Council Regulation (EC) 836/07 ([2007] O.J. L186/3). The cash changeover date for Slovakia was fixed at January 1, 2009: Council Regulation (EC) 693/08 ([2008] O.J. L195/1).

NOTE 33. The European Central Bank has issued guidelines to provide for the national central banks of future participating Member States to borrow Euro banknotes and coins from the Eurosystem. The purpose of the guidelines is to permit the frontloading of such banknotes and coins in order to facilitate a smooth cash changeover: European Central Bank Decision ECB/2006/9 ([2006] O.J. L207/39), as amended by ECB/2008/4 ([2008] O.J. L176/16). The Bank has also issued guidelines to ensure that national central banks make provision for the exchange of bank notes prior to the cash changeover date at par value: European Central Bank Decision ECB/2006/10 ([2006] O.J. L215/44).

**36–017** NOTE 54. Add: *Karafarin Bank v Dara (No 2)* [2009] EWHC 3265 (Comm.), [2010] 1 Lloyd's Rep. 236.

## 4. JUDGMENTS IN FOREIGN CURRENCY

**36R–081** NOTE 86. Add: Black, *Foreign Currency Claims in the Conflict of Laws* (2010).

**36–086** In *MK v JK (No.3)* [2006] IESC 4, [2006] I.R. 283, the Irish Supreme Court considered that, in matrimonial proceedings and in the maintenance of spouses and children, the trial judge had a discretion as to whether to award judgment in the currency of the payer or the payee. However, it would normally be proper to express an award in the currency of the country in which the payee resides, so that the wife or children, as the case may be, were not exposed to the risk of currency fluctuations.

**36–088** In the case of a bill of exchange, promissory note or cheque, the question whether the claimant is entitled to interest or instead to damages for late payment will be determined by the law applicable to the contract and, in general, awarded at the rate or in the amount applicable to the currency in question: *Karafarin Bank v Dara (No 2)* [2009] EWHC 3265 (Comm.), [2010] 1 Lloyd's Rep. 236.

**36–091** Section 2(5)(a) of the Companies Act 1985 has not been repeated in the Companies Act 2006. Instead, the point dealt with in para.36–091 is now the subject of express statutory provision. Section 542(3) of the 2006 Act provides: "Shares in a limited company having a share capital may be denominated in any currency, and different classes of shares may be denominated in different currencies." The subsection contains a cross reference to s.765, which makes provision in relation to the authorised minimum share capital of public companies. Section 765 provides that the initial requirement for a public company to have allotted a minimum share capital must be met either in sterling or in euros (but not in a combination of both, or in any other currency). This provision does not affect the right of a public company to denominate other shares in different classes in other currencies (as in the example given in the text).

NOTE 31. Applied in the case of a scheme of arrangement in *Re Telewest Communications Plc* [2004] EWHC 924 (Ch.). **36–094**

# Appendix 1

## REGULATION (EC) No 864/2007 OF THE EUROPEAN PARLIAMENT AND OF THE COUNCIL

### of 11 July 2007

### on the law applicable to non-contractual obligations (Rome II)

THE EUROPEAN PARLIAMENT AND THE COUNCIL OF THE EUROPEAN UNION,

Having regard to the Treaty establishing the European Community, and in particular Articles 61(c) and 67 thereof,

Having regard to the proposal from the Commission,

Having regard to the opinion of the European Economic and Social Committee ([1]),

Acting in accordance with the procedure laid down in Article 251 of the Treaty in the light of the joint text approved by the Conciliation Committee on 25 June 2007 ([2]),

Whereas:

(1) The Community has set itself the objective of maintaining and developing an area of freedom, security and justice. For the progressive establishment of such an area, the Community is to adopt measures relating to judicial cooperation in civil matters with a cross-border impact to the extent necessary for the proper functioning of the internal market.

(2) According to Article 65(b) of the Treaty, these measures are to include those promoting the compatibility of the rules applicable in the Member States concerning the conflict of laws and of jurisdiction.

(3) The European Council meeting in Tampere on 15 and 16 October 1999 endorsed the principle of mutual recognition of judgments and other decisions of judicial authorities as the cornerstone of judicial cooperation in civil matters and invited the Council and the Commission to adopt a programme of measures to implement the principle of mutual recognition.

(4) On 30 November 2000, the Council adopted a joint Commission and Council programme of measures for implementation of the principle of mutual recognition of decisions in civil and commercial matters ([3]). The programme identifies measures relating to the harmonisation of conflict-of-law rules as those facilitating the mutual recognition of judgments.

([1]) OJ C 241, 28.9.2004, p. 1.

([2]) Opinion of the European Parliament of 6 July 2005 (OJ C 157 E, 6.7.2006, p. 371), Council Common Position of 25 September 2006 (OJ C 289 E, 28.11.2006, p. 68) and Position of the European Parliament of 18 January 2007 (not yet published in the Official Journal). European Parliament Legislative Resolution of 10 July 2007 and Council Decision of 28 June 2007.

([3]) OJ C 12, 15.1.2001, p. 1.

(5) The Hague Programme ([4]), adopted by the European Council on 5 November 2004, called for work to be pursued actively on the rules of conflict of laws regarding non-contractual obligations (Rome II).

(6) The proper functioning of the internal market creates a need, in order to improve the predictability of the outcome of litigation, certainty as to the law applicable and the free movement of judgments, for the conflict-of-law rules in the Member States to designate the same national law irrespective of the country of the court in which an action is brought.

(7) The substantive scope and the provisions of this Regulation should be consistent with Council Regulation (EC) No 44/2001 of 22 December 2000 on jurisdiction and the recognition and enforcement of judgments in civil and commercial matters ([5]) (Brussels I) and the instruments dealing with the law applicable to contractual obligations.

(8) This Regulation should apply irrespective of the nature of the court or tribunal seised.

(9) Claims arising out of *acta iure imperii* should include claims against officials who act on behalf of the State and liability for acts of public authorities, including liability of publicly appointed office-holders. Therefore, these matters should be excluded from the scope of this Regulation.

(10) Family relationships should cover parentage, marriage, affinity and collateral relatives. The reference in Article 1(2) to relationships having comparable effects to marriage and other family relationships should be interpreted in accordance with the law of the Member State in which the court is seised.

(11) The concept of a non-contractual obligation varies from one Member State to another. Therefore for the purposes of this Regulation non-contractual obligation should be understood as an autonomous concept. The conflict-of-law rules set out in this Regulation should also cover non-contractual obligations arising out of strict liability.

(12) The law applicable should also govern the question of the capacity to incur liability in tort/delict.

([4]) OJ C 53, 3.3.2005, p. 1.

([5]) OJ L 12, 16.1.2001, p. 1. Regulation as last amended by Regulation (EC) No 1791/2006 (OJ L 363, 20.12.2006, p. 1).

(13) Uniform rules applied irrespective of the law they designate may avert the risk of distortions of competition between Community litigants.

(14) The requirement of legal certainty and the need to do justice in individual cases are essential elements of an area of justice. This Regulation provides for the connecting factors which are the most appropriate to achieve these objectives. Therefore, this Regulation provides for a general rule but also for specific rules and, in certain provisions, for an 'escape clause' which allows a departure from these rules where it is clear from all the circumstances of the case that the tort/delict is manifestly more closely connected with another country. This set of rules thus creates a flexible framework of conflict-of-law rules. Equally, it enables the court seised to treat individual cases in an appropriate manner.

(15) The principle of the *lex loci delicti commissi* is the basic solution for non-contractual obligations in virtually all the Member States, but the practical application of the principle where the component factors of the case are spread over several countries varies. This situation engenders uncertainty as to the law applicable.

(16) Uniform rules should enhance the foreseeability of court decisions and ensure a reasonable balance between the interests of the person claimed to be liable and the person who has sustained damage. A connection with the country where the direct damage occurred (*lex loci damni*) strikes a fair balance between the interests of the person claimed to be liable and the person sustaining the damage, and also reflects the modern approach to civil liability and the development of systems of strict liability.

(17) The law applicable should be determined on the basis of where the damage occurs, regardless of the country or countries in which the indirect consequences could occur. Accordingly, in cases of personal injury or damage to property, the country in which the damage occurs should be the country where the injury was sustained or the property was damaged respectively.

(18) The general rule in this Regulation should be the *lex loci damni* provided for in Article 4(1). Article 4(2) should be seen as an exception to this general principle, creating a special connection where the parties have their habitual residence in the same country. Article 4(3) should be understood as an 'escape clause' from Article 4(1) and (2), where it is clear from all the circumstances of the case that the tort/delict is manifestly more closely connected with another country.

(19) Specific rules should be laid down for special torts/delicts where the general rule does not allow a reasonable balance to be struck between the interests at stake.

(20) The conflict-of-law rule in matters of product liability should meet the objectives of fairly spreading the risks inherent in a modern high-technology society, protecting consumers' health, stimulating innovation, securing undistorted competition and facilitating trade. Creation of a cascade system of connecting factors, together with a foreseeability clause, is a balanced solution in regard to these objectives. The first element to be taken into account is the law of the country in which the person sustaining the damage had his or her habitual residence when the damage occurred, if the product was marketed in that country. The other elements of the cascade are triggered if the product was not marketed in that country, without prejudice to Article 4(2) and to the possibility of a manifestly closer connection to another country.

(21) The special rule in Article 6 is not an exception to the general rule in Article 4(1) but rather a clarification of it. In matters of unfair competition, the conflict-of-law rule should protect competitors, consumers and the general public and ensure that the market economy functions properly. The connection to the law of the country where competitive relations or the collective interests of consumers are, or are likely to be, affected generally satisfies these objectives.

(22) The non-contractual obligations arising out of restrictions of competition in Article 6(3) should cover infringements of both national and Community competition law. The law applicable to such non-contractual obligations should be the law of the country where the market is, or is likely to be, affected. In cases where the market is, or is likely to be, affected in more than one country, the claimant should be able in certain circumstances to choose to base his or her claim on the law of the court seised.

(23) For the purposes of this Regulation, the concept of restriction of competition should cover prohibitions on agreements between undertakings, decisions by associations of undertakings and concerted practices which have as their object or effect the prevention, restriction or distortion of competition within a Member State or within the internal market, as well as prohibitions on the abuse of a dominant position within a Member State or within the internal market, where such agreements, decisions, concerted practices or abuses are prohibited by Articles 81 and 82 of the Treaty or by the law of a Member State.

(24) 'Environmental damage' should be understood as meaning adverse change in a natural resource, such as water, land or air, impairment of a function performed by that resource for the benefit of another natural resource or the public, or impairment of the variability among living organisms.

(25) Regarding environmental damage, Article 174 of the Treaty, which provides that there should be a high level of protection based on the precautionary principle and the principle that preventive action should be taken, the principle of priority for corrective action at source and the principle that the polluter pays, fully justifies the use of the principle of discriminating in favour of the person sustaining the damage. The question of when the person seeking compensation can make the choice of the law applicable should be determined in accordance with the law of the Member State in which the court is seised.

(26) Regarding infringements of intellectual property rights, the universally acknowledged principle of the *lex loci protectionis* should be preserved. For the purposes of this Regulation, the term 'intellectual property rights' should be interpreted as meaning, for instance, copyright, related rights, the *sui generis* right for the protection of databases and industrial property rights.

(27) The exact concept of industrial action, such as strike action or lock-out, varies from one Member State to another and is governed by each Member State's internal rules. Therefore, this Regulation assumes as a general principle that the law of the country where the industrial action was taken should apply, with the aim of protecting the rights and obligations of workers and employers.

(28) The special rule on industrial action in Article 9 is without prejudice to the conditions relating to the exercise of such action in accordance with national law and without prejudice to the legal status of trade unions or of the representative organisations of workers as provided for in the law of the Member States.

(29) Provision should be made for special rules where damage is caused by an act other than a tort/delict, such as unjust enrichment, *negotiorum gestio* and *culpa in contrahendo*.

(30) *Culpa in contrahendo* for the purposes of this Regulation is an autonomous concept and should not necessarily be interpreted within the meaning of national law. It should include the violation of the duty of disclosure and the breakdown of contractual negotiations. Article 12 covers only non-contractual obligations presenting a direct link with the dealings prior to the conclusion of a contract. This means that if, while a contract is being negotiated, a person suffers personal injury, Article 4 or other relevant provisions of this Regulation should apply.

(31) To respect the principle of party autonomy and to enhance legal certainty, the parties should be allowed to make a choice as to the law applicable to a non-contractual obligation. This choice should be expressed or demonstrated with reasonable certainty by the circumstances of the case. Where establishing the existence of the agreement, the court has to respect the intentions of the parties. Protection should be given to weaker parties by imposing certain conditions on the choice.

(32) Considerations of public interest justify giving the courts of the Member States the possibility, in exceptional circumstances, of applying exceptions based on public policy and overriding mandatory provisions. In particular, the application of a provision of the law designated by this Regulation which would have the effect of causing non-compensatory exemplary or punitive damages of an excessive nature to be awarded may, depending on the circumstances of the case and the legal order of the Member State of the court seised, be regarded as being contrary to the public policy (*ordre public*) of the forum.

(33) According to the current national rules on compensation awarded to victims of road traffic accidents, when quantifying damages for personal injury in cases in which the accident takes place in a State other than that of the habitual residence of the victim, the court seised should take into account all the relevant actual circumstances of the specific victim, including in particular the actual losses and costs of after-care and medical attention.

(34) In order to strike a reasonable balance between the parties, account must be taken, in so far as appropriate, of the rules of safety and conduct in operation in the country in which the harmful act was committed, even where the non-contractual obligation is governed by the law of another country. The term 'rules of safety and conduct' should be interpreted as referring to all regulations having any relation to safety and conduct, including, for example, road safety rules in the case of an accident.

(35) A situation where conflict-of-law rules are dispersed among several instruments and where there are differences between those rules should be avoided. This Regulation, however, does not exclude the possibility of inclusion of conflict-of-law rules relating to non-contractual obligations in provisions of Community law with regard to particular matters.

This Regulation should not prejudice the application of other instruments laying down provisions designed to contribute to the proper functioning of the internal market in so far as they cannot be applied in conjunction with the law designated by the rules of this Regulation. The application of provisions of the applicable law designated by the rules of this Regulation should not restrict the free movement of goods and services as regulated by Community instruments, such as Directive 2000/31/EC of the European Parliament and of the Council of 8 June 2000 on certain legal aspects of information society services, in particular electronic commerce, in the Internal Market (Directive on electronic commerce) ([1]).

([1]) OJ L 178, 17.7.2000, p. 1.

(36) Respect for international commitments entered into by the Member States means that this Regulation should not affect international conventions to which one or more Member States are parties at the time this Regulation is adopted. To make the rules more accessible, the Commission should publish the list of the relevant conventions in the *Official Journal of the European Union* on the basis of information supplied by the Member States.

(37) The Commission will make a proposal to the European Parliament and the Council concerning the procedures and conditions according to which Member States would be entitled to negotiate and conclude on their own behalf agreements with third countries in individual and exceptional cases, concerning sectoral matters, containing provisions on the law applicable to non-contractual obligations.

(38) Since the objective of this Regulation cannot be sufficiently achieved by the Member States, and can therefore, by reason of the scale and effects of this Regulation, be better achieved at Community level, the Community may adopt measures, in accordance with the principle of subsidiarity set out in Article 5 of the Treaty. In accordance with the principle of proportionality set out in that Article, this Regulation does not go beyond what is necessary to attain that objective.

(39) In accordance with Article 3 of the Protocol on the position of the United Kingdom and Ireland annexed to the Treaty on European Union and to the Treaty establishing the European Community, the United Kingdom and Ireland are taking part in the adoption and application of this Regulation.

(40) In accordance with Articles 1 and 2 of the Protocol on the position of Denmark, annexed to the Treaty on European Union and to the Treaty establishing the European Community, Denmark does not take part in the adoption of this Regulation, and is not bound by it or subject to its application,

HAVE ADOPTED THIS REGULATION:

CHAPTER I

**SCOPE**

*Article 1*

**Scope**

1. This Regulation shall apply, in situations involving a conflict of laws, to non-contractual obligations in civil and commercial matters. It shall not apply, in particular, to revenue, customs or administrative matters or to the liability of the State for acts and omissions in the exercise of State authority (*acta iure imperii*).

2. The following shall be excluded from the scope of this Regulation:

(a) non-contractual obligations arising out of family relationships and relationships deemed by the law applicable to such relationships to have comparable effects including maintenance obligations;

(b) non-contractual obligations arising out of matrimonial property regimes, property regimes of relationships deemed by the law applicable to such relationships to have comparable effects to marriage, and wills and succession;

(c) non-contractual obligations arising under bills of exchange, cheques and promissory notes and other negotiable instruments to the extent that the obligations under such other negotiable instruments arise out of their negotiable character;

(d) non-contractual obligations arising out of the law of companies and other bodies corporate or unincorporated regarding matters such as the creation, by registration or otherwise, legal capacity, internal organisation or winding-up of companies and other bodies corporate or unincorporated, the personal liability of officers and members as such for the obligations of the company or body and the personal liability of auditors to a company or to its members in the statutory audits of accounting documents;

(e) non-contractual obligations arising out of the relations between the settlors, trustees and beneficiaries of a trust created voluntarily;

(f) non-contractual obligations arising out of nuclear damage;

(g) non-contractual obligations arising out of violations of privacy and rights relating to personality, including defamation.

3. This Regulation shall not apply to evidence and procedure, without prejudice to Articles 21 and 22.

4. For the purposes of this Regulation, 'Member State' shall mean any Member State other than Denmark.

*Article 2*

**Non-contractual obligations**

1. For the purposes of this Regulation, damage shall cover any consequence arising out of tort/delict, unjust enrichment, *negotiorum gestio* or *culpa in contrahendo*.

2. This Regulation shall apply also to non-contractual obligations that are likely to arise.

3. Any reference in this Regulation to:

(a) an event giving rise to damage shall include events giving rise to damage that are likely to occur; and

(b) damage shall include damage that is likely to occur.

*Article 3*

**Universal application**

Any law specified by this Regulation shall be applied whether or not it is the law of a Member State.

CHAPTER II

**TORTS/DELICTS**

*Article 4*

**General rule**

1. Unless otherwise provided for in this Regulation, the law applicable to a non-contractual obligation arising out of a tort/delict shall be the law of the country in which the damage occurs irrespective of the country in which the event giving rise to the damage occurred and irrespective of the country or countries in which the indirect consequences of that event occur.

2. However, where the person claimed to be liable and the person sustaining damage both have their habitual residence in the same country at the time when the damage occurs, the law of that country shall apply.

3. Where it is clear from all the circumstances of the case that the tort/delict is manifestly more closely connected with a country other than that indicated in paragraphs 1 or 2, the law of that other country shall apply. A manifestly closer connection with another country might be based in particular on a pre-existing relationship between the parties, such as a contract, that is closely connected with the tort/delict in question.

*Article 5*

**Product liability**

1. Without prejudice to Article 4(2), the law applicable to a non-contractual obligation arising out of damage caused by a product shall be:

(a) the law of the country in which the person sustaining the damage had his or her habitual residence when the damage occurred, if the product was marketed in that country; or, failing that,

(b) the law of the country in which the product was acquired, if the product was marketed in that country; or, failing that,

(c) the law of the country in which the damage occurred, if the product was marketed in that country.

However, the law applicable shall be the law of the country in which the person claimed to be liable is habitually resident if he or she could not reasonably foresee the marketing of the product, or a product of the same type, in the country the law of which is applicable under (a), (b) or (c).

2. Where it is clear from all the circumstances of the case that the tort/delict is manifestly more closely connected with a country other than that indicated in paragraph 1, the law of that other country shall apply. A manifestly closer connection with another country might be based in particular on a pre-existing relationship between the parties, such as a contract, that is closely connected with the tort/delict in question.

*Article 6*

**Unfair competition and acts restricting free competition**

1. The law applicable to a non-contractual obligation arising out of an act of unfair competition shall be the law of the country where competitive relations or the collective interests of consumers are, or are likely to be, affected.

2. Where an act of unfair competition affects exclusively the interests of a specific competitor, Article 4 shall apply.

3. (a) The law applicable to a non-contractual obligation arising out of a restriction of competition shall be the law of the country where the market is, or is likely to be, affected.

(b) When the market is, or is likely to be, affected in more than one country, the person seeking compensation for damage who sues in the court of the domicile of the defendant, may instead choose to base his or her claim on the law of the court seised, provided that the market in that Member State is amongst those directly and substantially affected by the restriction of competition out of which the non-contractual obligation on which the claim is based arises; where the claimant sues, in accordance with the applicable rules on jurisdiction, more than one defendant in that court, he or she can only choose to base his or her claim on the law of that court if the restriction of competition on which the claim against each of these defendants relies directly and substantially affects also the market in the Member State of that court.

4. The law applicable under this Article may not be derogated from by an agreement pursuant to Article 14.

*Article 7*

**Environmental damage**

The law applicable to a non-contractual obligation arising out of environmental damage or damage sustained by persons or property as a result of such damage shall be the law determined pursuant to Article 4(1), unless the person seeking compensation for damage chooses to base his or her claim on the law of the country in which the event giving rise to the damage occurred.

*Article 8*

**Infringement of intellectual property rights**

1. The law applicable to a non-contractual obligation arising from an infringement of an intellectual property right shall be the law of the country for which protection is claimed.

2. In the case of a non-contractual obligation arising from an infringement of a unitary Community intellectual property right, the law applicable shall, for any question that is not governed by the relevant Community instrument, be the law of the country in which the act of infringement was committed.

3. The law applicable under this Article may not be derogated from by an agreement pursuant to Article 14.

*Article 9*

**Industrial action**

Without prejudice to Article 4(2), the law applicable to a non-contractual obligation in respect of the liability of a person in the capacity of a worker or an employer or the organisations representing their professional interests for damages caused by an industrial action, pending or carried out, shall be the law of the country where the action is to be, or has been, taken.

CHAPTER III

**UNJUST ENRICHMENT, *NEGOTIORUM GESTIO* AND *CULPA IN CONTRAHENDO***

*Article 10*

**Unjust enrichment**

1. If a non-contractual obligation arising out of unjust enrichment, including payment of amounts wrongly received, concerns a relationship existing between the parties, such as one arising out of a contract or a tort/delict, that is closely connected with that unjust enrichment, it shall be governed by the law that governs that relationship.

2. Where the law applicable cannot be determined on the basis of paragraph 1 and the parties have their habitual residence in the same country when the event giving rise to unjust enrichment occurs, the law of that country shall apply.

3. Where the law applicable cannot be determined on the basis of paragraphs 1 or 2, it shall be the law of the country in which the unjust enrichment took place.

4. Where it is clear from all the circumstances of the case that the non-contractual obligation arising out of unjust enrichment is manifestly more closely connected with a country other than that indicated in paragraphs 1, 2 and 3, the law of that other country shall apply.

*Article 11*

***Negotiorum gestio***

1. If a non-contractual obligation arising out of an act performed without due authority in connection with the affairs of another person concerns a relationship existing between the parties, such as one arising out of a contract or a tort/delict, that is closely connected with that non-contractual obligation, it shall be governed by the law that governs that relationship.

2. Where the law applicable cannot be determined on the basis of paragraph 1, and the parties have their habitual residence in the same country when the event giving rise to the damage occurs, the law of that country shall apply.

3. Where the law applicable cannot be determined on the basis of paragraphs 1 or 2, it shall be the law of the country in which the act was performed.

4. Where it is clear from all the circumstances of the case that the non-contractual obligation arising out of an act performed without due authority in connection with the affairs of another person is manifestly more closely connected with a country other than that indicated in paragraphs 1, 2 and 3, the law of that other country shall apply.

*Article 12*

***Culpa in contrahendo***

1. The law applicable to a non-contractual obligation arising out of dealings prior to the conclusion of a contract, regardless of whether the contract was actually concluded or not, shall be the law that applies to the contract or that would have been applicable to it had it been entered into.

2. Where the law applicable cannot be determined on the basis of paragraph 1, it shall be:

(a) the law of the country in which the damage occurs, irrespective of the country in which the event giving rise to the damage occurred and irrespective of the country or countries in which the indirect consequences of that event occurred; or

(b) where the parties have their habitual residence in the same country at the time when the event giving rise to the damage occurs, the law of that country; or

(c) where it is clear from all the circumstances of the case that the non-contractual obligation arising out of dealings prior to the conclusion of a contract is manifestly more closely connected with a country other than that indicated in points (a) and (b), the law of that other country.

*Article 13*

**Applicability of Article 8**

For the purposes of this Chapter, Article 8 shall apply to non-contractual obligations arising from an infringement of an intellectual property right.

CHAPTER IV

**FREEDOM OF CHOICE**

*Article 14*

**Freedom of choice**

1. The parties may agree to submit non-contractual obligations to the law of their choice:

(a) by an agreement entered into after the event giving rise to the damage occurred;

or

(b) where all the parties are pursuing a commercial activity, also by an agreement freely negotiated before the event giving rise to the damage occurred.

The choice shall be expressed or demonstrated with reasonable certainty by the circumstances of the case and shall not prejudice the rights of third parties.

2. Where all the elements relevant to the situation at the time when the event giving rise to the damage occurs are located in a country other than the country whose law has been chosen, the choice of the parties shall not prejudice the application of provisions of the law of that other country which cannot be derogated from by agreement.

3. Where all the elements relevant to the situation at the time when the event giving rise to the damage occurs are located in one or more of the Member States, the parties' choice of the law applicable other than that of a Member State shall not prejudice the application of provisions of Community law, where appropriate as implemented in the Member State of the forum, which cannot be derogated from by agreement.

CHAPTER V

**COMMON RULES**

*Article 15*

**Scope of the law applicable**

The law applicable to non-contractual obligations under this Regulation shall govern in particular:

(a) the basis and extent of liability, including the determination of persons who may be held liable for acts performed by them;

(b) the grounds for exemption from liability, any limitation of liability and any division of liability;

(c) the existence, the nature and the assessment of damage or the remedy claimed;

(d) within the limits of powers conferred on the court by its procedural law, the measures which a court may take to prevent or terminate injury or damage or to ensure the provision of compensation;

(e) the question whether a right to claim damages or a remedy may be transferred, including by inheritance;

(f) persons entitled to compensation for damage sustained personally;

(g) liability for the acts of another person;

(h) the manner in which an obligation may be extinguished and rules of prescription and limitation, including rules relating to the commencement, interruption and suspension of a period of prescription or limitation.

*Article 16*

**Overriding mandatory provisions**

Nothing in this Regulation shall restrict the application of the provisions of the law of the forum in a situation where they are mandatory irrespective of the law otherwise applicable to the non-contractual obligation.

*Article 17*

**Rules of safety and conduct**

In assessing the conduct of the person claimed to be liable, account shall be taken, as a matter of fact and in so far as is appropriate, of the rules of safety and conduct which were in force at the place and time of the event giving rise to the liability.

*Article 18*

**Direct action against the insurer of the person liable**

The person having suffered damage may bring his or her claim directly against the insurer of the person liable to provide compensation if the law applicable to the non-contractual obligation or the law applicable to the insurance contract so provides.

*Article 19*

**Subrogation**

Where a person (the creditor) has a non-contractual claim upon another (the debtor), and a third person has a duty to satisfy the creditor, or has in fact satisfied the creditor in discharge of that duty, the law which governs the third person's duty to satisfy the creditor shall determine whether, and the extent to which, the third person is entitled to exercise against the debtor the rights which the creditor had against the debtor under the law governing their relationship.

*Article 20*

**Multiple liability**

If a creditor has a claim against several debtors who are liable for the same claim, and one of the debtors has already satisfied the claim in whole or in part, the question of that debtor's right to demand compensation from the other debtors shall be governed by the law applicable to that debtor's non-contractual obligation towards the creditor.

*Article 21*

**Formal validity**

A unilateral act intended to have legal effect and relating to a non-contractual obligation shall be formally valid if it satisfies the formal requirements of the law governing the non-contractual obligation in question or the law of the country in which the act is performed.

*Article 22*

**Burden of proof**

1. The law governing a non-contractual obligation under this Regulation shall apply to the extent that, in matters of non-contractual obligations, it contains rules which raise presumptions of law or determine the burden of proof.

2. Acts intended to have legal effect may be proved by any mode of proof recognised by the law of the forum or by any of the laws referred to in Article 21 under which that act is formally valid, provided that such mode of proof can be administered by the forum.

CHAPTER VI

**OTHER PROVISIONS**

*Article 23*

**Habitual residence**

1. For the purposes of this Regulation, the habitual residence of companies and other bodies, corporate or unincorporated, shall be the place of central administration.

Where the event giving rise to the damage occurs, or the damage arises, in the course of operation of a branch, agency or any other establishment, the place where the branch, agency or any other establishment is located shall be treated as the place of habitual residence.

2. For the purposes of this Regulation, the habitual residence of a natural person acting in the course of his or her business activity shall be his or her principal place of business.

*Article 24*

**Exclusion of renvoi**

The application of the law of any country specified by this Regulation means the application of the rules of law in force in that country other than its rules of private international law.

*Article 25*

**States with more than one legal system**

1. Where a State comprises several territorial units, each of which has its own rules of law in respect of non-contractual obligations, each territorial unit shall be considered as a country for the purposes of identifying the law applicable under this Regulation.

2. A Member State within which different territorial units have their own rules of law in respect of non-contractual obligations shall not be required to apply this Regulation to conflicts solely between the laws of such units.

*Article 26*

**Public policy of the forum**

The application of a provision of the law of any country specified by this Regulation may be refused only if such application is manifestly incompatible with the public policy (*ordre public*) of the forum.

*Article 27*

**Relationship with other provisions of Community law**

This Regulation shall not prejudice the application of provisions of Community law which, in relation to particular matters, lay down conflict-of-law rules relating to non-contractual obligations.

*Article 28*

**Relationship with existing international conventions**

1. This Regulation shall not prejudice the application of international conventions to which one or more Member States are parties at the time when this Regulation is adopted and which lay down conflict-of-law rules relating to non-contractual obligations.

2. However, this Regulation shall, as between Member States, take precedence over conventions concluded exclusively between two or more of them in so far as such conventions concern matters governed by this Regulation.

CHAPTER VII

**FINAL PROVISIONS**

*Article 29*

**List of conventions**

1. By 11 July 2008, Member States shall notify the Commission of the conventions referred to in Article 28(1). After that date, Member States shall notify the Commission of all denunciations of such conventions.

2. The Commission shall publish in the *Official Journal of the European Union* within six months of receipt:

(i) a list of the conventions referred to in paragraph 1;

(ii) the denunciations referred to in paragraph 1.

*Article 30*

**Review clause**

1. Not later than 20 August 2011, the Commission shall submit to the European Parliament, the Council and the European Economic and Social Committee a report on the application of this Regulation. If necessary, the report shall be accompanied by proposals to adapt this Regulation. The report shall include:

(i) a study on the effects of the way in which foreign law is treated in the different jurisdictions and on the extent to which courts in the Member States apply foreign law in practice pursuant to this Regulation;

(ii) a study on the effects of Article 28 of this Regulation with respect to the Hague Convention of 4 May 1971 on the law applicable to traffic accidents.

2. Not later than 31 December 2008, the Commission shall submit to the European Parliament, the Council and the European Economic and Social Committee a study on the situation in the field of the law applicable to non-contractual obligations arising out of violations of privacy and rights relating to personality, taking into account rules relating to freedom of the press and freedom of expression in the media, and conflict-of-law issues related to Directive 95/46/EC of the European Parliament and of the Council of 24 October 1995 on the protection of individuals with regard to the processing of personal data and on the free movement of such data (1).

*Article 31*

**Application in time**

This Regulation shall apply to events giving rise to damage which occur after its entry into force.

*Article 32*

**Date of application**

This Regulation shall apply from 11 January 2009, except for Article 29, which shall apply from 11 July 2008.

This Regulation shall be binding in its entirety and directly applicable in the Member States in accordance with the Treaty establishing the European Community.

Done at Strasbourg, 11 July 2007.

| *For the European Parliament* | *For the Council* |
| --- | --- |
| *The President* | *The President* |
| H.-G. PÖTTERING | M. LOBO ANTUNES |

(1) OJ L 281, 23.11.1995, p. 31.

# *Appendix 1*

**Commission Statement on the review clause (Article 30)**

The Commission, following the invitation by the European Parliament and the Council in the frame of Article 30 of the 'Rome II' Regulation, will submit, not later than December 2008, a study on the situation in the field of the law applicable to non-contractual obligations arising out of violations of privacy and rights relating to personality. The Commission will take into consideration all aspects of the situation and take appropriate measures if necessary.

**Commission Statement on road accidents**

The Commission, being aware of the different practices followed in the Member States as regards the level of compensation awarded to victims of road traffic accidents, is prepared to examine the specific problems resulting for EU residents involved in road traffic accidents in a Member State other than the Member State of their habitual residence. To that end the Commission will make available to the European Parliament and to the Council, before the end of 2008, a study on all options, including insurance aspects, for improving the position of cross-border victims, which would pave the way for a Green Paper.

**Commission Statement on the treatment of foreign law**

The Commission, being aware of the different practices followed in the Member States as regards the treatment of foreign law, will publish at the latest four years after the entry into force of the 'Rome II' Regulation and in any event as soon as it is available a horizontal study on the application of foreign law in civil and commercial matters by the courts of the Member States, having regard to the aims of the Hague Programme. It is also prepared to take appropriate measures if necessary.

# APPENDIX 2

## REGULATION (EC) No 593/2008 OF THE EUROPEAN PARLIAMENT AND OF THE COUNCIL

### of 17 June 2008

### on the law applicable to contractual obligations (Rome I)

THE EUROPEAN PARLIAMENT AND THE COUNCIL OF THE EUROPEAN UNION,

Having regard to the Treaty establishing the European Community, and in particular Article 61(c) and the second indent of Article 67(5) thereof,

Having regard to the proposal from the Commission,

Having regard to the opinion of the European Economic and Social Committee ([1]),

Acting in accordance with the procedure laid down in Article 251 of the Treaty ([2]),

Whereas:

(1) The Community has set itself the objective of maintaining and developing an area of freedom, security and justice. For the progressive establishment of such an area, the Community is to adopt measures relating to judicial cooperation in civil matters with a cross-border impact to the extent necessary for the proper functioning of the internal market.

(2) According to Article 65, point (b) of the Treaty, these measures are to include those promoting the compatibility of the rules applicable in the Member States concerning the conflict of laws and of jurisdiction.

(3) The European Council meeting in Tampere on 15 and 16 October 1999 endorsed the principle of mutual recognition of judgments and other decisions of judicial authorities as the cornerstone of judicial cooperation in civil matters and invited the Council and the Commission to adopt a programme of measures to implement that principle.

(4) On 30 November 2000 the Council adopted a joint Commission and Council programme of measures for implementation of the principle of mutual recognition of decisions in civil and commercial matters ([3]). The programme identifies measures relating to the harmonisation of conflict-of-law rules as those facilitating the mutual recognition of judgments.

(5) The Hague Programme ([4]), adopted by the European Council on 5 November 2004, called for work to be pursued actively on the conflict-of-law rules regarding contractual obligations (Rome I).

(6) The proper functioning of the internal market creates a need, in order to improve the predictability of the outcome of litigation, certainty as to the law applicable and the free movement of judgments, for the conflict-of-law rules in the Member States to designate the same national law irrespective of the country of the court in which an action is brought.

(7) The substantive scope and the provisions of this Regulation should be consistent with Council Regulation (EC) No 44/2001 of 22 December 2000 on jurisdiction and the recognition and enforcement of judgments in civil and commercial matters ([5]) (Brussels I) and Regulation (EC) No 864/2007 of the European Parliament and of the Council of 11 July 2007 on the law applicable to non-contractual obligations (Rome II) ([6]).

(8) Family relationships should cover parentage, marriage, affinity and collateral relatives. The reference in Article 1(2) to relationships having comparable effects to marriage and other family relationships should be interpreted in accordance with the law of the Member State in which the court is seised.

(9) Obligations under bills of exchange, cheques and promissory notes and other negotiable instruments should also cover bills of lading to the extent that the obligations under the bill of lading arise out of its negotiable character.

(10) Obligations arising out of dealings prior to the conclusion of the contract are covered by Article 12 of Regulation (EC) No 864/2007. Such obligations should therefore be excluded from the scope of this Regulation.

(11) The parties' freedom to choose the applicable law should be one of the cornerstones of the system of conflict-of-law rules in matters of contractual obligations.

(12) An agreement between the parties to confer on one or more courts or tribunals of a Member State exclusive jurisdiction to determine disputes under the contract should be one of the factors to be taken into account in determining whether a choice of law has been clearly demonstrated.

(13) This Regulation does not preclude parties from incorporating by reference into their contract a non-State body of law or an international convention.

---

([1]) OJ C 318, 23.12.2006, p. 56.

([2]) Opinion of the European Parliament of 29 November 2007 (not yet published in the Official Journal) and Council Decision of 5 June 2008.

([3]) OJ C 12, 15.1.2001, p. 1.

([4]) OJ C 53, 3.3.2005, p. 1.

([5]) OJ L 12, 16.1.2001, p. 1. Regulation as last amended by Regulation (EC) No 1791/2006 (OJ L 363, 20.12.2006, p. 1).

([6]) OJ L 199, 31.7.2007, p. 40.

(14) Should the Community adopt, in an appropriate legal instrument, rules of substantive contract law, including standard terms and conditions, such instrument may provide that the parties may choose to apply those rules.

(15) Where a choice of law is made and all other elements relevant to the situation are located in a country other than the country whose law has been chosen, the choice of law should not prejudice the application of provisions of the law of that country which cannot be derogated from by agreement. This rule should apply whether or not the choice of law was accompanied by a choice of court or tribunal. Whereas no substantial change is intended as compared with Article 3(3) of the 1980 Convention on the Law Applicable to Contractual Obligations ([1]) (the Rome Convention), the wording of this Regulation is aligned as far as possible with Article 14 of Regulation (EC) No 864/2007.

(16) To contribute to the general objective of this Regulation, legal certainty in the European judicial area, the conflict-of-law rules should be highly foreseeable. The courts should, however, retain a degree of discretion to determine the law that is most closely connected to the situation.

(17) As far as the applicable law in the absence of choice is concerned, the concept of 'provision of services' and 'sale of goods' should be interpreted in the same way as when applying Article 5 of Regulation (EC) No 44/2001 in so far as sale of goods and provision of services are covered by that Regulation. Although franchise and distribution contracts are contracts for services, they are the subject of specific rules.

(18) As far as the applicable law in the absence of choice is concerned, multilateral systems should be those in which trading is conducted, such as regulated markets and multilateral trading facilities as referred to in Article 4 of Directive 2004/39/EC of the European Parliament and of the Council of 21 April 2004 on markets in financial instruments ([2]), regardless of whether or not they rely on a central counterparty.

(19) Where there has been no choice of law, the applicable law should be determined in accordance with the rule specified for the particular type of contract. Where the contract cannot be categorised as being one of the specified types or where its elements fall within more than one of the specified types, it should be governed by the law of the country where the party required to effect the characteristic performance of the contract has his habitual residence. In the case of a contract consisting of a bundle of rights and obligations capable of being categorised as falling within more than one of the specified types of contract, the characteristic performance of the contract should be determined having regard to its centre of gravity.

([1]) OJ C 334, 30.12.2005, p. 1.

([2]) OJ L 145, 30.4.2004, p. 1. Directive as last amended by Directive 2008/10/EC (OJ L 76, 19.3.2008, p. 33).

(20) Where the contract is manifestly more closely connected with a country other than that indicated in Article 4(1) or (2), an escape clause should provide that the law of that other country is to apply. In order to determine that country, account should be taken, *inter alia*, of whether the contract in question has a very close relationship with another contract or contracts.

(21) In the absence of choice, where the applicable law cannot be determined either on the basis of the fact that the contract can be categorised as one of the specified types or as being the law of the country of habitual residence of the party required to effect the characteristic performance of the contract, the contract should be governed by the law of the country with which it is most closely connected. In order to determine that country, account should be taken, *inter alia*, of whether the contract in question has a very close relationship with another contract or contracts.

(22) As regards the interpretation of contracts for the carriage of goods, no change in substance is intended with respect to Article 4(4), third sentence, of the Rome Convention. Consequently, single-voyage charter parties and other contracts the main purpose of which is the carriage of goods should be treated as contracts for the carriage of goods. For the purposes of this Regulation, the term 'consignor' should refer to any person who enters into a contract of carriage with the carrier and the term 'the carrier' should refer to the party to the contract who undertakes to carry the goods, whether or not he performs the carriage himself.

(23) As regards contracts concluded with parties regarded as being weaker, those parties should be protected by conflict-of-law rules that are more favourable to their interests than the general rules.

(24) With more specific reference to consumer contracts, the conflict-of-law rule should make it possible to cut the cost of settling disputes concerning what are commonly relatively small claims and to take account of the development of distance-selling techniques. Consistency with Regulation (EC) No 44/2001 requires both that there be a reference to the concept of directed activity as a condition for applying the consumer protection rule and that the concept be interpreted harmoniously in Regulation (EC) No 44/2001 and this Regulation, bearing in mind that a joint declaration by the Council and the Commission on Article 15 of Regulation (EC) No 44/2001 states that 'for Article 15(1)(c) to be applicable it is not sufficient for an undertaking to target its activities at the Member State of the consumer's residence, or at a number of Member States including that Member State; a contract must also be concluded within the framework of its activities'. The declaration also states that 'the mere fact that an Internet site is accessible is not sufficient for Article 15 to be applicable, although a factor will be that this Internet site solicits the conclusion of distance contracts and that a contract has actually been concluded at a distance, by

whatever means. In this respect, the language or currency which a website uses does not constitute a relevant factor.'.

(25) Consumers should be protected by such rules of the country of their habitual residence that cannot be derogated from by agreement, provided that the consumer contract has been concluded as a result of the professional pursuing his commercial or professional activities in that particular country. The same protection should be guaranteed if the professional, while not pursuing his commercial or professional activities in the country where the consumer has his habitual residence, directs his activities by any means to that country or to several countries, including that country, and the contract is concluded as a result of such activities.

(26) For the purposes of this Regulation, financial services such as investment services and activities and ancillary services provided by a professional to a consumer, as referred to in sections A and B of Annex I to Directive 2004/39/EC, and contracts for the sale of units in collective investment undertakings, whether or not covered by Council Directive 85/611/EEC of 20 December 1985 on the coordination of laws, regulations and administrative provisions relating to undertakings for collective investment in transferable securities (UCITS) ([1]), should be subject to Article 6 of this Regulation. Consequently, when a reference is made to terms and conditions governing the issuance or offer to the public of transferable securities or to the subscription and redemption of units in collective investment undertakings, that reference should include all aspects binding the issuer or the offeror to the consumer, but should not include those aspects involving the provision of financial services.

(27) Various exceptions should be made to the general conflict-of-law rule for consumer contracts. Under one such exception the general rule should not apply to contracts relating to rights *in rem* in immovable property or tenancies of such property unless the contract relates to the right to use immovable property on a timeshare basis within the meaning of Directive 94/47/EC of the European Parliament and of the Council of 26 October 1994 on the protection of purchasers in respect of certain aspects of contracts relating to the purchase of the right to use immovable properties on a timeshare basis ([2]).

(28) It is important to ensure that rights and obligations which constitute a financial instrument are not covered by the general rule applicable to consumer contracts, as that could lead to different laws being applicable to each of the instruments issued, therefore changing their nature and preventing their fungible trading and offering. Likewise, whenever such instruments are issued or offered, the contractual relationship established between the issuer or the offeror and the consumer should not necessarily be subject to the mandatory application of the law of the country of habitual residence of the consumer, as there is a need to ensure uniformity in the terms and conditions of an issuance or an offer. The same rationale should apply with regard to the multilateral systems covered by Article 4(1)(h), in respect of which it should be ensured that the law of the country of habitual residence of the consumer will not interfere with the rules applicable to contracts concluded within those systems or with the operator of such systems.

(29) For the purposes of this Regulation, references to rights and obligations constituting the terms and conditions governing the issuance, offers to the public or public take-over bids of transferable securities and references to the subscription and redemption of units in collective investment undertakings should include the terms governing, *inter alia*, the allocation of securities or units, rights in the event of over-subscription, withdrawal rights and similar matters in the context of the offer as well as those matters referred to in Articles 10, 11, 12 and 13, thus ensuring that all relevant contractual aspects of an offer binding the issuer or the offeror to the consumer are governed by a single law.

(30) For the purposes of this Regulation, financial instruments and transferable securities are those instruments referred to in Article 4 of Directive 2004/39/EC.

(31) Nothing in this Regulation should prejudice the operation of a formal arrangement designated as a system under Article 2(a) of Directive 98/26/EC of the European Parliament and of the Council of 19 May 1998 on settlement finality in payment and securities settlement systems ([3]).

(32) Owing to the particular nature of contracts of carriage and insurance contracts, specific provisions should ensure an adequate level of protection of passengers and policy holders. Therefore, Article 6 should not apply in the context of those particular contracts.

(33) Where an insurance contract not covering a large risk covers more than one risk, at least one of which is situated in a Member State and at least one of which is situated in a third country, the special rules on insurance contracts in this Regulation should apply only to the risk or risks situated in the relevant Member State or Member States.

(34) The rule on individual employment contracts should not prejudice the application of the overriding mandatory provisions of the country to which a worker is posted in accordance with Directive 96/71/EC of the European Parliament and of the Council of 16 December 1996 concerning the posting of workers in the framework of the provision of services ([4]).

([1]) OJ L 375, 31.12.1985, p. 3. Directive as last amended by Directive 2008/18/EC of the European Parliament and of the Council (OJ L 76, 19.3.2008, p. 42).

([2]) OJ L 280, 29.10.1994, p. 83.

([3]) OJ L 166, 11.6.1998, p. 45.

([4]) OJ L 18, 21.1.1997, p. 1.

(35) Employees should not be deprived of the protection afforded to them by provisions which cannot be derogated from by agreement or which can only be derogated from to their benefit.

(36) As regards individual employment contracts, work carried out in another country should be regarded as temporary if the employee is expected to resume working in the country of origin after carrying out his tasks abroad. The conclusion of a new contract of employment with the original employer or an employer belonging to the same group of companies as the original employer should not preclude the employee from being regarded as carrying out his work in another country temporarily.

(37) Considerations of public interest justify giving the courts of the Member States the possibility, in exceptional circumstances, of applying exceptions based on public policy and overriding mandatory provisions. The concept of 'overriding mandatory provisions' should be distinguished from the expression 'provisions which cannot be derogated from by agreement' and should be construed more restrictively.

(38) In the context of voluntary assignment, the term 'relationship' should make it clear that Article 14(1) also applies to the property aspects of an assignment, as between assignor and assignee, in legal orders where such aspects are treated separately from the aspects under the law of obligations. However, the term 'relationship' should not be understood as relating to any relationship that may exist between assignor and assignee. In particular, it should not cover preliminary questions as regards a voluntary assignment or a contractual subrogation. The term should be strictly limited to the aspects which are directly relevant to the voluntary assignment or contractual subrogation in question.

(39) For the sake of legal certainty there should be a clear definition of habitual residence, in particular for companies and other bodies, corporate or unincorporated. Unlike Article 60(1) of Regulation (EC) No 44/2001, which establishes three criteria, the conflict-of-law rule should proceed on the basis of a single criterion; otherwise, the parties would be unable to foresee the law applicable to their situation.

(40) A situation where conflict-of-law rules are dispersed among several instruments and where there are differences between those rules should be avoided. This Regulation, however, should not exclude the possibility of inclusion of conflict-of-law rules relating to contractual obligations in provisions of Community law with regard to particular matters.

This Regulation should not prejudice the application of other instruments laying down provisions designed to contribute to the proper functioning of the internal market in so far as they cannot be applied in conjunction with the law designated by the rules of this Regulation. The application of provisions of the applicable law designated by the rules of this Regulation should not restrict the free movement of goods and services as regulated by Community instruments, such as Directive 2000/31/EC of the European Parliament and of the Council of 8 June 2000 on certain legal aspects of information society services, in particular electronic commerce, in the Internal Market (Directive on electronic commerce) ([1]).

(41) Respect for international commitments entered into by the Member States means that this Regulation should not affect international conventions to which one or more Member States are parties at the time when this Regulation is adopted. To make the rules more accessible, the Commission should publish the list of the relevant conventions in the *Official Journal of the European Union* on the basis of information supplied by the Member States.

(42) The Commission will make a proposal to the European Parliament and to the Council concerning the procedures and conditions according to which Member States would be entitled to negotiate and conclude, on their own behalf, agreements with third countries in individual and exceptional cases, concerning sectoral matters and containing provisions on the law applicable to contractual obligations.

(43) Since the objective of this Regulation cannot be sufficiently achieved by the Member States and can therefore, by reason of the scale and effects of this Regulation, be better achieved at Community level, the Community may adopt measures, in accordance with the principle of subsidiarity as set out in Article 5 of the Treaty. In accordance with the principle of proportionality, as set out in that Article, this Regulation does not go beyond what is necessary to attain its objective.

(44) In accordance with Article 3 of the Protocol on the position of the United Kingdom and Ireland, annexed to the Treaty on European Union and to the Treaty establishing the European Community, Ireland has notified its wish to take part in the adoption and application of the present Regulation.

(45) In accordance with Articles 1 and 2 of the Protocol on the position of the United Kingdom and Ireland, annexed to the Treaty on European Union and to the Treaty establishing the European Community, and without prejudice to Article 4 of the said Protocol, the United Kingdom is not taking part in the adoption of this Regulation and is not bound by it or subject to its application.

(46) In accordance with Articles 1 and 2 of the Protocol on the position of Denmark, annexed to the Treaty on European Union and to the Treaty establishing the European Community, Denmark is not taking part in the adoption of this Regulation and is not bound by it or subject to its application,

([1]) OJ L 178, 17.7.2000, p. 1.

HAVE ADOPTED THIS REGULATION:

CHAPTER I

**SCOPE**

*Article 1*

**Material scope**

1. This Regulation shall apply, in situations involving a conflict of laws, to contractual obligations in civil and commercial matters.

It shall not apply, in particular, to revenue, customs or administrative matters.

2. The following shall be excluded from the scope of this Regulation:

(a) questions involving the status or legal capacity of natural persons, without prejudice to Article 13;

(b) obligations arising out of family relationships and relationships deemed by the law applicable to such relationships to have comparable effects, including maintenance obligations;

(c) obligations arising out of matrimonial property regimes, property regimes of relationships deemed by the law applicable to such relationships to have comparable effects to marriage, and wills and succession;

(d) obligations arising under bills of exchange, cheques and promissory notes and other negotiable instruments to the extent that the obligations under such other negotiable instruments arise out of their negotiable character;

(e) arbitration agreements and agreements on the choice of court;

(f) questions governed by the law of companies and other bodies, corporate or unincorporated, such as the creation, by registration or otherwise, legal capacity, internal organisation or winding-up of companies and other bodies, corporate or unincorporated, and the personal liability of officers and members as such for the obligations of the company or body;

(g) the question whether an agent is able to bind a principal, or an organ to bind a company or other body corporate or unincorporated, in relation to a third party;

(h) the constitution of trusts and the relationship between settlors, trustees and beneficiaries;

(i) obligations arising out of dealings prior to the conclusion of a contract;

(j) insurance contracts arising out of operations carried out by organisations other than undertakings referred to in Article 2 of Directive 2002/83/EC of the European Parliament and of the Council of 5 November 2002 concerning life assurance (1) the object of which is to provide benefits for employed or self-employed persons belonging to an undertaking or group of undertakings, or to a trade or group of trades, in the event of death or survival or of discontinuance or curtailment of activity, or of sickness related to work or accidents at work.

3. This Regulation shall not apply to evidence and procedure, without prejudice to Article 18.

4. In this Regulation, the term 'Member State' shall mean Member States to which this Regulation applies. However, in Article 3(4) and Article 7 the term shall mean all the Member States.

*Article 2*

**Universal application**

Any law specified by this Regulation shall be applied whether or not it is the law of a Member State.

CHAPTER II

**UNIFORM RULES**

*Article 3*

**Freedom of choice**

1. A contract shall be governed by the law chosen by the parties. The choice shall be made expressly or clearly demonstrated by the terms of the contract or the circumstances of the case. By their choice the parties can select the law applicable to the whole or to part only of the contract.

2. The parties may at any time agree to subject the contract to a law other than that which previously governed it, whether as a result of an earlier choice made under this Article or of other provisions of this Regulation. Any change in the law to be applied that is made after the conclusion of the contract shall not prejudice its formal validity under Article 11 or adversely affect the rights of third parties.

3. Where all other elements relevant to the situation at the time of the choice are located in a country other than the country whose law has been chosen, the choice of the parties shall not prejudice the application of provisions of the law of that other country which cannot be derogated from by agreement.

4. Where all other elements relevant to the situation at the time of the choice are located in one or more Member States, the

(1) OJ L 345, 19.12.2002, p. 1. Directive as last amended by Directive 2008/19/EC (OJ L 76, 19.3.2008, p. 44).

parties' choice of applicable law other than that of a Member State shall not prejudice the application of provisions of Community law, where appropriate as implemented in the Member State of the forum, which cannot be derogated from by agreement.

5. The existence and validity of the consent of the parties as to the choice of the applicable law shall be determined in accordance with the provisions of Articles 10, 11 and 13.

*Article 4*

**Applicable law in the absence of choice**

1. To the extent that the law applicable to the contract has not been chosen in accordance with Article 3 and without prejudice to Articles 5 to 8, the law governing the contract shall be determined as follows:

(a) a contract for the sale of goods shall be governed by the law of the country where the seller has his habitual residence;

(b) a contract for the provision of services shall be governed by the law of the country where the service provider has his habitual residence;

(c) a contract relating to a right *in rem* in immovable property or to a tenancy of immovable property shall be governed by the law of the country where the property is situated;

(d) notwithstanding point (c), a tenancy of immovable property concluded for temporary private use for a period of no more than six consecutive months shall be governed by the law of the country where the landlord has his habitual residence, provided that the tenant is a natural person and has his habitual residence in the same country;

(e) a franchise contract shall be governed by the law of the country where the franchisee has his habitual residence;

(f) a distribution contract shall be governed by the law of the country where the distributor has his habitual residence;

(g) a contract for the sale of goods by auction shall be governed by the law of the country where the auction takes place, if such a place can be determined;

(h) a contract concluded within a multilateral system which brings together or facilitates the bringing together of multiple third-party buying and selling interests in financial instruments, as defined by Article 4(1), point (17) of Directive 2004/39/EC, in accordance with non-discretionary rules and governed by a single law, shall be governed by that law.

2. Where the contract is not covered by paragraph 1 or where the elements of the contract would be covered by more than one of points (a) to (h) of paragraph 1, the contract shall be governed by the law of the country where the party required to effect the characteristic performance of the contract has his habitual residence.

3. Where it is clear from all the circumstances of the case that the contract is manifestly more closely connected with a country other than that indicated in paragraphs 1 or 2, the law of that other country shall apply.

4. Where the law applicable cannot be determined pursuant to paragraphs 1 or 2, the contract shall be governed by the law of the country with which it is most closely connected.

*Article 5*

**Contracts of carriage**

1. To the extent that the law applicable to a contract for the carriage of goods has not been chosen in accordance with Article 3, the law applicable shall be the law of the country of habitual residence of the carrier, provided that the place of receipt or the place of delivery or the habitual residence of the consignor is also situated in that country. If those requirements are not met, the law of the country where the place of delivery as agreed by the parties is situated shall apply.

2. To the extent that the law applicable to a contract for the carriage of passengers has not been chosen by the parties in accordance with the second subparagraph, the law applicable shall be the law of the country where the passenger has his habitual residence, provided that either the place of departure or the place of destination is situated in that country. If these requirements are not met, the law of the country where the carrier has his habitual residence shall apply.

The parties may choose as the law applicable to a contract for the carriage of passengers in accordance with Article 3 only the law of the country where:

(a) the passenger has his habitual residence; or

(b) the carrier has his habitual residence; or

(c) the carrier has his place of central administration; or

(d) the place of departure is situated; or

(e) the place of destination is situated.

3. Where it is clear from all the circumstances of the case that the contract, in the absence of a choice of law, is manifestly more closely connected with a country other than that indicated in paragraphs 1 or 2, the law of that other country shall apply.

*Article 6*

**Consumer contracts**

1. Without prejudice to Articles 5 and 7, a contract concluded by a natural person for a purpose which can be regarded as being outside his trade or profession (the consumer) with another

person acting in the exercise of his trade or profession (the professional) shall be governed by the law of the country where the consumer has his habitual residence, provided that the professional:

(a) pursues his commercial or professional activities in the country where the consumer has his habitual residence, or

(b) by any means, directs such activities to that country or to several countries including that country,

and the contract falls within the scope of such activities.

2. Notwithstanding paragraph 1, the parties may choose the law applicable to a contract which fulfils the requirements of paragraph 1, in accordance with Article 3. Such a choice may not, however, have the result of depriving the consumer of the protection afforded to him by provisions that cannot be derogated from by agreement by virtue of the law which, in the absence of choice, would have been applicable on the basis of paragraph 1.

3. If the requirements in points (a) or (b) of paragraph 1 are not fulfilled, the law applicable to a contract between a consumer and a professional shall be determined pursuant to Articles 3 and 4.

4. Paragraphs 1 and 2 shall not apply to:

(a) a contract for the supply of services where the services are to be supplied to the consumer exclusively in a country other than that in which he has his habitual residence;

(b) a contract of carriage other than a contract relating to package travel within the meaning of Council Directive 90/314/EEC of 13 June 1990 on package travel, package holidays and package tours ([1]);

(c) a contract relating to a right *in rem* in immovable property or a tenancy of immovable property other than a contract relating to the right to use immovable properties on a timeshare basis within the meaning of Directive 94/47/EC;

(d) rights and obligations which constitute a financial instrument and rights and obligations constituting the terms and conditions governing the issuance or offer to the public and public take-over bids of transferable securities, and the subscription and redemption of units in collective investment undertakings in so far as these activities do not constitute provision of a financial service;

(e) a contract concluded within the type of system falling within the scope of Article 4(1)(h).

([1]) OJ L 158, 23.6.1990, p. 59.

*Article 7*

**Insurance contracts**

1. This Article shall apply to contracts referred to in paragraph 2, whether or not the risk covered is situated in a Member State, and to all other insurance contracts covering risks situated inside the territory of the Member States. It shall not apply to reinsurance contracts.

2. An insurance contract covering a large risk as defined in Article 5(d) of the First Council Directive 73/239/EEC of 24 July 1973 on the coordination of laws, regulations and administrative provisions relating to the taking-up and pursuit of the business of direct insurance other than life assurance ([2]) shall be governed by the law chosen by the parties in accordance with Article 3 of this Regulation.

To the extent that the applicable law has not been chosen by the parties, the insurance contract shall be governed by the law of the country where the insurer has his habitual residence. Where it is clear from all the circumstances of the case that the contract is manifestly more closely connected with another country, the law of that other country shall apply.

3. In the case of an insurance contract other than a contract falling within paragraph 2, only the following laws may be chosen by the parties in accordance with Article 3:

(a) the law of any Member State where the risk is situated at the time of conclusion of the contract;

(b) the law of the country where the policy holder has his habitual residence;

(c) in the case of life assurance, the law of the Member State of which the policy holder is a national;

(d) for insurance contracts covering risks limited to events occurring in one Member State other than the Member State where the risk is situated, the law of that Member State;

(e) where the policy holder of a contract falling under this paragraph pursues a commercial or industrial activity or a liberal profession and the insurance contract covers two or more risks which relate to those activities and are situated in different Member States, the law of any of the Member States concerned or the law of the country of habitual residence of the policy holder.

Where, in the cases set out in points (a), (b) or (e), the Member States referred to grant greater freedom of choice of the law applicable to the insurance contract, the parties may take advantage of that freedom.

([2]) OJ L 228, 16.8.1973, p. 3. Directive as last amended by Directive 2005/68/EC of the European Parliament and of the Council (OJ L 323, 9.12.2005, p. 1).

To the extent that the law applicable has not been chosen by the parties in accordance with this paragraph, such a contract shall be governed by the law of the Member State in which the risk is situated at the time of conclusion of the contract.

4. The following additional rules shall apply to insurance contracts covering risks for which a Member State imposes an obligation to take out insurance:

(a) the insurance contract shall not satisfy the obligation to take out insurance unless it complies with the specific provisions relating to that insurance laid down by the Member State that imposes the obligation. Where the law of the Member State in which the risk is situated and the law of the Member State imposing the obligation to take out insurance contradict each other, the latter shall prevail;

(b) by way of derogation from paragraphs 2 and 3, a Member State may lay down that the insurance contract shall be governed by the law of the Member State that imposes the obligation to take out insurance.

5. For the purposes of paragraph 3, third subparagraph, and paragraph 4, where the contract covers risks situated in more than one Member State, the contract shall be considered as constituting several contracts each relating to only one Member State.

6. For the purposes of this Article, the country in which the risk is situated shall be determined in accordance with Article 2(d) of the Second Council Directive 88/357/EEC of 22 June 1988 on the coordination of laws, regulations and administrative provisions relating to direct insurance other than life assurance and laying down provisions to facilitate the effective exercise of freedom to provide services ([1]) and, in the case of life assurance, the country in which the risk is situated shall be the country of the commitment within the meaning of Article 1(1)(g) of Directive 2002/83/EC.

*Article 8*

**Individual employment contracts**

1. An individual employment contract shall be governed by the law chosen by the parties in accordance with Article 3. Such a choice of law may not, however, have the result of depriving the employee of the protection afforded to him by provisions that cannot be derogated from by agreement under the law that, in the absence of choice, would have been applicable pursuant to paragraphs 2, 3 and 4 of this Article.

2. To the extent that the law applicable to the individual employment contract has not been chosen by the parties, the contract shall be governed by the law of the country in which or, failing that, from which the employee habitually carries out his work in performance of the contract. The country where the work is habitually carried out shall not be deemed to have changed if he is temporarily employed in another country.

3. Where the law applicable cannot be determined pursuant to paragraph 2, the contract shall be governed by the law of the country where the place of business through which the employee was engaged is situated.

4. Where it appears from the circumstances as a whole that the contract is more closely connected with a country other than that indicated in paragraphs 2 or 3, the law of that other country shall apply.

*Article 9*

**Overriding mandatory provisions**

1. Overriding mandatory provisions are provisions the respect for which is regarded as crucial by a country for safeguarding its public interests, such as its political, social or economic organisation, to such an extent that they are applicable to any situation falling within their scope, irrespective of the law otherwise applicable to the contract under this Regulation.

2. Nothing in this Regulation shall restrict the application of the overriding mandatory provisions of the law of the forum.

3. Effect may be given to the overriding mandatory provisions of the law of the country where the obligations arising out of the contract have to be or have been performed, in so far as those overriding mandatory provisions render the performance of the contract unlawful. In considering whether to give effect to those provisions, regard shall be had to their nature and purpose and to the consequences of their application or non-application.

*Article 10*

**Consent and material validity**

1. The existence and validity of a contract, or of any term of a contract, shall be determined by the law which would govern it under this Regulation if the contract or term were valid.

2. Nevertheless, a party, in order to establish that he did not consent, may rely upon the law of the country in which he has his habitual residence if it appears from the circumstances that it would not be reasonable to determine the effect of his conduct in accordance with the law specified in paragraph 1.

*Article 11*

**Formal validity**

1. A contract concluded between persons who, or whose agents, are in the same country at the time of its conclusion is

([1]) OJ L 172, 4.7.1988, p. 1. Directive as last amended by Directive 2005/14/EC of the European Parliament and of the Council (OJ L 149, 11.6.2005, p. 14).

formally valid if it satisfies the formal requirements of the law which governs it in substance under this Regulation or of the law of the country where it is concluded.

2. A contract concluded between persons who, or whose agents, are in different countries at the time of its conclusion is formally valid if it satisfies the formal requirements of the law which governs it in substance under this Regulation, or of the law of either of the countries where either of the parties or their agent is present at the time of conclusion, or of the law of the country where either of the parties had his habitual residence at that time.

3. A unilateral act intended to have legal effect relating to an existing or contemplated contract is formally valid if it satisfies the formal requirements of the law which governs or would govern the contract in substance under this Regulation, or of the law of the country where the act was done, or of the law of the country where the person by whom it was done had his habitual residence at that time.

4. Paragraphs 1, 2 and 3 of this Article shall not apply to contracts that fall within the scope of Article 6. The form of such contracts shall be governed by the law of the country where the consumer has his habitual residence.

5. Notwithstanding paragraphs 1 to 4, a contract the subject matter of which is a right *in rem* in immovable property or a tenancy of immovable property shall be subject to the requirements of form of the law of the country where the property is situated if by that law:

(a) those requirements are imposed irrespective of the country where the contract is concluded and irrespective of the law governing the contract; and

(b) those requirements cannot be derogated from by agreement.

*Article 12*

**Scope of the law applicable**

1. The law applicable to a contract by virtue of this Regulation shall govern in particular:

(a) interpretation;

(b) performance;

(c) within the limits of the powers conferred on the court by its procedural law, the consequences of a total or partial breach of obligations, including the assessment of damages in so far as it is governed by rules of law;

(d) the various ways of extinguishing obligations, and prescription and limitation of actions;

(e) the consequences of nullity of the contract.

2. In relation to the manner of performance and the steps to be taken in the event of defective performance, regard shall be had to the law of the country in which performance takes place.

*Article 13*

**Incapacity**

In a contract concluded between persons who are in the same country, a natural person who would have capacity under the law of that country may invoke his incapacity resulting from the law of another country, only if the other party to the contract was aware of that incapacity at the time of the conclusion of the contract or was not aware thereof as a result of negligence.

*Article 14*

**Voluntary assignment and contractual subrogation**

1. The relationship between assignor and assignee under a voluntary assignment or contractual subrogation of a claim against another person (the debtor) shall be governed by the law that applies to the contract between the assignor and assignee under this Regulation.

2. The law governing the assigned or subrogated claim shall determine its assignability, the relationship between the assignee and the debtor, the conditions under which the assignment or subrogation can be invoked against the debtor and whether the debtor's obligations have been discharged.

3. The concept of assignment in this Article includes outright transfers of claims, transfers of claims by way of security and pledges or other security rights over claims.

*Article 15*

**Legal subrogation**

Where a person (the creditor) has a contractual claim against another (the debtor) and a third person has a duty to satisfy the creditor, or has in fact satisfied the creditor in discharge of that duty, the law which governs the third person's duty to satisfy the creditor shall determine whether and to what extent the third person is entitled to exercise against the debtor the rights which the creditor had against the debtor under the law governing their relationship.

*Article 16*

**Multiple liability**

If a creditor has a claim against several debtors who are liable for the same claim, and one of the debtors has already satisfied the claim in whole or in part, the law governing the debtor's obligation towards the creditor also governs the debtor's right to claim recourse from the other debtors. The other debtors may rely on the defences they had against the creditor to the extent allowed by the law governing their obligations towards the creditor.

*Article 17*

**Set-off**

Where the right to set-off is not agreed by the parties, set-off shall be governed by the law applicable to the claim against which the right to set-off is asserted.

*Article 18*

**Burden of proof**

1. The law governing a contractual obligation under this Regulation shall apply to the extent that, in matters of contractual obligations, it contains rules which raise presumptions of law or determine the burden of proof.

2. A contract or an act intended to have legal effect may be proved by any mode of proof recognised by the law of the forum or by any of the laws referred to in Article 11 under which that contract or act is formally valid, provided that such mode of proof can be administered by the forum.

CHAPTER III

**OTHER PROVISIONS**

*Article 19*

**Habitual residence**

1. For the purposes of this Regulation, the habitual residence of companies and other bodies, corporate or unincorporated, shall be the place of central administration.

The habitual residence of a natural person acting in the course of his business activity shall be his principal place of business.

2. Where the contract is concluded in the course of the operations of a branch, agency or any other establishment, or if, under the contract, performance is the responsibility of such a branch, agency or establishment, the place where the branch, agency or any other establishment is located shall be treated as the place of habitual residence.

3. For the purposes of determining the habitual residence, the relevant point in time shall be the time of the conclusion of the contract.

*Article 20*

**Exclusion of *renvoi***

The application of the law of any country specified by this Regulation means the application of the rules of law in force in that country other than its rules of private international law, unless provided otherwise in this Regulation.

*Article 21*

**Public policy of the forum**

The application of a provision of the law of any country specified by this Regulation may be refused only if such application is manifestly incompatible with the public policy (*ordre public*) of the forum.

*Article 22*

**States with more than one legal system**

1. Where a State comprises several territorial units, each of which has its own rules of law in respect of contractual obligations, each territorial unit shall be considered as a country for the purposes of identifying the law applicable under this Regulation.

2. A Member State where different territorial units have their own rules of law in respect of contractual obligations shall not be required to apply this Regulation to conflicts solely between the laws of such units.

*Article 23*

**Relationship with other provisions of Community law**

With the exception of Article 7, this Regulation shall not prejudice the application of provisions of Community law which, in relation to particular matters, lay down conflict-of-law rules relating to contractual obligations.

*Article 24*

**Relationship with the Rome Convention**

1. This Regulation shall replace the Rome Convention in the Member States, except as regards the territories of the Member States which fall within the territorial scope of that Convention and to which this Regulation does not apply pursuant to Article 299 of the Treaty.

2. In so far as this Regulation replaces the provisions of the Rome Convention, any reference to that Convention shall be understood as a reference to this Regulation.

*Article 25*

**Relationship with existing international conventions**

1. This Regulation shall not prejudice the application of international conventions to which one or more Member States are parties at the time when this Regulation is adopted and which lay down conflict-of-law rules relating to contractual obligations.

2. However, this Regulation shall, as between Member States, take precedence over conventions concluded exclusively between two or more of them in so far as such conventions concern matters governed by this Regulation.

*Article 26*

**List of Conventions**

1. By 17 June 2009, Member States shall notify the Commission of the conventions referred to in Article 25(1). After that date, Member States shall notify the Commission of all denunciations of such conventions.

2. Within six months of receipt of the notifications referred to in paragraph 1, the Commission shall publish in the *Official Journal of the European Union*:

(a) a list of the conventions referred to in paragraph 1;

(b) the denunciations referred to in paragraph 1.

*Article 27*

**Review clause**

1. By 17 June 2013, the Commission shall submit to the European Parliament, the Council and the European Economic and Social Committee a report on the application of this Regulation. If appropriate, the report shall be accompanied by proposals to amend this Regulation. The report shall include:

(a) a study on the law applicable to insurance contracts and an assessment of the impact of the provisions to be introduced, if any; and

(b) an evaluation on the application of Article 6, in particular as regards the coherence of Community law in the field of consumer protection.

2. By 17 June 2010, the Commission shall submit to the European Parliament, the Council and the European Economic and Social Committee a report on the question of the effectiveness of an assignment or subrogation of a claim against third parties and the priority of the assigned or subrogated claim over a right of another person. The report shall be accompanied, if appropriate, by a proposal to amend this Regulation and an assessment of the impact of the provisions to be introduced.

*Article 28*

**Application in time**

This Regulation shall apply to contracts concluded after[1] 17 December 2009.

CHAPTER IV

**FINAL PROVISIONS**

*Article 29*

**Entry into force and application**

This Regulation shall enter into force on the 20th day following its publication in the *Official Journal of the European Union*.

It shall apply from 17 December 2009 except for Article 26 which shall apply from 17 June 2009.

This Regulation shall be binding in its entirety and directly applicable in the Member States in accordance with the Treaty establishing the European Community.

Done at Strasbourg, 17 June 2008.

| *For the European Parliament* | *For the Council* |
|---|---|
| *The President* | *The President* |
| H.-G. PÖTTERING | J. LENARČIČ |

---

1. The text was corrected in October 2009 to substitute "as from" in place of "after" ([2009] O.J. L307/87).